POSTWAR
HOLLYWOOD

To all my students – remembered, at hand, and anticipated – who give me immense joy

DREW CASPER

POSTWAR HOLLYWOOD

1946–1962

Blackwell
Publishing

BLACKWELL PUBLISHING

350 Main Street, Malden, MA 02148-5020, USA
9600 Garsington Road, Oxford OX4 2DQ, UK
550 Swanston Street, Carlton, Victoria 3053, Australia

First published 2007 by Blackwell Publishing Ltd

2   2008

Library of Congress Cataloging-in-Publication Data
Casper, Drew.
Postwar Hollywood, 1946–1962 / Drew Casper.
p. cm.
Includes bibliographical references and index.
ISBN-13: 978-1-4051-5074-3 (hbk. : alk. paper)
ISBN-13: 978-1-4051-5075-0 (pbk. : alk. paper)
1. Motion pictures—United States—History.   2. Motion picture
industry—United States—History.   I. Title.
PN1993.5.U6C34 2007
791.430973′09045—dc22

2006102880

ISBN-13: 978-1-4051-5074-3 (hardback)
ISBN-13: 978-1-4051-5075-0 (paperback)

A catalogue record for this title is available from the British Library.

Set in 11 on 13.5 pt Minion
by SNP Best-set Typesetter Ltd, Hong Kong

For further information on
Blackwell Publishing, visit our website:
www.blackwellpublishing.com

Contents

Acknowledgments

A book has many hands and hearts, voices and energies. *Postwar Hollywood: 1946–1962* is no exception. Ron Kirchoff, Ken Sanders, and Greg Schriefer made films available. From the archives, USC's Film/TV Special Collections Chief Ned Comstock secured photos that Charles Uy of USC's David Wolper Center reproduced. Techno wizards Bob Burkle and Dan Watanabe came to the rescue at all hours of the day and night. There at the gestation was USC colleague and trusty friend Rick Jewell who remained warmly encouraging. Blackwell's Ken Provencher, with his careful eye and organizational smarts, prepared the script for production, while Rebecca du Plessis, Lisa Eaton, and Juanita Bullough saw the book through to publication. Gifted with a poet's precision for words, a ballerina's flair for flow and an architect's structural savvy, executive editor Jayne Fargnoli made on-the-mark suggestions through all the various drafts, giving the project thrust and shape. Wittily sharp as a satirist, Fargnoli also made the collaboration downright fun. And then there's NYU colleague, mentor, nurturer, and friend Dana Polan. He resurrected the project. He guided it through several revisions, generously sharing with me his take on postwar Hollywood movies. He opened windows when doors slammed shut. He enlarged my academic perspective. With Polan, without whom this book, quite simply, never would be, you walk high above the world. I thank God for all of you.

Illustrations

Foreword

This book is the result of an escalating sense of frustration. Since the mid-1980s, I have taught a popular survey course in film studies, "The Postwar Years: 1946–1962," in which around 200 students enroll each year.

My frustration arises from the absence of adequate teaching books. Over the years, I have assigned Schatz's *Hollywood Genres*, Stanley's *The Celluloid Empire*, Bohn and Stromgren's *Light and Shadows*, Dowdy's *Films of the Fifties*, Biskind's *Seeing Is Believing*, and selected chapters from Sklar's *Movie-Made America*, Haskell's *From Reverence to Rape*, and Mellen's *Big Bad Wolves*. Robert Ray's largely theoretical *A Certain Tendency of the Hollywood Cinema, 1930–1980*, arriving at very general characteristics of the Hollywood film from a textual analysis of only some half-dozen works, was also used.

Most of these texts are, sadly, out of print. Further: while each has its strengths, none proves a satisfactory historical account of the development of the Hollywood fiction film within this extremely pivotal time. As for the large volumes of both international and/or American film history, they have all admirably served their purposes, outlining the century-long thrust and scope of movies but, alas, have not served mine, collapsing as they do this significant period into at most five to ten pages, covering only several issues. It is now time to fill in these outlines.

At the other extreme is the impressive *History of the American Cinema* series: meticulously researched, beautifully orchestrated, and well written by a group of first-rate scholars. But although it is an indispensable, encyclopedic reference work, it still doesn't meet the need for an undergraduate textbook. Furthermore, each volume, grand as it is, is generally bereft of any in-depth social and cultural history of the time covered. It's as if the film industry and its products existed in a vacuum. Also, the discussion of genres is much too general and limited, failing to appreciate the various subtypes that occurred within each genre, and why they did occur. (Author Peter Lev's volume 7, *The Fifties:*

Transforming the Screen, 1950–1959, actually admits to leaving out entire genres as well as omitting many films, while profligately devoting an entire chapter to science fiction.) The division, decade by decade from the thirties on, also creates overlaps and does not fully consider the periods and movements that start in one decade, continue in another, and spill over into a third, as for example, postwar Hollywood.

The period's significance is lost even in the impressive but reductive volume by Bordwell, Staiger, and Thompson, *The Classical Hollywood Cinema: Film Style and Mode of Production to 1960*, which argues that 1960 saw the end of the studio system mode of production and the classic Hollywood style and, incidentally, holds for an equally tendentious definition of "style" as solely a matter of narrative structure with little consideration of the ingredients of character representation, tone, and ideology. (Indeed, Bordwell's *The Way Hollywood Tells It: Story and Style in Modern Movies* goes on to contend that the classic Hollywood style has continued from the 1960s to the present, even in films that employ various new approaches in their constructions.) True, the studio-produced movie and the classic Hollywood style did continue to 1960 and even after (and is still in evidence today in some – but not all – films). But alongside these "classical" texts, many films, epicentered from 1946 to 1962, signaled a decisive break with "classical Hollywood cinema" whose heyday I would place between 1929 (the start of the Great Depression and the completion of the wiring of the American movie houses for sound) and 1945 (the end of World War II and the occurrence of the trial of the federal government's antitrust suit against the studios). Well-ordered stories with goal-oriented characters in action that proffered an ideal representation of life were not what many of these postwar films were about. The full-speed-ahead, no-nonsense thrust of story began to be undermined by moments of subjectivity and nuance. Clarity of character and meaning began to be muddied, intentionally and realistically, as the classical constructs of hero and villain became less and less applicable and the notion of absolute truth indefensible. Identification with the protagonist began to be threatened. Irksome questions, not tidy answers, were what moviegoers were being left with. Those assuring, optimistic, and feel-good classical finales were less and less in sight. And irony and self-reference abounded. Daring to violate strict narrative logic, more eager to plumb a below-the-surface realism, confident that entertainment could include the communication of ideas, and coming to believe that confrontation rather than comfort might be a viable, even longer-lasting effect, these films heralded something else. But the issue of style, more than just a matter of narrative structure, is only one difference between the postwar films and their antecedents.

Indeed, postwar Hollywood films bore witness to shifts in American politics, economics, societal issues, and the country's new forms of competing leisure activities. These works were also put together under a different set of business practices, and used alternate technologies that affected the narrative, visual, spatial, and temporal design of movies. Not as rigorously subjected to censorial structures as their forebears, these films also said new things and did things for the first time on the screen or took a bolder approach to what had already been spoken and done. Genre's classical mythologies began to be questioned; some even jettisoned and replaced, others hybridized. Tonal shifts within a movie were not that rare an occurrence anymore. To be sure, some works only partly embodied aesthetic differences from the "classical," but others disported these differences in a major way.

As such, claim could be made that these works (and there were a large number of them), in tilting with the prescribed tropes of the past, mark the start of something new in Hollywood picture making, one of those tantalizing phases of transition in the arts that British culture historian Raymond Williams talks of being a complicated blend of the residual and the emergent. Periodization, however, always presents problems. Historical eras as well as aesthetic periods just don't begin markedly and end neatly; they slop over and double back on one another in maddening fashion. And that holds true for my account of Hollywood's postwar years. Therefore, some of the films that form the basis of my argument came out shortly before 1946; some were made and released shortly after 1962. And certainly, resolutely classical film elements persist in this period.

Consequently, I feel strongly that a comprehensive history of the Hollywood fiction film, 1946–62, is warranted. The book can function as a text for my classes and similar classes around the world, whether their curriculums be devoted entirely to this period or be broad surveys in either the history of American or world cinema, for which this volume would be one in a series of texts. Moreover, this book will be of general interest for everyone who desires more knowledge of American pictures of this time, a period which is receiving new life and devotion in the rerelease of these films in the home viewing format.

The book is devoted exclusively to the Hollywood fiction feature film. Such important subjects as the American independent film, documentary, educational, experimental, avant-garde, sponsored, newsreel, cartoon, short subject, and foreign cinema will be incorporated only as they relate to or influence the theatrical feature film made by American picture outfits.

Six parts comprise the work, with the overall movement from context to text. Part I, "Cultural Overview: The Years of Change in America, 1946–1962," summarizes the nation's major historical events, its economic situation, societal issues, and other leisure activities with which movies were in competition. These aspects of culture were actual generators, explicitly and implicitly, of the way

Hollywood worked and consequently envisioned the world in its products. Avoiding the useless one-line time graphs or culture-bites of some film histories, an entire chapter is devoted to postwar American culture so that the reader can, in a deeper way, understand and appreciate how postwar movies said what they said, all the while noting their differences with what went before and why.

Part II, "Business," deals with the economic developments and business practices of the Hollywood film industry. Each of the industry's main components (production, distribution, and exhibition) is covered, with a view of seeing how industrial factors imprinted themselves upon the form and function of postwar films.

Part III, "Technology," surveys the medium's technological developments. In addition to covering the major shifts (from black and white to color, from Academy ratio to large screen, monaural to stereo, etc.), this part also details the more subtle changes in cameras, lenses, lighting, film stock, sound-recording equipment, and so on, that affected the kinds of pictures that were made and the style in which they were made.

Part IV, "Censorship," describes the censorship restrictions and, more importantly, the weakening of censorship that gave Hollywood pictures a freedom long denied. This freedom, of which Hollywood took full advantage, helped to make the films of this time unique. The content and presentational constraints imposed by the Production Code Administration, the Catholic Legion of Decency, state censor boards, obscenity prosecutions, extralegal devices of public officials, and foreign censors, as well as their evolving parameters, are profiled.

Just about all the salient genres are the concerns of Part V, "Genre." The myth, conventions, and iconography of the each respective genre are laid out. The directions in which each genre traveled are assessed: why, how, to what effect? Equally important is the consideration of the practitioners that fashioned these molds, be they independent producers, directors, or writers, tenuously associated with, turned loose from, or untouched by the studio.

The final Part VI, "Style," includes a discussion of Hollywood classical style, to better show Hollywood's departure with its excursions into expressionism and new degrees of realism, at times even modernism.

In these two aesthetic parts of the book (genre and style), extra-cinematic determinations or influences (major historical events, the economic situation, societal issues, other popular leisure activities) as well as cinematic determinations (the film business, technology, censorship) are shown to be pivotal in postwar genre configuration and reconfiguration and the embrace of certain styles.

Part I is, in a sense, the set-up. From Part II onward, film exemplification begins. In Parts III through VI, the heart of the matter, exemplification exists alongside the analysis of seminal films. These closely analyzed films are out-standing examples which illustrate the culture/filmmaking interface, or the tri-umphs and failures of Hollywood business, or developments in the technological area, or challenges to the prevailing censorship barriers, or the key artistic works in terms of genre and style (and sometimes all of the above). These films' seminal status also involves their slide from classical paradigms.

In the mention and discussion of films, the book is intended to be generous. By being so, it hopes to redress and make amends for the usual scanty, stereo-typic, and unfair exclusivity in the film selection that accompanies those sec-tions on postwar Hollywood in other textbooks, which ultimately belie the richness and diversity of this period.

Preface:
How to Use this Book

The book has three goals: (1) to impart some sense of the postwar culture as well as history of the industry's new way of doing business, its technological scramble, its sabotaging of censorship, and its preferred molds and styles; (2) to give an understanding of how interpenetrating extra-cinematic as well as cinematic factors determine a movie; and (3) to spot the significant differences between postwar films and their predecessors. The book ends with a select bibliography which, in addition to the endnotes, directs the reader to more information.

Now arises the question of how to use this book for a course: consecutively, not quite; hopping back and forth, well almost. A sample 16-week syllabus could go something like this.

Week 1 – Topic: Cultural Overview/Extra-Cinematic Determinations (Major Historical Events/Economic Situation/Societal Issues)
Screening: *A Place in the Sun* (P, 1950).[1]

First: discuss how major historical events, the economic situation, and societal issues constitute meanings in a film, while exemplifying such postwar issues as the Cold War, consumer culture and the American dream, middle-classness, the male in crisis, the female as stabilizer/destabilizer, etc., in the film. Second: address the issue of genre (male and romance melodramas) and signature of George Stevens. (Every week, an enumeration of the respective film's cultural determinations should precede delineation of genre.)
Readings: Part I/Chapter 1, Major Historical Events, Chapter 2, Economic Situation, Chapter 3, Societal Issues; Part V/Chapter 16.3, Male Melodrama, Chapter 16.4, Romance.

Week 2 – Topic: Cultural Overview/Extra-Cinematic Determinations (Other Popular Leisure Activities)
Screening: *Funny Face* (P, 1957)

After pinpointing the film's cultural determinants, discuss how popular leisure activities determine a film, with special emphasis on the musical stage. Focus then on the musical genre and the imprints of producer Roger Edens and director Stanley Donen.
Readings: Part I/Chapter 4, Other Popular Leisure Activities; Part V/Chapter 17.1, Musical Comedy and Musical Drama.

Week 3 – Topic: Business Practices/Independent Production,
UA and Runaway Production
Screening: *The African Queen* (UA, 1952)

Following an apprizing of the film's cultural determinants, show how business practices determine a film. Contrast independent production with the studio system, privileging UA and runaway production. Contrast UA with independent production at P (*A Place in the Sun*, an in-house independent feature). Finally, defend the film as an adventure and independent producer–director John Huston's distinctive traits.
Readings: Part II/Chapter 5.1–5.6, The Antitrust Suit Wrap-up and Fallout to Runaway Production; Chapter 5.8.2, Paramount; Part V/Chapter 11, Adventure.

Week 4 – Topic: Business Practices/The Industry and HUAC
Screening: *The Manchurian Candidate* (UA, 1962)

Narrow in on the film's cultural determinants, then the relationship of the industry and HUAC. Go on to present the film as a Cold War thriller–black comedy and the stylings of director John Frankenheimer.
Readings: Part II/Chapter 5.7–5.10, Diversification to Distribution Practices; Part V/Chapter 14.7, Black Comedy; Chapter 19.1, World War II and Cold War Thriller.

Week 5 – Topic: Business Practices/Diversification and Technology/1-Strip
Ansco Color and CinemaScope and Widescreen
Screening: *Love Me or Leave Me* (MGM, 1955)

After an illustration of the film's cultural determinants and industrial diversification with special emphasis on recordings and radio and MGM, discuss how technology determines a film. Next, set out the color situation and screen-shape revolution (multi-camera, anamorphic systems, widescreen, as seen in *The*

Manchurian Candidate), all the while contrasting these respective screen sizes with the classic ratio of *A Place in the Sun* and *The African Queen*. Define the film as a musical biography as well as director Charles Vidor's contributions.
Readings: Part II/Chapter 5.8.5, MGM, 5.7, Diversification; Part III/Chapters 7.1 to 8.3, Ansco Color and Metrocolor to Widescreen; Part V/Chapter 17.2, Musical Biography.

Week 6 – Topic: Technology/3-Strip Technicolor, Super Technirama 70, and Vista Vision
Screening: *Spartacus* (U, 1960)

Zero in on the film's postwar cultural issues, Kirk Douglas's independent company Byrna, and U. Next, discuss 3-strip color, Super Technirama 70, and Vista Vision (*Funny Face*). Then analyze the film as an historical spectacle as well as the shadings of director Stanley Kubrick and writer–adapter Dalton Trumbo.
Readings: Part II/Chapter 5.8.7, Universal; Part III/Chapters 8.4 to 8.5, Wide-Frame Systems to The 70 mm/Wide-Gauge Process; Part V/Chapter 13, Historical Spectacle.

Week 7 – Topic: Censorship
Screening: *From Here to Eternity* (C, 1953)

The film's addressing of postwar culture sets up a look at how censorial structures determine a film, the postwar transition in censorship, and Columbia. Next, consider the genre of male melodrama and director Fred Zinnemann's inflections.
Readings: Part II/Chapter 5.8.6, Columbia; Part IV/Chapters 10.1 to 10.11, beginning to *From Here to Eternity* (C, 1953); Part V/Chapter 16.3, Male Melodrama.

Week 8 – Topic: Censorship
Screening: *Anatomy of a Murder* (C, 1959)

Elucidate the film's take on postwar culture and the independent production scene at Columbia; and finish the discussion on the transition in censorship, highlighting the censorship problems with *A Place in the Sun*, *Love Me or Leave Me*, and *Spartacus*. Go on to define the genres of the social problem film and courtroom drama as well as independent producer–director Otto Preminger's voice; and title design.
Readings: Part II/Chapter 5.8.6, Columbia; Part V/Chapter 18, Social Problem and Courtroom Drama; Part VI/Chapter 24, Other Stylistic Devices (titles).

Week 9 – Topic: Genre/Family Melodrama
Screening: *Picnic* (C, 1955)

Underline the film's cultural references and the censorship problem. Discuss the concept of genre as a determination on a film. Finally, examine the genre of family melodrama as well as writer William Inge's trademarks.
Reading: Part V/Chapter 16.1, Family Melodrama.

Week 10 – Topic: Genre/Romantic Comedy
Screening: *Pillow Talk* (U, 1959)

How did postwar culture inscribe the film? How did it jump its censorial hurdles? What is romantic comedy (and how does it differ with other subforms of comedy)? What were producer Ross Hunter and writer Stanley Shapiro's inputs? Why the use of a theme song?
Readings: Part IV/Chapter 10.22, *Pillow Talk* (U, 1959); Part V/Chapter 14, Comedy; Part VI/Chapter 24, Other Stylistic Devices (theme songs).

Week 11 – Topic: Genre/Horror
Screening: *Psycho* (P, 1960)

Moving from a look at cultural determinants, old and new exhibition policies, and censorship obstacles, defend the film as a horror film while dissecting the thematics and formalities of producer–director Alfred Hitchcock.
Readings: Part II/Chapter 6, Exhibition; Part IV/Chapter 10.19, *Vertigo* (P, 1958); Part V/Chapter 15, Horror.

Week 12 – Topic: Genre/Female Melodrama
Screening: *All That Heaven Allows* (U, 1955)

How does the film address postwar concerns and redress the genre of female melodrama? What are producer Ross Hunter and director Douglas Sirk's innovations?
Readings: Part V/Chapter 16.2, Female Melodrama; Part VI/Chapter 22.1, Determinations and Practitioners.

Week 13 – Topic: Genre/Western
Screenings: *Stagecoach* (UA, 1939) and *The Searchers* (1956)

After appreciating *The Searchers* as a reflection of postwar culture, the censorship problems involved, and independent production at WB, contrast the differences between the two films and director John Ford's vision and its implementation.
Readings: Part II/Chapter 5.8.3, WB; Part V/Chapter 21, Western.

Week 14 – Topic: Style/Noir
Screenings: *Double Indemnity* (P, 1944) and *Invasion of the Body Snatchers* (AA, 1956)

Study each film's cultural markings; censorship battles in *Double Indemnity*; the concept of the B film and mini-major Allied Artists; and the relationship of style and meanings in a film. Next, analyze the noir style: its pure expressionist mode as seen in *Double Indemnity* and its hybrid expressionist–documentary-realist mode in *Invasion of the Body Snatchers*. Review the noir style in *Love Me or Leave Me*, particularly addressing the issues of noir and color/genre/period. Then, defend the first film as a crime thriller as well as the stamp of director–cowriter Billy Wilder and writers James M. Cain/Raymond Chandler; the second film as horror–sci-fi as well as the stamp of director Don Siegel. Exemplify the expressionism in *A Place in the Sun*, *The Manchurian Candidate*, *Spartacus*, *Anatomy of a Murder*, *All That Heaven Allows*, and *The Searchers*.
Readings: Part II/Chapter 5.3, The Decline and Shift in Product; Chapter 5.8.11, Monogram–Allied Artists; Part IV/Chapter 10.3, *Double Indemnity*; Part V/Chapter 19, Suspense Thriller; Chapter 15.1, Horror–Sci-Fi; Part VI/Chapter 22, Noir.

Week 15 – Topic: Style/Documentary Realism
Screening: *The Bridge on the River Kwai* (C, 1957)

From an unraveling of the film's cultural strands and the Hollywood–London connection, concentrate on the film's documentary realist style, all the while noting a new definition of entertainment. Present the work as a war film as well as independent producer Sam Spiegel and director David Lean's aesthetic personalities. Exemplify the documentary realism in *A Place in the Sun*, *The African Queen*, *The Manchurian Candidate*, *Spartacus*, *From Here to Eternity*, *Anatomy of a Murder*, and *The Searchers*.
Readings: Part II/Chapter 5.6, Runaway production; Chapter 5.8.6, Columbia; Part V/Chapter 20, War; Part VI/Chapters 23.1–23.2, 23.4, Documentary Realism.

Week 16 – Topic: Style/Psychological–Sociological Realism
Screening: *I'll Cry Tomorrow* (MGM, 1955)

After unpacking the film's cultural determinants and its psychological–sociological realist style, proceed to position the film as a biography with the distinct colorings of director Daniel Mann. Review the psychological–sociological realism of *Picnic*.
Readings: Part V/Chapter 12, Biography; Part VI/Chapters 23.3–23.4, Psychological–Sociological Realism.

Note

1   A film is characterized by its distributor and American release date. However, the first letter(s) of the studio stands in for the studio, as here, P/Paramount and thereafter, AA/Allied Artists, Buena Vista/BV, C/Columbia, EL/Eagle-Lion, M/Monogram, MGM/Metro-Goldwyn-Mayer, PRC/Producer's Releasing Corporation, R/Republic, RKO/Radio-Keith-Orpheum, SRO/Selznick Releasing Organization, TCF/Twentieth Century-Fox, UA/United Artists, U/Universal, and WB/Warner Bros.

Part I
Cultural Overview: The Years of Change in America, 1946–62

Introduction

The years 1946–62 in America were, most characteristically, ones of transition. World War II made just about everything come unstuck and begin to shift, giving a lie to the belief that, postwar, political ideology, family life, the role of the male and female, and morality were fixed. Both profound and pervasive, these changes set the stage for the tumultuous sixties and early seventies and continue to shape America and its people today. The attempt to sublimate, mask, even deny the dislocation that change inevitably prompts was also characteristic of this time. The suppression took many forms. Chief among them was the country's overcompensation in terms of conformity, which, in insisting upon an extrinsic model of behavior, blocked the unique self. Another form of suppression was the country's determinedly upbeat mood, whereby nagging doubts and worries were held in check, camouflaged, or transcended, at least for a while. Such instances of suppression, more than anything else, were responsible for the picture we still often endorse of the postwar era as one of halcyon bliss. It was anything but.

1

Major Historical Events

Introduction

Any investigation into the Hollywood fiction film, no matter the period, must begin with that period's historical events. So ours begins here. A key influence, though coming as it does from "outside" of cinema, historical events determine the medium at any given time and each individual text. They provide situations, stories, settings, and distinct types of people; issues and attitudes; images and sounds for films.

1.1 The Cold War

Journalists and politicians used the term "The Cold War"[1] to express the animosity between the United States (USA) and the Union of Soviet Socialist Republics (USSR), democracy and totalitarianism, and capitalism and communism, which escalated as World War II wound down. So far-reaching and enduring was this enmity that historians have often used the term to designate the entire postwar period.[2]

Shortly after the surrender of Germany, Premier Josef Stalin, having already annexed the Baltic States and parts of Poland, Finland, and Romania, began to set up communist governments in every Eastern European nation except Austria and Czechoslovakia. The Soviet Union was immediately perceived by most Americans as an imperialist nation set upon the complete domination of the world.

Democrat President Harry S. Truman (1884–1972), Roosevelt's Vice-President who succeeded him upon his death in 1945 and was reelected in a shock victory over Thomas Dewey in 1948, reorganized the nation's defense. The National Security Act of 1947 consolidated the Departments of the Army,

Navy, and Air Force into the Department of Defense, created the cabinet post of Secretary of Defense, and mobilized the Central Intelligence Agency (CIA). The two primary instruments of American foreign policy were the Truman Doctrine and the Marshall Plan (named after the Secretary of State). Promising assistance to any nation battling communism, the Truman Doctrine simplistically laid the cornerstone of American foreign policy for years to come: any government, no matter how fascist, dishonest, or incompetent, warranted America's aid, if it was hostile to the USSR. Equally an anti-communist ploy, the Marshall Plan pumped money into Western Europe to put it back on its economic feet, thereby aiding the economy of the USA, which looked to Europe for mutual trade.

In 1948, the Soviets seized Czechoslovakia and blocked all railroad, waterway, and highway routes through East Germany to Berlin's American, French, and British sectors, hoping to push the remaining allies out of the divided city. A gigantic airlift of supplies to Berlin frustrated the Soviet gambit, ending the blockade in 1949. In that year, the USA, along with Canada, Iceland, and 11 Western European nations, formed the North Atlantic Treaty Organization (NATO). Headed by the war's European Supreme Allied Commander, General Dwight D. Eisenhower (1890–1969), NATO began to pool armed forces powerful enough to withstand any attack from Eastern Europe. The myth of an isolationist America, free from foreign entanglements, was now a thing of the past.

In the Far East, communist revolutionary Mao Zedong brought a bloody three-year civil war to a climax by driving the Chinese Nationalists toward the South and proclaiming the existence of the People's Republic of China in 1949.[3] In the following year, North Korea, with Soviet planes, tanks, and trained officers, crossed the 38th Parallel which divided the communist North from the free South. The UN Security Council voted unanimously to dispatch a combined military force to repel the invading North Korean, and later Chinese, armies.[4] In the so-called Korean War (1950–53), 25,604 US troops were killed, 103,492 wounded, and 7,995 reported as missing in action. Truman sought a negotiated settlement. The Korean fracas, the first twentieth-century conflict the US did not win, shattered the myth of American invincibility, generating considerable anger and frustration at home.

Geneva was the site of the first US–USSR summit conference in 1955. President Eisenhower (Republican), who had trounced liberal Adlai Stevenson in both the 1952 and 1956 campaigns, reached an understanding with Premier Nicolai A. Bulganin and First Secretary Nikita S. Khrushchev.[5] Detente fizzled out in the following year when Soviet tanks pulverized the Hungarian revolution and the USSR threatened to send troops to assist Egypt against an Israeli attack. Alarmed at the spread of the Cold War to the Middle East, Congress passed the Eisenhower Doctrine in 1957, allowing the President to employ armed force to help any country which asked for assistance against armed aggression from a communist nation.

The Cold War spread to Latin America in 1960 when Fidel Castro seized American property and set up a communist dictatorship in Cuba with Moscow's imprimatur. Some 1,500 Cuban nationals, aided by the CIA and given the go-ahead by President John F. Kennedy (Democrat, 1917–63), who had defeated Eisenhower's VP Richard M. Nixon in the 1960 election, attempted to wrest Cuba from Castro. The Bay of Pigs invasion was a bust.

Despite the 1961 Vienna parley of Kennedy and Khrushchev on nuclear disarmament and troubles in Laos and Berlin, the USA escalated its military forces in Southeast Asia and the USSR erected the Berlin Wall, dividing the city into two distinct sectors. The US blockade of Cuba in 1962, though it brought the two megapowers to the brink of war, did force Cuba to dismantle its Soviet bases and strategically placed Soviet missiles.

The Cold War overseas made America paranoid at home. Adopting the consensus position, most Americans were skeptical about dissent. Faultfinding and derogation, they believed, made the country vulnerable to communist infiltration. Highly problematic was any deviation from Cold War orthodoxy, which came down to the fear, hatred, and eradication not only of the card-carrying, the fallen-away or, as in most cases, the suspected commie, but the foreigner, the intellectual, the radical and, warming the hearts of most anti-New Dealer politicos, the liberal as well.[6] Xenophobia riddled the land, setting off witchhunts, loyalty oaths, confessions, indictments, and restrictions galore.

The House of Representatives Un-American Activities Committee (HUAC), formed in 1938 to investigate subversive elements in all areas of American life and recommend legislation, was put on hold for the duration of the war. It returned to service in 1945. Labor unions were the initial target. In 1947, a loyalty security program was set up wherein the Federal Bureau of Investigation (FBI) began to check out government workers. Not one of the more than 15,000 in question was found to be an active party member. Two were dismissed as risks while 100 were suspected and lost their jobs.[7]

HUAC's main agenda in 1947, however, was "the communist infiltration of the Motion Picture Industry Activities in the United States." Chaired by J. Parnell Thomas and lasting two weeks, the probe charged ten witnesses, who refused to answer the question, "Are you now, or have you ever been a member of the communist party?" with contempt of Congress. All served jail sentences. The showbiz inquests, with their own built-in publicity, occupied HUAC's attention more or less for the next ten years.

HUAC went after communists in the State Department in 1948 when *Time* journalists Whittaker Chambers and Elizabeth Bentley confessed to espionage and named fellow communists. The Committee turned into a feeding-frenzy after Senator Joseph McCarthy's (Republican) speech to a woman's club in Wheeling, West Virginia in 1950 in which he claimed to have "a list of numerous communists known to the Secretary of State who are still working and making policy in the State Department – 205 to be exact." That year, the perjury conviction of former State Department official Alger Hiss, whom Chambers had named, was HUAC–McCarthy's one and only major coup.

The McCarran Act of 1950 (also known as the International Security Act) made communist and communist-front organizations register with the Subversive Activities Control Board. McCarran's follow-up measure of 1952 set immigration quotas, rejected subversives and aliens associated with totalitarian governments, and deported immigrants turned American citizens who joined communist organizations.

HUAC went on to ransack the legal, medical, and educational associations in the hope of smoking out communists. In 1952, the Supreme Court declared those "considered" subversives could be barred from teaching in public schools. The government set up bodies at state, county, and local levels to ban communist and subversive materials.

The year 1954 saw the end of McCarthy's career. The steely-principled TV journalist Edward R. Murrow and producer Fred Friendly had courageously indicted McCarthy as someone who unscrupulously preyed on the nation's fears for his own political aggrandizement. In the televised Army vs. McCarthy hearings, the vindictive, cruel demagogue from Wisconsin had been hoist by his own petard.[8] The Senate had chimed in with censure. The fires of hysteria were banked. Three years later, however, confessed Soviet spy Jack Sobel fanned the flames once again. That year, FBI chief J. Edgar Hoover's *Masters of Deceit*, a "non-fiction account of the insidious, imperialist maneuvers of communism," became a bestseller. In 1960, Air Force Secretary Dudley C. Sharp reported before HUAC that the American clergy was infested with communists, particularly the National Council of Churches (NCC).[9] In 1962, American communists were barred from traveling abroad.

Additionally, the battle of the bombs and the space race kept the Cold War hot. Four years after the USA dropped atomic bombs on Hiroshima and Nagasaki to force Japan's surrender and conclude the war in the Pacific, the USSR numbered an A-bomb among its possessions. The USA, in turn, developed more powerful bombs. Four times the power of the A-bomb, Edward Teller's hydrogen bomb was tested in 1952. The USSR exploded one in 1953. By 1960, the USA had stockpiled 18,000 nuclear weapons. In 1958, the US Air Force's Strategic Air Command mounted an intercontinental ballistic missile system, a year after the USSR had experimented with one. Civil defense exercises became part of the curriculum of every school. Kennedy enjoined families to add bomb shelters to their homes in case of atomic fallout. Science was now perceived as a mixed blessing. The naïve dream of atomic containment became a nightmare.

With its 1957 launch of *Sputnik I*, the USSR leapt ahead of America in the space race. This shocking development led to the establishment of the National Aeronautics and Space Agency (NASA) in 1958 and the passage of the National Defense Education Act, which provided substantial loans to college students. The Act encouraged graduate fellowship programs that prioritized science, mathematics, and foreign language studies. The same year, American put its first two satellites, *Explorer I* and *Vanguard I*, into orbit. In 1961, USSR's Yuri Gagarin orbited the globe, the first man to do so. US astronauts John Glenn, Scott Carpenter, and Walter N. Schirra made the trip a year later. Postwar experiments with rocketry and interest in the possibility of space travel, coupled with the Cold War fear of foreign takeover, had much to do with countless sightings of unidentified flying objects (UFOs) throughout the period. The year 1952 was a banner year, with 15,000 sightings,[10] and the Air Force's publication of photographs of the phenomenon.

1.2   Civil Rights

The embarrassing irony of the "separate but equal" status of black Americans in light of recently won battles against Hitler's theory of Aryan supremacy and Japan's elitist ideology contributed to a growing consciousness *of* and *in* minorities. The migration of blacks to northern industrial centers, which occurred immediately after the war and again in the mid-1950s, also played its part. Truman, seeing himself as an extender of Roosevelt's New Deal and angry at the HUAC brouhaha which infringed on civil rights, issued *To Secure These Rights* in 1946, a Presidential Committee report and dry run for his Fair Deal legislation. Aimed at toppling racial barriers and bolstering civil rights, the report declared, among other things, that segregated institutions would forfeit government financial support and, furthermore, the claims of Japanese Americans, evacuated in detention camps during World War II, would be settled. Congress consented to Truman's opening all jobs in the armed services to blacks and abolishing the military racial quota in 1948, but resisted most of the progressive legislation of his Fair Deal of 1949.

A Topeka, Kansas grammar school in 1950, not Washington's Oval Office, was the site of an unparalleled civil rights breakthrough. When his daughter Linda was barred from enrolling on the basis of her skin color, Oliver Brown confronted the Board of Education. The case wended its way to the Supreme Court. Four years later, America's highest court, with Earl Warren (Republican) in charge, in a single ruling that included four other similar cases, declared racial segregation in public schools unconstitutional.

After a black sit-in and boycott of buses in Montgomery, Alabama in 1955, segregation on buses in Alabama was deemed unconstitutional and the Interstate Commerce Commission banned segregation on interstate trains and buses. Black groups solidified, among them the Rev. Martin Luther King's Southern Christian Leadership Conference, advocating Gandhian nonviolent resistance. In 1961, seven black and six white "Freedom Riders" rode buses, defying segregation laws in transport terminals, diners, and gas stations in the upper and deep South. A year later, James H. Meredith, after being denied admission to the University of Mississippi, eventually registered. The Defense Department ordered full racial integration in its military reserve units, except for the National Guard. Segregation laws within and between state transportation facilities were ruled unconstitutional.

Many factors supported this burgeoning consciousness and helped readjust attitudes about blacks. Writings about the black man's struggle for identity reached a degree of popularity, such as Ralph Ellison's *Invisible Man* (1952). Jackie Robinson signed with the Brooklyn Dodgers, breaking professional baseball's color line in 1947. The New York Philharmonic's performance of Howard Swanson's "Short Symphony" in 1950 met with acclaim. Black rock-and-roll performers and their beat-conscious music made kids of all races shake their booties. In 1957, singer Nat King Cole hosted a TV network show; in 1959, Benjamin O. Davis, Jr. became the first black general in US history.

Conclusion

The Cold War affected business practices, especially in the industry's various responses to the HUAC witch-hunt and the slate of propagandistic anti-commie films. More importantly, however, the Cold War facilitated the industry's shift from a predominantly centrist conservative political ideology, adhered to and demonstrated by most studios (excepting WB and UA) to a predominantly liberal one. In addition, the industry's technological advances were egged on, in part, by the desire to show off the superiority of US technology over that of the USSR. The Cold War's indirect support of censorship naturally slowed, but did not stop the overhaul of the process. It particularly affected the genres of social satire, horror–sci-fi, family melodrama, the thriller, and the war film. Transgenerically, the dissent/consensus debate colored the conflictual strategy of most postwar films. Individuality – finding it; holding on to it – was a primary trait of the protagonist.

1-1   *Young Man with a Horn* (WB, 1950, p. Jerry Wald)
Blacks begin to make a notable entrance in postwar movies, as in this demythed musical biography, with Kirk Douglas's trumpeter sharing the frame with his black surrogate father-mentor-inspiration-friend (Juano Hernandez).

With the thrust of civil rights, more people of color, played by people of color, appeared on the screen, and not just in supporting roles. The racial stereotype became rare. The civil rights issue, particularly the race question, helped rid censorship of its miscegenation taboo. Race became an issue in most genres, and not just in the social problem film, constituting a character's identity problem.

Notes

1   American journalist Herbert Bayard Swope suggested the term "Cold War," initially used to characterize the Nazi way of taking over countries with little bloodshed, to statesman Bernard M. Baruch, who used it in a speech before the Senate Wars Investigating Committee in 1946. Journalist Walter Lippmann entitled a book *The Cold War* in 1947.

2   In the 1960s, Marxist historians took a revisionist stance on the Cold War, placing the blame principally at the door of the USA. John Patrick Diggins, in his excellent history *The Proud Decades: America In War and Peace, 1941–1960* (New York: Norton, 1988), repudiated the four main points of these revisionist histories on pages 67–72, namely: (a) America's failure to open a second front early in the war and lopping off lend-lease to Russia at the close of the war made Russia suspicious; (b) Truman's bombing of Hiroshima; (c) America's economic power over conquered Europe was a way of sustaining a capitalized system; (d) Soviet motivation was "defensive and cautious," not "radical and expansionist."

3   Chinese communism differed from the Eastern European brand. Rather than a satellite of the Soviet Union, China declared itself a nation alongside the USSR.

4   The Soviet Union staged a walkout during the discussion of the Korean situation in the Security Council. The vote, which required unanimity among the Council's members to send a combined force to Korea, was accomplished in the USSR's absence. This was the last time the USSR missed a Security Council vote.

5   After Stalin's death in 1953, Georgy M. Malenkov, Stalin's heir apparent, took over. Within the year, a power struggle developed between Malenkov and First Secretary of State Nikita S. Khrushchev, who got control of the party machinery and replaced Malenkov with his puppet Nicolay A. Bulganin. Khrushchev eventually became premier.

6   Some historians, as with I. F. Stone (*The Truman Era*, New York: Random House, Vintage Books, 1973), believed intramural fighting between the Republicans and Democrats was as responsible for the Red Scare in America, as were Soviet imperialist policies.

7   According to Allan Nevins and Henry Steele Commanger, *A Pocket History of the United States* (New York: Washington Square Press, 1986), 498, the American Communist Party numbered 75,000 in 1947, a dozen of whom were indicted each year between 1948 and 1952.

8   When G. David Schine, one of McCarthy's assistants, was drafted, McCarthy charged the army with undermining his search of communists in the military service. During the investigation, McCarthy attempted to besmirch the reputation of army special Counsel Joseph Welch by accusing Welch's law firm of having employed ex-communist Fred Fischer. Welch held his ground, saying that Fischer, when aware of the pro-communist activities of the Lawyers Guild which he had joined, left the organization. Welch then confronted McCarthy by asking the senator why he had now brought up the Fischer matter since he and his committee had been acquainted with Fischer for a long time.

9   Formed in 1950, the NCC comprised about thirty Protestant and Orthodox denominations which worked together educating, proselytizing, and providing social welfare and medical aid to people at home and in foreign countries.

10 David Michael Jacob, *The UFO Controversy in America* (Bloomington: Indiana University Press, 1975), 87.

2
Economic Situation

Introduction

A technology, an entertainment, an art form, a communication medium, and a cultural product, film is also a business connected with the economic situation of the country in which the industry is located and the film is produced. The state of a nation's economy can help explain a movie's specific financial outlay, along with its attendance record. The recessions of the late 1950s, for example, contributed to the industry's 1958–62 financial slump, resulting in, among other things, a cutback in the number of films in color.

2.1 Economic Resurgence

Despite increasing deficits owing to foreign aid and defense expenditure ($12.5 billion in 1958–9, a peacetime record), and slight recessions in 1949, 1953, 1954, and two in the late 1950s, this was a time of immense economic resurgence. With the veterans' return, the baby boom, and the influx of European refugees, which swelled the population (to 179 million by 1960 from 130 million in 1941), the demand for goods, housing, cars, health care, education, and many other services soared. Prices for these goods and services were inflated now that wage and price controls were continually being lifted. Wages in 1950 were up 130 percent from their 1939 level; average hourly earnings were rising at 2.5 percent annually. Money was available, whether from the interest accruing from deposits held by veterans and their families in banks, or from government loans, or the credit card, introduced in 1950. America's allies, too, wanted these goods and services. Conversely, America's fascination with European goods (German cars, Swiss watches, Italian films) also increased.

Technological advances modernized old industries (aircraft, locomotive, and construction) and launched new ones (electronics, communications, and plastics), while turning Americans into technophiliacs. Previously unheard-of products such as Dacron and chlorophyll flooded store counters. America's industrial output was two and a half times greater than it had been at the start of the Depression. Americans produced two-thirds of the world's manufactured goods. The economic gap between the North and the South closed. With the booming of the defense and space industries, the Sun Belt of New Mexico, Arizona, and Southern California became the new Eden. Dr. John W. Mauchly and J. Preper Eckert, Jr.'s demonstration of ENIAC in 1946 and their electronic digital UNIVAC in 1951 inaugurated the knowledge revolution in technology as well as the computer industry.

The alliance of the Eisenhower regime with industrialists abetted this economic upswing. Eisenhower believed a flourishing economy was a very effective defense against the Soviets, while keeping Americans' mind off Cold War tensions. Eisenhower's Federal Highway Act of 1956, in particular, called for $33.5 billion to be spent over a period of 14 years to build a national network of roads which energized the construction, engineering, and auto industries while altering the lifestyle of the nation.

2.2   Post-Industrial Society

The expansion of the professional spheres (banking, academia, health care, social services, and secretarial work) also excited the economy. The so-called "Madison Avenue" professions (marketing, advertising, sales, and public relations) crystallized, spurring on consumerism. The availability of money, a shorter working week with longer paid vacations, the emphasis on personal pleasure, and the emergence of "fun morality,"[1] partly a reaction to Depression deprivation and wartime rationing, generated a boom in leisure industries. Some leisure activities redefined themselves, while others came into being. This expansion, along with factory automation, which decreased the number of assembly-line workers as it increased the number of office workers, created, from 1956 onward, a "post-industrial society."[2] White collars now outnumbered the blue. In addition, big companies began to merge into powerful corporations, some of international scope.

At the war's end, the capital gains taxation was rolled out again. This measure, by removing certain monies from taxable-ness and applying a lower-rate tax to businesses, no matter how small, also fueled the economy as people began to incorporate.

Those who discounted fears of a postwar return to the Depression and bet on the American economy profited handsomely. The stock market performed strongly, with the Dow Jones Industrial average (DJI) posting gains in 11 of the 17 years. The DJI, which hit its post-1930 high of 212.50 on May 29, 1946, had climbed to 726.01 by January 3, 1962.

Conclusion

America's sound economic situation and the availability of money helped to keep the film industry afloat during two very rough patches. More than before, outside money flowed into the business, particularly in the area of independent production, energized by capital gains taxation. Following other businesses, studios reorganized for manpower profitability; updated their product, thematically and technologically; and diversified. One studio began to transform itself into a conglomerate. More money was spent on fewer productions than before. These productions, especially the pricey items, began vociferously to use their large expenditure as a marketing/advertising ploy, slyly implanting in the buyers' minds that quantity (the outlay of big bucks) insured quality. Foreign films made inroads commercially, affecting censorship and aesthetics. All the while, the burgeoning professional spheres and the post-industrial workplace and labor force, as well as the problems therein, provided new subject matter and conflict for movies.

Notes

1   See Martha Wolfenstein, "The Emergence of Fun Morality," *Journal of Social Issues*, 7:4, 1951.
2   Daniel Bell, *The End of Ideology: On the Exhaustion of Political Ideas In the 50s* (New York: Free Press, 1960).

3

Societal Issues

Introduction

Societal issues are yet another important extra-cinematic determinant of a film. They include cultural values; the image and function of the male/female/child; lifestyles, including sexuality; and the institutional interface. Moreover, as with historical events, societal issues provide topics for film.

3.1   Consumer Culture and Middle-Classness

The economic resurgence spawned a powerful consumer culture, nourished in part by the imminent possibility of a nuclear war: a nebulous future led Americans to prize acquisition and consumption in the here-and-now. A "middle-classness" solidified, designating an economic stratification (an annual income of $5,000 or over after taxes) as well as materialist and conformist attitudes. Described as the "American way of life," it was held up as an ideal: never had so many people (80 percent of whites fell into this category) had so much in the history of mankind. An emblem of this new class was the shopping mall, with its anchor department store that displaced a local government building or house of worship as the cynosure of the mushrooming suburban sprawl.

Journalist Vance Packard hurled a triple assault at the "American way of life." Big business/big government were *The Hidden Persuaders* (1957),[1] turning the public into Pavlovian animals through the tactics of motivation research. Americans were taught how and what to buy in terms of brand loyalties. *The Status Seekers* (1959)[2] theorized that all behavior was controlled by a drive for status, producing compulsive behavior and a concern for symbols of success in lieu of genuine achievement. *The Waste Makers* (1960)[3] argued that the American economy and the acquisition-relieving tension preached by Madison Avenue hatched a nation of gluttons. Products, built with planned obsolescence, were replaced by others. Newness was valued for its own sake. There were too many of the same kinds of everything.

3.2   The American Male

Consumer culture was not the only reason why many males were addled, insecure, and defensive. Veterans bore the physical scars (World War II left 670,000 wounded). Many were damaged psychologically, having experienced bombings and the death of comrades (400,000 were killed), and then having to face the bugbears of civilian readjustment (the loss of male bonding, for starters). As World War II gave way to the Cold War, particularly the Korean conflict and the defense and rebuilding of Europe, many wondered what exactly, if anything, victory had achieved. Another kind of totalitarianism, coupled with the threat of nuclear annihilation, now encircled the globe, endangering their own nation's freedom.

Assisted by the GI Bill of Rights of 1944–56, 7.8 million veterans enrolled in college or technical schools, less for an education than for the credentials that would help secure a high-paying job which would, in turn, enable them to start a family, buy a home, and be part of the new consumer class.[4] In the workplace, big business squeezed out the little man. Factory automation and corporate mergers fueled the fear of being laid off. Many who ventured into big business or any other bureaucratic system sadly experienced the diminution of self-reliance, creativity, and risk-taking in their jobs now that they were under the thumb of "the organization," wherein the administrative group mentality kept in check, if not subsumed, individual potential. The Social Ethic ("a belief in the group as source of creativity . . . in 'belongingness' as the ultimate need for the individual")[5] replaced the Protestant Ethic ("the pursuit of individual salvation through hard work, thrift, and competitive struggle").[6]

The first Kinsey report on *The Sexual Behavior in the Human Male*,[7] a nonfiction bestseller in 1948, also unnerved many men, less in terms of its statistics than in its enlightened conclusions. The "social significance" of the research flew in the face of existing moral and legal attitudes with regard to extramarital intercourse (a desirable part of growth) and homosexuality (an expression of capacities basic in the human animal).[8] The main gist of the report – that no two people are alike in sexual matters – was a slap in the face for the era's conformity code. The publication marked the beginning of the ubiquitously popular discussion of sex in American society.

The formation of the Mattachine Society, the first US gay rights organization, and ex-GI George Jorgensen's 1952 sex-change operation and subsequent emergence as "Christine" (and a celebrity to boot) gave many men concern. Civil rights breakthroughs caused many black men to painfully redefine themselves, while it forced many white males to perceive black people (and other people of color) differently.

From 1953, *Playboy*'s glossy advertisements of imported liquors, colognes, designer clothes, sport cars, and so on made its male readers feel special while broadening that particular market base. Its well-written articles, cartoons, and centerfolds (Marilyn was the first) valorized the single life, sex as play and an end in itself, thus opening up a new world.

Jack Kerouac's novel *On the Road* (1956) represented the road (not the home) and freedom (not responsibility) as sources of beatitude. Kerouac, along with poets Allen Ginsberg and Gregory Corso, was part of the Beatnik movement. Championing spontaneity, personal freedom, racial and sexual equality, self-exploration through meditation, and an acceptance of homosexuality, the beatniks offered an alternative lifestyle that included a look (beards, stringy long hair, black turtlenecks, sandals).

The medical profession shifted "from genetic to psychosocial explanations of men's biological frailty,"[9] dangerously signaling that too much responsibility with its attendant stress factors had caused a decrease in the male life span. Psychology, too, switched its axis, supplanting "maturity as the universal development goal"[10] and mark of adulthood involving, as it did, marriage, family, job, and civic duties with Abraham Maslow's doctrine of growth. Maslow advocated the goodness of basic instincts and spontaneity and saw life as an ongoing, ever mutating, endless adventure in the realization of one's potential. These factors contributed to "the collapse of the breadwinner ethic . . . a male revolt" against commitment and responsibility "well before the revival of feminism."[11]

The image and function of the American male that had evolved in American society and culture from its beginnings were no longer tenable. The male became detached from his moorings, drifting toward new, possible shores of relocation and redefinition.

3.3   The American Female

Another contributing factor to the tension of many males were females, many of whom found themselves in their own state of flux. Women's war effort at the front (100,000 nurses) and at home – where they constituted 36 percent of the work force and toiled more efficiently and carefully than men, though for less pay – gave many a woman a sense of herself.

Postwar, three million women were dumped from the work force. In many cases, believing their termination necessary (where would the men find work?) and accepting religious pronouncements that matrimony was sacred as well as Madison Avenue's representation of it as an ideal, many women opted for marriage, many of them at the remarkably young ages of 18 and 19. Were their true feelings submerged? By the early fifties, things changed. The female work force began to increase. While consumerism forced many into the marketplace, a sense of independence undoubtedly motivated others. Marriage did not seem to yield the full satisfaction promised. Many women's looks changed with their attitudes. Many shed their shoulder-length locks and upswept mound of hair for poodle clips and the shaggier Italian cuts, similar to the in-vogue, close-cropped male hairdo. Many also dyed their hair blonde in the hope of having "more fun," as the ad promised.

Kinsey's *The Sexual Behavior in the Human Female*,[12] an immediate 1953 page-turner, seemingly broadened the female viewpoint on premarital and postmarital sex and homosexuality.[13] Betty Friedan's seminal work on female consciousness, *The Feminine Mystique* (1963), depicted postwar American women as victims of a culture that convinced them that the fulfillment of their femininity was found in sexual passivity, male domination, and nurturing maternal love. This culture refused to allow women to grow and fulfill their potential as human beings. Woman's resultant disillusionment and malaise were relieved by a search for "strained glamor"[14] (another form of suppression).

3.4   The American Family

Suburbia was the symbolic setting for the middle-class family. The ex-GIs' need for room to raise their families, increasing automobile ownership, and the growing network of roads led to an urban-to-suburban exodus for many whites. The move of Southern blacks to Northern cities was an additional factor. Tracts of similar houses with two-car garages (one a station wagon) and similar barbecue pits in the backyard for sizzling steaks (the favorite meal) stood on similar tree-lined avenues, a mile or so from the spanking new mecca of department stores/supermarket/beauty salon/dentist office/movie theatre/gasoline station, and, a little further out, country club. Suburbia approximated the serenity, spaciousness, and greenness of country life (big bay windows and glass patio doors slid open to connect the suburban home directly to the outdoors) and guaranteed the conformity so dear to the spirit of the times. Conformity promised security; security, happiness.

But happiness came with a weird aftertaste. Locked in comfortable domains, many of these married males, bombarded by changes and options they never saw coming, agonized. Many females felt existential unease – although they could not put their finger on the cause of it just yet, it was, nevertheless, real. The couples' scramble for material goods became a lifestyle propelled by the drive to "keep up with the Joneses." Yes, the all-consuming material success ethic bred role-playing and other forms of hypocrisy, but it did provide another way to fit in, be accepted, and feel good – well, sort of. Additionally, it was a proof of accomplishment, a symbol of status and power, and an expression of one's identity. Or was it? Consumer indebtedness rose, three times as much as private income. Americans smoked, drank, and ate more than ever before. The nation's divorce rate also reflected societal pressures. After a record number of divorces in the immediate postwar years (610,000 in 1946), there was a decrease to 318,000 in 1951. After slight increases in 1952 and 1953, and slight decreases in 1954 and 1955, there occurred a steady rise from 381,000 in 1956 to 428,000 in 1962.[15]

With many dads working overtime or moonlighting and perhaps even moms working to maintain a standard of living they were accustomed to or expected to maintain, many children were neglected, left to map their own course through adolescence. The introduction of the TV dinner in 1954 (turkey, sweet potato, and pie cooked in a frozen-food container) meant that the family no longer needed to eat together. That and car availability made spatial fragmentation inevitable. The generation gap (the difference between the ethos of Depression-raised parents from that of their postwar offspring) resulted in temporal fragmentation. Most industries exacerbated this gap. Recognizing that, for the first time in America, youth as a group constituted a considerable and distinct market from adults, business catered to this new powerful class. Most diligent of all were the mass media, providing kids with a look and sound markedly different from those of their parents. Adolescence, as a social not biological fact, did not exist until the fifties.

3.5　Juvenile Delinquency

In cities, crimes by juveniles (18 or under), often organized in ethnic gangs undergoing acculturative angst, increased. Suburban juveniles engaged in drunkenness and disorder. Respect for authority appeared to be eroding among young people, and juvenile delinquency became the object of Senate Subcommittee probes in 1951 and 1954. President Kennedy signed a bill authorizing $30 million to fight juvenile delinquency in 1961. A new kind of doctor (the social worker/counselor/psychologist/psychiatrist) became an extended member of many families, dealing with juveniles and suburban parents as well. The psychiatrist, actually was accepted into society with the treatment of traumatized war veterans.

3.6   Sensuality, Sex, and Violence

Images of sensuality were more pervasive, compliments of Madison Avenue, *Playboy*, and the fashion world. Where the forties made female legs a fetish, the fifties fixated on breasts. Other parts of the female anatomy were not ignored, just relegated to a third glance, as with bare midriffs. The male torso also became an object of desire.

Sex outside of marriage was in many cases more mental than physical. Just because it was on everybody's mind, or seemed to be, and because it was now a favorite topic of conversation (thanks to Kinsey), it did not mean that everybody was doing it. By 1960, things started to change when the Food and Drug Administration approved an oral contraceptive known as "the pill," which was endorsed by Protestant leaders out of overpopulation fears. The 100th General Assembly of Southern Protestant Churches decreed that marital sexual relations without the intent of procreation were not sinful.

Newsreels and magazine/newspaper photos of World War II bombings and carnage as well as TV news coverage of the Korean War, racial outbursts, and football games made Americans at once curious about and inured to images of violence.

3.7   Social Morality

Concerning social morality, America turned inward. Frequently, "how to" tomes (*Look Younger Live Longer*, or *How I Raised Myself from Failure to Success in Selling*) became nonfiction bestsellers, all centered on the private sphere and the attainment of status and power. The "thingification" of American society also fostered a political and social quietism. So much of people's energy was invested in the accumulation of material goods that there was little time for anything else, let alone socially conscious pursuits. Besides, social consciousness ran the risk of defying conformity and thus easily could be construed as subversive. Such behavioral patterns, of course, were yet other instances of sublimation. More and more, the peer group, mass media, and society in general shaped America's value system, making an American less a person, more a personality.[16]

3.8   Crime

Organized crime received more press than before, simply because it turned most people on and sold papers. The larger-than-life figure of the criminal offered, vicariously, a refreshing antidote to the ordinary citizen. Mobster Bugsy Siegel opened the Flamingo Hotel in Las Vegas in 1946, substantiating the already suspect connection between the underworld and Las Vegas, the so-called "entertainment capital of the world." The outcome of Estes Kefauver's (Democrat) 1951 Senate Committee confirmed a rumor persistently denied by FBI head J. Edgar Hoover: the existence of nationwide criminal organizations. Called "syndicates," these organizations controlled gambling, labor racketeering, narcotics, prostitution, and were linked with boxing. White-collar crime grabbed the headlines every now and then: government graft and bribery; big business price fixing; TV quiz-show rigging and perjury; and "payola," the practice of record companies paying disc jockeys and other radio personnel to play their recordings on the air, thereby stifling competition.

3.9   Religion

Despite the US Supreme Court's abolition of the teaching of religion in the classroom in 1948, a religious revival permeated the land. A host of nonfiction religious books were continually spotted on the bestseller lists, including Protestant minister Norman Vincent Peale's *The Power of Positive Thinking*, Trappist monk Thomas Merton's bio *The Seven Story Mountain*, and the eight-times-listed Bible. In 1946, Pope Pius XII elevated to sainthood Mother Cabrini, the first American to enter this pantheon. Seminaries and convents had to find more room. Church and synagogue attendance continually rose, as did church construction. According to NCC's 1959 report, 64 percent of the population attended church. Polls, canvassing Americans' belief in God, registered in the 90th percentile.

But religion, for most, seemed to be a further instance of suppression and sublimation. Less a wrestling with mystery or an expression of the experience with a personal transcendent or immanent being, religion was a convenience. It provided assurance for those who clung to traditional values, surely being eroded by the creeping insinuations of the many "isms" in the air. Relativism, for example, denied all external standards of right and wrong. Positivism claimed the scientific-verifiable as the only sphere of valid knowledge. Materialism rejected the supernatural. Existentialism imagined a meaningless, absurd universe wherein the positing of man's free choice constituted the only value.

Religion also blessed the avid consumer with its gospel of positive thinking and steady industriousness that brought material success, a sign of God's blessing. Further, religion relieved Cold War tensions, assuring Americans that the Almighty was on their side since the Soviet Union was an atheist nation. But Americans were fundamentally secularist, "thinking and living in terms of a framework of reality and value remote from the religious beliefs simultaneously professed."[17] Institutional religion functioned for Americans as a mere "self-identification and social location."[18]

Conclusion

Societal issues affected film business. Suburbia was in part responsible for dwindling audiences and the modification of venues. The baby boom at first made yearly grosses decline significantly but eventually helped to stabilize them. Societal issues impacted upon aesthetics. The consumer culture/middle-classness supplied sharper arrows in social satire's quiver. The crisis in masculinity remapped adventure, shed a different light on bios, war, and the West while handing male melodrama a place in the sun. The besieged male, the "in-flux" female, and *Playboy* ignited romantic comedy. The female's burgeoning self-awareness empowered female melodrama. Infatuation with sensuality pumped the blood back into the anemic love story. Family melodrama bloomed while the nuclear unit withered. The teenager gave the musical a rock-and-roll twist and horror a youth spin. The religious revival kept fantasy and fantasy-comedy believable and hatched, in part, horror–sci-fi. Crime, the postwar kind, expanded the thriller's turf while the culture's inurement to violence rendered that turf harsh and brutal. As well, the films themselves, no matter the type, raised, debated, even grappled with these issues (especially sex), forcing censorship to rethink itself and forged new modes of representation. Sex had been the stuff of movies since the beginning, but the topic emblazoned postwar screens more than even in the pre-Code-enforcement decade.

Notes

1   Vance Packard, *The Hidden Persuaders* (New York: David McKay, 1957).
2   Vance Packard, *The Status Seekers: An Exploration of Class Behavior in America and the Hidden Barriers That Affect You, Your Community, Your Future* (New York: David McKay, 1959).
3   Vance Packard, *The Waste Makers* (New York: David McKay, 1960).
4   Diggins, 99.
5   William H. Whyte, *The Organization Man* (New York: Simon & Schuster, 1956), 14.

6 Ibid., 4.

7 Alfred C. Kinsey (1894–1956), Professor of Zoology at Indiana University, along with research associates Wardell B. Pomeroy and Clyde E. Martin, spent nine years of research in which 12,000 persons contributed case histories (a 300 to 500-question interview) and 5,300 males provided data from each and every age, every social level, several racial groups, and from all sections of the country, with a concentration in the Northeast. *About the Kinsey Report* (1948), a paperback of 11 essays by doctors, social scientists, theologians, and educators that offered positive commentary, outsold the report itself. Also that year, a simplified paperback version of the report, *American Sexual Behavior and the Kinsey Report*, appeared.

8 Alfred C, Kinsey, *The Sexual Behavior in the Human Male* (Philadelphia and London: W. B. Saunders, 1948), 559–662, 664.

9 Barbara Ehrenreich, *Hearts of Men: American Dreams and the Flight from Commitment* (Garden City, NY: Anchor Press/Doubleday, 1983), 70.

10 Ibid., 88.

11 Ibid., 12, 13.

12 Kinsey, along with research associates Pomeroy, Martin, and Paul H. Gerhard, carried out 15 years of research in which 5,940 white non-prison females contributed case histories (personal interviews) while 1,849 additional females, belonging to special groups not included in the statistical analysis, extended their observations. A decade later, another Kinsey report on female sexuality was published by the Kinsey Institute, contradicting some findings of the earlier work – none, however, that are listed in this chapter.

13 Alfred C. Kinsey, *The Sexual Behavior in the Human Female* (Philadelphia and London: W. B. Saunders, 1953), 328, 432–6.

14 Betty Freidan, *The Feminine Mystique* (New York: Norton, 1963).

15 See *Divorces and Divorce Rates, United States* (Hyattsville, MD: Department of Health, Education and Welfare, National Center for Health Statistics, March 1978).

16 David Riesman, *The Lonely Crowd: A Study of the Changing American Character* (New Haven, CT: Yale University Press, 1950). Riesman, with co-authors Nathan Glazer and Reuel Denney, revised the work in 1955.

17 Will Herberg, *Protestant–Catholic–Jew: An Essay in American Religious Sociology* (Garden City, NY: Doubleday, 1955), 14.

18 Ibid., 70.

4

Other Popular Leisure Activities

Introduction

Other leisure activities are yet another extra-cinematic determination of the industry and its products. As a competing leisure activity, film uses molds and materials from other popular leisure pursuits while enticing their personnel. More: film itself is a bastard phenomenon, made up of elements from other diversions. As such, film has continually trumpeted that what other entertainments, arts, and media do, it can do even better.

After the war, more leisure pursuits greeted Americans than ever before. Moreover, Americans had more time and the wherewithal to spend on amusements. Keenly aware of the stiffer challenges, Hollywood scrambled to compete.

4.1   Television

Postwar, television became *the* mass medium. It usurped this powerful role from radio, forcing radio to reformulate itself. It provoked a startling transformation in the nation's moviegoing habits. It cut into the theater and reading audiences. Television extended the spectator base for sports, allying it with the entertainment and advertising industries. It opened up the fashion world and, with its commercials, spurred on consumerism.

The high cost of a TV set (a 10-inch RCA Victor black-and-white (b/w), open-face console retailed at $375 in 1946) deterred only a few. In 1950, 9 percent of American households enshrined the box in their living room; four years later, 55.7 percent; and in 1962, 90 percent.[1] Broadcast hours expanded, infiltrating waking and sleeping hours as well as afternoons. At the start of 1948, 17 stations broadcasting in 8 cities mushroomed to 108 stations in 23 cities by the year's end. The Federal Communications Commission (FCC), after a four-year ban on station growth, permitted an increase in the number of stations to 1,051 – 809 commercial and 242 noncommercial or educational. Cable TV, first available in 1949, brought TV to homes outside the reach of stations through microwave-radio relay. American Telephone and Telegraph (AT&T) cables and microwave relays linked the East and West coasts in 1951. AT&T's orbiting satellite linked the globe in 1962.

TV technology continually improved. By 1956, shooting in high-fidelity videotape supplanted live recording and the airing of shoddy kinescope copies, made by filming in 16 mm film stock off a monitor and taking three days to reproduce. Networks and stations now had the ability to record and immediately reproduce picture and sound magnetically on tape. Over-the-air pay TV was a possibility by 1950. In 1953, the FCC gave RCA/National Broadcasting System's (NBC) compatible color system the green light. Only when the price of a color set dropped (a 15-inch RCA Victor open-face console sold for $1,100 in 1954) and the quantity of color programming rose (32 hours per week by 1960) did the sale of color TVs become a popular item.

Nightly 15-minute news broadcasts, begun by CBS News with anchorman Douglas Edwards in 1948,[2] and NBC's John Patrick Swayze in 1949, conferred eyewitness status of world events upon the viewer. The televising of Senate investigations and White House press conferences, as well as Edward R. Murrow and Fred Friendly's prototypical in-depth documentary series "See It Now" (1952–5),[3] raising such polemical topics as nuclear technology or hunger in America, kept people informed. The early-morning chatter of Dave Garroway on "The Today Show" (1952) and the late-night witty conversation of Steve Allen and Jack Paar – in 1954 and 1957, respectively – on "The Tonight Show" gave people company.

In documenting the Presidential Conventions of 1952 and 1956, TV helped win the election. The public opted for the image of the warmly smiling Eisenhower over the serious-visaged Stevenson even though the ex-military commander's rhetoric, unlike that of the focused senator, was vague. In the first of the four televised candidate debates in the 1960 election, Kennedy's aplomb and good bone structure gave him the edge on the perspiring, scowling, five-o'clock-shadowed Nixon, who was more adept at discussing the issues. The importance of image over issue in politics, TV confirmed, could not be overestimated.

Just about all of TV's formulas, including the aforementioned news and talk shows, came from radio. The majority of shows, no matter the genre, were transplanted radio programs and, in the very beginning, were simultaneously broadcast. Since radio broadcasting networks moved into TV first, it made perfect economic sense that they would use material and personnel already in place.

Appropriating the situation-comedy (sitcom) pattern of stereotypic characters getting in and then out of scrapes established by radio's "Amos and Andy" in 1928, most of the countless TV sitcoms centered around the middle-class family. "I Love Lucy" (1951–7), with Lucille Ball as a housewife always cooking up some plan, and real-life husband Desi Arnaz as her bandleader spouse, ruled the roost. "The Honeymooners" (1955–66), with bus driver Jackie Gleason, refreshingly dealt with the working class.

Crime series were another staple. Both the hardboiled school of detection of "Martin Kane, Private Eye" (1949–54) and the gentlemanly sleuthing of British homicide expert "Mark Saber" (1951–60) paved the way for the cool, glamorous, swinging detectives-in-exotic-locales of "77 Sunset Strip" (1958–64). While detectives dipped in popularity, flatfoots increased. The matter-of-fact style of "Dragnet" (1952–9), with Jack Webb solving cases from the Los Angeles Police Department files, set the standard. "Dragnet" spawned "The Lineup" (1954–60), whose actual case stories were produced with the San Francisco Police Department, and "The Untouchables" (1959–63), a breakthrough in its depiction of violence and detailed re-creation of the thirties.

Westerns were the leading action genre, from the radio transplant "The Lone Ranger" (1949–57) through the innovative adult westerns "Gunsmoke" (1955–75) to the parodic "Maverick" (1957–62). The "adult" sci-fi/fantasy anthology series, such as "Tales of Tomorrow" (1951–3) and Rod Serling's "The Twilight Zone" (1959–64), countered the juvenile "Captain Video and His Rangers" kind that appeared in the early years.

Live and New York-based (the move to Hollywood began in earnest in 1956[4]), TV's link with Broadway proved advantageous. The connection, involving as it did the appropriation of source material, actors, and craft, resulted in no less than two dozen drama anthology series, from the experimental "Kraft Television Theater" (1947–58) to the prestigiously mounted "Playhouse 90" (1956–60). Inspired by "Lux Radio Theater" and "Theater Guild of the Air," each series presented an adapted stage play, classical (*Twelfth Night*) or contemporary (*Dial M for Murder*); occasionally an adapted novel (*Wuthering Heights*) or film (*To Each His Own*); or an original teleplay in a weekly, bimonthly, or monthly 60- or 90-minute slot.

It was, however, in the area of the original teleplay that distinction arose. Writers appeared who respected the medium's penchant for intimacy and topicality, character and dialogue. Conceived at the outset with TV's time frame, small screen, and family viewership in mind, these usually family melodramas were comfortably right for the medium, unlike the works sourced from novels, plays, or films, more skeletal accommodations than adaptations. Paddy Chayefsky's "Marty" (1953), Rod Serling's "Patterns" (1955), Horton Foote's "The Trip To Bountiful" (1953), J. P. Miller's "The Days of Wine and Roses" (1958), Reginald Rose's "Twelve Angry Men" (1958), Robert Alan Arthur's "A Man Is Ten Feet Tall" (1953), and William Gibson's "The Miracle Worker"

(1957) held their own alongside the era's best-written theater pieces and screenplays.

Television produced its fair share of adapted musicals ("Peter Pan"), and occasionally fashioned musicals from the ground up ("Our Town," librettist David Shaw and tunesmiths Sammy Cahn and Jimmy Van Heusen's take on Thornton Wilder's revered play). The TV variety show emphasized either comic acts ("Your Show of Shows," 1950–4, with Sid Caesar and Imogene Coca) or piled on the musical numbers ("The Dinah Shore Show," 1949–63). Columnist turned host Ed Sullivan's "Toast of the Town" (1947–71) was a grab bag of the latest, most celebrated showbiz acts, including comic routines, songs and dances, stage interludes, animal acts, magic, acrobatics, clips from soon-to-be-released movies, and appearances by popular stars plugging themselves and their work.

Initially, TV converted radio's game-show formats ("Break the Bank," 1948–57), then came up with some of its own ("Pantomime Quiz," 1950–63, with theater folk playing charades). Uncle Bob Smith's "Howdy Doody" (1947–60) was a puppet show for kids while Dick Clark's "American Bandstand," which after local success in Philadelphia in 1952 went network in 1957, was a dance hall for teens. For sports enthusiasts, TV aired major league baseball's World Series, professional and collegiate football games, roller derbies, wrestling and boxing matches, and such special events as the 1956 summer and winter Olympics. And TV presented old movies, B films from the thirties and forties (westerns mostly) and some British films, occupying about one-fifth of broadcast time. Hollywood's pre-1948 A and B films appeared in 1956. The airing of Hollywood's post-1948 A films in prime time in 1961 considerably expanded the movies' rerun time on TV.

In its "try anything, hit or miss" infancy from 1948–56, TV showed such overall imagination and versatility that later critics called the period a "golden age," warranting the industry's own self-congratulatory Emmy Awards,[5] first presented in 1949. By the end of the fifties, however, East coast intellectuals and educators began to lash out at America's mass-media culture, targeting TV as the main culprit. They attacked TV's falseness, stereotyping, homogenization of reality, repetitiveness, and profit motive, all of which, they maintained, wreaked havoc on the artistic and intellectual life of the land. Harshest of all was FCC Chairman Newton Minow's description of TV as "a vast wasteland."

4.2   Recordings and Radio

Technological advances ushered in the high-fidelity/stereo era, boosting the industry's $200 million national gross in 1951 to $513 million in 1961.[6] Columbia's[7] development of the 33⅓ rpm long-playing record (LP) in 1948 delivered more sound (each 12-inch side held about 23 minutes of music), better sound quality (now that tape was used in recording), and durability (the record was made of sturdy Vinylite plastic). By the mid-fifties, the LP album had replaced the inferior-sounding 12-inch, 4-minutes-on-each-side 78 rpm record made of clay and shellac. Hi-fi consoles and/or component systems became part of the furniture in one of three homes in 1951; one of two, a decade later. In 1958, stereophonic or multichanneled records and phonographs appeared in stores.

Changes in pop music also contributed to this boom. Postwar, the spotlight shifted from the big bands and their swing music (Les Brown) to individual vocalists (Frank Sinatra) and their mellow pop sound. Pop was noted for its full-blown orchestrations, even rhythms, flowery verse, idealized view of life, and potent emotion. Disc jockeys, plugging songs on the radio while chatting about the singers, were hugely responsible for the switch. TV furthered this personalization by giving faces to voices ("The Perry Como Show"; the airing of 3-minute sight-and-sound tapes or "telerecords," a forerunner of MTV).

With the availability of portable magnetic tape equipment, innumerable small outfits emerged,[8] attuned to the country's diverse regional sounds. Country western was one such sound, with its spare fiddle/guitar/mandolin/bass fiddle accents, singsong rhythms, simplistic talk, earthiness, and shameless sentimentality. Another was the rhythm and blues (R&B) of urban blacks, with its equally spare instrumentation highlighting saxophone, piano, guitar, and drums; staccato rhythms; beats that overpowered words; sensuality, visceral affect, and blaring volume inviting people to move their bodies. Radio spinners were invaluable in getting this provincial music heard. Mainstream companies signed country artists and "covered"[9] R&B hits by having white contractees perform similar renditions.

If Bill Haley and the Comets' cover hit "Rock Around the Clock" broke down the door of white pop balladry, Elvis Presley's slew of hits ("Don't Be Cruel") tore the roof off. Presley's R&B/hillbilly/gospel sound made him the hottest thing in records from 1956 to 1963. Dark good looks topped by a head of glistening shoe-black hair and long sideburns; rhythm-shaking limbs and gyrating pelvis; and a respectful manner offstage, charmed. Gifted white artists, the wild Jerry Lee Lewis ("Whole Lotta Shakin' Goin' On") and the sweet Buddy Holly ("That'll Be the Day"), or black dynamos Chuck Berry ("Maybellene"), Fats Domino ("Blueberry Hill"), and Little Richard ("Tutti-Frutti") were mere princes in King Presley's realm of "Rock and Roll" (R&R), as DJ Alan Freed christened the "race" music, pushing it out of the ghetto and onto the white side of town.

By the early sixties, cover hits were passé as black R&R performers gained acceptance. From Berry Gordy's Motown Records came Mary Wells and the Contours and Martha and the Vandellas ("Heat Wave"). The "Motown

Sound," created by a talented group of musicians culled from jazz and blues clubs who called themselves "The Funk Brothers," was a distinctly slicker R&R sound.

The gigantic teen market, twelve million strong in 1955, essentially put R&R on the charts. It was their voice, a note-perfect expression of just how different they were from their parents. The outcry of the adult world, from church and civil officials to moms and dads, against this "jungle music" made this difference more resounding. The new sound, too, was an attack, albeit camouflaged, against the conformity surrounding the teens.

Original-cast, complete-score show albums and movie soundtracks came into fashion. The intellectual/college set grooved on jazz recordings: the stylings of saxophonist John Coltrane, Billie Holliday wailings, or the snappy Dave Brubeck Quartet.

The entry of chain stores, supermarkets, and major department stores into the retail record business kept the industry humming. With the growth of record clubs (mail-order merchandising where LPs were purchased by members at lower prices with a pledge to buy a certain number of records each year), the humming became a buzz. In 1958, the industry inaugurated the "Grammy Awards" as a badge of excellence.

However, the foremost advertiser and seller of records was radio, omnipresent in homes, cars, or dangling from a teenager's hand in the form of a transistor. Compelled to abandon its format of diverse types of programs for a mass audience because of TV's takeover, stations, by 1954, turned to broadcasting one of the many genres of music for a local audience. A disc jockey as emcee and chief reader of commercials interrupted the music half-hourly or hourly with a 5-minute news update.

4.3   Theater

Broadway showed signs of commercial curdling: fewer productions and hits than before, rising mounting costs and ticket price increases (the maximum of $3.50 for a drama or comedy and $4.85 for a musical in 1944 doubled to $7.15 and $8.60 by 1960). Aesthetically, though, it was a time of ferment. Electrifying audiences with their psychological-sociological realism were playwrights Tennessee Williams (*A Streetcar Named Desire*, 1947[10]), William Inge (*Come Back, Little Sheba*, 1950), and Arthur Miller (*Death of a Salesman*, 1949). Complementing this revered trio were Robert Anderson (*Tea and Sympathy*, 1953), N. Richard Nash (*The Rainmaker*, 1954), Carson McCullers (*A Member of the Wedding*, 1950), Michael Gazzo (*A Hatful of Rain*, 1955), and James Leo Herlihy and William Noble (*Blue Denim*, 1958). Linking arms with the new kids on the block were reemergents Lillian Hellman (*Another Part of the Forest*, 1946) and Clifford Odets (*The Big Knife*, 1949).

All bore the genes of America's first great dramatist Eugene O'Neill (1888–1953), who enjoyed rekindled interest. As with O'Neill, who brought Freud and Marx into American drama, they created complex people (the angel/superego and demon/id in each) and focused on inner conflicts, insisting upon the significance of dreams, the past, and sexuality, as well as the role of socioeconomic class in the makeup of a character. Following O'Neill, they contextualized their dramas in terms of the family in a particular region of the land.

The issues (psychic turmoil, family bust-up, repressive societal structures) were startlingly recognizable. The raw confessional mode, especially in dealing with rape, nymphomania, incest, homosexuality, castration, and drug addiction, was heart-rending, as was the Method, a new type of acting that proved a perfect fit for the playwrights' style.

The Method was a variation of Constantin Stanislavsky's (1863–1938) scientific system of behavioral realism,[11] practiced at the Moscow Art Theatre which he co-founded in 1897. For Stanislavsky, creating a character was the work of gathering the precious raw materials of emotive memory (dredging up an emotion similar to one in the play from one's own life), perceptual observation (carefully studying a character in real life similar to the one in the play), and ensemble playing (relating to the other actors on stage). Also part of Stanislavsky's theory and practice was the delineation of the director's functions as both mediator between playwright and actor and as chief orchestrator of a production.

In 1931, Lee Strasberg and Harold Clurman, who had studied Stanislavsky at the American Lab Theater along with Cheryl Crawford, formed the agitprop Group Theater (1931–41). For these radical lefties, theater was a means to social change and their take on the Method, a way to expedite their goal. Group Theater actor, writer, and director Elia Kazan, hand-in-hand with fellow alumni Crawford and Robert Lewis, opened the Actor's Studio in Manhattan in 1947, a place where an actor could begin or continue to learn his craft. By now, Kazan was a hotshot bicoastal director, nabbing in 1947 both the Tony for Miller's *All My Sons* (the first time the award, named after actress Antoinette Perry and founded by the American Theater Wing, had been given[12]) and the Oscar for *Gentleman's Agreement* (TCF). In 1948, Strasberg replaced Lewis as teacher of the Method.

The Studio trained a different kind of performer. To watch Marlon Brando or Joanne Woodward, among many others, was to believe in the character on stage as a living person. Directors such as Joshua Logan, Martin Ritt, and Daniel Mann appeared, who were sensitive to the new style of writing and acting, molding a production into an integrated entity.

Stage comedy, however, was in decline. Clichéd trifles, with hardly a thought in their heads or a sincere feeling in their hearts, ruled the day (Norman Krasna's *Who Was That Lady I Saw You With?*, 1958). Garson Kanin's *Born Yesterday* (1946), Moss Hart's *Light Up the Sky* (1948), George S. Kaufman and Edna Ferber's *Bravo* (1948), and Kaufman and Howard Teichman's *The Solid Gold Cadillac* (1953) did indeed shine, but hardly sparkled in the way their thirties satires did. Newcomer George Axelrod brought a raciness to his satires (*The Seven-Year Itch*, 1952; *Will Success Spoil Rock Hunter?*, 1955). Except for the Sidney Kingsley's daffy *Lunatics and Lovers* (1954), Thornton Wilder's smart overhaul of his *Merchant of Yonkers* (1938) into *The Matchmaker* (1955), and Jerome Lawrence and Robert Lee's madcap adaptation of Patrick Dennis's novel *Auntie Mame*, farce was moribund. As for romantic comedy (John Van Druten's *Bell, Book and Candle*, 1950), it was, at best, competent.

The musical, in a redefining frame of mind, also brought glory. The curtain raiser was *Pal Joey* (1940), a John O'Hara story of a vainglorious yet charming heel set to Richard Rodgers and Lorenz Hart's tunes and unsentimentally directed by George Abbott. *Lady in the Dark* (1941) followed, with Moss Hart guiding his own idea about a woman in the throes of analysis, articulated by Kurt Weill's melodies and Ira Gershwin's lyrics. Most influential was composer Rodgers, lyricist-librettist Oscar Hammerstein (R&H), and director Rouben Mamoulian's *Oklahoma!* (1943). Based on Lynn Riggs's play *Green Grow the Lilacs*, *Oklahoma!* topically captured an America in transition while allegorically justifying the slaughter of Nazis with the self-defense exoneration of the protagonist's murder of a bully.

Librettos now boasted of pedigree, having descended from a solid novel, play, and, ever so frequently, a film. Librettos prided themselves on their abilities to mold engagingly lifelike characters and address present-day tensions, even when period (sexism in *Annie Get Your Gun*, 1947) or fantasy (racism in *Finian's Rainbow*, 1947). These librettos were then used to set the show's overall tone and style, fusing visual design, music, and dance. The R&H shows (from *Carousel*, 1945 to *The Sound of Music*, 1959) were fine instances of "integrated" musical drama and textbooks for many music men. Tunesmith Frederick Loewe and lyricist-librettist Alan J. Lerner even surpassed their mentors with *My Fair Lady* (1956), an almost exact translation of Shaw's *Pygmalion* save for the finale.

Other practitioners retained the concept of a solid book as source of integration but chose a satiric, knockabout attitude. Composer-lyricist Frank Loesser was the standout talent of "integrated" musical comedy, especially with Jo Swerling and Abe Burrows's Runyonesque *Guys and Dolls* (1950). *Gypsy* (1959), with Arthur Laurents's retooling of stripper Gypsy Rose Lee's nostalgic and acidic memoirs of her bulldozing stage mama and composer Jule Styne and lyricist Sondheim's *ne plus ultra* of musical scores, proved an intoxicating blend of musical drama and musical comedy.

Spearheading the choreographer-director movement that was to enlist Bob Fosse in *Redhead* (1959) and Gower Champion in *Carnival* (1961), Jerome Robbins with *West Side Story* (1957) made the choreographer a key shaper of a show. Set designers Boris Aronson, Jo Mielziner, and Oliver Smith competed with movie technology and bested TV's unimpressive visuals with spectacularly designed full sets, which took their cue from the book. Making it all come alive were the show-stoppers: singers Ethel Merman and John Raitt; singer-clowns Carol Channing and David Wayne; singer-dancers Gwen Verdon and Ray Bolger; and actors Rex Harrison and Richard Burton, who poignantly spoke the songs.

4.4   Adult Popular Fiction

The second breath of the paperback revolution revitalized the sale of adult pop fiction. Soft-covered, fit-in-your-back-pocket-sized, produced at a lower cost but in a much greater volume than its hardcover cousin and invented with the GIs in mind, Robert Fair De Graef's "Pocket Books" were priced inexpensively at 25 cents as opposed to the $2.00–$2.75 hardcover range. By 1962, paperbacks cost 95 cents; hardcovers, $7.95.

After the war, new houses sprang up. By 1960, established hardcover publishers jumped on the paperback bandwagon, turning out trade (quality-line) paperbacks alongside the 6-to-12 months' bestseller reprint. Paperbacks became the fastest growing branch of the publishing business, their sales volume eventually exceeding that of adult hardcover books.[13]

Also catalyzing the fiction boom was the proliferation of outlets and book clubs. Intermedia energization played its part too. Mika Waltari's *The Egyptian*, 1949's number one bestseller,[14] turned up in fifth place in 1954, the year of the film version's release. Social pressure of the "You-haven't-read-*The Cardinal*-yet?" variety (another instance of conformity) was a factor, as was the sharp increase in college graduates[15] in the immediate postwar years (from 186,000 in 1940 to 432,058 in 1950).[16]

The most prevalent genre of bestselling adult popular fiction[17] was male melodrama, contemporary (Herman Wouk's *Youngblood Hawke*, 1962) or period, usually set against a time of national crisis, such as Frank Yerby's *Foxes of Harrow* (1946). The "gendered" male adventure magazines (*Argosy*, *Male*, etc.), with their stories, essays and interviews, were pulpy counterparts. Much more luridly sensational and fantastic and couched in low cult prose, the well-liked entries were cheaper too, at about 35 cents a pop.

Female melodrama (Kathleen Winsor's contemporary *Star Money*, 1950; Anya Seton's period *The Winthrop Woman*, 1958) shared the second-favorite spot with family melodrama (Elizabeth Goudge's present-day set *Pilgrim's Inn*, 1948; Frances Parkinson Keyes's past-located *Blue Camellia*, 1957.) They were better written, longer versions of the short stories anthologized in *Modern Romance* and *True Confessions*, dog-eared female magazines, which sold for around 35 cents.

Only five works could be classified as historical novels, researched re-creations of actual events, such as MacKinlay Kantor's *Andersonville* (1955), capturing the life in and around a prison during the Civil War. World War II stories (Leon Uris's *Battle Cry*, 1953), however, abounded in hardcover and paperback. The social problem novel appeared sporadically with racism, the most hotly argued topic (Jerome Weidman's *The Enemy Camp*, 1958). Religious and inspirational works firmly bracketed the era (Russell Janney's *Miracle of the Bells*, 1946/7; Taylor Caldwell's *Dear and Glorious Physician*, 1959) and were, in the main, anti-science, anti-liberal, and theologically bankrupt.

Detective stories and mystery thrillers, courtroom dramas, westerns, and sci-fi, considered second-rate genres, were grist for the paperback mill. Mickey Spillane's reactionary Mike Hammer punching and lusting his way through *I, the Jury* (1947) to *Kiss Me Deadly* (1952)[18] drew a large following but nowhere near that of Erle Stanley Gardner's Perry Mason, a suave lawyer from the classical school of detection, who first entered a courtroom in 1933. By war's end, he had solved 8 mysteries; 13 years later, he could file away another 54. Gardner was *the* bestselling author. Mass-market paperback editions of thrillers, comic books which grew up with William Gaines's E.C. line (*Crime Suspensestories*, 1950), and TV wiped out all 178 crime pulp magazines by 1951. Rarely did hardcover handle mysteries (Daphne Du Maurier's *My Cousin Rachel*, 1952) and courtroom dramas (Meyer Levin's *Compulsion*, 1957), while the paperback attempted to keep the western alive, especially Louis L'Amour's 24 works (*Hondo*, 1953). Paperbacks, along with the 31 sci-fi pulp magazines (*Galaxy*) kept sci-fi robust, both in short-story and novel-length forms.

The vogue for the confessional mode of dark secrets coming to light, frank discussions of forbidden topics, intimate scenes of smoldering sexuality, also part of the stage's psychological-sociological realist melodrama, were characteristic of pop fiction and nonfiction bestsellers (madam Polly Adler's *A House Is Not a Home*, 1953). Its most lurid expression, however, was found in 1952's *Confidential* magazine which fathered twin sisters *Whisper* and *Exposed*. Blazoned with sleazy showbiz, political, and sport celebrity scandals in minimum-print-but-maximum-photo format, these magazines, seminal in the tabloidization of American culture, were towel-wrapped in nightstands or hidden under the bed by avid male and female subscribers alike.

Bestselling fiction, on the whole, reaffirmed middle-class manners and values: heterosexual romantic love, culminating in marriage; the safeguarding of the family seen as the basis of society and source of individual happiness and security. Optimism about human nature was pervasive: every problem had a solution. The individual had to triumph over conformity, though the victory did not necessarily preclude the notion of being well liked. The urge to follow one's heart rather than one's head in important matters[19] was espoused. Existential unease, despite and sometimes because of cohesive social structures, also cropped up (Sloan Wilson's *The Man in the Gray Flannel Suit*, 1955). Elaborate plotting, a result of a seemingly endless round of actions in addition to the paralleling or contrasting of the major plot strand, had much to do with the bestseller's undue length.

There were exceptions to the embrace of middle-classness (James Jones's *From Here to Eternity*, 1951/3; John O'Hara's tomes; J. D. Salinger's *Franny and Zooey*, 1962 – his influential *Catcher in the Rye*, 1951, never attained bestseller clout). Translated French bestselling novels (Simone de Beauvoir's *The Mandarins*, 1956; Françoise Sagan's *Bonjour Tristesse* and *A Certain Smile*, both 1958) were similarly iconoclastic.

Comic novels, unsurprisingly in an era of conformity, were scarce. Satire was warmly urbane (Frederick Wakeman's takeoff on radio advertising in *The Hucksters*, 1946) or interlarded with farce, blunting its sting (William Brinkley's Navy press officers in the Pacific in *Don't Go Near the Water*, 1956). In the end, these novels usually came around to embracing the middle-class values that they set out to sport with (the wedding ritual in Edward Streeter's *Father of the Bride*, 1949). Russian émigré Vladimir Nabokov's *Lolita* (1958/9) was a rarity, a highbrow hit that was anarchic and vitriolic, akin to the sensibility of other artistic, but non-bestselling, writers (Saul Bellow, *Henderson, the Rain King*, 1957; John Barth, *The End of the Road*, 1958). Most likely, *Lolita*'s suggestive situation of a middle-aged professor's obsession with a near-pubescent girl sold copies, not its blackly comedic vision or quality of its prose.

4.5   Sports, Travel, and Home Improvement

Americans took to outdoor and indoor sports, new as well as old ones, as never before.[20] Swimming, fishing, hunting, boating, and waterskiing (due to the increased production of artificial lakes and reservoirs) were popular unorganized outdoor activities. Tennis, skiing, and golf, in the main pursuits of those on upper incomes, and bowling and softball, the lure of those on lower incomes, were popular, organized open-air activities. All were part of the new postwar "fun morality." By 1962, the sporting goods industry was worth $2 billion.[21]

Consumers also spent more money attending professional and collegiate sporting events which were now firmly spectator- rather than player-centered: $116 million in 1945; $326 million by 1962. College football was the favorite, followed by major league baseball, professional football, and lastly, basketball.

Television considerably extended the spectator base for sports. The Sports Broadcasting Act of 1961 provided for the negotiation of packages between network and sports organizations which replaced the haphazard process of individual franchises negotiating separate television contracts. TV likewise enthroned professional football as the chief of American sports. Unlike baseball, football was better suited to the medium because its action was more focused, concrete, and engaging, and violent as well. Baseball's evocation of the past turned youth off. Its slow, dignified style was out of sync with modern life. America's summer vacations, built around tourism, the road, and the car, disrupted the baseball season which, for another thing, was longer and required more games than either football or basketball. The rising popularity of summer sports, such as golf and tennis,[22] also undermined the nation's "favorite pastime." Football became so popular that another league (American Football League) made a go of it.

The war created an infatuation with foreign lands. The expansion and streamlining of passenger planes made foreign travel a possibility for many people who had never previously considered it. American travelers increased from 435,000 in 1947 to 1,999,000 by 1963. Europe (before all else the Mediterranean) was the preferred destination, with the West Indies and Central America second, and South America third. The war also opened up the South Pacific as a tourist hotspot, as did Hawaiian statehood in 1959, the year that Alaska, too, was admitted into the Union. For low-income families, however, travel usually meant a trip to a US national or state recreational park, the seashore, or Disneyland in Anaheim, California, the first theme park which opened in 1955. Still many Americans' idea of a "getaway" was jumping in the car on a Sunday afternoon and driving outside the city limits to look at the endless tracts of new homes in the orderly new neighborhoods that were springing up. For these Americans, home improvement would also become a significant leisure-time activity. By the end of this period, most Americans owned their own home.

Conclusion

Other popular leisure activities influenced every aspect of film. For starters, the highly rated TV program, the SRO Broadway show, and the bestseller energized the industry's adaptation syndrome, promising, as they did, financial glory. Television and home improvement were contributing factors to shrinking audiences. The recording industry's move to stereo revolutionized sound technology. Controversial writers such as Tennessee Williams and James Jones helped to unravel the thick skein of censorship, upping the stakes of screen realism and sensationalism. Most of all, aesthetics were affected. The family sitcom kept family comedy alive; the recording industry, the musical. The theater was instrumental in the crystallizations of family melodrama and psychological-sociological realism. Print media made the thriller rougher and more real while pulling male melodrama out of its corner. Participant and spectator sports took biography along a new route, as did the tell-all nonfiction bestsellers. Travel influenced narrative (the way the story is told). It also encouraged location shoots, giving postwar films a backdrop different from the hitherto usual studio-hothouse look. Talent and craft came to the movies from television, theater, fiction, and records, altering the look, sound, and feel of movies. All along, the incorporation of other leisure pursuits convinced the industry that it was holding its own and, in some cases, besting the competition.

Notes

1   Corbett Steinberg, *TV Facts* (New York: Facts on File, 1985), 86.

2   Only prime-time network shows are considered in this description.

3   The dates of each series, from Tim Brooks and Earle March's The *Complete Dictionary of Prime Time Network Shows: 1946–Present* (New York: Ballantine Books, 1981), designate the first and last original telecasts, reruns excluded.

4   Renting space in the film studio and purchasing Los Angeles real estate did begin as early as the late forties.

5   At first called "Immy," after the "image orticon tube," an improved iconoscope or television camera picture tube, it became known as "Emmy" thereafter owing to a typographical error, which consensus felt sounded better than its original name.

6   Figures come from the Basic Industry Association of America's tabulations: *The First Four Hundred Years: III, From 1900–1984* (New York: Oxford University Press, 1988).

7   Columbia Phonograph Records is an entity distinct from the Columbia Broadcasting System and Columbia Studio.

8   Robert C. Toll in *The Entertainment Machine: The American Show Business in the Twentieth Century* (New York: Oxford University Press, 1982), 116, insightfully maintained that portable magnetic tape equipment allowed "small companies to enter the business, travel to regional musical centers, and inexpensively record and edit songs."

9   In 1951, a Chicago federal judge declared that musical arrangements were not "copyrighted property" and therefore not subject to the protection of the law.

10   The date indicated – and every subsequent date – is the date of the play's production on Broadway.

11   Stanislavsky's codification of his famous system occurred in 1909. His subsequent books on the subject: *An Actor Prepares* (New York: Theater Arts, 1936), *Building a Character*

(New York: Theater Arts, 1949), and *Creating a Role* (New York, Theater Arts, 1961) witnessed to the various emphases and thrusts the system took through the years.

12   The Tony Committee comprised theater actors, writers, and producers.

13   An excellent historical overview of the paperback, which has provided some of the facts in this section, is Kenneth C. Davis, *Two-Bit Culture: The Paperbacking of America* (Boston: Houghton, Mifflin, 1984).

14   Unless otherwise indicated, the date of the work is that of its appearance on the hardcover bestseller list.

15   Bernard Berelson, "51 Study of Reading Habits," in Bernard Rosenberg, ed., *Mass Culture: The Popular Arts in America* (Glencoe, IL: Free Press, 1965), 119–25, argued that education was the chief factor in the constitution of readership.

16   *The Statistical Abstract of the United States* (87th ed., Washington, DC: US Department of Commerce, 1966), 130.

17   The works cited have been culled from the ten bestselling hardcover fiction lists of each year, all of which found their way into paperback, as well as from significant paperback bestsellers, invariably works in the so-called "B" genres which never had a hardcover lineage. When considering hardcover bestselling fiction up to 1959, it is important to keep in mind that sales volume and longevity at times took a back seat to moral and, to a lesser extent, aesthetic decorum. Paperback bestselling lists were free of this prudery. A devastating blow was dealt to literary censorship in 1959 when, concerning Grove Press's unexpurgated version of D. H. Lawrence's *Lady Chatterley's Lover* for American audiences, Supreme Court Justice Frederick Van Pelt Bryan ruled that the postmaster was neither a specialist nor an arbiter in matters of obscenity, that the book was not obscene by the prurient interest rule, and that books must be judged as a whole, not from isolated passages.

18   Spillane's first four works appeared initially in hardcover. Sales were modest. When reprinted in paperback, however, sales went through the roof. *The Big Kill* and his subsequent work premiered in paperback. Spillane's conversion to the Jehovah's Witnesses in 1952 ended a successful career that made him the number two bestselling author.

19   William Darby, *Necessary American Fiction: Popular Literature of the 1950's* (Bowling Green, OH: Bowling Green State University Press, 1987), 3.

20   Foster Rhea Dulles, *A History of Recreation: America Learns To Play* (New York: Appleton-Century-Crofts, 1965), 347. Dulles's observations reiterated those of Robert H. Boyle in *Sport: Mirror of American Life* (Boston: Little, Brown, 1963).

21   Boyle, 174–5.

22   Benjamin Rader, *American Sports: From the Age of Folk Games to the Age of Spectators* (Englewood Cliffs, NJ: Prentice Hall, 1983), 285–6.

Part II

Business

Introduction

Postwar, Hollywood's business practices underwent seismic changes. Unprecedented not only in terms of quantity, these changes were also unique in regard to their encompassing nature. No part of the industry, from mode of production to the foreign market, from production slate to diversification, from political ideology to exhibition format, went untouched. The changes were, finally, resounding. They had crucial repercussions that steered the industry in other directions while offering a glint of contemporary procedures. Such a shift as this argues for the demarcation of these postwar years as a period distinct from the initial buildup and subsequent stabilization of Hollywood's commercial enterprise.

5

Production and Distribution

5.1   The Antitrust Suit Wrap-Up and Fallout

The government's antitrust legislation against the Big Five (Paramount Pictures, Inc.; Radio-Keith-Orpheum Corp.; Loew's, Inc., aka Metro-Goldwyn-Mayer; Twentieth Century-Fox Film Corp.; and Warner Bros. Pictures, Inc.) and the Little Three (Universal Corp.,[1] Columbia Pictures Corp., and United Artists Corp.), as well as First National Exhibitors Circuit, Inc., moved inexorably toward the final rounds. It flashpointed the beginning of the end of the studio system, auguring something new in Hollywood's way of doing business.

As far back as 1921, the Federal Trade Commission had been aware of the monopoly in the movie business, whether it be the vertical integration of the studios that brought together production, distribution, and exhibition concerns under one roof or the large exhibition circuits that cold-shouldered the small-fry independent exhibitor. In 1938, the Department of Justice filed an antitrust suit against the Big Five and the Little Three. Though Universal, Columbia, and UA did not own an exhibition empire (hence the designation "little"), they operated in collusion with the majors. The studios, along with First National, were charged with 28 separate offenses. Settled out of court, the Consent Decree of November 20, 1940 found the defendants making various concessions that would be in place for three years. In 1944, the assistant Attorney General moved for a new trial since the concessions were never meant to be remedies. For example, in 1945, the Big Five owned 3,137 of the 18,076 venues across the land. Of these 3,137 houses, 70 percent were first-run city-center movie houses that commanded 47 percent of the yearly box-office take.

On December 31, 1946, the Federal Court for the Southern District of New York handed down its final decision. Figuring that the Big Five *in toto* owned little more than one-sixth of all US houses, the court deemed that this ratio in no way could be construed as a monopoly of exhibition. It therefore found no reason to order the majors to divorce themselves from their exhibition wings, as the government had urged. The court did, however, go along with the government in charging the distributor-defendants[2] with eight counts and the exhibitor-defendants with four counts of unreasonable restraint of trade and attempt at monopoly.

These abuses were to be corrected by a new code of practices that, in the main, extended the terms of the 1940 consent decree. Distributor-defendants were forbidden to "fix minimum prices." Also disallowed was a system of "clearances" (the designation of the amount of time between showings of the same movie within a particular geographical area). Existing or future "franchise agreements" that extended the showing of pictures beyond one movie season were outlawed. "Formula deals," the determination of a license fee of a given picture by a specified percentage of the picture's national gross, were also *verboten*. Gone, too, was the practice of "master agreements," which covered feature exhibition for an entire circuit of theaters. Likewise axed was the policy of licensing a picture upon licensing another picture. A 20 percent cancellation was allowed for contracted pictures not "trade shown" (screened in advance for the exhibitor). If trade shown, cancellation was to be exercised ten days afterward. Banned, finally, was the arbitrary refusing of an exhibitor's demand to license a picture.

Further: the code laid out selling practices involving theaters the distributor did not own. A license was to be offered on each feature, notifying all exhibitors not less than 30 days in advance of the date of bids, except in a competitive area where the distributor owned a theater. The offer was to state the amount of flat rental as minimum for a specific playing time and the picture's availability. Within 15 days of receiving notice, any exhibitor might bid for the film, stating terms of the run, acceptable price, and clearance, as well as play date. Terms might be flat rental, percentage of gross, or any other form. The distributor could reject all offers, but if any were accepted, a license had to be granted to the highest responsible bidder who possessed a theater, location, and equipment adequate enough to bring about a reasonable financial return.

As far as the exhibitor-defendants went, franchise agreements, formula deals, master agreements, and any type of "pooling arrangements" (agreements between competing exhibitors and their affiliates to operate a number of theaters as one unit under common management, sharing profits by percentage) were forbidden. Theaters could not be leased to another defendant or independent operating a theater in the same competitive area for a share in the profits. Also discountenanced was the joint ownership with another defendant or independent where the interest was greater than 5 percent and less than 95 percent. Companies in this 6-to-94 percent ownership situation had to acquire from or sell to the co-owners the difference in interest within two years. If a company wished to buy out another to have the required 95 percent ownership, the company had to prove that such acquisition would not unduly restrain competition. The expansion of current theater holdings without the court's permission was also gainsaid. Finally, the booking of features through any agent known to be also acting in such manner for any independent or affiliated exhibitor was frowned upon.[3]

The 1946 decision made none of the parties completely happy. Because the decree sidestepped the issue of divorcement, the government planned to appeal. The Big Five did consider the retention of their exhibition wings a victory. True, about 1,292 jointly owned theaters were affected, but this was no great financial shakes except for Paramount and RKO who owned, wholly and jointly, most of the houses. Yet, they believed the government would appeal, pressing for complete divorcement and a ban on "cross-licensing," an agreement between companies to play each other's product. In the event, they determined to counter-appeal. They worried also about present and past damage claims that the independent exhibitor might bring against them now that some of their "practices" were deemed monopolistic and illegal.[4] That the majors could retain their theaters while they themselves were forbidden to build any more without court approval miffed the Little Three. Ironically, independent exhibitors, whose grievances the new code was meant to redress, complained most, fearing rental increases, bidding wars, and inflated real-estate costs in acquiring theaters.[5]

The government did appeal, the defendants cross-appealed, and on May 3, 1948, the Supreme Court delivered its verdict, upholding most of the points of the 1946 decree. Additionally, it nixed competitive bidding,[6] "conditional" block booking (the selling of blocks of pictures with strings attached), cross-licensing, and joint ownership of theaters. Believing the monopoly unresolved, the court found the majors guilty of restraint of trade and ordered divorcement of one of their enterprises (which came down to relinquishing their theater circuits) and divestiture (the sale of their theater holdings). The majors were to come up with a divorcement plan in one year (with full divorcement to be completed in five years) and to dispose, at once, of interest in about 1,000 theaters.[7]

On November 8, 1948, RKO appealed for a consent decree, calling for the creation of two separate entities: RKO Pictures Corp., headed by Ned E. Depinet, and RKO Theaters, with Sol J. Schwartz in charge. The division was completed on December 31, 1950. The decree also ordered the disposal of 241 jointly owned houses and the selling of its stock in 30 more. After divestiture, the RKO Theaters Corp., eventually sold to New England industrialist Albert A. List in 1953, numbered around 89 houses.[8] In this and all subsequent consent decrees, the government ruled that the newly formed theater corporation was to number no administrative personnel, in common with the disaffiliated distribution organization, and must create limited trusteeships to keep stockholders from controlling both companies.

Paramount filed on March 3, 1949 and on December 31 split into Paramount Pictures Corp., a production-distribution complex steered by Barney Balaban, and United Paramount Theaters, Inc. (UPT), with ex-attorney Leonard Goldenson in charge of 650 houses after divestiture. In 1953, UPT merged with the American Broadcasting Company (ABC) and became known as American Broadcasting-Paramount Theaters (AB-PT), with Robert E. Kintner commanding the TV division,[9] which comprised 5 TV stations, 6 FM/AM radio stations and, through affiliations, 355 radio outlets and 81 TV outlets. Thus far, it was the biggest transaction in broadcasting history. Eventually Goldenson became president and set out to bring Hollywood to television.

WB, TCF, and MGM appealed. In a final decree on February 8, 1950, the court ordered complete divorcement within three years with a proposed divorcement plan to be submitted within six months. In a separate judgment, C, U, and UA were allowed to pursue theater acquisition.

On January 4, 1951, WB obeyed, divesting itself of 56 to 77 theaters within two years. On February 28, 1953, the outfit split into Warner Bros. Pictures, Inc. with fraternal rulers Jack, Harry, and Albert, and the Stanley Warner Corp. of 334 houses sold to Simon H. Fabian and Samuel Rosen.[10]

Though Fox's Skouras brothers had vowed never to capitulate unless they retained charge of both new companies, Spyros, Charles, and George did enter a consent decree on June 7, 1951. Fox was to divest itself of some 100 of its 541 theaters within two years and diversify another 57 in specified localities if competition failed to develop there in a given time.[11] On September 27, 1952, Fox split into a production-distribution firm Twentieth Century-Fox and National Theaters, Inc., which, after diversification, numbered 356 venues. Spyros ran the studio while Charles defiantly continued on as boss of the theater organization until his death in 1954. National Theaters' VP John B. Bertero became chief two years later.

Holdout MGM, which, as late as 1950, still argued that integration was not wide enough to warrant divorcement, issued its consent decree on February 7, 1952. Outright divestiture of 24 houses and provisional divestiture of 50 others, subject to product limitation, was ordered.[12] On August 30, 1954, the firm split into Loew's/MGM, Inc. production and distribution center with Nicholas Schenck prevailing, and Loew's Theaters, Inc., comprising 112 venues which Joseph R. Vogel governed. Divorcement, however, was not completed until March 12, 1959.

Appeals, stockholder approvals, the creation of trusteeships, and financial considerations slowed down divorcement, completed only in 1959. Rising theater remodeling costs and a sagging box office caused divestiture to drag on until 1957. Divestiture was to leave the five disaffiliated circuits with half of the 3,137 theaters the majors controlled but by 1957, the circuits actually had disposed of more theaters than they were ordered to − 1,903 houses in all. The capitulation erased the former difference between the Big Five and the Little Three. Now all eight were on a par as production-distribution centers.

5.2   The Loss of the Audience

The dwindling of the audience occurred simultaneously with divorcement and divestiture. After the peak year of 1946, when 90 million Americans attended the movies every week,[13] 1951 saw 64 million; 1956, 46,530,000; and 1961, 41,634,000. These figures were even more unsettling when seen against the population upswing and soaring national income. What happened?

The exodus to suburbia and the baby boom, severing a part of the population's link with the downtown movie palaces and the neighborhood houses, while turning that sector into stay-at-homes having and caring for babies, had much to do with audience erosion. Television and, as the period rolled on, other competitive leisure activities (records, spectator and participant sports, travel, and home improvement) also chiseled away at the block of moviegoers.

Consequently, the studios saw capitulation in a new light. True, there now would be no guarantee of a run, no matter how good, bad, or indifferent a picture was, and exhibition profits could not be used, as they often were, to offset production losses. On the other hand, exhibitors faced a financially rough time. Most theaters sold off by the studios were the city-center showcases, too big and geographically undesirable owing to the urban decampment of the white middle class. Moreover, the studios still controlled distribution, a rarely unprofitable phase of the business, since distribution revenue came "off the top" of movie grosses and was determined by the amount of earnings rather than the cost of production. And the studios felt they would continue to hold sway since distribution was an extremely costly area to break into. To make a go of it, for instance, a newcomer would have needed an international network of exchanges; money to finance about 30 films a year which, at this time, came down to about $50 million; not to mention yearly overhead expenses in the neighborhood of $25–$30 million.

5.3   The Decline and Shift in Product

Minus a guaranteed outlet and audience, the studios, wisely, cut back on product. By 1962, the majors produced a mere 102 films,[14] a significant drop from a total of 362 in 1936, for instance. With supply reduced, the companies also knew that demand from exhibitors increased. This basic rule of economics gave the studios more leverage.

The outfits also pursued a policy of concentrating on A features. "Make 'em big" was a pretty good, though not sure, bet of exhibitor bidding and crowd turnout. This came down to spending more money on fewer films in terms of more production values, multiple star casts, and top directors. After 1953, the use of the latest technologies was added to the mix. Such ploys as these were enlisted to make a movie markedly different from what people got free at home. "Movies are better than ever," the companies sloganized, urging: "Don't Be a Living Room Captive – Step Out and See a Great Movie."

A fifties spin in terms of casting involved the pairing of established players with newcomers to tap both the middle-aged and youth markets (Spencer Tracy and Joan Bennett for the elders and Elizabeth Taylor and Don Taylor for the teens in *Father of the Bride*, MGM, 1950). Another casting wile was to costar a Hollywood commodity with a foreign player to beef up the film's international revenue (Clark Gable and Sophia Loren in *It Started In Naples*, P, 1960).

Adaptation of a previous sourced work was yet another financial ploy. The practice was always around, but this period chalked up more adaptations than any previous time. In pre-divorcement days, two-thirds of the product was original; 15–20 percent based on novels, 5–6 percent on plays.[15] In a 1957 statement the Writers Guild of America/West (WGA) decried the lack of original scripts, which the group figured decreased from 65 percent between 1938 and 1952 to 28 percent between 1953 and 1956.[16] The years 1957–62 saw an approximate 52 percent adaptation–48 percent original split.[17]

A bestseller, a hit show, and, additionally, a highly rated teleplay came with a presold aura, an intermedia charge. Having either been taken up by the public or, at least, talked about, these financial behemoths had "penetration": they had embedded themselves in the mind of the public. Those who had read or seen the product would buy into it again to relive the experience and/or see what the movies had done with the material. "You've read the book, now see the movie," became one of the industry's frequent selling bylines. Those who had only heard about it were now given the opportunity to see what all the fuss was about and thus, be "with it" (conform).

In addition to providing the industry with a pretty good possibility of a financial return, adaptation clearly was a way of meeting the competition from fiction, stage, and TV. If the adaptation turned out to be a commercial plum then that was, in the industry's mind, a decided case of having a leg-up on the competition. Adaptation also endowed the product with "pedigree": a proven financial and/or artistic track record. "Pedigree" further contributed to the "bigness" of a movie. Product that had credentials was also easier to get backing from bankers.

Studio consolidation, involving as it did cutting back on house-writers who had, in a most cost-effective manner, turned out scripts during the heyday of the studio, also energized the adaptation syndrome. Independent production, wherein a commercially proven novel, stage play, or teleplay was often a key element in getting the production off the ground, was equally influential.

The price of a bestseller or play naturally skyrocketed, driving up production costs. TCF shelled out $500,000 for *The Razor's Edge* (1946), Somerset Maugham's 1944 powerhouse novel. In 1961, WB purchased the musical *My Fair Lady* (1964) for $5.5 million and 47.5 percent of the film's gross over $20 million. The pre-sold aura of redoing a popular film from the past (there now was such a thing as a studio library) and the cost-saving deletion of a pricey acquisition fee expectedly increased the number of remakes.

Product was also given an international appeal, a *sine qua non* in this era when the foreign market began to count as never before. An adventure film on the recent American Air Force dropping supplies in defiance of the USSR blockade, *The Big Lift* (TCF, 1950), shot entirely in Berlin, had only two American actors in the German cast.

"Make 'em real" was yet another way to go, also mobilizing modes of production and technological factors, while influencing content and style. Such a practice plugged into, while actifying, the specialized audience of educated adults the industry decidedly started to acknowledge only in 1951 with the commercial successes of *A Streetcar Named Desire* (WB), whose $1.25 million negative cost (the price of producing a picture, minus advertising and distributor costs) snowballed into $4.8 million in rentals (the money returned to the distributor minus the exhibitor's expenses); *A Place in the Sun*'s (P) $2.3 million return on a $3.5 million investment; and *Detective Story*'s (P) $2.8 million on an average Paramount $1.1 million production.[18] "Make 'em real" was also a way to keep in step with the novel, stage play, and teleplay, all parading a new realism.

Though A features took prominence, the production of Bs was stepped up. (The war had undermined the production of B movies when cutbacks were the order of the day and pictures enjoyed extraordinarily long runs.) In fact, B movies underwent a budget upgrade from their former $400,000-and-under level. Their non-star casting practice was no longer in effect. Even their usual one-to-four week shooting schedule was lengthened. The 1946 consent decree's ban on block booking made this makeover inevitable. Now, every picture (no distinction was made between As and Bs) had to be sold individually, on its own merit and hence, competitively.

The market for Bs was still there. Audience attrition lessened the length of a run for an A, making more available playing time on the nation's screens that Bs could and did fill. Often a B (the 68-minute thriller *Jeopardy*, MGM, 1953, with Barbara Stanwyck) soloed in a first-run house for a week's run, returning a percentage of the house rental fee in lieu of the usual flat fee charged for Bs. In small towns where everyone could see an A in three days, the need for filler was even more acute. A considerable percentage of patrons in urban and rural areas were attracted to genres typical of B production: the western, thriller, or musical for the oldsters; horror and sci-fi for the youth. Bs met the double-bill format that still existed in some parts of the country (notably the Northeast) and at the faddish drive-ins. B production also kept the soundstages in Hollywood this side of desertion.

Only in the early sixties did the B film die. The simultaneous release of a movie in two or more first-run theaters in three dozen or so markets, thus upgrading second-run theaters and drive-ins to first-run status, was bone-crunching. The folding of poverty-row B mills Monogram, Producer's Releasing Corporation, and Republic also did damage. But public indifference dealt the lethal blow. Audience attrition continued and, when people did eventually go out and see a movie, the "big" A film was the draw. After all, they could see old Bs on TV. Eventually, television resurrected the B movie with its made-for-TV-movies, inaugurated by MCA/Universal/Revue Studios in 1964 with the NBC airing of the thriller *See How They Run*.

5.4   Consolidation

With fewer movies produced, consolidation seemed in order. Administration, business personnel, and staff regrouped. Layoffs and salary cuts became routine. Publicity departments were streamlined. Services, from mogul's barber to actor's elocutionist, were discontinued. To minimize the fixed payroll and reduce overhead expenses even further, talent and craft were pink-slipped. The 598 actors under contract in 1946, alas, dwindled to 207 in 1962.[19]

The popular player or key technician, of course, was retained if he wished to be, but under very different circumstances. Since the war's end, the rankling of the high-priced talent over the long-term exclusive contract in which a studio held all the trump grew bitter. Olivia de Havilland, with lawyer Martin Gang, had won her suit against Warners' contract system. (The decision was handed down in 1944 and went unreversed in Warners' appeal a year later.) No longer could a studio add 4 months without pay to a contract's length if an actor went on suspension. Also, a studio contract could run no more than seven years.

The non-exclusive contract was in (a certain amount of player-selected pictures over a certain period along with a percentage-of-profit deal). The deal often involved the talent's incorporation into a company to take advantage of capital gains tax. Talent would invest just enough money (usually talent's deferred salary) to qualify for the special taxation while the studio picked up the rest of the tab. In this way, top earners could reduce income tax by almost 20 percent.

Creative freedom added to a star's power, though the pressure to provide a hit and return a profit was still there. Autonomy likewise foregrounded the importance of the star's agent, business manager, or lawyer in wheeling and dealing (as did independent production) with the Music Corp. of America (MCA), the William Morris Agency, and Charles K. Feldman's Famous Artists controlling the talent pool. MCA ten-percenter Lew Wasserman, the man behind James Stewart's sweet 50 percent-of-the-profit-after-costs Universal deal in 1950 (*Winchester 73*), received as much press as the actor. George Chasin got Tyrone Power $250,000 upfront plus 50 percent of the net profits for *Mississippi Gambler* (U, 1953). For *Bridge on the River Kwai* (C, 1957), William Holden received 10 percent of the worldwide gross. Some stars held out for considerable upfront fees (Doris Day's $250,000 for *The Pajama Game*, WB, 1957). The surrealistic spiraling of stars' salaries began, way out of sight of an actor's weekly pay stub at a set contracted amount with slight raises every six months, as in the bygone days.

The unions' battles with studios for better wages and benefits for workers aggravated the consolidation. Cost of living increases were a major factor in rising production costs. In 1946, the negative cost of an average A feature was $900,000. By 1950, it had edged up to $1 million; jumped to $1.5 million in 1956; and hit the $2 million mark by 1961.[20] In 1932, an average A came in around $153, 000; in 1940, $304,000.

5.5   The Mode of Independent Production

With product decline and consolidation, the studios, reversing their former policy to keep independents out, increasingly welcomed them. And there were many to be welcomed,[21] now that the antitrust ruling opened up the possibility of venues and the "independent producer/corporation" bug bit house producers, players, and directors, itching for a creative say and more money. Businessmen outside the industry also galvanized the independents. Serge Semenenko, for instance, got the First National Bank of Boston to bankroll independent Hal. B. Wallis's Paramount productions in a revolving fund of $2.5 million, thus introducing New England investment bankers to movies. In addition to providing studios with additional product and income, the alliance with independents restored some of the control the rulings took from them in terms of booking product, now that *they* also distributed independent films.

In 1949, 20 percent of the 234 major studio films were independently produced. By 1957, of the 291 releases, 58 percent were indies. Quantity-wise, RKO came second; WB and C, third; P, fourth; TCF and MGM, fifth; and U brought up the rear. UA was out front.

A distribution firm founded for independents back in 1919 by Charles Chaplin, Douglas Fairbanks, D. W. Griffith, and Mary Pickford, UA[22] came into its own. The outfit set the standard other companies matched or even bettered, presaging what was to come in the industry.

To attract an independent with a "package" (a script and perhaps bankable star or director), UA honchos Arthur B. Krim and Robert G. Benjamin offered full financing (some studios promised only partial financing) for a standard distribution fee of 30 percent of the box-office "nut" (box-office gross minus exhibitor's fee) in the USA, Canada, and England; 40 percent elsewhere. They also promised a good deal of autonomy, which encouraged the personal (the Wayne-produced/directed/starred *The Alamo*, 1960); the controversial (*Night of the Hunter*, 1955, from Paul Gregory, about a greedy, murdering preacher), or the hitherto forbidden (the drug-addiction angle of *Monkey on My Back*, 1957, from Edward Small). In addition, they embraced experimentation along formal lines, which, they believed, would further distinguish UA product. The nifty B *Vice Squad* (1953), from the Sequoia-Sol Lesser group, unclassically juxtaposed two alternating but eventually intersecting stories (one: a day in the life of a police captain; the other, a crime caper).

After Benjamin and Krim and the respective producer mutually agreed upon story, casting, director, and budget over which, once set, the company kept a tight control, the independent was left alone. The film could be shot anywhere the story warranted – an inevitable decision, since UA owned no studio. (At other firms, the independent could rent soundstages and equipment, using the retained talent and craft.) The independent had the final cut, unless censoring boards' feathers were ruffled. He could review exhibition contracts and renegotiate them, and pocketed a 50 percent share of the profits (box-office gross minus the exhibitor's fee, 30 percent distribution tariff, and money borrowed from UA and its accumulating interest). In time, the rights to the product reverted to the independent (with other studios, the ownership was a matter of negotiation). UA (and the other studios) would eventually buy back those rights, certainly from the financial winners. A deal usually involved the production of several films and cross-collaterization (making up the losses of one production from the profits of another).

Sam Spiegel and director John Huston's Horizon-Romulus Pictures' *The African Queen* (1951), Huston's Romulus Pictures' *Moulin Rouge* (1952), and Stanley Kramer's Screen Plays Corp.'s *High Noon* (1952) were impressive commercial and critical starters. Kramer had had a berth at UA since 1948. After a brief desertion to Columbia, he returned in 1955 as producer-director of *Not as a Stranger*. Impresario Michael Todd realized his dream with the $6 million Oscar-winning *Around the World in Eighty Days* (1956), which raked in $22 million, becoming number 3 in the decade's top hits.

The Mirisch Co., Inc., including brothers Harold (president), Marvin (VP/secretary/treasurer), and Walter (VP/Production), along with a production manager, lawyer, and publicist, was a prominent unit. To hand a top director the best material and surround him with the best talent available while varying the product were goals manifested in some 67 features within a 15-year span, as with the distinctive *Some Like It Hot*, 1959, made by director Billy Wilder in tandem with Marilyn Monroe's Ashton Prods., co-starring Tony Curtis and Jack Lemmon.

Established and new directors alike gravitated to UA: Frank Capra (*A Hole in the Head*, 1959, in association with Frank Sinatra) and Stanley Kubrick (*Killer's Kiss*, 1955), as did actors: Bob Hope (*Paris Holiday*, 1958) and Robert Mitchum (*Thunder Road*, 1958). Harold Hecht and Burt Lancaster's 1953 deal was enviable (75 percent profits, 25 percent distribution fee, overhead allowances). And their unit did deliver the goods at the outset: *Apache* (1954); *Vera Cruz* (1954); *The Kentuckian* (1955), which Lancaster also directed; *Trapeze* (1956); and particularly *Marty* (1955), a $350,000 investment that returned $2 million and four Oscars for production/direction (Delbert Mann), acting (Ernest Borgnine), and adaptation (Paddy Cheyefsky). *Marty* was also the first American film to receive the Grand Prize at the Cannes International Film Festival. Hecht-Hill–Lancaster's new deal in 1956 (story head James Hill was promoted to full partner) was even more mouthwatering (a bonus plan based on sales volume), but their choices were too innovative (character studies, downbeat endings, the ironizing ploy) even for the adult majority for whom they were intended. With the exception of *Run Silent, Run Deep* (1958), all were financial flops: from *Bachelor Party* (1957) to *Summer of the Seventeenth Doll* (1960).

This mode of production was in marked contrast to the studio system in place since the late 1910s wherein the VP/Production chose the material and assigned it to a contract producer who would oversee contract writer/s in the development of the scenario. The VP/Production and producer would decide upon the contract director, one most suited to the material, mostly in terms of his financial success with previous similar efforts. All three would decide on the cast, choosing from the list of contractees before considering players contracted to rival studios or freelancers. After principal photography, the producer would again take the reins; rarely did a director have the right of a first cut. Of course, the studio owned the film.

Besides spreading the profits around, this alternative way of picture-making came with the possibility of the product being individually handcrafted instead of factory manufactured. Personal vision, now more than ever before, could subsume corporate industrialism. In innumerable cases, this is exactly what transpired. Independent production eventually eclipsed the studio system and house style: a distinct thematic and look that each studio bore, eventuating from the respective studio's use of actors, genre invocation, and approach to visual/ aural design.

5.6   Runaway Production

Runaway production – the making of a picture, wholly or in part, outside the USA – was another aspect of the production scene. It usually involved the use of location shooting, such as the Australian backdrop of *Kangaroo* (TCT, 1952). Runaway production, with its location shooting, was an attempt to counter early TV's single-set, inside-the-studio look, in the hope of seducing people away from the tiny box. It also outdid a stage production's full sets and turned the novel's prose setting into flesh and blood. Further: runaway production was a way to compete with the voguish leisure activity of travel, by taking the audience, minus the discomfort and princely cost, to any part of the globe.

Technological and aesthetic factors kicked in, of course. Color, large-screen formats, and stereo sound, as well as story values and the new styles of realism were best served by location shooting. Egypt, Hong Kong, the Tobago Keys, and Israel contributed considerably to the achievement and appeal of *Valley of the Kings* (MGM, 1954), *Love Is a Many-Splendored Thing* (TCF, 1955), *Heaven Knows, Mr. Allison* (TCF, 1957), and *Exodus* (UA, 1960). The actual world became Hollywood's soundstage, another clear affront to the studio hothouse look of the past. Runaway production also afforded more freedom to the creators since the filmmaking process took place away from the supervising money men.

But runaway production was, primarily, a matter of sound economic sense. Studio dismantling and cheaper production costs overseas put Hollywood on the go. Foreign crews, not enmeshed in restrictive union practices, actually worked anywhere from 20 to 50 percent below US scale, and materials were less costly. Rome's newly rebuilt Cinecittà studios became one of Hollywood's homes away from home. The near-guarantee of a larger foreign market in showcasing native talent in native settings was also a consideration. Also,

5-1   *The Nun's Story* (WB, 1959, p. Henry Blanke)

Even female melodramas gravitated toward location shooting, as here with Audrey Hepburn as Sister Luke in the Congo-shot documentary-realist runaway production in Widescreen and Technicolor.

independents found it easier to raise money when runaway production was part of the package.

Filming overseas also brought with it the possibility of American companies taking advantage of "frozen funds" and/or national subsidies. Other national cinemas had been devastated not only by the economic chaos of getting out from under the rubble of war but also by popular taste that preferred the polish and pretense of formerly blocked classic Hollywood films to their own country's products. To rebuild and protect their respective national film industries, Europe, and later Asia and Israel, took measures to curtail the enormous amount of American imports. Import quotas (the relationship of nationally produced films to films produced outside the country), as well as screen-time quotas (a portion of domestic films, as opposed to imports, reserved for a theater's screen time) were introduced. The transfer of American film earnings was restricted. Government subsidies were arranged for native filmmakers and/ or productions.

Take England as an example. Similarity of language made the country Hollywood's most valuable overseas customer. In addition to the quota system (20 percent domestic vs. 80 percent foreign in 1947; 45 percent domestic a year later; 40 percent domestic in 1949; then 30 percent in 1950) which, if truth be told, really did not help British cinema find its distinct voice, the Labor government, on August 7, 1947, slapped a stiff 75 percent ad valorem tax on imports. This meant that 75 percent of the expected earnings of the imported film were to be paid in advance. Up in arms, the Yanks imposed a boycott. On March 11, 1948, a compromise was reached. After subtracting the permissible amount of receipts, Hollywood could withdraw a flat $17 million annually for a period of two years. This figure could be increased by the equivalent of British film earnings in the States and indeed, in 1950, there began a $3 to $4 million yearly increase in blocked remittances. All other earnings were frozen. The money could be spent, however, by investing in British productions, coproducing with the British on native soil (RKO/Disney British Prods., Ltd.), purchasing studio real estate (but not theaters), or investing up to $2.5 million outside the film industry.

Additionally, in 1949 Parliament set up the National Film Finance Corporation as a way to funnel money to British filmmakers. In 1950, the governing body initiated the Eady Plan, whereby, through the adjustment of the entertainment rate tax, money would be rebated to producers of British productions. Though never intended to help finance US runaway production, both subsidy programs, employing extremely liberal criteria in the determination of what constituted a "British" production, did not exclude them, provided quota laws were met. This scenario (specifically, blocked foreign currency) was roughly played out in other countries as well.[23]

An amendment to the 1951 income tax law also encouraged filming overseas. To entice engineers, carpenters, and other skilled laborers to work on economic development programs overseas, Congress, in a Marshall Plan state of mind, exempted from paying tax on their earnings any US citizen who spent 17 out of 18 consecutive months abroad. Some actors (Gene Kelly), producers (Pandro S. Berman), and directors (John Huston) happily interpreted the ruling to their own advantage.

Runaway production contributed to labor unrest at home, continually shouldering the blame for the rising percentage of unemployed craft. In 1953, Roy M. Brewer, IATSE's international representative and the president of the Hollywood American Federation of Labor Film Council, claimed that 50 percent of the craft (up 25 percent from 1948) was out of work and pointed his finger at the culprit – runaway production.[24] Two years later, the Council denounced runaway production as "un-American." The Screen Actor's Guild (SAG) pointed out that of the 467 US releases in 1946 (including the product from major studios and independents), 378 were made in that country; in 1960, of the 387 releases, only 154 were home grown.

5.7 Diversification

As with many postwar industries where staying alive depended upon diversification, the studios branched out into TV and music. Competition now mutated into alliance.

5.7.1 *Television*

TV diversification divided the industry. Some, from the start, championed an immediate tie-up with TV. Paramount's TV investments started back in 1938 with the purchase of a sizable share of DuPont, manufacturer of TV equipment, and its application for experimental TV licenses in New York City. Paramount established the first station in Chicago in 1940, and another in Los Angeles in 1943. The company would have expanded into TV had not the pending anti-trust suit made the FCC look askance at its TV foray. Disney, in 1945, talked of TV's "tremendous impact." Fox's Skouras, who hailed TV as the greatest boon to pictures since sound, had in 1948, unsuccessfully negotiated with Edward J. Noble for the acquisition of ABC, offering $15 million – $6 million short of the asking price.

Others were smug, despite the gigantic yearly leaps in the sale of TV sets and the considerable dip in movie attendance during telecasts such as the 1947 Yankees–Dodgers World Series which drew 700,000 viewers. In 1950, RCA's General David Sarnoff approached MGM to become a producing partner. The company told him to get lost. By creating unmatched entertainment with the help of the competitive onslaught of new technologies and adapting the new medium for use in theaters as a supplementary activity (a concession of sorts), the diehards reckoned that movies would clobber the upstart medium, just as it had done with radio back in 1925. By 1956, when the bloom was off the technological rose, the optimism curdled, forcing the industry into an if-you-can't-lick-'em-join-'em mindset.

The industry's inroads into TV took five directions: Theater TV, Toll TV, the use of TV to sell movie product, the sale or lease of film libraries to TV, and the formation of TV subsidiaries to produce TV shows.

Theater TV, the televising of major sporting, political, or theatrical events (*Carmen* at the Met) on the big screen, started up in 1948 with New York's Paramount Theater's 18-minute live programs transmitted by Paramount's Intermediate Large Screen System ($35,000 installation cost) and Philadelphia's

Fox Theater's televising the Louis–Wolcott fight with RCA equipment. (Unlike Paramount's 1-minute, 6-second time lapse in which incoming images were photographed, developed, then projected, RCA's system was instantaneous, using a receiver much like the home TV set in addition to a projector that threw images on the screen as they were recorded.) That year, the industry appealed to the FCC for a national system of Theater TV. The FCC would eventually deny the request. By 1950, 16 theaters were equipped with Theater TV; a year later there were 40, despite the problems of loop connections with AT&T's national TV relay facilities and exhibitors' gripes about monthly charges by the phone company.

Except for P and TCF, the industry's policy was one of wait-and-see. In 1952, Paramount purchased 50 percent of Chromatic Lab, which developed a new color-convertible TV receiver that used 35 mm film, throwing an image on the screen less than one minute after the reception of the TV signal. In 1950, TCF picked up an option for the Swiss Eidophor System, an instantaneous color system, and in the following year, co-obtained rights to CBS color TV. Theater Network Television, Inc. came up with program and distribution practices. Though a couple more systems arrived, Theater TV was dead by 1954, when movie technology seemed to come to the rescue.

Toll TV's life span was longer, roughly a dozen years. In 1950, the studios applied as a unit for a block of 10 to 12 channels on the ultra high-frequency range to be known as "the Movie Band" and decided to make product available for the experimental run of Zenith Radio Corp.'s "Phonevision." For this "pay-as-you-look" system, a special unit, linked up with a special telephone circuit, was installed on a TV set. After a household called an operator on the telephone circuit to order a movie, a signal key came over the telephone activating the unit to unscramble the picture. The 90-day test runs involved televising 90 features to 300 selected Chicago families on a 3-per-day basis from a downtown transmitter at a charge of $1 per picture. January 1, 1950's inaugural program included *April Showers* (WB, 1948) at 4:00 p.m., *Welcome Stranger* (P, 1947) at 7:00 p.m. and *Homecoming*, (MGM, 1948) at 9:00 p.m. (Offering product more than two years old prevented any bites out of current box office.) The $6,750 receipts (around $22.50 per family) were solid, if not shattering.

Paramount bought 50 percent of International Telemeter Corporation's "Telemeter," a coin-operated home box office attachable to any TV receiver which, in turn, permitted a transmitting station to charge patrons for programs. Its hookup with 70 homes in Palm Springs in 1953 premiered with the new release *Forever Female* at a cost of $1.35, while the picture simultaneously screened at the downtown Plaza for $1.15. Matty Fox, head of Motion Pictures For Television, Inc. and financial/personal consultant of UA's Krim and

Benjamin, purchased an alternative system called "Subscriber Vision" from Skiatron Electric and Television Corp. (formerly the Scophony Corp. of America).[25] The rival process transmitted scrambled signals over the airwaves which a decoder unscrambled, utilizing a perforated card and connected to a TV. After a successful test in New York City via closed circuit on WOR-TV, Fox, deciding to aggressively pursue distributing old movies to TV, let it die.

Toll TV, forerunner of cable TV, didn't sail. Economic data never proved conclusive enough in its favor, and the system was unable to duplicate the latest film technologies. Further, the FCC never decided whether Toll TV was broadcasting or a common carrier service, whether in the public interest or not, and which parts of the crowded radio spectrum could be delegated to it.

Spot announcements and/or TV trailers to hype its upcoming product was a third way the industry was going to harness TV to its own use. The Academy Awards telecast, begun in 1953, functioned, of course, as one glorious three-hour-plus spot. That the telecast was paid for by advertisers outside the industry made it even more glorious.

By selling or leasing its libraries to TV, the fourth movie–TV liaison, the industry knew it was playing into the upstart's hand. No longer could it lay sole claim to superior entertainment. Yet there was nothing the industry could do in the light of severely needed capital. That the policy incurred the ire of the exhibitors, as did Toll TV, worried the industry far less, if at all.

Small outfits and British producers made the first move. In 1948, Monogram sold CBS rights to its three-or-more-year-old Bs while the *New York Daily News* TV station WPIX secured rights to 24 major Alexander Korda releases. J. Arthur Rank sold 70 of his movies the following year. In 1951, Republic's new subsidiary, Hollywood Television Service, distributed the studio's older pictures, selling rights of some 175 features to KTTV for $225,000. Wising up the next year, Republic leased (not sold) to major market stations 104 westerns, some of which were post-1948.[26] (In the long run, leasing brought in more money than outright selling.) In 1951, recent Lippert films, the Bs of UA's Edward Small and Hal Roach, Jr. and those of Paramount's Pine-Thomas found their way onto TV. That year, Matty Fox, by advancing UA $0.5 million to buy Eagle Lion, secured TV distribution rights to its 200-picture library, which included the PRC and UA libraries.

By 1955, giant steps had been made. Save for Howard Hughes's *The Conqueror* (1956) and *Jet Pilot* (1957), RKO leased in perpetuity the TV rights of its entire library of 740 features for $15.2 million to the newly formed C. & C. Television Corp., a subsidiary of the parent C. & C. Super Corp., which controlled various businesses and whose largest stockholder and president was Matty Fox. (However, General Teleradio, Inc., RKO's new owner, held TV rights to the pictures in six cities where it owned TV stations.) A total of 123 of

Republic's popular Gene Autry and Roy Rogers oaters galloped down MCA's TV trail to the happy tune of $3 to $4 million. NBC hosted the American premiere of Korda's *The Constant Husband*, a Technicolor comedy with Rex Harrison. Through its own subsidiary Screen Gems, formed in 1949 to make commercials for national TV sponsors, Columbia released 104 pre-1948 titles, the first time a major company had marketed its product both for the theater and home screens.

The following year, MGM made 725 of its pre-1948 films available for a period of 7 years for $60 million, entering into a number of leasing deals, several of which gave the company 25 percent ownership of 5 VHF and 2 UAF stations in 21 TV markets. MGM made a killer $900,000 deal with CBS for four showings of its evergreen *The Wizard of Oz* (1939). In a $21 million, no-strings-attached pact, WB sold outright negatives and residual rights of 850 pre-1948 features to Associated Artists Prod., Inc. TCF gave 20-year leasing rights of 156 pre-1948 films to National Telefilm Associates (NTA). Earlier, NTA had acquired 52 Fox films. As part of the agreement, TCF acquired a 50 percent stock interest in NTA Film Network, a NTA subsidiary. Korda's highly anticipated Technicolor production of Shakespeare's *Richard III* with Laurence Olivier was televised on NBC three hours before its American premiere at New York's Bijou Theater. By 1956, 13 percent of TV programming was given over to the airing of movies.

In 1957 Screen Gems took over the TV distribution of Universal's pre-1948 backlog of some 600 titles for a 7-year period, guaranteeing Universal a minimum of $20 million, and becoming, up to that time, the biggest distributor of theatricals for TV. Paramount sold all of its pre-1948 pictures to MCA for $50 million. UA's new subsidiary Gotham Television Film Corp. purchased 700,000 shares of stock in Associated Artists Prod., Inc. for $27 million; two years later, in 1959, it purchased domestic residuals to the RKO library from Matty Fox for $3.7 million. Through another subsidiary ZIV Prods., UA in 1960 began leasing its pre-1948 library, bought back from Matty Fox. That year, too, the entire Republic library became available to TV.

NBC's prime time "Saturday Night at the Movies"' airing of *How to Marry a Millionaire* on September 23, 1961 inaugurated a new era. A 1953 release and TCF's second film in the large-screen process of CinemaScope/Technicolor,[27] it was a lushly mounted comedy with the megawatt power of Betty Grable, Marilyn Monroe, and Lauren Bacall. The showing of the first post-1948 A in prime time[28] sent ratings soaring and hatched the post-1948 movies-on-TV series "ABC Sunday Night at the Movies," "NBC Monday Night at the Movies," and eventually seven others by the end of the sixties. TCF immediately sold 30 of its post-1948 pictures for $6 million and an additional 88 to Seven Arts Prods. Allied Artists and Embassy followed suit.

The TV airing of movies opened up the question of "residuals," the schedule of extra payments to talent for repeated use of its work on TV. "Residuals" became a hotly debated topic among movie companies, owners of TV rights (of pre-1948 movies), and the guilds from 1950 on. The inability to work out residuals was one of the main reasons post-1948 features were kept off the air. By 1955, however, "August 1, 1948" was established as the date after which movie companies were obliged to work out with guilds a payment schedule for additional performances.

In 1960, the one-month actors' strike and five-month writers' strike brought the issue to a head. Actors and writers waived rights to share in any income from the sale or lease of movies to TV made *between 1948 and 1960* in exchange for settlement deals involving pension, health, or welfare plans. Further, producers promised an increase in salary minimum of all classifications of actors and writers. But, for any picture started *after January 31, 1960*, the producer was to pay 6 percent of receipts for TV display to the actor and 2 percent to the writer, after deducting 40 percent for distribution expenses, if the producer assumed distribution costs. If the picture were sold outright, the producer deducted 10 percent before the payments.[29]

The formation of TV subsidiaries to produce and/or distribute "telefilms," the last of the film–TV connections, began in 1948 with UA's TV department. In 1949, Monogram's Interstate Television Corp. produced and distributed TV product. Columbia's Screen Gems organized a production department in 1951 under the supervision of Harry Cohn's nephew Ralph, turning out "Cavalcade of America," "The Adventures of Rin Tin Tin," and "Father Knows Best." The first major to produce episodic TV, Columbia also introduced motion-picture budgeting to TV. Universal's inroad occurred in 1949 with the promos *Hollywood Flashes* (10 stills of current activity on the lot; a 10-stills movie preview) and *Movie Star Albums* (a 20-stills chronicle of a star). Once Universal's subsidiary United World Films began TV production in 1951, film and TV production were combined under one roof. The MCA takeover of Universal between 1959 and 1962 solidified the TV operation, which became known as MCA Television. In 1953, Republic organized Studio City TV Production, Inc., renting space and equipment to TV companies.

TV production was for Disney a way to come up with $7 million seed money for Disneyland, another avenue of diversification. In exchange for 34.48 percent stock in the park and guaranteed loans up to $4.5 million, AB-PT produced "Disneyland" (later called "Walt Disney Presents"), an hour-long weekly program for seven years beginning in 1954.[30] The show's subjects varied from a behind-the-scenes look at a forthcoming theatrical to the showing of the 1951 animated feature *Alice in Wonderland*. No subject, however, was as successful as the three-part life of Davy Crockett. The high-rater generated a $10 million merchandizing bonanza that included the sale of coonskin caps, guitars, and a hit record. This instance of synergy, the spinning-off of related commercial enterprises/products from a film within the company, was something which had been familiar to Disney since the thirties with their animated Mickey Mouse figure and would, of course, become a salient feature of postmodern Hollywood picture-making. Additionally, lead actor Fess Parker became a household name. *Davy Crockett, King of the Wild Frontier* (1955), compiled from the three telefilms, was released theatrically, as was the sequel *Davy Crockett and the River Pirates* (1956), compiled from two later telefilms. "The Mickey Mouse Club," a daily children's show that aired for a full hour (1955–7), then half an hour (1957–9), brought fame to Mouseketeer Annette Funicello. The "Zorro" series (1957–9), with Guy Williams as the masked avenger in nineteenth-century California, spawned a mini-industry of capes, swords, and water pistols. These shows rounded out Disney's stay at ABC. In 1961, the entrepreneur switched to NBC with "Walt Disney's Wonderful World of Color," a potpourri of promotion documentaries, live action shorts, TV adaptations of Disney movies such as *Pollyanna* (1960), and two- or three-part telefilms which received theatrical release in Europe.

Jack's son-in-law William T. Orr and ABC shook hands in 1955 with "Warner Brothers Presents," three alternating series based on the studio's past films, *Kings Row* (1942), *Casablanca* (1943), and the sole crowd-pleaser *Cheyenne* (1929, 1947). In 1956, Jack announced that studio facilities would be available for the production of telefilms for ABC and in the following year came up with another long-running western series, "Maverick," and went on to score with "Sugarfoot," "Lawman," "Colt 45," and the detective show "77 Sunset Strip."

Two years after "MGM Parade," a half-hour studio advertisement featuring star contractees, film clips, and behind-the-scenes glimpses of current productions, aired on ABC in 1955, MGM resurrected its "The Thin Man" series. Between 1955 and 1957, "The Twentieth Century-Fox Hour," an anthology of new properties and adaptations of old movies, ran on CBS. In 1957, the entire RKO studio converted to TV production. UA-TV produced five series in the 1959–60 season and acquired ZIV TV Programs, the largest syndication company outside network TV, for $17 million. Though Paramount announced its ingress in 1952, purchasing the WB's Sunset plant in 1953 for that very purpose, the studio began distributing "Wrestling from Hollywood" over local KTLA/Channel 5 only in 1956 and entered production with the game show "Make Me Laugh" in 1958. Players (Bing Crosby's Lanier Prods. in 1952) and producers (Hitchcock's Shamley Prods. in 1955) also formed TV production units.

5.7.2   *Music*

To capitalize on its production of musicals through the issue of soundtracks, MGM formed MGM Records in 1946, the first alliance between movie making and record manufacturing. Down the line, MGM Records acquired performers for its label, other than those featured in its musicals (Joni James, Hank Williams). The move was profitable (in 1958, the $5.52 million earnings[31] helped offset severe production-distribution losses) and inspired the company's take-over of Verve Records in 1960, a popular jazz label featuring the likes of Ella Fitzgerald and Charlie Parker.

From the other direction, in 1951–2 Decca Records chief Milton Rackmil procured 43.3 percent of Universal stock. In Rackmil's studio-record combine, movies would sell records; records, movies. Besides Universal soundtracks ("The Glenn Miller Story") and those of Columbia, which Decca also published beginning with "The Jolson Story" in 1946, Decca released countless single hits from popular recording artists (Bing Crosby, the Four Aces).

After purchasing RKO in 1955, the General Tire and Rubber Co. purchased 25 percent of the Unique Record Co. and the Lamas Music Corp. UA teed off in 1957 with two subsidiaries: UA Records Corp. (featuring Steve Lawrence and Diahann Carroll) and UA Music Corp., which licensed music from UA's pictures for performances in various media. In 1957 Paramount acquired Dot Records, where Pat Boone and Paul Anka reigned. WB Records, Jack's dream of added exposure to recently acquired contractees such as Connie Stevens, and additional income from the soundtracks of its TV series, lost money in the first four years since its 1958 inception. But with the added repertoires of comedy albums by Bob Newhart and folk group Peter, Paul, and Mary, the company changed its financial tune. In 1958, TCF started up a record company, as did Columbia, which also purchased a music publishing house in 1959 ("Gower Music Corp."). Even AIP came to the party with a newly formed record company in 1959, premiering with the "Goliath and the Barbarians" soundtrack.

5.8   Company Profiles: The Administrative and Financial Picture

The industry, as a whole, survived the loss of its exhibition wing and audience downsizing as well, largely through changes in production strategy, diversification, and sale of their assets as well as technological and aesthetic shifts (as we shall see). However, the years 1948–50, when buyer attrition was first felt and the foreign market was in turmoil, and 1958–62, when the divorcement tab was finally in and the customers wearied of techno-razzmatazz, were financially wobbly.

5.8.1   Radio-Keith-Orpheum (RKO)

RKO's golden period climaxed in 1946 with a $12.2-million profit, a picture Oscar for *The Best Years of Our Lives*, and other box-office dazzlers (*Notorious, The Spiral Staircase, Till the End of Time*). *Best Years*, posting a $10.4 million take, was the top performer of the decade. The deal, however, enormously favored independent Goldwyn.

At the death of VP/Production Charles Koerner in 1946,[32] company president N. Peter Rathvon took over until socially conscious producer-writer Dore Schary, fresh from the Selznick Organization, was selected the following year. Despite rising production costs – which were acutely felt at RKO, where the average negative cost for a production was lower than at the other majors – the studio managed pretty well. But in 1948, when Floyd Odlum's Atlas Corp. sold its shares to the pathologically peculiar billionaire Howard Hughes, RKO steadily declined. A dabbler in movies since the late twenties, Hughes had produced five movies for UA, including *Hell's Angels* (1930), which he also directed, *The Front Page* (1931), and *Scarface* (1932).

Cantankerous Hughes made Ned E. Depinet president in 1948, while producer Sid Rogell ran production from 1948 to 1950 and was, in turn, replaced by producer Samuel Bischoff, who lasted till 1951. Hughes laid off employees, cutting in-house productions down to the bone (in 1950, 13; by 1953, a mere 5). Unprofitable product, the severing of its mighty theater chain, a heap of lawsuits, and the consequent departure of prestigious independents Selznick, Goldwyn, and Disney, performers Cary Grant and John Wayne, and directors John Ford's Argosy Co. and Howard Hawks's Winchester Prods. resulted in a loss of $5.8 million in 1950 and $10.2 million in 1952.

In 1952 Hughes and Depinet unloaded their stock on a syndicate comprising Chicago businessmen Ralph Stolkin and Abraham Kovlish, Texas oil operators Raymond Ryan and Edward Burke, and Los Angeles theater owner Sherrill Corwin. The adverse publicity elicited by the *Wall Street Journal*'s investigation of three of the group's questionable backgrounds caused the syndicate to return the stock to Hughes the following year. Hughes appointed Republic's VP/Distribution James P. Grainger president. Grainger attempted to turn the company around through more color (*Sea Devils*, 1953; *Susan Slept Here*, 1954); and 3-D (*Louisiana Purchase*; *Devil's Canyon*, both 1953) movies, but it was no go. In 1954 Hughes sought to purchase all RKO's assets for $23.5 million. Floyd Odlum grudgingly had prevented Hughes from obtaining the necessary 95 percent for a tax write-off. In 1955 Hughes sold RKO Radio Pictures[33] for $25 million to Thomas F. O'Neil's General Teleradio, Inc., a subsidiary of the General Tire and Rubber Co. RKO Radio Pictures, now known as "RKO Tele-radio Pictures, Inc.," became a division of a company which owned, among other things, countless radio stations and six TV stations. It was the first example of a film company becoming a subsidiary of a non-theatrical conglomerate.

VP/CBS Daniel O'Shea became president while William Dozier, ex-associate of Koerner, stepped in as production head. Departments were restructured. Key craft and staff, let go in 1954, were brought back. Flickering stars Claudette Colbert and Dana Andrews were cajoled; would-be stars Anita Ekberg and Richard Egan enticed. With the releases of the Jane Russell adventure *Underwater!* (1955) in SuperScope/Technicolor, the John Wayne–Susan Hayward $6 million historical spectacle *The Conqueror* (1956) in CinemaScope/Technicolor, and America's newly-wed sweethearts Debbie Reynolds and Eddie Fisher's *Bundle of Joy* (1956), a color remake of its 1939 hit comedy *Bachelor Mother*, it looked like the company might make a go of it. But, as with most of its 25-films-per-year-slate, these were second-rate imitations of what the competition was turning out. Save for *The Conqueror's* $4.5 million loot, the other two tanked.

RKO Pathé in New York closed its doors in 1956, consolidating production at Culver City. The music business diversification proved a bust. In 1957, production and distribution ceased and the 11 unreleased films were distributed by others. Desilu Productions, Lucille Ball and Desi Arnaz's TV company, bought the Gower Street and Culver City physical plants for $6.1 million.

5.8.2 Paramount

Paramount, posting profits of $39.2 million in 1946, $28.2 million in 1947, and $22.6 million in 1948, easily won the fat years' sweepstake. Through the sensible, stable management of president Barney Balaban from 1936 to 1966 and studio administrative head Y. Frank Freeman from 1938 to 1959, the studio continued to operate in the black, though the gains were dramatically less: $5.5 million in 1951, $8.7 million in 1956, and $5.9 million in 1961.

Screenwriter and ex-MGM associate Don Hartman was buttonholed in 1951. He, along with Freeman, encouraged the move to independent production and profit sharing. Hartman, in Hollywood, looked after what went on the screen while Freeman, largely in New York, held the purse strings. On Hartman's sudden death from a heart attack in 1958, Balaban put Freeman in Hartman's shoes while legal affairs officer Jacob H. Karp stepped in for Freeman.

The management also pursued a "less but better" picture policy, averaging only 22 films a year. In addition to the catch of distinguished independent producers such as the topical and diverse Hal Wallis, William Perlberg-director George Seaton, pioneers in star-power packaging (Bing Crosby, Grace Kelly, and William Holden in *The Country Girl*, 1954), Alfred Hitchcock at his peak, special-effects enthusiast George Pal (*When Worlds Collide*, 1951), and Italian producers Carlo Ponti, Dino De Laurentiis, and Marcello Girosi, who brought along Ponti's wife Sophia Loren, management also went after respected directors by offering them the cachet of producing their own works in-house. This policy of in-house producing kept contractees Cecil B. DeMille on the lot up to his death in 1955 and Billy Wilder until *Sabrina* (1954). Ex-WB wunderkind Michael Curtiz was invited, as was John Ford. Part of the reason for buying out the failed independent Liberty Films on a stock-exchange basis was to acquire the services of its three eminent founders: William Wyler (from *The Heiress*, 1949, to *The Desperate Hours*, 1955); George Stevens (*A Place in the Sun*, 1951, and *Shane*, 1953), and Frank Capra (*Riding High*, 1950, and *Here Comes the Groom*, 1951). Management also kept its eye out for talented TV directors, signing up Robert Mulligan, who worked with his producer-partner Alan J. Pakula (*Fear Strikes Out*, 1957) and saw to it that the best of its contractee directors stayed on: Mitchell Leisen, John Farrow, and ex-WB whiz William Dieterle. Such ace directors, the management correctly reasoned, attracted top players (Montgomery Clift, Olivia de Havilland, Clark Gable, James Stewart, John Wayne).

Having helped discover the comedy goldmine in the thirties, the brass saw to it that the comedy continued by retaining director George Marshall (from Dean Martin/Jerry Lewis films to *Papa's Delicate Condition*, 1962, starring TV sensation Jackie Gleason). The execs encouraged comedy writers to direct, such as Frank Tashlin (from *Son of Paleface*, 1952, to *The Disorderly Orderly*, 1964), Melville Shavelson (from *The Seven Little Foys*, 1958, to *A New Kind of Love*, 1963), and Melvin Frank and partner Norma Panama (*Knock on Wood*, 1954). Contractee comic Bob Hope was retained; Martin/Lewis and Danny Kaye signed. Though Paramount kept up its heavy supply of comedy, the quality of former years wasn't there.

From the late forties through the mid-fifties, Paramount was fortunate to have four top box-office males on its roster (Hope, Martin/Lewis, Crosby, Alan Ladd), and had the insight to develop Holden – whose contract was shared by Columbia – and Elvis Presley into box-office contenders.

Though Paramount's own first-rate large-screen process of VistaVision was short-lived, it did boost the sales of the Curtiz/Crosby musical *White Christmas* (1954) to the tune of $12 million and showman DeMille's *The Ten Commandments* (1956), the studio's most expensive production to date at $13 million and its biggest financial success, boasting $34.2 million in rentals, the second mightiest earner of the fifties. All of DeMille's spectaculars helped keep the studio in the black: *The Unconquered* (1947), with a $5.3 million take; *Samson and Delilah* (1949), with $9 million, the third fattest calf of the forties; and best picture

Oscar-winning *The Greatest Show on Earth* (1952), with $12.8 million – the seventh top grosser of the decade.

5.8.3   Warner Brothers

Warners' profits reached $19.4 million in 1946, peaked at $22.1 in 1947, then shriveled to $9.4 million in 1951 and $2.1 in 1956 and recovered to $7.2 million in 1961, after declaring a $1 million loss in 1958, the first of its kind since 1934. Despite labor relations fights in which the company was continually vilified, Jack "The Colonel" and his production chief Steve Trilling ruled with a tight fist. There was a decided move to independent production (the Charles K. Feldman Group introduced Tennessee Williams to the screen; Hitchcock/Sidney Bernstein's Transatlantic, Elia Kazan's Newton, as well as a flock of actor units including James Cagney, John Wayne, and TV star Jack Webb). Budgets, on which Jack kept a close eye, were, overall, reasonable, never profligate. Ex-contractee directors Curtiz, Delmer Daves, Irving Rapper, and Raoul Walsh, all of whom had complied with Jack's demands, were rehired for a one- or two-picture deal. A concerted remake policy was intensified. A slate, averaging 22 films a year, aped Paramount. The production of TV series was encouraged.

In 1956, Jack, Harry (who died two years later), and Albert sold their 800,000 shares for around $22 million to an investment company headed by bankers Serge Sememenko and Charles Allen, Jr. As hush-hush as it was immediate, Jack bought back his shares and usurped Harry's job as president while continuing to run the studio, now free of his siblings' influences. With an outside group as co-owner, however, Jack did forfeit some control.

The new partner-investors unloaded holdings (land, labs, Britain's Teddington Studios) and skewed Jack's course, directing him to snap up "certified" novels and plays, however pricey, and place them in capable hands. Rehired producer-director Mervyn Le Roy, after 16 years at MGM, turned out high-blown yet solid works such as *The Bad Seed* (1956) and *The F.B.I. Story* (1959). Stanley Donen, coproducing with George Abbott, delivered nifty musicals *The Pajama Game* (1957) and *Damn Yankees* (1958). Elegance marked Fred Zinnemann's *The Nun's Story* (1959) and George Cukor's *My Fair Lady* (1964). Broadway's Morton da Costa restaged his *Auntie Mame* (1958) and *The Music Man* (1962). *Sayonara* (1957), *Tall Story* (1960), and *Fanny* (1961) were trusted to acclaimed theater man Joshua Logan who, though he never really knew how to make a play or novel cinematic, did know how to elicit performances.

Warners had no films in the top-ten echelon. *Life with Father* (1947), *Giant* (1956), a Stevens-directed bestseller, *Sayonara*, and *Auntie Mame*, however, made the next 11-to-20 tier. The outfit scored the biggest 3-D hit ever with *House of Wax* (1953). Yet its CinemaScope/Warnercolor extravaganzas (the

$2.85 million production tagged *King Richard and the Crusades*, 1954; the $3.2 million *The Silver Chalice*, 1954; the $3.1 *Land of the Pharaohs*, 1955) all came a cropper though the $4 million *Helen of Troy*, 1956), eked out $3.2 million. Though top contractees cleared out by the early fifties, fiscal luminaries Gary Cooper, Doris Day, Randolph Scott, and John Wayne had Warners as their home base for a while, as did teen attractions James Dean, Troy Donahue, Tab Hunter, Connie Stevens, and Natalie Wood.

5.8.4   Twentieth Century-Fox

Twentieth Century-Fox's profits climbed to a record $22.6 million in 1946, slipped to $4.3 million in 1951, and rose slightly to $6.2 million in 1956. The house's fortunes, however, tumbled to a $2.9 million loss in 1960, $22.5 million in 1961, and a staggering $39.8 million in 1962.

As long as Zanuck ran things, the company made a go of it. The commercial failure of the exorbitant bio of President *Wilson* (1944) and his own war experience caused Zanuck's interest in period Americana to take a back seat to searingly topical social concerns. This, along with the trimming of a picture's budget from an average $1.8 million to $1.2 million by 1952, paid off. *The Razor's Edge* (1946), *Gentleman's Agreement* (1947), *Apartment for Peggy* (1948), *Calling Northside 777* (1948), *A Letter to Three Wives* (1949), *I Was a Male War Bride* (1949), *Pinky* (1949), *The Snake Pit* (1949), *All About Eve* (1950), *Broken Arrow* (1950), *Twelve O'Clock High* (1950), *The Desert Fox* (1951), *Monkey Business* (1952), and *The Snows of Kilimanjaro* (1952) were money-makers. These were critically acclaimed feats as well, which had something to do with Zanuck's continuing respect for writers and directors. He encouraged scribes Philip Dunne, Nunnally Johnson, and Joseph Mankiewicz to direct. He kept premier house director Henry King on, along with Henry Hathaway, Walter Lang, and Otto Preminger, while contracting Elia Kazan, Samuel Fuller, Howard Hawks, and ex-WB Jean Negulesco.

Zanuck's penchant for showmanship did not wane either. Betty Grable musicals continued. New players, groomed for stardom in molds that had clicked previously, took over, with the molds topically updated. Marilyn Monroe was a sensual Grable; Jennifer Jones, a more neurotic Gene Tierney. Susan Hayward was Linda Darnell on speed. Gregory Peck was a complicated Tyrone Power. Grable was belle of the box-office ball six times; Monroe and Hayward each thrice. For the adults, Gary Cooper, Bette Davis, and Cary Grant were red-carpeted while for youth, such hopefuls as Jeffrey Hunter, Terry Moore, and Robert Wagner were ushered in.

Bankrolled by Rockefeller organizations, owner Spyros Skouras, in an attempt to brighten the financial picture, purchased Swiss Dr. Henri Chrétien's patent for the large-screen process "Anamorphoscope" after J. Arthur Rank's option ran out in late 1952. The studio renamed it "CinemaScope." The initial venture *The Robe* (1953) racked up $17.5 million, placing #4 in the decade's top box office. CinemaScope helped double the profits to $8 million by 1954, which hovered in the $6 million range for the next three years, and rose to $7.6 million in 1958. Fox was enabled to purchase a record company, 191,000 outstanding shares of company stock owned by Hughes for $5.1 million, and a substantial interest in TODD-AO and the Magna Theater Corp., with whom Fox co-produced *South Pacific* (1958), which amassed $16.3 million in rentals and placed #5 in the decade's top box office draws.

As with Skouras and the public, Zanuck, too, was so swept up by the novelty of CinemaScope that the 1953–6 anamorphic product was, on the whole, aesthetically inferior to that of their pre-anamorphic years. Bogged down by a problem-beset industry and fired up by a desire to make the kind of money independents were making without the stress, Zanuck stepped down in 1956, joining the ranks of independents. Ironically, Zanuck, during his tenure, eschewed outside influences, keeping independents out unless they tilled B soil.

Spyros's subsequent replacements were, quite simply, disasters. Buddy Adler, C's former executive producer who became in-house Fox producer in 1955, wore Zanuck's hat from 1956 to 1960, or rather tried to. Unable to spot good material, Adler seemed daunted by the task and, unlike his predecessor, was never really around to supervise production. At Adler's death from cancer in 1960, Bob Goldstein, head of Fox's European operations, took over, and was replaced by VP/TV division Peter G. Levanthes, whose policy of fewer but more ambitious pictures never paid off.

After Zanuck's abdication, the product,[34] commercially and aesthetically, was the worst in Fox's history. B-meister Robert Lippert and his Regal Films helped to offset the fiscal busts (in 1960 alone, the $5 million musical *Can-Can* and the $3.6 million Monroe comedy *Let's Make Love*). Only a handful of movies were artistically meritorious (*Compulsion*, 1959, *Sons and Lovers*, 1960, *The Hustler*, 1961, *The Innocents*, 1961) but not cash champs, except for Jerry Wald's *Peyton Place* (1957). Much earnest work turned out artistically mediocre (*The Young Lions*, 1958, *The Diary of Anne Frank*, 1959, *Wild River*, 1960). Non-stars Pat Boone, Stephen Boyd, Joan Collins, Bradford Dillman, Fabian, Hope Lange, Don Murray, Suzy Parker, and Stuart Whitman were promoted. Fox lost credibility with its 35 films-per-year slate, the same number as that of the Zanuck reign. The Adler–Goldstein–Levanthes tenure was also responsible for that vast sinkhole *Cleopatra* (1963).

Begun as a typical $4 million fifties historical spectacle, *Cleopatra* turned into a media event that almost toppled the studio. Four years in the making at a cost of around $40 million (the most expensive film to date), the folly courted disaster after disaster. There were innumerable rewrites. Producer Walter Wanger departed. Joseph Mankiewicz replaced him and director Rouben Mamoulian. Elizabeth Taylor supplanted Joan Collins for $2 million, $3,000 weekly living expenses for four months, an additional $50,000 per week if the production spilled over, and 10 percent of the gross. Richard Burton stepped into the sandals of Peter Finch, who himself had superseded Stephen Boyd. Sets were built, razed, then built again in Hollywood, London, Rome, Egypt, and finally Spain. Taylor's ailments, among them a near-death tracheotomy, resulted in an off-and-on-again shoot. An adulterous affair between the leads that broke up Taylor's recent marriage with singer Eddie Fisher and Burton's with his long-standing wife sent the paparazzi sniffing the set like wolves. Countless lawsuits ensued. A $12.5 million loan from Metropolitan Life Insurance Co. and the sale of its land (384 acres with 75 leased back) and its post-1948 library kept the gates open. Wall Street's Carl M. Loeb, Rhoades & Co., and Treves & Co.'s acquisition of 22 percent interest pumped in more needed cash, as did the god-favored release of Zanuck's war film *The Longest Day* (1962), doubling its $7.75 million investment.

In 1961, Zanuck was asked to straighten things out. He shut down *Cleopatra* for 8 months and cut 300 workers to assess the damage. Skouras was bumped up to titular Board Chairman, a position he was forced by the Wall Street contingent to vacate the next year, while Zanuck became president and his 27-year-old producer son Richard, VP/Production. Green-lighting an additional $2 million, Zanuck managed to finish the grand-looking *Cleopatra*, which accumulated underwhelming reviews and rentals ($26 million). Taylor's hairstyles, makeup, and costumes, however, did influence fashion, while her on-set romps helped usher in the sexual revolution.

5.8.5   *Metro-Goldwyn-Mayer*

After an all-time-high profit of $18 million in 1946, president Nicholas Schenck did not relish the downward slide ($10.5 million in 1947, $4.2 million in 1948, MGM's lowest since the Depression). That the Tiffany of studios placed behind P, WB, and TCF in profits rubbed salt into the wounds. Schenck dogged factory foreman Louis B. Mayer to get another expert cohort like Thalberg who had died in 1936 at the age of 37. In 1948, Mayer chose Dore Schary, eliminating the top-heavy group of elderly exec producers (known as "The College of Cardinals") whom he supervised. Schary had actually worked at MGM as a writer in the late thirties and as exec producer on small budgeters in the early forties before his Selznick stint and his RKO rout with Hughes. Mayer would continue as VP/Studio; Schary as VP/Production. Schary's artistic control, however, would be subject to Mayer and Schenck.

The union between the fanciful paterfamilias Mayer and the feet-on-the-ground stepson Schary began on a happy note. Schary was a company man, trusting and enforcing Metro's policy of huge amounts of production value, star quality and, of course, a strong producer answerable to the VP/Production, thus harnessing a director's individuality. The relationship, however, mutated into an armed neutrality, caused principally by disagreement about what kind of pictures to make. Mayer was locked into the past; Schary wanted Metro pictures to mirror current societal problems. Elaborate, glossy Technicolor productions, cut from the studio cloth, continued: the historical spectacle *Quo Vadis* (1951), minus Schary's suggestion of Nero as a fascist dictator, the adventure *Ivanhoe* (1952), and the musical *Show Boat* (1951). So, too, did the gritty war film *Battleground* (1949) and that slice of Tinsel Town's underbelly, *The Bad and the Beautiful* (1952). Both types of star-filled pictures made money, though profits were never that large since MGM pictures were expensive to mount.

Mayer and Schary alike relied on stars to sell pictures. Even when technology became the in-thing, the stars continued to take precedence. That is why MGM held its people in place well into the mid- to late fifties. Clark Gable and Greer Garson left in 1954; June Allyson, Lana Turner, and Esther Williams in 1955; Ava Gardner in 1956; Fred Astaire, Gene Kelly, and Van Johnson in 1957; Robert Taylor in 1958. Eleanor Parker, twice box-office winner Debbie Reynolds, and four-time victor Elizabeth Taylor stayed. Down the road, pecuniary proven Glenn Ford (from 1953), Doris Day (from 1955), and Yul Brynner (from 1957) were placed under nonexclusive contract.

When Mayer vetoed Schary's *The Red Badge of Courage* (1951), the relationship turned hostile. Schary's insistence sent Mayer appealing to Schenck who, in the end, let Schary have his way. As Mayer predicted, the picture laid an egg. Without consulting Mayer, Schenck announced to the press that several West/East coast execs would be receiving profit-sharing options. (The boon to the West coast execs, actually Mayer's suggestion, went unacknowledged.) When Mayer badmouthed the New York office and Loew's stockbrokers, Schenck severely reprimanded him. All along, Mayer, sensing a loss of control, called a showdown. Again, Schenck sided with Schary. Mayer, after a resplendent 27-year reign, resigned in 1951.

To increase profits, Schenck and sole chief Schary inaugurated cuts in production costs and salaries. In 1952, the B unit was galvanized and a one-year pay cut went into effect for officials and executive staff members in a $1,000-or-over-a-week bracket. The $4.7 million profit in 1952, the $4.5 million in 1953, and the $6.3 million in 1954 were still not good enough for stockholders. Schenck, rapped for poor management and a failure to meet the postwar challenges, was retired in 1955, after a half-century in the industry. Arthur M. Loew, son of the founder and successful head of Loew's International, reluctantly succeeded him. The disgruntled Wall Street board, feeling that junior dragged his feet, precipitated his resignation in less than a year. Shortly after Joseph R. Vogel, ex-president of Loew's theaters, was elected president in 1956, a fierce struggle for control erupted between Vogel and the Joseph Tomlinson–Stanley Meyer bloc on the board of directors. Meyer's ambitious ideas impressed major stockholder Tomlinson, as did his enlisting the support of Mayer, whose last hurrah it proved to be. (Mayer was to die in 1957.) The infighting and management disarray cost the firm dearly: a $0.5 million loss in 1957, the first ever for MGM, and a tepid $0.8 million profit in 1958.[35]

Victorious, Vogel began to clean house. He dismissed Schary in 1956,[36] paying off the balance of his $200,000-a-year contract, and appointed casting director Benjamin Thau as studio administrator and in 1958, house-producer Sol C. Siegel as VP/Production. With the studio facilities able to accommodate 40 to 50 productions a year but with a yearly average of only 28, thereby accruing an approximate $10 million yearly overhead, Vogel tightened budgets, allocated space for TV production, and steered the studio toward independent production. Vogel also slated a star-studded bracing range of audience-nabbers: *Cat on a Hot Tin Roof* and the Oscar-winning *Gigi* (both 1958), Hitchcock's *North By Northwest* (1959), *Please Don't Eat the Daisies* and *Butterfield 8* (both 1960), and the decade's #1 victor *Ben-Hur* (1959), which brought in $36.7 million on a record $15 million outlay and 11 Oscars, including best picture.

An expansive ego from escalating profits ($7.7 million in 1959, $9.6 million in 1960, and $12.7 million in 1961 – the best in town) brought with it expensive deals that naively gambled on sumptuous productions. In 1959, a long-term multiple picture deal with Cinerama, Inc., with Siegel exercising complete supervision, yielded the large-scale *How the West Was Won* (1962), which clicked, and the bloated *The Wonderful World of the Brothers Grimm* (1962), which did not. Samuel Bronston's 70 mm Technirama production of *King of Kings* (1961) crashed, so did Marlon Brando's remake of *Mutiny on the Bounty* (1962), which only asked for trouble with its $20 million budget. European co-production deals with Italy's Titanus Film, Ltd. in 1959 and France's Gaumont Productions in 1961 yielded zilch. By 1962, the danger signs flashed – a mere $2.6 million profit and TV's Robert Weitman's monicker replacing that of Sol C. Siegel.

5.8.6   *Columbia*

With record profits of $3.5 million in 1946 and $3.7 million the next year, Columbia was on its way to major status. *The Jolson Story* (1946) outperformed any Columbia release ever: a $7.6 million take and #6 in the decade's top moneymakers. *Gilda* (1946) proved Rita Hayworth could sell tickets. Equal access to theaters naturally helped. The studio jettisoned its B series by the late forties, save for *Jungle Jim* (1948–55). The company was now in a position to take a chance on such carefully mounted topicals as *All the King's Men* (1949), the studio's first Best Picture Oscar in 11 years; *Born Yesterday* (1950); *Death of a Salesman* (1951); *From Here to Eternity*, the Oscar-winning picture of 1953 and #10 in the decade's top hits with a $12.2 million take; *The Caine Mutiny*, 1954; best picture Oscar-winning *On the Waterfront* (1954); and *Picnic* (1955). The gods smiling, Columbia crossed over: its $4.9 million profit in 1955 was the fourth highest industry total.

In the early fifties, owner/president Harry Cohn's aggressive inroads into independent production (Randolph Scott and Harry Joe Brown Productions of ten shoot-'em-ups) and TV, as well as his acquiescence to the New York front office's demand of feature cutback (the average 52 films per year from 1946 to 1951 was reduced to 38 from 1952 to 1956), kept the grin on the management's face. Other right moves included the grooming of sexpot Kim Novak to replace Hayworth and compete with Fox's Monroe, the enlistment of clowns Judy Holliday and Jack Lemmon, the build-up of versatile Glenn Ford and William Holden, and erecting ex-WB Bogart's Santana tent on the lot.

In 1958, Cohn died (brother Jack had succumbed two years earlier). Samuel J. Briskin, Harry's former associate in charge of Bs, was selected to run the place while another old-timer Abe Schneider was to be president, with Leo Jaffe as VP. Cohn's will left the voting control of his 193,000 shares to three trustees: wife Joan, attorney Mendel Silberberg, and ex-MGM director George Sidney, who began his tenure there with the mega-hit *The Eddie Duchin Story* (1956).

Management uncertainty, along with the tepid reception of prestigious As (*Bell, Book and Candle* and *Bonjour Tristesse*, both 1958) and freeze-out of big-rollers (*Porgy and Bess* and *They Came to Cordura*, both 1959; *Pepe* and *Song Without End*, both 1960; *The Devil At 4 O'Clock*, 1961), caused Columbia's $5 million nosedive in 1958, a $2.9 million loss in 1959, and a $2.1 million recovery in 1960, but another $1.4 million loss in 1961. Though 1957's Oscar-winning picture *The Bridge on the River Kwai* accumulated $18 million and was placed #6 in the decade's roll call, half the profits reverted to the independent Spiegel, as was the case with other commercial champs at the time (Sinatra and Essex Co.'s *Pal Joey*, 1957, and Otto Preminger and Carlyle's *Anatomy of a Murder*, 1959). Independent production kept profits modest.

The new regime did carry over Cohn's profitable British connections by making deals with Hammer (minus the horror product which Universal distributed) and Open Road Productions (*The Guns of Navarone*, 1961, blasting out a $12.5 million niche) while continuing with Spiegel (*Lawrence of Arabia*, 1962, seizing a $16.7 million haul and a #17 spot in the decade's box-office loftiest as well as another best picture Oscar). From 1956, Columbia went on a selling spree (Pathé, 24.5 acres in Burbank, the Sunset Boulevard operation). In 1960, management allowed the public to purchase stock in its TV subsidiary while retaining 59 percent. By 1962, the lady with the torch again stood tall, posting a $2.6 million profit.

5.8.7   Universal

Raking in its highest profits ever at $4.6 million in 1946 and merging with International Pictures, formed in 1943 by former Fox exec William Goetz and lawyer/ex-RKO president Leo Spitz, Universal aimed to be respected. Goetz and Spitz ran the studio while industrialists John Cheever Cowdin and Nate J. Blumberg headed up the New York office. The number of As increased, such as *The Egg and I* (1947), an adaptation of Betty McDonald's bestseller with Claudette Colbert and Fred MacMurray that netted $5.5 million, entitling it to the twelfth rung on the decade's box-office ladder. A-budgets, too, moved up to the $1–$1.5 million neighborhood.

Bs were to be cut. What this really came down to, however, was less a lopping off of Bs, except in the instances of westerns, musicals, and horror films, than an upgrading of them so as to pass as As, such as *Slave Girl* (1947), a Technicolor adventure with Yvonne de Carlo, George Brent, and a talking camel, directed by B-meister Charles Lamont. Except for its illustrious productions, Universal features went out in a double-feature format – not one A and one B, as this format signified – but rather, according to management, as two top films for the price of one.

Encouraged by the equal access to theaters, Goetz and Spitz kept things rolling in the good old studio way by retaining a stable of players (Bud Abbott and Lou Costello, Ann Blyth, Donald O'Connor, Jeff Chandler, Shelley Winters) and, in the main, in-house productions. Independents who did land on the lot were small-time and unable to enlist stars, but their efforts were intriguingly different from the typical Universal fare (producer Mark Hellinger's hard-hitting thriller *Brute Force*, 1947). The reciprocal trade pact with Brit J. Arthur Rank was renewed.

Goetz and Spitz's strategy failed. With the market shriveling, Universal's prestigious As had a tough time competing with those of the majors due to their inability to line up stars. In 1948, for example, *A Double Life* succeeded with waning Ronald Colman whereas the adaptations of Lillian Hellman's *Another Part of the Forest* and Arthur Miller's *All My Sons* failed. The lavishly mounted but star-less adaptations of the Broadway musicals *One Touch of Venus* and *Up in Central Park* and the original musical *Casbah* also took the count. As for the Rank films, they made no significant fiscal inroads on Yankee shores, though many were critically striking (1948's *Hamlet*, the firm's first best picture Oscar since 1929). In 1948, Universal posted a $3.2 million loss. Production ceased after U's $1.1 million loss in 1949.

When production started up again, Bs were increased, especially westerns. Series were reinstated: *Ma and Pa Kettle* (1949–57), *Francis, The Talking Mule* (1950–6). The horror cycle revivified in 1953. Studio manager Edward Muhl, on the lot since 1927, was responsible for these changes. Muhl knew that these types of features would be gobbled up by neighborhood movie houses, most of them in rural areas, where TV had not as yet made an incursion.

In 1951–2, Decca Records pumped much-needed money into the company ($3.75 million), eventually acquiring Rank's large block of 134,375 shares as well as Goetz and Spitz's 150,000 shares. Decca honcho Milton Rackmil succeeded Blumberg as president (Cowdin had resigned in 1950) and gave Goetz and Spitz's job to Muhl. Players were groomed with the teen market in mind: Tony Curtis, Piper Laurie, Audie Murphy, John Saxon, even a home-grown Monroe named Mamie Van Doren, and box-office bloomers Sandra Dee and Rock Hudson. Stars were borrowed: Gregory Peck (*A World in His Arms*, 1952); Tyrone Power (*Mississippi Gambler*, 1953). Percentage deals were cut with independents (Stewart). Fading ladies were given a two- or three-picture deal: Anne Baxter, Jeanne Crain, Ann Sheridan, Barbara Stanwyck, Jane Wyman, and later, June Allyson, Susan Hayward, and Lana Turner. Most came under the wand of producer Ross Hunter who, in dollying up old fashioned formulas, amassed the bucks. By the early fifties, the company combined film and TV production under one roof.

All went well until 1957, when production again ground to a halt and 25 percent of its employees were laid off. A $10 million loan under a new credit agreement with the First National Bank of Boston and the Guaranty Trust Co. of New York got things going again but the studio suffered a $2 million loss in 1958, rendering it vulnerable to takeover.

By this time, MCA, founded in 1924 by ophthalmologist-musician-band booker Jules C. Stein, had become the premier talent agency for all media under the shrewd guidance of president Lew Wasserman. In 1950, MCA had moved into TV production-distribution under the Revue Productions banner. In 1957, MCA had acquired the Paramount film library. By 1959, Revue Productions, outgrowing the old Republic studio space, began the takeover of the 420-acre Universal studio lot for $11.25 million, shelling out an additional $10 million for capital improvements. Lawyer Sidney J. Sheinberg, who joined Revue in 1959, had much to do with MCA's expansion. Universal Pictures Corp. was now a tenant at the studio it sold to MCA/Revue, paying a $1 million yearly rent.

In 1962, after having acquired the parent Decca Records and becoming Universal's leading stockholder, MCA completed the takeover and the Department of Justice served MCA with divestiture papers. MCA surrendered its talent representation wing, deciding solely to pursue TV production-distribution. The consent decree further stipulated that for a period of seven years MCA was forbidden to acquire any major film, TV, or recording company. Exempt from this provision were Universal Pictures Corp., which it acquired completely in 1964 and the formerly acquired Decca Records, with which it merged to form MCA Records, also in 1964. That year, Revue Productions began to be known as "Universal Television." Finally, the decree forbade MCA, for a period of five years, from distributing any 1948–56 Universal picture to TV.

Wasserman, the first instance of an agent running a studio and a hint of what was just around the corner, continued with the Rackmil–Muhl combo but inaugurated some changes. Production output was just about halved (from 1946 to 58, Universal averaged 35 to 36 pictures a year; from 1959 to 62, about 18 to 19). Concentration was on outfitting A pictures which had to hold their own with any other studio's product. These pictures would, therefore, involve not only top stars and splendid production values but proven directors as well. Independent productions were preferred. The coffers filled: female powerhouse Doris Day and her indie company Arwin with the $7.5-million trove *Pillow Talk* (1959), marking the return of blacklisted director Michael Gordon; the Blake Edwards-led *Operation Petticoat* (1959), with Cary Grant, for his Granart Productions, adding $9.3 million; and Kirk Douglas/Bryna Production of the Stanley Kubrick-directed *Spartacus* (1960). Starring Douglas, *Spartacus*, which at $12 million was the most expensive film the studio ever mounted, grossed $14 million, placing it at #7 on the decade's top box-office roster. By 1959, Universal was in the black, declaring a $4.7 million profit, which ballooned to $6.3 million in 1960, $3 million in 1961, and $4.4 million in 1962.

5.8.8   United Artists

The new management team of Gradwell Sears and Arthur Kelly was put in place in 1947. As with their predecessor Edward C. Raffery, who called the shots from 1941 on, they were unable to fill the slots of the departed independents of popular quality pictures such as Disney, Goldwyn, Korda, Wanger, and Selznick. Being sued for breach of contract for using RKO as distributor on some of his pictures, Selznick disposed of his holdings in the corporation for $2 million in 1947. The new independents, including Benedict Bogeaus, Sol Lesser, David Loew, Seymour Nebenzal, and Hunt Stromberg, were just not in their forbears' class. Worse, the public shunned producer/director/star/stockholder/ HUAC suspect Charles Chaplin's *Monsieur Verdoux* (1947). Sears/Kelly were unable to hold the company with its modest profits of $0.4 million in 1946 and $0.5 in 1947 and reverse the steady losses of $0.5 million in 1948, $0.2 million in 1949, and $0.9 million in 1950. Another team, headed by Paul McNutt, took over in 1950 and proved equally ineffectual. The next year, McNutt allowed entertainment lawyer Arthur B. Krim, who had wheeled and dealed at low-rent Eagle-Lion, access to major stockholders Mary Pickford and Chaplin. He pitched his terms. They accepted.

Krim and partner Robert G. Benjamin felt they had a pretty good chance. Independent fever was in the air. Quality venues were open to non-major product. Pictures came in cheaper at UA than at other companies due to the lack of studio overhead that could add 20 to 40 percent to a picture's budget. So, to attract power players, Krim and Benjamin drastically revamped company policy by offering full financing, profit sharing, and creative freedom. Chicago financier Walter Heller put up a $3-million line of credit; Fox's Skouras lent $0.5 million. Matty Fox gave UA $0.5 million to buy Eagle-Lion in exchange for TV rights to the UA and EL libraries.

For operating the company in the black for one year within a three-year period (a feat Krim and Benjamin accomplished by their first year in office with $0.3 million profit), 50 percent of the stock passed into their hands. In 1953, the Bankers Trust, the Chemical Corp. Exchange Bank, the Bank of America, and the First National City Bank of New York started to invest in the company. In 1955, Chaplin sold his 25 percent for $1.1 million; a year later, Pickford sold her 25 percent for $3 million. In 1957, after 38 years as a privately owned outfit, UA went public, offering $17 million in stock and debentures, and began a program of expansion. In 1959, UA entered into a $15 million financial agreement with Prudential Insurance Co. of America and Boston's Puritan Fund, Inc.

By the mid-fifities, UA was a major player and an industry leader as well, with its increasing number of pictures (an average 22 films from 1946 to 1950 to an average 39 from 1951 to 1962), snowballing profits (a smashing $4.3 million in 1961), and four best picture Oscars.

5.8.9   Disney

Expanse of product pushed Walt Disney's company, of which he was president and executive production manager, into profit, while laying the foundation for major studio status. Hybrid animation-live action features (*Song of the South*, RKO, 1946) appeared. Nature shorts (*Seal Island*, RKO, 1946) expanded to feature-length documentaries (*The Vanishing Prairie*, BV, 1954). Live-action adventures (*The Sword and the Rose*, BV, 1953) and, eventually, comedies (*The Shaggy Dog*, BV, 1959) and musicals (*Babes In Toyland*, BV, 1961), arrived. Such fare complemented the animated features, which, in this time of spiraling production costs, came in at around $4 million and hence, were extremely risky and foolhardy to concentrate upon. The number of features released, including an occasional pick-up and "telemovie," which played overseas as a theatrical, gradually rose from two in 1946 to nine by 1962.

The inevitable formation of its own distribution company Buena Vista also augmented Disney's cachet. From the start of its RKO association in 1937, brother Roy, exec VP/business manager, chafed at the way RKO handled Disney product as well as its 30 percent distribution fee, which, by the way, was standard. Since Hughes's takeover of RKO, Roy's gripes became more frequent. A hassle over the length of the nature documentaries and the proposed feature's topic (desert animal life) forced Roy to establish BV with the release of *The Living Desert* (1953). In this way, the company controlled its own product in terms of packaging. Disney would now offer a feature, short, and cartoon as a unit to the exhibitor, determine the time of release, and settle on tie-ins. Best, the company halved its distribution expenses to 15 percent.

Getting the show on the road was financially rough. Expenditure guidelines were strict. A 34 percent reduction in payroll accounts occurred in 1949. Another roadblock was the $4.2 million debt to the Bank of America and the RKO loans in return for extension of its distribution rights. Disney's first postwar profits of $717,542 did not occur until 1950, largely due to the financial success of the animated *Cinderella* (RKO) and the live-action *Treasure Island* (RKO). TV diversification in 1954, *20,000 Leagues under the Sea* (1955), *Old Yeller* (1957), and *Lady and the Tramp* (1955), hitting the animation high mark of $6.5 million, sweetened the kitty. Boosting profits to a record $4.4 million in 1961 was a string of promoted-on-TV hits: *The Absent-Minded Professor*, *The Parent Trap*, and the animated *101 Dalmatians*. The success of Disneyland from 1955 on, for which the new subsidiary WED Enterprises was formed with Walt as president and brother-in-law Bill Cottrell as VP, were also responsible for the company's euphoria. The 22-year-old Bank of America debt was paid off by 1961. Only 1960 saw a loss of $1.3 million due primarily to the lavish $6 million expenditure on the animated *Sleeping Beauty* (1959) and its subsequent baffling first-release gross of only $5.3 million. In 1961, VP Bill Anderson began to run the day-to-day studio activity, allowing Walt more time with Disneyland and TV.

5.8.10   Republic

Many ailments abetted Republic's demise in 1958. Foremost was owner/studio head Herbert J. Yates's dottiness in making Vera Hruba Ralston, who became his wife in 1953, a star.[37] Of her 26 films spanning 1941–58, financed by the profits from the Bs, few paid back their investments. In 1956, investors sued Yates for squandering the firm's funds on his wife's career.

Barring director Allan Dwan's *Sands of Iwo Jima* (1950) and John Ford's *Rio Grande* (1950) and *The Quiet Man* (1952), all starring John Wayne, Republic's prestige productions just could not hold a candle to even the majors' B fare. This had something to do with Yates's antiquated tastes. The burgeoning vogue for in-your-face realism was simply beyond him.

TV undermined Republic's Bs by putting the Saturday kiddie matinee at the neighborhood houses out of business where Republic product often filled the bill. Republic's TV subsidiary failed to come up with a winner and, in releasing its films to TV (some post-1948), Republic incurred the wrath of the exhibitors, who retaliated by not giving its pictures a fair circulation shake.

With a 1957 loss of $1.3 million and $1.4 million in 1958 (except for a $349,990 debit in 1948, every year showed under a million dollars' profit), Yates retired in 1958, selling to banker-realtor Victor M. Carter for $6 million. Carter made the studio available for film/TV production.

5.8.11   *Monogram–Allied Artists*

In 1946, Monogram, the site of B westerns/gangster thrillers and series (*The Bowery Boys*), formed a subsidiary Allied Artists Prods., Inc. with S. Steve Broidy as president and Monogram founder W. Ray Johnston as board chairman. Broidy's aim was to bring out a quality line to compete with the majors, such as the romantic comedy *It Happened on Fifth Avenue* (1947) with Don Defore, Ann Harding, and Victor Moore, helmed by ex-MGM contractee Roy del Ruth. From 1947 to 1952, the subsidiary increased its output from 3 to 8 films per year and, after a sound $375,895 profit in 1946, incurred losses for the next four years before recording a 1951 profit of just over a million dollars. In 1953, AA subsumed Monogram, increased its offerings (an average 36 films per year from 1953 to 1958) and continued in clover with a 1958 high of $1.1 million. Its slate consisted of upgraded Bs, built around a premise an audience could immediately grasp and identify with (a newspaper headline often was used as source). These upgrades utilized recognizable players and no-nonsense directors who took a voguish documentary realist·approach. Many such AA features played as singles in first-run situations: director Don Seigel's *Riot in Cell Block 11* (1954) with Neville Brand and *Crime In the Streets* (1956) with James Whitmore and Sal Mineo. Its horror–sci-fi line (*Attack of the Crab Monsters*, 1957) provided drive-in double-feature fodder.

By the mid-fifties, Broidy got quixotic with the $3 million William Wyler Technicolor production of *Friendly Persuasion* (1956), headlining Gary Cooper and Dorothy McGuire and Billy Wilder's *Love in the Afternoon* (1957) with

Cooper, Audrey Hepburn, and Maurice Chevalier, filmed on location in Paris and at the Studios de Boulogne where art director Alexander Trauner built the most expensive sets ever on a French soundstage. Both critically reputable enterprises were financially nerve-racking: *Persuasion*'s $4 million; *Love*'s $2 million. Both had, in part, contributed to the losses of $262,499 in 1959 and a considerable product cut (an average 13 films per year from 1959 to 1962). The staggering $1.5 million loss of 1962 put the outfit into a tailspin.

5.8.12   American International Pictures

In 1954, Realart Pictures' sales manager James H. Nicholson and showbiz-bitten lawyer Samuel Arkoff formed American Releasing Corp. Expanding two years later as "American International Pictures," the outfit had its headquarters at Chaplin's former Sunset/La Brea studio. There president Nicholson and VP Arkoff devised a winning policy that kept the company in the black.[38] The movie was to have an audience-grabbing title, capitalized upon in the advertising, thus preselling the product. Who could resist the copy for *It Conquered the World* (1956): "every man its prisoner, every woman its slave?" No one. In fact, only after the title and advertising had been decided upon was a writer enlisted to provide the script. In this respect, AIP (and to a lesser extent, AA) was a forerunner of the high-concept approach to filmmaking that infected Hollywood from the late seventies on (subject matter immediately understood that could be succinctly captured in a logo, TV commercial, and preview). AIP also anticipated the new Hollywood in its emphasis on marketing strategy, often shelling out more money in advertising than its customary $40,000–$100,000 production outlay.

AIP's fare of a yearly average of eight items was exploitable and highly saleable: westerns (*Five Guns West*, 1955), war films (*Submarine Seahawk*, 1958), rock-and-roll musicals (*Shake, Rattle, and Rock*, 1956), horror (*Voodoo Women*, 1957), drag-racing adventures (*Dragstrip Girl*, 1957), and social-problem films of the juvenile delinquency ilk (*Diary of a High School Bride*, 1959). Even when the company elevated its product, the fare had the same enticingly sleazy aura, such as the Roger Corman/Edgar Allan Poe horror series or the spectacular *Sign of the Gladiator* (1959), boasting a $0.5–$1 million advertising budget. With its dive into exploitational waters, this minor held the dubious distinction of contributing in a major way to the tabloidization of the screen.

The continual relegation of its product to the bottom half of a double bill forced the company to send out its films in pairs. The back-to-back presentation of its horror–sci-fi *The Day the World Ended* (1955) and *The Phantom from 10,000 Leagues* (1956), both unfurling the threat of nuclear power gone amok, clicked, setting the standard of thematic combos.

The drive-in effusively embraced the AIP product since it conferred first-run status upon this modish form of exhibition and was perfectly suited to the large percentage of its teenage clientele. At the outset, Nicholson and Zarcoff were cognizant of the youth-market potential and geared their product accordingly. And all the independents who had a hand in the AIP stew (producers Alex Gordon, Sid Pink, Herman Cohen, and Bert I. Gordon) were of the same mind.

Initially, the company also bucked the majors' distribution policy by renting its product for double bills directly to about two dozen regional sub-distributors in the country. These mini-outfits paid a flat fee for exclusive rights for a limited time to show the product in a designated area. With Corman's *House of Usher* in 1960, the percentage system went into effect.

5.9   The Industry and HUAC

The first HUAC investigation of communist infiltration in the movie industry in 1947 set off several responses. Of the 42 subpoenaed, 19 were considered "unfriendly." Eleven were called to testify in the second week of the hearings (the other eight were never called). Ten were accused of being in contempt of Congress: writers Alvah Bessie, Lester Cole, Ring Lardner, Jr., John Howard Lawson, Albert Maltz, Samuel Ornitz, and Dalton Trumbo; writer-directors Herbert Biberman and Edward Dmytryk; and producer Andrew Scott. Bertolt Brecht, after answering questions and denying membership, left for Europe. These men saw the proceedings as an infringement of the Bill of Rights. Two were given prison terms of six months; the remaining eight served one year.[39]

A brigade of patriots cooperated with the Committee. Among them were leaders Disney, Mayer, and Warner; actors Gary Cooper (who claimed he turned down scripts because of their inherent communist propaganda), Adolph Menjou, Robert Montgomery, George Murphy, Ronald Reagan, and Robert Taylor; directors Leo McCarey and Sam Wood; and writers Ann Rand and Morrie Ryskind. Some named names. Warner told the Committee that his dismissal of 16 writers at the end of their contracts was because of their communist affiliation.

Ultimately fearing public opprobrium that could easily result in a financial boycott of its pictures as well as government intervention (at no time did the industry countenance the indictment of being taken over by communists), 50 top guns of the Motion Picture Association of America (MPAA), impelled particularly by Paramount's Balaban, Loew's Schenck, and Fox's Skouras, held a two-day meeting at New York City's Waldorf Astoria Hotel, where they drafted the so-called "Waldorf Statement." The meeting was convened on the very day

(November 24, 1947) the House cited the "Hollywood Ten." In the main, the document supported the Committee's decision in regard to the "unfriendly" witnesses, immediately discharging or suspending all without compensation. The statement, further, formalized the promise of not employing a communist or any other kind of government subversive and invited the various talent guilds and trade unions' cooperation in eliminating subversives. (Communists, actually, were interested in infiltrating the unions.) Lastly, the statement asked Congress to pass a law to help American industries shake themselves free of disloyal elements.

A third response swelled from the industry's liberal conscience. "The Committee for the First Amendment" draft was signed by 500 producers, directors, writers, and actors. The brainchild of heavyweights Huston, Wyler, and Philip Dunne, the document excoriated the Committee for its violation of the civil rights of citizens, use of guilt by association rather than "individual account-ability," disallowance of the rights of a "criminal" on trial, and the destruction of reputations.[40]

Huston, along with performers Lauren Bacall, Humphrey Bogart, Paul Henried, Danny Kaye, Gene Kelly, and others, chartered a plane to Washington, DC and aired their views in two national broadcasts on ABC radio on October 26 and November 2. Their presence vied with the Committee's for news head-lines, allowing the country to hear and read about the other side.

Of the 90 witnesses in the 1951–2 inquest, about half took the fifth amend-ment (actor Howard Da Silva, producer-writer Sidney Buchman, director Joseph Losey, writers Paul Jarrico, Abraham Polonsky, Lillian Hellman, and Carl Foreman, who testified later in 1956). Others (performers Lee J. Cobb and Sterling Hayden, director Elia Kazan, and writers Clifford Odets and Budd Schulberg) admitted past membership and named names. Dmytryk also became "friendly." Some performers such as José Ferrer and John Garfield cleared their names.

From this and the subsequent 1953–5 inquiry, the Committee compiled a roll call of "unfriendlies" as well as a list of about 314 names cited as communists by cooperative witnesses.[41] The studios set up "clearance men"[42] to check out employees' past and present political references, "blacklist" or, at the very least, put on the back burner names that did not clear. The studios also abided by the names provided by such conservative assemblages as the American Legion which, in 1951, published the names of over 300 industry workers with alleged communist associations;[43] the Motion Picture Alliance for the Preservation of American Ideals, organized in 1944 to smoke out commies; Myron C. Fagants' Cinema Educational Guild which published *Documentation of the Red Stars In Hollywood* and *Red Treason In Hollywood*; and a group started by three ex-FBI men which distributed *Red Channels: The Report of Communist Influence In*

Radio and Television. The paradigmatic *Red Channels*, published in 1950,[44] reaching out primarily to the business community, had a foreword by J. Edgar Hoover, pointing out that the communists had supplanted the printed word with airwaves as *the* medium of propaganda. *Red Channels* also set forth an index of names, occupations, and organizations of "possible" communists as well as of organizations and publications found to be communist or communist fronts prepared and released by HUAC in 1948. Additionally, a gray list, mostly the work of the American Legion, took shape, warning studios of the strong leftist ideology of directors (Lewis Milestone and Vincent Sherman) and writers (Michael Blankfort and Dore Schary).

The investigations resulted in interrupted and/or ruined careers. Europe became the refuge of actors Larry Parks and Chaplin. Chaplin refused to challenge the Department of Justice's attempt to seek his exclusion from the States because of alleged subversive activities. Directors Jules Dassin, Cy Enfield, Bernard Vorhaus, and John Berry, whose 16 mm documentary *The Hollywood Ten* (1951) raised money for the defense of those cited for contempt of Congress, also fled to Europe, as did writers Carl Foreman and Donald Ogden Stuart. For those suspected writers who wished to work in Hollywood, the resorting to a "front" (the use of a pseudonym) and working at a reduced fee were necessities. (Directors were too high-profile for "fronts.") "Robert Rich," Oscar-winning author of *The Brave One* (RKO, 1956), was actually Dalton Trumbo. In Mexico since 1948, Trumbo had been working under a variety of names and occasionally employing fronts, as for *Roman Holiday* (P, 1953), for which Ian McLellan Hunter won an Oscar.

The probe also caused red labeling of pictures such as *The Best Years of Our Lives* (RKO, 1946), because of its delineation of a postwar America rife with problems. Quite a few films came from Zanuck's social-conscious roster, such as *Apartment for Peggy* (1948), an affecting social satire-male melodrama set against the postwar housing shortage or the sci-fi *The Day the Earth Stood Still* (1951), that argued for acceptance of a peaceful outsider. Director Frank Capra (*Mr. Smith Goes to Washington*, C, 1939) was hounded. Picketing from right-wing groups outside a theater showing an "un-American" film (*Death of a Salesman*, C, 1951) or a film that involved a communist maker (Losey's *M*, C, 1951) were common.

To appease the public, the industry produced about 200 blatant, anti-commie films. Centered around the period 1948–53, these mostly B spy thrillers were commercially and aesthetically negligible. Even major films failed to find an audience, the #1 male box-office star John Wayne as *Big Jim McLain* (WB, 1952) an exception. *I Was a Communist for the FBI* (WB, 1951) did, however, ignite a cycle of FBI thrillers (*Pickup on South Street*, TCF, 1953) and eventually spawned the popular TV series "I Led Three Lives" in 1953. Of course, communism

5-2 *Trial* (MGM, 1955, p. Charles Schnee)

In this courtroom drama, a law professor (Glenn Ford), set up by communist lawyer (Arthur Kennedy) into arguing the case of a 17-year-old Mexican youth accused of murdering a white girl, begins to see the light at a rabble-rousing rally.

as a background, catalyst, or antagonist cropped up in every genre. This Hollywood ploy to keep topical and realist, while assuring the public that it was indeed vigilant in exposing the enemy, usually took a *Sturm und Drang* tone as in the courtroom drama *Trial* (MGM, 1955). Occasionally, however, Hollywood gambled with a lightly satiric tone and suggested a "cooperation" option (the musical *Silk Stockings*, MGM, 1958, or the social satire *One, Two, Three*, UA, 1961). Some films took an allegorical approach, as with a host of horror–sci-fi films or the historical spectacle *The Ten Commandments* (P, 1956) in which producer-director DeMille's prologue tells us that Moses' story embodies the conflict between freedom (the Israelites) and totalitarianism (the Egyptians as embodied by dictator-like Rameses).

Most pertinent is the fact that HUAC caused the gradual political ideological shift from centrist Republican to liberal Democrat. In the light of decades of movies in which America, democracy, and the family were lionized and the American Dream illustrated, the industry felt this relentless searching out and questioning were senseless and stressful. Even when it was a matter of a thirties social-problem film exposing some injustice in the land, especially taken up at WB where VP/Production Jack, a Democrat, ran the studio (other studio heads were Republicans), the solution was, more often than not, presented as achieved, or at the very least, forthcoming. The HUAC brouhaha was a betrayal by the government, so thought the industry at large. The Waldorf Statement, remember, was a grandstanding gesture to stave off any financial retaliation.

Other factors undoubtedly pitched in: the aggregation of liberal Jewish activists from the East coast; the exodus of European émigrés who fled Nazi nightmares; and the sobering experience of the industry people who served during World War II. But it was mainly HUAC that changed old Hollywood's political drift, sending up another flare marking a new period.

The last four investigations (1953–5, 1954, 1957, and 1958) were pale reprises. The industry had more important things to worry about and besides, the emphasis shifted to the New York stage and TV. The end was definitely in sight by 1959 when the Academy nullified its rule that a person who had admitted membership in the party or had declined to refute charges of such membership would be refused an Oscar[45] and Trumbo admitted that he was, indeed, Robert Rich. The following year, Preminger announced he would give screen credit to Trumbo for *Exodus*. Producer-actor Kirk Douglas seconded the motion, trumpeting Trumbo's name for *Spartacus*, while Stanley Kramer credited Ned Young for the adaptation of *Inherit the Wind*.

5.10   Distribution Practices

Foreign-market expansion was a key policy that became, by the early fifties, a necessity. All eight major distributors in 1946 organized the Motion Picture Export Association (MPEA) to pursue this very thing. It addressed four problems: foreign government cartels, the selection of pictures that would fairly represent American life and in no way offend foreign sensibilities, the repair of the pre-war distribution mechanism, and lastly, the handling of the large number of not-yet-spooled-abroad 1939–45 films which could not just be dumped en masse. The MPEA was equally aggressive at acquiring new overseas markets. In 1946, the markets in Egypt, the Middle East, India, China, and South America expanded from 35 percent to 50 percent. Ten years later, sales pitching began to the Iron Curtain countries of Hungary, Poland, the former Czechoslovakia,

East Germany, and Romania. In 1947, the foreign market contributed 40 percent of the total US revenues, up from the 25–35 percent prewar range. By 1954, the percentage increased to 45 percent and reached 52 percent in 1962.[46]

The distribution of foreign films, the province primarily of small independent outfits, was another avenue. In 1946, the majors picked up 13 foreign films; 60 by 1962. Companies even formed subsidiaries to handle overseas product. By the end of the fifties, it was not unusual for the majors to advance a portion of the expected box-office revenues to foreign producers in return for distribution rights in certain markets. Additional new markets included 16 mm versions for educational purposes, hospital showings, and the airlines' In Flight service, which commenced in 1961 with the New York–Los Angeles flight showing of *By Love Possessed* (UA).

To compensate for the loss in profits from theater divorcement/divestiture, the distribution charge increased roughly from 30 percent to 36 percent by the mid-fifties. Since each film was now sold on its own merits, a sliding scale was set up whereby a percentage due a distributor could change weekly, depending upon the take at the tills. Also introduced were guarantees (the practice whereby the distributor collected money up front from the exhibitor to play the film with recoupment only from the distributor's share, if and when earned), advances (again, exhibitor's money up front, but refundable if the film failed), and extended playing time.

While the number of picture engagements was reduced, their types increased. The roadshow, a special first-run, exclusive engagement that catered to the "big" picture became popular. Resembling the presentational format of the legitimate theater (8:30 p.m. performances, 2:30 p.m. Wednesday, Saturday, and Sunday matinees, reserved seats at considerably higher admission prices in the $2–$3 range, souvenir programs sold in the lobby, a 2½-hour or more running time relieved by an intermission), the roadshow turned moviegoing into an event, conferring further luster upon an already illustrious picture. Still-standing movie palaces in big cities were the usual spots for a 2–6-month road-show run. With some clearance time, the film then wended its way into second runs with the roadshow 70 mm versions reduced to a 35 mm anamorphic format.

In 1962, UA introduced a new release pattern in the New York area known as "Premiere Showcase," opening *The Road to Hong Kong* in 11 suburban runs simultaneously with the picture's downtown first run. In line with TV's summer repeat policy, stage revivals, and paperback reprints, rereleases became more frequent than before. *Best Years of Our Lives* (RKO, 1946) reopened in 1953. By 1958, the industry began releasing its major films during the summer, not as before, in winter. The record business's summer slump and the TV summers of inferior substitutes and reruns made this season less competitive.

Marketing strategies were Neolithic. Males attended more than females. It was not until the mid-fifties that the industry paid attention to changing audience demographics. The more educated and well-to-do people were, the more they went to the movies. Youth went more than adults (AIP had to teach the majors this lesson). There was very little, if any, consideration of the black audience.

The industry enlisted opinion Research Corp. of Princeton, New Jersey to conduct a market research project in 1957 (hard to believe the first of its kind) which concluded that teenagers constituted 52 percent of the audience while 72 percent of the audience was under 29.[47] Though a program was devised, none of the points was carried out. Only the slogan: "Get More Out of Life – Go Out To A Movie" was used for a short time. The sneak preview, whereby a selective audience was polled by response cards, was enlisted more and more.

The cost-effective coming attraction; the use of print, radio, and TV; and word of mouth became marketing mainstays. In 1946, the industry spent a total of $65.7 million in intermedia advertising; in 1956, $69.5 million.[48] Newspaper advertisements received the heftiest outlay ($50 million) with radio and then, of course, radio and TV receiving the next biggest chunk and largest increases (from $2 million in 1946 to $15 million in 1956). Magazines ranked third, with outlay decreasing ($5 million in 1946 to $2.6 million in 1956), due to the 13 or so very popular fanzines (*Modern Screen*, *Photoplay*) losing their audience by the early sixties. On accessories like one sheets (an advertising poster used in a theatre's lobby or display cases outside), lobby cards, posters, and stills, the $5 million outlay in 1946 dwindled throughout the period, as did outdoor advertisement (billboards, posting) from $1.7 million in 1946.

The pre-sold-aura mentality and diversification energized cross-promotion. Novel-sources and movie soundtracks/singles were promoted to sell a movie. Novelizations of original films were also written, flooding bookstores before, during, and after the film's release. With the advent of the newly revised technologies (to be seen) and the undaunted move into honestly human, controversial, or forbidden subject matter (as we shall see), the industry began more intensely to use technology and subject matter as selling points, expanding on its former parading of star, genre and/or lavish production values/budget as audience magnets.

Notes

1   On November 12, 1946, Universal merged with independent studio "International Pictures" and became known as "Universal-International" until 1963, when new owner Music Corporation of America (MCA) decided to drop the surname. Throughout, the studio will be referred to as "Universal."

2 The court dismissed complaints against all the studio defendants upon their acts as producers.

3 Statutory Court Decision Text: US District Court Southern District, New York: USA, Plaintiff against Paramount Pictures, Inc., et al., Defendants, Dec. 31, 1946, Equity No. 87–273.

4 In his capsule essay "United States Versus Hollywood: The Case Study of an Antitrust Suit," in *Sight and Sound*, 19 (February, 1951), 418–20 and (March, 1951) 448–50 (reprinted in Tino Balio, ed., *The American Film Industry*, Madison, University of Wisconsin Press, 1985, 449–62), Ernest Borneman stated that the majors worried if smaller distribution companies such as Republic, Monogram, and SRO, not named in the decree, might be allowed to beat them at their own game. Yet the reaction from counsels and heads of these companies invariably revealed that they, too, understood that they would be prevented from the very monopolistic practices that the majors were accused of and that they would comply.

5 *Hollywood Reporter*, 91(44–50), Jan. 2, 3, 6, 7, 8, 9, 10, 1947 and 92(1), Jan. 13, 1947. *Variety*, 165(5), Jan. 8, 1947. *Motion Picture Herald*, 166(1), Jan. 4, 11, 1947. Jack Alicoate, ed., *The 1947 Film Daily Year Book of Motion Pictures* (29th ed., Fort Lee, Chicago, and Hollywood: J. E. Brulatour).

6 Though banned by the Court, the distributor still practiced competitive bidding, where two exhibitors wanted a picture in the same run and bid financially for it.

7 *Hollywood Reporter*, 93(36–9), May 4, 5, 6, 7, 1948. *Variety*, 170(9), May 5, 1948. *The 1948 and 1949 Film Daily Year Books of Motion Pictures*, 30th and 31st eds.

8 *Motion Picture Herald*, 173(6), November 6, 1948, 13–14.

9 *Motion Picture Herald*, 174(10), March 5, 1949, 12–13, 16–19, 22, 24, 26–7.

10 *Motion Picture Herald*, 182(2), Jan. 13, 1951, 7 and 190(10), March 8, 1953, 13.

11 *Motion Picture Herald*, 183(10), June 9, 1951, 15–17.

12 *Motion Picture Herald*, 186(5), Feb. 7, 1952, 20–1, 24.

13 This was a 10-million-a-week gain from the average weekly audience of 80 million during the heyday of the classical period.

14 Figures come from the yearly *Film Daily Year Book of Motion Pictures*.

15 Leo A. Handel, *Hollywood Looks at Its Audience: A Report on Film Audience Research* (Urbana: University of Illinois Press, 1950), 22.

16 Gene Brown, ed., *New York Times Encyclopedia of Film*, 1952–7, Vol. 6, August 11, 1957 (New York: New York Times Books).

17 In compiling the 1957–62 statistics, all features, co-productions, and foreign pick-ups included, released by the eight majors, were considered. In the case of RKO, features released by other distributors for the years 1957 through 1960 were tabulated. In terms of "story" source, only if the screenplay was derived from a previously *published* story was it considered an adaptation.

18 All film box-office figures in this book come from *Variety* and hence, are ballpark figures. Unless otherwise noted, box-office receipts are for US and Canadian (North American) rentals only.

19 *The 1946 and 1963 Film Daily Year Books of Motion Pictures*.

20 Figures from yearly *Film Daily Year Book of Motion Pictures*.

21 According to Michael Conant, *Antitrust In the Motion Picture Industry* (New York: Arno Press, 1978), 113, the number of independent producers of As went from 40 in 1945 to 70 in 1946, 100 in 1947 and 165 by 1957.

22 For a fuller account of UA, see Tino Balio's *United Artists: The Company That Changed the Film Industry* (Madison, University of Wisconsin Press, 1987).

23   For a detailed account of the US–British situation and accounts of the Hollywood industry's working relationship with France, Italy, Spain, and West Germany, see Thomas H. Guback, *The International Film Industry: Western Europe and America since 1945* (Bloomington, Indiana University Press, 1969), 16–36. Poland, Yugoslavia, Chile, Israel, Pakistan, Turkey, Burma, Indonesia, Formosa, Vietnam, and the Philippines were other countries that blocked foreign currency.

24   *New York Times Encyclopedia of Film*, 1952–7, Volume 6, June 3, 1953.

25   Through General Precision Corp., which owned both American Scophony and 11 percent of TCF stock, the studio had an oblique connection with this form of Toll TV.

26   Republic western stars Gene Autry and then Roy Rogers fought to prevent the studio from releasing their pictures to TV. For one thing, they argued, it would mean their endorsement of the respective sponsor's products. On June 13, 1954, the US Court of Appeals, Ninth District, San Francisco, in a decision of industry-wide importance, cleared the way for Republic to release to TV the Autry/Rogers oaters.

27   Though the movie's advertisements in the papers and on the TV highlighted the fact that *How to Marry a Millionaire* would be shown in CinemaScope, no one really saw the irony of this. Most viewers, of course, did not see the film in color either.

28   NTA had already acquired 30 late fifties RegalScope theatricals which Fox independent Robert L. Lippert sold to clear his Regal Co. of debts, but these B movies were not shown in prime time.

29   All studios were affected by these strikes, save Universal, which, along with many independent production companies, had already signed residual agreements with actors and writers.

30   Actually, Disney's TV debut was "One Hour in Wonderland" in 1950, an extended studio promo built around a party. Disney mounted another promo special in 1951.

31   Russell Sanjek, *American Popular Music and Its Business: The First Four Hundred Years, III, From 1900 to 1984)* (New York: Oxford University Press, 1988), 349.

32   For a fuller account of RKO history, see Richard B. Jewell (with Vernon Harbin), *The RKO Story* (London: Octopus Books, 1982) and Barbara Lasky, *The Biggest Little Major of Them All* (Englewood Cliffs, NJ: Prentice Hall, 1984).

33   RKO Radio Pictures was a distinct entity from RKO Corp., which was restructured as a holding company for the money owed to stockholders.

34   Product was judged from 1958 on, since films released in 1956 and 1957 were Zanuck's babies.

35   For a detailed account of the proxy fight, consult Emmett John Hughes, "MGM: War Among the Lion Tamers," 1957, reprinted Gerald Mast, ed., *Movies in Our Midst: Documents on the Cultural History of Film in America* (Chicago: University of Chicago Press, 1982), 652–66.

36   The company had not made enough money under Schary. Also, his extremely active participation in the Democratic Party campaign for Stevenson throughout California and production of a film on the history of the Democratic Party shown at the Chicago Democratic convention were an embarrassment to the largely Republican makeup of the Loew board.

37   For a fuller account, see Maurice Richard Hurst, *Republic Studios: Between Poverty-Row and the Majors* (Metuchen, NJ: Scarecrow Press, 1979).

38   Financial figures are unavailable, since AIP published no fiscal report.

39   In 1948, Gordon Kahn published *Hollywood On Trial* (New York: Boni & Gaer) to explain and defend the actions of "the Hollywood Ten" to the American public.

40   Frank J. Donner, *The Un-Americans* (New York: Ballantine Books, 1961) is an excellent work on HUAC's abuses of power.

41   In his succinct article "The Mass Hearings" reprinted in Balio, *The American Film Industry*, 425, John Cogley came up with 212 actual studio workers. The others, Cogley stated, were wives of studio employees, trade and union personnel, and communist party functionaries who had never held jobs in the industry. The essay is part of a two-volume work *Report on Blacklisting* (Fund to the Republic, 1956) helmed by Cogley, an ex-editor of the Catholic weekly periodical *Commonweal*. The study, which comprised interviews from 500 persons who had firsthand knowledge of the situation in Hollywood and New York, was supplemented by a legal study by Harold W. Horwitz and two sociological studies, propaganda-analyst Dorothy B. Jones's *Communism and the Movies: A Study of Film Content* and New York University's Dr. Marie Jahoda's *Anti-Communism and Employment Practices in Radio and Television*.

42   As Cogley noted in his study, the program for clearing accused persons was suggested by national syndicated newspaper columnist George E. Sokolsky, who was concerned over what would happen to ex-communists, liberals, and persons innocent of left-wing affiliations. The studios' self-policing programs, however, unleashed a host of private accusations and lengthy lists.

43   Upset with the industry's seeming insouciance, the Legion published the names in *The American Legion* magazine. At a meeting of March, 1952, the Legion told the industry to check out the list. Most producers did not and went on to use the list as a criterion for employment rather than as a basis for further investigation.

44   Cogley pointed to the appearance of *Red Channels* as the point when the blacklist took on an institutional fervor.

45   The Academy voted the anti-Communist ban in effect in 1957 to block the recognition of Michael Wilson as contributing writer on *Friendly Persuasion* (AA, 1956). Wilson had invoked the 5th in the 1951 hearings.

46   Figures are from yearly *Film Daily Year Book of Motion Pictures*.

47   A year earlier, U's David Lipton, the first advertising-practices studio executive, who countenanced the employment of market research as a selling guide and claimed that the awareness of trends and public dispositions could be helpful advertising tools, had stirred the waters.

48   Figures, which come from the yearly *Film Daily Year Book of Motion Pictures*, are unavailable from 1959 on.

6

Exhibition

Though the number of suits filed by the independent exhibitor against the studios steadily declined after 1954, the relationship between production-distribution and exhibition was anything but rosy. The exhibitors' continual attempt to replace an arbitration system that had expired in the 1940 consent decree came to naught. Exhibitors also decried the lack of major studio product, proposing many solutions that ranged from investing in film companies as a means of gaining a voice in management to an American version of Britain's Eady Plan. Even the studio release pattern bothered exhibitors, urging an orderly release of quality product in lieu of bunching top pictures for tested peak business periods. Though the antitrust decision resulted in bumping up the status of exhibitors (first-run houses increased while third and fourth-run houses moved up to second runs), exhibitors resented the open bidding system that increased the prices for film rentals, forcing many small fry (those not part of a mighty circuit) out of business. In addition, the exhibitors, lambasting the majors for giving TV stations new product, took action against the practice of Toll TV, filing a protest with the FCC. Exhibitors were also up in arms over the studios' sale of their film libraries to TV, especially the post-1948 batch. When all seemed lost, they urged companies for a reasonable clearance for TV showing and in 1960 formed an agency to negotiate post-1948 films for theatrical rereleases.

Even with the declining audience and the splintering of the formerly homogeneous mass audience into specialized ones, the audience movie-going pattern remained roughly the same: in 1946, 40 percent of the business from Monday through Thursday, 15 percent on Friday, 20 percent Saturday and 25 percent Sunday; by 1961, 50 percent, Monday through Friday, 30 percent Saturday, 20 percent Sunday.[1] At the behest of exhibitors, the Oscar night ceremony was switched to Monday, the slowest night at the movies.

The loss of patrons, lack of product, and shifting demographics forced many hardtop (indoor) theatres to close. Only 9,150 hardtops, down from 17,811 in 1948, survived in 1963.[2] Hardest hit were the city-center palaces, the tiny neighborhood houses and, with the desegregation of theaters in the South in the early sixties, the so-called "Negro" theaters.

The figure would have been bleaker had not exhibitors come up with alternatives and compensations. One such alternative was the "art house," mushrooming in numbers from 50 in 1946 to 395 by 1962.[3] The "art house," either a refurbished intimate city-center house or the newly built venue located at a city's limits, contained anywhere between 200 to 500 seats. Brazilian coffee was served in the lobby along with program notes. There was a slightly higher admission price than mainstream hardtops. The "art house" primarily accommodated the increasing influx of foreign films (89 in 1946; 331 by 1961).[4] Postwar fascination with all things foreign, exacerbated by travel overseas, stirred interest in the foreign film. The antitrust decree, product decline, the flourishing adult audience, the J. Arthur Rank–Universal connection, and Italian neo-realism (cf. Chapter 23) that sent up critical huzzas and forced the Academy to inaugurate a special award in 1947 for *Shoe Shine*[5] added to the vogue. With the 1960 roadshow presentation of director Federico Fellini's *La Dolce Vita* (Italy/France) in large city-center houses, the foreign film increasingly appeared in major circuit theaters. The "art house" catered also to risky Hollywood productions (*Lust for Life*, MGM, 1956), revivals of Hollywood classics (*Rebecca*, UA, 1940), documentaries (*Kon-Tiki*, RKO, 1951), and American independent films (Shirley Clarke's *The Connection*, 1960).

The intimate hardtop, built in a suburban shopping mall, thus foregrounding movies as a consumer product, was another alternative. Of the 278 hardtops constructed between 1960 and 1962, more than one-third were located in malls. Still another venue was the Cinerama New Dome Theater, located in the hub of large cities to show productions in the Cinerama process (see Chapter 8.1.1). By 1962, 60 Domes existed in America; 40 overseas.

The drive-in, springing up on the edge of cities all over America (not just in the rural South and West), compensated somewhat for the decrease of the hardtops. A cynosure for youth who saw it as a form of dating with a built-in sofa on which to make out, the drive-in also proved attractive for the large family, which, not having to pay babysitting or parking fees, found it an extremely cheap evening out. Numbering 820 in 1948, the drive-in peaked at 4,063 a decade later.[6] The brainchild of Richard Hollingshead, Jr., who opened the first one in Camden, New Jersey in 1933 with a 3-year-old B picture, the drive-in finally showed major studio releases in 1938 with the development of the car speaker. Other exhibitor compensations included the concession stand (with ice-cream, cold sodas, buttered popcorn, and hot dogs popular items) and higher admission prices, which rose from \$.65 to \$1.80 for adult after-5:00 p.m. performances at city-center venues.

Psycho (P, 1959) reconfigured the exhibition format. Fearing that the film's suspense and understanding might be compromised if the audience came in late or at any old time, producer-director Hitchcock insisted on the policy of staggered performances in which the public entered only once at the film's start and cleared out at the film's end. This still-in-effect policy flew in the face of the continuous, enter-whenever-you-want format of previous decades.

Conclusion

Hollywood's commercial makeover which, remember, came with no money-back guarantee, kept the industry not only above water but sailing the waves. Disney's rise, in a sense, canceled RKO's demise; AIP's opening offset Republic's closing. Exhibitors had compensations.

But that's not the whole picture. The loss of the exhibition wing eventuated in a more selective approach to A features (now that product had to be cut) and the upgrading of B items. The reliance on proven source material from fiction, the stage, and TV's dramatic anthology series brought solidity to Hollywood films. The plugging into an acknowledged adult audience, a profitable ploy to boot, raised the intellectual, emotional, sensual, and visceral bar in films. The concentrated effort to give the product an international appeal as well as runaway production, involving a location shoot and the creative input of native talent and craft as well, endowed features with an unparalleled frankness and freshness. Often independent productions revealed a unique perspective, a distinct voice. The shifting in political ideology instilled a deeper passion and earnestness. This refashioning, as we shall see, affected censorship, genre, and style.

Notes

1 Figures are from the yearly *International Motion Picture Almanac*, ed. Charles S. Aaronson (New York: Quigley Publications), which based its percentages on data from the Department of Commerce.
2 Lists of movie houses in the US are inconsistent. The figures quoted come from "the most detailed and accurate data" drawn from the *Census of Selected Service Industries* and recorded in Christopher H. Sterling and Timothy R. Haight, *The Mass Media: Aspen Institute Guide to Communication Industry Trends* (New York and London: Praeger, 1978), 34.
3 Figures are from yearly *Film Daily Year Book of Motion Pictures*.
4 Ibid.
5 The Academy continued with its special award for foreign language film until 1956, when the board created the "Best Foreign Language Film Award" category.
6 Sterling and Haight, 34.

Part III
Technology

Introduction

Whether reintroducing and refining technologies which had been around, or developing others, the postwar film industry was remarkable in its emphasis on, even flaunting of, technology both within the movie's text and in a movie's advertising. This, of course, was in line with the trend of just about every old industry technologically updating itself and the nation's resultant technophilia. America bought into technology since it energized the surface optimism, the deliberate cheerfulness of the time. Technological advances were a testament that the "American way of life" was the best, and ultimately a proof of the superiority of the US over the USSR.

The foregrounding of movie technology, more pertinently, was a means to compete with other leisure activities: TV certainly, but also stereo recordings/ phonographs, spectator/participant sports, and travel. To reclaim the deserters while retaining the faithful was the objective.

Color, large screens, stereo, 3-D, and special effects became part of what going to the movies was about. Technology, in fact, became another route, in addition to the time-honored uses of star and genre and the touting of production values, which postwar Hollywood used as an advertising charm. As we shall see also, the film that dealt honestly with achingly human, hair-triggering topical, controversial, and/or forbidden matter was still another side of moviegoing as well as an exploitable one, as in *Baby Doll* (WB, 1956), which purposely avoided techno-pizzazz. Some films, such as *Picnic* (C, 1955), had it both ways, enticing the spectator with both technology and thematics.

7

Color

In 1940, 4 percent of the product was in color; in 1954, 58 percent. With 1958's financial crunch, color's use dropped to 25 percent but the decrease proved to be short-lived. The continually increasing deployment of color marked another difference with the preceding years' patchy use.

Color countered the b/w TV image and rendered actual locations, where movies were increasingly being shot, more involving. The federal antitrust decree of 1950[1] that broke up Technicolor's monopoly on color photography also contributed to the hike in color movies. Its patents now had to be licensed to other manufacturers and producers. Companies inevitably turned aggressive in marketing a one-strip color system ("monopak") which the industry took up.

Monopak, based on the wartime introduction of "integral tripak," was a three-color subtractive process that eliminated the use of separate negatives by containing its three layers of color dye (red/blue/green) within the same emulsion and coupling them in the developing process.[2] Technicolor, on the other hand, was an additive process which used three separate negatives, each containing a color dye (red/blue/green). It required a special camera and a complicated developing process. With monopak, color movies could now be made from a single negative with an ordinary camera and a compact printing process that any studio was able to set up on its premises, and hence, more cheaply. (Color stock cost twice as much as that of b/w. Also, color movies were more time-consuming to shoot owing to the changing light and color values which had to be regulated on the set and matched on the editing table or in the lab.)

Not only was it cheaper, but monopak facilitated location shooting. The single compact camera it called for dispensed with the extremely heavy, bulky Technicolor machine that accommodated three separate negatives. For *King Solomon's Mines* (1950), MGM shot the Kenya/Uganda/Belgium Congo/Tanganyika exteriors in monopak and the few interiors at Culver City in Technicolor.

Further, monopak, faster to process than Technicolor, made film dailies available in less time.

7.1 Ansco Color and Metrocolor

During the war, General Aniline and Film Corp. developed the monopak commercial film process Ansco Color, based on the German process Agfacolor. *Sixteen Fathoms Deep* (M, 1948) was the first feature in this process. By 1950, Ansco had introduced 35 mm negative-positive color print, supplanting the reversal type, which proved too contrasty. Whereas RKO and UA's interest in Ansco Color was sporadic, MGM's was ardent, from *The Wild North* (1952) through its 3-D specials (*Escape from Fort Bravo*, 1953) to its CinemaScope musicals (*Brigadoon*, 1954), though it still used Technicolor. With Ansco's improvement in 1955, boasting finer grains, higher speeds, and far superior color reproduction, MGM made the process its own, rechristening it "Metrocolor." Debuting with *Lust for Life* (1956), Metrocolor became a studio signature.

7.2 Eastman Color, Warnercolor, Color By Deluxe, Columbia Color

Marketed in 1950, Kodak's monopak Eastman Color became the preferred process by 1956. That the color values of all monopak processes lacked staying power did not deter the industry. Monopak's chemicals deteriorated over time with a significant loss of color fidelity: the blue/green/yellow spectrum practically disappeared, leaving the print a rosy purple.[3] Nor did the decision makers mind that monopak could not hold a candle to Technicolor's lush, saturated color range. Monopak was cheaper. That was reason enough for its use.

Various labs (some on the studio lots) were associated with the Eastman process. They invariably put their respective names on the processed films. At WB, pictures shot in the Eastman process carried the credit "Warnercolor," starting in 1952. TCF's Eastman color prints of its CinemaScope productions from 1954 were made at its Deluxe Lab, bannering the credit "Color By Deluxe." (Fox's early 'Scope releases had a "Technicolor" credit line since the Technicolor lab made the prints from Eastman Color negatives.) UA's productions, processed at Fox's DeLuxe lab, also ran the Color By Deluxe tag – part of UA's payback for Fox's President Skouras's $5 million loan. The Pathé Lab's version of Eastman Color was called "Pathécolor," later "Eastman Color by Pathé," and was used occasionally by UA (*Adventures of Robinson Crusoe*, 1954), RKO

(*Louisiana Territory*, 1954), and ARC (*Apache Woman*, 1955). "Columbia Color" showed up as a credit around 1958–9 but ceased thereafter when Columbia referred to the process as "Eastman Color." When MGM (*Love Me or Leave Me*, 1955) and U (*Pillow Talk*, 1959) used Eastman Color, they called it "Eastman Color."

Buena Vista, Paramount, and Columbia (despite its short-lived "Columbia Color" and "Eastman Color" tags) shot their product in the Eastman process but had Technicolor do the printing. As such, the color of their prints, which were labeled "Technicolor," had relative staying power. Warners followed in the early sixties.

7.3 Trucolor by Consolidated and Cinecolor/Natural Color/Super Cinecolor

Cheaper (only 25 percent more than the cost of b/w stock) and faster to develop (24 hours), but inferior (unable to produce all the colors of the spectrum), color processes continued to be rolled out until the mid-fifties. The two-color process "Trucolor," converted by Consolidated Film Lab into the three-color process "Trucolor by Consolidated" with the use of the new Dupont color positive stock in 1951, was the mainstay at Republic, its *Johnny Guitar* (1954) considered its finest 110 minutes. The other two-color process was "Cinecolor," developed by the Cinecolor Corp. in 1950. Cinecolor was eventually refined into a three-color process, first called "Natural Color," and then "Super Cinecolor." A staple at the bush-league outfits (Monogram, Producers Releasing Corporation, Allied Artists), all eight majors dabbled in it for their B projects.

Directors, cinematographers, production designers, and costumiers deployed color more and more to reveal rather than record reality, often to express subjectivity. Color, at this time, became an important vehicle for thematic values. Red was the predominant hue of the aliens in *War of the Worlds* (P, 1953), honing the allegorical aliens = communists (with their red flag) equation of the horror–sci-fi films. Bleaching out primary colors, *Track of the Cat*'s (WB, 1954) look was a correlative of the icy familial relationships within the snowed-in farmhouse of 1880s Northern California as well as a conveyor of atmosphere. *Moby Dick* (WB, 1956) superimposed a b/w negative of the completed color print over a color negative to give the appearance of old nineteenth-century whaling prints of the film's setting. Each of *Lust for Life*'s five movements, built around a predominant tone/s, encapsulated Van Gogh's emotional states while designating a particular period of his work. The opening's inky blacks and ghostly grays characterized the bereft, despondent artist and his socially conscious paintings in the Borinage where he worked in the mines. Dark greens suffused the film's second part, when the sick painter went to Holland and immersed himself in the countryside. The brilliant reds and blues of the next phase spoke of a Vincent who was strong and hopeful while depicting the Impressionistic influence of Paris. The yellows, subdued reds, and greens marked his period at Arles and St. Rémy, as his demons approached. The final movement, detailing life at Auvers outside Paris when madness took hold, contained a riot of color, suggesting the combination of many influences in the last stage of his work. The use of DayGlo colors provided an ironic contrast with the dark, dastardly doings in *A Kiss Before Dying* (UA, 1956). *Bonjour Tristesse* (C, 1958) juxtaposed monochrome with color sequences, contrasting the narrator's physical and psychological space.

Notes

1   Filed on August 19, 1947, the suit alleged that Technicolor, Inc. did more than 90 percent of all business in commercial color movies. The suit also included Eastman Kodak, alleging that Technicolor, Inc. had entered into a series of agreements with Eastman whereby patents, new developments, and technological information relating to color photography would be reserved for Technicolor's exclusive use in the professional market.
2   Technicolor monopak was first used for exteriors in *Lassie Come Home* (MGM, 1943) and entirely for *Thunderhead, Son of Flicka* (TCF, 1945).
3   The question of whether the color companies and studios knew of monopak's unstable quality is tricky. Eastman Kodak always printed a warning to this effect on its label. Those who did pay attention (and many did not quite simply because they did not believe movies had any long-term financial value) knew that, while the prints were unstable, the negative was not. And this was no great shakes since a print could always be struck from a negative. By 1960, it was generally known that the shelf life of a color print was 10 years; that of the negative, 25 years; and that if the storage temperature of the negative was lowered by five degrees, its life could be doubled.

8

Screen Shapes and Accompanying Sound Systems

8.1 Multi-Camera Systems

8.1.1 Cinerama and Interlocked Six-/Seven-Track Magnetic Stereo Sound

On September 30, 1952, *This Is Cinerama* premiered at Manhattan's Broadway Theater to wild applause from critics and public alike, triggering the large-screen revolution. The process, developed by engineer-photographer-boatsman-special effects expert Fred Waller, had already been exhibited as "Vitarama" at the 1939 New York World's Fair and used as a gunnery trainer for the army and air force during World War II. Since the late forties, Cinerama had been offered and turned down by practically every major studio. A group of independents subsequently formed Cinerama, Inc.: newscaster Lowell C. Thomas, producer Merian C. Cooper, showman Mike Todd, and a subsidiary of the Fabian–Rosen Stanley Warner Corp.

A most elaborate technology with, on the whole, awesome results, Cinerama employed a single 35 mm camera with three 27 mm lenses (about the focal length of the human eye) set at 48-degree angles to each other. Each lens, with its separate negative, photographed a different area of the scene (the middle lens shot straight in front; the right lens, scene left; the left lens, scene right) while a single rotating shutter made sure that each negative was exposed simultaneously. A large auditorium with three projection booths, each with an oversized reel of film that held 7,500 feet running up to 50 minutes, was required to show the image, which ran at 26 frames per second, as opposed to the usual 24 (each

8-1 *Caged* (WB, 1950, p. Jerry Wald)

Classical Ratio (1.33:1) – that is, four units of width (horizontal, left to right) to three units of height (vertical, bottom to top).

8-2 *How the West Was Won* (MGM, 1962, p. Bernard Smith)

Multi-camera system Cinerama (2.76:1)

8-3 *Bad Day at Black Rock* (MGM, 1954, p. Dore Schary)
Anamorphic system CinemaScope (standardized at 2.35 : 1)

8-4 *Operation Petticoat* (U, 1959, p. Robert Arthur)
Widescreen (standardized at 1.85 : 1)

8-5 *One-Eyed Jacks* (P, 1961, p. Frank P. Rosenberg)
Wide-Frame System VistaVision (1.66:1; 1.85:1; 2:1 but usually presented 1.85:1)

8-6 *Legend of the Lost* (UA, 1957, p, Robert Haggiag, Henry Hathaway)
Anamorphic/Wide Frame System Technirama (2.34:1)

8-7   *West Side Story* (UA, 1961, p. Mirisch Bros., Robert Wise
70 mm/wide-gauge process Super Panavision 70 (2.05 : 1)

frame contained six instead of four sprocket holes). While the center booth projected the image onto screen center, the right booth lighted screen left; the left booth, screen right. Onto a concave screen of about 1,110 vertical slats (strips of perforated tape), a gigantic image 76 feet wide and 24 feet high appeared, covering 146 degrees peripheral and 55.5 degrees vertical vision. To keep each picture together, a vibrating device ("gigolo") was in place while the projectors were synchronized by a mechanism operated by still another projectionist. Half of the film had to be loaded on one reel (changeovers were out of the question), requiring an intermission and a running time of two hours maximum.

To intensify the illusion of reality and sense of participation, sound engineer Hazard E. Reeves's six-track stereo sound accompanied the image. Five speakers were located behind the screen and others on the sides and at the rear of the house.[1] A separate 35 mm film recorded the magnetic track, transcribed on location by means of multi-microphones as well as post-produced. Reproduced through interlock with the projector, this stereo system required the services of a sound-control engineer who was also in charge of the mechanism that kept the projectors in sync. Opening and closing the curtain and dimming and raising the lights involved a fifth projectionist.

Stereo, too, had been around before the adoption of Cinerama. In addition to Bell Telephone's recording and reproducing experiments in the thirties, WB tried out a two-channel system for *Four Daughters* (1938) and *The Santa Fe Trail* (1941). Disney's *Fantasia* (1940) was equally impressive for its successful integration of RCA's "Panoramic Stereo Sound System."

Cinerama came with definite drawbacks. Despite the "gigolo" device, the two "joins" in the picture were visible and image matching remained a problem, especially due to variations in projection illumination. (Mis-sync between the interlocked picture and sound rarely posed a problem.) Unless the spectator sat in an auditorium's center or rear-center, some degree of distortion was inevitable. Theater conversion cost between $75,000 and $140,000. (Eventually, special "Cinerama Dome" theaters were built.) The projection crew was drastically increased. As a result, only 22 US theaters were equipped to roadshow[2] Cinerama movies. The production of a feature, however, came down to a then average of $1 million.[3]

Subject matter was problematic. Quite simply, what could a producer put on a screen with an aspect ratio (ratio of picture's width to its height) of 2.76 units of width to every 1 unit of height (2.76:1)? Eschewing plot, Cinerama took the travelogue/cultural event documentary route (Venice's canals, a snippet of *Aida* at the La Scala Opera House), veering off, now and then, into chills and spills (a roller-coaster ride at Rockaway's Playground). *Cinerama Holiday* (1955), *7 Wonders of the World* (1956), *Search for Paradise* (1957), and *Cinerama South Sea Adventure* (1958) traveled the initial Cinerama documentary route, which, as we shall see, was not as much a stretch now that the documentary mode and sensibility hovered heavily over postwar Hollywood.

By 1958, the public's support for Cinerama withered.[4] After a pact with MGM and adjustment (increase of screen size, use of one booth for all projections,[5] reversion to 24 fps to facilitate conversion to 35 mm or 70 mm, the move to 7-track sound), Cinerama (now called "Super Cinerama") turned to storytelling with *The Wonderful World of the Brothers Grimm* and *How the West Was Won* (both 1962), while never forsaking its travelogue and chills-and-spills origins.

With *It's a Mad, Mad, Mad, Mad World* (UA, 1963), Cinerama introduced 70 mm single-lens projection ("70 mm Super Cinerama"). Filmed in Ultra Panavision 70, the movie was projected though an enlarging lens specially made for the company.[6] Cinerama's last revision ("New Super Cinerama Process") sounded its death knell: reduction of screen curve to 120 degrees, use of standard material for the screen, an aspect ratio comparable to that of standard 70 mm, and the shooting of all films in 70 mm with no optical correction.[7]

8.1.2   Cinemiracle

Louis de Rochemont, producer of *Cinerama Holiday*, unveiled another multi-camera system called "Cinemiracle" on April 8, 1958 at Grauman's Chinese Theater in Los Angeles. Developed by National Theaters, Inc., the Smith-Dietrich Corporation, and de Rochemont himself, Cinemiracle was an improvement on Cinerama with its elimination of the "joins" and the consolidation of all three projectors interlocked with seven-channel magnetic stereo in one booth. Only one feature, *Windjammer*, was filmed in Cinemiracle. An extremely impressed and stressed-out competitor, Cinerama, Inc.,[8] snapped up the process.

8.2   Anamorphic Systems

8.2.1   *CinemaScope and Mag Optical Stereophonic Sound; RegalScope; CinemaScope 55*

Galvanized by Cinerama yet hoping to skirt its elitism, Fox came up with CinemaScope. Debuting with the historical spectacle *The Robe* at Manhattan's Roxy Theater on September 16, 1953, CinemaScope was a smash.

CinemaScope was a system in which the camera's anamorphic lens, covering a large field of vision, virtually compressed the picture to fit a 35 mm frame. A compensating lens on the projector then expanded the picture. CinemaScope produced an image 2⅔ wide as it was high on a surface composed of highly reflective material embossed with thousands of tiny, concave mirror elements. Its initial aspect ratio of 2.66:1 was reduced to 2.55:1 and then standardized to 2.35:1 to accommodate its sound component. Three microphones on the set furnished the sound carried by three house speakers. An additional track recorded the reproduced sound effects.

Anamorphosis, patented in Great Britain as early as 1862 by Sir David Brewster, had already undergone about half a dozen variations when Fox optioned Henri Chrétien's Hypergonar Lens. Fox technicians Earl Sponable, Sol Halprin, Lorin Grignon, Herbert Bragg, and Carl Faulkner refined the system while the enlisted optical firm of Bausch & Lomb improved on Chrétien's lenses.

This less costly process, with an economically feasible $10,000–$25,000 installation fee, was presented on a continuous, no intermission policy by one projectionist. Also, unlike Cinerama's sound-image interlock system, Fox introduced MagOptical Stereophonic Sound, a four-track magnetic sound system on the film strip that offered a backup optical head for mono use if a house were not equipped for stereo or if its stereo system went out.

Yet CinemaScope did have quite a few wrinkles to iron out. Subject matter could be daunting. Though used initially for large-scale genres (adventure, musical), CinemaScope became at home with intimate ones as well (romantic comedy, romance melodrama).

Directors were chagrined at the "mail-slot" shape. They wondered what to frame and how to stage (keep the camera distant from the players who were horizontally arranged across the frame?). How to control an audience's eye, how to compose a close-up were equally puzzling. What about cutting? With so much detail (and money) spent on the set, shouldn't the audience be allowed to savor it? Besides, quick cutting could disorient the viewer. Was a long-held shot really the solution? (The large screen shape did result in less cutting in pictures than in the previous period, but this occurrence was also motivated, as we shall see, by the prevalent documentary realist and psychological-sociological realist styles that favored working within the frame.) Textures were blurry. Colors appeared muddy. Horizontal-line staging seemed warped, especially when photography involved a short focal-length lens.

The recording and reproduction of magnetic stereophonic sound was no piece of cake either. Cutting and matching stereo sound with the image was hairy business. With continual use, a magnetic track became less and less effective in sound reproduction. It also had a tendency to litter itself with ambient noise. And it cost twice as much to produce than optical monaural.

Despite these problems that were eventually solved, producers and public rallied behind CinemaScope. Exhibitors, only after realizing they had lost the screen shape battle, joined the ranks. By the end of 1953, 1,500 theaters were equipped; by 1954, when a quarter of the product was in CinemaScope, 11,000 theaters converted.

For approximately the first two years,[9] 'Scope films were produced in two versions, anamorphic and flat. The flat renditions were to accommodate "unequipped" theaters. This, of course, meant shooting a scene twice, the second time invariably involving a restaging, which sent time, production costs, and tempers mounting. Frank Sinatra, for example, walked off the set of *Carousel* (TCF, 1956) when informed that director Henry King planned to restage and reshoot a scene. After all, he argued, he was not getting paid twice.

Leased for a $25,000 fee per picture to all studios, some of which developed their own anamorphic processes (WB's "WarnerScope," RKO's "SuperScope," AIP's "Superama," R's "Naturama")[10] but in the end yielding to Fox out of a need for standardization, CinemaScope was a package that included color, four-track stereo, and the replacement of a "Miracle Mirror" screen that reduced unnecessary reflections. When WB wanted to shoot its CinemaScope-planned *Rebel Without a Cause* (1955) and MGM *Trial* (1955) in b/w, Fox threatened a lawsuit. WB acquiesced; MGM produced its film flat. Only with the company's *Teenage Rebel* (1956) did Fox drop the color obligation. Earlier in May, 1954, Fox relaxed the sound requirement, allowing exhibitors, who fought stereo conversion through their union IATSE, the choice of either mono optical or one-track hi-fi magnetic minus the stereo (the latter for exhibitors who converted to mag without adding the stereo channeling). Fox backed off also from its special screen demand. Not to associate its system with anything inferior,

Robert E. Lippert's B movies for Fox, shot in CinemaScope, received the credit "RegalScope," after the independent's Regal Films banner.

To produce "superspecials" with sharper definition, greater depth of field and less distortion, Fox decided to increase the actual width of the film stock to 55 mm. This warranted a special camera (the Fox 4 × 55 with the image area of the negative four times that of 35 mm), special processing equipment, and a special projector. The 55 mm prints included seven-channel stereo sound (five behind the screen, one for special effects, and a control track regulating the sound's movement). Though *Carousel* and *The King and I* (both 1956) were filmed and advertised in this new format, called "CinemaScope 55," Fox decided to distribute 35 mm reductions to spare exhibitors any more conversion costs. (*The King and I*, however, did play a few engagements in CinemaScope 55.) Then, too, Fox was already eyeing a merger with Todd-AO.

8.2.2   Panavision 35

In 1953, Robert E. Gottschalk formed Panavision, Inc. to manufacture anamorphic projection lenses for CinemaScope. Unlike exclusive suppliers Bausch & Lomb's cylindrical lenses, called "baltar," Panavision's optics were prismatic, thus enabling a change in the lenses squeeze ratio by a turning of the knob on the lens itself. The "panatar" lens caught on.

While designing a wide-gauge system for MGM, Panavision created a new photographing lens designed for 35 mm photography that reduced CinemaScope's distortion while enhancing definition. MGM showcased this improved anamorphic process with the Presley musical *Jailhouse Rock* (1957) and, in no time, every studio converted. Begrudgingly, Fox threw down the gauntlet in 1966. By the late sixties, Panavision 35 became the industry's standard anamorphic process and is still in use today.

CinemaScope/Panavision 35 (and other large-screen formats) did affect narrative. The large screen shapes vitalized the trend of multiple (usually three) protagonists. The use of several protagonists, especially when seen at the same time, seemed an ideal way to fill the large screen space. The commercial incentive to "make 'em big," which involved many stars in one picture, was also an impetus. The adaptation of the multi/subplotted novel as well as the stage play, each with its host of major characters, must also be factored in.

A mere sampling includes the three protagonists of *Woman's World* (TCF, 1954), where the wives came with respective husbands; *Les Girls* (MGM, 1957); and *The Young Lions* (TCF, 1958). Four suburban couples populated *No Down Payment* (TCF, 1957); four siblings, *Until They Sail* (MGM, 1957). *The Long Hot Summer* (TCF, 1958), culled from five short stories of Faulkner and his novel *The Hamlet*, had four pairs of protagonists: a drifter and a schoolteacher, a patriarch and his mistress, newlyweds, and a gay man and his doting mother. Five major characters take the lid off the Senate in *Advise and Consent* (UA, 1962). The use of multiple protagonists encouraged a narrative of alternating parallel or contrasting scenes of what each protagonist was up to and episodic structuring. These were shifts from the classical paradigm of the use of one central action thrust and the preference for linear structure. Genre and style experimentation, to be discussed later, also affected such narrative and structural shifts.

CinemaScope/Panavision 35 affected narrative in other ways. Often starting or finishing a scene and sprinkled generously throughout, especially if the film was location shot, was a slow dolly out to or a leisurely pan of or a bold cut to an extremely long vista shot, held for a noticeably lengthy interval. Basically descriptive, such shots were usually unaccompanied by character point of view. *The Bridge on the River Kwai*'s narrative is flecked with such shots (the surrounding hills of the Ceylon jungle viewed from an office perched high up; thousands of bats disturbed by explosives going off; the completion, then destruction of the impressive bridge).

Another narrative trope, which found its way into the historical spectacle and adventure, was the shot of someone opening a curtain onto a vast space beyond, loaded with buildings and/or casts of thousands. A crimson drape parts to reveal the splendor of the imperial city of Rome in *The Robe* while VistaVisioned *The Ten Commandments* (P, 1956) has Moses drawing back a curtain to display for the pharaoh the city being erected by the Israelite slaves.

In imitation of Cinerama, the maneuver of interspersed scenic tours and cultural presentations was constant, deployed by a camera placed on or in a moving vehicle, tracking in front of a moving vehicle, or just statically recording. In *How to Marry a Millionaire* (TCF, 1953), the camera is placed on the dashboard of a snow tractor as it heads up the hills of Maine and later, in the plane's cockpit as it lands in Kansas City. A couple of descriptive passages of New York City (one in which the Staten Island ferry crosses the screen horizontally, left to right) also bejewel this social satire. In *Love Is a Many-Splendored Thing* (TCF, 1955), the camera is placed on the hood of the ambulance as it races through Hong Kong's main drag. *The Ambassador's Daughter* (UA, 1956), shot entirely in Paris, has more camera descriptions and accompanying commentary of the City of Light, including two fashion shows at Dior, the "Swan Lake Ballet" at the Place de l'Opéra and (would you believe) a stroll through the sewers, than it has plot. Tours of Tokyo actually interrupt the mystery in *Stopover Tokyo* (TCF, 1957) while Kabuki and the Matsubayashi Girls' revue stall *Sayonara*'s (WB, 1957, in Technirama) twin romances.

In addition to their descriptive function, such shots and travelogue scenes were meant to fill the spectator with awe. They "self-reflexively" commented on technology's ability to make the location, in all of its myriad detail, palpable. Such shots and scenes so consciously revealed and foregrounded the very operation of film's formal strategies and materials (here, the large-screen presentation of story and composition) that the very operation became part of the film's meaning and affect. "Self-reflexivity" did break plot cohesiveness, undermining the "transparency" of the Hollywood classical style. In lieu of erasing a film's formal properties while the film presented itself ("transparency"), these films grandstanded their techniques, revealing their method of construction, allowing the spectator to see the films actually making themselves.

Large screen shapes influenced visual design. Sets, on the whole, were more spatially encompassing and more realistically detailed, whether studio built or location shot, and usually peopled by groups of extras. (As a contrast with classic design, compare the visual design of *Ivanhoe*, 1952, shot in 1.33:1 aspect ratio and that of the CinemaScoped *Knights of the Round Table* the following year, both adventure films made by MGM on locations in Britain by the same producer, director, photographer, production designers, and even with the same star.) The camera often noted the design, holding on the set or moving around it, as it does during the astronomy lecture at the Griffith Park Observatory in *Rebel Without a Cause* (WB, 1955) or the tour of the huge Kansas granary in *Picnic* (C, 1955). At once, thematic and showy, visual design warranted long takes and less cutting into bits and pieces. Rapid montages threatened to upend the set's grandeur.

Framing and staging were also affected. Sportingly self-reflexive, *It's Always Fair Weather*'s (MGM, 1955) "I Shouldn't Have Come" number musicalized the changes from flat to large screen. Continually throughout the musical, co-directors Stanley Donen and Gene Kelly divided the frame in three panels to tell the stories of the three ex-GIs with each panel simultaneously and ironically commenting on the other two. Director Rouben Mamoulian musically parodied new framing and staging strategies in the "Stereophonic Sound" number in *Silk Stockings* (MGM, 1957). Tashlin began *The Girl Can't Help It* (TCF, 1956) in 1.33:1 b/w/monaural and then added the new technologies until the screen became 'Scope, color, and stereo. *Pillow Talk* (U, 1959) split the frame for its antagonistic party-liners. Throughout *Lust for Life* (MGM, 1956), various screen shapes showcased Van Gogh's works.

Large screens encouraged same-shot action and reaction. In *Love Me or Leave Me* (MGM, 1955) Doris Day, on the frame's extreme left side, is shown from neck to knee with her breasts thrust out and wiggling rear as she warbles "Everybody Loves My Baby" while on the frame's right side, James Cagney lasciviously locks in on her body. In the thirties, Wyler and a few others used this architecture occasionally, rendering a more complex image. Now, the exception became the rule.

Accommodatingly, the large screen shape often included leads and supports within the frame at one and the same time, acting and reacting to each other. In *Picnic*, eight members and friends of the Owens family assemble in the parlor before heading out to the Labor Day festivities. This type of framing and staging strengthened ensemble performance, which, conversely, also warranted this mode of visual structuring. Postwar films, on the whole, tended to be more ensemble pieces than the hitherto star-vehicles. The documentary realist and psychological-sociological realist styles (as we shall see) also played their parts in this switch.

With Wyler, Hitchcock, and Welles's perfected use of vertical depth of field (foreground, middle ground and background of actor/set/prop in focus), which made these directors' films so uncharacteristic of the thirties and early forties staple, CinemaScope/Panavision 35 played a variation by adding extended movement among the vertical planes. *East of Eden* (WB, 1955), for example, has Raymond Massey and James Dean foregrounded on the frame's left side watching a train moving diagonally left to right in the middle ground toward the background. Not surprisingly, this type of shot was held interminably.

The new screen shapes activated horizontal depth of field with actor/set/prop visible across left, center, and right frame, as, for example, golddiggers Betty Grable, Marilyn Monroe, and Lauren Bacall relaxing in their rented Manhattan penthouse in *How to Marry a Millionaire*. The new screen shape also brought about an emphasis on horizontal staging, particularly, having an actor sprawled across a bed, his/her face on one side, legs on another (Lee Marvin across Spencer Tracy's bed in *Bad Day at Black Rock*, MGM, 1955). *King of the Khyber Rifles* (TCF, 1953) sported hand-to-hand sparring in a prone position. In *Violent Saturday* (TCF, 1955), Victor Mature slithers, from right to left edge of the frame, underneath a car while aiming his rifle at the robbers. Burt Lancaster and Tony Curtis's *Trapeze* (UA, 1956) act is often shown horizontally across the screen, with the camera positioned alongside or from below looking up. Her hands tied, Debbie Reynolds shimmies on the floor to get loose in *The Gazebo* (MGM, 1959).

Additionally, the new spatial formats encouraged diagonal depth of field – with actor/set/prop in focus along a diagonal line from frame's corner to corner – as well as spherical depth of field – with actor/set/prop on varying height levels, in focus in low- or high-angled right/left foreground corner, through lower- or higher-angled middle ground center, to even lower- or higher-angled right/left background corner. *Carmen Jones* (TCF, 1954) relished the latter combination, with Harry Belafonte on a second-floor landing foregrounded in the frame's right corner peeking down at Dorothy Dandridge on a pay phone backgrounded in the frame's left corner with two flights of stairs between the estranged lovers in the center middle ground. *Exodus* (UA, 1960) turned this

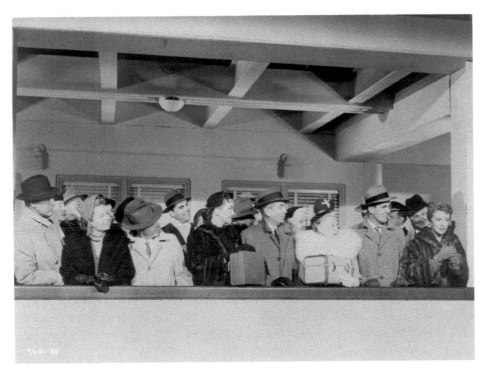

8-8   *An Affair to Remember* (TCF, 1957, p. Jerry Wald)

CinemaScope's decentering with Cary Grant on the frame's left edge with Deborah Kerr on the frame's right edge as recent lovers, each affianced to another, in this romance melodrama.

visual maneuver into a suspense-producing gambit: often, someone on a mountaintop, roof of an abode, or building ledge in the foreground right corner of the frame observes some figure or action below in the middle ground center and still another figure or action even further below in the background left frame corner.

A good deal of unclassical decentering within the frame, which came with the screen's new terrain, functioned as a succinct icon for the contretemps between two characters (*A Kiss Before Dying*, UA, 1956), loneliness (the terminal and bar encounters between Paul Newman and Piper Laurie in *The Hustler*, TCF, 1961), or to hint of a world about to come apart (the backstage standoff between James Cagney/Jane Greer and Dorothy Malone in *Man of a Thousand Faces*, U, 1957). Director Anatole Litvak pulled off a nifty variation in *Anastasia* (TCF, 1956), when he played a scene between Ingrid Bergman and Yul Brynner with neither actor within screen space. Instead, her voice is heard coming from her bedroom door on the right edge of the frame while his voice comes from his bedroom door on the left edge, signaling, in this use of offscreen space, how miles apart they are in regards to their professional and personal lives.

The use of multiple protagonists, the inclusion of descriptive shots and travelogue scenes, the same-shot action/reaction, ensemble staging, and the various depth-of-field compositions, all of which demanded a long take for the audience to assess meaning, extended movies' running time. In 1937, a midpoint in the classical sound years (1929–45), the average running time of an A feature at the five major and three minor movie combines was approximately 89 minutes. In 1954, the halfway mark of postwar years (1946–62), the average length was 98 minutes.

8.3   Widescreen

A counter to the radically elaborate, expensive multi-camera and anamorphic systems, widescreen, with aspect ratios ranging from 1.66:1 to 2:1, became fashionable. Lorenzo del Riccio's 1924 Magnascope process[11] was still occasionally trotted out for a movie's climactic sequence, as in *Portrait of Jenny*'s (SRO, 1948) hurricane, where it was accompanied by an audio expanding system advertised as "Cyclophonic" sound. MGM presented in its entirety *Ivanhoe* (1952) and Shakespeare's *Julius Caesar* (1953) in 1.75:1 aspect ratio for some engagements. Universal presented *Thunder Bay* (1953) in 1.85:1.

It was, however, Paramount that pushed the so-called "Panoramic Screen" with its 1953 product, hoping that the 1.66:1 aspect ratio would become an industry standard. Any flatly shot movie in the classic 1.33:1 aspect ratio could grow in size, the company advertised, by spreading the image over a larger area by means of a wide-angle lens attachment to a standard projector, a special aperture plate, and the installation of a concave screen. Deciding against copyright, Paramount urged exhibitors to obtain the equipment, which ran from an inexpensive $600 upwards, directly from the manufacturing companies. From 1954, practically all films, not shot in a special process, were shown in the Panoramic Screen format. Eventually, the widescreen aspect ratio became a constituent in the film's production, thus avoiding the graininess and compositional problems (image top and bottom slightly cropped) inherent in its use at the beginning when films were shot in the 1.33:1 aspect ratio and enlarged. By the early sixties, the 1.85:1 ratio became the standard for flat widescreen and has remained so.

8.4   Wide-Frame Systems

8.4.1   *VistaVision and Perspecta Stereophonic Sound*

Paramount, abandoning its widescreen pitch and dissatisfied with Fox's CinemaScope, sought another solution. Reenter del Riccio, who developed for the studio a "Lazy 8 Butterfly Camera" in which 35 mm film passed through the bulky camera horizontally instead of vertically, exposing eight perforations or two frames to record one image. This process necessitated a modified camera aperture and claw device. The image produced was twice as wide as that of 35 mm film and slightly taller, with a 1.85:1 ratio. Refined further by Loren L. Ryder and John R. Bishop, the system was baptized "VistaVision: Motion Picture High Fidelity."

VistaVision was projected in three formats: the infrequent horizontal double frame; regular 35 mm reduced with a 1.85:1 aspect ratio; and the anamorphic mode using SuperScope's variable projection device with aspect ratios of 1.66:1, 1.85:1, and 2:1.[12] The musical *White Christmas* (1954), the initial presentation, was, according to the studio, shown in an anamorphic format.[13] *Strategic Air Command* (1955) was the first film in which VistaVision prints were released in the horizontal double-frame format.

Paramount almost exclusively used the genre-friendly process which afforded great clarity of definition, even when presented in regular 35 mm reduced format (as it usually was). By 1961, Paramount began phasing out this expensive process, requiring twice the amount of negative film in addition to a special camera, for the cheaper anamorphic Panavision 35.

Perspecta Stereophonic Sound accompanied VistaVision prints. Developed by Robert Fine, this system, boasting remarkable sound fidelity and compatible mag/optical formats, included three low-frequency tones heard only by an "integrator" which automatically controlled the sound's volume and direction. Perspecta was a less elaborate, cheaper system to mix sound and to install. For houses equipped with stereo, only the "integrator" was needed while, in addition to the "integrator," conventional houses needed some amplifiers, loudspeakers, and a multiple gang fader. The cost: a trifling $990. MGM was first to realize Perspecta's potential with *Knights of the Round Table* (1953).[14] By 1960, MGM discontinued its use, along with Warners, Columbia, and Paramount. Exhibitor indifference matched industry shortsightedness.

8.4.2   *Technirama and Super Technirama 70*

An anamorphic system/VistaVision/three-strip Technicolor combo, Technirama was the brainchild of the Technicolor Corp. Photographed in double-width negative, 50 percent of the image was squeezed during shooting (as opposed to 'Scope's 100 percent), while the other 50 percent was squeezed during printing. Though depth of field and image definition enormously improved while distortion and graininess for exteriors and interiors were reduced, pricey Technirama with a 2.34:1 aspect ratio did not sell. Universal (which debuted the process in 1957 with the western *Night Passage*), Paramount, and Columbia's use was sporadic (RKO even used it once); UA used it six times; WB, seven. Undeterred, the company upped the stakes with Super-Technirama 70 in which the horizontal 35 mm was decompressed and printed directly onto 70 mm stock. Designed for blockbusters, the system made its bow in 1959 with UA's *Soloman and Sheba* and Buena Vista's animated *Sleeping Beauty*. Three years later, it was retired.

8.5   The 70 mm/Wide-Gauge Processes

8.5.1   Todd-AO

Michael Todd, one of Cinerama's risk takers, became impatient with the system's inherent problems, especially the sync lines. Selling his stock and breaking with the company in 1953, Todd sought out the brilliant optical scientist Dr. Brian O'Brien, head of Rochester University's Institute of Optics, to develop a process with Cinerama's pluses but not its minuses. O'Brien, together with the American Optical Co., which had tagged him to head its research program, came up with Todd-AO. The impressive technology utilized 65 mm wide-gauge film stock with a five-sprocket hole frame in lieu of the usual four[15] and with magnetic stripes along the edges for the six-track sound system (five channels behind the screen while the sixth supplied the surround sound on both sides and rear of the auditorium). Release prints were 70 mm wide to provide the extra space needed for the sound striping.

The Mitchell Camera Co. refined its old 70 mm camera to shoot the wide-gauge stock, concocting a 4-lens apparatus: the extreme wide-angle 128-degree lens, 64-degree, 48-degree, and 37-degree. Holland's Phillips Co. developed the projector, compatible with other large-screen processes as well as standard 35, to show wide-gauge film with its aperture four times that of the standard 35 mm projector, thus allowing more light to hit the screen, composed of a light-reflecting plastic fabric with aluminum squares. The resulting 90-degree image arc, with a generally 2.05 : 1 aspect ratio, was three and a half times greater than the standard 35 mm image.

For Todd-AO's premier, Todd secured the rights for $1,020,000 to the then longest running Broadway musical, *Oklahoma!* (Magna, 1955).[16] Todd's personally produced *Around the World in Eighty Days* (UA, 1956)[17] was a follow-up commercial smash, as was *South Pacific* (Magna, 1958). Fox purchased major stock in both Todd-AO and Magna, releasing *Can-Can* (1960) and *Cleopatra* (1963) in the process. The studio would continue to use Todd-AO for its out-of-the-ordinary offerings throughout the sixties. Goldwyn employed it for *Porgy and Bess* (C, 1959); John Wayne for *The Alamo* (UA, 1960). Eventually, Todd-AO became the wide-gauge standard.

8.5.2 Camera 65 and Ultra Panavision 70; Super Panavision 70

To trump Fox's CinemaScope, MGM commissioned Panavision, Inc. to come up with a system for a 65 mm wide-gauge film format. MGM had employed "Realife-70 mm" for its westerns *Billy the Kid* (1930) and *The Great Meadow* (1931) but had abandoned the process due to exhibitor expense, prohibitive during the Depression.[18] What the Panavision boys devised was a photographic process that utilized a "revolutionary" optical system, "incorporating a spherical objective lens and an anamorphic element (wedged prisms) that imparted a slight horizontal squeeze to the image . . ."[19] A new projecting lens, an optical printer to produce 35 mm prints from the original 65 mm negative, and five channels of sound were also part of the system which MGM labeled "Camera 65." The process was arrayed for MGM's male melodrama *Raintree County* (1957) and *Ben-Hur* (1959) and BV's *The Big Fisherman* (1959).

Streamlining the large, heavy camera and refining the prismatic compression device while standardizing it at 1.25:1, Panavision renamed the system "Ultra Panavision 70," which MGM used for its adventure-male melodrama *Mutiny On the Bounty* (1962). A further variation was Panavision's own 65 mm wide-gauge film format. Tagged "Super Panavision 70," it registered an extremely sharp, bright image with an aspect ratio of 2.35:1 with four-channel magnetic sound for 35 mm prints and a ratio of 2.05:1 with six-channel magnetic sound for 70 mm. UA's historical spectacle *Exodus* (1960) kicked off this imperially arresting system.

Notes

1 According to Robert E. Carr and R. M. Hayes, *Wide Screen Movies: A History and Filmography of Wide Gauge Filmmaking* (Farland & Co., Inc.: Jefferson, NC and London, 1988), 15, the most definitive book on the subject, Cinerama used both six- and seven-channel systems: it was "a matter of patching the appropriate channels to speakers from the projection booth sound system."

2 *This Is Cinerama* premiered overseas as the government's official exhibit at the International Trade Fair held September 2 to October 1, 1954 in Damascus, Syria. Eventually, Cinerama was shown in eight foreign countries.

3 Cinerama's financial figures used in this section are from *Film Daily's Special 10th Anniversary Edition*, Jan. 21, 1963, 26, a special issue devoted to Cinerama.

4 The premier Cinerama attraction grossed $32 million; all five around $82 million. The last travelogue did poorly.

5 Actually, the first installation of a single-booth Cinerama occurred in August, 1960 at Cinerama's own Claridge Theater in Montclair, New Jersey.

6 Ibid., 28.

7 Ibid., 28–30.

8   For other multi-camera systems, such as Thrillarama, Wonderama, etc., see Carr and Hayes, 53–4.

9   The approximation was derived from the production dates of the first CinemaScope movie *The Robe* (February, 1953) and one of the last to be reshot twice, *Carousel* (Spring, 1955).

10   For other anamorphic systems, see Carr and Hayes, 67–143.

11   The screen opened out by hauling away the black borders at the top and sides, producing an image four times that of a regular screen. Two reels of the same film were run simultaneously through the projector. At the designated sequences, one reel was shut down while the other, with an enlarging lens now attached, took over.

12   Ibid., 144.

13   Possibly, but not everywhere. Ryder claimed the film played two Los Angeles engagements in the horizontal format. See Carr and Hayes, 145.

14   Evidently, the in-production date of *Knights* preceded the formulation of Fox's rigid CinemaScope package.

15   With the increase of sprocket holes, the film's speed is faster, creating a sharper, steadier image. The first two Todd-AO releases were seen at 30 fps instead of the customary 24 fps but with *South Pacific* (1958), the frame rate returned to the standard 24 fps. See Carr and Hayes, 168.

16   The Magna Theater Corp. was formed in 1953 to use the Todd-AO process and distribute Todd-AO features. In addition to Todd, industry head Joseph Schenck, music men Rodgers and Hammerstein, producers Arthur Hornblow, Jr., and Edward Small, Broadway theater owner and producer Lee Shubert, UA theater chain head George P. Skouras, New York University law professor Charles Seligson, and Judge M. Landis were members.

17   Todd died an untimely death at 51 in a light plane crash in 1958. He was in the midst of preparing *Don Quixote* in Todd-AO.

18   At the start of the thirties, wide-gauge processes were in the air. Some of these short-lived systems included Fox's 70 mm Grandeur Screen, Paramount's 56 mm process, and the 63 mm Spoor Natural Vision.

19   Carr and Hayes, 173.

9

Three-Dimension, Special Effects, and Film Production Refinements

9.1 3-D

"Natural Vision" was a reconstruction by brothers Milton and Julian Gunzberg of a system first displayed by the Polaroid Co. in 1939, which took its inspiration from a stereoscopic cine camera patented by Englishmen William Friese-Greene and Mortimer Evans in 1889. (Actually, in the early thirties, MGM had produced 3-D Metroscopix shorts, but they never caught on.) Natural Vision's camera had two lenses fairly close together (about the extent of the distance between two eyes) that focused at slightly different angles upon the same object. Two not quite superimposed images resulted, beamed onto the screen by two projectors. By means of Polaroid filters on the projectors and Polaroid glasses (one eyelid green, the other red) worn by the spectator, the two pictures became one, resulting in an illusion of depth. Presentational requirements, consisting of a high-intensity reflective screen and an interlock system for the two projectors, cost exhibitors around $2,000.

Radio dramatist Arch Oboler, reckoning that the process would excite the public, put up his own $300,000 to make a B adventure *Bwana Devil* in 3-D. Since no major distributor would take a risk, he arranged for the movie's simultaneous booking at the Paramount in Los Angeles and Hollywood in November, 1952. Notwithstanding the muffled critical voice, consumer response was loud and clear (a $2.7 million take). Bids for distribution rights poured in. Oboler favored UA. During 1953–4, 69 features from every studio were produced in 3-D. Before the end of 1953, however, the 3-D boom had gone bust and roughly one-third of the pictures were released flat.

With 3-D's aura of exploitation, most 1953 features were quickly and shod-dily made Bs in the horror (the remake *House of Wax*, WB's mightiest recoup of the year at $5.5 million), western (*Fort Ti*, C), adventure (*Sangaree*, P), or thriller molds (*Second Chance*, RKO). They concentrated not on depth but sensational effects and tricks: spitting on audiences, hurling knives at them, kicking them in the face, shooting them point-blank, and plunging them in an actress's décolletage. Even director George Sidney was not above it all in encour-aging Ann Miller to throw scarves out at audiences during the "Too Darn Hot" number in MGM's *Kiss Me, Kate*, an adaptation of Cole Porter's showpiece. Hitchcock's *Dial M For Murder* (WB, 1954) was a rare exception. Other things also hastened 3-D's demise. Glasses were discomforting, especially for members of the audience who already wore spectacles. The 15-minute intermission, necessitated by the simultaneous use of two projectors that had to be kept from overheating, annoyingly interrupted the story and broke the film's rhythm. Exhibitors squawked at the conversion fees. The public flurry over Cinema-Scope, seen *without* glasses, finally buried the gimmick.[1]

9.2   Special Effects

Special effects (f/x) make-up (Charles Parker's mangled Massala/*Ben-Hur*, MGM, 1959) proceeded apace. Mechanical special effects, those staged before the camera (A. D. Flowers's explosives/*Battleground*, MGM, 1949) also advanced. In-camera effects, those involving a camera crew, and post-production effects/ opticals, those done in a laboratory, however, made significant leaps. In these areas, traveling matte work, model animation, and stop-motion photography were the showpieces.

Traveling matte work on the screen (two separately recorded on-the-set images, usually one foreground, one background, combined in the lab) regis-tered far more realistically than rear projection (live foreground combined with rear screen on-the-set projection), and began to be used more frequently. The move to color generated new types of traveling mattes while large frame sizes, which provided larger elements and sharper images to work with, made lab work easier. Of the various systems, such as the blue-screen process and WB's ultraviolet process, the sodium vapor process, which used a beam-splitting camera, proved the best. Developed by the Rank Organization in 1956, it was refined by Disney Company's Ub Iwerks (*Darby O'Gill and the Little People*, 1959). Ray Harryhausen and George Pal were other standout f/x contributors.

Harryhausen (1920), with an interest in sculpture, anatomy, paleontology, and the dinosaur paintings of Charles R. Knight, was one of 25 assistants on

Willis O'Brien's *Mighty Joe Young* (RKO, 1949). O'Brien, who had revolution-ized model animation and stop-motion photography (*The Lost World*, First National, 1925; *King Kong*, RKO, 1933), was Harryhausen's idol and inspira-tion. On *Mighty*, O'Brien passed the torch, assigning Harryhausen the creation of the gorilla puppets' arms and 85 percent of the hands-on animation. Both shared the f/x Oscar for it.

Harryhausen then signed on for a series of horror–sci-fi monster movies, giving monsters "character," as *The Beast from 20,000 Fathoms* (WB, 1953) which, when trapped in a burning amusement park, spits out roller-coaster cars in desperation. *It Came from Beneath the Sea* (C, 1955), which cinched Harry-hausen's 30-year-plus relationship with producer Charles H. Schneer, had a giant octopus attacking San Francisco. Next up were the fantasy adventures for Columbia. From *The Seventh Voyage of Sinbad* (1959) on, the wizard advertised his technique as "Dynamation" to distinguish it from animated drawings, car-toons, and puppet work. Dispensing with expensive glass paintings and rear projections, Dynamation, relying on a front projection system of twin 45-degree prisms, achieved dimensional perspective and registration. One of the 90 f/x in the flashy *Jason and the Argonauts* (1962) showed seven skeletons, each with five appendages, wielding swords and spears against the embattled Jason and his two cohorts.

George Pal (1908–80), a Hungarian trained as an artist illustrator at the Budapest Academy of Arts and Sciences, worked at Germany's UFA and designed commercials in Paris and Holland, where he also made some "Puppetoon" shorts, which he transplanted to Paramount (1939–47). Surrounding himself with the very best f/x craftsmen, producer Pal launched a series of features that reaped six f/x Oscars. For *Destination Moon* (EL, 1950), Pal insisted on a scien-tifically accurate rendition of a trip to the moon and got it from Lee Zavitz's mechanical effects and John Abbott's animation. Along with Paramount's f/x expert Gordon Jennings, Pal depicted the destruction of the world by a wander-ing star in *When Worlds Collide* (1951) and Martian war machines in *War of the Worlds* (1953), as well as an infestation of Amazon red ants (*The Naked Jungle*, 1954). In addition to supervising Gene Warren and Tim Baar's creepy f/x (moldy books decomposing, snide sphinxes), Pal also directed *The Time Machine* (MGM, 1960).

Other significant contributors in mechanical and optical effects were John B. Fulton, who burned oil wells in *Tulsa* (EL, 1947), blew up *The Bridges at Toko-Ri* (P, 1954), and parted the Red Sea for *The Ten Commandments* (P, 1956); Robert A. Mattey and Ralph Hammeras, whose giant squid battled with the crew of the Nautilus in *20,000 Leagues under the Sea* (BV, 1954); and MGM's A. Arnold Gillespie, whose tidal wave/earthquake appeared in *Green Dolphin Street* (1947).

9.3   Film Production Refinements

Magnetic sound recording came into use in 1949. Initially, the film stock was coated with a magnetic iron oxide stripe on the edge opposite the sprocket holes but by year's end, full coating of the stock, creating a much smoother surface and richer sound quality, became the way to go. After 1950, quarter-inch tape recorders supplanted magnetic recorders in recording sound at once with the camera's photographing. Instant playback and enhanced sound quality were important advantages of magnetic over optical tracks. Even with the magnetic to optical transfer on the print for exhibition, the sound quality was noticeably better than mere optical sound recording.

In the late forties, Universal sound engineer Jack Foley began experimenting with the performance of sound effects in post-production dubbing sessions. It was much easier to achieve clarity, texture, and nuance of sound effects in this way rather than recording the sounds on the set or inserting them into the track from the studio library of pre-recorded sounds.

By 1951, cellulose acetate and in 1954, cellulose triacetate were used as a film stock base in lieu of cellulose nitrate.[2] Though nitrate produced sharp images, picking up a wealth of details, it was flammable, shrunk over time (requiring large sprocket holes), was non-resistant to moisture, and had a one-to-two-decade life span. Inferior to nitrate in its image registering, triacetate was, however, inflammable, unshrinkable, warp-free, and required smaller sprocket holes.

Kodak developed faster b/w and color stocks. Faster film stocks encouraged location shooting and the use of night-for-night shots (*Touch of Evil*, U, 1958), not the usual day-for-night.

Location shooting and even studio interiors, which now were being built to real-life- specifications (the home in *The Desperate Hours*, P, 1955) rather than on the extravagant scale of the bygone years, resulted in a cutting back of lighting units.[3] For locations, lighting units such as Colortan, available in 1949, were designed to be compact, lighter in weight, yet still effective. Reduced personnel and the need to economize were also behind this streamlining.

With more and more location shooting and its logistics made smoother by technology, less second-unit location process photography occurred. *The Big Sky* (RKO, 1952), filmed in the Grand Teton spread, boasted that it was the first film to forgo process exterior shots.

The reflex camera, a fifties innovation, allowed a cameraman to forgo the viewfinder and compose shots directly through the lens. This narrowed the distance between the photographer and director's intentions and execution.

Wider lenses appeared (a 14 mm lens in 1959), promising to encompass a wide area and a sharper depth of field than the human eye could achieve.[4] This refinement gave an image complexity with multi-vertical and horizontal planes in focus, thus helping to make possible the realism the period craved (cf. the constant use of an 18mm lens for *Touch of Evil*). The zoom lens debuted in 1947 and more sophisticated ones became available (the Pan-Cinor in 1956 with a zoom ratio of 4 to 1), emphasizing the subject by zooming in or contextualizing the subject by zooming out in a more direct, rapid way than a moving camera. A boon to location shooting and cost cutting, the zoom could emphasize, shock, and ironize, as in Hitchcock's work.

Introduced in 1946, the crab dolly, a four-wheeled mount in which a camera could be placed, afforded even more camera maneuverability: the possibility of movement towards/away-from/and now parallel with the action, allowing the change in spatial organization within the frame to be more fluent, frequent, longer, and above all, lifelike. A miniature crab dolly, able to move through normal-sized corridors and doorways, was on the market four years later.

Conclusion

Technology has always been a vehicle for film's matter and manner. With its emphasis, aesthetics changed. Spatial reconfigurations within the frame were the result of larger aspect ratios. F/x advances were important factors in the formation of the sci-fi genre and its hybrids and in more graphic depictions of catastrophes in historical spectacles and battles in war films.

Moreover, the period witnessed, in an unprecedented way, the foregrounding of technology not only in the presentation of the film but in the very fabric of the film itself, disrupting Hollywood's classic style's seamlessness of story and transparency. Sometimes, this self-reflexivity unstrung film's literary bindings (*Escapade In Japan* (RKO/U, 1957).

Technology-privileging was also seen, more aggressively than ever before, in the marketing and advertising of a film, extending the pitch of a movie beyond star, genre, and production value. As such, the period 1946–62 in American film marked the start of the industry's pinpointing of technology in the production and consumption of a film. This emphasis was part of an unexpressed but nevertheless felt collusion with the audience.

Notes

1   Smell-O-Vision, the addition of smell to sight and sound, was yet another techno-gimmick. An advance over previous attempts that invariably involved a single odor emitted from a

single source (Aromarama), Smell-O-Vision, developed by Swiss osmologist Hans Laube and presented by Mike Todd, Jr., synchronized the odor machine to a picture's action by means of a magnetic track. Many distinct odors from a console-type machine played by impulses from the soundtrack were piped through plastic tubes located in the back of every theater seat. After a $23,000 installation fee, Todd's own Cinestage Theater in Chicago premiered the first and only feature in this process, the British-made *Scent of Mystery*, a Hitchcockian *Around the World in Eighty Days* pastiche, in January, 1970. The 30 scents (rose, orange, pipe smoke, shoe polish, perfume, port wine, coffee, lavender, peppermint, etc.) uncorked throughout the movie were sniffed insouciantly by critic and consumer alike.

2   Small-gauge amateur and noncommercial cinematography had been using acetate cellulose safety base stock for quite some time.

3   Barry Salt, *Film Style and Technology: History and Analysis* (London: Starwood, 1983), 312.

4   Each lens has its own focal length, which equals the number in millimeters used to express a lens's respective width or length. In other words, a focal length refers to its range of focus (above 50 mm equals very long; below 50 mm equals very wide). A normal/middle focal-length lens is approximately 50 mm.

Part IV
Censorship

Introduction

In 1908, the film industry formed the National Board of Censorship to address the public outcry over the lack of morality in movies and keep the federal government's nose out of its business. In 1922, when public furor heated up again, Will H. Hays, conservative postmaster general of the Harding administration, became president of the Motion Picture Producers and Distributors of America, later shortened to the Motion Picture Association of America (MPAA). His job also entailed casting an eye over film content. Two years into his tenure, Hays drew up "The Formula," which requested studios to submit a summary of a play or novel they intended to produce for possible objections. In 1927, the MPAA outlined a "Don'ts and Be Carefuls" list of 11 topics and 26 themes to be treated with sensitivity and caution. Three years later, the catalog was fleshed out into the Production Code by Catholic Martin Quigley, publisher of the trade journal *Motion Picture Herald*, and Jesuit priest Daniel A. Lord. Only in 1934, when the Catholic Church's effectual Legion of Decency (LD), with its ratings A-1 (Morally Unobjectionable For All), A-11 (Morally Unobjectionable For Adults), B (Morally Objectionable In Part For All), and C (Condemned), materialized to do what the Production Code Administration (PCA) was supposedly doing but was, in fact, not doing, was the Code rigorously enforced. The PCA now entered into all phases of filmmaking (script selection, drafts, finished film), seeing that all was in line, slapping a $25,000 fine on disobedient studios. More specific and stricter caveats on crime, clothing, profanity, and animal cruelty were tinkered with between 1938 and 1940.

Things went on, predictably, with the PCA reining in films that strayed. Then, in the postwar years, resistance mounted. Confrontations with the PCA and LD resulted in an overall begrudging accommodation on the part of both bodies with a resultant diminution in their power. In addition, the eight states which had censorship laws and the almost 200 municipalities, with their respective regulations that controlled the theatrical showing of certain subject matter, increasingly lost battles in the higher courts and were continually reprimanded to better define their terms. Obscenity prosecutions and instances of extralegal devices of public officials protecting film content also declined while pressure groups ran out of steam. Even HUAC's decade-long heyday, shoring up the conservative supports in the land, could not stem the tide.

Why? Most obviously, the culture was changing. The postwar adult male/female, youth, family, how they looked and, more pertinently, how they behaved, were different from the past. A turning toward private pleasure brought sensuality out in the open and it hadn't been out there since the Jazz Age. Sexual morality was being profiled and discussed, its traditional parameters questioned and broadened by Kinsey, *Playboy*, *Confidential*, and the beatniks. Images of the Korean conflict and racial turmoil, in newsreels, newspapers, and TV broadcasts, desensitized Americans to violence while stirring up a curiosity about it. The documented vicious tactics of juvenile gangs and crime syndicates had the same effect.

The antitrust decree enforcement and the switch to independent production also undermined censorship. Independents now had a guaranteed venue, whether or not the picture came stamped with a PCA "Seal." (Though the Supreme Court in 1942 ruled that circuits were allowed to show pictures without a "Seal," a gentlemen's agreement existed between these circuits and the MPAA to show only "Sealed" pictures. Now that the circuits were no longer owned by the majors, the fear of retaliation from the majors if an exhibitor, especially an independent, did not book a "Sealed" picture, was a thing of the past.) As such, not only did independents enervate the major studios' hold on enforcing the Code and, consequently, on screen content, but they were able to challenge, and in some cases, buck the Code entirely.

The adaptation syndrome also palsied censorship's grasp. The industry consistently scoured stage and fiction for material because of the "penetration" factor, promising a possible financial guarantee. Postwar, the play and novel were discovering new shores of topicality, controversy, and sensation. Unlike movies, theater and publishing's lack of censorship other than vague state/city ordinances regarding obscenity, pornography, and immorality enabled a play and novel to be hip to the new cultural clime.[1] Their refreshingly bold thematic sophistication likewise attracted the industry and became a further incentive in its hot pursuit. Recalling the Depression, when a daring screen basted a tattered box office, producers hoped history would repeat itself.

Television, too, did its part. By becoming *the* mass medium and relegating movies to a relatively elitist position, TV lifted from movies the onus of censorship that went hand in hand with being number one. The more audience-encompassing a medium was, the safer its subject matter had to be. TV, by becoming #1, could say less; movies, by becoming #2, could say more. (A play and novel's elitism was another factor in these media's ability to tell it like it is.) Representations on the screen that could not be beamed into a family's living room, naturally, were a way to compete with TV and, hopefully, keep the invader at bay.

The influx of European films and, conversely, the need for American movies to appeal to the foreign market brought further thematic sophistication to the product, giving censorship a run for its money. Old-world culture and its representations were far more sophisticated than the naively optimistic, provincial, bourgeois, chauvinistic, puritan American culture and its artifacts. The foreign film showed the industry what the screen was capable of in terms of subject matter (markedly in the areas of sensuality/sexuality, moral attitudes, and values). More: instances of these imports' solid commercial reception in the States further convinced the industry that it had ignored the American movie-going public's desire and devalued its intelligence.

Aesthetic factors must not be lost sight of in regard to censorship's turmoil. Many producers/directors/writers/actors, loosened from the studio's ideological bonds and functioning as independents, now had a chance to say what they wanted to say, often in an uncompromised way. Thus, postwar picture-makers began looking at film less and less in terms of sheer entertainment–escape (as formerly), and more and more as an entertainment that could communicate human values and ideas, depict lives as lived, and lay bare what was specially urgent in their own minds and hearts. Still countenancing the Code's general dictums ("movies should not lower moral standards"), the industry began rejecting its list of "Thou Shalt Nots." Such commandments, it opined, kept American movies from being complexly human, real, and personal.

That said, it is time to examine the influential films that weakened censorship, filling the screen with words, actions, and attitudes not heard or seen before or if so, not quite in the same way.

Note

1 The US had no general censorship, though several particular censoring bodies existed: a customs censorship over the importation of obscene literature; a post-office censorship over the use of the mails to distribute immoral writings or photos; a variety of state and local organizations that kept an eye out for immoral publications and stage productions.

10
Test Cases

10.1   *The Outlaw* (UA, 1946/RKO, 1950)

In 1946, the PCA removed the Seal from the second release[1] of independent Howard Hughes's *The Outlaw*, a Jules Furthman original which director Howard Hawks started. Forced out, Hawks relinquished the baton to Hughes himself. The humorous advertisements, obsessively foregrounding 20-year-old lead Jane Russell's 38–24–36 physical endowments ("What are the two great reasons for Jane Russell's rise to stardom?") were deemed brazenly offensive by the Advertising Code Administration (ACA), which worked in tandem with the PCA. Hughes sued, charging the PCA with conspiracy to suppress competition.

Both sides called a spade a spade. Indeed, Hughes and publicity man Russell Birdwell's ads flagrantly bucked the ACA's rules and for sure, the major studio-backed PCA did indeed control screen content, which was yet another way of keeping independents and foreigners out. Hughes lost. With ads toned down and more revisions, the polemical work left the RKO gate in 1950 with Seal restored and the LD's modified C to B rating "glamorizing crime and immorality."[2]

Hughes's *The Outlaw* was one of the first films brazenly to plug into the postwar vogue for images of sensuality. While not overlooking her legs, the movie concentrated on Russell's décolletage, signaling that part of the female anatomy that would reach a fetishistic height during the era. As such, Hughes, Russell, and their movie helped open the screen in terms of a much more sensual representation of women while questioning and, ultimately, sabotaging the Code ruling against "indecent or undue exposure."

10.2   The Jane Russell Syndrome: Rita Hayworth, Marilyn Monroe, Cyd Charisse, Sophia Loren, and Gina Lollobrigida

Russell continued to exploit her assets in practically all her subsequent work. In the Russell tradition were the curvaceous, well-endowed figures of Columbia's Rita Hayworth and Fox's Marilyn Monroe. As *Gilda* (1946), Rita's strapless torso, bared leg, and glove-removed-arms gyrated through "Put the Blame on Mame." In *Down To Earth* (1947), she pranced as gossamer-garmented Terpsichore. Only her dance of the seven veils enlivened *Salome* (1952). As *Miss Sadie Thompson* (1953), a somewhat scrubbed version of Somerset Maugham's story "Rain," Rita bumped and grinded her way through "The Heat Is On" in 3-D, no less, encircled by ogling Marines, one of whom jerks his bottle of beer that explodes with foam. In *Pal Joey* (1957), her "Zip" number, more rotation than strip, was the best thing in the show. *Niagara* (1953) found Marilyn singing over a phonograph rendition of "Kiss" in a fuchsia knot-over-the-braless-breast sheath, "cut down so low in the front, you can see her kneecaps," as hubby Joseph Cotton growls. *Gentlemen Prefer Blondes* (1953) teamed her with Russell. As a chanteuse in *River of No Return* (1954), she straddled an onstage beam, shimmying up and down. With a shoulder bra, bare waist, and a thigh-revealing slit skirt, she caused a "Heat Wave" in *There's No Business Like Show Business* (1954). She was up to her old tricks in *Some Like It Hot* (UA, 1959), warbling "I'm Through With Love" in a sheath that sported a net bodice revealing braless bosoms with sequins embroidered over the nipples, rimmed by a baby spot.

In most of these ladies' work, it was their suggestive dancing and costumes that bordered and, at times, crossed the border of undue exposure that triggered alarms. Though given a Seal (the musical genre or musical sequence in dramatic films took the heat off), Hayworth and Monroe's pictures were, however, LD-rated B. The Legion knew full well that the scanty clothes of see-through material that outlined the bodies and the dance movements (the surface) were actually codes of arousal, foreplay, the sexual act, and post-coital glow, brought home even more by the continual cutaways during the dance to the males' reactions, be it the turn-on, the grin, the leer, the approval, or the satisfaction (the substance).

Statuesque Cyd Charisse, reigning danseuse of the MGM musical, should not be overlooked in this regard either. It's hard to believe, but *Singin' in the Rain* (1952), *Meet Me in Las Vegas* (1956), and *Silk Stockings* (1957), along with the gangster film *Party Girl* (1958), though Sealed, were rated B by the Legion owing to Charisse's "indecent" costuming and dancing. Italian imports Sophia Loren, popping out of the Adriatic in a braless flesh-colored dress in *Boy on a Dolphin* (TCF, 1957), and Gina Lollobrigida, with breasts swimming on bathwater in *Solomon and Sheba* (UA, 1959), extended the sensual representations of women on the American screen.

10.3   The Adaptation of Controversial and Sensational Novels: *Double Indemnity* (P, 1944), *Leave Her to Heaven* (TCF, 1945), *The Postman Always Rings Twice* (MGM, 1946), *Duel in the Sun* (SRO, 1946), *Forever Amber* (TCF, 1947), and *Flamingo Road* (WB, 1949)

The Seal-approved and lucrative *Double Indemnity*, from hardboiled writer James M. Cain's 1936 magazine serial novelized in 1940, greenlighted another Cain sensation, *The Postman Always Rings Twice*, on Metro's shelf since its purchase in 1934. Notwithstanding Harry Ruskin and Niven Busch's laundered rewrite, *Postman*'s murderous lovers emerged sympathetic (the Lana Turner/ John Garfield casting helped enormously) and the satire of the two corrupt district attorneys remained stinging. In addition, sexual references (the sizzling hamburgers on the grill) spiked the potion. *Double Indemnity*'s low-key lighting was eschewed in favor of high-key to help alleviate, not compound, the aura of scum. Unlike *Double Indemnity*'s A-II rating, however, *Postman* was slapped with a B on "insufficient retribution" grounds. Nevertheless, *Postman* went on to exceed *Indemnity*'s torrid box office, both kicking off the fearless rush to snap up salacious bestsellers.[3]

Duel in the Sun, independent Selznick and H. P. Garrett's sculpting of a Niven Busch potboiler, was not as lucky as its trendsetters. Premiering in Los Angeles in December, 1946, the Code-approved *Duel* was denounced by Archbishop Cantwell as "morally offensive and spiritually depressing," while representatives of 13 women's clubs met for a discussion sponsored by the MPAA. Selznick himself made 56 cuts to receive a Legion B: "immodestly suggestive sequences, glorification of illicit love" in lieu of the organization's threatened C before widely releasing the $5.25-million valentine to his inamorata Jennifer Jones. Despite the capitulation, Lewt's (anti-cast Gregory Peck) rape of Pearl (Jones) still remained, as did her enjoyment of it. In fact the sadomasochistic tone of their fornication remained intact.

Forever Amber also had a hard time of it. (Fox's *Leave Her to Heaven* in 1945, with the murder of a crippled teenager, the killing of an unborn baby, and a suicide retained from Ben Ames Williams's lurid 1944 bestseller and an A-II rating, was a piece of cake compared to *Amber*'s reception.) Philip Dunne's adaptation of Kathleen Winsor's 1944 account of the career of a courtesan in the era of the Restoration Court of Charles II of England underwent a good deal of Breen bowdlerization to get a Seal, but not enough to escape a Legion C ("glorified immorality") and clerical thunder and lightning.

Six weeks into the run, president Skouras, hoping to head off any possible financial downturn on the $4.6-million production with contractee Linda Darnell in her first big role, had the film's prologue and epilogue revised. "This is the story of Amber St. Claire," the film now began, "slave to ambition, stranger to virtue . . . fated to find the wealth and power she ruthlessly gained wither to ashes in the fire lit by passion and fed by defiance of the eternal command . . ." For the finale, the voice of male lead Cornel Wilde repeated lines spoken earlier: "In heaven's name, Amber, haven't we caused enough unhappiness? May God have mercy on us both for our sins." The old DeMille trick of having your cake and eating it too suckered the Legion into a B.

The Fox bigwig worried needlessly since business, before and after the revisions, was just as brisk. Contractee director Otto Preminger knew the public was ready for *Amber* ($6 million-worth of admissions) but was powerless to do anything about the moral brouhaha, although he did attempt to point out to Legion reviewers, to no avail, what could be shown on the screen.

Another steamy novel, though somewhat cooled down to Code standards, was *Flamingo Road*, a nasty slice of American politics adapted by novelist Robert Wilder himself from his 1943 work. Curiously, most of the objectionable items listed in the PCA correspondences were actually ignored. Joan Crawford's frequent undressing was earmarked for deletion, yet in an early scene, she's seen fidgeting with her garter high on her shapely thigh. Suggestive lines stayed in (customer to waitress: "You're a good girl"; waitress: "Yeh, good and ready"). Suicide, a Code taboo, did, in fact, transpire. The "roadhouse" still resembled a brothel where the madam gets a friendly pinch on the ass. This irony between the censor's underlined objections and a producer's ignored responses was not peculiar to *Flamingo Road* but rather paradigmatic of many contested films at this time. Despite the disregard for the red-inked items, *Flamingo Road* did get a Seal, though the Legion countered with a B for its "low moral tone."

10.4   Racism: *Pinky* (TCF, 1949) and *Curley* (UA, 1947)

Pinky, Philip Dunne and Dudley Nichols's tailoring of Cid Ricketts Sumner's 1946 novel, dealt with miscegenation, a Code taboo and a contentious topic (the picture was the year's second highest grosser). That white actress Jeanne Crain played the light-complexioned black woman passing herself off as white and falling in love with William Lundigan was indeed a capitulation, but this was the only way, in 1949, to get a Seal. Until the mid-fifties, many movies defied the taboo in the same white-playing-people-of-color way: from *Devil's*

Doorway's (MGM, 1950) "Indian" Robert Taylor in love with Paula Raymond to *Love Is a Many-Splendored Thing*'s (TCF, 1955) "Eurasian" Jennifer Jones–William Holden liaison.

Some films thumbed their noses at the proscription and got away with it. *Japanese War Bride* (TCF, 1952), with Don Taylor marrying a Nipponese played by Japanese Shirley Yamaguchi, was one of these films, undoubtedly ignored owing to its B-picture status. (Code people paid less attention to Bs since their audience was much less than for As.) Mexican Kathy Jurado played the mistress of support Lloyd Bridges in *High Noon* (UA, 1952) and the second wife (an Indian) of patriarch Spencer Tracy in *Broken Lance* (TCF, 1954). Jurado's supporting role status in both films took the edge off. *House of Bamboo* (TCF, 1955) passed muster since its romance between Robert Stack and Yamaguchi remained chaste. The work of Mexican Ricardo Montalban at MGM from 1947 to 1954, including romancing Esther Williams in *Neptune's Daughter* (1949) and Lana Turner in *Latin Lovers* (1953), was a harbinger.

Pictures about miscegenation touched on the subject of racism and were usually suppressed by Southern censors. State and city censorship, up to this time supported by the MPAA, was becoming an embarrassment, never more so than in the instance of *Curley*, banned by Tennessee censors for its scene of a desegregated class of schoolchildren (but not miscegenation, mind you). After UA lost its appeal in the Tennessee Supreme Court, MPAA President Eric Johnston appealed the decision in the US Supreme Court, which refused even to hear the case.[4]

10.5   *The Bicycle Thief* (1949)

Art houses were customarily the province of foreign films where, unable to pass the Code test, they played without a Seal. After the antitrust decree settlement, foreign film distributors pursued a wider, more prestigious showcasing. In rare instances when a foreign film showed legs, a major distributor stepped in, promising even more saturation. For such a thing to happen, however, a Seal, though not essential, was extremely helpful and encouraged.

Foreign film distributor Joseph Burstyn latched onto a gem, *The Bicycle Thief*. Trailing clouds of critical glory, the picture was doing solid business in Manhattan when WB came to call. The studio offered to enter into a deal with Burstyn, contingent on the film getting a Seal.

Two scenes in this tale of a father and son's search for a stolen bicycle (the bike was necessary for the father's job and family livelihood) offended PCA's Catholic honcho Joe Breen. One involved the lad's pausing alongside a wall to relieve himself (he never does, owing to his father's insistence that they lose no time); the other is set in a bordello, where their quest has led them (it is morning, and we see the bathrobe-clad ladies of the night at breakfast). The first went up obliquely against the Code's notion of "good taste"; the second, its warning against "the limited use of places of sex." Breen asked for cuts. Burstyn held his ground.

Foreign producers and distributors saw this as another instance of the industry's blocking foreign films' entry and wide accessibility through the PCA. Such a charge was harmful to the PCA's authority, particularly now with the industry's monopolistic practices still fresh on the government's mind; the nation rebuilding Europe, including its film industries; and the possible threat of a renewed backlash from foreign countries with their oodles of Hollywood imports.

Burstyn campaigned, urging the MPAA, which had, prior to the fanfare, reviewed the film as "a picture for everyone," to countermand Breen's intransigence. More harm was done to the PCA's image when the Legion gave the film a B: "material unsuitable for entertainment motion pictures" (which was never specified), not the usual C for pictures without a Seal, thus severing the PCA–LD union. Adding insult to injury, the Academy awarded it a foreign film Oscar in 1949. Controversy, as it had in the past, so stoked the box-office fires that eventually four out of five MPAA theater circuits booked the show. To play a picture without a Seal, which major circuits had not done since 1934, put into question exhibitor support of the PCA and the Code.[5]

10.6   *Stromboli* (1950)

Protestant and Catholic Churches, communities across the land, and Colorado's senator Edwin C. Johnson (Democrat) raised a good deal of sound and fury over *Stromboli*. (The politico went on to propose the federal licensing of film actors, producers, and distributors for a nominal fee which could be revoked whenever a holder was convicted of a crime involving moral turpitude or admitted conduct of such nature, as in the case of Ingrid Bergman.) Recut by director Alfred Werker for its American coproducer/distributor RKO and given a Seal and the Legion's A-II designation, the movie's content, a story of spiritual rejuvenation of a refugee who decides to stick with her poor fisherman husband and make the best of her squalid life on the bleak island of Stromboli, did not offend. What did, however, was the fact that *Stromboli* was the collaboration of one of Hollywood's most popular stars and her director, lover, and eventual second husband Roberto Rossellini. With the images of her nun (*The Bells of St. Mary's*, RKO, 1945) and canonized saint (*Joan of Arc*, RKO, 1948) still in America's mind, Bergman, enamored of Rossellini's neo-realist *Open City* (1946), and eventually of the director himself, had abandoned her dentist husband and her 10-year-old daughter. A child out of wedlock (her husband at first refused to grant Bergman a divorce) and *Stromboli* were the first fruits of their unholy union. Offensive, too, was RKO's advertising ("Raging Island . . . Raging Passions . . . This is it!") that milked the scandal for all it was worth. Not content to call on exhibitors to ban the film (as most bluenoses did), the Birmingham Alabama Protestant Minister Association and the Memphis, Tennessee Censorship Board voted to ban all films in which Bergman appeared – and all films Rossellini directed.[6]

10.7 *The Miracle* (1950) and the US Supreme Court Decision of 1952

Italian cinema's momentous affront with censorship occurred when the intrepid Burstyn opened the 41-minute *The Miracle* in Manhattan, one of a trio of short features under the omnibus title *The Ways of Love*. Approved as a solo by US Customs and as part of the trio by the New York State Board of Censors, *The Miracle*, directed by Rossellini, blithely recounted the fancies of a mentally unbalanced peasant woman who, drunk with wine and in a transport of religious fervor, is seduced by a bearded vagrant she believes to be St. Joseph. Upon bearing a child, she further believes the birth to be the result of an immaculate conception.

On December 23, 11 days after its inauspicious opening, the city's Department of Licenses Commissioner Edward T. McCaffrey ordered a halt, finding the picture "officially and personally blasphemous." Warned by Burstyn that the picture's withdrawal violated contractual agreements, theater manager Lillian Gerard continued to exhibit the film. McCaffrey suspended the theater's license while threatening any other New York theater that showed the film with license revocation. The Legion concurred, handing the omnibus *The Ways of Love* (it did not single out *The Miracle*) a C rating: "a sacrilegious and blasphemous mockery of Christian and religious truth." Further support for McCaffrey's decision came from the Catholic War Veterans and the Chancellor of the New York Archdiocese, who declared the movie "an open insult to the faith of millions of people in [the] city and hundreds of millions throughout the world."

Following the State Supreme Court's warning to sign a temporary injunction, McCaffrey, on December 30, lifted the ban pending further adjudication. Two immediate problems confronted the Court: the right of the License

Commissioner to censor and the desirability of censoring a film about which there was an honest divided opinion. The fear of thought control in this heyday of HUAC must also have weighed in. In early January, the Court ruled against the Commissioner.

On January 7, 1951, while the Catholic War Veterans and the Holy Name Society picketed in front of the theater, Cardinal Spellman asked Catholics nationwide to boycott the picture. On January 23, the New York Film Critics switched the location of its awards ceremony, at which *The Miracle* was to receive the best foreign film citation, from Radio City Music Hall to the Rainbow Room of the RCA Building, fearing picket lines and a Catholic boycott of the Music Hall.

On February 16, the State Board declared the film "sacrilegious." Theaters cancelled showings. Burstyn pressed. On October 16, the Court of Appeals, in a 5-to-2 decision, upheld the right of the State Board to ban the film. Burstyn was undaunted, taking the case (*Joseph Burstyn, Inc. vs. William V. Wilson, Commissioner of Education of New York, et al.*) to the US Supreme Court, the first film censorship case tried there since 1915's *Mutual vs. Ohio*. In a landmark decision on May 26, 1952, all nine justices reversed the New York State Court of Appeals and, what is more, overturned the 1915 decision which held that the exhibition of movies was a "business pure and simple" and, as such, not included in the constitutional guarantees of free speech and press. Moreover, the Court found the word "sacrilegious" in regard to *The Miracle* to be a vague test, too susceptible to various meanings to constitute a satisfactory standard. The industry hailed the decision, which was a blow to various state and municipal censoring boards and the Legion, as well as to Catholic pressure groups. Burstyn felt that the decision "clears the way for the motion picture to take its rightful place as a major and adult art form, as a medium of expression and communication of ideas on all facets of our life and society."[7]

10.8.   *Detective Story* (P, 1951), *Beyond the Forest* (WB, 1949), *The Doctor and the Girl* (MGM, 1949), *A Place in the Sun* (P, 1951), *People Will Talk* (TCF, 1951), and Code Amendments of 1951; *A Streetcar Named Desire* (WB, 1951)

The stage significantly impacted upon movie censorship in 1951 when revered William Wyler sought to film Sidney Kingsley's 1949 play *Detective Story* and in-demand Elia Kazan agreed to steer Tennessee Williams's Pulitzer

Prize-winning *A Streetcar Named Desire*, which Kazan himself staged in 1947. Liberal directors both, committed to screen honesty, they had already butted their heads against censorship's wall: Wyler with *These Three* (UA, 1936), a version of Lillian Hellman's 1934 play *The Children's Hour*; Kazan with *Pinky*.

Detective Story had two, possibly three (depending on one's interpretation), objections: the cop's Catholic wife's abortion; the cop's murder, with its hint of suicide as he masochistically walks directly toward the suspected criminal's gun. While the murder of a police officer and the representation of suicide became taboos with the 1938 Code fiddling, the subject of abortion was not actually found in the Code, for it was assumed to be unsuitable screen material.

The Legion had already been instrumental in excising the abortion plot point in *Beyond the Forest*, sourced in Stuart Engstrandt's 1948 shocking novel, and consequently changed the film's rating from C to B. When MGM had confronted Breen with regard to *The Doctor and the Girl*, refashioned from Maxene Ven Der Meersch's 1948 polemical fiction, by pointing out that the abortion prohibition was nonexistent, he worked out a swap ("illegal surgery" in lieu of the word "abortion"). The abortion subplot in *A Place in the Sun*, a translation of Theodore Dreiser's 1924 novel *An American Tragedy* and Patrick Kearney's 1926 stage version, had already been approved (a Seal and an A-II). No wonder. The word "abortion" was never uttered. The doctor not only refused to perform the operation but was shown to be repelled by the very idea. When the pregnant girl and her boyfriend discussed the doctor's decision, their exchange was whispered; the scene shrouded in shadows. The finale, in which the girl drowned and the boy was escorted to the electric chair, was construed as punishment for the transgression, an instance of "compensating moral values," a principle so dear to the Code's heart. At Fox, *People Will Talk* deleted the entire discussion of abortion, though the Legion smacked its knuckles with a B for condoning extramarital pregnancy.

Wyler expunged all mention of "abortion" and "abortionist," substituting "baby-farm grist mill" in reference to the doctor's illegal operation. Satisfied, Breen did not raise a stink about the cop-killing and glossed over, as did the Legion with an A-II, the suicide implication (not only a taboo, but in Catholic morality, the one "unforgivable" sin). In fact, after niggling with *Detective Story*, Breen softened the Code's implied cop-killing taboo with a tacked-on clause: "unless such scenes are absolutely necessary to plot" and the suicide proscription as well, adding that suicide, when shown, "should never be justified, glorified, or used to defeat the . . . law."

Two other emendations went into effect in 1951. Abortion was added to the list of forbidden subjects in a series that included nudity, sex hygiene, and venereal diseases. Also enjoined were the depictions of drug use and illegal drug trafficking, added at the request of the Federal Narcotics Bureau, concerned over illegal traffic in narcotics and an increase in addiction. Up to 1946, the Code banned films dealing with narcotics. In 1946, however, an amendment was passed permitting such films, provided they did not "stimulate curiosity concerning the use of, or traffic in, such drugs, or . . . show in detail the effects of the use of narcotics," thus paving the way for the release of *To the Ends of the Earth* (C, 1948) about a T-man ferreting out opium smugglers.

After Williams toned down *Streetcar*'s language ("goddamns," "ass," racial slurs such as "greaseball"), other crimps had to be ironed out. The husband's rape of his sister-in-law going unpunished flew in the face of the Code's "compensating moral values" dictum. Further, the in-law's account of her marriage to a homosexual and her nymphomaniac fondness for young boys were instances of the "sexual perversion" no-no. Kazan agreed to scrap the perversion bits but stood adamant about the rape. A bruising round of battles later, Breen allowed the rape, if done obliquely, and if the ending, wherein the wife rushes back into her husband's arms, be changed.

What Kazan agreed to and what he did through innuendo were, fortunately, two different things. The rape scene: husband grabs in-law; cutaway to a smashed mirror; direct cut to a torrent of water gushing from a hose. The sexual metaphors were as arousing as any shots of two bodies lolling about. True, in the end, the wife takes refuge in the neighbor's second-floor apartment after telling her baby: "We're never going back there, never." But we never really believe it. The wife's behavior seems a spur-of-the-moment reaction. In fact, this very situation occurred previously when, after a quarrel with her husband, the wife sought her neighbor's refuge. But then (and presumably now), the wife, heeding her mate's bellowing "Stella," slowly descended the stairs and allowed herself to be taken up in his brawny arms.

As for the deletion of the "perversions," the in-law does narrate the story of a young, sensitive soul, whom, on her wedding night, she reviled as weak. That night, she continues, he put a gun in his mouth and blew his brains out. No stretch of the imagination was needed to deduce that the fellow was homosexual. His suicide method, in fact, was a metaphor for fellatio. Her insatiable taste for young men, truth to tell, was peppered throughout, and heartily at that. She gives a young sailor the once-over within the film's first minute. She asks the time of day and a light for her cigarette from a teenage paper-carrier whom she kisses. Other narrated back stories involve her being evicted from a semi-disreputable hotel for moral turpitude in bringing men there and being dismissed from school because of her liaison with a 17-year-old.

To avoid a C and cop a B, the Legion demanded 12 cuts. Executed by independent producer Charles K. Feldman at the distributor's urging and unknown to Kazan, who was understandably miffed, the excised four minutes did not harm the movie's integrity.[8] *Streetcar* proved that any subject could be proper material for the screen, if treated properly.

10.9   *The Moon Is Blue* (UA, 1953)

F. Hugh Herbert's romantic comedy about the attempt of two wolves to seduce a miss whose virtue wins out in the end and who even leads one of the roués to the altar bored critics but titillated Broadway in 1951. Breen, however, did not crack a smile. In fact, he strenuously objected to the piece's frivolous attitude toward sex, seduction, and virginity (she: "Do you mind if I take my shoes off?"; he: "Take anything off you like").

Breen's grumblings scared the majors away so director Preminger, the stage version's coproducer, decided to take the independent route. As a selling point, Preminger nabbed star William Holden in a delayed salary and percentage deal to play the wolf turned sheep.

Preminger was no stranger to censorship. Prior to *Forever Amber*, he had besieged the PCA to permit a scene in which husband and wife were seen sleeping in the same bed for *In the Meantime, Darling* (TCF, 1944). Permission denied, he managed to get the male hunched over on the right side while the female sat up on the left side of the same bed. Now in control, Preminger was itching to demand his constitutional rights. He made only one concession: a reference, at the movie's end, by the older wolf to his lifestyle as an "immoral philosophy of life."

Unimpressed, Breen refused the Seal, despite second-in-command Geoffrey Shurlock's alternate opinion that *Moon* was indeed a moral movie. Fearing the Code could be smashed if the Seal-less movie found an audience, the Legion backed Breen by slapping a C in lieu of its initial B on the picture: "tends to deny Christian and traditional standards of morality . . . and dwells hardly without variations upon suggestiveness in situations and dialogue."

UA's bosses decided to go for broke. The movie, after all, cost a piddling $450,000 to produce and besides, all the censorship scrimmages could be an audience magnet. Waiving the "Code-approved" regulation of Preminger's contract, UA got the picture to market where it made a whopping $3.5 million, playing three of the five recently divorced theater chains, all MPAA members. Lo and behold, a picture made money, lots of it, without a Seal, condemned by the Legion, declared "an occasion of sin" by Church cardinals, and banned in Kansas, Ohio, Maryland, Wisconsin, Jersey City, and Milwaukee. Preminger and *The Moon Is Blue* eviscerated the Code and Legion as well,[9] while further enervating state and city censorship.

10.10   *The French Line* (RKO, 1953)

Hughes and Russell reunited for the musical *The French Line*. Mary Loos and Richard Sale's old-fashioned libretto posed no problems. It was a cliché about a Texas oil heiress whose wealth so intimidated American men that she ventured to Paris in the guise of a struggling model and there found a husband. (In the pre-production stage, Hughes deleted some suggestive gestures and jokes that displeased Breen.) Russell's costumes were entirely another matter. Throughout, Michael Woulf and Howard Greer's shockingly low-cut outfits foregrounded Russell's world-famous chest. The *pièce-de-résistance* was a corset with strategically placed cut-out circles (one revealing her navel) for the appropriately titled "I'm Looking for Trouble" number. The bubble-bath number forsook salacious clothes entirely: in this sequence, Russell's bosoms floated on water. Color, dance movements, lascivious reactions from the menfolk, and 3-D (one ad promised: "J.R. in 3-D. It'll knock BOTH your eyes out") further accentuated Russell's trademarks.

Inspired by Preminger's intrepid stand, Hughes refused to cut. Breen, in turn, withheld the Seal. Archbishop Ritter of St. Louis, locus of the film's premiere, was enlisted to back Breen. Ritter's first letter, read from every pulpit, urged the faithful to shun the film. Ritter's second letter placed the city's hefty Catholic population under the penalty of mortal sin if they embarked. Disparaging reviews, clerical fulminations, and police threats to raid the theater did not keep people away. It appeared that Hughes, too, had broken the Code and hit pay dirt.

Despite the Legion's C: "grossly obscene, suggestive and indecent action, costuming and dialogue . . . capable of evil influence upon those who patronize it," Hughes went wide with the film. State censors in New York, Pennsylvania, Kansas, and Ohio banned it. Catholics picketed. Hughes made cuts for a general release. Reviews and word of mouth continued to be awful but the public turned out to see what the fuss was about.

10.11   *From Here to Eternity* (C, 1953)

Director Fred Zinneman and adapter Daniel Taradash trimmed the sensationalism of James Jones's well-written 1951 bestseller. Even the army applauded the reworking and agreed to cooperate. The profanity of pre-Pearl Harbor military men was excised. The brutality, as in the stockade incident, was off screen. The adulterous relationship between the captain's wife and the sergeant, who works for the captain, and the fornicating affair between the private and the hostess at a social club, however, remained. Though whitewashed in its resemblance to an USO club, the club still had brothel overtones, including its name "The New Congress Club" (one of the designations of the word "congress" is that of sexual intercourse). The novel's nude bathing scene, though now with the sergeant and captain's wife in bathing suits, still aroused. The buildup of the rationale for the wife's adultery (the loss of her child; a callous husband who also had his own string of extra-curriculars), an admission of regret on her part, and the captain's comeuppance (not the novel's ironic twist of his promotion), along with the deleted profanity and muted violence, did not undermine the film's probity. Nor did the Legion's B: "reflects the acceptability of divorce, tends to condone immoral actions; suggestive situations" keep *Eternity* from cinching eight well-deserved Oscars, including that for best picture, and record rentals.

10.12 Shurlock's Reign and Code Readjustments of 1954; *La Ronde* (1950) and *M* (C, 1951)

In 1954, Shurlock, an English Protestant educated at Dartmouth who had been with the PCA since its inception, replaced the retiring Breen, a conservative Catholic. The appointment of the moderate liberal, sympathetic to the idea of movies for adults, displeased the Legion, fearing that its mutual reciprocity with the PCA might be jeopardized.

One of the first things that Shurlock did was ease Code taboos relating to the representations of miscegenation ("a special subject to be treated within the careful limits of good taste"), liquor, and some profane words. Only a year before, for instance, the word "hell" had to be deleted from *Cease Fire* (P, 1953) while now, the stevedore's "go to hell" – to a priest, no less – in *On the Waterfront* (C, 1954) was sanctioned.

On the state scene, the Supreme Court ruled that New York had exceeded its power in labeling the French import *La Ronde* "immoral," in categorically declaring that the film "would tend to corrupt morals," and refusing it a license. The Court also overturned Ohio's ban of *M* (C, 1951) on the grounds that the movie tended "to incite crime." The Court accused the respective censor boards of not providing clear-cut standards in what constituted an "immoral" picture or one that "incited to crime."

10.13   Backlash; *The Man with the Golden Arm* (UA, 1955) and *Picnic* (C, 1955)

A momentary backlash occurred in 1955 when Senator Estes Kefauver (Democrat) formed a subcommittee to investigate the proliferation of sex and violence in current fare and plumb the nebulous area of the effects of these images on children.[10] Children aside, the growing concern over the possible negative impressions of America these controversial movies might give foreigners (something to be circumvented at all costs during the Cold War chill) undoubtedly ignited the probe. The foreign movie critics' outcry over the frequency and intensity of violent images in American movies alarmed the government. To make matters worse, various overseas government censors were snipping, in part or entirely, fight scenes.

The Senator singled out seven films. *The Wild One* (C, 1953), based on a real-life incident in 1947, followed the Black Rebels, a band of young leather-clad motorcyclists terrorizing a suburban town – its homosexual subtext went unnoticed. *The Blackboard Jungle* (MGM, 1955), derived from Evan Hunter's 1954 trailblazing book, looked unflinchingly at juvenile delinquency in a New York City high school. *Kiss Me Deadly* (UA, 1955) was a translation of one of Mickey Spillane's sadistic vigilante detective Mike Hammer pulps. The last four 1955 movies were all gangster films: *New York Confidential* (WB), *Five Against the House* (C), *Violent Saturday* (TCF), and *The Big Combo* (AA). That *Combo*'s mobster had two hit men who were lovers astonishingly failed to raise any censor's eyebrows. The notorious seven were branded B by the Legion for "excessive brutality," "low moral tone," and too detailed methods of crime.

Another Kefauver subcommittee had Hollywood nabobs and laymen opine about the link between on-screen sex, violence, and crime and off-screen juvenile delinquency. Additionally, questionnaires were sent to 180 clinical psychologists, medical men, and psychiatrists for their opinions about this possible connection. The 1956 report declared that overly violent or sadistic films might "initiate and provide the content for anti-social behavior on the part of emotionally disturbed children," a conclusion heard every time such a study was conducted.

While the iron was hot, the Legion implored the PCA to strengthen enforcement. In response, the PCA denied a Seal to a rendition of John Van Druten's play *I Am a Camera* (1955) about the amoral Sally Bowles who, among other frivolities, postpones an abortion of what turns out to be a false pregnancy. The Legion tagged the British import with a C: "wholly unsuitable on moral grounds." Startling figures were disclosed: in 1955, 82 films or 30 percent merited an A-I;

97 or 35 percent made the A-II cutoff; while 92 or 33 percent fell into the B category, an increase of 11 percent from the previous year.

Obstacles from the right, however, did not hinder breakthroughs from the left. Independent Preminger, along with chosen adapters Walter Newman and Lewis Meltzer, cinematized Nelson Algren's hard-edged 1949 novel *The Man with the Golden Arm*, about a Chicago gambler who becomes a drug addict. The PCA refused the Seal despite the film's strong anti-drug sentiment. Drug addiction, no matter the picture's attitude, was *verboten* and that was that. The cagey showman then kowtowed to the Legion's objection to the protagonist preparing heroin in a spoon by cutting the 30-second shot. Feeling that it was calling the shots metaphorically and literally, the Legion, instead of the expected C (the pro forma category of any picture without a Seal), rated the film B: "minimizes the characters' moral obligations." Preminger had caused a tear between the PCA and Legion, one much more severe than *The Bicycle Thief*'s rip.

UA pushed ahead with distribution. After all, the un-Sealed *The Moon Is Blue* hadn't kept the customers away. Furthermore, Preminger had, in a sense, financially insured his movie by casting three popular players (addict Frank Sinatra, his wheelchair-bound wife Eleanor Parker, and his mistress Kim Novak) and changing Algren's downbeat ending to a happy one. Bingo – $4.3 million in the tills.

William Inge was another playwright whose translations, while sending censors' blood pressure up, delivered something new. When his 1953 Pulitzer Prize-winning *Picnic* opened, the PCA told interested buyers Paramount and Fox that a Seal would be withheld because of the play's "treatment of illicit sex without compensating values." The PCA suggested the death of either Hal, the aging stud who has his way with 18-year-old Madge, or both their deaths as a solution. Two years later, when Columbia's Cohn snapped up the rights for $500,000, the objection was never mentioned, owing to the Breen-to-Shurlock change of command at the fort.

What was mentioned, however, was the profanity, which stage director Joshua Logan and *Eternity*'s adapter Daniel Taradash erased. Three other items, also red-circled, did remain: Hal's hitchhiking story in which he tells of ambidextrously servicing two females; Madge's mother who encourages her daughter to sleep with her rich boyfriend to get him to marry her; and the sexual liaison of Hal and Madge bringing home the salvific power of sex. Moreover, at every turn, sensuality went unabated: broad-shouldered Hal stripped to the waist and later in a bathing suit; Madge in undergarments and bathing suit; female legs shimmying out of swimsuits while male torsos were towel-dried side by side; schoolteacher Rosemary continually smoothing out her woolen skirt over her derrière. Though Legioned B ("emphasis on lustful actions, situations and dialogue . . . tends to debase the virtue of purity"), *Picnic* netted $6.3 million.

10.14   The Code Revision of 1956

In January 1956, Eric Johnston appointed a "watchdog" committee (himself as head, Paramount Chief Balaban, Columbia VP-Treasurer Abe Schneider, and Daniel O'Shea, reorganized RKO's boss) to reexamine the Code and process of its administration, particularly its appeal methods. By December 11, 1956, the committee's revision was finalized, the first comprehensive changes since the Code's 1930 adoption had gone into effect. Four absolute taboos were abolished: the portrayal of illicit narcotics practices (though the former list governing its presentation was expanded);[11] the portrayal of abortion (though "the subject shall be discouraged, shall never be more than suggested, and when referred to, shall be condemned"); the portrayal of prostitution, "the methods and techniques of (which) and white slavery shall never be presented in detail, nor shall the subjects be presented unless shown in contrast to right standards of behavior"; and the portrayal of kidnapping. Scenes of childbirth and surgical operations, formerly prohibited in fact and in silhouette, were permitted to be treated "within the careful limits of good taste." Miscegenation could now be handled, at the producer's discretion.

On the other hand, the use of racial slurs was discouraged (formerly, the Code told producers to "take cognizance" of the fact that such terms were offensive to movie patrons). A stronger stand against cruelty and brutality was also urged, banning "all detailed and protracted presentations of physical violence, torture, and abuse." As a capitulation to the Legion and *The Miracle* decision, the word "divine" was added to the proscription: "Law – natural or human – shall not be ridiculed, nor shall sympathy be created for its violations," and blasphemy was banned: "Ministers of religion, or persons posing as such, shall not be portrayed as comic characters or as villains so as to cast disrespect on religions."

So as to seem less an abrogation than contemporization of the Code, the revision reiterated its continued espousal of the sanctity of marriage and home: "adultery and illicit sex, sometimes necessary plot material, shall not be explicitly treated, nor shall they be justified and made to seem right and permissive." As for membership, the PCA made a move to include representatives of both exhibitors and independent producers on its appeal board.

10.15   *Baby Doll* (WB, 1956), *Tea and Sympathy* (MGM, 1956), and *The Bad Seed* (WB, 1956)

As an example of its new, progressive thrust, the Code found no fault with Kazan's *Baby Doll*. An amalgam of two of Tennessee Williams's one-act plays,

27 Wagon Loads of Cotton and *The Unsatisfactory Supper*, it was fraught with desperate types and situations. A middle-aged alcoholic Mississippi cotton-mill owner (Karl Malden) had married white-trash 18-year-old (Carroll Baker). Though married for two years, the girl was still a virgin. Her husband had promised her dying father that he would not touch her until she was "ready." Financial problems and sexual frustration force him to burn the mill of a young, virile Sicilian competitor (Eli Wallach). Seeking revenge, the Sicilian, through foreplay, manipulates the girl into signing a confession of her husband's guilt. More egregious, it was played in a satiric, at times farcical manner.

The Legion, fearing what the revised Code would be like in the light of' *Baby Doll's* Seal and chagrined at not being asked for its input during the revision, strapped *Baby Doll* with a C: "morally repellent both in theme and treatment." The Legion went on to castigate the PCA for approving the picture. The PCA remained silent; not so Cardinal Spellman, who warned Catholics that they would be committing a sin if they cast their eyes *Baby Doll's* way.

Independent now with the right of final cut, Kazan refused to make any changes. His intention was not in portraying what was moral or immoral, he countered, but only the truth. He was particularly outraged at Spellman's charge that the picture was "unpatriotic." Spellman claimed that he made his statement, not only as a protector of souls, but also as a "loyal citizen in defense of America." Spellman was alluding to Kazan's prior communist ties.

Williams demurred: "I can't imagine that an ancient and august branch of the Christian faith is not larger in heart and mind than those who set themselves up as censors of a medium of expression that . . . extends the world over." Also foiling Spellman was the Episcopalian Rev. Pike: "the Church should not suppress statements of human problems but rather it should provide solutions for them." Pike further questioned the theological correctness of Spellman's position while railing at the assorted attempts of minority groups to impose their will on the community. Pike also remarked that he found more gratuitous sensuality in the Church-endorsed *The Ten Commandments* (P, 1956) than in *Baby Doll* which, incidentally, he had seen, unlike Spellman, who had only a second-hand report. Pike even hoisted Spellman on his own petard when he declared that the suppressions of free expression of ideas and free description of the real situation smacked of communism. Pike did, however, concur with Spellman on one point – the brazen logo (Baker, in baby-doll pajamas, sucking her thumb while lying on her side in a crib), which was Hollywood's first attempt to sell the image of the "nymphet."

Neither circuit cancellation nor mixed reviews but word of mouth choked *Baby* financially. The initial crowds perceived the movie as dreary, strained, and odd; its star-less cast, a turn-off.

10-1   *Tea and Sympathy* (MGM, 1956, p. Pandro S. Berman)
Semi-bowdlerized stage-to-film family melodrama adaptation that takes on the subject of homo-sexuality, as town slut (Norma Crane) shouts "Sister Boy" at shy, sensitive Chilton preppie (John Kerr).

Two other stage adaptations that year were further witnesses of the Code's liberalization. Robert Anderson's groundbreaking 1953 *Tea and Sympathy* con-cerned the boarding-school simpatico between a sexually frustrated coach's wife (her husband is a latent homosexual) and a "sissy" student perceived as gay (he prefers classical music to physical sports, enacts the female lead in the school play, sews, cooks). Their reciprocal understanding climaxes with her taking him to bed. Except for the subtraction of the coach's closeted homosexuality and addition of a coda in which the woman claims adultery ruined her life, adapter Anderson's values came through. Even the Legion's explanation for its B-rating recognized that "the solution of the plot still tends to arouse undue sympathy for and to condone immoral actions."

John Lee Mahin's screen treatment of Maxwell Anderson's 1955 footlight version of William March's 1954 novel *The Bad Seed* also contained deletions (the talk about homosexuality and Freudian complexes) and changes (the 8-year-old murderess struck by lightning replaced the play's ending in which the child ironically survives her own mother's attempt to dispatch her with sleeping pills). Yet the film emerged as a chilling portrait of an amoral child murderess who even causes her mother's suicide attempt.

Despite the code restriction ("pictures dealing with criminal activities in which minors participate . . . shall not be approved if they incite demoralizing imitation on the part of the youth") and the board's fear that such a character with no regret or guilt could have a very powerful effect on impressionable child viewers, *The Bad Seed* got a Seal. WB promised in the ad campaign to indicate that the film was "recommended for adults only." The Legion, seeing the finale's bolt from the blue as proof of God's existence and justice, rated the movie A-II.

10.16 *Giant* (WB, 1956), *Serenade* (WB, 1956), *Island in the Sun* (TCF, 1957), and *Sayonara* (WB, 1957)

The year 1956 saw a miscegenation breakthrough. *Giant*, a transcription of Edna Ferber's 1952 bestseller, had support Dennis Hopper marrying Mexican Elsa Cardenas. *Serenade* (WB, 1956), a sanitized scenario of Cain's 1937 novel, went further by having protagonist Mario Lanza married to Mexican Sarita Montiel. Boldest of all, *Island In the Sun* (TCF, 1957), condensed from the 1955 novel by Alec Waugh, foregrounded two black–white relationships (lovers Joan Fontaine and Harry Belafonte; marrieds John Justin and Dorothy Dandridge) while backgrounding a third (James Mason is one-sixteenth black). *Sayonara* (WB, 1957), drawn from James A. Michener's 1954 tome, also dealt with two interracial couples (Marlon Brando/Miko Taka; Red Buttons/Miyoshi Umeki). Enlighteningly, the Legion, interpreting Buttons/Umeki's double suicide as "behavior patterns indigenous to a pagan culture," handed *Sayonara* an A-II. Except for *Serenade*, all films cleaned up at the box office.

10.17 Legion Expansion: *Peyton Place* (TCF, 1957)

With the accession of liberal clerics and laymen as reviewers, the Legion got into the cultural swing of things by expanding its classification with an A-III designation: morally unobjectionable for adults. A-II now signified "morally unobjectionable for adolescents." Jerry Wald's independent production of Grace

Metalious's 1956 notorious bestseller about a New England college town called *Peyton Place* was first to fly the new label. John Patrick Hayes's screen version did not pull back from the novel's contentious situations: an illegitimate daughter's anger with her frigid mama; a stepfather's rape of his stepdaughter and her consequent murder of him; and a mama's boy's trauma (coded homosexual).

10.18   *Roth vs. US* and *The Game of Love* (1954); *The Garden of Eden* (Excelsior Pictures, 1957)

In 1957, the US Supreme Court handed down a definition of "obscenity" which further throttled state and city censorship, thus opening up the screen's sensual and sexual parameters. A year earlier in New York City, Samuel Roth, known since the late twenties in the East coast publishing world as a publisher of "obscene" books and magazines, was again convicted of violating a postal statute regarding the mailing of "obscene" materials. After the Federal Court of Appeals for the Second Circuit confirmed the judgment, Roth and his lawyers argued the conviction in the Supreme Court. The august body decided that "obscenity" was not protected by the freedoms of speech and press and also, that explicit sex was not necessarily obscene. Further, the court enumerated that three elements constituted "obscenity." First, it had to be established that the dominant theme of the material taken as a whole appealed to prurient interest in sex. Secondly, the material had to be patently offensive because it affronted contemporary community standards relating to the description or representation of sexual matters. Last, the material had to be utterly without redeeming social value. Roth was vindicated.

In 1956 Chicago's Censor Board banned the French import *The Game of Love*.[12] This adaptation of Colette's contumacious 1933 novel centered on a pair of teenagers who, disturbed by the emotions developing in them, finally consummate their union, after the 16-year-old boy has been initiated by an adulterous older woman. The censors flatly stated that the film was "not acceptable to standards of decency, with immorality featured and dialogue unfit." The District Court overturned the decision initially but, in review, decided to uphold the censors' verdict. US distributor Times Film Corp. fought back. The US Court of Appeals for the Seventh Circuit affirmed the lower court's decision but the US Supreme Court, instancing the case of "*Alberts vs. California*," a companion state case to the benchmark "*Roth vs. US*," reversed it. For the first time ever, the Supreme Court judged a specific artistic work was not obscene and entitled to constitutional protection. Seal-less and clobbered by a Legion C, the film made money.

The stink over *The Garden of Eden* evaporated before it reached the level of the Supreme Court. This American independent film followed a stressed-out widow who flees the home of her stern father-in-law. When her car stalls, inhabitants of a nudist colony come to her rescue. Witnessing the wholesome way of life in the colony, her peace is restored. When her father-in-law arrives, he, too, undergoes a conversion. "Indecent!" yelled the New York censors, banning the film. The New York State Supreme Court transferred the case to the Appellate Division, which annulled the censor's verdict, declaring that "indecent" was too general and vague a term to constitute a valid censorship standard. Additionally, the lawmakers declared that nudity in itself without smuttiness was not obscenity in law or common sense.

10.19   *Vertigo* (P, 1958), *Bonjour Tristesse* (C, 1958), and *Cat on a Hot Tin Roof* (MGM, 1958)

Hitchcock deleted the Code's crime-doesn't-pay ending of *Vertigo* in which James Stewart and Barbara Bel Geddes listen to a radio report about the apprehension of the murderer. It was another case of the maestro ignoring, sidestepping by means of coding, trading (my concession for your concession) or, at most, paying only slight obeisance to the Code. *Notorious* (RKO, 1946) featured a kiss between principals Cary Grant and Ingrid Bergman that reached the level of a set piece, exceeding the Code's 30-second limit by 150 seconds. Bergman's character was more gold digger than prostitute, according to the PCA's interdictions, but she did come across as someone who had been around the sexual block many times. *Rope* (WB, 1948) featured two homosexual protagonists, completely uncoded. *Strangers on a Train* (1951) retained Laura Elliot's extramarital pregnancy and Robert Walker's demonstration of murder at a cocktail party, both PCA remonstrances. Oddly, the PCA did not ax the homosexual dimension of Walker's character. True, in *Rear Window* (P, 1954), Miss Torso did wear more than just black panties (her sole attire in the script). In compliance with the Code, she was given the addition of a bra, but the business Hitch gave her with that extra bit of clothing was just as humorously risqué. While exercising with her back to the audience, her bra falls off and she bends below the screen frame to retrieve it. Other boldly underlined items in the script, however, did remain in the film: the character of the estrous, newly married woman in a neighboring apartment and Grace Kelly's display of overnight-implied peignoir and slippers. In *Psycho* (P, 1960), the graphic depiction of violence was what Hitch intended.

The year 1958 saw the Legion complimented on its A-III ratings. Foremost was *Bonjour Tristesse*. Censorship's bête noire Preminger guided the adaptation of Françoise Sagan's 1954 Gallic romp, eschewing any kind of bowdlerization. Present and accounted for were a sybaritic father and his equally amoral 17-year-old offspring who enjoy living together (he's her "darling"), never more so than when they are deliciously using "corruptible" people as ego-stroking distractions. Also on hand was a divorced woman, the pawn in the father/daughter's current diversion that ends with the woman's suicide made to look like an accident: "her gift to them," as the teenager concludes. The father's bubble-headed mistress and the daughter's hormonal 25-year-old guy next door, whom the high-schooler sleeps with as part of the game, complete the quintet. Set on the French Riviera, with our clique wearing bathing suits and shorts while continually eating, drinking, and fornicating, the film oozes with sensuality. Preminger also audaciously retained the sprightly tone of the memory, forgoing any *Sturm und Drang* and observed, never evaluated, the situation. Compensating moral values are not found – well, at least not the kind we've come to expect. Yes, the daughter is melancholic, bored, and self-pitying ("Will I ever be happy again?"), but solipsistic as ever in recalling the summer of the woman's death. And, truth to tell, she and her father are still up to their old tricks, even planning next summer's jaunt on the Italian Riviera.

Next came *Cat on a Hot Tin Roof*, director-writer Richard Brooks's sly version of Tennessee Williams's 1955 play with Brick's homosexuality not quite transformed into hero worship for his football buddy. Brooks, who liked to tackle disputatious subject matter (*The Blackboard Jungle*, *Elmer Gantry*, Williams's *Sweet Bird of Youth*) became censorship's bête grise.

10.20   *Lady Chatterley's Lover* (1957), *And God Created Woman* (1958), *Room at the Top* (1959), and *Never on Sunday* (1960)

In 1959, the foreign film turned a corner in America. Showing the industry just how sensually and sexually sophisticated movies could be while decimating state and city censorship, the foreign film finally began to be booked in major venues, impressively amassing bucks.

French import *Lady Chatterley's Lover*, based on D. H. Lawrence's novel privately published in 1929,[13] was denied a license in New York by the state censors: the "whole theme of the picture was immoral," presenting adultery "as a desirable, acceptable, and proper pattern of behavior." While the New York Courts upheld the ban, the Supreme Court in 1959 ruled the government could not interfere with the exhibition of films because it disapproved of an idea expressed, even if it were a sexual one. The ruling forced the New York State Board of

Censors to liberalize its policies concerning nudity and illicit love. Art houses and a few major downtown houses did nicely with *Lady*, due to her notoriety, lack of a Seal, and Legion C.

Philadelphia's DA found that another French import, *And God Created Woman*, violated a state law. The conte of a whimsical, liberated coquette who marries one brother but goes off with the other brother and eventually with a wealthy yachtsman starred Brigitte Bardot, France's Monroe, in various states of *déshabille*. When two exhibitors cancelled their contracts, distributor Kingsley-International, Columbia's art house subsidiary, brought a suit in Philadelphia's Court of Commons for an injunction to prevent the DA from blocking exhibition. While the Court considered the distributor's request, the film was shown, but when the Court refused to issue a preliminary injunction, the film was seized and the exhibitors arrested. The state's Supreme Court reversed the decision, pointing out that the lower court erred in dismissing the distributor's request. Bardot's fling, forfeiting a Seal and branded "C," played major houses. One of the most successful foreign films up to this time, it cleared $4 million.

Room at the Top, a faithful rendering of John Braine's 1957 novel, arrived from Britain. It followed an ambitious, cynical boy from the modern industrial slums of Yorkshire to making it in London, his success having most to do with his performance between the sheets. Along the way, he becomes involved with an older married woman who, when replaced by the boss's daughter, commits suicide. The lack of retribution (the boy does not get his comeuppance), the frank language (a telephone operator was called a "constipated bitch"), plus the explicit love scenes and suicide, Continental Distribution reasoned, would preclude a Seal, so the film was not even submitted to the PCA. The Legion, surprisingly, gave it a B: "gross suggestiveness in costuming, dialogue and situations...[and tendency] to arouse undue sympathy for an adulteress." Not only a commercial success, *Room* picked up best actress (Simone Signoret) and adapted script (Neil Paterson) statuettes at the Academy Awards as well as a best picture nomination.

Following Continental's lead, Lopert, UA's foreign subsidiary, avoided submitting *Never on Sunday* to the PCA. The Greek import was ex-blacklisted producer-director-writer Jules Dassin's showcase of his wife Melina Mercouri as a prostitute teaching an expatriate American academic (Dassin himself) to share her zest for life. Despite sporting the scarlet letter C[14] and being banned in Atlanta in 1961 (upheld by Georgia's Supreme Court on a technicality), the film garnered $4 million, two Oscar nominations (best actress, best direction), and one win (best song).

10-2   *Anatomy of a Murder* (C, 1959, p. Otto Preminger)

Real-life judge Joseph N. Welch asks a defense lawyer (James Stewart), district attorney (Brooks West), and prosecutor (George C. Scott) if a word other than "panties" can be found for "undergarments" – director Preminger's ploy of self-reflexively foregrounding the courtroom drama's daring language.

10.21   *Anatomy of a Murder* (C, 1959)

Graphic language was a defiant element in Preminger's presentation of Robert Traver's 1958 bestseller *Anatomy of a Murder*. The PCA made no fuss, though words such as "rape," "sperm," "spermatogenesis," "panties," "bra," "contraceptive," and "climax" (as in sex) and such lines as "kick that bitch from here to kingdom come" jumped out from the soundtrack. In fact, Preminger self-reflexively privileged the word "panties" in the film by having the judge ask if there's another word for "undergarments" other than "panties." Crosby and Sinatra had gotten away with the Cole Porter lyric "Have you heard/That Minsey Starr/She got pinched in the Ass-tor Bar" in the musical *High Society* (MGM, 1956) and the word "whore" was heard for the first time on the screen in Selznick's production of Hemingway's 1929 novel *A Farewell to Arms* (TCF, 1957). What came from *Anatomy*'s mouth was, however, unheard of.

Despite the problematic words, the Legion resorted to a "Separate Classification (SC)":[15] "the clinical analysis with which the subject matter of this film (rape) is so explicitly and frankly detailed is judged to exceed the bounds of moral acceptability and propriety." That was OK by Preminger, who believed polemic was an audience aphrodisiac. The picture was a howling financial success ($5.5 million), though Chicago censors refused to give the film a license until the District Court overturned their judgment.

10.22   *Suddenly Last Summer* (C, 1959), *Some Like It Hot* (UA, 1959), and *Pillow Talk* (U, 1959)

Three films defied, more boldly than before, the Code taboo of sexual perversion in deed or inference. Implications of homosexuality and cannibalism were the kinks in *Suddenly Last Summer*, Williams and Gore Vidal's screen version of Williams's one act play which, along with another one-acter, *Something Unspoken*, was a must-see off-Broadway show in 1958. The PCA had problems but the Appeal Board promised a Seal if independent producer Sam Spiegel would delete certain scenes and some dialogue, which he agreed to do. The Legion gave out another SC. *Suddenly* captured over $2 million in ticket sales.

Producer-director-co-writer Billy Wilder's *Some Like It Hot* and producer Ross Hunter's *Pillow Talk* employed the same climactic conceit in which a straight male insinuates that he is homosexual in the hope that the female will turn aggressive, either initiating him into the ecstasy of heterosexual sex (*Some*) or making the moves on him (*Pillow*). No problem with Seals, though the Legion slapped *Some* with a B for its "suggestiveness in costuming, dialogue and situations" while it exonerated *Pillow* with an A-III. This, undoubtedly, had much to do with casting since an actor's persona (as well as genre) affects perception. *Some*'s personas of Tony Curtis and Marilyn Monroe made the material seem dirty. *Pillow Talk*, which also imaged the male as satyr and sex as fun and games and was equally imbued with double-entendres and suggestive situations galore, got away with them because of the spanking-clean personas of Rock Hudson and Doris Day. Also, *Some* was in b/w, *Pillow* in color – an indelicate conceit always appears shabby in b/w, sparkling in color. Both films were box-office wildfire.

10.23   *Blue Denim* (TCF, 1959) and *A Summer Place* (WB, 1959)

The subject of teenage pregnancy, with its attendant discussion of abortion marked *Blue Denim*, taken from the 1958 play by James Leo Herlihy and

William Noble, and *A Summer Place*, director Delmer Daves's rewrite of Sloan Wilson's 1958 bestseller. Both films received Seals. While the Legion categorized *Blue* as A-III material, it went on to give *Summer* a B, not for its teenage pregnancy plot turn but the portrayal of the acceptability of divorce and justification of remarriage (as seen in the teenagers' parents).

10.24   *Happy Anniversary* (UA, 1959)

Happy Anniversary, a rendering of Joseph Fields's 1954 play, bothered the Code. Here, the slant was on the troubles that arise when a married man reveals that he and his wife have had premarital sex. The PCA refused a Seal. In yet another instance of a rift, the Appeal Board countered, promising a Seal if independent producer Ralph Fields, who still refused to cut several scenes, added a few lines "to morally compensate for what transpired." The addition: "I was wrong. I never should have taken Alice to that hotel room before we were married. What could I have been thinking of?," was placed over an already shot scene in which the husband is sitting sadly on the stairs, rejected by his spouse and in-laws after his drunken revelation of the premarital liaison. (A similar situation had occurred in 1953 when the PCA withheld its Seal from the British farce about a bigamist, *The Captain's Paradise*. An added prologue and epilogue in which the protagonist's voice-over warned the audience not to emulate him ended the standoff.) Unappeased, the Legion doled out a B. Its objection included the film's "highly suggestive" advertising (copy jokingly heralded a new photographic process: "Sin-a-Scope").

In a move against proposed state and municipal regulation of motion pictures and in response to the flak from the NCC's Broadcasting and Film Commission and the Catholic Episcopal Committee which charged the PCA with relaxation, the MPPA studied, throughout most of 1959, the feasibility of an industry self-classification system to rate pictures for adults and general audiences. Deemed inadvisable and capable of creating more problems than it solved, the idea was abandoned. This decision did not lessen the religious groups continually badgering the industry over the next few years to adopt a ratings system, arguing that the breach might be filled by the public's demand for classification by law. Looking back at the 1959 releases, the Legion pointed to alarming statistics: a 14.59 to 24.33 percent jump in B-rated movies. Films making the A-I category numbered 66; A-II, 47; A-III, 51; and B, a shocking 54.

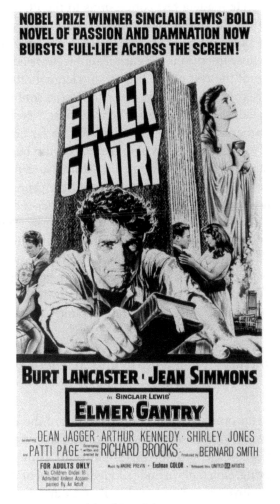

10-3 *Elmer Gantry* (UA, 1960, p. Richard Brooks)

The start of the Rating System with the "For Adults Only" tag at the bottom left of the advertising copy for this contentious male melodrama of a fundamentalist preacher.

10.25 *Elmer Gantry* (UA, 1960)

Writer-director Brooks, now independent producer, was back, this time turning the board apoplectic with a version of Sinclair Lewis's polemical work of 1927, *Elmer Gantry*, which, up to now, Hollywood had refused to consider. With the help of maverick UA and iconoclastic Burt Lancaster, the book had a second life. Though the translation was considerably pared down, Brooks retained the heart of the matter. He made a few concessions to the PCA. For example, the characters of Pengilly, the one Zenith minister who objects to his colleagues' obsession with the bottom line, and Sister Rachel, the only member of Sister Falconer's group whose intentions are entirely noble, were added to balance the base representation of the rest of the Protestant clergy. Pretty much, however, Brooks stuck to his guns. His Gantry, a shyster in the soul business, and Falconer, a somewhat delusional miracle worker revivalist, were both ambassadors of American consumerism. Their delineations were a far cry from the Code's 1930 dictum and 1956 caveat ban on blasphemy. No film had ever quite represented the clergy and religion as this one did. More: *Gantry* was claim-staking in its blatant depiction of prostitutes as well. And the censor-circled dialogue remained, as with whore Lulu Bains's recounting of her seduction by Gantry: "He got to howlin' 'Repent! Repent!' And I got to moanin' 'Save me! Save me!' And first thing I knew he rammed the fear of God into me." For his efforts, Brooks received a mighty $10.4 million box-office donation, despite the "For Adults Only!" warning displayed in bold type at the bottom of the ads and a Legion B: "negative atmosphere which does not clearly distinguish between true and sincere religionists and those who would exploit."

10.26   *Sanctuary* (TCF, 1961) and *Splendor in the Grass* (WB, 1961)

The two-version syndrome (one for US consumption; the other intended for foreign markets) went into overdrive and was profiled, making the industry come off as downright schizophrenic. British director Tony Richardson, in his first American offering, *Sanctuary*, a hodgepodge of several of William Faulkner's short stories, shot a love scene between Lee Remick and Yves Montand twice, the second version spectator-arousing. At WB, Kazan and William Inge's original *Splendor In the Grass* featured two bathtub flip-out scenes: one with Natalie Wood's almost exposed derrière; the other with Wood totally bare-assed. Both versions, however, came with a handful of stimulating scenes: Wood and Warren Beatty's wet underwear opener; stripped Beatty and other football jocks in the locker room; suggested fellatio (Beatty presses Wood to her knees with her face before his crotch, asking her to be his slave); Beatty's nymphomaniacal sister (Barbara Loden) gang-raped at a New Year's Eve party. Though the film was Sealed, the Legion was perturbed: "The visual eroticism . . . is excessive . . . its theme presents a confused pattern of moral behavior to young adults." To go with a Legion B rather than C, the film's advertising carried the notation: "No one under 16 will be admitted unless accompanied by an adult." A similar sop to the Legion occurred with Inge's adaption of James Leo Herlihy's 1960 novel

All Fall Down (MGM, 1962). To get an A-III, and not a B, the film had to be advertised as "adult" entertainment.

10.27   *Lolita* (MGM, 1962) and the Code Amendment of 1961

Vladimir Nabokov's novel *Lolita*, an account of a middle-aged academic's obsession with a 12-year-old who, ironically, seduces him, was considered pornographic when first published in 1954. US-printed in 1957, the black comedy remained a bestseller during 1958–9. Independent producer-director Stanley Kubrick and partner James B. Harris, backed by TV production company Seven Arts, which had a deal with MGM, guided Nabokov in the adaptation. The producers, desiring a wide audience, needed a Seal. Changes were made: Lolita's age was upped a few years to 15; the more outrageous double-entendres toned down (though a good deal remained, as did the movie's invention of Quilty's spicy search with his girl for a sexual threesome). Casting was understated (James Mason/Professor; newcomer Sue Lyon/Lolita; Shelley Winters/Lolita's mom). Code coauthor Quigley was enlisted to run interference between the PCA and LD. All forbiddances were complied with. Still, *Lolita* stumbled over the "sex perversion" taboo.

Pressure mounted from other studios in varying stages of production on big-budgeted pictures that dealt with "sex perversion." Because of the hefty investment involved, these companies also wanted a broad-based market and, therefore, needed a Seal. Over at UA, William Wyler had finished his second stab at *The Children's Hour* (1962), tackling the repression of a lesbian teacher's love for another teacher at an academy for young girls. UA had also bought Gore Vidal's 1960 play *The Best Man* (1964), which turned on the dilemma of what one possible presidential candidate would do with the damaging information about the accusation of homosexuality leveled at a rival candidate. At Columbia, Preminger was imaging the script of Allen Drury's 1959 Pulitzer-Prize-winning novel *Advise and Consent* (1962), which had already been adapted for the stage in 1960 by Loring Mandel. In this, some senators dig up dirt (a month-long affair with a fellow combatant in Hawaii during World War II) in the hope of blackmailing a principled senator/family man into withdrawing his block of the President's nomination of a new Secretary of State. The unearthing of his homosexual tryst eventually drives the tortured senator to suicide. Preminger also inserted scenes at a gay dating service and gay bar, neither of which appeared in the novel or play. Also at Columbia, producer Sam Spiegel and director David Lean were in the process of mounting a biography of *Lawrence of Arabia* (1962), who was reputedly a homosexual. Universal had *Freud* (1962) in the works, producer and co-writer Wolfgang Reinhardt's account of the psychiatrist's early case histories of sexual aberration.

Besides these pressures, agonizing memories still haunted the PCA. For all the endless go-rounds and deletions on Kubrick's *Spartacus* (U, 1960), Dalton Trumbo's adaptation of Howard Fast's 1952 novel,[16] the sexual preference of Crassus (Laurence Olivier) for Antoninus (Tony Curtis) unmistakably came through. Despite all the raised eyebrows over *Exodus* (UA, 1960), Trumbo's rendition of Leon Uris's 1958 bestseller, Preminger got away with freedom fighter Sal Mineo's graphic confession of being used as a woman in a Nazi concentration camp. A Seal was denied, however, to the British import *Victim* (1962), a responsible, socially relevant film about a closeted barrister fighting the British law on homosexuality, and, in retrospect, should not have been. Even the Legion had doled out a SC for *Victim*. Further: much heated discussion arose from handing a Seal to *The Last Sunset* (U, 1961), Dalton Trumbo's rendering of Howard Risby's 1957 pulp *Sundown at Crazy Horse*, which featured a gunslinger drawn to the 16-year-old daughter of his former lover who turns out to be his child.

Something had to be done, and so the Code was amended on October 3, 1961. It was now permissible to consider approving references to the subject of sexual aberration, "provided any references are treated with care, discretion and restraint and in all other respects conform to the Code." Only the taboos of the depiction of nudity and venereal disease remained.

Lolita was Sealed. Though 2 out of 12 Legionnaires wanted a C rating, the organization decided on a SC with the provisos that it would have veto power over advertising materials and MGM would add two captions to the ads: "This movie has been approved by the MPAA" and "For persons over 18 only."[17]

Besides the amendment, the PCA, that year, gave a Seal to both *The Moon Is Blue* and *The Man with the Golden Arm*. UA had resubmitted the films uncut, planning to reissue the films on a double bill and eventually lease them to TV, which shied away from pictures without a Seal. Shurlock acknowledged that the moral police had erred in not granting Seals previously.

10.28   *Don Juan* (1959)

Anti-censorship advocates hoped that the *Don Juan* case would demolish state and local censorship once and for all. The Chicago Police Commissioner denied a license to this adaptation of Mozart's opera *Don Giovanni* about an obsessive womanizer who gets off on conquering and humiliating women and their menfolk because its distributor Times Film Corp., after paying the required licensing fee, refused to submit the Austrian film for examination by censors.

The District Court for the Northern District dismissed the complaint – "no justifiable controversy existed" – and the Court of Appeals for the Seventh Circuit confirmed the judgment. In a narrow decision, the Supreme Court upheld the constitutionality of prior restraint. (At this time, 4 states and 11 cities[18] still had movie-licensing laws.) Though the case opened up the question of the discrepancy between movie censorship and that affecting other media, the Court never gave an answer. In light of the surprising decision, the National Association of Broadcasters, the American Book Publishers Council, and the Authors League, fearing future restrictions in their own domain, joined the MPAA in Washington, DC, hoping to end movie censorship on a state and city level. The hope was in vain, well, at least for a time. In 1993, the last remaining local film board (Dallas) would close its doors.

Conclusion

The PCA would be terminated much sooner, in 1968. The postwar years started the pot boiling, all the while turning up the heat. Once that happened, it was inevitable that the lid would pop off. Even the Legion, its ground made fallow by postwar happenings, renewed itself eventually. And, all along, these postwar Code and Legion stirrings, which were considerable, were instrumental in making imagined reality closer to actuality.

Notes

1 Finished in 1941, *The Outlaw* was given a trial run in San Francisco only in 1943. Hughes, devoting all his energies to make a fighter-bomber plane for war use, shelved the picture, though it was commercially successful. In 1948, the picture was sold to RKO after UA's previous distribution in 1946 and was released for the third time in 1950. For a fuller account of *The Outlaw* controversy, see Leonard J. Leff and Jerold L. Simmons, *The Dame in the Kimono: Hollywood, Censorship, and the Production Code from the 1920s to the 1960s*, 2nd ed. (University of Kentucky Press, 2001, 113–44.

2 All the Legion's classifications and respective reasons came from *The National Catholic Office for Motion Pictures* (New York: National Catholic Office For Motion Pictures, 1966).

3 For a fuller account of *The Postman Always Rings Twice* controversy, see Leff and Simmons, 132–44.

4 Edward de Grazia and Roger K. Newman, *Banned Films: Movies, Censors and the First Amendment* (New York and London: R. R. Bowker Co., 1982), contains an historical account of state and local censorship cases.

5 For a fuller account of *The Bicycle Thief* controversy, see Leff and Simmons, 145–66.

6 A similar situation occurred with the release of Chaplin's *Limelight* (UA, 1952). Under the threat of picketing by the American Legion, the Fox West coast theatres in Los Angeles, as

well as Loew's circuit in New York, at the urging of the Kiwanis Club and the American Legion, refused to play the film, pending the outcome of the investigation by the Justice Department concerning the granting of reentry privileges to Chaplin owing to his suspected communist allegiance. Chaplin gave up his residency in the USA before the verdict was in, bitterly declaring in London: "Since the end of the last World War, I have been the object of lies and vicious propaganda by powerful reactionary groups who by their implications and by the aid of America's yellow press have created an unhealthy atmosphere in which liberal-minded individuals can be singled out and persecuted" (*New York Times Encyclopedia of Film*, Vol. 6, April 18, 1953).

7   *The Miracle* case was taken from clippings collated in *The New York Times Encyclopedia of Film*, Vols. 5 and 6, Dec. 24, 25, 30, 31, 1950; Jan. 2, 23, Feb. 17, Oct. 19, 1951; and May 27, 1952.

8   For fuller accounts of both *Detective Story* and *A Streetcar Named Desire* controversies, see Leff and Simmons, 167–89.

9   For fuller accounts of both *The Moon Is Blue* and *The French Line* controversies, see Leff and Simmons, 190–218.

10   Here was a rare instance in which images of sex and violence as well were targeted. Unlike Europeans, Americans, in general, are less bothered by screen slaying than laying.

11   *The Man With the Golden Arm*'s financial success plus studio muscle (TCF was in preproduction with the adaptation of Michael Gazzo's 1955 stage success, *A Hatful of Rain*, 1957, for which it shelled out $250,000 while UA was readying another tale of drug addiction, *Monkey on My Back*, 1957, a true account of world welterweight champ and addict Barney Ross) forced the drug issue.

12   Court rulings in both Massachusetts and Maryland lifted Boston and Baltimore's bans on the movie.

13   *Lady Chatterley's Lover* was published in an expurgated version in 1932. An unexpurgated version appeared in 1959.

14   The prostitute-protagonist no longer gave the PCA sleepless nights, as witnessed in *The World of Suzie Wong* (P, 1960), an adaptation of Richard Mason's 1957 novel and Paul Osborn's 1958 play starring Hong Kong-born Nancy Kwan, and *Butterfield 8* (MGM, 1960), a reworking of John O'Hara's 1935 novella with Elizabeth Taylor. (Technically, Taylor is not a prostitute but rather a nymphomaniac model who gives it away for nothing.) The Legion, however, was still bothered, putting both films on its B list. Yet, when director Leo McCarey recounted *An Affair to Remember* (TCF, 1957), a romance melodrama with Cary Grant and Deborah Kerr as two high-class whores, or when producer Arthur Freed dealt with the grooming of a Parisian demimondaine (Leslie Caron) in the musical *Gigi* (MGM, 1958), or when director Blake Edwards presented a romantic version of Truman Capote's *Breakfast At Tiffany's* (P, 1961), featuring two prostitutes (Audrey Hepburn and George Peppard), the Legion rated the first A-II; the other two, A-III. Actor personas and genre cannot be discounted in the perception and moral evaluation of pictures.

15   Instituted in 1958 for producer Louis de Rochemont's independent *Martin Luther*, the "Special Classification" category was applied to movies, which, while not morally offensive per se, required, so the Legion deemed, caution and some explanation so that the uninformed be safeguarded from wrong interpretation and false conclusions.

16   *Spartacus* was privately published in 1951.

17   For a fuller account of the *Lolita* controversy, see Leff and Simmons, 219–46.

18   Kansas, Maryland, New York, and Virginia were the states; the cities included Atlanta, Chicago, Fort Worth, Kansas City, Newark, Pasadena, Portland, Providence, Sacramento, San Antonio, and Wichita Falls.

Part V

Genre

Introduction

Genre is a category of film in which many individual movies can be grouped together because they share essentially common characteristics. For example, for the most part, we all know a western when we see one. The question arises as to what these essentially common characteristics are. First, the similarity includes particular kind of characters, dialogue/actions, and conflicts. Other demarcating elements include the particular persona of actor called for; spatial and temporal setting; mood and atmosphere; kind of sound design, specifically music; subject matter and themes. These elements constitute the genre's "myth," or story. Furthermore, each genre has certain ways of doing things peculiar to itself, or "conventions," another criterion that can help lump individual films together as a genre. Most obviously, the musical uses song and dance to tell its story. Gaslight lingo pops out of a gangster's mouth. Finally, a set of images and sounds shared by a cluster of films ("iconography") can also help identify a group of films as a genre. The American Frontier brings to mind a western; the blast from a spaceship as it leaves its launch pad, sci-fi; a map, an adventure film. Iconography derives from the genre's respective myth. Myth or story, conventions, and iconography are the constituents of genre.

From its inception, the American film industry used genre, following in the footsteps of the stage, vaudeville, popular song, the circus, fat Victorian and slim dime novels, comic strips, and painting. The industry learned early on that genre was a socially understood and accepted way of selecting and ordering societal tensions, whether overt or suppressed. Genre – its respective myth, conventions, and iconography – came from a culture to embody that culture so the culture could understand itself better.

Moreover, the use of genre in all these entertainment media/arts, and now film, was a financial necessity. Quantity led to formulation. Genre provided selling elements on the part of the producer and an assurance for the buyer. Genre minimalized production costs. Some variation, however, was allowable since controlled innovation sold just as well as strict regularity. The use of genre could also be an aesthetic boon. Repetition on the part of the maker, quite possibly, could assure quality. An established formula could lead to economical storytelling that was lean and immediate, which, in the case of movies, was a large part of its appeal. In addition, the use of genre flattered the American penchant for parameters in cultural representations wherein clarity rather than ambiguity, action rather than contemplation, termination rather than questioning (and a happy termination rather than sad) were preferred.

In the Silent Period (1896–1928), genres in American films began to emerge. Genres crystallized in the Classical Period (1929–45). During the postwar years (1946–62), genres were in transition, signaling a break with what went before. Events, aesthetic or otherwise, do not begin or end definitively; it is a matter of anticipation and spilling over. Therefore, the history of every genre during the period 1946–62 is not unadulteratedly transitional. Nevertheless, there are enough changes going on in genres at this time to see a discontinuity with their classical embodiments.

How could there not be? If a culture significantly changed (and American culture did just that between 1946 and 1962) and if genre reflected and expressed culture, genre ferment was inevitable. Competition with other leisure activities, which went into overdrive, also did its part in genre unrest. Now that other art forms/media were updating themselves, it was imperative movies did the same. Even more, the broadcasting of old movies on the tiny screen made the consumer want and expect something different on the large screen. Aware of this desire and hope, moviemakers eagerly obliged. Competition with aformulaic European product exposed and disposed the consumer to material off the beaten track, further inciting Hollywood to play around with formula, cautiously but sometimes daringly. And if the thematics happened to be transgressive, censorship was ready to make concessions.

Likewise, with the mode of independent production supplanting the studio system's generic approach to rolling out movies, filmmakers, as never before, were able to individualize the product. Even when working on a studio film, they were generally given some leeway, especially if they had already proven themselves commercially. Furthermore, the industry's burgeoning perception that they were working in a medium that not only could entertain but could entertainingly communicate ideas and raise issues made many infuse a genre's familiar parameters, which immediately took an audience in, with social and personal concerns. Therefore, the dialectic between genre and auteur (producer/director/writer able to incarnate through film's formal systems a distinct vision or sensibility in film after film), noticeably heating up, was a significant part of the life of just about every genre during these years. Laced throughout this discussion on genre, therefore, are biographical–artistic sketches of these architects who used genre structures not as an evasion from but rather an egress into meaning.

Some genres reached their classical height and at the same time crossed borders, moving in other directions. Topical accommodation of subject matter, attitudes, even conventions was one such direction. Demythology or turning the classical paradigm inside out was a more radical route. Another was the appropriation of genre as a vehicle for the airing, even debating of social issues; hybridization, still another. Genre appropriation and hybridization, of course, had occurred in the classical phase but not to the degree of its postwar frequency. Appropriation was enkindled by the trumpeting of realism; hybridization by TV segmenting (10 minutes of a brooding thriller gave way to a bright 30-second toothpaste jingle) and formatting (an evening at the tube offered news, followed by a western, a musical variety, sitcom, then a cop show.) Parody, also given a boost by TV showing old movies, was another recourse. Some genres crystallized. Instances of these "latest" forms had isolatedly cropped up before, but there was no evidence of a steady stream then as now, designating the respective genre in full flourish, boasting an inordinate number of aesthetically shining examples, and, most significantly of all, defining a cultural period. Other genres went into decline.

Since creator and consumer alike were pretty sure of the way forward by this time, the pleasure, they knew, lay in the detours, the devilish curves, the surprising vagaries. This was also part of what going to the movies was like back then.

11

Adventure

The adventure film's third flourish (1945–62), salvoed by *The Spanish Main* (RKO, 1945) and *The Bandit of Sherwood Forest* (C, 1946), was also its climax.[1] Columbia and Universal's A and B units, for the first time, offered stiff competition to leaders MGM, TCF, and WB.

The industry's "make 'em big" maxim, the possibility of a location shoot, often involving the use of blocked funds, and the deployment of refined and new technologies proved immeasurably redounding. The color, large-screen, stereo embodiment of the genre's unfamiliar, inhospitable, remote yet colorful and exotic locale (sea/island, jungle/forest, desert, mountain/wild north, which now was extended to include the sky), entered into the construction of the narrative, as the genre devoted more time than ever to the description of, and the conflicts arising from, its respective location. Moreover, this location was more often than not actual. The approach was modeled after the documentary travelogue, a short-subject staple studios churned out to accompany their features, and eventually the money-making Cinerama travelogues. It was practiced either discreetly (*The White Tower*, RKO, 1950; *Safari*, C, 1956; *Action of the Tiger*, MGM, 1957) or immoderately (the virtually plotless *Around the World In Eighty Days*, UA, 1956; the Baedeker-like *Escapade in Japan*, RKO/U, 1957; and the day-at-the-zoo *Hatari!*, P, 1962). The fashionable documentary-realist style, as we shall see, gave this approach legitimacy. This emphasis on actual locations was also an antidote to the travel bug.

Public domain and previously purchased source materials were additionally conducive. Circulating in studio conference rooms were works by Daniel Defoe (*Robinson Crusoe*, C, 1952), Alexandre Dumas (*The Return of Monte Cristo*, C, 1946), H. Rider Haggard (*King Solomon's Mines*, MGM, 1950), Rudyard Kipling (*Soldiers Three*, MGM, 1951), Raphael Sabatini (*The Fortune of Captain Blood*, C, 1950), Walter Scott (*Ivanhoe*, MGM, 1952), Thomas Malory (*Knights of the Round Table*, MGM, 1953), Robert Louis Stevenson (*Rob Roy, Highland Rogue*,

BV, 1954), and Jules Verne (*20,000 Leagues under the Sea*, BV, 1954). With the genre's past heydays in 1920–9 and 1934–42 providing a lengthy index of sources and models, remakes were equally tempting (*The Spoilers*, U, 1956).

The easing of censorship proved to be a further incitement. Countenanced now were graphic depictions of violence, especially in torture scenes with their sadomasochistic clinches. Suggestive costuming was legitimized, especially period pieces that invoked historical accuracy. In the desert tales, for example, the female midriff went uncovered and often included a display of the navel while the drapery across the female breasts was nothing more than a bra.

Counterpointing end-of-career adventurers (Douglas Fairbanks, Jr., Clark Gable, Errol Flynn, Tyrone Power) and aging actors reinventing themselves as adventurers (Louis Hayward, Paul Henried, Robert Taylor, John Wayne) was a band of unlined faces and taut bodies who additionally helped to keep the genre flying (Jeff Chandler, Tony Curtis, Kirk Douglas, Stewart Granger, Alan Ladd, Burt Lancaster, Victor Mature, Gregory Peck, Richard Widmark, Cornel Wilde). Notably new in making the female the protagonist of a dominantly male-centered genre were *Anne of the Indies* (TCF, 1951), with Jean Peters as the feared captain of the Spanish Main battling the French; *Against All Flags* (U, 1952), with Maureen O'Hara as a buccaneer saving an eighteenth-century British navy officer (Flynn) wrongly accused of being a spy; *Sea Devils* (RKO, 1953), with Yvonne de Carlo as a British operative during the Napoleonic Wars; *Miss Robin Crusoe* (TCF, 1954), a distaff variation of Defoe with Amanda Blake; and *Princess of the Nile* (TCF, 1954), with Debra Paget rousing her people against the Bedouins in the thirteenth century.

The besieged postwar male necessitated the image of the adventurer hero, which provided guidance and helped suppress what in reality was happening to him. One type is the extraordinary male, charged with (or in the process of attaining) exceptional courage, practical competence, discipline, endurance, self-sufficiency, an ability to lead, moral certitude, and optimism. He overcomes seemingly insurmountable obstacles in accomplishing some critical mission that, in the end, restores order. Basically a loner, he sometimes separates himself from a corrupt society and goes outside the law (becoming an outlaw) to bring back justice. In some instances, a band of followers form around him. One of his followers or supporters is invariably a woman, who, with her love and the hero's reciprocal response, brings a dimension of warmth to his character, while offering needed respites from the scenes of political discussion and practical action. Sometimes the woman comes on board because her rescue is part of the mission. As a fiercely individual risk-taker, the figure stirred up quixotic energies or, at least, longings the conformist era tried to quash.

The figure, however, is no revolutionary. After excising society-threatening elements, the adventurer restores the status quo, never once questioning it. In

Two Years Before the Mast (P, 1946), Harvard student/sailor (Ladd) does decry the working conditions at sea in the 1830s. Additionally, *Captain from Castile* (TCF, 1947), Kipling's *Kim* (MGM, 1950), *King of the Khyber Rifles* (TCF, 1953), and *Seven Cities of Gold* (TCF, 1955) were revisionist, undermining a long-standing, entrenched perspective about history, politics, societal issues, and culture. Characters in these films voice their critique of colonialism, especially its inherent racism (*Seven Cities*' Father Junipero Serra/Michael Rennie), or characters are shown to be victims of racism. As the son of an English Protestant father and Indian Muslim mother who fights for the British, *Khyber*'s half-caste (Power) is not fully trusted by them. When his commanding officer's daughter moons over him, her father ships the girl to England.

The extraordinary male type (be he knight, pirate/buccaneer, naval captain, brigade leader, or explorer) inhabits the swashbuckler cycle (the late Middle Ages to the nineteenth century in Europe, the Empire, and the New World).[2] The cycle's period setting involves a time of war or societal upheaval and, as such, includes many battle sequences. Britain extricating itself from Roman rule and the internal dissension resulting from the debated kingship (Arthur or Mordred?) backgrounds *Knights of the Round Table*. A written or voice-over prologue, sometimes reappearing through the film to bridge spatial-temporal intervals, is used to contextualize the setting, placing the audience *in media res*.

The other type, equally nourished by the postwar male malaise, is the flawed hero, with abilities and attitudes scaled down to audience size, even simmering with inner turmoil. Though part of a group that comprises a gamut of folk forming a societal microcosm, he stands above it, at the very least in his ability to mold the group into derring-do. The group always includes a female as a love interest who, additionally, spurs on a doubting hero or corrects a self-interested one. The group as value never eclipses the hero's individuality. As such, this type also played into many postwar males' longing for a vanished time when individualism was cherished and possible. This figure populates the fortune-hunter cycle (as explorer-entrepreneur, safari guide, smuggler, insurance adjuster, engineer, archeologist, gambler, war profiteer, art dealer), concerned with finding and restoring treasure or loved ones. He's also at home in the disaster cycle (as sea/sky pilot, escaped POW), engaged with survival. In the wartime mission series (as soldier of fortune, mercenary), he can be counted on to fight for a cause and/or make a quick buck.

The fortune hunter/disaster/wartime mission cycles were usually set in the industrial present. Fortune-hunter tales revolved around such characters as an ex-Navy vet (Chandler) who dives for illegal gold in Macao (*Smuggler's Island*, U, 1951), a Kenyan white hunter (Gable) leading a safari among hungry animals and equally hungry females (the remake *Mogambo*, MGM, 1953), an engineer

(Stewart Granger) mining for emeralds in Columbia amid natural disasters (*Green Fire*, MGM, 1954), or an American captain of a cargo boat (Van Johnson) getting a French woman's blind brother out of communist-occupied Albania (*Action of the Tiger*).

The fortune-hunter cycle was not immune to period, however. Tyrone Power, shifty at cards, fisticuffs, and women, turns up as a *Mississippi Gambler* (U, 1953) in antebellum New Orleans. An anti-social nineteenth-century English gentleman (David Niven) takes up a wager to go *Around the World in Eighty Days*, the era's most lucrative adventure film ($22 million). *The Big Sky* (RKO, 1952) recorded one of the "great first times" in American history: a 2,000-mile trek on a 63-foot hand-operated keel boat up the unexplored Missouri River from St. Louis to Montana to expand the trade route with the Indians for pelts and open the Great Northwest in 1832. Director Howard Hawks's band of hunters this time are Kentucky mountain folk (Kirk Douglas, Dewey Martin) and some Frenchmen who, in defiance of the established trading "Company," bravely do it on their own. Besides the individual (free traders) versus the con-formist ("the Company") overlay, the film resonates with an homoerotic aura with Dewey's eyes, at every turn, fixed on Kirk, Kirk's arm around Dewey's shoulder while tussling his hair, Dewey's tender hold on the wounded Kirk's neck, etc. And to have a Hawksean male of action wonder about God and the afterlife as Douglas does, is a side of the male adventure protagonist Hawks never revealed in his classic heyday.

Garden of Evil was another nineteenth-century fortune-hunter tale that played a couple of variations. Here, a plucky woman (Susan Hayward) rounds up four mercenaries (Gary Cooper, Richard Widmark, Cameron Mitchell, Victor Manuel Mendoza) who, for $2,000 apiece, follow her into an Apache-infested land to rescue her husband. He has been trapped in a mine while plundering gold at her instigation ("I wanted gold and all the things it could buy"). Disil-lusioned and remorseful, she fends off dangerous terrain and rape and offers to stay behind to divert the Apaches so the men, with her maimed husband in tow, have a better chance of escape. Only in the film's last quarter does Cooper take the narrative's reins from Hayward. Unique also in its dour (not the genre's usually buoyant) tone, initially set by the title, the film spent less time on the mission's "adventures" than disasters with their underlying critique of the pursuit of money, thus subverting the genre while stinging the skin of postwar culture.

With Barry Storm's novel as guide, *Lust for Gold* (C, 1949)'s tone was even more downbeat, its denunciation of the obsession with money more scathing, its story completely given over to the quest's calamitous outcome, as its aclas-sical narrative flip-flopped between past and present, paralleling the tale of a prospector (Glenn Ford) who comes upon a $20-million cache of ore in the

11-1   *Garden of Evil* (TCF, 1954, p. Charles Brackett)

The female (Susan Hayward) as initiator and leader of a demythed adventure with males (from left to right) Gary Cooper, Richard Widmark, Victor Manuel Mendoza, and Cameron Mitchell.

Superstition Mountains outside of Phoenix in 1866 and that of his contemporary grandson and fellow avaricious risk-takers who attempt to find the missing gold. Moreover, the characterization of the prospector as an unmitigatedly greedy and treacherous human being, murdering his partner and destroying a money-crazed married woman along with her spineless husband (the present-day counterparts were not that much better) was also something new. *Lust for Gold*, similarly *Garden of Evil*, demythed the adventure film.

John Wayne at WB was continually put in charge of disasters and wartime missions. He headed a civilian crew of an Army Transport Command that crash-landed in Labrador (*Island in the Sky*, 1953). He piloted a Honolulu-to-San Francisco passenger plane that lost an engine (*The High and the Mighty*, 1954). His German sea captain maneuvered a rickety freighter from Sydney to the North Sea during World War II (*The Sea Chase*, 1955). As an escapee from a communist prison in Amoy, he guided 89 persons in a ferry boat to freedom (*Blood Alley*, 1955). Richard Widmark gave Wayne a run for his money at Fox as a whaling ship's first mate rescuing a lad in *Down to the Sea in Ships* (1949); a Navy man marshaling a group of weather observers across 800 miles of Mongolian desert with the Japanese hot on his trail (*Destination Gobi*, 1953); a venal American commander who rents a submarine to a group of scientists and military to stop communist atomic plans in the northern Pacific (*Hell and High Water* (1954); and the aforementioned *Garden*. So did Peck, whose quartet included the gainful adventure in which Allied saboteurs infiltrate a Nazi-held Greek island to blow up *The Guns of Navarone* (C, 1961).

A handful of directors were continually attracted to the genre. At MGM, Richard Thorpe's remake *The Prisoner of Zenda*, *Ivanhoe*, and *Knights of the Round Table*, as well as George Sidney's remakes *The Three Musketeers* (1948)/ Dumas and *Scaramouche* (1952)/Sabatini were, more or less, factory fashioned. Thorpe's *Knights*, however, was one of the first features to free the initially staid CinemaScope camera with its plethora of magnificent tracking-alongside-the-action shots: leisurely traveling through a forest; processing down the aisle in a cathedral for a wedding; cantering during falconry; and, best of all, furiously advancing with the hordes of knights into battle. Sidney did contribute a decided lyricism and fun while infusing the romance with heartfelt emotion, especially Eleanor Parker's unrequited love for Granger's *Scaramouche*. At Paramount, John Farrow skillfully fashioned *Two Years Before the Mast* and *Botany Bay* (1953); for Warners, *Plunder of the Sun* (1953) and *The Sea Chase*; at RKO, the remake *Back from Eternity* (1956). For Fox, Henry Hathaway's *Down To the Sea In Ships*, *The Black Rose* (1950), and *Prince Valiant* (1954) and for UA *Legend of the Lost* (1957), with Wayne, exuded his customary brio while playing it somber in *Garden of Evil*. Raoul Walsh, a genre-diverse pillar at WB since 1939 (*Captain Horatio Hornblower*, 1951, with Peck) and freelancer from 1952 (*Blackbeard the Pirate*, RKO, 1952, *The World in His Arms*, U, 1952, with Peck and *Sea Devils*), vivified professional, pragmatic men who welcomed, even thrived on the dangers that came their way and the self-reliant women of the world who shared the dangers.

John Huston's (1906–87) imprint, however, was indelibly personal. As a dialogue writer at Universal in 1931, he nestled under William Wyler's wing. He moved to WB as a contract writer in 1938 where he meritoriously was promoted to writer-director status three years later. After his 1948 departure, he went independent. All tall tales, Huston's adventures fixed on a group of nononsense, resourceful guys (often fortune hunters) who invariably failed at what they set out to do, through their own flawed natures as well as fate's heartless twists. The contrast between the rigid process of the quest itself involving as it did structure, stamina, and steadfastness and its accidental, sudden unraveling constituted the hair-raising tension in his demythed pieces. Huston's world was essentially (and unclassically) absurd.

11-2   *The Treasure of the Sierra Madre* (WB, 1948, p. Henry Blanke)

Director John Huston's demythed adventure with three avaricious prospectors (from left to right): Walter Huston, Humphrey Bogart (playing against type), and Tim Holt.

The Treasure of the Sierra Madre (WB, 1948), Huston's faithful draft of B. Traven's novel, dogged three avaricious prospectors, each suspicious of the other (Humphrey Bogart, Tim Holt, and Oscar-winning support Walter Huston), all the while mordantly assessing the changing power plays among them. A timely, uncompromised critique of the capitalistic mentality and its effect on the male psyche brought no gold at the box office but did earn Huston Oscar gold as director and writer. Huston's lighter, lucrative ($4.2 million booty), and first color feature *The African Queen*, (UA, 1951), a coadaptation with James Agee of C. S. Forester's novel set in German East Africa during World War I,[3] was loaded with auteur variations and generic anomalies. One of the navigators in a dilapidated riverboat attempting to blow up a German gunboat was a skinny, prim missionary spinster (Katharine Hepburn). Women usually occupied the fringes of Huston's world and the genre as well. The other was a boozy, craven skipper with a gurgling stomach and bad teeth (Oscar-winning Bogart). Both unattractive and middle-aged, Hepburn and Bogart were oceans apart from the customary young, dashing/pretty, lithe/shapely genre habitués. A good part of the running time was devoted to the old biddy's browbeating of the gone-to-seed boatman to get him in shape. This stabilization, moreover, turned to affection and love, emotions Huston's people don't easily come by. *Heaven Knows, Mr. Allison* (TCF, 1957), with Charles Shaw's novel inspiring Huston and co-writer John Lee Mahin, was somewhat of a replay of *Queen*. The survival escapades of a rough, crafty World War II marine (Robert Mitchum) and a refined but good-sport religious (Deborah Kerr) are now transposed to a Japanese-occupied Pacific isle and interwreathed with a romance melodrama.

Interesting in regard to Huston's imagistic dialogue, densely textured frames that energized offscreen space as well, though not in *Treasure, Queen,* or *Allison*'s class, were Huston's other adventures. Sourced in Robert Sylvester's novel and cowritten with Peter Viertel, *We Were Strangers* (C, 1949) fixed upon John Garfield leading a group of Cuban rebels in building an underground tunnel in an attempt to assassinate a dictator. Remake *Moby Dick* (WB, 1956) stretched Peck as Melville's tormented Ahab. In *The Roots of Heaven* (TCF, 1958), with Romain Gary reworking his novel with Patrick Leigh-Fermor, an idealistic dentist (Trevor Howard) inspires others to join him in his quest to preserve elephants in French Equatorial Africa where tusks were sold profitably, thus showing a more enlightened side of fortune hunting.

Coadapter Truman Capote (from the James Helbick novel) encouraged the outrageous situations and tongue-in-cheek tone of Huston's *Beat the Devil* (C, 1953), in which a pathological liar who tells the truth for once, a dead man back in Soho, and a supposedly drowned one off the Amalfi coast upend the project of a criminal quartet (among them Huston favorite Bogart) to swindle the British government of its uranium deposits in East Africa. Such shenanigans and ironic distancing illustrated another *au courant* trend. What with the protagonist's extravagant actions, which often included outlandish disguise (sometimes drag) in the accomplishment of the mission, the genre always had displayed a fair share of humor (*The Adventures of Robin Hood*, WB, 1938). Postwar, however, the humor was sustained and turned self-conscious, festooning adventures with a level of parody. Emblazoning the way was the Lancaster trio: *The Flame and the Arrow* (WB, 1950), *Ten Tall Men* (C, 1951), and *The Crimson Pirate* (WB, 1952), with Burt's pre-credit address to the audience to believe only half of what it sees and plot-busting with his and friend/colleague Nick Cravat's actual circus routines. Also veined with parody were producer Sam Katzman Bs starring Henried (*Thief of Damascus* C, 1952), *Around the World In Eighty Days*/Verne, Hathaway/Wayne's *North to Alaska* and Hawks's jokey *Hatari!*, among others. While clearly attesting to the plethora and popularity of adventure movies whose conventions had to be known for this added level to work, the trend also pointed to the genre's finale – to send-up a genre was to send it on its way.

Notes

1 The adventure film's cycles are crisply outlined in Brian Taves, *The Romance of Adventure: The Genre of Historical Adventure Movies* (Jackson: University Press of Mississippi, 1993).

2 This is an extension of John G. Cawelti's periodic designation of the swashbuckler in *Adventure, Mystery and Romance* (Chicago: University of Chicago Press, 1976).

3 The making of *The African Queen* became the subject of Peter Viertel's novel *White Hunter Black Heart*, which was filmed in 1990 by Warners with Clint Eastwood giving an eminently watchable turn as the outlandishly waggish Huston.

12

Biography

The year 1955 witnessed a quintuple summation of the classical bio which every studio continued to turn out (with MGM, WB, UA, and TCF luminaries). From Fox came *A Man Called Peter*, with Richard Todd as Scottish preacher/US Senate chaplain Peter Marshall, derived from his wife's profile. It was the first of three bios directed by Henry Koster. In the Universal entry *To Hell and Back*, Audie Murphy played himself, the most decorated soldier in US history as recounted in his autobiography. Warners emblazoned *The McConnell Story* with Alan Ladd as World War II/Korean War ace flyer; Paramount, *Strategic Air Command* with James Stewart as General Curtis Le May, whose bomber force was a deterrent to the communist domination of the world. Columbia offered director John Ford's *The Long Gray Line* with Tyrone Power as West Point athletic instructor Marty Maher, inspired by his memoirs.[1]

Classical bios dealt with the lives of the actual great and famous, whose names were used: people from the past recognized as displaying some excellence that was important to national history/culture. Also accounted for were medics (*Sister Kenny*, RKO, 1946, with Rosalind Russell as the early 1900s Australian nurse who ushered in a new treatment for infantile paralysis, and culled from her autobiography); inventors (*The Iron Mistress*, WB, 1952, with Ladd as early nineteenth-century knife designer Jim Bowie and adapted from Paul I. Wellman's historical fiction); politicians (*The Magnificent Yankee*, MGM, 1950, with Louis Calhern as 1902–30 Supreme Court Justice Oliver Wendell Holmes, based upon the Emmet Lavery play); and royalty (the Koster-directed *The Virgin Queen*, TCF, 1955, with Bette Davis as England's Elizabeth).

Alongside these works, aclassical bios appeared and became the dominant mode after 1955. These bios departed from the genre's classical myths and iconography while varying its conventions. Definitely more interested in contemporary figures than historical relics, they factored in the greatness and fame criteria halfheartedly, if at all. They also extended the types to include, in a nod to the growing importance of the media, media-constructed personalities.[2]

The athlete was the most frequently portrayed biographee. No surprise here, since the athlete-bio was a way to compete with the rise of spectator/participant sports with the narrative constructed in large part around the feats themselves and a mise-en-scène providing the moviegoer with the best stadium or ringside seat to view exciting displays of individual prowess. Other prevalent new or revamped types included the artist, the entertainer (especially the movie star, with postwar cinema yet again recognizing its history), the infamous, and the heroic ordinary citizen, such as *The True Story of Lynn Stuart* (C, 1958), with Betsy Palmer as a housewife who volunteered to smoke out a drug gang. The revolutionary (Elia Kazan's *Viva Zapata!*, TCF, 1952, with Marlon Brando; *Seven Angry Men*, AA, 1955, with Raymond Massey as John Brown; *Villa*, TCF, 1958, with Rudolpho Hoyas) was the new bio's restyling of the classical figure of the statesman/politician. In deference to the postwar religious revival, the religious person also was held over, but now drawn along social worker lines, such as *The Inn of the Sixth Happiness*'s (TCF, 1958) English missionary Gladys Aylward (Ingrid Bergman) ministering to children in 1930 war-torn China, adapted from Alan Burgess's historical fiction, or *The Hoodlum Priest*'s (UA, 1961) Jesuit Charles Dismas Clark (Don Murray) rehabilitating ex-cons.

When dealing with contemporary celebrities (athletes, painters, entertainers, the infamous, heroic citizens), the new bios often forsook the classical hagiographical approach, finding more interest in the private drama behind, or in place of, the public achievement. The biographee wrestling with his/her demons – the more sordid, the better – was the preferred stratagem, quite in tune with the voguish confessional mode and an indicator of realism. This practice held true even when the updates occasionally dealt with historical figures (the aforementioned bios on revolutionaries; the mistress bios such as *Desiree*, TCF, 1954, with Koster directing Jean Simmons as Napoleon's paramour from Annemarie Selinko's historical fiction and *Diane*, MGM, 1956, with Lana Turner as Henry II's lover).

Jim Thorpe – All American (WB, 1951) presented Burt Lancaster as a demoralized 1912 American Indian Pentathlon/Decathlon winner who takes to the bottle. Throughout the Robert Wise-directed *Somebody Up There Likes Me* (MGM, 1956), the juvenile delinquent-hoodlum-convict roots of Rocky Graziano (Paul Newman) turned fifties middleweight boxing champ were never forgotten. Graziano's own tell-all bestseller was the film's source. The mental instability of Boston Red Sox Jimmy Piersall (Anthony Perkins) was director Robert Mulligan's pitch in *Fear Strikes Out* (P, 1957).

Director Huston's *Moulin Rouge* sketched Jose Ferrer as the vinegary Toulouse-Lautrec, a self-loathing, cognac-addicted, café-and-brothel habitué.

Director Vincente Minnelli's *Lust for Life* (MGM, 1956) limned Kirk Douglas as the crazed nineteenth-century Van Gogh and Oscar-winning support Anthony Quinn as the tempestuous irritant Gauguin. In Koster's *The Naked Maja* (UA, 1959), Anthony Franciosa emerged certifiably manic as eighteenth-century painter Francisco Goya.

Nearly all entertainer entries were whiskey-soaked: *Jeanne Eagels* (C, 1957), with Kim Novak; *The Buster Keaton Story* (P, 1957), with Donald O'Connor; and *Too Much Too Soon* (WB, 1958), with Dorothy Malone and Errol Flynn as Diana and John Barrymore, based on Diana's heart-to-heart memoirs. *Prince of Players* (TCF, 1955), from Eleanor Ruggles's historical fiction, reached back into time, documenting the Booths, America's first major family of actors, with Raymond Massey as the dipsomaniacal father, Richard Burton as son Edwin, and John Derek as son John, who shot Lincoln. Juiciest of all was *I'll Cry Tomorrow* (MGM, 1955), with Susan Hayward as Lillian Roth and based on Roth's frank journal, taking the entertainer from her 10th Avenue tenement beginnings with her smooth/slimy Jewish stage mama through hapless romances to her battle with booze. The film's last quarter veered off into a social problem film and ended with Roth's appearance on Ralph Edward's then popular TV show "This Is Your Life."

Though *Man of a Thousand Faces* (U, 1957) may not have drowned his troubles in booze, James Cagney's Lon Chaney is majorly problemed. The matter of Chaney's art was pretty much given the brush. Instead, the 122-minute account spotlighted the star's solipsism. He keeps secret his parents' deafness from his pregnant wife, who, when she finds out, wants an abortion. His refusal to allow her a career causes her to attempt suicide by swallowing acid in the middle of his vaudeville act. He initiates a divorce. He lies to his son, telling him that his mother is dead. Affection to the winds, he treats his second wife as a caretaker. All along, he punches his way out of arguments. Though rigid and unforgiving, Chaney emerges as a decent fellow while his first wife, though victimized, is self-absorbed. The characters' ambiguity, as in most post-classical bios (even Bob Hope as hedonistic mayor James J. Walker in *Beau James*, P, 1957), was at odds with classical bio's character clarity.

Of course, in turning to the infamous as subject, the biographee's nasty private side was a given. *Black Magic* (UA, 1949) told of the eighteenth-century Count Cagliostro (Orson Welles), who used his hypnotic and conjuring abilities in the pursuit of power and wealth. *The Great Jewel Robber* (WB, 1950) reconstructed the life of satyr Gerald Dennis (David Brian) who, during 1947–8, stole over $1 million in valuables from society homes. *The Girl in the Red Velvet Swing* (TCF, 1955) rehashed the lurid 1906 scandal in which obsessively jealous millionaire Harry Thaw (Farley Granger) mortally shot playboy-architect Stanford White (Ray Milland) who flirted with his showgirl wife Evelyn Nesbit

12-1   *I'll Cry Tomorrow* (MGM, 1955, p. Lawrence Weingarten)
Biography's female icon Susan Hayward as alcoholic entertainer Lillian Roth.

(Joan Collins), who, in turn, lied at the trial to save her husband. *I Want to Live!* (UA, 1958) wondered whether prostitute-thief Barbara Graham, in robbing an old lady, ever pistol-whipped her to death and thus merited the gas chamber. Cobbled together from magazine articles by San Francisco reporter Ed Montgomery, *Live!* raised issues, as did every Wise movie – here: capital punishment and media abuse. In her Oscar-nabber, Susan Hayward remarkably went from flippant cynicism though excruciating terror to limp acquiescence. With three bios to her credit, Hayward emerged as the genre's female icon.

Most impressive of the infamous lot was *Birdman of Alcatraz* (UA, 1962), with Lancaster as Robert Stroud, a bitter lifer for a double murder who, in the course of his 53 years behind bars, became an expert in bird disease. Set for practically all of its 148-minute running time in a prison cell, *Birdman* was riveting, as it painstakingly documented human regeneration within, ironically, the inhuman penal system. Chalk it up to Guy Trosper's astute adaptation of Thomas E. Gaddis's book; Lancaster's minutely detailed, unshowy rendering of a dour, antisocial man; and John Frankenheimer's committed direction.

Frankenheimer (1930–2001), a New York City kid of German Jewish-Irish Catholic heritage, was a Williams College theater major. In the Air Force (1951–3), he studied Eisenstein and made documentaries. He went into TV, clocking in 152 broadcast series/dramas before going to RKO in 1957 to turn his TV piece "Deal a Blow" into *The Young Stranger*. Frankenheimer was something new, part of a group of filmmakers who apprenticed in documentary and TV (not the studio system), carting a bag of documentary (hand-held camera, use of fast stock for grainy effect, location shoot) and early TV tricks (talking heads, dissolve/superimposition to show time's passage, dialogue patching scenes, shock cuts).

With *Birdman* and all of Frankenheimer's works, the destabilized male, of all ages, with parental problems, in unsatisfactory or nonexistent love relationships, was paramount. The Frankenheimer male did try to get it together with a display of valor he never even realized he was capable of. Sometimes he was successful, though victories were purely Pyrrhic as here; most often, he failed.

The aclassical bios' behind-the-scenes perspective snagged the intertwined dual conflicts of classical bios (the new vs. the old; the private vs. the public). The struggle to overcome life's inevitable, yet unforeseen, personal tragedies (one's inner demons) now took precedence over the struggle to overcome resistance to the community in ushering in the new and the attendant self-doubt and temptation to compromise (the classical bio's innovator-vs.-establishment clash). The innovator-vs.-establishment conflict was still there, though faintly, as in *Moulin Rouge*, which flirted with the issues of Parisian lowlife as the proper subject matter of painting and the use of the lithographing process in duplicating painting, two bold innovations of Lautrec. The inclusion of such a conflict, naturally, set off the postwar individual–conformity vibe. The concentration on the biographee's underside, however, fairly eclipsed the other conflict in classical bios: the struggle on the part of the biographee between duty to self or others (the private-life-vs.-public-career debate). More than not, the protagonists were seen primarily, sometimes only, as suffering victims, their survival celebrated more than their achievement.

Two motifs still remained from the classical bios, though now reconstituted as the protagonist's further demons. Victimization by disease continued. In addition to Van Gogh's madness in *Lust for Life*, baseballer Monty Stratton (male icon James Stewart in one of four bio appearances) loses his leg in *The Stratton Story* (MGM, 1949). The traditional accident was equally retained, as with golfer Ben Hogan's (Glenn Ford) car crash (*Follow the Sun*, TCF, 1951) or *Moulin Rouge*'s Lautrec stumbling down the staircase, a fall that stunted his growth.

As far as demons went, aclassical bios focused, time and again, on victimization by alcohol (as already seen) and added victimization by drug addiction, such as *Monkey on My Back* (UA, 1958), with Cameron Mitchell as thirties welterweight champ/Guadalcanal war hero Barney Ross. Crisis situations such as wars also created victims. In *Above and Beyond* (MGM, 1952), Col. Paul Tibbets (Robert Taylor), in charge of the atom-bombing of Hiroshima, borders on a nervous breakdown. The traditional victimization by an uncomprehending society that felt threatened by the innovative accomplishment, however, underwent a variation. In *The President's Lady* (TCF, 1953), Hayward is hounded as the notorious divorcee who became the First Lady when marrying Andrew Jackson. In *The Outsider* (U, 1961), Tony Curtis, as the Pima Indian flag-raiser on Mount Suribachi, is unable to cope with fame in a white man's world and drinks himself into an early grave. Here the victimizations resulted not from what the characters accomplished but from who they were.

Most common, however, was the victimization by parents: *Moulin Rouge*, *I'll Cry Tomorrow*, *Somebody Up There Likes Me*, *Fear Strikes Out*, and *Too Much Too Soon*. *The Miracle Worker* (UA, 1962), which William Gibson adapted from his play, balanced the oppression of Oscar-winning support Patty Duke's deaf and dumb Helen Keller by the enlightenment of Anne Bancroft's Oscar-winning teacher. Deserting spouses also played a part: *Jim Thorpe – All American*; *The Winning Team* (WB, 1952), with Ronald Reagan as baseball great Grover Cleveland Alexander; and *Man of a Thousand Faces*. Here too was another sabotage of the classical bio in which parents or spouses helped rather than hindered.

The revamped bio also broke the rigid white American/European male/female prototype (though male representations were twice that of female). Lives of Native Americans turned up (*Jim Thorpe – All American*, *The Outsider*). Also appearing were accounts of blacks (*The Jackie Robinson Story*, EL, 1950, with the baseball great playing himself; *The Joe Louis Story*, UA, 1953, with Coley Wallace as the heavyweight boxing champ); and Mexicans (*Viva Zapata!*, *Villa*).

Conventions were toyed with. In lieu of a series of significant episodes in a life covering a considerable time span, the new bios concentrated on one or two events. *The Spirit of St. Louis* (WB, 1957), based on Lindbergh's own account of the first nonstop New York to Paris flight in 1927, was the most condensed, spending practically all of its 135 minute duration in a cockpit. Stewart plunged us into an unhinged state of soul. *Sunrise at Campobello* (WB, 1960), with Dore Schary adapting his own play, kept in eyeline Franklin Roosevelt's (stage repeat Ralph Bellamy) physical and psychological struggle with poliomyelitis. Similarly designed was Huston's trio. The heart of *Moulin Rouge* was Lautrec's hopelessly tortured relationship with a petulant, tormenting prostitute that kept the crippled dwarf from responding to the model who truly loved him. *The Barbarian and the Geisha* (TCF, 1958) sighted the frustrating attempts of Captain Townsend Harris (Wayne), first US Consul to Japan in 1856, to be accepted by the insular kingdom and the equally frustrating consequences involving a resourceful native woman. *Freud* (U, 1962) fixated on the years 1890–5 wherein the doctor (Montgomery Clift) laid the foundation of his psychoanalytic theories, working out his neuroses through those of a single patient. Adventures of the spirit that halted on an ironic note, the trio bore the Huston imprint.

A trial scene, usually the final movement in classical bios, comprised almost half of the Otto Preminger-directed *The Court Martial of Billy Mitchell* (WB, 1955), with Gary Cooper as the whistleblower Brigadier General who argues for the buildup of air power in 1921. Other trial-laden works included *St. Joan* (UA, 1957), based on the George Bernard Shaw play, with Jean Seberg as the fifteenth-century Maid of Orléans (also directed by Preminger, who reveled in the clash of controversial points, as only a trial can provide); and *I Accuse!* (MGM, 1957), with José Ferrer as nineteenth-century Dreyfus up against anti-Semitism.

In fact, the new bios were not that reliant on classical plotting, materializing more from character analysis (and a smudged character at that) and less from a story's arc, often privileging the biographee's subjectivity in the telling. They often forfeited the customary heterosexual romance, dollops of action (even the cutting off of the ear occurs below the frame in *Lust for Life*), and a happy ending.

Huston's *Moulin Rouge* and Minnelli's *Lust for Life* went even further with their modernist narratives. With Pierre LaMure's historical novel as a basis, Huston opened with an enthralling 20-minute description of Lautrec's favorite haunt and inspiration, the Moulin Rouge of 1890: the décor; the performers flaunting their talent; the customers, watching, conversing, and dancing. As Lautrec leaves the nightclub and walks home through an alley lined with whores (yet another inspiration for this "painter of the streets and gutters"), a subjective memory montage takes us from Lautrec's privileged upbringing through his accident to his leavetaking. Interweaving his frustrated love life is a detailed description of the process of lithographing and two choreographed montages of his work that invest the paintings with an exuberant lyricism, emotions that Lautrec must have felt while capturing his subjects on canvas. Throughout, the spatial perspective of the camera set at 4′6″ from the ground (Lautrec's actual height) undermined the camera's classical 5′5″ stance.

Adapted by Norman Corwin from Irving Stone's historical fiction, Minnelli innovatively used a five-part narrative for *Lust*, each section visually designed in terms of Van Gogh's emotional bearings and various styles (see Chapter 7). The film, covering Van Gogh from age 25 to his demise at 37, comprised brother Theo's voice-over readings of Vincent's letters from his tortured soul (subjectivity once again). The events described in the letters were objectified and interspersed with instructional passages about art. Throughout the unfolding of these events occurred the continual alternation of Vincent's perceived reality, as when he opens the bedroom shutters on his first morning in Arles, to his

12-2 *Lust for Life* (MGM, 1956, p. John Houseman)

Another instance of director Vincente Minnelli's preoccupation: the transformation of reality. In this biography, painter Vincent Van Gogh (Kirk Douglas) reconstructs "observable" reality into an "imagined" one on canvas.

re-creation of that reality on canvas (the real–imagined dialectic cuts through Minnelli's work). Shuffled through these events were shots of a finished Van Gogh now hanging on a museum wall, which, by film's end, constituted a full CinemaScope-framed catalogue of the artist's oeuvre.

A startlingly new attitude toward biographical material appeared with Ford's tribute to naval hero-scriptwriter-friend Frank W. "Spig" Wead in *The Wings of Eagles* (MGM, 1957). Its light, whimsical tone, secured by Wayne's breezy portrayal and the farcical concocting of incidents (a dashed reconciliation with wife ends with a phonograph spitting records at her) was a far cry from the gravitas of Ford's classical *Young Mr. Lincoln* (TCF, 1939) or *Madame Curie* (MGM, 1943). *The Great Imposter* (U, 1961) reprised this attitude, with director Robert Mulligan playfully recounting the lives of Ferdinand Waldo Demara, Jr. (Curtis): schoolteacher/Trappist novice/prison warden's assistant/surgeon.

Less so than their ancestors, the new bios were still mediated, determined by factors that made the "reality" of the subject questionable. True, with the studio's collapse, biographee choice depended less on whose life would best represent or could best be tailored to the worldview of studio head and persona of star contractee.[3] Now, independents selected a life for its already financially successful showings as a novel or play, which often fell into the heavily mediated class of historical fiction and autobiography. Newspaper headlines and featured articles in magazines, equally mediated sources, also drew producers. About half of the film bios were previously sourced, evidencing again the competition with other leisure activities. If an actor was in charge, the subject's possibility as a vehicle for the actor's talent was considered. The genre, both classically and aclassically, highlighted the solitary performance wherein the lead actor was on the screen for most of the film's span. Such a convention invariably garnered an acting Oscar nomination, if not a win. The input from the biographee, if alive, or his/her family/estate, always on the lookout for anything truly image-damaging, also weighed in.

True, strict historical research was not the intent of the new bios, just as they were not in the ken of their forebears. Yet, rather than the classical bio's hagiographic tone, the new bios did attempt a no-holds-barred, tabloid approach, which could/did ensure more (not total) honesty in representation. Abetting the expose approach were censorship's pliancy and the use of the documentary realist style.

Notes

1   In this discussion, the biography is considered distinct from crypto-bios, which avoid the use of real-life names and are mediated along other generic lines, such as *Rope* (WB, 1948), a thriller suggested by the crime of Leopold and Loeb. Also, when a film contains an actual figure, past or present, as protagonist, yet embodies more of the mythology of a genre other than that of biography, it is considered as an example of that other genre, as the gangster film *The Rise and Fall of Legs Diamond* (WB, 1960). The lives of musical entertainers/entrepreneurs, wherein musical mythology equals and/or surpasses biographical mythology, are defined as "musical biographies" and discussed in the Genre/Musical section.

2   Leo Lowenthal, of the Frankfurt School persuasion, in his significant 1944 essay "Biographies in Popular Magazines," in Paul F. Lazarsfeld and Frank N. Stanton, eds., *Radio Research, 1942–3* (New York: Duell, Sloan & Pearce), noted this shift (he used the then popular *Collier's* and *Saturday Evening Post* for his data) and went on to distinguish between bios of people of production from postwar bios of people of leisure consumption. George F. Custen, in his remarkable study on *Bio/Pics: How Hollywood Constructed Public History* (New Brunswick, NJ: Rutgers University Press, 1992), expanded on this shift and offered extended analysis of the genre.

3   For an impressively detailed account of this process and how it works, see Custen.

13

Historical Spectacle

The "make-'em-big" edict, along with the possibility of an unparalleled representation owing to technological advances, revived the historical spectacle. As with the musical, the historical spectacle launched several processes. (Fox's CinemaScope innovation and the TODD-AO buy-out contributed to that studio's towering number of productions.) The possibility of lowering the exorbitant financial outlay by filming abroad and foreign audience interest were also energizers, resulting in many co-productions, usually involving European producers (Dino De Laurentiis/Carlo Ponti) and a location shoot in Italy or Spain. Also, the genre's material had "penetration." Often in the public domain, the material forwent a pricey bid for rights. And these tales were full of sex and violence – potent consumer catnip.

In its re-creation of events significant to a nation's history, culture, or religion (usually in the founding stage), the genre's span was panoramic, anywhere from Greek (*Helen of Troy*, WB, 1955), Macedonian (*Alexander the Great*, UA, 1956), Jewish (*Esther and the King*, *The Story of Ruth*, both TCF, 1960 and anomalistically female-centered), and Christian mythology (*King of Kings*, MGM, 1961). The matter of Britain (*The Vikings*, UA, 1958) was considered, as were twelfth-century Asian history (*The Conqueror*, RKO, 1956) and early American history (*John Paul Jones*, WB, 1959). The genre's view encompassed even the post-World War II establishing of the nation of Israel (*Exodus*, UA, 1960), with which the spy thriller mixed easily and social problem film (WASP ex-nurse from Indiana finds Jews "strange") uneasily. Nonetheless, the genre had a fondness for Old and New Testament and early Christian religious history, encouraged, no doubt, by the postwar religious revival and the fact that movies that invoked God sanctioned, in the censors' mind at least, suggestive situations, costume, dancing, and other code taboos.

Unlike the bio, the historical spectacle welcomed folkloric figures (*The Prodigal*, MGM, 1955, an embellishment on the biblical parable), fictive ones in an historical event (*Exodus*), as well as actual ones as protagonist. Whether imagined or existent, the protagonist was a leader or, in the course of the story, on his way to becoming one. Skirting psychology, the genre was interested in the actions of the leader and those of the people he led. Prototypically, its plot and conflictual strategy involved a macro-culture persecuting a micro-culture which fought through to freedom. Military battles and/or athletic contests alternated with victory celebrations, which for the ruling class came down to orgies; for the dispossessed, liturgical worship. Pageantry (marches, parades, entrances to cities, coronations of the conquerors) vied with pain (humiliation, torture, the sacking and burning of cities, subjugation of the underprivileged). Romance countered renunciation; lust, repentance. Portents were dissected; dreams interpreted. Tight spots gave way to miracles. The historical spectacle opened its mouth during meetings of the large council, or when delivered messages were proclaimed, or when the solitary leader prayed out loud to God. From time to time, impassioned speeches to stir the troops or followers could be counted upon from both sides, delivered from a height with thousands of attentive ears below. Stirring stories from the nation's past invariably interspersed the speeches. And, if you were lucky, the grave, stentorian male voice of God could be heard from time to time (*Solomon and Sheba*, UA, 1959, had three such emanations).

In the religious items, God's support for the underclass was a given, evinced especially in causing calamities for the disbelieving ruling class. Most amazing was the *Solomon and Sheba* sequence of countless Egyptians being blinded during their battle charge by the sun flashing on the shields of the sparse Jewish fighters, thus being forced to plunge to their deaths by tumbling into a hidden, deep gorge. Echoing the male melodrama, many religious epics also filigreed the "sensitizing" of its male protagonist in terms of his conversion to the "true" faith (*Quo Vadis*, MGM, 1951).

The historical spectacle, mounted on a grand scale, had the dubious distinction of being the most expensive genre to produce. The cast, both principals and supports, was large; the amount of extras gargantuan. *Land of the Pharaohs* (WB, 1955) boasted 9,787 extras in one scene alone. Many foreign players, especially English ones, found work in the form owing to the foreign shoot and to their unknown faces and accents immediately reinforcing the setting's unfamiliarity. Visual design was historically researched and sumptuously re-created. Boris Leven's production design for *The Silver Chalice* (WB, 1954), however, was an eye-arresting surprise. Through his use of spare set-dressing and bold colors, Leven inventively took a pop-art approach to early Christian myth. In the area of female costume, authenticity was undermined by capitulation to the player's physicality and contemporary fashion. Fifties décolletage, for example, appeared in whatever era the story was set, in keeping with the standard

13-1   *The Ten Commandments* (P, 1956, p. Cecil B. DeMille)
Israelite slaves build an Egyptian temple in the "cast-of-thousands" historical spectacle.

Hollywood practice of accenting the historically accurate silhouette with the then contemporary fad/s. Elaborate musical scores (Miklós Rózsa, Franz Waxman), colored by chants and hymns, pulsated throughout the piece. The genre's running time clocked in anywhere between two and four hours.

Epicentered between 1949 (*Samson and Delilah*, P) and 1966 (*The Bible: in the Beginning*, TCF), the religious historical spectacle was just as literarily bankrupt as its financially less successful secular counterpart (starting in 1954 with *King Richard and the Crusaders*, WB/twelfth century and ending in 1965 with *The Agony and the Ecstasy*, TCF/fifteenth-century Pope Julian uniting Italy and *Khartoum*, UA/nineteenth-century standoff of the British in the Sudan). And rarely did the films manifest a sense of the spiritual. *David and Bathsheba* (TCF, 1951), with writer Philip Dunne's focus on David's guilt-ridden affair with one of his soldiers' wives and director Henry King's simpatico understanding, was an exception.

So was *Ben-Hur*, the most lucre-and-laurel accoladed of the pack. Karl Tunberg's script was multi-strand. Amid the culture clash and romance, a son searched for his mother and sister while homoerotically bonding with a friend (via gay contributor Gore Vidal's touches) and, every so often, came into sensitizing contact with Christ. The film also boasted a state-of-the-art rendition of four spectacular sequences in Camera 65/Metrocolor (a sea battle, the

Crucifixion, the miraculous cure of leprosy, and a chariot race). Spectacular sequences, be they disasters, miracles, battles, or agonies, were a genre staple.

Ben-Hur, too, had a William Wyler-modulated performance by Oscar-winning Charlton Heston, the male most associated with the genre (Yul Brynner, Richard Burton, Kirk Douglas, Rex Harrison, and Victor Mature each did three). In addition to the seeker of Christ, Heston was Moses/*The Ten Commandments* (P, 1956); John the Baptist/*The Greatest Story Ever Told* (UA, 1965); and in its secular counterparts, the explorer Lewis/*The Far Horizon* (P, 1955); Andrew Jackson/*The Buccaneer* (P, 1958); the eleventh-century Spanish knight *El Cid* (AA, 1961); a marine opposing the Boxer Rebellion of 1900/*55 Days at Peking* (AA, 1963); Michelangelo/*The Agony and the Ecstasy*; and British General "Chinese" Gordon/*Khartoum*.

The genre, however, was not known for scaling thespian heights except as far as its villains went. The turns of George Sanders's Saran of Gaza (*Samson and Delilah*); Peter Ustinov's Nero and Patricia Laffan's Poppaea (*Quo Vadis*); Charles Laughton and Judith Anderson as the Herods (*Salome*, C, 1952), another female-constructed work; and Jay Robinson's Caligula in *The Robe* and its sequel *Demetrius and the Gladiators* (TCF, 1954) overpowered their respective pictures. Equally mesmerizing was Yul Brynner's chilly intransigent Rameses in *The Ten Commandments*. Even Brynner's shaded good guys, his *Solomon* and the pirate Lafitte who comes to the rescue of Andrew Jackson in *The Buccaneer*, are bullheaded. Right up there, too, were Jack Palance's fifth-century Attila the Hun (*Sign of the Pagan*, U, 1954), his sorcerer revolutionary (*The Silver Chalice*), and his sadistic gladiator (*Barabbas*, C, 1962).

When the postwar generation held the directorial reins (Robert Aldrich/*Sodom and Gomorrah*, Richard Fleischer/*Barabbas*, John Huston/*The Bible*, Nicholas Ray/*King of Kings*), things still stayed the same as they did when the genre was placed, as it customarily was, in the hands of the very respected, end-of-career old guard (Cecil B. DeMille of *Samson and Delilah* and *The Ten Commandments*), except for Robert Rossen. Producer-writer-director Rossen turned the first half of the 141 minutes of *Alexander the Great* into a family melodrama of intergenerational conflict wherein an ambitious son (Burton) is caught between a bitter, grasping, loony mother and a lubricious, paranoid barbarian of a father while imbuing the entire enterprise with his customary preoccupation: the self-destruction of a gifted idealist by the corrupting influences of society. Marxist Rossen's Alexander was a capitalist, pressing on in Asia Minor, Persia, and India, less and less interested in his dream of unification than in the acquisition of riches.

A duo, however, soared above the rest. *Spartacus* (U, 1960) and *Lawrence of Arabia* (C, 1962), bio-historical spectacle hybrids, psychologically probed their protagonists' underside in addition to carefully detailing the momentous events of which they were the center. All along, the films conjoined the private and public, an individual conscience and a nation's culture.

Insurrectionist *Spartacus*, who spearheaded the revolt of Roman slaves in the first century BC, was a perfect subject for blacklisted Dalton Trumbo who, skimming Howard Fast's novel, concentrated on leftish clichés: the oppression of the disenfranchised, the moral decadence of political rulers (bisexual patrician general Crassus), and the idealistic socialist community formed by the slaves where love, even altruism, blossomed. Fortunately, the self-taught Stanley Kubrick (1928–98), in what was only his fifth feature, made time for the things on his mind: the obsessional side of the slave turned gladiator in his pursuit of justice (his demons), the nightmare side of human existence, and the havoc-wreaking effects of the breakdown in communication. Had Kubrick been given complete control, the film might have been even better. Producer-star Douglas, ousting Anthony Mann and instating the neophyte, who had directed him impressively in *Paths of Glory* (UA, 1957), remained the dominant voice. Nevertheless, Kubrick's developing ability to tell a story visually and aurally, assisted by Russell Metty's Super 70 mm Technirama/Technicolor photography and Alex North's complex score, alternately witty and elegiac, introspective and thundering, made much of the film visceral (the warrior-training program; the slaves vs. Roman legions battle enlisting 10,000 extras; the crucifixions along the Appian Way).

Lawrence of Arabia was even more impressive. From the British archeologist – soldier-writer's own *The Seven Pillars of Wisdom*, the British Robert Bolt (and an uncredited Michael Wilson), under British director David Lean's (1908–91) guidance, molded an unfathomably dimensioned figure. Despite raging private demons (eccentricity, the need to be a loner, the inability to handle authority, identity – his homosexuality was skirted) and public ones (the incompetence of confreres), here was a man who never wavered in his far-fetched resolve to unite warring Arab tribes during World War I to foment a successful revolt of the Arabs against the Turks. Intriguingly unassuming and grandiose, Bolt and Lean's Lawrence was also delineated as a diminished, though never defeated, figure as he watches, years later, the unraveling of the Arab Council in Damascus and eventually returns to England.

The character Lawrence was an epitome of Lean's pessimistic view of very adventuresome people striving to flee their humdrum lives that placed them in metaphorical (and sometimes literal) prisons where none of their intellectual/emotional fire was allowed to burn. It was, to be sure, another take on the over-riding individual-vs.-conformity dialectic that riddled postwar films, but Lean's take was ambiguous. The setting, too, was pure Lean: a society in crisis.

From British newcomer Peter O'Toole, Lean exacted a shaded performance, as befitting the legend he played, while mediating powerful turns from an international cast. With the assistance of trusty cameraman Fred A. Young, who shot in Super 70 mm Panavision/Technicolor on location in Jordan, Lean made the desert setting as ambivalent a character, sometimes benign, sometimes hostile, as Lawrence himself. Lean's eye for composition, his cutting ability (his first creative job was as an editor in the British cinema), and his uncanny knack of inlaying Maurice Jarre's surging score made the images appear choreographed. Check out the meeting with Ali who first appears as a speck on the horizon, the capture of the train, or the Battle of Aqaba. Or most indelible, the jump cut of the close-up of Lawrence in an office lighting a match, watching it burn, and blowing it out, and the darkness being instantly replaced by a long shot of a pre-dawn desert horizon with the sun peeping out: a succinct metaphor of the extinction of Lawrence's life as a rank-and-file soldier to his rising as a charismatic warrior of the sands. The pinnacle of Lean's poetry, *Lawrence* earned seven Oscars, including that for best picture/director. It was released in three versions (222-minute road show, 202-minute select theatres, 187-minute general release).

14

Comedy

Comedy came down somewhat from the highs of the silent twenties and squawking thirties. The Cold War mentality made satire's subversion suspect while deeming the disorder of farce frivolous. Stage and fiction comedy was mediocre and, hence, unreliable. Many contract merrymaking writers, who had expertly crafted comic engines from the ground up, were terminated. The industry's emphasis on the latest technologies undermined word and performance, essentials in a comic text's construction. And the trend toward realism made comedy's convention of exaggeration and stylization chancy.

Also, many classical comedy auteurs were in decline. Charles Chaplin (1889–1978), the only slapstick clown holdover, was ahead of his audience with the black comedy *Monsieur Verdoux* (UA, 1947), sunk into bathos with *Limelight* (UA, 1952), and was definitely passé in *The King in New York* (Archway, 1957). With the flat *Cluny Brown* (TCF, 1946) in release, Ernst Lubitsch (1892) died in 1947.

Frank Capra's (1897–1991) *It's a Wonderful Life* (RKO, 1946) marked a transition in his populist comedies. Instead of continuing to move on, Capra reverted. He stayed in the game until *Pocketful of Miracles* (UA, 1961), his *Lady for a Day* (C, 1933) redo, which played to empty houses. A thirties staple, populist comedy peaked with director Leo McCarey's Father O'Malley duo with Bing Crosby: Oscar-winning *Going My Way* (P, 1944) and *The Bells of St. Mary's* (RKO, 1945). Postwar populist comedy, often reconstituted with a female crackerbarrel Yankee philosopher protagonist, was sporadic and had a patchy financial record. People embraced Oscar-winner Loretta Young as *The Farmer's Daughter* (RKO, 1947) and were respectful to Judy Holliday's *The Solid Gold Cadillac* (C, 1956), but snubbed Doris Day's *It Happened to Jane* (C, 1959).

Preston Sturges (1898–1959) left Paramount after a series of glittering gems from 1941's *The Great McGinty* to 1944's *Hail, the Conquering Hero*. A heady mélange of farce, screwball romance, social satire, and parody, with intertextuality galore and narrative subversion, Sturges's films stood classical comedy on its head. His last labors were lackluster: *Unfaithfully Yours* (TCF, 1948), *The Beautiful Blonde from Bashful Bend* (TCF, 1949), and *The Sins of Harold Diddlebock/a.k.a. Mad Wednesday* (RKO, 1950) which did, however, flaunt one of his outrageous conceits. The film opened with the last reel of the 1925 slapstick classic *The Freshman* in which Harold Lloyd wins the football game. A businessman then offers him (ditto Harold) the chance to get ahead in the good old American way. Twenty years later, he is a failure, even though he followed the rules and practiced the virtues. By madly renouncing the conformist ways, Harold, by the final reel, becomes a success.

14.1   Social Satire

Social satire is a subform of comedy with a humorously critical focus on instances of contemporary societal fragmentation, limitation, incongruity, or deviation from the norm. This deviation is pointed out by the authorial voice within the story (some character) or outside the story, in the hope (presumably) that the audience takes note and brings about a correction. Writer-directors Billy Wilder, Joseph Mankiewicz, Howard Hawks (director only), and Frank Tashlin made it memorable. All topically accommodators of this durable subtype, Wilder also made it shiver with thrilleresque frissons, as did Mankiewicz, who further added melodrama. Tashlin played with conventions, making his films resemble real-life cartoons. Further: they refused to toe the Cold War line which preferred satire to stay only in the private sphere, exuding a warm, urbane wishy-washiness that, in the end, embraced the sported-with values.

Wilder (1906–2002), a Viennese Jew who fled the German film industry in 1934, had been co-writing comedies at Paramount and on loanout since 1938 until his co-writing/directing calling card *The Major and the Minor* (P, 1942). Honing his thriller skills for a while, Wilder returned to social satire.

A Foreign Affair (P, 1948) appeared first. In this one, a black-market entrepreneurial army captain (John Lund), his cabaret-singer mistress who had also pussyfooted with Hitler (Marlene Dietrich), a repressed Corn Belt congresswoman investigating army morale (Jean Arthur), and a Machiavellian colonel (Millard Mitchell) play dangerous games amid the ruins of postwar Berlin.

Whether self-interested con-artist, or self-absorbed romantic who is conned, or a combination personality, Wilder's people were all masqueraders for money and/or lust. His clear-eyed understanding, precise specification, and dispassionate exposure of them ensured objectivity, a necessity if the satire is to remain biting and funny. Character contextualization, the authenticity that resulted from an accumulation of details, and strong, cohesive plotting gave Wilder's satires, co-written pre-1950 with Charles Brackett and post-1957 with I. A. L. Diamond, texture. The witty, rueful ironies recalled Lubitsch; the droll, acerbic perversities, Von Stroheim. The tough dialogue had a visual quality about it, full of similes, metaphors, and characters telling stories. Dialogue, for the most part, dictated camerawork, cutting, and pace.

Some Like It Hot (UA, 1959) and *The Apartment* (UA, 1960) took their places alongside of *A Foreign Affair* as vintage Wilder. Equal parts social satire, farce, and parody (of the gangster film), the iconoclastic *Some Like It Hot* tracked a pair of down-on-their-luck jazz musicians (Jack Lemmon and Tony Curtis). After inadvertently witnessing the St. Valentine's Day Massacre, the duo flee in bras and high heels as "Daphne" and "Josephine," the bass and sax in the "Sweet Sue and her City Syncopaters" all-girl band, where they hit on a ditsy, dipso-maniacal chanteuse (Marilyn Monroe), who's into her own game of pretense to marry a millionaire. *The Apartment*, winner of five Oscars including picture, director, and writer honors, was a West 60s pad belonging to Consolidated Insurance Co.'s "desk number 861" (Lemmon). To get ahead, the clerk loans his place to execs for their extramarital affairs, particularly the VP/Administra-tion (Fred MacMurray), who's stringing along the head-over-heels-in-love-with-him elevator operator (Shirley MacLaine).

Wilder's other satires, if not dazzlers, did sparkle. William Holden, snatching the Oscar as the self-serving POW trading with the Nazis and engineering an escape, inhabits *Stalag 17* (P, 1953), based on Donald Bevan and Edmund Trzcinski's stage success. Subtly but ever so scathingly, the film also attacked the McCarthy era witch-hunts as the majority of soldiers metaphorically put on trial one of their nonconforming own. Tom Ewell, with his family away on summer vacation, breaks out with *The Seven Year Itch* (TCF, 1955), which he hopes the curvaceous Marilyn Monroe upstairs will scratch. Ewell had origi-nated the part in George Axelrod's hit show. *Sabrina* (P, 1954), from Samuel Taylor's play, is Audrey Hepburn, a Long Island Cinderella with two Prince Charmings on a string (Bogart and Holden). *Love in the Afternoon* (AA, 1957), based on Claude Anet's novel, comes down to the mutual "fascination" of middle-aged playboy millionaire (Gary Cooper) and a dewy-eyed cello student (Hepburn). A revamp of Alexandre Breffort's international musical success minus the numbers, *Irma la Douce* (UA, 1963) reunited *The Apartment*'s MacLaine and Lemmon as a prostitute and her police protector, respectively. *Irma la Douce*, as with *Sabrina* and *Love in the Afternoon*, blended social satire with romantic comedy. Cream of the second-string crop, however, was *One, Two, Three* (UA, 1961), Ferenc Molnár's one-acter totally refitted for the Cold War climate and perpetual-motion machine James Cagney as an unscrupulous, womanizing Coca Cola exec in West Berlin called upon to (1) camouflage the boss's daughter's marriage to a communist; (2) sweet-talk his wife into a reconciliation now that she's sure of his affair with his pert blonde secretary; and (3) hawk the wonders of the famous soft drink to the city's eastern sector.

Mankiewicz (1909–92), born of eastern Jewish ancestry in Wilkes Barre, Pennsylvania, was both educated (a BA degree from Columbia) and cultured (he was a theater devotee). He joined older brother Herman in Hollywood in 1929 after a stint in Berlin translating UFA titles from German to English. He became an in-demand intertitler and scriptwriter at Paramount and wrote and produced at MGM before arriving at Fox in 1943 where Zanuck was luring comedy writers with the bait of allowing them to direct their work as well. (From the mid-forties on, Fox rivaled, and even bettered, classic comedy champ Paramount up to the advent of CinemaScope in 1953, when the genre hit a low point, not only at Fox but at every studio, until the producers' and public's hot affair with technology cooled down around 1958.) Here Mankiewicz peaked with back-to-back screenplay/direction Oscars for *A Letter to Three Wives* (1949), a Vera Caspary story from a John Klemper novel, and *All About Eve* (1950), based on a story by Mary Orr.

Class stratification, suburbia and the country-club set, marriage, and pop culture were pilloried in *A Letter to Three Wives* as three young married women (Jeanne Crain, Ann Southern, and Linda Darnell), about to embark on an all-day riverboat outing, receive a note from their best friend who confesses she just ran away with one of their husbands (might it be Jeffrey Lynn, Kirk Douglas, or Paul Douglas?). The news makes each wife dispiritingly flash back on her respective relationship. Oscar-winning best picture *All About Eve* had a go at the theater profession, aging, ambition, egoism, and the female in the workplace as a series of Eve's friends – footlight prima donna (Bette Davis), bitchy critic (George Sanders), playwright's dilettante wife (Celeste Holm) – flash back on how Eve (Anne Baxter) received her theater award.

People Will Talk (1951) scowled at the smug conformist attitude, particularly in the medical profession, where science precluded faith; narrow-minded, petty academia; and the social stigma of the unmarried pregnant woman. Starring Cary Grant as the sourball-dispensing, orchestra-conducting doctor and Crain as his troubled patient, the film, though bravely intelligent, was not as focused as *Letter* and *Eve*. Mankiewicz's iconic suspenseful rummaging into the past of his people's lives was handled here in purely verbal flashbacks. With his independent *The Barefoot Contessa* (UA, 1954), Mankiewicz got long-winded, heavy blows replacing his usual light jabs as he took on the movie profession (cynical writer-director/Bogart; lying press agent/Oscar-winning support Edmund O'Brien; sad star/Ava Gardner; heartless producer/Warren Stevens) and the international jet set (impotent count/Rossano Brazzi). The piece, still marked with gorgeously witty dialogue (and speeches), contained Mankiewicz's characteristic signature mystery-thriller element, the alternating voice-overs filling in the past, and the surprising final fillip, all of which adoring Joe remembered from brother Herman's script of *Citizen Kane* (RKO, 1941). Also characteristic was his works' hybridization with melodrama which, for one thing, made the characters more humanly dimensioned than satire's usual ploy of type-characters. For another: melodrama's attendant pathos gave Mankiewicz's satires heft.

Hawks (1896–1977), an Indiana WASP who graduated Cornell in mathematical engineering, entered the movies humbly in 1917 as a prop boy and went on to work as writer, editor, and finally director in 1926. He operated independently, working at practically every factory and working almost every genre quite niftily. *I Was a Male War Bride* (TCF, 1949), with a Charles Lederer, Leonard Spigelgass, and Hagar Wilde script, needled the efficient, pushy female (Ann Sheridan), the put-upon male (Grant), and institutional bureaucracy (the army). *Monkey Business* (TCF, 1952), a Ben Hecht/Charles Lederer/I. A. L. Diamond concoction, skewered America's obsession with staying young. Both films contained Hawks's usual sexual push–pull and the professional–irresponsible dialectic. These conflicts interlaced a clean, simple storyline set within a short span of time and presented in an unfussy, medium-shot way. Speaking of spare storylines, in *Bride*, an American WAC officer accompanies a French military man on an unimportant mission in postwar Germany, marries him, then gets around the Congressional Act regulating war brides' (but not war husbands') entry into the States. In *Monkey Business*, an anti-aging drug accidentally enters a water cooler and is ingested by the chemist (Grant), his wife (Ginger Rogers), and his colleagues, turning the lot into feckless kids.

Frank Tashlin (1913–72) replaced the strong literary trait of Wilder, Mankiewicz, and Hawks's satires with a cartoon-like quality which made his canon unique to the times as well as the genre. Passionate about cartoons, the New Jersey teenager took a correspondence course in drawing. After work for animators Max and Dave Fleischer, WB's Leon Schlesinger, Disney, and UPA, which he helped form in 1941, Tashlin started writing for human actors (1945–51) and directing them from 1952. In *The Lieutenant Wore Skirts* (TCF, 1955) a civilian writer (Ewell) brainwashes his wife (Sheree North) so that she be declared insane and unfit for military duty, thus putting an end to sexual apartheid. Adapted from George Axelrod's play, *Will Success Spoil Rock Hunter?* (TCF, 1957) deals with a New York advertising account exec (Tony Randall) who, in an attempt to retain a dissatisfied lipstick manufacturer client, cajoles a Junoesque movie queen (Jayne Mansfield) into pushing the product. *Bachelor Flat* (TCF, 1962), from the Budd Grossman play, catches a disturbed teenager (Tuesday Weld) moving into an archaeologist's (Terry-Thomas) Malibu pad without informing him she is his fiancée's daughter.

Tashlin's episodic sketches were replete with some of the most clinically disturbed middle-class professionals in all postwar cinema, be they the shy, the dismissed, the maladroit, the anally compulsive, the hypochondriac, the sexually challenged, the over-sexed, the fey male, or the macho female. Their problems were partly caused and totally exacerbated by the pressures of modern living. Drawn as caricatures, sometimes grotesques, in which instances the creator's objectivity spilled over into dislike, Tashlin's people became unwitting perpetrators and/or victims of an interminable series of violent, invariably vulgar events which made for the dollops of farce in his work. With the action staged horizontally across one plane, often with color as background and cutting principle, his frames resembled cartoon panels; his people, animated figures. Unselfconsciously modernist, Tashlin's comedies were so extremely stylized that the spectator was aware of watching a movie, not a representation of life.

An odd yet searingly topical entry that added new targets was John Deighton and Roland Kibbee's tailoring of George Bernard Shaw's play *The Devil's Disciple* (UA, 1959) for Kirk Douglas as the atheist-rapscallion who sacrifices his life, Burt Lancaster as the ineffectual pastor turned fighting rebel, and Laurence Olivier as British General Burgogne, more gentleman than warrior. Set in 1777 when the colonial wars were drawing to a close, the film sharply pilloried Christianity, marriage, the writing of history, and the military on both sides (particularly in its interlarded scenes of puppet animation). These institutions, the film disclosed, were not all what they purported to be; their surface belied their substance.

Social satire hybridized frequently and fluently with melodrama, a nod to realism's favor. In addition to the Mankiewicz set, the New York psychological–sociological playwrights and telewriters were largely responsible for the quantity and distinction of this mix, none more so than Paddy Chayefsky (1923–82). In *Marty* (UA, 1955), winner of four Oscars (picture, script, actor, and director Delbert Mann) and Chayefsky's best, a lonely, 34-year-old Bronx Italian Catholic butcher, heavy-set and hard on the eyes (Ernest Borgnine), finally breaks away from his manipulative mama and the boys on the corner when he decides to make a date with the shy, unadorned Irish teacher he meets at a dance. *The Catered Affair* (MGM, 1956) is what an Irish Catholic Bronx battle-ax (Bette Davis) is determined to give her daughter, though she and her cabbie husband (Borgnine) can ill afford it. A big wedding, it seems, is the only way to squelch the gossip of her daughter being knocked up, which spread throughout the neighborhood when the daughter planned an inauspicious but financially practical exchange of vows in the rectory. Five Gotham accountants comprise *The Bachelor Party* (UA, 1957), more commiseration than celebration as they ritualistically make their stops at assorted watering holes. Progressively drunker, they get more in touch with their angst-ridden souls which they ventilate non-stop. The newlywed (Don Murray) fears the added expense of a baby on the way. Abortion might be the answer. Old benedict (Larry Blyden), straddled with a couple of kids, envies the guy who's hitting on a "dish" in the subway. Asthma forces the senior (E. G. Marshall) to rethink his life. The swinging middle-aged single (Jack Warden) is still frightened to go home alone at night. The probable homosexual (Phillip Abbott), a 32-year-old virgin contentedly living with his mother, is now being pushed into an arranged marriage with a widow.

Existential problems were at the core of Chayefsky's films, all based on teleplays. How does the common man make his life amount to something or, at least, experience the illusion of meaning? How does he break with routine; how does he enjoy; how does he deal with loneliness? What is this thing called marriage with its boundaries and burdens? Airing such concerns naturally sabotaged the classical conception of goal-oriented characters. Character, melodramatically layered, unclassically prevailed over plot. In fact, Chayefsky's pieces, built from a situation in which characters interacted, were plotless. Dialogue, full of nuances and rhythms of everyday urban speech, overlapped, and was set on the city's sidewalks and subways, or in markets and tenements where nylons were strung on a rope across a parlor to dry. Dialogue also unclassically eclipsed actions.

14.2 Farce

Farce prefers a series of episodes rather than the usual tight, cohesive plot of the best social satires to tell its story. The characters and situations in these episodes are more exaggerated (sometimes to the degree of caricature and grotesque) than those in comedy's other subforms. (Exaggeration is a necessity in comedy so that the distance such exaggeration ensures would enable the audience to laugh and see the point. And, as with all forms of comedy, farce believes there is nothing like laughter to make the point about man's fragmentation, limitation, incongruity, or deviation from the norm easily digestible.)

Farce sticks to the least severe instances of man's fragmentation, relegated as it is to instances of man's physical fragmentation, the realm of the body. Social satire, on the other hand, deals with spiritual fragmentation, the realm of the mind and heart. A man who doesn't duck in time and gets a pie in the kisser is not as serious or significant an instance of fragmentation than, say, a man who ruins another's reputation. In farce, the protagonist can fall into and/or instigate this fragmentation that brings about bodily discomfort, even harm on occasion, to himself and/or others. The essential method of farce is physical humor, relying as it does on actions, whereas social satire scores with verbal humor elicited through dialogue. A farce may contain some social satire, while social satire is not immune to bits of farce.

Besides *Some Like It Hot*, only two other farces hit their marks and, incidentally, were the period's number one and two top-grossing comedies. *Auntie Mame* (WB, 1958), Betty Comden and Adolph Green's expansion of the Jerome Lawrence and Robert E. Lee play based on Patrick Dennis's bestseller, pummeled the values of orthodoxy and conformity as it traced the adventures of free-spirited Mame Dennis from Hoover to Eisenhower. This monument to the avant-garde admonishes the young, the frightened, the mean: "Live, live, live. Life is a banquet and most poor suckers ["bastards" on the stage] are starving." Sophisticated clown Rosalind Russell incandescently enshrined her bravura stage role. Footlight director Morton Da Costa and photographer Harry Stradling used Technicolor's palette and Technirama's large space humorously (the blackouts on Mame's droll reactions and suggestive details, as the bouquet of forget-me-nots pinned atop the derrière of Mame's black, backless widow's weeds).

In *Operation Petticoat* (U, 1960), Stanley Shapiro and Maurice Richlin spun a yarn of a naval commander (Grant) who gets his ramshackle "moanin' and groanin'" submarine back to active duty in the Pacific, notwithstanding his supply officer (Curtis) bringing a quintet of female nurses, a couple of pregnant village women, and a goat on board. Furthermore, the submarine returns to safety by means of a brassière. The writers and director Blake Edwards (1922) charged the World War II tale with Cold War palpitations: fear of the stranger (professional and competent women, minorities, a "pink" submarine); the corporate mentality vs. individual initiative; and, above all, the crisis in masculinity (the commander's one chance of destroying a Japanese tanker is dashed by a female's throwing a lever that results in torpedoing a beached truck). Consumer culture was also given a yank with the lead characters' contrast coming down to a traditional man (Grant) who holds out for the values of honor and duty, and the fifties man (Curtis) with a talent for selling himself and for shopping. Edwards's first major directorial job paraded his knowledge of gag construction learned from silent slapstick, whether it be a ladies' girdle used as a valve spring in the engine room or the pig successfully passed off as a drunken Seabee. Edwards also knew how to use on-screen and off-screen space for surprisingly hilarious effect, as when Grant collects Curtis's creature comforts – that fill a golf bag – from the frame's edges. Most stunning was Edwards's audacious tonal shifts throughout. In the sick bay below, Grant's derrière is being bandaged after he has sat on the nurse's hot curling iron. Cut to the flat deck above where, at a New Year's Day luau, the military men and women sing, a cappella, "Auld Lang Syne," and heartfully mean every word when, out of the blue, a surprise air attack blasts the party to pieces.

14-1 *Auntie Mame* (WB, 1958, p. Morton Da Costa)
Deconstructor of conformity Mame Dennis (Rosalind Russell) welcomes her nephew Patrick (Jan Handzlick) under the disapproving gaze of his guardian Nora (Connie Gilchrist).

Petticoat was the top of the line of military farces, instancing the lingering memory of World War II though replayed in a zany mode from *Operation Mad Ball* (C, 1957) through *Don't Go Near the Water* (MGM, 1957) to *The Wackiest Ship in the Army* (C, 1961). This farcical tone, in lieu of the usual grave handling of World War II subject matter, was daringly new.

14.3 Romantic Comedy

The besieged male, the grappling female, and the resulting tension between the sexes topically energized romantic comedy, dealing as it does with foolishness, fancies, rivalries, and cross-purposes (all instances of fragmentation) of the male and female encountering each other under the romantic moon. The fact that there are *two* different species out there, who find themselves on *one* similar, all-consuming plane of eros, gives rise to the foibles erupting in a battle that must be waged to achieve, maintain, and restore a state of harmony. The move toward realism and the easing of censorial structures also gave "the battle of the sexes" an immediacy and sophistication.

The husband-and-wife team of writers Garson Kanin and Ruth Gordon, director George Cukor (1899–1983), and performers Spencer Tracy and Katharine Hepburn arrived first with the intelligent *Adam's Rib* (MGM, 1949). Through the ingenious conceit (romantic comedy's linchpin) of a defense lawyer (Hepburn) arguing against her assistant DA husband (Tracy) the case of a woman with three kids who shot at her philandering husband and his mistress, American society's skewed attitude toward gender, pleasure, and sex, marriage and family, justice and morality, and the professional sphere (the law) was gleaned. Furthermore, *Adam's Rib* played the situation on the marital plane where the union is endangered (not the usual courtship one) and in the middle-class professional sphere that many of the audience recognized and most aspired to. And it flecked the plane (a career couple, mind you, without kids or dog) with intimate, heretofore-unseen-on-the-screen interactions such as her satisfied squeals after being grabbed and pulled behind a wall by him – one time emerging with a slipping décolletage.

Cukor's observant eye and spatially whole, long-take *mise-en-scène* that eschewed close-ups and rarely resorted to medium shots favored performance in rhythm. This type of visual structure came naturally to Cukor, who had apprenticed as a stage director at Rochester's Lyceum Stock Theater before making his Broadway debut in 1925. Part of the Manhattan tide that washed upon Los Angeles shores as dialogue directors when sound arrived, Cukor moved from Paramount contractee to Selznick's director of choice at both RKO and MGM. As an independent hire-out in the postwar years, Cukor's comedies came into their own, because he had more control in choosing material that rang a bell with him, as *Rib*'s female crossing over the accepted societal limits. And *Rib*'s characters' profession and class and the courtroom setting were conversant with him, having been reared in an upper middle-class Hungarian-Jewish family headed by papa, the lawyer. So familiar, in fact, that he saw the courtroom as pure theater with lawyers as actors, whose quality of performance decided the case's win or loss on the part of the audience of judge, jury, and movie spectator. A gay man, Cukor was given an alter ego with the character of the gay neighbor (David Wayne) who fulfills the genre's convention of the confidant.

Equally strong actor personas, each able to hold the screen, each playing equally strong characters, each protagonist as well as antagonist, were as essential to romantic comedy as charming ones. (Romantic comedy was one of the few classical genres to represent the female as equal and/or superior to the male.) Furthermore, both actors must create an on-screen chemistry. In the above tests, Tracy and Hepburn scored A-pluses.

The team's follow-up *Pat and Mike* (MGM, 1952) maintained the standard. She's a phys-ed teacher and zealous athlete; he, a crusty sports promoter who becomes her manager. Minus Cukor and the Kanins, however, *Desk Set* (TCF, 1957), Phoebe and Henry Ephron's go at William Marchant's play under Walter Lang's baton, with Hepburn as a TV researcher who fears the computer will replace workers and Tracy as the computer designer, was below par. First-rate, however, were Cukor and Kanin's adaptation of Kanin's Broadway hit *Born Yesterday* (C, 1950), with Oscar-winning stage-repriser Judy Holliday as the mistress of a war profiteer (blowtorch Broderick Crawford) who hires a liberal reporter (Holden) to educate her, and Cukor and writers Brackett, Richard L. Breen, and Walter Reisch's *The Model and the Marriage Broker* (TCF, 1951), with matchmaker (Thelma Ritter) arranging career girl's (Jeanne Crain) romance, and vice versa.

Practically every other romantic comedy that followed was fair to middling, except *The Quiet Man* (R, 1952), a one-of-a-kind from writer Frank Nugent and Oscar-winning John Ford about the courting and marriage of a retired, peace-seeking American boxer (Wayne) to a fiery, mind-of-her-own Irish lass (Maureen O'Hara). The proletarian Irish Roman Catholic landscapes and county customs, which grounded and contributed to the duo's nonconformist pigheadedness, were accurately detailed. The film also contained farce galore, hilariously climaxing with Wayne shoving, dragging, even kicking O'Hara from the train through the village onto the farm some five miles away. There she collects her dowry from her recalcitrant brother and a donnybrook involving an entire village erupts. Continually, Victor Young's airs made satiric points, as when a jig's beat and tempo underline the free-for-all. A far cry from the off-the-studio-assembly-line jobs, *The Quiet Man* was as lovingly handcrafted as the best of the postwar films. It was also one of the visual glories of the genre (and postwar cinema as well). Comedy was not known for its look until the postwar period, thanks especially to the romantic comedies of Minnelli (*Designing Woman*, MGM, 1957) and Stanley Donen (the London-shot *Indiscreet*, WB, 1958).

Pillow Talk (U, 1959) recorded a seismic jolt. Shapiro and Richlin penned an Oscar-winning lollapalooza. In the conning of a decorator (Doris Day) by a songwriter (Rock Hudson), social, gender, and sexual issues spiraled, the very ones that Kinsey, Hefner, and Maslow were raising, which happened to be on most adults' minds. Not only topical, it was forthrightly risqué, with repartee or verbal skirmishing (another convention) replete with double-entendres and indelicate puns ("There are some men who don't end every sentence with a proposition"). As such, *Pillow Talk* brought full circle its two worthy predecessors: the Norman Krasna play rescript *Indiscreet*, with an actress (Ingrid Bergman) actually sleeping with a businessman (Grant) who's pretending to be married so he won't get hooked; and *Teacher's Pet* (P, 1958), a Fay and Michael Kanin original directed by George Seaton, in which veteran reporter (Gable) hoodwinks journalism lecturer (Day) into thinking him a cub writer so he can get under her skirts.

Gay Ross Hunter (1920–96), who started out as an actor in 1945 and switched to producing at Universal from 1953, was responsible for the inspired casting of the relatively young Hudson and Day (rather than middle-agers Tracy and Hepburn). As such, the film's appeal was to a younger crowd as well. Moreover, their playing with each other was perfectly pitched. So, too, were their respective confidants – Tony Randall and Thelma Ritter, equally his and hers. Designer clothes and accessories were siren songs and battle cries, as with Doris's white, backless sheath outlining a derrière in rumba time that elicits Rock's sigh: "So that's the other end of your party line." Sets were places of allurement (Rock's bachelor pad) and bickering (Doris's bedroom); props, as with the telephone, at once aphrodisiacs and clubs. Ex-stage/blacklisted director Michael Gordon's imaginative split-screen *mise-en-scène*, illustrating the conceit of two antagonistic people sharing the same party line, made CinemaScope a thematic necessity, while imparting sexual ironies, as in the bathtub scene where Doris and Rock take a bath together and self-reflexively comment about it (". . . most people [are] willing to meet you halfway"). And Frank De Vol's bouncy score contextually joked and winked in all the right spots.

Pillow Talk's roaring success created an almost exclusive Universal franchise, lasting until 1968. Hudson and Day reunited for *Lover Come Back* (1962), self-consciously sporting a cleverer, racier Shapiro and Paul Henning script about two competing Madison Avenue ad execs and sharper direction, this time by Delbert Mann. *Lover* also served up some tantalizing satire on advertisers and consumers as Hudson sells a product, VIP, that doesn't actually exist. In their final outing, *Send Me No Flowers* (U, 1964), with Norman Jewison steering Julian Epstein's amusing conceit, Hudson's a hypochondriac searching for a mate for his wife Day when he erroneously believes he's going to die. The rest of the franchise was a matter of fits and starts, even when starring one of the prototypical players and penned by Shapiro (Hudson and Gina Lollobrigida in *Come September*, 1961, or Day and Grant in *A Touch of Mink*, 1962). Bobby Darin and Sandra Dee were a cut-rate Hudson and Day in *If a Man Answers* (1962).

Additionally, romantic comedy–romance melodrama was a winning combo, once again the special province of New York stage and TV writers. The Kanin–Gordon and Cukor original *The Marrying Kind* (C, 1952) was a his (Aldo Ray) and hers (Holliday) flashback version of marriage dissolution transpiring in the presence of a divorce court judge. Throughout, each's voice-over verbal memories on the soundtrack counterpointed the visual incarnation, resulting in some

14-2 *The Marrying Kind* (C, 1952, p. Bert Granet)
Tonal shifts pervade director George Cukor/writers Ruth and Garson Kanin's romantic comedy-romance melodrama as picnicking wife Judy Holiday sings the ukulele-accompanied "Dolores" to husband Aldo Ray as kids run to the lake, the source of distressed cries.

gleeful ironies. Tonal shifts occurred smoothly, as when Holliday strums "Dolores" on a ukulele at the family picnic while a commotion, set off by their drowned son, brews. Playwright William Inge and adapter George Axelrod's *Bus Stop* (TCF, 1956) touted Monroe's multifaceted performance, funny yet poignant, as a mediocre chanteuse sidetracked on her way to Hollywood by a rodeo rider-rancher (Don Murray). In N. Richard Nash's tele/stage play *The Rainmaker* (P 1956), an itinerant con-artist (Lancaster) promises to bring rain to a drought-stricken farm where an uncomely spinster (Katharine Hepburn) cares for her father and brothers. Garson Kanin's teleplay *The Rat Race* (P, 1960) involved a cynical dance-hall hostess (an against-type Debbie Reynolds) sharing her West Side cold-water flat with a still-wet-behind-the-ears jazz musician hopeful (Curtis). In playwright William Gibson and adapter Isobel Lennart's *Two for the Seesaw* (UA, 1962), a Greenwich Village Jewish kook (MacLaine) keeps the loneliness at bay with a married WASP (Robert Mitchum).

14.4   Family Comedy

Family rumblings and the ticks of suburbia where the postwar family hung out provided recognizable instances of fragmentation. As such, it was material perfect for satire and kept family comedy, a Hollywood staple since 1934, riding the crest. The effort to compete with TV's extremely popular sitcoms, even to the extent of producing sequels to duplicate TV's see-you-next-week open-ended structure, also determined the subform's longevity. Also, the casting ploy of old and new players could be neatly accomplished by the subform's parents/children inhabitants. Its conservative ideology, fluently spouted by the iconic wisdom-dispensing Yankee figure embodied in either parent or child, went hand in hand with the era's overall conservative ideology in which traditional values of the home were affirmed despite and/or because of the tremors. (The least anarchic of the various branches of the comedy tree, family comedy's satire is gentle, ultimately proffering a celebration of the American family as the basic unit of democracy.) Except for the switch from the country to suburbia, family comedy stayed pretty much, but not quite, the same with its episodic plot built from incidents that revolve around problem solving and/or getting out of scrapes to the end of keeping the family intact.

Hooking the audience was *The Egg and I* (U, 1947), Chester Erskine and Fred Finklehoffe's version of Betty McDonald's bestseller in which city slickers (Claudette Colbert and Fred MacMurray) buy a farm where they meet indigent hicks (Marjorie Main and Percy Kilbride as Ma and Pa Kettle, with 15 kids). Main and Kilbride walked away with the picture, consequently spawning a successful B series, a total of nine entries from 1949 to 1957. Paramount's *Dear Ruth* (1947), Arthur Sheekman's adaptation of a Norman Krasna play with father (Edward Arnold) and sisters (Joan Caulfield and Mona Freeman), also cleaned up at the turnstiles, resulting in sequels *Dear Wife* (1949) and *Dear Brat* (1951).

Fox produced a spate of family comedies, notable for the wryly amusing performance of the persnickety, didactic, so-pleased-with-himself Clifton Webb. As suburban boarder-babysitter Lynn Belvedere who pours a bowl of porridge on a mischievous baby's head in *Sitting Pretty* (1948), F. Hugh Herbert's screenplay of Gwen Davenport's novel, Webb caused audiences to cheer so much that Fox placed him at the center of *Mr. Belvedere Goes to College* (1949), where academia becomes his metaphorical home, and *Mr. Belvedere Rings the Bell* (1951), set in an old folks' home. Webb was limelighted again as a stern industrial engineer and father of 12 in *Cheaper by the Dozen* (1950), Lamar Trotti's reworking of novelists Frank B. Gilbreth, Jr. and Ernestine Gilbreth Carey's memory of their upbringing that did not fall into the nostalgic trap. Since

Cheaper by the Dozen climaxed with his death, his wife (Myrna Loy) carried on in his spirit in the 1952 sequel *Bells on Their Toes*. In *Mr. Scoutmaster* (1953), on the other hand, Webb is taught by his metaphorical children; in *Holiday for Lovers* (1959), Luther Davis's version of Ronald Alexander's play, he finds he cannot teach his pubescent daughters anything. As *The Remarkable Mr. Penny-packer* (1959), Walter Reisch's working of Liam O'Brien's 1890s-set play, a nonconforming Webb is a paean to liberalism: a Darwinian; feminist; situation ethicist; a believer of instinct, not reason; and a bigamist to boot, running two households totaling 17 kids.

Pennypacker swerved from the well-trodden trail. In a sense, Minnelli's MGM efforts did too, when he turned his attention to the middle-class suburban family, observing the species at critical ritual points where the discrepancy between the ideal and real (a Minnelli trademark) and insecurities were most telling. A daughter's marriage (Elizabeth Taylor) turns the *Father of the Bride* (Spencer Tracy) apoplectic in husband-and-wife writers Albert Hackett and Frances Goodrich's 1950 adaptation of Edward Streeter's novel. The arrival of the first grandchild creates major stress in the same cast-and-crew sequel *Father's Little Dividend* (1951). The honeymoon is bolixed in *The Long, Long Trailer* (1954), which Hackett and Goodrich knitted with farce to accommodate the talents of TV's most popular sitcom couple Lucy and Desi. A coming-out unravels father (Rex Harrison), stepmom (a deliciously zany Kay Kendall), and offspring (Dee) in *The Reluctant Debutante* (1958), William Douglas Home's own adaptation of his stage work that sent Minnelli across the Atlantic and up in class. *The Courtship of Eddie's Father* (1963), John Gay's reworking of Mark Toby's novel, induces more perspiration than usual from widower Glenn Ford with a precocious 6-year-old by his side. Permeated with disturbing undertones throughout (even at the pictures' close), Minnelli's comedies jabbed at the cul-de-sac of conspicuous consumerism; irksome role-playing with its attendant hypocrisies; and stifling bourgeois morality, all of which brought the era's conformist bugaboo in focus. Often parents acted like kids; kids, adults. Nightmares (from the bride's father mired in the church aisle through the storm-beset honeymooners to the tyke's shriek at the dead goldfish, which reminds him of his dead mother) continually erupt, making the home anything but safe.

Recent Universal contractee Douglas Sirk (1900–87) also both espoused and subtly subverted the family with mocking humor and funny, though stinging, irony. Born in Hamburg of Danish parents and sporadically studying law, philosophy, and the history of art, Sirk emerged an important stage director in German theater in the twenties and thirties while directing German films at UFA from 1934 to 1938, before immigrating to France. WB invited him to remake a German film for them in 1939, which never materialized. Relegated to Bs in the forties, mostly for UA, he switched to Universal in 1950. Still saddled with Bs, all types, he made them special. Three years later, he was the premier director on the lot.

The power of children over parents, the infantilization of grownups and the sophistication of kids, the discrepancies of the generation gap, the games of pretense, the relentless monetary pursuits, and the empty, dehumanizing social rituals came to light in his entries. *Has Anybody Seen My Gal?* (1951), where a $100,000 inheritance discombobulates a middle-class family, and the period *Take Me to Town* (1952), in which a widowed preacher and his sons take in a shady lady in a narrow-minded town, were tops.

14.5   Fantasy Comedy

The insertion or interruption into the real world of a figure or occurrence, alternative and radically distinct from the human, or the reverse, the positioning of the human in an extra-worldly modality, are fantasy's *modi operandi*. In both instances, an effortless or an uneasy acceptance of this counter-reality on the part of a protagonist occurs. The acceptance renews the protagonist's life, which is in need of any help it can get in both spiritual and/or material matters. Fantasy uses the "alternative" world not only as a way of offering insights about the real world and its wonders, but more, its woes, and one's place in it.

Melodramatic fantasy renewed itself in 1939 with *On Borrowed Time* at MGM. What had been a trickle before now became a steady stream for the next 15 years, even branching out in that very year with the fantasy comedy *Topper Takes a Trip* (MGM), a sequel to *Topper* (MGM, 1937), and the musical fantasy *The Wizard of Oz* (MGM). In melodramatic fantasy, the unknown is highlighted with its attendant fear and stress, as we shall see. Fantasy comedy, on the other hand, revels in the incongruity in the juxtaposition of two different realms, pointing up the deviation of the real from the ideal in the belief that what hopelessly is (the real) can come closer, approximate, or even match what hopefully could or should be (the ideal). The juxtaposition also encapsulates the conformity/real world-uniqueness/ideal world debate. In musical fantasy's agenda, alternative reality is presented as the transformation of the real world shown to be in the protagonist's reach.

The hybrid fantasy-melodrama/comedy/musical went into high gear throughout the forties until the mid-fifties when religious fervor was high. World War II and its aftermath nourished belief or, at the very least, the desire to believe in the reality of an afterlife, presented as having definite connections with our own world, in order to assuage the death of loved ones in the war and provide clear-cut guidelines, especially moral ones, in the postwar time of shifting values. Fantasy's inhabitants (God and Satan/angels and devils/

incarnated consciences/ghosts or the dearly departed/miracle workers/religious people/Kriss Kringle) and/or its settings (Heaven, Hell) often operated as a metaphor for the highly popular Freudian superego–id construct within the protagonist.

Capra's 1946 career-peaking and period-demarcating *It's a Wonderful Life* at once epitomized his utopian populist vision and soberly questioned it while spilling over into fantasy. Clarence, an angel in need of wings, is sent by St. Joseph to answer the fervid prayers of the folks in Bedford Falls. There, friends and family are worried about crazed George Bailey who, on this snowy Christmas Eve, stands on a bridge, eyeing the roiling black waters below.

Effectively refashioned by Capra and Goodrich and Hackett from a story by Philip Van Doren Stern and stirringly brought to life by a postwar redefined James Stewart, the suicidal common man Bailey captured the locked-away frustration, desperation, and hysteria of the American male at this time when things were becoming too much to bear. A tale in which the starry heavens mixed easily with a down-to-earth small town, where reality was at once past, present, and possible, *It's a Wonderful Life*, idealistic and sardonic, sentimental and clear-eyed, jabbed at the very classical norms it embraced.

Fox's dozen or so fantasy-comedies were the most heartfelt. In *The Ghost and Mrs. Muir* (1947), Philip Dunne's adaptation of the R. S. Dick novel immaculately incarnated by Mankiewicz, the spirit of a deceased sea captain (Harrison) materializes to aid financially and romantically a widow (Gene Tierney) who had bought his former home. *The Miracle on 34th Street* (1947), director Seaton's own Oscar-winning adaptation of Valentine Davies's story, was blessed with a genial old man (Oscar-nabbing support Edmund Gwenn) who seems actually to be whom he claims to be – Kriss Kringle. Seaton's documentary-realist style, including actual footage of the Macy's Thanksgiving Day parade, grounded the fantasy, making the outrageous conceit appear at least probable. In *Come to the Stable* (1949), Oscar Millard and Sally Benson's screenplay of Clare Boothe Luce's story, two French nuns (Loretta Young and Celeste Holm) keep their promise to God and build a hospital in Bethlehem, Connecticut in return for a children's hospital being spared from the war's bombing. In *For Heaven's Sake* (1950), Seaton's adaptation of a Harry Segall play, an angel (Webb) patches the marital rift of a childless theater couple (Robert Cummings and Joan Bennett) and, in turn, is saved from the road to perdition by a fellow angel (Gwenn). Fox director Henry Koster was most associated with the subform. In addition to *Stable*, and *The Luck of the Irish* (1948) in which a leprechaun (Cecil Kellaway) embodies a newsman's conscience (Tyrone Power), Koster went on loanout to RKO for the Fox-like *The Bishop's Wife* (1947), where an angel (Grant) answers a cleric's (David Niven) call for guidance, then to Universal for *Harvey* (1950).

Avoiding Fox's whimsy and the light satire of both the ardent believer and agnostic, Universal opted for the wacky, wherein the collision of the "impossible" with the human sets off farcical sparks. For *Mr. Peabody and the Mermaid* (1948), Fox's Nunnally Johnson retailored Guy and Constance Jones's novel about a staid married Bostonian (William Powell) hooking and falling in love with a mermaid (Ann Blyth). In the *Francis* series (seven of them in 1950–6), David Stern's adaptation of his own novel, Donald O'Connor interacts with a mule who talks. *Harvey*, Mary Chase's own reworking (with Oscar Brodney) of her Pulitzer Prize-winning stage success, deals with an inebriate (Stewart) and his constant companion, a six-foot rabbit inhabited by a pooka (a spirit in animal form that appears every now and then, especially to nonconforming crackpots). *You Never Can Tell* (1951) was Lou Breslow's account of a murdered dog which returns to earth in human form (Dick Powell) to trap his killer. In the Fox facsimile *Sally and St. Anne* (1952), a James O'Hanlon and Herb Meadows tale, the mother of the Blessed Virgin saves an Irish family (Gwenn as head) from losing its home. In *It Grows on Trees* (1952) by Leonard Praskins and Barney Slater, Irene Dunne owns a $10-sprouting backyard tree.

By the early fifties, fantasy-comedy's deus ex machina increasingly involved material gain and success, and the films pointed out that the wish come true was not all that it was cracked up to be. Later, the subtype took a scientific and technological spin wherein the academic/inventor protagonist comes up with some far-fetched concoction. *The Absent-Minded Professor* (BV, 1961) invents a gooey, gravity-resistance substance, "Flubber," that makes things fly. Relying on farce and special effects, this modification severed the subform's spiritual roots, pointing to the secular direction it was to take.

14.6   Comedian Comedy

Uttering its last gasps was comedian comedy, in which a pre-filmic popular comedian, retaining aspects of his persona and performance, is placed in a loose fictional context. Affronting classical notions of plot and characterization by having the comedian incarnate the preexisting persona while barely attempting to portray the story's character, comedian comedy also undermined movies' representational acting style by encouraging active spectatorship with the performer's asides and address to the camera.[1]

Holdover Bob Hope continued at Paramount until 1957, but his 13 straight years as box-office heavyweight ended in 1953. His postwar movies (particularly *The Great Lover*, 1949, and *The Lemon Drop Kid*, 1951), though essentially Hope vehicles, with his assumption of the cowardly pose and masterly delivery of one-liners, were attempts at plot and character solidity intended to extend his range. More successful in this crossover from comedian to comic actor was Danny Kaye, exceptional as the daydreaming milquetoast whose nagging mother, pouting fiancée, and Air Force-reject status undermine his masculinity in *The Secret Life of Walter Mitty* (RKO, 1947). Producer Goldwyn overdecorated James Thurber's *New Yorker* story with fantasy sequences galore (each a parody of a film genre) in which Kaye showcased his forte (mimicry, tongue-twisting songs, rubber puss, and posture) while interweaving a spy thriller that caricatured the dream sequences. By the time of the social satire *Me and the Colonel* (C, 1958), based on Franz Werfel and S. N. Behrman's play, in which Kaye's Jewish refugee from the Nazis is stripped of all his shtick, the switch was complete.

Dean Martin and Jerry Lewis, the new duo on the Paramount block succeeding Crosby and Hope, stayed in the groove – a decision undoubtedly dictated by their fiscal clout. Through 16 films from *My Friend Irma* (1949) to *Hollywood or Bust* (1956), their crooning straight-man/schlep buddy routines, dotting a flimsy plot with little wit, were aesthetically zilch. Lewis's persona of a manic weakling, however, brought male emotion and insecurity out in the open, in his duos with Martin and his subsequent solo work (*The Delinquent Debutante*, 1957, through *The Family Jewels*, 1965).

On an even lower rung of the aesthetic ladder were holdover buddies Bud Abbott and Lou Costello, who made 29 movies at Universal from 1940 to 1955 strictly for the GI, adolescent, and kiddie trade. Lean and tall, Abbott was the straight man, forever grumbling about and chastising short, tub-of-lard Costello, a cowardly, nervous, easily frightened pantywaist prone to all sorts of perils from encountering Frankenstein through being auctioned as a slave girl to being caught up in a hillbilly clan war. This Laurel and Hardy retread repeated their four times box-office win between 1941 and 1944 in 1948–51.

14.7   Black Comedy

Black comedy, gaining steam, points its finger at those situations and institutions meant to help, heal, bring humans together (friendship, sex, marriage, family, religion, small-town communities, government, the military, a country's defense systems, a hospital, the media, a death in the family, etc.), and proceeds to show how these very structures not only pull humans apart, but fragment them in the severest way possible. Black comedy fixates on this shocking irony, with utmost glee and dispassion (extreme exaggeration and distance are prerequisites). As such, it displaces the *Sturm und Drang* tone of essentially melodramatic material with a ghastly funny, contemptuously cool one. Implying that nothing can be done about these appalling instances of fragmentation except laugh at them, black comedy is extremely cynical.

Chaplin's *Monsieur Verdoux* (UA, 1947) tells of a modern-day Bluebeard. In director-writer Claude Binyon's *Stella* (TCF, 1950), based on Davis Miles Disney's novel, an alcoholic uncle fatally hits his head on a rock while punching out a relative at a family picnic. An impromptu burial and coverup follow to avoid murder charges and funeral expenses. Upon discovering that the uncle carried a double-indemnity insurance policy, measures become even more desperate for the family. In *The Gazebo* (MGM, 1959), George Wells's adaptation of Alec Coppel's play, a TV writer-director of mysteries shoots (or presumes to shoot) a blackmailer and hides the corpse after self-reflexively gaining advice from a criminal lawyer friend and colleague Hitchcock. In *Lolita* (MGM, 1962), Nabokov's own film rendition of his novel directed by Kubrick, obsession mistaken for love leads to all kinds of death.

14.8   Parody

Parody is an affectionate shafting of cinematic manners (not social ones, as in satire) which also are exaggerated in presentation, ripping classic Hollywood style's seamlessness (the adventure film send-up *Double Crossbones*, U, 1951, with Donald O'Connor). Part of film comedy's silent and classical past, parody continued, now that the industry and audience were enlarging their knowledge of film history through TV reruns and its variety shows which usually offered a condensed movie parody. To wring some variation from the formula, parody often infused comedian comedy, as in Abbott and Costello's *The Wistful Widow of Wagon Gap* (U, 1947) – the western – or Bob Hope's *My Favorite Spy* (P, 1951) – the thriller. More and more, parody found its way into sequences of films (Wilder's *From Here to Eternity* beach scene in *The Seven Year Itch*; throughout Tashlin's work).

Note

1   Steve Seidman, *Comedian Comedy: A Tradition In Hollywood Film* (UMI Research Press, 1981) isolated and defined the subform.

15

Horror, Science Fiction, and Fantasy

Except for Universal, horror was not a priority A or B item at the majors during the thirties. With the studios' collapse and decline in product, the making of horror films was even less on their minds. For instance, RKO's Val Lewton B-horror unit, responsible for nine shivery works that at once recalled the genre's past and anticipated its future, came to a screaming halt with *Bedlam* in 1946, four years after the series began. In addition, the heightened "realisms," the in-vogue styles of postwar Hollywood, as we shall see, clashed with horror's "expressionism." Literal statements on man's tangible, verifiable societal relations were "in." "Out" was horror's purview of man treading unknown, forbidden, repressed, and infrequently delved-into waters, be they physical, psychological, supernatural, preternatural, or post-natural, wherein the would-be knower encounters "the monstrous," as either part of life or having created the monstrous or becoming the monster. Only when the unknown involved the scientific was interest sparked, resulting in an alliance with *au courant* science fiction that trotted out the trendy documentary realist style and occasionally resorted to 3-D. Horror also submitted to a cheap, strictly-for-the-kids AIP rejuvenation. Finally, taking hold of itself, it went existentially modern: recognizably real, engagingly topical.

15.1   Horror–Science Fiction

Both the monster horror–sci-fi hybrid (an update of the creator–creature myth, as in the Frankenstein cycle) and the end-of-the-world horror–sci-fi hybrid shared the same plot and conflictual strategy. Crises such as scientific research and technology (atomic energy testing or space exploration) gone amok, or an invasion from outer space, or nature out of kilter, produce a monster (a species of spider, sea inhabitant, prehistoric beast, space alien, or unfortunate human

205

being) and/or the world's termination. Going up against the monster, or attempting to keep the planet from exploding, or coping with survival after an atomic holocaust that must be attended to post haste constitute the various conflicts. Scientist, politician, journalist, military policeman, FBI agent, sheriff, religious leader, and scientist's daughter or female student people the monster horror–sci-fi cycle. A gamut of types (consistently, a religious person, pregnant woman or mother with a child, a black man) inhabits the end-of-the-world edition. The films' conservative ideology took a negative view of science (actually, the use of hard science and logical speculation were negligible), urging a return to traditional values, especially religious ones. Feeding off fifties' xenophobia and the resultant valorization of conformity, particularly Cold War/atomic bomb paranoia, these movies functioned allegorically, the monster a metaphor for the stranger, specifically the bomb-possessing, atheistic commie "from another world" bent on America's annihilation.

The Thing (RKO, 1951), directed by Christian Nyby under producer Hawks's substantive guidance, kicked off the monster cycle. Inspired by John W. Campbell, Jr.'s story, *The Thing* turned out to be a vegetative alien threatening a party of military, scientists, and press in the Arctic. A disembodied eye embedded in a block of ice, a severed hand that moves, sled dogs drained of blood, breath vapors from the humans, and the stentorian voiceover of the finale warning us to "watch the skies" chilled the bones. The plot was given an ambivalent twist with the Don Siegel-directed *Invasion of the Body Snatchers* (AA, 1956). Based on a popular serial in *Collier's* magazine and Jack Finney's novel, the invasion in question occurs in the small community of Santa Mira, California where alien pods, empowered to replace human beings with soulless simulacra, take over. Allegory certainly, but did the aliens stand for the communist takeover of the US or the dehumanizing evil of fifties' conformism, or both?

Jack Arnold (1916–92), ex-actor turned documentary filmmaker before signing on with Universal in the early fifties, established himself as a director who brought something passionately personal with the 3-D *It Came from Outer Space* (1953), the second Ray Bradbury adaptation that year following *The Beast from 20,00 Fathoms* at WB. Arnold followed his commercial hit with the 3-D *The Creature from the Black Lagoon* (1954), the 3-D sequel *Revenge of the Creature* (1955 – the third entry *The Creature Walks Among Us*, 1956, was directed by John Sherwood), *The Incredible Shrinking Man* (1957), *Monster on the Campus* (1958), and *The Space Children* (P, 1958). Without heart and mind, Arnold implied, technology could undermine a person's humanity, especially wiping out the idiosyncrasies that make one a unique individual (here again, the straying or staying option). Science and technology were a mixed blessing for Arnold, as they were for many Americans by mid-decade.

Marking the monster horror–sci-fi cycle's popularity, along with Arnold's work, was *Them!* (WB, 1954). The Ted Sherdeman original, matter-of-factly directed by Gordon Douglas, featured desert ants made gigantic and ravenous after atomic bomb testing. *The Fly*, a James Clavell contrivance directed by Kurt Neumann in CinemaScope/Deluxe Color, about a scientist who reintegrates himself with the head of a fly that intruded upon his teleportation experiment, was Fox's sleeper of 1958, spawning two sequels, *Return of the Fly* (1959) and *Curse of the Fly* (1965).

Neither as plentiful nor as exciting as the monster cycle, the end-of-the-world horror–sci-fi series was ignited by producer-director Arch Oboler's *Five* (C, 1951), depicting nuclear holocaust survivors. Producer George Pal's Paramount duo, *When Worlds Collide* (1951) and the H. G. Wells-rooted *War of the Worlds* (1953), added heat to the cycle with the addition of Technicolor, crisp direction by Bryon Haskin, and elaborate effects. Of *War's* $2-million budget, $1.3 million, in fact, were blown on Gordon Jennings's Oscar-winning special effects. Pal went for the visceral, whereas the nuclear holocaust-themed *The World, the Flesh and the Devil* (MGM, 1959) with Harry Belafonte and producer-director Stanley Kramer's *On the Beach* (UA, 1959), with Gregory Peck, from Nevil Shute's disquieting novel, opted for the didactic ("there is still time . . . brother").

15.2   AIP Teenage Horror

AIP's economical take ($100,000 a pop) was to tailor the classic myths for the emergent teenage market. A troubled youth regressed by a shrink was the nub of *I Was a Teenage Werewolf* (1957). With a $1 million gross, despite its distribution on the lower half of a double bill with the upper *Invasion of the Saucer Men* and its Legioned B rating, the film instated the teen monster cycle. Fast on its heels followed *I Was a Teenage Frankenstein* (1957), in which the creature was assembled from bodies of dead hot-rodders. Next up, *I Was a Teenage Mummy* (1962). Even in AIP's version of the current horror–sci-fi flicks, teen-ager protagonists went to battle to save the earth (*Attack of the Giant Gila Monster*, 1959).

Producer-director Roger Corman's (1926) line, however, was noteworthy, shot though with a wry humor that turned self-reflexive at times. In *A Bucket of Blood* (1959), an inept busboy's critically-acclaimed "work of art" (he had covered in clay a cat he accidentally impaled) inspires a series of killings. A goofy florist's assistant nurtures a carnivorous plant who talks real mean in *The Little Shop of Horrors* (1961). It was, however, with the reimagining of Edgar Allen Poe (seven items, from *The House of Usher*, 1960, to *The Masque of the Red Death*, 1964) that Corman's style became more distinctive.

In the series, Corman centered upon the crumblings of a degenerate adult world of power and privilege, invariably presided over by that figure of authority Vincent Price. Price's handsome visage, impeccable manners, and eloquence delivered in a beguilingly gentle voice belied demons that raged within – a cultural surface–substance metaphor, this. Corman's use of Price clinched the actor's status as the era's definitive horror presence. Of course, it was all overripe and amusing (parodic on one level) but a heartfelt respect for the spirit of what Poe intended was never lost. In addition to the depiction of decadence, despair, and the fatality of evil, the Corman/Poe lot affectively broached the awful meaninglessness of people's lives.

15.3   Modern Horror

Hitchcock's landmark *Psycho* (P, 1960) revolutionized horror by putting the modern detective and middle-class felon thrillers into a haunted house, causing it to rattle with pertinent existential concerns. Further: by extending the boundaries of the representation of violence, *Psycho* dropped the major studio film smack dab into the exploitational arena where it has since burrowed in. And by spicing the mix with an outré black humor that demythified sex, marriage, capitalism, the American home, mom, cops, car salesmen, and, self-reflexively, the genre itself and classical narrative (with its handful of unsympathetic characters, its continual stopping and starting up again, emphasis on subjectivity, and no ending), *Psycho* changed the very axis of horror and American movies as well. Recall: it also altered exhibition.

The nature of horror was no longer external to man or metaphorical.[1] It was here, now, real. Set in present-day Arizona and California, *Psycho* dealt with the devastating effect of the implosion of an all-American boy-next-door type in a crew-neck sweater (Anthony Perkins) munching candy corn, the kind of person that crosses our paths several times a day. No typical monster, he. As a matter of fact, Robert Block's novel, *Psycho*'s source adapted by Joseph Stefano, was based on the actual 1959 crimes of Ed Gein, a harmless Wisconsin handyman, middle-aged and overweight, discovered to be a serial murderer, grave robber, and cannibal, complete with a mother problem. Obviously, in making the protagonist young and attractive and in the use of constant point-of-view shots, Hitchcock began the process of identification with Perkins. As the film proceeds, however, the process is shattered by second thoughts and misgivings. Ploys such as these, of course, made the film even more stressfully unsettling.

In *Psycho*, additionally, the explanation of horror did not reside, as in the classics, with the invocation of God or science (Derry) or even with the psychological, for that matter. Yes, the film's finale did have a shrink go on and on about Oedipal trauma, sexual repression, and identity confusion but in such a dull, facilely clinical fashion that it came off as too pat (and darkly satirical) to accept, let alone pay attention to after the shocking penultimate scene. No, the protagonist's own pop-philosophizing: "we all go a little mad sometimes" was a more believable explanation, supported as it was by the film's sudden shifts. But, if you come right down to it, his pronouncement was no explanation at all. Quite matter of factly, things just happen, and if they do (and the film implied they did), then closure, upbeat conclusion, and logical explanation are inoperative. At the film's heart was a cynical vision of a meaningless, absurd universe in which God's providence and retribution were nowhere to be found.

The graphically presented shower, staircase, and cellar mayhem, coming out of nowhere, also unnerved, causing in the spectator not only the genre's usual horror or shudder affect but shock as well. Here was the unmistakable start of the film-as-sensation aesthetic that would eventually grip Hollywood. This was something new, as was the use of five unsympathetic leads (Perkins is an anally-fixated psychotic; Janet Leigh a fornicator and a thief; the detective Martin Balsam a cellophane man; Leigh's lover John Gavin and sister Vera Miles, who wears a hideous wig, wooden and leaden) and a gallery of dislikable supports, from the crass millionaire to the gruff sheriff. There is no one in the film to sympathize with, no one to open our hearts and minds to. And yet, this is what going to the movies was supposedly all about, becoming one with the people on the screen, making pacts, forging alliances, forming community at least for a little while. Well, with *Psycho*, Hitchcock changed all that. He disconnected us, severing our relationship to the people on the screen, setting us adrift, just as he did with all his characters (Perkins to Leigh: "We're all in our private traps and not one of us gets out"). In so doing, Hitchcock sabotaged the moviegoing experience in yet another way.

Business-wise, Hitchcock, in the late fifties, had been intrigued by AIP's upward spiraling stock from its production of cheapie exploitational horrors. When Paramount agreed to distribute what they labeled "lurid and trashy" only after Hitchcock agreed to finance the film himself via his TV banner Shamley Prods., the maestro decided to indulge his intrigue and keep costs down. Eschewing the Vista Vision/Technicolor-location splendors of his previous Paramounts, Hitchcock shot the film small screen/b/w on Revue's soundstages (Universal's TV subsidiary), essentially with his TV show crew, wannabes, and an on-the-wane leading lady.

A slew of exploitative rip-offs (William Castle's *Homicidal*, C, 1961) and imitations (the remake *The Cabinet of Dr. Caligari*, TCF, 1962) immediately trailed in the dust of *Psycho*'s commercial stampede (an $800,000 investment netted $11.2 million first time around). Director Robert Aldrich's *Whatever*

Happened to Baby Jane? (WB, 1962), with Bette Davis and Joan Crawford as has-been movie star sisters locked in a sick sadomasochistic relationship, extended the *Psycho* formula with its self-conscious use of Gothic grotesquerie, movie history, and the spectator's apperceptive mass of the actors involved. Because of *Psycho*, horror films were headed uptown: A actors, craftsmen, and budgets.

15.4   Science Fiction

The strong showing of three films galvanized the possibility of A status for relatively new sci-fi. First off the pad came independent Robert Lippert's *Rocket Ship X-M* (Lippert, 1950), director-writer Kurt Neumann's tale of the first manned rocketship to the moon that goes off course and lands on a devastated Mars. Having an even bigger impact was Pal's Technicolored *Destination Moon* (EL, 1950), directed by Irving Pichel. Robert Heinlein coauthored the screenplay based on his own novel. Most compelling of all was *The Day the Earth Stood Still* (TCF, 1951), Edmund H. North's adaptation of Harry Bates's space-age Christ story, directed by Robert Wise. Their B budgets ($74,000, $600,000, and $960,000, respectively) saw A recoups ($2 million, $2.5 million, and $1.85 million). The postwar intrigue with technology, experiments in rocketry, the mushrooming space industry, UFO sightings, and the youth market which had already made sci-fi pulp and sci-fi comic books successful literary enterprises, explained, in part, sci-fi's appeal. Special effects advances in model animation, stop-motion photography and traveling matte work ensured this appeal. The genre's commercial and (at times) critical stature notwithstanding, the industry continued to perceive the genre primarily for young people. Kubrick's *2001: A Space Odyssey* (MGM, 1968) would eventually change their minds.

Despite the similarity of sci-fi's conflictual strategy with that of horror, they are distinct forms, as scholars John Baxter, who also noted a difference between sci-fi literature and sci-fi film, Bruce Kawin and Vivian Sobchack have eloquently demonstrated.[2] The object of the unknown is different. Sci-fi's realm deals with the possible, whether future technology, space/time exploration, or the existence of the inhuman/alien. Its scientific premise is backed by a reasonable amount of hard science and logical speculation. Its plot gives way to an adventurous exploration of some kind. All this assails horror's focus on the scientifically suspect regions of the supernatural/primordial/unconscious or subconscious. Furthermore, the attitude toward the unknown is different. In sci-fi, curiosity is positive and the danger lies in the irresponsibility of a closed mind whereas in horror, curiosity is negative, concerned as it is with the dreadful consequences of knowing. A reversal of horror's situation, sci-fi's liberal

15-1 *Destination Moon* (EL, 1950, p. George Pal)

The crystallization of science fiction enlarges the terrain of postwar Hollywood movies.

faction wipes out the conservative side. Lastly, the relatively new genre is to some extent ideational: issues and ideas are equal to or, sometimes, take precedence over individuals in action.

Sci-fi's ideational bent explains in part why major players rarely appeared. The genre's preponderance of f/x was another. Its ideational bent, which runs the risk of being too talky, was also the reason behind the industry's preference for sci-fi hybrids rather than the real thing.

Besides mixing with horror, sci-fi also got hooked into adventure, as with *This Island Earth* (U, 1955), Franklin Coen and Edward O'Callahan's adaptation of Raymond F. Jon's novel directed by Joseph Newman in Technicolor, where aliens from Metaluna come to earth to recruit scientists to help them find a new source of atomic energy, or *Journey to the Center of the Earth* (TCF, 1959), Walter Reisch and Charles Brackett's reworking of Jules Verne, directed by Henry Levin in CinemaScope/Deluxe Color. A mystery structure (who is the monster?) was added to *Forbidden Planet* (MGM, 1956), Cyril Hume's space-age *The Tempest*, set in a colony on the star Altair IV in AD 2200 featuring Robbie the Robot (think Ariel); so was Freud (the monster is none other than Walter Pidgeon/Prospero's id). Despite the ingredients, the film, directed by

Fred M. Wilcox, got soporific at times with its elaborate explanations of futuristic technology. Its use of color, however, to show technology's function as well as to depict the monster was eye-alerting, as was the occasional decentering within the CinemaScope frame.

15.5　Fantasy

Most fantasies were mired in pietism (*The Miracle of the Bells*, RKO, 1948), didacticism (*The Boy with Green Hair*, RKO, 1949, a soapbox for producer Schary's anti-war polemic), or sentimentality (*I'll Never Forget You*, TCF, 1951, a remake of *Berkeley Square*, Fox, 1933). Two were exceptional. In *Portrait of Jennie* (SRO, 1949), an artist (Joseph Cotten) with not "a drop of life in his paintings" finds his inspiration in a spectral figure (Jennifer Jones aging convincingly from teenager to young woman) who materializes in and out of Central Park looking for someone to love. Peter Berneis and Paul Osborn's adaptation of Robert Nathan's novel, deliberately skirting cause and effect and explanations, perturbed. Equally so did the eerie expressionist rendering of Gotham locations by ex-German expressionist William Dieterle; the color experimentation at the climax of the b/w film (a green-tinted hurricane, an orange-tinted recovery, a Technicolor portrait of Jennie); Dimitri Tiomkin's tinkly scoring of Debussy, and the atypically placed credit sequence at the film's end. *Alias Nick Beal* (P, 1949) was Jonathan Latimer's modern Faust tale, convincingly executed by John Farrow, in which an upright politician (Thomas Mitchell) is tempted by a mysterious stranger who happens to be the devil incarnate (Ray Milland) to give up his anti-crime campaign. This noir blend of gangster underworld and spirit netherworld intoxicated.

Notes

1　Chuck Derry, in his seminal work on horror films of the sixties and seventies, *Dark Dreams: A Psychological History of the Modern Horror Film* (Cranbury, NJ, 1977), called this new type of horror film "the horror of personality."

2　For a fuller appreciation of sci-fi and its distinction from horror, see John Baxter, *Science Fiction in Cinema* (New York: A. S. Barnes, 1970), Bruce Kawin, "Children of the Light," in *Film/Genre/Reader*, ed. Brian Keith Grant (Austin: University of Texas Press, 1986, 236–57), as well as Vivian Sobchack, *Screening Space: the American Science Fiction Film* (New York: Ungar, 1980).

16

Melodrama

16.1   Family Melodrama

Between *A Tree Grows in Brooklyn* (TCF, 1945) and *Who's Afraid of Virginia Woolf?* (WB, 1966), Hollywood's infatuation with the social institution of the family itself as subject and conflict reached an obsessional level. In fact, it was *the* defining genre of the time.

Actually, *The Little Foxes* (RKO, 1941) was the curtain-raiser. Crafted by leftist playwright Lillian Hellman from her stage smash and directed by Wyler, *The Little Foxes* are the Hubbards, second-generation Southern carpetbaggers around the turn of the twentieth century (bachelor brother, married brother and his son, and their married sister). With an unbounded greed, they use all others, even their own family, for profit. The film's coruscating portrait of capitalism, class stratification (from aristocrat sister-in-law to the "yes-suh" black servants), and the American family was hailed as something new. Its wartime release made the film shocking and that shock was not ameliorated by the adaptational addition of the character of a young reporter for comic relief and a heterosexual romance with the sister's daughter.

Since fiction, stage, and TV found family roilings a topic that paid dividends, all the competitively concerned studios (independents too), through adaptation and imitation, bought shares. MGM, C, TCF, WB, and P (in that order) led the way, with U and UA not far behind, while RKO brought up the rear. In addition, the genre had possible appeal to both males and females in just about every age group, comprising, as it did, the senior-to-kid character spectrum and a conflict colored by the clash of people of different generations locked in the same space. The genre, too, was a shoo-in for the industry's business scheme of pairing established performers (parents) with newcomers (children) within the same movie.

Material from the likes of Tennessee Williams and John Steinbeck endowed the product with cultural prestige – after money, the industry's second most doggedly pursued item. That the material was hawked as an example of the "new realism" sweeping American arts and the media, which the industry took to mean also "controversial" and "steamy," added further incentive. To the liberally enlightened, material such as this also provided a legitimate way to loosen the hold of censorship, helping movies grow up. The critically acclaimed Method provided a perfect conduit for the presentation of this material on stage and TV and many Method actors were part of the film package, bringing a mesmerizing type of acting and player to the screen. The movie mounting often involved lionized stage and TV directors reprising their original work. Staying on and shoring up the eroding Hollywood ranks, many pursued the form. The genre's wide appeal soon encouraged Hollywood alumni and newcomers to try their hands at it as well.

Family melodrama sired five basic plot and conflictual strategies, at times intertwined within the same film. Predominant was the outsider as disruptive element, stirring up sub rosa tensions within and between family members, forcing festering, below-the-surface issues out in the open, all the while offering a critical perspective on the unit. A metaphor for the era's xenophobia and the surface–substance dialectic, the outsider, through interpersonal and intra-personal confrontations and evaluation, brings about family realignment or destruction. Family melodrama, as with the female and romance branches, tends to unfold within the private space of the family or that of the romantic couple, with only nods to the workplace (a constant setting in the male melodrama). Within that private space, family melodrama, as with other subforms, is primarily concerned with the highs and lows of personal feelings.

The stranger, the most severe instance of outsidedness, proved the family's sharpest critic. From the vantage points of distance (coming as he or she did from the outside) as well as class, sensibility, and sometimes age differences, the stranger pointed up the soul-withering effects of patriarchal capitalism on the family unit, with women as second-class citizens and children as parental extensions, often reckoned as objects for the accumulation of wealth, security, and power. The stranger found the family stagnating in the outmoded, valueless beliefs of the community in which it was inscribed, a hotbed of provincialism, intolerance, hypocrisy, and repression, especially sexual. The stranger could spot, often illuminate, and invariably aggravate the cracks in a marriage. A modified countercultural figure, the stranger who, it is to be noted, did not arrive on the doorstep problem-free, anticipated the sixties hippie.

The stranger could be an itinerant. In the Nicholas Ray-directed *The Lusty Men* (RKO, 1952), penned by cowboy David Dortort and Horace McCoy, an over-the-hill Texas rodeo star (Robert Mitchum) attaches himself to a married couple (Susan Hayward and Arthur Kennedy), igniting the husband's dream turned obsession of quick bucks on the rodeo circuit (to hell with the farm and his wife's desires). The stranger even makes a play for the wife. A roving reporter (Rock Hudson) covers a family of flyers performing in a New Orleans air show in the Sirk-guided *The Tarnished Angels* (U, 1958), George Zuckerman's transformation of Faulkner's *Pylon*. Out for "a human interest story," the journalist offers his apartment to the troupe of gypsies, comprising an ex-World War I flying ace/husband (Robert Stack), his parachute-jumping wife (Dorothy Malone), and a mechanic (Jack Carson) who has fathered a boy with the wife. The encounter dredges up bitter memories, nostalgia for one's roots, jealousies, and identity realignment. A wandering guitarist (Marlon Brando) is directed to a dingy Mississippi five-and-dime as a possible clerk in Sidney Lumet's *The Fugitive Kind* (UA, 1960), Williams's co-adaptation of his stage piece. While attempting to rescue the shopkeeper wife (Anna Magnani) from her hellish existence, he sets free the town's alcoholic tramp (Joanne Woodward).

Most famously of all, foolhardy hobo-gigolo (William Holden) wakes up the white picket-fenced home of mother, daughters, and spinster schoolteacher-boarder (Betty Field, Kim Novak, Susan Strasberg, and Rosalind Russell) in a sleepy Kansas town in *Picnic* (C, 1955), Daniel Taradash's respectful version of William Inge's (1917–73) masterwork. *Picnic* was vintage Inge territory: the Midwest, lower middle-class people living lives of quiet desperation. The grand-motherly neighbor, who cares for her own invalid mother, is the unofficial spokeswoman: "I feel sort of excited . . . I think we plan picnics just to give an excuse – to let something thrilling happen in our lives." In this four-generational "family" of ladies (within the house and next door), each is isolated, quietly fearful that more of the same is to come, sad that the past can't be retrieved and lived again, this time in a different way. Each hides the stress from observing the day-in-day-out routine and putting on appearances. Sex can relieve the tedium for a while; love for even longer. But sex and love, as these ladies know, require compromise and humility.

The specificity could only have come from someone who was there, and Inge was. Born in Independence, Kansas, he was raised primarily by his mother; his traveling salesman father took to the road. Sensitive, introspective, and gay, Inge sought escape in school dramatics and silent movies before studying at the University of Kansas. After some years as a teacher and newspaper arts critic, he took a crack at stage writing. *Picnic* was only his second play.

As with his other work, *Picnic* was all character, human behavior, and motivation, carefully caught in everyday life, each character complete with backstory and dream life. These characters, invariably a family, become shaken up by a stranger (the prototypical Inge situation). Moreover, there were no villains; no heroes either. As such, Inge's work witnessed a break with classical Hollywood storytelling with its driving thrust of a strong plot and good guy–bad guy demarcation.

From a potpourri of Method players (Field, Strasberg, and Cliff Robertson as Novak's beau), seasoned performer Arthur O'Connell as Russell's gentleman, Hollywood professionals (Holden and Russell), and new studio contractee Novak, Joshua Logan (1908–88), director of the footlight version, who had studied under Stanislavsky in Russia, molded a masterful ensemble, each member adhering to the measured Midwest intonation and pace. Russell's schoolteacher, in particular, unfalteringly brought home Inge's character complexity. Arousedly pulling up Holden's pants to see his legs, she showed the desperation behind the drollery. And poignancy never undermined the rage as she faced up to her aging: "Look at that sunset . . . it's like the day didn't want to end, like the daytime was going to put up a big scrap to keep the night from coming on."

Master cinematographer James Wong Howe guided Logan's eye (it was Logan's first solo movie). Both registered ineffaceable Technicolor location-shot images that understood CinemaScope, as with the blend of actors and actual locals during the picnic. *Picnic* was one of the first works to eschew the genre's usual b/w/flat-screen/studio-shot format. Equally pleasurable and commercially savvy was George Duning's lush, wistful score that interlaced the old standard "Moonglow" during the sensuous Holden–Novak dance on the dock, strung with Japanese lanterns against a pitch-black sky. All melodrama indulges in full-bodied musical scores that punctuate the scene's emotional aura. Such a convention is intended to lock in the audience's identification with character, particularly by getting the audience to feel what the character feels. The excess of emotion and affect is one of the melodrama's intentions, be it in terms of music or sound effects or other formal elements such as visual design (here with décor and color), composition, and/or editing. In melodrama, formal hyper-reality is at the service of rendering thematic reality more significant and absorbing while objectifying the subjective.

Family melodrama's outsider could also be a co-worker, as in Williams's *The Glass Menagerie* (WB, 1950), or director-writer George Seaton's reworking of Clifford Odets's play *The Country Girl* (P, 1954), in which a director (Holden) stages the Broadway comeback of an aging, alcoholic musical actor (Crosby, playing against type) while making a play for his wife (Oscar-winning Grace Kelly). Sometimes, the stranger was a new neighbor (newlyweds Jeffrey Hunter and Patricia Owens; Japanese-American Aki Aleong) on a Southern California suburban block (*No Down Payment*, TCF, 1957). In director Martin Ritt and writer Philip Yordan's incisive reworking of John McParland's novel, the confrontation exposes the angst brought on by credit-card debt to keep up with the Joneses, sexual repression, promiscuity leading to rape, and prejudice.

The relative of a neighbor (Burt Lancaster) stirs the pot in *The Rose Tattoo* (P, 1955), set in a seedy Sicilian village on the Gulf Coast, palpably rendered by Oscar-winning lenser Howe. Looking for an older, established woman to give him a home, he unlocks the repression of a widow (Oscar-winning Magnani, in her American debut), imprisoned for three years within her foolish dream of her late husband that has soured her life and that of her high-school daughter (Marisa Pavan). The interloper's irrepressible humor and unbridled sensuality make the widow face facts: her "wild-as-a-gypsy" husband had been having a year-long affair, and was a smuggler; she has been repressing her daughter. Melodrama loves to reveal secrets, which come in all shapes and sizes (adultery, criminality, murder, a sexless marriage, or one of convenience, illegitimacy, perjury, alcohol/drug addiction, insanity, financial failure, injustice, etc.).

This Williams coadaptation with Hal Kanter, directed by Daniel Mann, who piloted the play, even added more iconic moments of "hysteria" to which melodrama is prone. In addition to the widow's fainting, screaming, suicide attempts, madness, and the bruising bachelor's falling on his knees asking forgiveness, *The Rose Tattoo* flaunts a slugfest between the widow and the mistress at a local bar's blackjack table. Williams even parodies the genre's convention of hysteria by having the daughter's teacher reprimand the widow: "Let's have no outbursts of emotion." In melodrama, hysteria occurs when a character is most suppressed, and usually in the most public of places, where many people observe the private moment. Such an irony only heightens the hysteria.

The boarder was another breed of outsider: the Arthur Miller-sourced *A View from the Bridge* (Cocinor, 1961); Briton Peter Shaffer's schematized play *Five Finger Exercise* (C, 1962), where the boarder is a tutor; the Inge-based *The Stripper* (TCF, 1962) and, most touching of all, his *Come Back, Little Sheba* (P, 1952), interpreted again by Howe, writer Kitti Frings, and original stage director Daniel Mann, also responsible for *Five Finger Exercise*. Here, a collegian (Terry Moore) rents a room in the achingly drab Midwest clapboard home of middle-aged Lola and Doc (Oscar-winning Shirley Booth, reprising her stage role, and Lancaster, playing against type). The nubile newcomer energizes Lola's memories of losing their little white fluffy dog "Sheba" and of once being pretty. She goes on to bring about Lola's confrontation with her own dreary, slovenly existence and, worst of all, the realization that the past is gone forever. The art student's carrying on with the lascivious football hero, in particular, brings to the fore Doc's bottled-up rage of having impregnated Lola and of having abandoned medical school to support her (the secret). Settling on chiropractic, Doc went on to piss away his inheritance on booze (yet another secret). Though sober for a year, the alcoholic is about to explode once again (hysteria). Probably the most pathetic aspect of this childless couple (Lola's miscarriage had messed up her chances of having kids) is her calling him "Daddy;" he countering with "Baby."

Besides the revelation of secrets and hysterical outbursts, melodrama indulges in the conventions of accident (losing the dog); coincidence (Doc coming home when the athlete is posing in his shorts for the student); the ironic reversal of fortune (Lola and Doc's); the sudden interruption of crucial moments (the young couple coming upon the old folks' dancing); and the triumph of the good. In postwar melodrama, the notion of the "good" came down to propriety and the way things should be or are expected to be in addition to morality, as here with Doc enjoining Lola: "We got to go on."

The outsider could come courting, sometimes marrying into the family. When he or she did, the courter challenged the family's comfortable encrustations of habit, notions of class distinction, and racial prejudice, often bringing to light deep-seated resentments and what the period considered aberrant sexuality (usually incest, but sometimes homosexuality or lesbianism). The courter set up a rivalry between him/herself and the family spokesman that often turned violent.

Giant (WB, 1956), Fred Guiol and Ivan Moffat's rewrite of Edna Ferber's bestseller, contained a series of courters. The unlettered Texas cattle baron Bick Benedict (Hudson) carries off affianced Leslie (Elizabeth Taylor) from her Maryland country manor. The liberated, socially conscious Leslie bursts upon the Victorian Texan spread, noting that her sister-in-law Luz (Mercedes McCambridge) is mother, wife, and colleague to brother Bick. Ranch-hand become millionaire Jett Rink (James Dean) becomes infatuated with Leslie and then, out of frustration and spite, with the Benedicts' daughter Luz II (Carroll Baker). A Chicana (Elsa Cardenas) marries the Benedicts' doctor son (Dennis Hopper); an experimental farmer (Earl Holliman), the other Benedict daughter (Fran Bennett).

George Stevens (1904–75) won his second Oscar for his flawless direction of *Giant*. With photography as his hobby, he had gone into movies as a cameraman for Hal Roach in 1922, and began shooting and directing shorts in 1930 and features by 1933. He had one of the most elegant eyes in the business. His World War II experience and his recognition of America's drastic change after the war gave his vision complexity and sophistication. He now saw more of reality and penetrated rather than merely observed relationships and situations. His former idealist view of life became realistically tempered. His people who used to have no mind for issues were supplanted by people facing issues (*The Talk of the Town*, C, 1942, a dry run). Films that usually ended with a marriage vow were now concerned with what happens after the marriage vow (the last part of his *Woman of the Year*, 1942, also a harbinger). Sentiment replaced sentimentality. Though his output was much less (8 features between 1948 and 1970, unlike the 17 between 1933 and 1943), the films were much more heartfelt, an accomplishment occasioned by his postwar independent producer status.

From *Giant*'s series of disruptive suitors that spanned several decades, Stevens unearthed another plot/conflictual strategy of the genre: the painful growth, development, and coming to terms with life within the family unit. This transition is reflected in all the characters except Luz and Jett, who refuse to change, and the state of Texas, as it uneasily moves from cattle to oil and the landed gentry give way to the nouveaux riches. Likewise, the sprawling 198-minute opus embodies the transitions of postwar America: the crumbling of the tradition-encrusted husband–father; the independent wife–mother who doesn't bend to Texas but bends Texas to herself; the children who will pursue their own dreams rather than those of their parents; and the incursion of people of color, a fact cemented by that final shot of the blue-eyed, white baby alongside the white/Hispanic brown-eyed baby in the same playpen.

In this his second color film, Stevens made the on-location colors thematic: Texas's yellows and mustards assaulted Maryland's greens and lavenders; Jett, covered with black oil, announces his strike against the white columns of the Benedict spread. Color encouraged Stevens's knack with stark, elemental, formal contrasts. *Giant*'s $5.1 million budget returned $14 million.

Written on the Wind (1957), sourced from Robert Wilder's book and directed by Sirk, was Universal's spin on a Texas dynasty. In this one, Hadley Oil Enterprises' playboy heir (Robert Stack) brings home a Manhattan bride (Lauren Bacall) to his father (Robert Keith), sister (Oscar-winning support Dorothy Malone), and best friend/metaphorical brother/firm's geologist (Hudson). And the dynasty comes crashing down. Sensing that the love of her life, Hudson, is in love with Bacall, Malone's nymphomania goes into high gear, occasioning her father's fatal heart attack. (In a remarkable montage of hysteria and coincidence, Malone's masturbatory rumba to a phonograph recording in her bedroom actually causes the father to collapse on the staircase.) Furthermore, Malone lies to her brother that Hudson and Bacall have had relations. Stack takes to the bottle again and begins wielding the gun he keeps under his pillow. When Stack, who suffers from a "weakening" (not the book's "sterility"), learns of his wife's pregnancy, he concludes Hudson is the father and sets out to kill him.

As with his already-noted family comedies, director Sirk's contribution to melodrama was big-time. Whatever the subtype, Sirk stitched the paradigmatic plots with personal concerns. Throughout, there were the natural/artificial, focused/aimless, the aware/unaware, parent/child dichotomies. Unhappy people were nostalgic for what had been (Malone and Stack's "river" haunts). Happiness, when it occurs, is soon shattered. People keep going around in circles, repeating the same mistakes, getting nowhere. And also, Sirk's canon is replete with unclassically double-edged endings, sour twists on melodrama's triumph of good/propriety convention. Here, the business-suited Malone stroking a replica of an oil well (phallic symbol) at her father's desk, with a large portrait of her father looking down on her, counterpoints Hudson leaving the mansion with Bacall. Postwar melodramas, in general, did not conclude on the "happily-ever-after" note of their silent and classical predecessors. And no melodramas exemplified this more than those of Sirk, who managed to ironize, criticize, even subvert his movies' final moments.

At the extreme of Stevens's nuanced, measured rendition, German Expressionist Sirk's approach was blatantly telescopic (the film runs for 99 minutes), seen in his over-the-top use of formal systems (especially color) wherein meanings were straightaway and unequivocal. Adapter George Zuckerman followed suit (brushing her hair, Bacall dismisses Malone: "I just brushed you out of my hair").

The Eugene O'Neill-sourced trilogy *Mourning Becomes Electra* (RKO, 1947); *That Forsyte Woman* (MGM, 1949), based on the first book of John Galsworthy's saga; the Françoise Sagan-adapted novel *Bonjour Tristesse* (C, 1958); Chayefsky's teleplay/stage play *Middle of the Night* (C, 1959), in which arguments about class and ethnic, religious, and age differences swirl around the dining-room table; the Joseph Stefano teleplay *The Black Orchid* (P, 1959); the Nelson Algren novel *Walk on the Wild Side* (C, 1962), with a whorehouse as metaphoric home; and the Hellman play *Toys in the Attic* (UA, 1963), where a nephew's rich child bride exposes his spinster aunts' unnatural love toward him; all contain courters. With the European as courter, the Jamesian clash between Old-World sophistication and New-World naiveté riddled *Wild Is the Wind* (P, 1957), O'Neill's *Desire under the Elms* (P, 1957), and *Light in the Piazza* (MGM, 1962), the last derived from a Elizabeth Spencer novel.[1]

The outsider could also be a family member who had abandoned the unit, voluntarily or through necessity, and who now returns (the wives and mothers of the Kazan-directed *Sea of Grass*, MGM, 1947/Conrad Richter novel and the Sirk-directed *All I Desire*, U, 1953/Carol Brink novel; or the stepson of *Phaedra* (Lopert, 1962), director-co-writer Jules Dassin's update of Euripides). The outsider could also be the former lover of a family member who reappears, as with the poor ex-lifeguard turned rich chemical engineer in director-writer Desmond Daves's retelling of Sloan Wilson's novel *A Summer Place* (WB, 1959), or the aging gigolo in director-writer Richard Brooks's pasteurization of Williams's *Sweet Bird of Youth* (MGM, 1962) – his sweetheart's abortion replaces her hysterectomy in the play; his facial disfigurement, the play's castration. In either case, the returnee exposes some festering secret that has kept the family members locked in ignorance, fear, hatred, and misery. The returnee goes on to warn of the deleterious effects of living in the past and provinciality (family and community view the return as a scandal and the exposure as further scandal). Revealing the family as a forcing bed of hypocrisy and deceit, the returnee argues for an openness and honesty, a starting over that involves forgiving and forgetting. In *Desire in the Dust*'s (TCF, 1960) variation, from Henry Whitting-ton's novel, the Southern redneck, returning from prison, turns the tables on his wealthy, manipulative girl and her father. They had reneged on their promise of social acceptability after he took the rap for their car accident that killed the scion's son.

The traumatization of one family member by another and the subsequent working through the trauma was the genre's second standard plot and conflic-tual strategy. The Minnelli-directed *The Bad and the Beautiful* (MGM, 1952), Charles Schnee's Oscar-winning screenplay, was prototypical. In this meta-phorical family (movie studio/home, various contractees/children, producer/father, and studio head/grandfather), director (Barry Sullivan), actress (Lana Turner), and writer (Dick Powell) successively work through their victimization by an unscrupulous producer (Kirk Douglas) who dishonored the director; used, not loved the actress; and ultimately caused the death of the writer's beloved wife.

Dredging up the past, each relives the hurt through memory in an office session guided by the studio head. The film also contained, though metaphori-cally here in the figure of the studio head, a character resident to the cycle – the psychiatrist/psychologist, who took over for the classic family doctor/clergy-man. Also, the film exemplified the analyst–analysand structuring of scenes common to this cycle, in part or, as here, overriding the entire work. No sur-prise, with the genre's image of the home as the site of individual breakdown and neurosis as a pervasively normal condition of family life.

Whether with family comedy (as we have seen), the musical (as we shall see), or melodrama, Vincente Minnelli (1903–86), MGM's premier house director from 1944 on, suffused genres with his sensibility. As Minnelli's people attest time after time, one can move on, if one confronts the past trauma that has caused the present torment, reliving the pain to understand and thereby control it rather than allowing the trauma to have its way. This new state, achieved through self-confrontation, is unmistakably the triumph of individuality. As such, his canon provided a cultural touchstone with its individual–conformist cleft running through it.

Minnelli was so committed to his people's inner life that he embodied it – here, not only by the three memory flashbacks that constituted practically the entire film but within each flashback, by the illustration of the revelatory, life-changing moment of a bruised psyche. In the film, no moment was more telling than the actress's discovery of the producer's philandering and her hallucinatory drive away. By means of the excess of performative, visual, and compositional sound codes (throbbing upper body, uncontrollable crying, passing lights, swerving car, jittery camera moves, blaring traffic noise), subjectivity at its most traumatic is objectified, relived, and mastered.

As with *The Bad and the Beautiful*, Minnelli's *Tea and Sympathy* (MGM, 1956), scripted by the author of the play, Robert Anderson, is a memory flashback, this time of a "sissy" son (John Kerr, encoring his stage role) psychologically brutalized by his father and fellow students while in prep school (metaphorical home). The ministrations of the headmaster's wife (Deborah Kerr, consigning her stage performance to celluloid), which include having relations with him, begins the healing.

In some films, the healing of the traumatized person was ambivalent. Minnelli's majestic *Home from the Hill*, husband and wife Harriet Frank and Irving Ravetch's update of William Humphrey's autobiographical East Texas thirties-set novel, narrows its sights on 17-year-old Theron (George Hamilton). Distantly fathered by the rich macho Wade Hunnicutt (Robert Mitchum), with a yen for hunting wild animals and women, and suffocatingly mothered by the coldly genteel Hannah (Eleanor Parker), who has ended all intimacy with her husband four months into her pregnancy, Theron has been used by his parents as a pawn in their power plays. "They tore me in half this way every day of my life," he intimates to his girl, Libby (Luana Patten). Minnelli inspired designers to create a house that had no flow, a space all chopped up, cluttered, and oppressive (especially through the preponderant use of the color red) as an emblem of family life and Theron's state of soul. Upset by Theron's naïve "gentleness" (a product of his mother), Wade shows his son "how a man lives" (the issue of masculinity is a transgeneric concern of postwar Hollywood). The wild boar hunt, all tracking shots, yellow fumes, and yelping dogs tossed in the air, is Theron's baptism of fire (here, another generic pattern asserts itself – the coming of age). Theron is further conflicted by his mother's revelation of his father's promiscuity and "the secret" that Rafe (George Peppard) is Wade's bastard son (the pattern of outsider as intruder). Even more, Theron is upset by his father's refusal to acknowledge Rafe as his son (here, the film touches on yet another generic thrust – generational confrontation). Theron is unable to commit to Libby, even after having sex with her, for he doesn't want to go the way of his parents. He avenges Wade's murder by killing Libby's father (Theron has now become a hunter of men) and runs away into the woods. He has turned his back on the old world to create a new one. At the film's end, Hannah accepts Rafe, who has married Libby and given her (and Theron's) child a home. (Rafe and his actions have provided the film with a fifth definition of masculinity, in addition to those of Theron, Wade, Libby's pathologically insecure father, and the gaggle of joke-playing, rumor-mongering old-timers – a switch from the usual band of small-town, gossipy old biddies.) As such, the film invokes yet another generic strategy, that of family restoration. The acceptance scene burns in the memory with its decentered CinemaScope frame: Wade's red grave marker on the left; Hannah and Rafe's walk away on the right. The finale's reversals of

16-1   *A Streetcar Named Desire* (WB, 1951, p. Charles K. Feldman)

Another of playwright Tennessee Williams's signature cruel confrontations between characters –
here, boyfriend Mitch (Karl Malden) subjects Blanche (Vivien Leigh) to the scrutiny of a light
bulb to determine her age.

fortune are multi-toned: problematic in Theron's case, happy for Rafe, sad for
Wade on the brink of reconciling with Hannah, and simultaneously up-and-
down for Hannah.

In *A Streetcar Named Desire* (WB, 1951), healing is nowhere to be found. The
film climaxes with brutish Stanley's (Brando) rape of his fragile sister-in-law
Blanche (Vivien Leigh) and concludes with her being led to an asylum. Com-
mencing as it does with Blanche's unexpected arrival at her sister Stella's (Kim
Stanley) flat, the film also interweaves the outsider–intruder pattern.

Streetcar retained the ambiguity of the characters, situations, and even ending
of Williams's Pulitzer Prize-winning masterpiece. As in Inge's work, classically
melodramatic cheerable heroes and hissable villains were absent. Williams
(1911–83) also was committed to the portrayal of human beings, each capable
of healing and hurting. More: his compassion for his people (Stanley also) was
enormous. "The unlocking and lighting up and ventilation of the closets, attics,
and basements of human behavior" was what he said his writing was all about.

At age 14, writing became for him a way to cope with life's discomfort: an overbearing mother, a lobotomized sister, a homophobic father who called him "Miss Nancy."

Co-adapter Williams (with Oscar Saul) and play's *régisseur* Kazan did not impose classical Hollywood plotting in the transfer, concerned solely with characters enclosed in a ground-floor tenement in the working-class district of New Orleans. Stanley, Blanche, Stella, and Stanley's co-worker Mitch (Karl Malden), who comes to call on Blanche (another instance of the outsider–intruder pattern), sniff each other out and attempt to reach forth, all the while silently crying out for understanding, some gentleness, and sexual renewal but, alas, only proceed to cruelly confront each other and end up, in some respect, locked in a prison of loneliness. Notice how Kazan, photographer Harry Stradling, and the production designers made the set get smaller and smaller, an objective correlative of the characters' psychological states.

By the beginning of the fifties, Kazan (1909–2003), a Greek émigré from Turkey, the Yale Drama School, and the Group Theater, was riding the crest of a wave. Committed to realism, his camera checked out a character's class, ethnic, and regional status, manners, and habits, intensely sympathetic to those who were struggling and disenfranchised (Blanche as well as Stanley). Kazan knew how to breathe life into a performance, concretizing a character's inner life by showing the actor how to use a prop. Kazan weighted reactions, often holding on an actor being talked to or watching. He believed in the transforming power of the ensemble. All except Leigh were Method and had come from the Broadway version. (Leigh had played Blanche in London's West End under husband Laurence Olivier's guidance – New York saw Jessica Tandy.) But the acting was all of a piece, meriting three Oscars (Brando had to be content with a nomination), and memorializing Leigh's towering performance. Turned on and repulsed by Stanley, creating illusion all around her while sinking deeper and deeper into delusion, she is the family's unerring, articulate conscience: "What's straight? A line can be straight or a street. But the heart of a human being?" *Streetcar* was the film that made the Method known to film audiences. After *Streetcar*, acting would never be the same again in Hollywood pictures.

Curiously, from the same studio and year came *Storm Warning*, a Richard Brooks and Daniel Fuchs "original." Hybridized with a woman-in-distress thriller (Ginger Rogers witnesses a murder and is coerced into not testifying) and a social-problem film (Ku Klux Klan), *Storm Warning*'s family melodramatic pattern was a carbon copy of *Streetcar*. Rogers arrives unannounced at the home of younger pregnant sibling Doris Day. Day's thuggish husband Steve Cochran rapes Rogers (or begins to).

Most films in this cycle centered equally on victim/s and victimizer – the latter, in no less a way, was also a victim of a pathological drive to control others, springing from great insecurity, fear, even self-loathing. Edna Lee's novel-sourced *Queen Bee* (C, 1958) was a case study with control-freak Joan Crawford causing her husband's alcoholism, son's nightmares, niece's cynicism, and sister-in-law and fiancé's suicides while making herself sick with guilt, obsessively vain, flirtatious, and jealous, promiscuous and, alas, a victim of murder. Sometimes, the instance of a parent or guardian's need to control a child masked a perverse desire to couple with the child. The desire was acted upon in *The Story of Esther Costello* (C, 1958)/Nicholas Monsarrat bestseller in which a husband actually rapes the rescued blind, deaf, and dumb girl who has come to live under his roof. In most cases, it remained a sin of thought (*The Strange One*, C, 1957, Calder Willingham's novel/play set in a Southern military academy – metaphorical home – where the senior cadet – metaphorical parent – lusts for his underlings). When power plays happened between familial coevals, desire spilled over into deeds (*Streetcar*, *Storm Warning*).

Family traumatization also appeared in *Harriet Craig* (C, 1950)/George Kelly's Pulitzer Prize-winning play *Craig's Wife*, first filmed in 1936; *Home Before Dark* (WB, 1958)/Eileen Bassing novel; the Delbert Mann-directed *Separate Tables* (UA, 1958), Terence Rattigan's own revamp (with John Gay) of his West End success where two of the residents of a seaside hotel are a domineering mother and her spinster daughter; *Go Naked in the World* (MGM, 1960)/ Thomas Chameles novel; and the bowdlerization of D. H. Lawrence's tome *Sons and Lovers* (TCF, 1960). The Wyler-guided *The Children's Hour* (UA, 1962), playwright Hellman's reworking with John Michael Hayes of her stage hit first filmed by Wyler in 1935, played a variant with a student traumatizing two teachers at a New England private school (metaphorical home). The cycle also pointed out how lovelessness between parents can incite great turmoil in children, as in *The Decision of Christopher Blake* (WB, 1948)/Moss Hart play and the Sidney Lumet-directed O'Neill drama *Long Day's Journey into Night* (Embassy, 1962).

Generational confrontation, due to ethical disparity, partisan love, or lack of communication, was the genre's third basic plot and conflictual strategy. Frequently involving a youth's traumatization that sets off a rebellion or some dastardly act, the confrontation might end with reconciliation, but more often, with the overthrow and death of the old coupled with a leavetaking. This subtype flattered the youth market.

In the Miller-derived play *All My Sons* (U, 1948), a son (Lancaster) discovers that his father (Edward G. Robinson) had been a dealer in faulty war goods, causing the death of 21 pilots during World War II. Even when the son points out the horrendous nature of his irresponsibility, the father is unable to fathom it. Yul Brynner, Richard Basehart, and William Shatner are *The Brothers Karamazov* (MGM, 1958), who take a stand against the unbridled lust, anti-intellectualism, and greed of their father (Lee J. Cobb), eventually killed by the bastard son (Albert Salmi) in Brooks's stab at Dostoyevsky. *Parrish* (WB, 1961) is Troy Donahue, who revolts against his stepfather's (Karl Malden) ruthless business practices by starting his own Connecticut tobacco farm in Daves's reworking of Mildred Savage's novel.

Son-versus-father conflicts could be metaphorical, as with the Wise-directed *Executive Suite* (MGM, 1954), Ernest Lehman's shapely retailoring of Cameron Hawley's novel set in a furniture company's boardroom. Here, a young, idealistic design engineer (Holden) comes up against a middle-aged unconscionable comptroller (Fredric March) who opts for efficiency and profit. In order not to load any side and to make the audience do some thinking, VP/Production Schary decided to forego any musical scoring. The film's other anti-classical innovation, the opening sequence's subjective camera rendition of the boss (who is never seen) going about his business and suddenly suffering a fatal heart attack, was entirely Wise's idea. Rod Serling's teleplay-derived *Patterns* (UA, 1956) transpired in a Wall Street corporation; *The Young Doctors* (UA, 1961), from Arthur Hailey's novel, in a hospital.

Not only a case of sons versus fathers, the cycle also cast its eye on a daughter (Paulette Goddard) thwarting her father (Oskar Homolka) and brother-in-law's (Broderick Crawford) theft in *Anna Lucasta* (C, 1949), Philip Yordan's coadaptation of his play (with Arthur Laurents) set among the working-class Polish community in Pennsylvania. UA remade it with an all-black cast in 1958, with Eartha Kitt as Anna. An illegitimate daughter (Diane Varsi) rebels against her mother's (Lana Turner) double standards in a New England small town while another daughter (Hope Lange) kills her rapist stepfather (Arthur Kennedy) in *Peyton Place* (TCF, 1957), John Michael Hayes's canny yet feeling adaptation of Grace Metalious's sizzling bestseller. The Ida Lupino-executed *Hard, Fast and Beautiful* (RKO, 1951) and *Claudelle English* (WB, 1961), based on an Erskine Caldwell novel, showed the devastating effects that come from bitter, acquisitive mothers using their daughters to gain monetary stability.

Another Part of the Forest (U, 1948), Hellman's prequel to *The Little Foxes*, flipped the coin, making the children (Edmond O'Brien, Dan Duryea, and Ann Blyth) even more amoral than their father (Fredric March), the rich Alabamian who sold smuggled Union salt at $8 a pound to the Confederates (the secret). The Martin Ritt-directed *Hud* (P, 1963), Ravetch and Frank's attentive translation of Larry McMurtry's novel, followed suit, pitting Homer, a tradition-bound, morally upright patriarch of a cattle ranch (Oscar-winning support Melvyn Douglas) against his son Hud (Paul Newman), who sleeps around and has no qualms about selling off an infected herd. Between them stands Homer's 17-year-old grandson Lon (Brandon de Wilde), who must choose which way to go. Housekeeper/substitute mother Alma (Oscar-winning Patricia Neal), after a near-rape by Hud, chooses to leave. After the grandfather bites the dust, so does Lon, who now shares in the secret of his father's death. Interlacing *Hud*'s generational conflict were the patterns of the initiation of youth (Lon) and its reverse, the arrested growth of an adult (Hud), motifs close to Ritt's heart, appearing in all of his family melodramas.

Being as socially conscious as he was, Ritt (1920–90) always contextualized his stories within a transition point in society (here, it's the immense change in America after the war.) Further contextualization was seen in Ritt's insistence on the ethic, racial, religious, socioeconomic, typological dimensions of a regional America. By means of the b/w photography of Howe, *the* cameraman of family melodrama, who lit the characters in unflatteringly direct light, filtered out the cloud cover, and made the barren landscapes even bleaker by shooting in anamorphic Panavision, Ritt caught the parched, circumspect, empty quality of middle-class WASP life in a Texan cattle community.

Ritt shaped performances that got under the audience's skin, their authenticity clinched by his long-take, composition-in-depth visual trope. This was his forte, having been a stage actor himself, Method at that (here, Newman and Neal are of the same persuasion). After legal studies at New York City's St. John University, Jewish Ritt joined the Group Theater. A stint in World War II interrupted his career, but he went back to acting upon his return, even lecturing at the Actors Studio. Eventually, he moved into direction – stage, TV, then film. His film debut, *Edge of the City* (MGM, 1956), was a happy fault. Administrative and financial disarray caused MGM to overlook Ritt's blacklisted status.

Partisan love also caused the generational rift in this cycle, invariably causing aftershocks of sibling rivalry. In the Mankiewicz-directed *House of Strangers* (TCF, 1949), Philip Yordan's go at Jerome Weidman's novel, the head of a New York Italian banking family (Edward G. Robinson) favors one son (Richard Conte), sending the other three boys at their brother's throat.

In the Fred Zinnemann-crafted *A Hatful of Rain* (TCF, 1957), Michael V. Gazzo's coadaptation (with Alfred Hayes and an uncredited Carl Foreman) of his play that is essentially a character study, it's the same old story, though this one is set in a low-rent Gotham housing project. The blustering Italian father (Lloyd Nolan) worships his married Korean War hero son Johnny (Don Murray, married to pregnant Celia/Eva Marie Saint) who, unbeknown to Pop, is addicted to morphine (the film is hybridized with the social problem film). On the other hand, Pop contemns his bar-bouncer bachelor offspring Polo (Anthony Franciosa), who does not come through with the promised $2,500 needed to refurbish a Palm Beach bar the father has just bought. If truth be known, it was the promised money that occasioned Pop's visit north. As such, the film is plaited with the disruptive outsider thread. In the 24-hour visit, lifetimes of secrets bubble to the surface: the father's running out on the boys when his wife died,

16-2   *A Hatful of Rain* (TCF, 1957, p. Buddy Adler)

The family melodrama's iconic dinner scene with (from left to right), brother Johnny (Don Murray), brother Polo (Anthony Franciosa), Johnny's wife Celia (Eva Marie Saint), and the brothers' Pop (Lloyd Nolan) in a low-rent New York City housing project.

putting them into orphanages; his self-centeredness (he didn't even make it to Johnny's wedding); Johnny's marriage at breaking point; Polo's love/lust for his sister-in-law and his cockeyed way of helping his brother's fix by financing his drug habit; and, of course, guilt-ridden confessions all around. Imbricating this living-room tumult is the craziness of the street, which also invades the home from time to time. While suppliers hound Johnny for the $500 arrears, Johnny aims to steal money to satisfy his twice-a-day fix and attempts suicide in the front seat of Polo's car while it is moving in downtown traffic (hysteria at its height). The actual wintry New York interiors and exteriors in CinemaScope/ b/w, endlessly decentered and often diagonally multi-planed, aggravate the gut-wrenching situations.

In Kazan's mounting of *East of Eden* (WB, 1955), Paul Osborne's reduction of Steinbeck's 602-page tome to its last fourth, a morally rigid, Bible-spouting Mr. Trask (Raymond Massey) loves his obedient son Adam (Richard Davalos) as much as he chastises his wildly independent, mischievous son Cal (Dean in his first and best performed role). Hurt, Cal even tries to buy his father's love: the $5,000 he made from his bean investment, the exact amount his father lost in shipping lettuce, is a birthday present for the old man.

As with the smattering of period family melodramas (practically all transpire in contemporary times), *East*, though set in 1917, was fifties in spirit, epitomizing the male identity crisis ("Talk to me father," Cal pleads, "I got to know who I am"); the female's (Julie Harris) stabilization of the male; prejudice and especially, domestic trauma. Dean even sports fifties haircut, chinos, and white bucks.

Kazan's macro–mini culture clash, this time, is seen in the dichotomy of the farming community of Salinas, where the Trasks live, and Monterey, a rough-and-tumble port where mother and wife Kate (Oscar-winning support Jo Van Fleet), who had abandoned the family years before, runs a brothel-saloon. The Salinas' citizenry's violence toward the German shoe-repair man also exemplifies Kazan's clash.

Lack of communication, particularly because preoccupied parents have no time for their offspring or because they are just plain unable to raise children (dote on them, spoil them, live through them, yes, but not raise them) also fanned intergenerational fires. Parents' (Melvyn Douglas and Lynn Bari) neglect turns their 16-year-old (Joan Evans) into a juvenile delinquent and suicide victim in *On the Loose* (RKO, 1951). In attempting to understand the problem of teenage suicide (as director Ida Lupino tells us is the intent of her production company's film, in voice-over during the pre-credit sequence), the film has a tinge of the social problem genre about it. In *The Young Stranger* (RKO, 1957), brought to the screen by the original TV director John Frankenheimer and writer Robert Dozier, a 16-year-old (James MacArthur) struggles to make his prominent film exec father and social-butterfly mother (Jim Daley and Kim Hunter) hear, let alone believe, his side of the delinquency report, so out of touch are they with him. Teenagers (Brandon de Wilde and Carol Lynley) plan an abortion in *Blue Denim* (TCF, 1959), Edith Sommer and Philip Dunne's adaptation of James Leo Herlihy and William Noble's play. These middle class kids (he's 16; she's 15) cannot take their problem to her widowed professor father (Vaughn Taylor) or his military dad (MacDonald Carey), fixated on past glories. Mother (Marsha Hunt) is no help either, preoccupied with her elder daughter's wedding. Edith Sommer's play *Teenage Rebel* (TCF, 1956) altered the formula. The film starts with the damage already done to the 15-year-old daughter of divorced parents (Betty Lou Keim), then tracks the hostile girl as she goes from living with her father when he takes a new wife to living with her remarried mother (Ginger Rogers).

Painful growth, development, and coming to terms with life through or despite the family was the genre's fourth strategy. Whether abandoning

solipsistic attitudes and letting in more of the outside world or replacing denaturing traditions with values attuned to reality, the protagonist moves on. The
rite of passage is embodied by a child's move to adolescence or that of an adolescent to young adulthood. An adult being dislodged from a state of arrested
growth or childhood reversion and getting on with a productive life as well as
the reverse, the adult being stuck, unable to grow up, were other manifestations.

A *Tree Grows in Brooklyn* (TCF, 1945) was a signal film in the genre and a
period-defining one as well. Though set in the early 1900s, *Tree* graphically
delineated the postwar family, the European ethnic rise from lower to middle
class, the female coming into her own, and the male in crisis.

Tess Slesinger and Frank Davis's adaption of Betty Smith's gargantuan
bestseller measures the growth of young teenager Francie Nolan ("Special"
Oscar-winning Peggy Ann Garner) in a household of women: her fanatically
penny-pinching scrub-lady mother (Dorothy McGuire), so exacting of her; her
sexually insatiable aunt (Joan Blondell); and her instructive grandmom (Ferike
Boros). The males are there but ineffectually off-center. Francie's good-hearted
singer-waiter father, whom she adores, is a hopeless drunk and eventually succumbs to pneumonia (Oscar-winning support James Dunn). Little brother
Neeley (Ted Donaldson) is someone she has to look out for, especially, late on
Christmas Eve, when she and Neeley withstand the customary hurling of unsold
Christmas trees at the poor to get a free tree. As for the Irish cop (Lloyd Nolan)
who's smitten with her mother, he only looks on from the sidelines, smiling. In
her journey from squalor to respectability, from a kid to a young girl with a
high-school diploma, from resentment to acceptance, Francie must weigh heart
(her father's dreams) with head (her mother's practicality) and come to terms
with his death and her mother's obduracy.

In his direction of the poor Irish immigrant class, Kazan eschewed classical
Hollywood glamour with his non-stellar casting. Also avoided was the usual
Hollywood folksiness (the opening objective track of a city block teeming with
people, activity, and noise) and sentimentality (the unforced naturalness of the
scenes involving the film's central metaphor of the ailanthus tree springing out
of the cracks of the cement sidewalk). And moralizing was nowhere in sight.
The overt moralizing of traditional melodrama of the D. W. Griffith ilk was
generally thrown out in the postwar variety, largely due to the genre's disbelief
in a clearly demarcated world of good and evil. Such a world was less tenable,
if at all, in light of a culture's weighing in of relativism. Postwar melodrama was
still concerned with morality, however, as it continued to expose problematic
aspects of social interaction.

Teenager Brandon de Wilde in *All Fall Down* (MGM, 1962), an Inge adaption
of James Leo Herlihy's novel directed by Frankenheimer, undergoes an agonizing readjustment in his middle-class Cleveland suburban household, generating

a major transition in his life. He wisely comes to realize that his mother's (Angela Lansbury) dominating ways are brought on by a sense of her own uselessness. His dad's (Karl Malden) alcoholism, he deems, is a needed crutch in the face of his pummeling wife. Seeing his folks for what and why they are, he is able to deal with them better. Idolatry that turned to murderous thoughts finally melts into pity for his selfish, irresponsible, sexually swaggering older brother (Warren Beatty). And the crush on the spinster house guest (Eva Marie Saint, who commits suicide because of Beatty) is finally deemed, by him, adolescently foolish.

The Zinnemann-made *A Member of the Wedding* (C, 1952), Edward and Edna Analt's remolding of Carson McCullers's novella/play, Julie Harris, committing her stage role to film, is a 12-year-old who feels disjoined during this transition from childhood to adolescence in the household of the black family cook (Ethel Waters), a 7-year-old cousin (Brandon de Wilde), and an absentee widowed father. Her older brother's refusal to take her along on his honeymoon becomes the turning point in her life.

Director Stevens added two memorable portraits. In *I Remember Mama* (RKO, 1948), DeWitt Bodeen's faithful rendering of John Van Druten's play based, in turn, on Kathryn Forbes's novel, a daughter (Barbara Bel Geddes), reading her autobiographical memoirs, flashes back to the crises of her Norwegian family when she was a 15-year-old schoolgirl in 1910 San Francisco. Through the recollection, which Stevens leavens with humor to avoid sappiness, the distaff Boswell charts her growth into a young adult and successful novelist. Though period, the piece gave off postwar vibes of the increasing centrality of the American female (mama Irene Dunne) and the male's periphery within the home. In the road-showed *The Diary of Anne Frank* (TCF, 1959), Goodrich and Hackett's version of their play grounded in Frank's nonfiction account, the home is a cramped attic hideout in Nazi-occupied Amsterdam. (Parodoxically, the CinemaScope frame made the attic even more confining.) The Franks share their tiny nest with the Van Daans (Oscar-winning support Shelley Winters as Mrs. Van Daan) and a dentist (a career reversal for clown Ed Wynn). During the tumultuous years of infighting and gift-giving at Hanukkah, bitter resentments and sweet dalliances with the Van Daan boy (Richard Beymer), and the final arrival of the Gestapo presaging sure extinction for these Jews, Anne blossoms from a young girl into a woman, unshakeable in her faith: "In spite of everything, I still believe that people are really good at heart." The film also shows the Van Daan boy maturing, through Anne's influence. First-time-out Millie Perkins's merely adequate lead performance, despite Stevens's guidance and the film's exorbitant length (170 minutes), kept the work from soaring.

Cat on a Hot Tin Roof (MGM, 1958), a coding of Williams's drama by director Brooks, who coadapted with James Poe, deals with the growth of a

30-year-old adult. On a Mississippi plantation, the emotionally arrested son Brick (Newman) fixates on his college football days when he bonded with fellow athlete Skip. Brick blames Skip's suicide on his wife Maggie (Taylor), whom he believes seduced Skip, and on himself for not taking Skip's telephone call prior to the suicide. He drinks all day. He has ended all sexual intimacy with Maggie, despite her continually peeling off and putting on clothes right in front of his very blue eyes. On top of that, he shows no interest in taking over the estate from Big Daddy (Burl Ives's stage reprise). Big Daddy gave him only "things," while Skip gave him "love." These issues cloak Brick's sexual-identity angst (emblematized by his use of a crutch), though they don't dislodge it.

Cat seethes with the genre's every other conflictual strategy as well: outsider–intruder (Skip); traumatization (Big Daddy sets off Brick's hysteria, tearfully shouting while smashing antiques in the cellar); generational confrontation (the ethical disparity of Big Daddy and older avaricious son Gupper/Jack Carson; Big Daddy's preference for Brick); and family restoration (Maggie's got a lot on her plate – the problem of sex, the issues of succession and inheritance – and she's not about to excuse herself from the table). The disclosure of secrets that clears the air of "mendacity" (Brick tells Big Daddy that he has terminal cancer, not a spastic colon, as he was led to believe; Daddy calls Skip a rotter and castigates Brick for never growing up) is accompanied by visual excess: gusty wind, pelting rain, French doors bursting open, shears blowing every which way, a convertible stuck in the mud, a broken crutch.

Cat proved a career-turning film for Brooks. A graduate of Temple's School of Journalism, the Philadelphian Brooks (1912–92) toiled as a sportswriter and NBC radio newscaster/writer before his 1941 Universal arrival where he penned B films. After the publication of his 1945 novel *The Brick Foxhole*, Brooks moved up, assisting producer Mark Hellinger in story construction and dialogue (*Brute Force*, 1947). Brooks's liberal social consciousness appealed to MGM's Schary, who, while at RKO, had produced Brooks's novel, and he was given a writer-director berth. From 1950 to 1958, Brooks's array of transgeneric adaptations at MGM was impressive. Even when it was a matter of an original (*Crisis*, 1950), his films wore their social consciousness on their sleeves, catching people at a moral crossroads as they faced a social inequity. His dialogue, however, could at times become rhetorical and his *mise-en-scène* obvious (Brick smashing the blowup of himself as a football hero and hurling the trophy into a corner).

In *Raisin in the Sun* (C, 1961), Lorraine Hansberry's own screen treatment of her play about a South Side Chicago black family, directed by TV and stage expatriate Daniel Petrie, the adult son (Sidney Poitier) finally becomes a man. On the other hand, *Summer and Smoke* (P, 1956), James Poe and Meade Roberts's clean-up of Williams's play directed by stage Brit Peter Glenville, etched the stunted growth of two next-door neighbors (Laurence Harvey, and Geraldine Page cementing her off-Broadway success).

The genre engaged itself, lastly, with family restoration and reinvention. Whether harmful or, at best, ambiguous, restoration and reinvention prove well nigh impossible.

An embodiment of the restoration strategy traced the desperate drive, engineered by guilt over some past hidden fault (the secret) to hold the family together, usually in the name of "honor," at whatever cost (always hypocrisy and lies, sometimes a crime). This pattern reverberated with the era's obsession with conformity and camouflage. *Suddenly Last Summer* (C, 1959), Williams's own adaptation (with Gore Vidal) maneuvered by Mankiewicz, was paradigmatic. In this, a Southern matriarch (Katharine Hepburn) bribes a hospital head with $1 million to perform a lobotomy on her niece (Taylor) in the hope the girl will excise the memory of her beloved gay son who fell victim to his own flesh-procuring tactics. The bitch mother (Mary Astor) of *Stranger in My Arms* (U, 1959), from a Robert Wilder novel, will stop at nothing to see that her cowardly son, who actually despised the old lady, receives posthumously the Medal of Honor. Shirley Booth's hands are full, keeping a husband from flying the coop while coping with some sleazy adult children in *Hot Spell* (P, 1958), taken from Lonnie Colman's play. To keep the family blood pure, pineapple plantation tycoon (Charlton Heston) of *Diamond Head* (C, 1963)/Peter Gilman novel thwarts the marriage of his sister (Yvette Mimieux) to an Hawaiian, going so far as to stab him not so accidentally. Behind closed doors, the fulminating patriarch keeps a Chinese mistress (Frances Nuyen). Proper dowager Bette Davis of *Where Love Has Gone* (P, 1964) goes to improper lengths to hush up granddaughter Joey Heatherton's knifing of her mother Susan Hayward's lover. The film also takes up the pattern of traumatization: Davis's indulgence and meddling in Hayward's life have turned her into a rebellious nymphomaniac who eventually turns to suicide as a way out. Hayward's depravity, in turn, drives Heatherton to murder. John Michael Hayes's adaptation made presentable the Harold Robbins potboiler, which was inspired by the 1958 Lana Turner scandal in which the movie star's daughter Cheryl stabbed her mother's gangster lover Johnny Stompanato.

In *Death of a Salesman*'s (C, 1951) variation, with Stanley Roberts adapting Miller's lauded work, a proud father (Fredric March) refuses to admit that the values he taught his sons (Arthur Kennedy and stage-holdover Cameron Mitchell) were false and damaging. Ashamed to tell his wife (Mildred Dunnock, willing her brilliant stage turn to posterity) that he has lost his poorly paid job and accepted a family offer to start a new life in Alaska, he drives to his death in his dilapidated car. The $20,000 insurance policy can now pay off the mortgage, thus retaining family "honor."

Another embodiment of the restoration strategy concerned itself with the search for a child whose loss was due to some transgression on a father's part (once again, the male in crisis). Only in this instance was restoration sometimes presented as a possibility. In *Little Boy Lost* (P, 1953), director-writer Seaton's reworking of Marghanita Laski's teleplay, Crosby (in his first dramatic role) returns to Paris to find the bastard child he sired during the war. Searching for an illegitimate son he abandoned 20 years before, James Cagney in *These Wilder Years* (MGM, 1956) winds up with a teenage mother and her baby. Crosby, bitter over his wife's adultery, is a *Man On Fire* (MGM, 1957), embroiled in a harsh custody battle for his son whom he even kidnaps despite a court order.

Reinvention was another way to go, involving as it did the rejection of the "real" family and the subsequent formation of a substitute "ideal" one, which, in the end, is destroyed by societal pressures. In the Ray-directed *Rebel Without a Cause* (WB, 1955), a Stewart Stern original from Ray's own story, high-schoolers (James Dean, Natalie Wood, and Sal Mineo) leave their respective Los Angeles homes and form an alternative family. Dean's decision-making and protective measures, in contrast to the inaction of his weak, self-deprecating father emasculated by a shrewish wife, hold the unit together. Dean welcomes rather than eschews Wood's kisses, unlike her father, who, embarrassed by the girl's blossoming into womanhood and his own incestuous feelings toward her, cuts off her displays of affection, calling her a "tramp." One occasion excepted, Dean is always there for Mineo, a child of divorced parents whose mother is absent and whose father sends checks to his well-appointed home which has only a black servant (substitute mother) in residence. With a picture of movie star Alan Ladd in his school locker and attachment to Dean, Mineo is also troubled by a problem of sexual identity. Wood, unlike her insensitive mother, understands and responds to the needs of both her "husband" (Dean) and "child" (Mineo).

Ray (1911–79) came of filmic age postwar after working in architecture (he was a protégé of Frank Lloyd Wright) and theater. As such, his work evinced a sensitivity to story structure (*Rebel*'s orchestration of three parallel teenage lives, the three alternating night/day sequences), thematic use of décor (students viewing the exploding universe in the Griffith Park Planetarium), and thematic compositions (unbalanced staging and movements of the camera that do not follow through – both aclassical gambits).

Ray's genre-diverse films seethed with the postwar existential blues, whether contemporary or period, whether situated in middle-class households and apartments or the outposts of civilization. His principals, usually male, pretty much feel out of context, both familially and societally. They feel alone (*Rebel*'s Mineo editorially comments on an instructor's lecture on man in the universe: "What does he know about man alone?"). No extrinsic structures support them.

They are on their own, making a stab at finding meaning and value in and by themselves. Often, his people gravitate toward a personal relationship, hoping for answers therein. *Party Girl* (MGM, 1958) tells the mouthpiece for the mob: "When we're not together, we're nothing." Some relationships show signs of working; others come apart. Hand in hand with the male's sense of aloneness in Ray's works is a questioning by the male himself of the societally accepted notion of macho masculinity. Some even abandon it, undergoing the throes of sensitivization.

In the Minnelli-directed *The Cobweb* (MGM, 1955), John Paxton's adaptation of William Gibson's novel, a clinical psychiatrist (Richard Widmark), escaping from his self-absorbed, nymphomaniacal wife (Gloria Grahame) and two whining kids, has a liaison with the sanatorium's crafts director (Lauren Bacall). Their devotion to a disturbed adolescent painter/metaphorical son (John Kerr) solidifies the union. The film also entwines the disruptive outsider strand as the wife intrudes upon the metaphorical family of asylum staff and patients with her designer drapes to hang in the rec room.

Also Minnelli-signed, *Some Came Running* (MGM, 1958), John Patrick and Arthur Sheekman's downsizing of James Jones, an ex-vet writer (Sinatra) accidentally returns to his Indiana hometown. He seeks out his older brother (Arthur Kennedy), who had shunted him off to an orphanage when their parents died (the secret). The writer, disillusioned, blocked, lonely, seeks some understanding and connection. The brother now successfully runs a jewelry store, inherited from his wife's father (did he marry for money?), and is a respected board member of the bank. But he is a "dull, greedy, small" social-climbing individual with no thoughts for anyone but himself. Though obsessed with appearances, as is his shriveled-up, sexless wife, he is having an affair with his young bookkeeper (another secret). When his high school-age daughter coincidentally comes upon her father making out in a lovers' lane, she is traumatized, turning to booze and sex. This is the writer's upper-middle-class family, ensconced in an icily formal colonial manse way out in the country where modish Manhattans are served in proper cocktail glasses and no welcome mat graces the entrance. Contemning what he sees, the writer forms an alternative unit with a classless gambler (Dean Martin) and a prostitute (MacLaine clutching a purse in the form of a stuffed animal, typifying the child she craves). Seedy hotel rooms and garish bars constitute their abodes, where the writer is warmed by the gambler's friendship, the whore's devotion, and tumblers of bourbon. Here, and in *The Cobweb* and *Home from the Hill*, Minnelli saw the substitute family as an "ideal" one, having been re-created by the protagonists' inner needs and imagination due to their eviscerating "real" family.

Minnelli braided a triangled romance within this striking contrast of families, in which the writer is caught between the puritanical, dubious, brainy schoolteacher (Martha Hyer, with her long golden hair upswept in a tight chignon) and the generous, trusting whore who has found a job in the brassière factory (Maclaine, in pixie-cut red hair). In a reverse of the usual deployment of all-stops-pulled-out formal systems during the many minor and major climaxes that pepper melodrama (here with the "After You're Gone" nightclub scene or the whore's ex-boyfriend's hunt to shoot the writer at the town centennial celebration), Minnelli shuts down all systems during the writer's seduction of the schoolteacher. The CinemaScope/Metrocolor frame is cloaked in shadows; the two characters are silhouetted; and Elmer Bernstein's pounding score is reduced to muted violins. Such deprivation of excess, of course, only goes to heighten the scene's emotionality and the audience's identification and affect.

A Miller adaptation of an *Esquire* story written specifically for his then wife Monroe and manned by Huston, *The Misfits* (UA, 1960) are a sad, unemployed lot. A nervous recent divorcee who's been put through the wringer (Monroe) naïvely still expects to find kindness around every violent corner and just as naïvely tries to protect every hurt human and animal. An anachronistic rugged individualist and divorced man (Clark Gable, in his screen adieu) plays around and wants nothing to do with earning "wages." A widower shaken by his wife's death in childbirth and his experience of World War II bombing raids (Eli Wallach) totters with self-pity. A sexually confused bachelor (Montgomery Clift) still calls his mother, wanting her approval. Badly scarred and incessantly using alcohol to ease the pain, all these nonconformists come together momentarily as a family in an "unfinished" house, ironically in Reno, the graveyard of families. (A fifth member, a sharp-tongued middle-ager – Thelma Ritter – leaves the group when she bumps into her ex-husband with his new wife at the rodeo.) Plotless, *The Misfits* is structured as an alternating series of duets, trios, quartets, and quintets that dredge up the bruising past, raise issues about life in the present, and worriedly image the future. At the roping-of-the-wild-stallions climax (the film's one action sequence), the "family" go their separate ways. Only the neurotically sensitive naïf and the over-the-hill cowboy have a chance at repair as their finale probing suggests. She: "How do you find your way home in the dark?" He: "Just head for the big star – the highway's right under it."

Family melodrama brought literary distinction to Hollywood not only in the representation of "eminent authors" on the screen but in these authors' approach to writing which, if it did not exactly assail classical storytelling, tweaked it. In the cases of Inge, Williams, and Miller's adaptations and imitations such as *Hot Spell*, there was indeed a clear break with the classical mold.

Psychologically and sociologically detailed characterizations took precedence over action. A character's inner conflict was the heart of the matter. The classical divide between heroes and villains was no longer tenable. Though *Home from the Hill*'s parents have just about destroyed their kid with their passive aggression, they are shown with reasons for acting as they do, and in acknowledging their enormous shortcomings, come off also as decent and sensitive. Dialogue was attuned to the diction and patterns of speech corresponding to the respective characters' regionality, class, ethnicity, and religion. Poetic titles were metaphoric. The use of structuring metaphor-motifs raised questions in the audience's mind: the significance of the hunt in *Home* or the rounding-up of the mustangs in *The Misfits*. Melodrama had come a long way from *Broken Blossoms* (UA, 1919) and *Lilly Turner* (WB, 1933), where characters resided in a world unmitigatedly split between good and evil. and conflicts were mostly exterior as the characters went up against an opposing force outside themselves. Then, everything was pretty much spelled out; there was no question about whose side you were on or what anything meant.

The subtype also shattered the American screen's parochialism. Unlike regional-flavored classical cinema, it raised regionality to character status, giving over a chunk of narrative time to the description of a specific locality's traditions (the barbecue of the boar and the spring-cleaning of the graveyard outside the East Texas town in *Home*). It talked of all classes and types: the poor, the nouveau riche, the disenfranchised, the racially diversified, and such hitherto unmentionables as lesbians and gays (repressed or coded/*The Long Hot Summer* but not always/*Suddenly Last Summer*), prostitutes, foreigners, the handicapped, the ugly, in addition to the middle class, the wealthy, the socially accepted, the comely. It pitted one class against the other, as with the cushioned legitimate son Theron and the hardscrabble bastard, visually encapsulated by the two different cemeteries across the road in *Home*. The genre often raised class issues, such as the sexual arousal when one class encountered a totally different class (*Streetcar*'s Stanley and Mitch's yen for Blanche). Characters' various ethnic backgrounds and religious affiliations imaged a heterogeneous land, something that classical cinema merely hinted at.

Family melodrama's thematic sophistication brought distinction as well. The family was seen as ambivalent but, more usually, problematic. This kind of portrait was, on the whole, at odds with the one that emerged in classical cinema. A space and structure that harmed rather than healed, the family was a site of breakdown and estrangement, hostility and unhappiness, loneliness, and dysfunctionality, sending its members to the release valves of memory, dream, illusion, alcohol and sometimes drugs, indiscriminate sex, violence, suicide, or just making them hit the road and get the hell out. The genre was sensitive to the harmful effects upon the family unit of patriarchal capitalism, middle-classness, Puritan repression, and propriety, all with their consequent conforming and camouflaging patterns of behavior. The genre also pinpointed the crisis in masculinity and the clash of macro- and mini-cultures in a melting-pot America. Without being tedious, the genre captured the tedium of everyday life. In addition to addressing the awkward move from teenager to young adult, which classic Hollywood also talked about, the genre took up the fears attendant on moving into and/or just being middle and/or old-aged, which classic Hollywood seldom entertained. In these portrayals of age issues, the genre afforded a second spring for such seasoned actors as Katharine Hepburn, Barbara Stanwyck, Joan Crawford, Fredric March, and Edward G. Robinson. The veterans' renaissance, along with Method newcomers, raised the level of screen acting.

Family conflict, so much on everyone's mind, became interwoven, as expectedly, with the male, female, and romance melodramas. Surprisingly, it bled into other genres as well: adventure (*The Sundowners*, WB, 1960/restoration), biography (*Fear Strikes Out*, P, 1957 and *Man of a Thousand Faces*, U, 1957, both instances of traumatization), social satire (*Marty*, UA, 1955/outsider, *The Catered Affair*, MGM, 1956)/generational confrontation), and courtroom drama (*To Kill a Mockingbird*, U, 1962/growth). Even horror was not immune, as with Ray's *Bigger Than Life* (TCF, 1956), in which a cortisone-overdosing father turned monster (and hence outsider) traumatizes his kid to the point of offering him up for slaughter to an unknown god, in the manner of the biblical Abraham whom the father delusionally believes he is. Family melodrama crossed over musical lines (*Young at Heart*, WB, 1955, *The Pajama Game*, WB, 1957, with factory workers as metaphorical family, and *The Music Man*, WB, 1962, all instances of the outsider; *Just for You* (P, 1952), *Flower Drum Song*, U, 1962/ generational confrontation; and *Gypsy*, WB, 1962/traumatization and generational confrontation). Nor was the thriller spared (*The Desperate Hours*, P, 1955/outsider and *The Man Who Knew Too Much*, P, 1956/outsider, traumatization and restoration; *The Wrong Man*, WB, 1957/traumatization). The frequent hybridization of family melodrama with the western formed a distinct cycle, as we shall see.

16.2   Female Melodrama

Though fewer films of the genre appeared than before (with TCF outstripping U three to one and WB two to one and running neck-and-neck with MGM), and though it trod a well-worn path, female melodrama made significant topical swerves while appropriating new conventions along the way. The series of financially successful remakes spruced up by Universal producer Ross Hunter clearly exemplified these aspects: *Magnificent Obsession* (1954), Robert Blees's adaption of Lloyd C. Douglas's novel with Jane Wyman, first made in 1935; *Imitation of Life* (1959), Eleanore Griffin and Allan Scott's update with Lana Turner of Fannie Hurst's novel and 1934 movie; *Back Street* (1961), Eleanore Griffin and William Ludwig's adaption of Hurst's novel with Susan Hayward,

16-3 *All That Heaven Allows* (U, 1956, p. Ross Hunter)

Director Douglas Sirk's unequivocal style is captured in this female melodrama as elder, bourgeois-encrusted Jane Wyman is transplanted into a world of youth (baby fir tree held by a young Rock Hudson) and nature (trees, stream, wooden bridge).

varying the 1932/1941 versions; and the warhorse *Madame X* (1966), Jean Holloway's reworking of Alexandra Bisson's play with Turner, made in 1915, 1920, 1929, and 1937. The Hunter canon also included first-timer *All That Heaven Allows* (1956), Peg Fenwick's take on Edna and Harry Lee's serial in *Women's Home Companion*, which also starred Wyman. Each film played true to form: a plot and conflictual strategy revolving around a woman's problems, cares, and worries that call for a difficult moral choice or two. The crucial decisions also elicit a good deal of suffering for her and others and, in the end, some form of renunciation.

But that was not the whole picture. The woman emerged not so much as victim but rather victim–victor, a nod to the female's postwar transitional status and slew of contemporary bestselling fiction. And the icon of hysteria, though present, was not as frequent now that the protagonist was more in control than before. This is best seen in *Back Street*, where Hayward, though abandoning respectable marriage for her married lover, parlays a successful, fulfilling career as a fashion designer. In *All That Heaven Allows*, middle-aged Wyman ruffles the judgmental feathers of her social set and grown children and returns to her gardener Rock Hudson, 15 years her junior and a nonconformist. OK, director Sirk's finales are double-edged. Wyman, last seen ministering to Hudson after his accident, does have the aura of a mother tending her child, suggesting also a return to a role she supposedly abandoned.

Victim–victor was now the rule. Unwed mothers, for instance, no longer gave up their child for its own good, as Bette Davis did as *The Old Maid* (WB, 1939). The period/genre heralder *To Each His Own* (P, 1946), director Mitchell Leisen's affecting embodiment of Charles Brackett and Jacques Thery's script, was transitional. The lovesick girl (Oscar-winning Olivia de Havilland) does give up her son but 30 years later, while heading up a lucrative cosmetics industry and doing volunteer work as a bomb spotter in London during World War II, she arranges for his wedding and, in so doing, is revealed as his mother. *Three Secrets* (WB, 1950) finds Eleanor Parker, Patricia Neal, and Ruth Roman ready to claim the child they abandoned years ago. In *The Sins of Rachel Cade* (WB, 1960), taken from Charles Mercer's novel, the eponymous heroine (Angie Dickinson) keeps the child and, further, refuses to leave her nursing career in an African mission to return to England with the child's father. This was not a demonstration of the typical giving-up-love-for-a-career motif but rather a case of having both a career and love, for the film's ending suggests that Rachel will respond in kind to the love of the resident doctor. In *Susan Slade* (WB, 1961), based on Doris Hume's novel, "a girl of great courage" (Connie Stevens) admits that the baby she had before she could marry its father is really hers, not her mother's. After her lover impregnates her and goes off to sea, Leslie Caron's distressed *Fanny* (WB, 1961), Julius Epstein's non-musical movie transfer of S. N. Behrman's libretto, marries a wealthy, older man to care for herself and her child. Eventually, she comes to love her provider. *Paula*'s (C, 1952) variation had a suburban wife (Loretta Young) nursing the little boy she harmed in a hit-and-run accident and eventually adopting him.

Other victim–victors included the wealthy, pampered sisters on the English Channel island of St. Pierre in the nineteenth century ("bold, scheming, and not so nice" Lana Turner and her opposite Donna Reed) in *Green Dolphin Street* (MGM, 1947), Samuel Raphaelson's telescoping of Elizabeth Goudge's volume. Victim of her own God-complex, Turner courts the dissolute, slovenly neighbor while relentlessly molding him into an officer and a gentleman. Further victimization comes to her (and her sister too) when the drunk, feckless fellow mixes up their names ("Marianne" and "Marguerite") in a love letter which erroneously professes his beloved to be Turner, not Reed. A mere "accidental" slip of the pen reverses fortunes. Oblivious to the real state of affairs and in defiance of her father, Turner follows the fellow halfway round the globe. Triumphing over the rigors of life in untamed New Zealand as his wife and mother of his child (a native uprising, an earthquake, a tidal wave), she uses her savvy in the merchant shipping business to remake her husband into a financial success, first at lumber, then at raising sheep and exporting wool. Once again, she's the stabilizer of the male – a motif that consistently surfaces, constituting part of her "victor" status. Her focus, stamina, faithfulness (in resisting the blandishments of a suitor), and "learned humility" (in discovering her husband's long-ago proposal to her sister – the secret hidden away in a desk drawer) win her mate's love in the long run. Spinster Reed, back home, contentedly finds fulfillment as a nun. All along, Turner is proactive, thumbing her nose at her parents and neighbors' criticism that girls are not supposed to act as she does.

Equally focused, assertive, positioned, and rich, Barbara Stanwyck as *B. F.'s Daughter* (MGM, 1947) remakes a free-and-easy assistant professor of economics at Columbia University, whom she marries, into her idea of a great man: an economic theorist who writes books, gives lectures, and works for the Roosevelt administration during the war. Her program backfires. He turns on her, ashamed that he has not done it on his own. Through tenacity and humility, she fights to get him back. Distinctly, Luther Davis's rendition of John Marquand's bestseller was saturated with social satire that pitted conservatives against liberals, rugged individuals against socialists, *nouveau riche* against middle class, and wisely unearthed the follies of both camps. Stanwyck again, in *East Side, West Side* (MGM, 1949), Isobel Lennart's svelte upholstering of Marcia Davenport's bestseller, ends up a winner. This time, however, she leaves her alcoholic hubby, who just can't stay away from temptress Ava Gardner. Despite years of humiliation, she exits with grace, thanking him for all the good things. Jeanne Crain moves from espouser to exposer of a college sorority's hypocrisy, prejudice, and sadism in *Take Care of My Little Girl* (TCF, 1952), the Epstein brother's version of Peggy Goodwin's novel directed by able craftsman Jean Negulesco (1900–93), who devoted himself to both female and romance melodrama.

In *Elephant Walk* (P, 1954), informed by Robert Standish's novel, the young wife (Elizabeth Taylor), refusing the sensitive arms of another, sticks by her husband, helping to free him from the domination of his father while nursing the Indian colony in Ceylon through a plague and taking charge of the restoration after an elephant stampede. Out on a 1901 cocoa plantation in South America in the midst of *The Naked Jungle* (P, 1954), the proxy bride from New Orleans (Eleanor Parker) stamps out her egotistic, insecure husband's fear of her. He wanted a lifeless "ornament" to fill the impressive compound he has built. What he got instead was a humorous, accomplished, sensual, and experienced "woman" (she had been married before and he resents her not being "new"). Tellingly, he (not she) becomes hysterical, dousing her with cologne, throwing her against the bedroom's columns. Further: she has a mind of her own that interrupts, contradicts, and dispenses good advice about the invasion of the soldier ants. Associated with the genre after the war, disaster sequences, enlisting the deployment of special effects (here, *Green Dolphin Street*, *Elephant Walk*), became another witness to the female's victor status.

Natalie Wood as *Marjorie Morningstar* (WB, 1958) walks away from her ill-fated brush with showbusiness and first love, a self-absorbed, bohemian song-writer and social director of a summer resort. She faces up to her modicum of talent (by means of the conventional accidental eavesdropping scene). She comes to realize her beloved is self-destructive and a scattered dilettante, not the genius she imagined. (Here again, the genre, postwar, touches upon the female remake of the male, her misperception owing to love, her subsequent readjustment.) Painfully, she grows up and is happily hopeful during the bus ride back into the city with the smart, talented stage writer who had always adored her.

This adaptation of the hefty Herman Wouk bestseller, with a thirties-to-fifties-setting makeover, introduced the Jewish American princess: a female with a large ego, supported by a well-to-do family, buying into conspicuous consumerism and the good life (a perfume credit made its debut in this film). Further: Central Park West Marjorie does not subscribe to her parents' hand-me-down notion that an illicit love affair or two can ruin a girl's life but follows the advice of the iconic confidante (Carolyn Jones), a promiscuous girl with a taste for wealthy older men who give her a lifestyle her parents can't afford. The entire movie, in fact, revolves around the question: will 18-to-25-year-old Marjorie lose her virginity? As with romantic comedy, quite a few female melodramas contained a scene or two constructed around the *au courant* sexual morality debate. In the Somerset Maugham story remake *Miss Sadie Thompson* (C, 1953), an evangelist castigates the doctor for his embrace of Freud in sexual matters.

In *Butterfield 8* (MGM, 1960), a somewhat cleaned-up take on a John O'Hara novella, a high-living model's (Oscar-winning Taylor) loss of a father at an early age, a week-long molestation as a 13-year-old by her uncle and her reaction: "I loved it. I loved every minute of it" (another first), and a delusional mother has turned her into a promiscuous good-time girl. By falling in love with a married lawyer, she does free herself from her dissolute life and sessions with the shrink, while instilling in her mother a sense of reality. Realizing the man is too insecure to commit (female projection again dashed), she drives away to Boston. Though he follows in a speeding car to stop her and causes an accident in which she dies, she has won and, in death, has finally stabilized her man.

The Heiress (P, 1949), Wyler's entry in the victim–victor stakes, was a genre milestone and memorably kickstarted his career's third phase: Paramount in-house producer-director, 1949–55. Melded with family melodrama (the outsider as courter), Ruth and Augustus Goetz's cinematization of their play based on Henry James finds handsome Morris Townsend (Montgomery Clift) setting his sights on homely spinster Catherine Sloper (de Havilland), who resides with her widowed doctor father (Ralph Richardson) and her aunt/confidante (Miriam Hopkins) in a tony 1850s Washington Square brownstone.

This situation sets off a heated war between daughter and father and a cold one between daughter and suitor. The caution that the father feels toward his ingenuous, gauche daughter's welfare emerges eventually as control and revenge on his part. The pain and anger over losing his wife in childbirth make him resent, even despise his child: "What I lost when she died, what I got in her place." This renders him heartless as he sets his daughter straight: "You got one virtue that outshines them all – your money. You got nothing else . . . one exception – you embroider neatly." Learning that she has been denied her inheritance because of her defiance of her father's wishes to delay the marriage, the suitor's fire is cruelly dampened and when eventually recharged years later, after the father's death, it is just as cruelly extinguished by the daughter. "Yes, I can be very cruel," she tells her aunt, "I have been taught by masters." Though uncharacteristically period, the film echoed the father–daughter dynamic and the male manipulation and domination of the female in many American households.

More ambiguous than in the play and novella due to Wyler's input, Clift is genuinely charming, naïve, and vulnerable (he's right upfront about his aims, as he tells the father: "I'm looking for a position . . . I'm fit for nothing . . . a little inheritance and I spent it") and, above all, shows unquestionable affection for the daughter (how else to explain the lifting up of the woman's spirits?). Wyler also saw to it that the father is softened and hence more ambiguously human than in the first two iterations. Mannered and witty, he *is* protective of his daughter. Both actors hit their marks resoundingly.

But it is de Havilland, through a deep rapport with Wyler, who not only holds her own with the males but delivers the performance of a lifetime, justifying a second Oscar. As she sits waiting in the parlor late at night, she realizes that she, once again, has been the plaything of someone who supposedly loved her. It is here that her transformation from victim to victor begins as she trudges up the staircase, lugging her suitcase containing her hurriedly packed honeymoon trousseau. When next seen, her shyly retiring, ungainly carriage has given way to an erect posture that speaks of self-possession. Her large, supplicating, dull orbs now sparkle. Her once soft voice has grown harsh, noticeably loud; the words come out gravely, meditatively. Formerly ill-fitting clothes are exchanged for perfect tailoring. No longer will she take, but she will give (she goes one better with her ailing father as she tells him: "Don't be kind, it doesn't become you."). The transformation is, in a word, chilling. Incidentally, her character, too, was tampered with by Wyler: she's more appealingly alive (even before the change) and hence, more sympathetic.

Sliding mahogany doors, mirrors, the staircase of this well-appointed but icy abode, and the daughter's embroidery were structuring metaphors–motifs in Wyler's layered *mise-en-scène* that visually encapsulated the thematics. The preference of using two actors in the same frame (one full-faced, the other profiled), in lieu of the classical shot–reverse shot construction, helped preserve both wars' immediacy and the rhythm of the performances.

In Wyler's other period piece *Carrie* (P, 1952), an admirable rendition by writers Ruth and Augustus Goetz of Theodore Dreiser's litigious novel, the female (Jennifer Jones) starts out as disadvantaged, naïve thing from a Missouri farm who journeys to Chicago where she works for a dollar a day sewing in an ill-lit shoe factory and boards with her sister and brother-in-law, who demands $5 a week rent. Seduced by a glib traveling salesman (Eddie Albert) into cohabitation, falling in love with a respected restaurant manager (Laurence Olivier) who keeps mum about his wife and children, eventually marrying him after he lies about his divorce, and even losing her child during pregnancy, she rises above all these selfishly manipulating males, making herself into a successful second lead in stage comedies.

When the genre did concentrate upon suffering victims, the females, to whom the genre was primarily geared, stayed away. The postwar woman knew she had come a long way from the masochism of Joan Fontaine (*Letter From an Unknown Woman*, U, 1948), or that of Lizabeth Scott (*Paid In Full*, P, 1950). Lana Turner's naïve, small-town girl eaten up by New York's fashion mill (*A Life of Her Own*, MGM, 1950) was equally a flop, as was Loretta Young's gangster's moll turned nurse who marries a neurotic pilot with whom she has a child, only to be abandoned by him when he catches her with her ex-lover (*Because of You*, U, 1952). No one bought into Olivia de Havilland's dethronement and death in *That Lady* (TCF, 1955), taken from Kate O'Brien's novel, either.

The other line of female melodrama that proved financially iffy was one in which the woman was portrayed as unredeemably evil, her choices (greed, adultery, deliberate miscarriages, even murder) unquestionably immoral, and her destruction (suicide or an ironic accident) a certainty, as with *The Strange Woman* (UA, 1946) with Hedy Lamarr and *Beyond the Forest* (WB, 1949) with Bette Davis. The representation was too unflattering for the female audience. Only when placed in the formula of the gender-nonspecific thriller did this kind of woman and her shenanigans stand a chance of making a buck. However, *Leave Her to Heaven* (TCF, 1945), from Ben Williams's bestseller, savvily megaphoned by genre pro John M. Stahl, was a booming success. But, take note, the portrait of the pathologically jealous, murdering protagonist (Gene Tierney) was balanced by the supporting one of her sensitive, alert stepsister (Jeanne Crain) who, in the end, wins her brother-in-law's heart.

Hunter's initial three (*Magnificent Obsession, All That Heaven Allows, Imitation of Life*) were remarkable, too, because of director Sirk's *mise-en-scène* privileging a society and a culture, even the woman's own family, that causes, aggravates, or at the very least, remains insensitive to her trouble. Patriarchal capitalism, small-town provincialism, crushing class structures, the conformist state of mind, the material success ethic, the spurious suppression-anodyne, and spoiled, insecure offspring stifled the female. Racism was added to the maelstrom in *Imitation of Life*, with its twinning of two mother–daughter stories, one Caucasian and one black. The ending was true to Sirkian form, with Lana Turner bringing the black girl into the funeral car, which can be construed as just another career move on the part of the actress-character who, after all, performs this deed before a crowd (think audience) of watchers. Also, the black girl has finally achieved her misguided goal – she now has a white mother.

When socially acute directors came to the form – such as Minnelli, King Vidor (*Beyond the Forest; Ruby Gentry*, TCF, 1952), and Walsh (*The Revolt of Mamie Stover*, TCF, 1956) – they also stressed the link between the female's trouble and society/culture/family. Most telling in this regard was Minnelli's *Madame Bovary* (MGM, 1949), with Jones as a farm girl turned village doctor's wife and mother of his child turned mistress of a wealthy man in Robert Ardrey's adaption of Gustave Flaubert's scandalous novel. In fact, *Bovary*'s framing device of author Flaubert (James Mason) on trial for the publication of his novel that is seen as "an outrage against public moral and established custom" explicitly states that society/culture/family had caused an Emma Bovary and "thousands like her in the world." As Flaubert recalls his so deemed "monstrous creation of a degenerate imagination," we are privy to the conditions that produced an Emma. The rigid class system, the repressed convent education, the stultifying routine of village life, and the sentimental novels and operas she devours are there from the start. Later on, unscrupulous usurers take advantage of her financial naïveté – for her wardrobe, the perpetually over-flounced Emma racks up 15,000 francs of debt. A dull, uncomprehending, unambitious husband; a nanny who righteously judges her unorthodox ways; and the disadvantaged state of the female in the nineteenth century, brought home by Emma's wish for a male child for if "a man wants to change, he can," further play their part. Though she ends her life by taking poison, the film ends on a triumphant note or two. Flaubert is exonerated because of the "truth" of the character and he, in writing the novel, and we, the audience at the novel's replay on the screen, never condemn Emma.

Warners' genre-sensitive Vincent Sherman also made the connection in his retelling, seven years later, of Somerset Maugham's *The Letter*, now called *The*

Unfaithful (1947), with Ann Sheridan, but more especially in *The Damned Don't Cry* (1950). In this Gertrude Walker novel inspired by the Bugsy Siegel–Virginia Hill hookup, a scornful father-in-law, irate husband, and the death of her son cause Crawford to bolt from the shack that looks out over oil derricks. In her drive "to get more out of life" and "to kick and punch and belt [her] way up 'cause nobody's gonna give you a lift" (as the world has taught her), she ends up in the arms of a ruthless syndicate boss, allowing him to refashion her as a socialite heiress to better do his dirty work.

These directors, as with Daniel Mann (*Butterfield 8*) and Irving Rapper (*Marjorie Morningstar*), also delved into the female's sensual/erotic side, another acclimatization. *Until They Sail* (MGM, 1957), playwright Robert Anderson's deferential adaptation of James Michener directed by Wise, made female sexuality its center. Here, four New Zealand sisters are left behind while the town's males go off to fight in World War II and a battalion of sexually frisky marines arrive. Each female, in her own way, secretly smolders for (Joan Fontaine), remembers and longs for (Jean Simmons), outrightly lusts for (Piper Laurie), and continually talks about (Sandra Dee) sex. All along, the gals acknowledge that their behavior, involving as it does fornication, adultery, promiscuity, cockteasing, and a suggested masturbation, assails the way they have been brought up and taught (again, the sexual morality debate). Even bolder, Cukor's *The Chapman Report* (WB, 1962)/Irving Wallace novel studied female sexuality in the suburbs.

The Hunter series further added full-bodied romance to the stew, bucking the more often than not classical convention of the flat, wooden male figure on the story's periphery. Postwar, the male moves toward the center, part of the female's vexation as well as victory, while fleshing out female eroticism.

Also in evidence in the Hunter series was the motif of a menopausal woman with a much younger man, still another postwar bow, this one to the issues of female longevity and male biological frailty. Hunter's handling of the motif was an affront to the usual transgeneric practice at this time of casting a middle-aged male with a young female, which made no plot point, only a financial one (58-ish Astaire and 28-ish Audrey Hepburn in *Funny Face*, P, 1957). Age discrepancy as well as the issues of female sensuality and the sadomasochism of the heterosexual coupling hang over *Autumn Leaves* (C, 1956). Rendered by iconoclastic director Robert Aldrich in the noir style, the shadowed, awry-angled piece suspensefully unfolds as if it were a mystery with mature Joan Crawford (50 at the time) as detective trying to figure out her immature lover (Cliff Robertson, a mere 31). *About Mrs. Leslie* (P, 1955) was a refreshing change, not in its story of a woman abandoning the prospect of respectable marriage because of her already married lover, but in the middle age of its couple (Shirley Booth and Robert Ryan).

Identity crisis was yet another topical adjustment, countenancing the era's increase in mental health problems. Freudian psychology, of course, provided a vocabulary to dramatize a bruised psyche. Identity crises, too, cropped up in the Hunter series. Those frequent mirror shots in the Sirk trilogy visually but silently put the question in the mind of its ladies: who am I? In *Imitation of Life*'s second plot strand, race is the culprit. Race similarly conflicted Jeanne Crain in the Kazan-directed *Pinky* (TCF, 1949)/Cid Ricketts Sumner novel; Ava Gardner as the Anglo-Indian in the Cukor-fashioned *Bhowani Junction* (MGM, 1956)/John Masters novel; and Yvonne de Carlo as a Southern belle with "negro" blood in her veins in Walsh's *Band of Angels* (WB, 1957)/Robert Penn Warren novel.

Nervous breakdowns, even psychosis, became de rigueur. In director Curtis Bernhardt's noir-drenched *Possessed* (WB, 1947), derived from Rita Weiman's novel, Crawford, through narcosynthesis and from a hospital bed, recalls her past to psychiatrists in order to pierce her catatonic stupor. A victim of *amour fou* who desperately wants an engineer to have the same feelings for her as she for him, she manipulates, schemes (marries an older man), and lies. Her sense of reality gradually evaporates, as she is unable to distinguish between real and misplaced guilt (as a live-in nurse, she believes she assisted in her patient's suicide) and real and imagined crime (she spies on her stepchild and subsequently hits the girl, knocking her down the stairs to her death). In Arthur Laurents's breezy tailoring of Marcelle Maurette and Guy Bolton's international stage hit, Oscar-winning Ingrid Bergman is *Anastasia* (TCF, 1956), a consumptive who also suffers from bouts of amnesia and who roams the streets of Paris. A trio of *déclassé* Russian money-grubbers intent on cashing in on the Romanov inheritance gruelingly manipulate the woman into claiming she is indeed the Romanov princess. Multiple personality disorder was treated in *The Three Faces of Eve* (TCF, 1957), taken from an account of the actual case compiled by doctors Corbett H. Thigpen and Hervey M. Cleckley, with Oscar-winning Joanne Woodward as a Georgia woman with three distinct personalities (irresponsible party girl/Eve Black, a defeated housewife/Jane, and a pleasant thing who has no memory/Eve White). The traumatic childhood experience of being forced to kiss her dead grandmother in her coffin incited Eve's splintering. MGM's similar and simultaneous version was called *Lizzie*/Shirley Jackson novel, with Eleanor Parker's mental disorder triggered by rape.

Along these lines, director/co-writer (with Collier Young and Malvin Wald) Ida Lupino came up with the intriguing independent programmer *Outrage* (RKO, 1950). A newly affianced girl (Mala Powers) is raped, resulting in shock, paranoia, identity problems (she runs away and suppresses what has happened to her), and violence (with a wrench she hits a guy who wants to dance with her, almost killing him). Eliciting much of the intrigue was Lupino's interest in the victim's subjectivity made palpable by the use of subjective shots; multi-planed compositions in which the foregrounded girl reacts to the backgrounded situation; verbal flashbacks; and expressionistic sounds. Self-reflexively, Hollywood stardom was the cause of the mental disorder of Bette Davis in *The Star* (TCF, 1952) and Kim Stanley in Cheyefsky's Monroe-inspired *The Goddess* (C, 1958). In all of these, apart from *The Goddess*, the ladies end up in recovery.

The Nun's Story (WB, 1959) emerged as the most intelligent of the identity-crisis cycle. Following Kathryn Hulme's bestselling autobiography, Robert Anderson never once let go of a woman's struggle with her voluntarily embraced vows of poverty, chastity, and obedience which place one's right to possess, love, and choose in the hands of another, threatening the very notion of individuality. Undoubtedly, Anderson was also encouraged by director Zinnemann, who staked out the terrain of identity as his own, whether it be a fragmented individual who tries to get it together (*A Hatful of Rain*) or here, where a strong personality runs the risk of losing her identity due to conformist attitudes.

One of the few American directors able to capture spirituality, Zinnemann exacted a performance from Audrey Hepburn that never left any doubt that this was a soul wrestling with itself: her pride at being smarter and prettier than her fellow nuns, her acknowledgment of the medical mission doctor's love for her, her desire to stay in the Congo, her need to avenge the death of her brother in the war by assisting the underground. These situations flew in the face of her vows, her commitment to God, and the neutral war stance of her order. Franz Planer's Belgium/Congo location shoot and Franz Waxman's starkly dramatic score made indelible impressions. Anomalously for the genre and all Hollywood films, no end music was used. Zinnemann insisted that the nun's decision to leave the convent after some 17 years be not colored by music; the right or wrong of her decision left to the audience.

Producer Hunter wisely knew that a female star – her appearance and performance – was at the center of female melodrama and that many of his ladies were in their careers' second spring. He also knew that his colleague Sirk could pull all sorts of thematic values and ironies literally out of a hat or gloves or a mink coat, so he costumed (often Jean Louis), bejeweled (Leykin et Cie), and coiffed the girls to the hilt. Capitalizing on the emergence of high fashion among the middle class because of Madison Avenue and TV and, naturally, the availability of money, high fashion continued to play a significant role in the genre. Rightly, wardrobe and jewelry contributions began to be given a separate card during the opening credits, no longer hidden away in the card that listed about a dozen credits. *Lucy Gallant* (P, 1955) went so far as to insert a fashion show into its story, self-reflexively hosted by Paramount's actual reigning couturier Edith Head, who designed the costumes for the film. (Postwar plots, no matter the genre, were noticeably interrupted by fashion shows.)[2]

By the time Wyman came under Hunter's wing, she was the acknowledged genre queen. No one suffered and emerged triumphantly as she did. The crease between her eyebrows that became more pronounced as her tribulations mounted and relaxed as she transcended adversity was proof of that. In *Johnny Belinda* (WB, 1948)/Elmer Harris play, she's a deaf mute who is raped. She goes on to kill her violator, is found innocent of the crime, keeps the baby, marries the town's doctor, and wins an Academy Award. She is a lifetime nanny of other people's babies who has won their respect and love in *The Blue Veil* (RKO, 1951). As a schoolmarm, she also devotes herself to her farmer husband and son in the third remake of *So Big* (WB, 1953)/Edna Ferber novel. A hiatus from Hunter finds her as *Lucy Gallant*/Margaret Cousin novel, who, abandoned by the groom when her father was indicted for embezzlement (the secret), makes a profit in selling her trousseau in an oil-rich Texas boomtown in 1941 (a literal reversal of fortune). Riding out the economic rainbow and plying her sense of style, she opens an expensive dress shop. Refusing to settle down with a chauvinist rancher ("Haven't I the right to do two jobs at once?" she asks) and bucking the advice of her confidante (Thelma Ritter), she goes on to build up a swanky department store. Lucy winds up with both career and marriage which, incidentally, she proposes.

Back Street's Hayward challenged Wyman's title (Jones, Turner, and Crawford were mere ladies-in-waiting). In *Smash-Up – The Story of a Woman* (U, 1947), a social-problem blend that takes up the issue of alcoholism, she's a nightclub singer turned wife and mother who hits rock bottom, sobers up, and gets her sense of inadequacy in hand. Her small-town college kid, pregnant in Manhattan, marrying someone she doesn't love when her military sweetheart dies, and once again taking to the bottle is the predicament in *My Foolish Heart* (RKO, 1949)/J. D. Salinger story. As a one-quarter Indian firebrand who's ambitious, smart, and "hard as a driller's fist," she's an oil baron in *Tulsa* (EL, 1949) who braves a conflagration (disaster sequence). Though *I Can Get It for You Wholesale* (TCF, 1951) was an unfortunate softening by leftists writer Abraham Polansky and director Michael Gordon of Jerome Weidman's tome of a ruthlessly ambitious fashion designer in Manhattan's garment district, Hayward's career woman has a rollercoaster go of it. As a pampered city girl married to a dedicated preacher assigned to a backward rural Georgia village in the early twentieth century in the location-shot *I'd Climb the Highest Mountain* (TCF, 1951)/Corra Harris novel, she learns to cook, pulls the community through an epidemic, suffers her child's death, confronts narrow-mindedness, sends on her way a rich married woman with designs on her husband, and takes charge of her husband's finances. *Untamed* (TCF, 1955)/Helga Moray novel, reuniting her with *I'd Climb*'s director Henry King, asked even more of her as a forthright miss in Ireland's County Limerick of 1847 who, when the potato famine hits, crosses the sea to South Africa (Zululand location). And she was, singlehand-edly, up to it, whether facing a Zulu attack or a farm destroyed by a storm (disaster sequence). Her *Woman Obsessed* (TCF, 1959)/John Mantley novel is a pioneer woman in the Canadian Northwest wilderness who endures farm work, a surly second husband who slaps her, an 8-year-old son who runs away, a miscarriage, a forest fire, and a blizzard (disaster sequences). As *Ada* (MGM, 1961)/Wirt Williams novel, her call girl turned politician's wife becomes the power behind the throne. And no one belted an interfering female or male better than Hayward.

Most of Hayward's films and others as well (*Green Dolphin Street, Elephant Walk, The Naked Jungle, Lucy Gallant, The Sins of Rachel Cade*, etc.) evinced a postwar convention in which the female was dropped in an extremely unfamil-iar, brutalizing, masculine environment, thus expanding the genre's terrain to include areas well beyond the home. Such a setting, intensified by the prevalent use of color and locations, made the female's victory even more resounding. In fact, *Three Came Home* (TCF, 1950)/Agnes Newton Keith autobiography directed by the reliable Negulesco, drops its American wife/mother (a daunting Claudette Colbert) in a Japanese prison camp on an island of Borneo. Merging with the war genre, the film did not shrink from depicting the debasements she undergoes. Nevertheless, the victim emerged unvanquished, particularly in not signing the false statement about the rape attack.

The Hunter series added a couple more genre conventions. The deployment of color as thematic indicator was a constant. A lush musical score, often with a theme song popping up over the opening/end titles or during the film, was relied upon to wring yet more tears and/or make hearts beat more joyfully and sell a single or soundtrack as well.

16.3 Male Melodrama

By taking an interest in his angst, male melodrama made the male seem special, as with many other items, from *Playboy* to spectator sports. (Still, it was non-sexist in its appeal to both men and women, unlike its female counterpart.) The genre's pertinence and its status as fiction's leading form explained, in large part, its evolvement. The genre's quantity, with Fox's output far surpassing its WB/MGM/UA competitors, as well as its quality went, simply, unchallenged. In the classical period, WB, with its bent toward male-oriented genres, was an admirable leader, however, in codifying the genre from *The Man Who Played God* (1932) through *Anthony Adverse* (1936) to *Kings Row* (1942).

Whether period (*Foxes of Harrow*, TCF, 1947/Frank Yerby novel, *The Black Rose*, TCF, 1950/Thomas B. Costain novel, *Les Misérables*, TCF, 1952/the fourth version of Victor Hugo's standby) or contemporary (*Any Number Can Play*, MGM, 1949/E .H. Heth novel, *Slattery's Hurricane*, TCF, 1949/Herman Wouk novel, *Youngblood Hawk*, WB, 1964/Wouk), the genre traces a series of adventures, professional labors, and sexual episodes of an unfulfilled and/or disturbed male protagonist through which he comes to some understanding and readjustment about himself, the meaning of life, and his place in it. This comes down to embracing spiritual values: love, altruism, honesty, mercy, seeking forgiveness, repentance, even an ennobling concept of God, as in *The Egyptian* (TCF, 1954)/Mika Waltari novel. Here was a genre, along with family and female melodramas, certain thriller subtypes, the war film, and the western, that emblazoned the burning postwar issue of the crisis in masculinity and further, offered a mildly psycho-religious sensitivization solution. Thus, it needfully counterbalanced the classical male-in-action prototype with the male as contemplative-in-action, a male at once riddled with strength and softness, imperviousness and vulnerability, the kind of male that fit the Method actor to a T.

The protagonist can be an unwitting discoverer of this wisdom or higher state. Indian doctor-prince (genre icon Richard Burton), giving up a wealthy woman, stays on to minister to his people in *The Rains of Ranchipur* (TCF, 1955)/Louis Bromfield novel first filmed in 1939 as *The Rains Came*. An unbridledly ambitious racing driver (Kirk Douglas), assessing the estrangement from his friends and beloved, has a change of heart in *The Racers* (TCF, 1956)/Hans Ruesch novel. Argentinean playboy (Glenn Ford), who initially believes one doesn't "have to right the world's wrongs," turns French underground spy in *The Four Horsemen of the Apocalypse* (MGM, 1962). Writers Robert Ardrey and John Gay and director Minnelli updated *Apocalypse*'s source, a Vicente Blasco Ibáñez novel and a Valentino vehicle way back in 1921, from World War I to World War II, and portrayed the wastrel's conversion as the realization of his ideal self. In Minnelli's *Two Weeks in Another Town* (MGM, 1962), Charles Schnee's reinvention of Irwin Shaw's novel, a manic depressive, psychotic, alcoholic actor (Douglas), after three years in a sanitarium, answers the distress call of his former director. In doing so, he attempts to make a comeback but further, to understand the past when his promiscuous wife seduced the director (the secret). Casting aside suicidal thoughts, he comes through a night of the director's further betrayal and liaison with his ex-wife. To become whole again, he realizes he must rid himself of his codependent, parasitic entourage and rely on his inner vision and strength.

Often the protagonist can be a conscious pursuer of spirituality, as in the period- and genre-defining *The Razor's Edge* (TCF, 1946), Lamar Trotti's effective version of Somerset Maugham's bestseller. Genre icon Tyrone Power plays ex-flier Larry Darrell who, returning disturbed from World War I, loses confidence in the accepted values of the culture. Desiring to do more with his

16-4   *The Razor's Edge* (TCF, 1946, p. Darryl F. Zanuck)

In this male melodrama, Larry Darrell (Tyrone Power in a career stretch) searches for Sophie (Anne Baxter, on sofa) in an opium den, a locale rarely seen on the screen.

life than sell bonds (a cultural touchstone for the postwar ex-serviceman and an emblem of the individual vs. the group mentality), he journeys to the Himalayas to seek spiritual guidance from a Hindu mystic. "Real happiness comes from within . . . the path to salvation is as hard to travel as the sharp edge of the razor," the holy man instructs him. (That Hinduism rather than Christianity provides "the way" is a startling switcheroo.) Along his enlightened path to find out "what life is all about," Larry rejects the seductions of married Isabel (Gene Tierney manically acknowledging female sexual desire), cures the severe headaches of Isabel's industrialist husband Gray (John Payne), and rehabilitates alcohol/drug/rough trade addict Sophie (Oscar-winning support Anne Baxter).

The Razor's Edge was Fox's primo male attraction first film after serving in World War II and a decided career switch from his classical persona of a dashing lover and/or peerless wielder of derring-do. (In *The Rains Came*, Power was more engaged in being in love than in soul searching.) Finally, he had something to play and ex-MGM/WB director Edmond Goulding, known as an actor's director, brought it out of him. Power's career about-face mapped the direction of many actors after the war.

Counterpointing but, in the end, paralleling Larry's development was Elliott (Clifton Webb). On his deathbed after receiving Extreme Unction, the snobbish Elliott, whose life has been one dreary round of cocktail parties and superficial chatter, wisely wonders what his blessed Lord will say to him. Elliott, too, was something new in male representation, an unmistakable homosexual, irate that the tassel of his bathrobe does not come down to his knees and therefore sway. Also new was the character of the coal miner, who is a defrocked priest, as he ironically confesses to Larry.

Narrative-wise, Herbert Marshall starts out (and continues) as a disembodied commentative first-person voiceover but unconventionally enters into the proceedings as the character Maugham, the source's actual author, and a confidant to Larry (the genre also welcomes the confidant). Unconventional, too, and unsettling was the film's non-closure. Last but not least was the matter of the film's theme, which displaced the culture's traditional criteria for male maturity. The embrace of a well-paid job, marriage, fatherhood, religion, civic duty, and patriotism was not what it was all about, the film implied. The continual search for the meaning of life (an adventure of the spirit, if you will), which in the protagonist's case encompasses thus far the virtues of altruism, self-sacrifice, and celibacy, brings fulfillment.

Whether an unwitting or a very decided seeker of the light, physical pain (sometimes) and psychological anguish (always) wrack the protagonist's bones, as with the big game hunter/writer Gregory Peck, felled by a wound, agonizing over his life in *The Snows of Kilimanjaro* (TCF, 1952)/Hemingway short story. Dissatisfaction with the self and/or the societal construction of the self; lack of fulfillment at work; guilt over a past trespass, usually sexual extracurriculars or some kind of stealth (the secret); the loss of a male buddy or sweetheart; the annoying intrusion and uncomfortable readjustment of true love (here, the stabilizing female appears); the acknowledgment of having behaved badly (whether selfishly, cowardly, dishonestly, harshly, judgmentally, or irresponsibly) are the usual pangs occasioning the male's humanization. At the end, a conversion occurs, involving confession or redress of the "terrible" past thing and/or restitution. Crying or perspiring, a signaler of breakthrough, is a genre icon.

Estranged from his parents, a fidgety longshoreman (John Cassevetes), who has caused his older brother's death by reckless driving and who has busted out of the army because of a brutalizing sergeant (the secrets), comes to the New York docks in director Ritt's debut *Edge of the City* (MGM, 1956), Robert Alan Arthur's enlargement of his teleplay. A black stevedore (confidant Sidney Poitier) befriends him, even interceding for him in a fight with a racist boss.

Unfortunately, the intercession results in the black man getting a hook in his back. The longshoreman, now even more troubled, refuses, along with his co-workers, to tell the investigating detective what happened (still another secret). He calls home and talks to his parents (previously, he would call but never talk). Finally, with the prodding of the black man's wife and his girlfriend's outrage (female stabilization), he decides to come clean. The film startles with its racially integrated Gotham locations and situations.

Sometimes the conversion comes down to reconciliation with a wife after a sexual fling. The return is usually seen as the right course (doctor Robert Mitchum in *Not As A Stranger* (UA, 1955)/Morton Thompson bestseller) Many films (Fox's *The View from Pompey's Head*, 1955/Hamilton Basso novel with Richard Egan and *Ten North Frederick*, 1958/John O'Hara novel with Gary Cooper), however, presented the mending as problematic, imbuing the work with turbid undercurrents. The unappreciated husband/father (Fred MacMurray) in *There's Always Tomorrow* (U, 1956), producer Hunter/director Sirk's remake of a 1934 film, compares himself to his latest manufactured toy, "Rex, the walkie-talkie robot" (one of Sirk's explicit visual correlatives). He comes alive only when an old flame hits town. Feeling he is "trapped in a tomb of his own making," he decides to divorce his wife and marry his former girl. The son's confrontation with the woman forces her to reassess the situation and return to her Manhattan routine (another robot). Father goes back to his suburban life with an equally robotic wife, still absorbed with her schedule and children. In true Sirk fashion, the film ends where it began, his people indeed moving but, alas, in circles, making no progression whatsoever. Sirk's typically double-edged last shot is of the three offspring behind the stairway's balustrade, suggesting that they and their concerns will still predominate in the household and, thus, continue to eclipse the father and his needs and, appropriately, should be behind bars (Sirk's problematic child). In *From the Terrace* (TCF, 1960)/John O'Hara novel, an investment banker (Paul Newman), upending "the attainment of wealth and high position," actually leaves his promiscuous wife, who wants an "open" relationship.

Body and Soul (UA, 1947) and *The Hustler* (TCF, 1962) were kings of the hill, an achievement primarily due to director Robert Rossen (1908–66). Raised by Jewish parents in a hardscrabble quarter of New York's East Side, schooled at New York University, and working with agitprop theater groups gave Rossen an activist liberal bent. An avowed communist by 1937, he drifted from the party seven years later, though his Marxist perspective remained. During HUAC's initial probe, Warner named Rossen as one of his writers (1936–42) dismissed because of communist affiliation. Rossen was the first of 19 "unfriendly witnesses." After the outing of the first 10, the Committee recessed. When it resumed, the Committee never bothered to call the others, among them Rossen.

But by 1947, *Johnny O'Clock* (C) was in release, Rossen's first writer-director credit. (A letter of testimony to Columbia's Harry Cohn got him the job.)

Both Charley (Garfield) in *Body and Soul*, an Abraham Polonsky original, and Eddie (Newman) in *The Hustler*, Rossen's co-adaptation (with Sidney Carroll) of a Walter Tevis novel, are compromisers too (as with Rossen who eventually named names), victims of the corrupting capitalist system. They use others and allow others to use them, denaturing their talent into a craving for money and insensateness that is, in the end, self-annihilating.

Charley is from the slums: "I just want to be a success." As a boxer, he becomes money-obsessed, dishonest, and callous, destroying his relationships with his mother and girl. Pool shark Eddie is so hungry to become a rich, respected winner that nothing stands in the way, even his mindful lame girl's warning of his gambler-manager's perfidy. To convince him of what is what, the girl allows the manager to have his way with her and then, after scribbling "perverted/twisted/crippled" in lipstick on the bathroom mirror, cuts her wrists. Self-awareness comes to both only after a terrible personal loss.

Rossen's Oscar- winning *All the King's Men* (C, 1949) split his canvas by countering two males. Jack Burden (John Ireland) undergoes an appraisal of himself. The rich boy turned working reporter turned political hatchet man finally comes to believe that politician demagogue and friend Willie Stark (Oscar-winning Broderick Crawford) is totally evil. By being his right-hand man, Jack also realizes he is perpetuating that evil. He walks away. On the other hand, Willie, the impoverished farm hick who puts himself through law school and eventually runs for governor, falls deep into the capitalist-political bog while contributing to it. At first, he spouts off about "getting the truth out," and he does. Yet, even at this early stage, Willie's idealism is clouded by his concern for materialism and his own pleasure, evinced in that medium shot of him gnawing at a chicken wing, oblivious to his wife's importunateness about service. A believer in the end justifying the means, Willie leaves a sordid trail of lies, graft, and revenge. He commits adultery with his secretary (Oscar-winning support Mercedes McCambridge) and Jack's society girl. He becomes a drunk (he starts out as a teetotaler). He is guilty of murder, an honest judge's suicide, intimidation, and slander. Moreover, he busts up with his wife and occasions the paralysis of his adopted son when he makes the kid play in the football game even though the boy is suffering from severe headaches.

Collapsing Robert Penn Warren's almost 500-page novel into a mere 109-minute running time, the movie unfolds like gangbusters, with its overlapping dialogue, cluttered frames that privilege foreground dressing and use of off-screen space. Most of all, however, it is the montage structuring of the entire film (not just the passage-of-time sequences) which makes the film play *furioso*, emblematic of Willie's rise to power and his sock-it-to-'em approach.

So atypically classical, Rossen's narrative construction presaged what was to come in filmmaking while his documentary realist style gave the work a blistering immediacy. *The Hustler*'s narrative also breached tradition with its five pool games suspending the story's thrust, each immersing us into Eddie's emotional state. Assembled by editor Evan Lottman, the passages had a meditative feel and lyricism, unlike the rest of the film edited by Dede Allen.

Body and Soul's writer Polonsky, coadapting Ira Wolfert's novel with the novelist himself, delivered a facsimile of the Charlie, Eddie, and Jack characters in *Force of Evil* (MGM, 1948). In this, Garfield as a pricey gambling syndicate lawyer legitimizes the city's independent numbers racket outfits into a sleek conglomerate, with his client as head and him on the take. Joe's brother, however, is a holdout and is eventually thrown in the river for bucking the syndicate. Embittered over the murder of his brother, who took care of him as a kid (the secret), and guided by the woman (female stabilization) who worked for his brother, Joe exposes the scheme and culprits by means of a tapped phone off the receiver and turns himself in.

The repentance is deathbed in *Death of a Scoundrel* (RKO, 1956), and in Philip Yordan and Robert Wyler's close refit of Sidney Kingsley's play *Detective Story* (P, 1951), unfalteringly discharged by Wyler. A police officer (Douglas) is morally indignant at his wife's premarital indiscretion that resulted in an abortion and her subsequent inability to conceive (the secret). He plays judge and jury and takes the law into his own hands, beating up suspected criminals. An abusive criminal father who drove his mother insane, as well as his erroneous judgment in letting go two boys who eventually robbed and killed a butcher (other secrets) explain, in part, his obsessive, borderline psychotic intransigence. Mortally shot in the stomach, the detective tells a reporter to help his wife forgive him, drops charges against a thief whose girl has promised to make restitution, and murmurs: "Oh my God, I am heartily sorry for having offended Thee."

A spate of male melodramas concludes with an unredeemed protagonist, one who becomes increasingly aggressive, acquisitive, power-mad, selfish, and/or deluded. In the end, he is left with nothing; he is materially and/or spiritually bankrupt. He may or may not realize his screw-up but if he does realize it, it is too late to do anything about it. *The Champion* (UA, 1949), the creation of writer Carl Foreman, director Mark Robson, and actor Douglas, is a blood-brother of *All the King's Men*'s Willie. Here, an up-from-the-gutter boxer of unbridled ambition and pride ("I want people to call me mister") and lust for the good life ("We're on that gravy train and there are no stops") uses people as stepping stones – wife, manager, no matter who. A screenwriter on the comeback trail (Bogart) allows his anger and aggressive nature get the better of him in the Ray-directed *In a Lonely Place* (C, 1950). That he has been unable to work since the war and is suspected of the murder of a hatcheck girl he picked up one night (the film is part mystery thriller) add stress to his serious relationship with a caring neighbor. Realizing she is pulling out of the planned marriage and leaving town, he begins to strangle her. In *Shakedown* (U, 1951), Howard Duff is a conscienceless news photographer who, career-wise, works both sides against the middle. Also on his way to hell was Broadway gossip columnist (a bespectacled Lancaster) in *Sweet Smell of Success* (UA, 1957), a scalding Ernest Lehman/Clifford Odets brew. The control-freak scribe enlists, on a quid-pro-quo basis, an ambitious publicity agent (Curtis), who has "the scruples of a guinea pig and morals of a gangster," to destroy his sister's love for a jazzman. The agent, the film's other unredeemed reprobate, plants a calumnious item in the newspaper condemning the musician as a marijuana-smoking commie. After stashing some dope in the musician's overcoat pocket, he tips off the police. The ruse wrecks the relationship but also renders the sister suicidal, while turning the columnist and his stooge against each other. Never once does the columnist, who lives with his sister and has a silver-framed picture of her on his desk, face the fact that he is in love with her. Never once does the agent question his Machiavellian tactics. Even Spencer Tracy, in an outing against type, added to this gallery of scoundrels in *Edward, My Son* (MGM, 1949), Donald Odgen Stewart's engrossing version of Robert Morley and Noel Langley's stage hit. Unscrupulous and delusional, businessman Tracy cheats an insurance company ("I did it because I was pushed"); blackmails a headmaster who wants to expel his son who has a corrupting influence on the rest of the boys ("When I fight, I fight with anything I can lay my hands on"); sells out his business partner, who jumps from a roof because of the betrayal; takes a mistress; and refuses his wife a divorce. He is the reason for his wife's alcoholism and his son's devolvement into an unmitigated rotter who meets his death at age 23. At the film's end, this "Napoleon of finance" still believes what he did was best for his son and plans to take his son's bastard child under his wing.

A genre variation fastens upon the "focused" male, defined in a series of films as someone who, come what may (even death), stays true to himself. The conflict comes down to a male holding onto his individual integrity against a conformist society which undermines or destroys (or attempts to), deliberately or accidentally, this connection to his inner core, this rigorous "sensitivity."

Zinnemann (1907–97) returned to this concern repeatedly. A Viennese Jew who had studied at the Technical School of Cinematography in Paris and had assisted the famous cameraman Eugene Schuftan in Berlin, he began making documentary shorts for MGM (1937–9), then moved into B features (1942–9) before graduating to A pictures, as with his Oscar-winning *From Here to Eternity* (C, 1953), Daniel Taradash's canny collapse of Jones's 859-page eye-opener. *Eternity* turned out to be another of Oscar-winning Zinnemann's sensitive renderings of this bout with integrity (cf. the female melodrama *The Nun's Story*), a film that brimmed over with feeling without a glint of sentimentality. Despite his outfit's "treatment," Pvt. Prewitt (genre icon Montgomery Clift) refuses to enter the middleweight boxing tournament, having sworn, after blinding an opponent in the ring, never to fight again. Though he is told "A man's gotta play ball," it falls on deaf ears, as he replies: "If a man doesn't go his way, he's nothing." Furthermore, he keeps his promise to avenge his friend Maggio's death. And, on the evening of the Pearl Harbor attack, neither his girl's protest nor his gaping stomach wound prevent his return to the base: "They need every guy they can get . . . I'm a soldier." Sgt. Warden (Lancaster) forsakes acquiescing to the woman he loves, refusing to go to officer-training school: "I'm not an officer. I'm an enlisted man. I can't do it. I would be putting on an act." Completing the male trio is Maggio (Oscar-winning support Sinatra), who never once gives the sadistic stockade sarge the satisfaction of knowing he is hurting him: "He asks me if it hurts. And I spit at him."

Eternity's women were in dire contrast. Karen (Deborah Kerr) sails home with her philandering husband whom she despises while Alma/Loreen (Oscar-winning support Donna Reed) is steeped in her fantasy of "being proper" (that is, conforming) because "when you're proper, you're safe."

Clift reprised the mold in *Raintree County* (MGM, 1957), Edward Dmytryk's sprawling rendition (2 hours, 46 minutes) of Millard Kaufman's adaption of Ross Lockridge, Jr.'s unwieldy novel set in 1858–65 Indiana against the background of Civil War and Reconstruction. When any form of melodrama is set against a crucial time in a nation's history, as here, the emphasis still remains on the individual's psychic state. How the event affects the character's personality, relationships, and situations is central, not the event itself.

Bearing the same DNA were textbook writer Walter Pidgeon in *If Winter Comes* (MGM, 1948)/A. S. M. Hutchinson novel; whiskey priest Henry Fonda in *The Fugitive* (RKO, 1948)/Graham Greene novel; architect Gary Cooper in *The Fountainhead* (WB, 1949)/Ann Rand novel that enshrines self-integrity and a man's right to exist for himself; tank-town boxer Robert Ryan in *The Set-Up* (RKO, 1949)/Joseph Marsh's narrative poem; power-cruiser skipper John Garfield in *The Breaking Point* (WB, 1950)/Hemingway novel and its remake *The Gun Runners* (UA, 1958) with Audie Murphy; small-town barber David Wayne in *Wait Till the Sun Shines, Nellie* (TCF, 1951)/Ferdinand Reyher novel; managing editor Humphrey Bogart in *Deadline U.S.A.* (TCF, 1952); journalist Tyrone Power in *The Sun Also Rises* TCF, 1957)/Hemingway novel; columnist Clift in *Lonelyhearts* (UA, 1958)/Nathaniel West novel; undeterred actor Anthony Franciosa in *Career* (P, 1959)/James Lee play; doctor Paul Muni in *The Last Angry Man* (C, 1959)/Gerald Green novel; and obsolete cowboy Douglas in *Lonely Are the Brave* (U, 1962)/Edward Abbey novel.

The Big Knife (UA, 1955), Odets's play translated by James Poe and director Aldrich, and *Requiem for a Heavyweight* (C, 1962), Rod Serling's movie acclimation of his telefilm directed by TV's Ralph Nelson, altered the protagonist's customarily ennobling last stand. *Knife's* movie star (Jack Palance), to stop hurting those he loves, slashes himself fatally in the bathtub while *Requiem's* over-the-hill-at-age 37 boxer (Anthony Quinn), out of loyalty to his manager, agrees to wrestle, entering the ring as "Big Chief Mountain Rivera," complete with Indian headdress, tepee blanket over his shoulders, and hatchet. Both finales were ambiguous: at once admirable and ignoble. Both films were also unusual in that they were essentially character-studies.

Male melodrama often hybridized with the adventure film along the lines of *Thunder in the East* (P, 1951)/Alan Moorehead's novel in which the pilot-mercenary (Ladd) stops charging refugees from Peking his exorbitant fees and sacrifices his life to stay with the blind girl he loves. Others include *Kangaroo* (TCF, 1952); *They Came to Cordura* (C, 1959), Rossen's reimaging of Glendon Swarthout's novel; *The Devil at Four O'Clock* (C, 1961)/Max Catto novel; and remake *Mutiny on the* Bounty (MGM, 1962)/Charles Nordhoff and James Hall novel. The genre, additionally, crossbred with family melodrama, as with *The Man in the Gray Flannel Suit* (TCF, 1956)/Sloan Wilson novel where public relations man (Peck) turns down a career-changing business trip with his boss so he can spend more time with his family and draws up an agreement to send $100 each month to the bastard son he sired during the war (the outsider motif). In *By Love Possessed* (UA, 1961), a shamelessly disrespectful skeletization and rearrangement of James Gould Cozzens's 1957 novel that highlighted the sensational aspects, small-town upper-middle-class Massachusetts lawyer (Efrem Zimbalist, Jr.) in the end faces up to the chaos in his own seemingly ordered life – his own adultery with his partner/friend's wife; his own unhappiness; his rebellious son accused of raping a tart and causing the suicide of his proper girlfriend (she swallows cleaning fluid); an embezzling older partner; and another partner turned bitter alcoholic. Realizing the difference between "real right and wrong" as opposed to "legal right and wrong," the lawyer breaks off the affair, reconciles with his family and advises his partners (the "growth of the adult" motif).

16.4   Romance Melodrama

The eros in heterosexual coupling, invariably during the wooing stage, is the genre's subject; its conflict: the obstacles to union, creating passion and suffering that are the heartbeat of romance. Romance melodrama is all about not getting what you want – until the end, sometimes.

The formula still worked. Postwar culture was, in the main, sanguine about love in the bud, less so about married love, as seen in family/female/male melodramas. The noir thriller's representation of erotic un-togetherness (as we shall see) voiced the culture's faint though increasing cynicism about romance before and after marriage. Along with the culture's sunny slant on romance, contemporary thematic tune-ups, spurred on by the industry's adaptation overdrive, its remake policy, the possibility of soundtrack and single-disc energization, location shooting, and the new technologies helped leader TCF and second-placed P and MGM to keep the genre agleam in the public's eye. Jennifer Jones, Deborah Kerr, and Elizabeth Taylor were female icons, while their male matches included William Holden, Van Johnson, and Rossano Brazzi.

The married status of one of the lovers remained the most frequently invoked obstacle. In *September Affair* (P, 1950), fellow Americans Joan Fontaine and Joseph Cotton miss a plane back to her career and his family, respectively (thank God, because the plane crashed), and spend stolen time together in Naples, Capri, and Florence, underlined by the old standard "September Song." *Indiscretion of an American Wife* (C, 1953) was a neo-realist (see Part VI) spin on the old chestnut by writers Cesar Zavattini and Truman Capote and shepherded by Vittorio de Sica, with Jones's married woman and Clift's professor hooking up in Rome's train station. *Summertime* (UA, 1955)/Arthur Laurents's play brought together a needy spinster secretary from Ohio (Katharine Hepburn) and a married Italian shopkeeper and father (Brazzi). To have the romance transpire against real-life Venice in Eastmancolor, director David Lean made the heartbeat and heartbreak more haunting. An orchestra conductor (Brazzi) with a mentally impaired wife entrances American tourist (June Allyson) against CinemaScope/Technicolor Bavarian locations in Sirk's *Interlude* (U, 1957), retooled from *When Tomorrow Comes* (U, 1939)/James Cain story. In *Strangers When We Met* (C, 1960)/Evan Hunter novel, married architect Douglas has an affair with equally married neighbor Novak. *Beloved Infidel* (TCF, 1960)/Sheila Graham autobiography unveils the columnist's (Kerr) liaison with married writer F. Scott Fitzgerald (Peck).

The twist in Huston's *Heaven Knows, Mr. Allison* (TCF, 1957), with Kerr and Mitchum, and *Sea Wife* (TCF, 1957)/J. M. Scott's novel, with Joan Collins and Richard Burton, was that the female was a nun married to Christ. Both films were hybridized with adventure, being also World War II survival tales: the first set on a South Sea island; the other on a raft in the Indian Ocean after the sinking of a freighter carrying refugees from Singapore. *The End of the Affair* (C, 1955)/Graham Greene novel comes about when a married woman (Kerr) vows to Christ to give up her soldier lover (Johnson) if his life is spared in a bombing. The reverse situation of a woman in love with a priest occurred in *Winter Meeting* (WB, 1948)/Ethel Vance novel, with Bette Davis and James

Davis (on his way to become a priest) and *The Angel Wore Red* (MGM, 1960), with Ava Gardner and Dirk Bogarde.

In every case, lovers returned to their spouses and kept their vows, since the era valorized marriage and religion. These were not completely unhappy endings since nothing ensured passion's endurance more than renunciation. In about two-thirds of postwar love stories, the lovers were star-crossed, yet still believed in love and, no matter the suffering involved (especially at the end), never expressed regret.

Separation and/or death, usually because of war, constituted other obstacles. Hemingway's *A Farewell To Arms* (P, 1932) was loosely remade as *Force of Arms* (WB, 1951), with lovers William Holden and Nancy Olsen, World War II substituting for World War I, a male melodrama redemption subplot, and a reimagined finale. Selznick's *A Farewell to Arms* (TCF, 1957) stuck close to the original, with the ambulance driver (Hudson) rowing out of the war zone with the pregnant nurse (Jones) who dies in childbirth, as does the baby, against the Italian Alps in CinemaScope/Deluxe Color. Also filmed on location in Cinema-Scope/Eastman Color, *A Time to Love and a Time to Die* (U, 1958)/Erich Maria Remarque novel told things from the German side with Nazi private (John Gavin) and garment-factory worker (Lilo Pulver) in love. Knowing that the lovers' first encounter (usually fortuitous) and last goodbye (usually unrecognized as such by the lovers) are a relationship's privileged moments, director Sirk underlined these conventions with Miklós Rózsa's music and emblematic elements of staging and visual design (through an opened door, Gavin lays eyes on Pulver for the first time at the far end of the room; Pulver looks through the broken pane of a bomb-blasted station at a departing train taking her husband away). Sirk's ironically circular finale found Gavin once again at the Russian–German front. Now, an act of mercy (he allows enemy prisoners to flee) leads to his death.

In *Act of Love* (UA, 1954)/Irwin Shaw novel, set in 1944 wartime Paris, military bureaucracy and middle-class sensibility, not war's destruction, wreck the union. The commander refuses to give an American soldier (Douglas) permission to marry the French girl (Dany Robin) he's sleeping with. Devastated that the police have marked her as a prostitute and full of remorse at offending God by her fornication, the girl drowns herself in the Seine. *D-Day, the Sixth of June* (TCF, 1956)/Lionel Shapiro novel with Dana Wynter, Robert Taylor, and Richard Todd and shot in England in CinemaScope/Deluxe Color intertwined the separation/death-by-war pattern with the standard triangle situation of two people in love with the same person. (The triangle situation still proved popular: *Stallion Road*, WB, 1947/Stephen Longstreet novel, *Flame and the Flesh*, MGM, 1954, *One Desire*, U, 1955/Conrad Richter novel.) *Miracle in the Rain* (WB, 1956)/Ben Hecht novella added a miraculous touch. A medal which a secretary

(Wyman) had given to a GI reporter (Johnson) comes back into her hands in St. Patrick's Cathedral, New York, after she has been informed of his death, thus bringing home the constant generic refrain of love's endurance after death. The film also foregrounds the iconic use of personal objects (here, a medal) to anthropomorphize lovers.

Separation by an accident was yet another time-honored pattern. A car hits a pedestrian (Kerr at her staunchest best) running against the light to meet her beloved (Grant, allowing feeling to seep through his veneer) at the top of the Empire State Building in *An Affair to Remember* (TCF, 1957). Leo McCarey's heartrending remake in CinemaScope/Deluxe Color of his own *Love Affair* (RKO, 1939) also employs two sets of love triangles. Ex-nightclub singer Kerr, "with expensive tastes," is the mistress of a prosperous businessman to whom she's engaged while suave gigolo Grant is being kept by a well-off socialite whom he has promised to marry. *Affair*'s dicey tonal shifts into farce and satire miraculously enhance (not undermine) the romantic mood through contrast while keeping the sentiment from turning into sentimentality. The title song, introduced by Vic Damone over the credits, is heard twice within the film (sung by a dubbed Kerr) and played on a piano by Grant's grandmother (the genre's iconic spokesman of destiny and fate). A genre convention, a theme song may provide music for lovers to dance to (another iconic situation). Here, Kerr and Grant do dance, but to another song. When used for underscoring, the title song is an instance of melodrama's "excess," here lifting the audience to the romantics' highs or plummeting them to their lows. Title songs went into overdrive thanks to the booming recording industry.

Similar to *Affair*'s situation and tonal shifts but smarter and sleeker was *Breakfast at Tiffany's* (P, 1961). Playwright George Axelrod and director Blake Edwards transmogrified Capote's novella into a swooning romance, studded with incisive satire and bright farce. High-class whore Holly Golightly (Givenchy-dripping Audrey Hepburn) makes us laugh at her sincere phoniness and alarming behavior. At the same time, she makes us feel the heartache of a girl who is made even more addled, insecure, and frightened by love's responsibility in the figure of another whore, a reformed one (George Peppard). And there's heartache in the emergence of Holly's hayseed "husband" who separates the lovers. The balance of such tonal contrasts was not to be believed, as was Edwards's Manhattan location shoot in VistaVision/Technicolor that reeked with grit and glamour. Inlaying the wittily elegant images with Henry Mancini's score, featuring the dreamily melancholic "Moon River," Edwards lifted the enterprise to lyrical loftiness, thus hitting the genre's emotional bull's-eye.

That old female-destabilizing-male standby was still invoked (*Of Human Bondage*, WB, 1946/Maugham novel with Eleanor Parker and Paul Henried first made at RKO, 1934), but was box-office iffy. Its opposite and topically in-tune female stabilizing male (*From This Day Forward*, RKO, 1946)/Thomas Bell novel with Fontaine and Mark Stevens) sold. The financially successful *Rhapsody* (MGM, 1954)/Henry Handel Richardson novel played it both ways while adding a variation. A wealthy, spoiled girl (Taylor) clings smotheringly to Italian violin student (Vittorio Gassman). His first love, however, is the violin. Her all-consuming "need-love" as well as his independence destabilize *her*, resulting in a suicide attempt. Though she marries an adoring American piano student (John Ericson), she at best tolerates him. Her father and the violinist have taught her to "be the loved one, never the lover." Expectantly, the aspiring pianist gives up his lessons, lives off her, and becomes an alcoholic. To prove her worth to the now famous violinist, she rehabilitates the pianist, planning to divorce him when he's a success and begin anew with the violinist. Well, her rehabilitation, which involves her discovery of "gift-love" and how transforming that kind of love can be, extends to her staying with the pianist. Played against the South of France, Zurich, the Swiss Alps, and Paris in Technicolor (second unit) and flooded with lushly romantic airs from Tchaikovsky and Rachmaninov, the film's representation of love's types and vagaries engrossed. Taylor's follow-up with Johnson, *The Last Time I Saw Paris* (MGM, 1954)/F. Scott Fitzgerald story, also played it both ways. When concerning itself with destabilization (whether of the male, or the female in *Rhapsody* or *Carnival Story*, RKO, 1954, or both mates as in *Gilda*, C, 1946, with its out-of-sorts gambler, Ford, reigniting an old flame, Hayworth, now married to his boss and friend, George Macready), the genre flirted with love's sadomasochistic aspect.

The genre ignored other types of love. Other- and same-sex friends and same-sex lovers as protagonists (homosociality was suspect; homosexuality was considered, on the whole, aberrant) were given the fisheye. No, the genre consistently and complacently proclaimed that the true self was found through heterosexual coupling, the most transcendent thing in life that can happen to an individual. However, *Trapeze* (UA, 1956)/Max Catto novel with Paris's Cirque d'Hiver locations in CinemaScope/Deluxe Color was a wake-up call. Whether intended or not, the male bonding between Lancaster and Curtis had more ardor as mentor and student worked together to perfect "the triple" somersault on the bars, and more anguish when Gina Lollobrigida become a destabilizing wedge between them than that of the triangle situation of two guys falling for the same gal.

The genre did, however, update itself. The icon of gorgeous landscapes (even in wartime) that pluck the lovers out of the everyday, thereby highlighting the specialness of romance, was given a boost by its embrace of location shooting, large screen, and color. Typically, against Rome's architectural glory in 'Scope and color, the American secretaries' affairs (Dorothy McGuire/Clifton Webb,

Jean Peters/Brazzi, Maggie McNamara/Louis Jourdan) in *Three Coins in the Fountain* (TCF, 1954) seemed to transcend the mortal.

Class as obstacle continued and was nothing new (*Roman Holiday*, P, 1953/ Oscar-winning Audrey Hepburn as a princess and Peck as a reporter under Wyler's direction shot on location in the Eternal City; *The Swan*, MGM, 1956/ Grace Kelly as the princess and Louis Jourdan as the valet in a CinemaScope/ Eastmancolor remake of *One Romantic Night*, UA, 1930; and *That Kind of Woman*, P, 1959/Sophia Loren as a woman of the world and Tab Hunter as a naïve soldier, a refurbishing of *The Shopworn Angel*, P, 1929 and MGM, 1940). Race as obstacle, however, was. And no film did it as sentiently as *Love Is a Many-Splendored Thing* (TCF, 1955), playwright John Patrick's simpatico rendering of Han Suyin's autobiography. But *Love's* racial chasm between Eurasian Suyin (Jones at her career best) and Caucasian Mark Elliott (Holden) is complicated by several factors. Their nationalities are different (though mixed, she's Chinese in her heart; he's an American through and through). Marital status likewise separates them (she's a recent widow – her Nationalist general husband had been killed by the communists; he's married). And they do not share the same political ideologies (she's a doctor in the thick of the communist infiltration of the mainland while he's an outside reporter covering the fray).

Jones and Holden's in-tune-with-each-other performances; Leon Shamroy's sumptuous CinemaScope/Deluxe Color lensing in Hong Kong; and the Oscar-winning Paul Francis Webster–Sammy Fain mellifluent title song, heard no less than ten times during the film (the lovers dance to it twice) had much to do with the film's profound affect. Director Henry King's handling, however, had most to do with it.

King (1888–62), an entertainer in stock since receiving a high-school diploma, ambled over to the other side of the proscenium and eventually began directing shorts in 1915, features four years later. After a Goldwyn tenure (1925–7), he signed with Fox in 1930, becoming its premier house director for some thirty years. Though proficient in all genres, it was his heartfelt, multifaceted rendering of love and lovers, as here, "The Gift of the Magi" sequence from the omnibus *O. Henry's Full House* (TCF, 1952) with the reciprocally sacrificing marrieds Jeanne Crain and Farley Granger, *Beloved Infidel*, and *Tender Is the Night* (TCF, 1961) with Jones and Jason Robards, Jr., that sent him and the audience.

King portrayed love's deference. Suyin tells Mark that she will let him decide about continuing their affair since he is stronger: "But you are gentle . . . there's nothing stronger in the world than gentleness." Love involves sacrifice, King conveyed, as Suyin resignedly accepts her hospital dismissal because of her indiscreet affair. Love's sensuality was not ignored, as when bathing-suited Suyin lights her cigarette from the cigarette of bathing-suited Mark. King limned

16-5   *Love Is a Many-Splendored Thing* (TCF, 1955, p. Buddy Adler)
Postwar, sensuality returns to the romance melodrama (as in the pre-Code days) while interracial coupling becomes a constant, as with star-crossed lovers Jennifer Jones and William Holden.

love's transcendence in four major scenes on the grassy hillside behind the hospital. Even part of the lovers' Macao rendezvous was set on the hotel balcony looking down on the street below. Places of height to which lovers gravitate, emblematic of their separation from and ultimate transcendence of the everyday, is a genre icon.

Love's permanence was insisted upon. After news of Mark's death, Suyin hears him rereading his letters, recalls his words, even sees him on the hillside. Repetition of lines (*The Last Time I Saw Paris*'s "take me home now"), songs (*Three Coins in the Fountain*'s Oscar-winning title tune), objects (*Summertime*'s gardenia, *Miracle in the Rain*'s medal) and places (*A Time to Love and a Time to Die*'s apple-blossom tree on the hillock, *Affair*'s Empire State Building) is a generic trademark, acting as memory which is so important to the sustaining of romance, especially after separation or, as here, after death. Building the case for love's spirituality, King filled his film with talk of destiny and the signaling of omens (the clear sky with a bright moon; butterflies; the fortune-telling by beetles; the funeral procession parade). With the use of these generic icons, King made us believe that God was watching over his lovers.

The genre convention of having lovers talk in aphorisms (she: "I have such an awareness," he: "There's nothing fair or unfair under heaven" or "God has been good to us . . . we have not missed the many-splendored thing" – even the title of this love story is an aphorism) did not call attention to itself, as it was likely to do in many romance melodramas (*Summertime*'s "Everything happens sooner or later"; *An Affair to Remember*'s "Winter must be cold for those who have no warm memories"; *A Time to Love and a Time to Die*'s "Trust life and go on," a film that also contains an aphoristic title).

Many love stories also bridged, or tried to bridge, the racial divide: the Technicolor *Foxfire* (U, 1955)/Anya Seton novel, *Kings Go Forth* (UA, 1958)/Joe David Brown novel, *Island in the Sun* (TCF, 1957)/Alec Waugh novel filmed on a West Indian island in CinemaScope/Deluxe Color, *Sayonara* (WB, 1957)/ James Michener novel taking the Technirama/Technicolor-location-shoot-in-Japan route, *The World of Suzie Wong* (P, 1960)/Richard Mason novel/Paul Osborn play with Technicolor Hong Kong locations. Not only was the race issue raised in these films but the lovers, more often than not, got each other at the end. (*Kings Go Forth* and one set of lovers in both *Island* and *Sayonara* were the exceptions.) These lovers were seen as people exploding bourgeois sensibility, bucking convention and conformity.

The genre cross-mated with family melodrama, most significantly in *Splendor in the Grass* (WB, 1961). Inge's Oscar-winning original, willfully directed by Kazan in Technicolor, showed how sexual repression, promulgated by a conformist Puritanical Midwest society in the twenties, the Church, and, above all, by ignorant but well-intentioned parents, can not only pose obstacles to union but bring about promiscuity and mental collapse. *Splendor* was seminal also in dealing with the plight of teenage love (Natalie Wood, and Warren Beatty in his film debut). It spoke to both the adult and teenage audience, raking in $4.7 million, three times its budget. A decade before, Goldwyn had produced a teenage love story *Roseanna McCoy* (RKO, 1949), with his protégés Joan Evans and Farley Granger, but no one turned out. In *A Summer Place* (WB, 1959), teenage love shared the center with an adult affair; here, it was the center. *Splendor* also brazened raw scenes of sensuality which postwar romance melodrama (*Carnival Story*) had a hand in bringing back after the Code's enforcement when wholesomeness replaced eroticism.

A Place in the Sun (P, 1951) was another milestone in the genre and another densely textured work by Oscar-winning director Stevens. Along with adapters pre-blacklisted Michael Wilson and Harry Brown, Stevens transformed and updated Theodore Dreiser's naturalistic novel *An American Tragedy* (1925), a textbook on environmental and economic determinism, and Patrick Kearney's

16-6　*A Place in the Sun* (P, 1951, p. George Stevens)

Conflicted about his pursuit, George Eastman (Montgomery Clift) cannot quite believe that he's holding his dream come true (Elizabeth Taylor) in his very arms in the romance–male melodrama.

1926 play into a dark, brooding contemporary love story–male melodrama where choice, for better or worse, was possible. "It is not what has been done to you that matters," Stevens argued in the film and all of this postwar efforts, "but rather what you do with what has been done to you."[3] Director Josef Von Sternberg's version of 1931 had turned the one-note novel into a routine courtroom drama.

The film blended classical concerns (the triangle situation; capitalistic-engendering class differences) with postwar topicality (increased sensuality, fornication, abortion) and meshed them with issues of the male melodrama. Thus, the film broadened the appeal of an essentially female-skewed genre.

In romance melodrama, the chemistry between two physically and personality-engaging performers is a necessities, for the audience must be convinced of the players' mutual attraction. Also, the audience must fall in love with them and desire their union. Further: since it is an intimate genre enlisting a small cast, most of the running time is given over to the lovers, usually in close-ups and/or extreme medium shots. Therefore, the spotlighted duo had better be attractive to avoid tedium. In these matters, the genre was lucky during this time for in most cases, casting sent sparks flying. Here, the casting and playing of Clift and Taylor turned chemistry into magic. That they looked similar was intentional. That no one else in the film came close to their good looks was also intentional (Keefe Brasselle as Clift's cousin was a pallid imitation; Shelley Winters as the other woman was way out of range). Their physical resemblance to each other clinched the fact that, despite their coming from two different sides of the tracks, they belonged to each other. Just so, it compounded the sense of transcendence that the love story claims to be the effect of the specialness of romantic love. Love's transcendence was also suggested by the lovers' drive in the convertible to a remote hilltop. Driving in the front seat of a convertible is an iconic postwar site (*Rhapsody*, *Love Is a Many-Splendored Thing*, among others).

Under Stevens's wing, Method newcomer Clift delivered the most complex performance of his career as the outsider seeking to fit in (a Stevens concern). Though ashamed and insecure about his class (a dirt-poor son of a street evangelist mama who runs a homeless shelter), Clift is timidly ambitious and calculatedly impetuous and eventually, hesitatingly deceitful in his pursuit of the American dream. He does find love and position and he truly is in love and is bright enough to make good in the job but all along, he is deeply conflicted about his pursuit and cannot quite believe the dream is in his grasp (at one point, he sheepishly asks Taylor: "And you love me?"). Alas, he is unable to stand up for it, let alone fight for it when the dream is threatened because he guiltily knows that he himself is a large part of that threat. Notice that Clift never stands up straight, continually bends his head, and mumbles a lot. His entrance locks this in: his back is toward us as it advances nearer and nearer and finally turns, revealing his face, slightly bent, and a crooked smile. His exit, however, countermands this stance: face-forward, he walks toward us, forthrightly, his head is up and his countenance relaxed, as he has assumed the responsibility of his actions. Taylor, after a decade of screen work, came of dramatic age. With her varied repetition of "seems we always spend the best part of our time saying goodbyes," the poignancy increases.

Stevens's long takes and slow pace were necessary to absorb the layered images. Close-ups of the lovers removed them from the surrounding space, making them transcend the context. The continued close-ups of Clift's face put us through his shifting emotions and mental processes as he tries to figure things out: "In the back of my mind, I wanted to drown her but I didn't want to think such things." The staging often caught the lovers, when alone, off-center; when together, centered in the frame, as with their dancing to Franz Waxman's sad undertones that held the love motif in check and gave off a sense of heartbreak. The fluid visual and aural dissolves whispered of the associations between actions and events. This technique was surely Stevens's analogue of the genre's fate/destiny icon. The film's visual motifs had the same effect. Two policemen break up the Clift/Winters lovemaking in the car, causing the couple to seek the privacy of a bedroom. Later, a policeman tickets a speeding Taylor with Clift in the convertible; and eventually takes Clift into custody, thus severing his relationship with Taylor. Turning off an ear-splitting radio on Winters's window ledge gets Clift inside her bedroom; later on, a radio on the dock blares out the accident/crime (Winters's drowning). The patterns continue with shots of mama at the mission and shots of Clift's former bed at the mission and the one in Winters's flat. Images of the lake, birds of all kinds (loons, pigeons, canaries), and Stevens's iconic window frame were also interwoven.

Notes

1   In *Light*, the comeuppance is also reversed for the younger son of an Italian Catholic shoe-store owner has fallen in love with the 26-year-old daughter of a wealthy WASP family who – because of a kick in the head from a pony in childhood – has the mental capacity of a 10-year-old (the secret).

2   Tips of the iceberg include social satire *How to Marry a Millionaire* (TCF, 1953); romantic comedies *The Ambassador's Daughter* (UA, 1956), *Designing Woman* (MGM, 1957), and *That Touch of Mink* (AP, 1962) and musical comedies *Neptune's Daughter* (MGM, 1949), *Lovely To Look At* (MGM, 1952), and *Funny Face* (P, 1957).

3   Donald Richie, *George Stevens: An American Romantic* (New York: Museum of Modem Art, 1970), 58.

17

Musical

The Cold War climate, with its valorization of consensus and the group as well as the era's economic sunburst, nourished the musical's paean to togetherness and success. Keeping skies blue were the prescriptive business policies of turning out spectacular entertainment and adaptation, especially in regard to the Broadway musical, now in a grace period ushered in by Rodgers and Hammerstein (R/H) and Frank Loesser's integrated book–musical approach. Adaptation also came down to the thriftier musicalization of comedies and melodramas from movies' own history. The roadshow exhibition format and the conversion to color, stereo, and large-screen formats[1] were equally conducive, as was the possibility of a top-of-the-charts soundtrack album or single, which was a selling magnet. And caring directors arrived, some of whom plied the genre personally, able to use film's formal systems to render songs in cinematic fashion, choreograph space, lyricalize time, and create cine-dances.

Simultaneously, however, clouds began to dot the horizon. Studio breakup with craft disbanding was hard on the musical, which thrived in a studio hothouse where the many various technical units needed for its production were in place. Independents, by and large, shied away due to the exorbitant outlay for rights to a show, the large numbers of personnel required, and techno costs. Also, producers, foolishly believing locations undermined the genre's intention and affect, never really gave it a chance to cash in on the runaway production sweeps until the late fifties. More: the product's international slant undercut the musical's indigenously American makeup. For one thing, how do you dub or subtitle a musical sequence into a foreign language? Foreign countries refused to import musicals or, when they did reluctantly, the musicals either flopped (*Lil' Abner*, P, 1959) or played with numbers deleted (*The King and I*, TCF, 1956).

The stage adaptation was a double-edged sword. With a prestigious property (prestige varying directly with purchasing price), a sacrosanct attitude set in.

Translation, not reformulation, became the rule. Prestigious directors, no matter how unattuned they might be to the genre's lyricism, recorded the enterprises (Fred Zinnemann's *Oklahoma!*, Magna, 1955). To secure the investment, stars (so what if they couldn't sing or dance) were dubbed (Deborah Kerr/*The King and I*); dances either cut or performed by doubles (Kim Novak/*Pal Joey*, C, 1958).

As if this weren't enough, TV variety shows began taking the place of musicals for many of the middle-aged to older audience while the new R&R sound made Tin Pan Alley uncool for youth, the considerable new consumer class. Makers of musicals steered clear of R&R, perhaps knowing full well that the new sound undermined how music functioned in the book musical. Rock was too limited a form of expression for all that songs and dances must do. Lyrics fell by the wayside in rock since the beat, rhythm, and earsplitting orchestration were more important than words. Nor did rock lend itself to variations within a score. When the industry did cross over, it was in a condescending way, as with the prototypal *Rock Around the Clock* (C, 1957). Cheesily produced by Sam Katzman and directed by Fred F. Sears in b/w flat, the 77-minute B musical contained about 80 percent music (Bill Haley and the Comets, the Platters, etc.) and 20 per cent plot (how a R&R band made it to the top). About twenty of these revue-like musicals were made. Throwbacks to primitive-sound musicals, they showed a profit and caused dancing in the aisles, an occasional riot, and the denunciation of the Catholic Church. Director-writer Tashlin's *The Girl Can't Help It* (TCF, 1956) did, however, sport some nifty satire of the music industry and gangsters.

17.1   Musical Comedy and Musical Drama

The epicenter of the musical was MGM, where three musical units (Arthur Freed, Joe Pasternak, and Jack Cummings) made more of the best musicals than any other studio, so much so that their work became industry standards. The most accomplished Freed unit came up with a line of attack. Composer Freed (1894–73) arrived in 1929, along with his partner lyricist Nacio Herb Brown, to score *The Broadway Melody* (1929). From composing, in 1939 he shifted into producing *Babes In Arms* and, with Mervyn LeRoy, *The Wizard of Oz*. He differentiated between the typical musical, a kind of variety show with a backstage setting (*Babes*) and the preferable *Wizard*, an engrossing story about everyday people with everyday concerns in which the potential of song and dance to do much more than make an audience merry was tapped. He knew talent and surrounded himself with the best, among them, his associate Roger Edens (1903– 76), a gay man of impeccable taste who had come to Metro in 1933 as composer-lyricist-music adapter. Freed knew that a singer and dancer had to be cast since the musical depended largely on performance in the construction of its text. Most especially, he allowed the talent freedom to create.

Meet Me in St. Louis emerged in 1944. Its folkloric simplicity about a family's need to hold onto its roots and remain united tapped a psychic nerve during wartime. Its approach to the form, blocked out in *Wizard* and filled in by R/H's 1943 *Oklahoma!*, made the tale unfold as unselfconsciously as life.

For *St. Louis*, writers Fred Finklehoffe and Irving Brecher took Sally Benson's loose, episodic, day-to-day activities in the life of the Smith family, circa 1903, which had appeared as a series in *The New Yorker*, and tightly structured them around the four seasons, arranging them to climax with the family's uprooting to New York City. Vincente Minnelli (1903–86), Freed's white-haired boy, who had reanimated the Broadway revue in the thirties with his ingenious visual design and staging and had fulfilled Freed's hope with his feature debut *Cabin in the Sky* (1943), was selected to direct.

Minnelli's dramatic sense was evinced in his focus upon the felt pressures of experience that sent the characters (daughters Esther and Tootie; Mr. and Mrs. Smith) deep within themselves, where they derived their beau ideal that energized the reshaping of their lives. He believed the genre could be psychological as well as subjective and topical, with his take on the individual–conformity rift. This thrust appeared in all of his subsequent musicals and, as already seen, in his family comedies and melodramas as well. Minnelli's vision, consequently, gave ballast to the genre's archetypal plots and subjects. Pro forma, *St. Louis* delineated getting the girl/boy or "romance" (Esther/John, Rose/Warren, Lon/Lucille, even the rejuvenated Mr./Mrs.) and keeping the family or "community" together (the Smiths stay put). Also present was putting on the show or "production," exemplified metaphorically by the family attending the World's Fair, and its corollary: don't lose your sense of beauty or "dressing-up," as sisters Esther and Rose continually do, and eventually, so does the town, in hosting the fair. The film likewise reveled in the protagonist/s achieving name, fame, and fortune or "rags-to-riches" (the city and, by extension, the Smith family "is headed for a boom . . ."). All these typical affairs of the form result in "transformation" and "transcendence" (St. Louis in springtime, its World's Fair, the Smith family in white). These generic patterns were now made more believable and involving since they sprang ultimately from the characters' respective life renewals. For a director to impose his personality on MGM product, and on the musical genre no less, was in itself an achievement and an indication of something new happening at that most lock-step of studio factories and in the most collaborative and routine of all genres.

Such heed was taken in the ensemble playing that Judy Garland as Esther gave her first assured performance, while Margaret O'Brien as Tootie became a criterion to measure all child performances. Guided by period photographs of the town and American Gothic painting which painter manqué Minnelli researched and held up as models, *Oklahoma!*'s designer Lemuel Ayers, joining house designers, costumiers, and Technicolor cameraman George Folsey, revived the overstuffed, curlicued shape of people's lives at the time. The art of production design was reanimated at MGM; other studios took note.

Seamlessly woven into the story were Hugh Martin and Ralph Blane's ingenuous original score ("The Trolley Song"), some period airs, and choreographer Charles Walters's waltzes and cakewalks. And Minnelli's *mise-en-scène*, which rendered space musically, released, rather than merely recorded meanings. The $1.7 million budget returned $7.5.

Here was clearly a decided break with the past: the fifth-row-center-photographed Broadway show, the studio revue, Berkeley's kaleidoscopic montages tossed into Depression-flavored shyster satire, the recording of Astaire and Rogers's remarkable dances flimsily interlacing a screwball romance or an Eleanor Powell fantasia. It had even surpassed its anticipations whispered by Ernst Lubitsch in *The Love Parade* (P, 1929) and Rouben Mamoulian in *Love Me Tonight* (P, 1931). Postwar, this is how the musical remained: expanding conventions, reality-attuned, even striking a demythological note now and then.

The Freed/Minnelli connection made aesthetic waves with other originals. *Yolanda and the Thief* (1945) was seminal in its extended Eugene Loring/Fred Astaire/Lucille Bremer psychologically accurate dream ballet "Will You Marry Me?" (Yet another lift from *Oklahoma!* and the homogenization of Freud in American pop art, the dream ballet would become such a staple in film musicals that some, as Donald O'Connor in *Something in the Wind*, U, 1947, spoofed the convention.) *The Pirate* (1948) was a neat S. N. Behrman Freudian farce outfitted with Cole Porter ditties and Robert Alton's dances for Garland and Gene Kelly, who were in top form as the repressed maiden and strolling player. The musical self-reflexively had a whack at actors' unmitigated egoism, "the profession," even Judy and Gene themselves eager to entertain and be applauded. Concocted by Alan Jay Lerner, *An American in Paris* (1951), arguably an inferior effort, was awarded best picture Oscar. Presumably, Kelly's audacious 17-minute climactic daydream ballet set to Gershwin's tone poem which appropriately invoked Dufy, Renoir, Rousseau, Van Gogh, and Lautrec in sight, sound, and movement, fitted the voters' idea of culture. *The Band Wagon* (1953), Betty Comden and Adolph Green's playful jab at the New York theater scene and, in particular, the "realism" of the serious R/H musicals with its dwindling "fun" quotient, contained Astaire's best (and self-reflexive) performance as an addled, over-the-hill performer warbling Arthur Schwartz and Howard Dietz's melodies and moving to Michael Kidd's choreography. With the traditional musical's myth and conventions probed and shown to be silly and irrelevant (the musical as a swirl of unrelated gags, songs, and dances merely to give the audience a good time), *The Band Wagon* then proceeded convincingly to remyth the classical form as an expression of genuine creator passions and audience longings. The Colette-inspired *Gigi* (1958) was Lerner and Loewe's ho-hum *My Fair Lady* duplicate about the grooming of a *fin-de-siècle* demimondaine (Leslie Caron), this time played against knockout Impressionist-inspired, Paris-lensed Cinema-Scope/Metrocolor locations. Roadshowed *Gigi*'s eight Oscars included ones for Freed and Minnelli. Its $13.2 million take quadrupled its price tag.

Throughout these originals and his Broadway babies (*Brigadoon*, 1954; *Kismet*, 1955; *Bells Are Ringing*, 1960), Minnelli played with conventions – love at first sight, luck, coincidence, serendipity, apocatastasis, magic, colossal derring-do, divine providence, and miracles – and got away with it. His vision of the unlimited imagination of a human being and its ability to remold reality, along with his belief in the musical's myth, were that ardent; his mechanical know-how, that good.

On The Town (MGM, 1949) resulted in a quantum leap for the unit and genre. Here was an adaptation of a 1944 stage show that was truly rethought for film, a model for all adapters. Comden and Green, the show's original librettists who had been part of Freed's enclave since *Good News* (MGM, 1947), revamped the tale of three sailors on 24-hour-leave in New York City. The writing, as with all of their librettos, was smart, counterpointing bright satire and roistering slapstick with pathos. It was also strikingly contemporary, reverberating with the postwar shifts in American society: most notably the anachronistic males, children really, adrift in a sophisticated metropolis; and the mod females: hootch dancer, cabbie, anthropology grad, each aggressive, savvy, responsible. The ensemble playing of gobs (Gene Kelly, Frank Sinatra, and Jules Munshin) and gals (Vera-Ellen, Betty Garrett, and Ann Miller) was perfect.

On the Town's most significant breakthrough came from the director-choreographer team of Stanley Donen (1924) and Gene Kelly (1917–96). The Broadway chorus boy and leading man found themselves together in *Pal Joey* (1940), eventually bonded, and began collaborating in Hollywood with Kelly's solo and ensemble numbers in *Cover Girl* (C, 1944), Pasternak's *Anchors Aweigh* (MGM, 1945), *Living in a Big Way* (MGM, 1947), a comedy with three numbers, and Freed's *Take Me Out to the Ball Game* (MGM, 1949). The apprenticeship, which also involved each working separately, paid off, contributing to a work that pushed the boundaries of the dance musical well beyond that of Berkeley and RKO Astaire. Dance's dramatic possibilities were plumbed further – it took to the streets, for one thing. The prevalence of dance in the text was bold. Dramatic passages and songs were choreographed, linking these sections with the abundant dance passages, giving the entire piece flow, lilt, deftness. Even more:

dances were made cinematic, achieving their three-dimensional effect on stage in the two-dimensional medium of film by means of visual design (the use of décor and props as part of the dance), framing (the most expressive part of the dancer's body), staging (privileging vertical and diagonal lines), camerawork (follow the dancer, open up space on emotional highs, close it down on lows), editing (cut on the next development of the dance and always on music beats to preserve continuity), and sound design (accentuate a dancer's intricate steps or bravura movement by some orchestral instrument).

Two things kept *On the Town* this side of paradise: the schizophrenic visual design and substituted score. Donen and Kelly had fought to shoot the entire film on location. Freed allowed the parvenus only a week's shoot which they blew on the film's opening and closing scenes.[2] Donen and Kelly also went the mat to retain Comden and Green/Leonard Bernstein's dazzlingly sophisticated score, to no avail, for only three songs and some dance music were retained. Songs had to be more accessible for moviegoers, the powers-that-be opined, and MGM presses would make more money from the sale of records and sheet music if the songs were owned outright. After all, the film cost $2.2 million. Eden's airs, supporting Comden and Green's lyrics, had to make do. The public didn't mind, purchasing $4.5 million-worth of tickets.

Donen/Kelly/Comden-Green's next outing was the masterpiece *Singin' in the Rain* (1952). A cockeyed valentine to Tinseltown and the movies during the tumultuous transition from silents to talkies, the musical featured the period Freed/Brown repertoire and Kelly, side by side with the talented hoofer Donald O'Connor and the obliging, quick study Debbie Reynolds. The team brilliantly used the genre's thematics and conventions and, in a breathtakingly self-reflexive modernist manner, the medium's technical vocabulary as the film's raw material while Donen and Kelly's "cine-dances" were even more assured. The crowd-pleaser's $2.5-million investment recouped $7.6 million.

It's Always Fair Weather (1955), the final Donen/Kelly/Comden and Green/ Freed hookup, was a melancholic sequel to *On the Town* with a navy-to-army switch of uniforms. Here, three army buddies (Kelly, Dan Dailey, and Michael Kidd) reunite, as they had promised, 10 years later at Tim's Bar in New York City, only to discover they have nothing in common except their lost ideals. In fact, they don't even like each other anymore. Kelly is a fast-living hustler managing a two-timing boxer with nothing to show for it. Ulcer-ridden Dailey has sold out his painterly talent for cartooning TV commercials. Kidd's flipping hamburgers in a greasy joint is about as far cry from his hope of being a world-famous chef. The situation of sadly compromised and disillusioned males had an authentic ring to it. True, the musical was brightened with an on-target lampoon of TV (Dolores Gray's gushing hostess of a maudlin program) and Madison Avenue (Cyd Charisse's career woman) and a farcical, wartime-reminiscent battle in which the ex-friends momentarily help each other and bond. Nevertheless, at the film's end, the guys, now sadder but wiser, go their separate ways without a promise to meet again, anticipating Stephen Sondheim's dispiriting cynicism. Donen and Kelly's CinemaScope *mise-en-scène* was as adroit as it was funny and sad at the same time. The character-dancing was peerless. Despite the many assets and one liability (the mediocre Comden-Green/André Previn score), the demythed musical's reception was underwhelming.

Donen's solos added to the "cine-dance" vocabulary with Freed's *Royal Wedding* (1951), starring the director's idol and inspiration Astaire, and Cummings's *Give a Girl a Break* (1953) with dancers Marge and Gower Champion, Debbie Reynolds, Bob Fosse, and Helen Wood. With *Seven Brides for Seven Brothers*, 1954) and *Funny Face* (1957), however, Donen perfected the vocabulary.

Cummings's *Seven Brides* was Hackett and Goodrich's romantic coming-of-age adaptation of Stephen Vincent Benet's "Sobbin' Women," a tall tale tilting with the frontier ethic. Composer Gene de Paul and lyricist Johnny Mercer's felicitously varied score, approximating frontier diction and rhythms, was passionately rendered by baritone Howard Keel and soprano Jane Powell. The musical also vaunted Kidd's robust choreography – its highlight, the "Hoedown and Barnraising Ballet," involved a large ensemble of about 19 people. A potpourri of square dancing, modern jazz, acrobatic stunts, slapstick, and fisticuffs, reinforced by Donen's camera movements and furioso cuts on music beats, howls, hammer blows, and thudding punches until the building's ominous creak freezes all movement, the corker remains the most integrated ballet in film musicals. Neither excrescence (*Rain*'s "Broadway Rhythm–Broadway Melody") nor regurgitation (*Town*'s "A Day in New York"), the ballet initiates the brothers into the courtship ritual and brings the town males' jealousy to a head while painting, in moving colors, a frontier social. Donen's first CinemaScope venture became a textbook on how to distribute the vast horizontal space. Denied location money (the hothouse exteriors were the movie's only flaw), the sleeper was one of year's biggest grossers ($4.7 million).

For *Funny Face* (1957), Edens's production unit moved to Paramount and then to Paris so Astaire could dance with studio plum Audrey Hepburn. Leonard Gershe's piece in which a mousy bookclerk becomes a high-fashion model crossed Cinderella with Galatea and was set against the razzed milieux of haute couture and the beatnik counterculture. Four Edens–Gersche songs alloyed the score of Gershwin gold. But nothing marred its intertextual look that appropriated, while spoofing, the high jinks of slick glamour photography (fashion photographer Richard Avedon's actual life inspired the libretto).

Throughout all his partnered and solo work, the Donen signature was unmistakable. The camaraderie, fun, and romance arising from a shared effort; the proletarian status of his skylarking people seen against recognizable landscapes; the naïve males' cockiness and savvy females' craftiness, which cause pretense, hypocrisy, and deception at every turn, were pure Donen. His preference for irony over sentiment; his satiric etching of characters, the genre, the medium itself; and his generous doses of farce hoisted the genre's hilarity bar. The librettos that made essential points with dispatch; the brief, on-target dialogue; the lyrical blending of choreographed book passages and songs with "cine-dances" created a pell-mell pace that went unsurpassed. The exuberant exploration of film technique and the prevalence of f/x gave rise to yet another motif, the magic of movies. Donen's work was intelligent, lean, robust, traits uncharacteristic of a genre often associated with mushiness and indulgence. Post-classical/modernist Donen undermined the MGM house style and redefined the genre, as did Minnelli.

Three other stylists were associated with Freed. Dancer-choreographer Charles Walters (1911–82) of *Easter Parade* (1948) fame was Minnelli's disciple, never more so than in *Lili* (1953) for producer Edwin Knopf. Helen Deutsch's libretto followed Paul Gallico's novel about the transition of a 16-year-old orphan (Caron) to a young adult working a carnival act wherein she talks to puppets. With only one song, two Freudian dream ballets, and a magic show as a musical number, the slight (80 minutes), intimate (a cast of five) musical's focus was on the book. Ex-musician George Sidney's (1916–2002) showstoppers included *The Harvey Girls* (1946) and *Show Boat* (1951). Broadway wunderkind Rouben Mamoulian (1897–1987)'s beauts were *Summer Holiday* (1948) and *Silk Stockings* (1958).

Pasternak (1901–81), Universal producer of teenage soprano Deanna Durbin musicals from 1936 to 1942, transferred to MGM in 1942. Enamored with singing, all kinds from operatic to pop, his musicals were, generally, singing-star vehicles dotted with specialty acts (pianist Jose Iturbi, Wagnerian tenor Laurence Melchior, bandleader Xavier Cugat) that, occasionally, threatened the integration scheme. A preserver of musical tradition not only in the type of loose musical he produced, Pasternak also groomed performers in molds which had already been set (Jane Powell/*A Date with Judy*, 1948, took over for Durbin; coloratura Kathryn Grayson and tenor Mario Lanza /*That Midnight Kiss*, 1949, were the new Jeanette MacDonald and Nelson Eddy; tenor Johnny Johnston/ *This Time for Keeps*, 1946, recalled Crosby; Vic Damone/*Rich, Young, and Pretty*, 1951, Sinatra). Capitalizing on the postwar fascination with Europe and the R/H style of writing that tended toward arioso and minimalized dance, he had much to do with the short-lived revival of operetta, none more royally lucrative than *The Student Prince* (1954) with Ann Blyth and Edmund Purdom, the latter lip-synching to Lanza's voice. Cummings (1900–89), who had headed a unit since 1934, aped Freed.

17-1   *The Shocking Miss Pilgrim* (TCF, 1947, producer William Perlberg)

For this feminist musical comedy, "integrated" Betty Grable is in character as Boston's first type-writer and unflappable suffragette and in an outfit buttoned up to her neck.

At MGM's closest rival TCF, Betty Grable was still the most financially successful exponent of its typical musical, built around a WASP singing female star in a showbiz setting, studded with specialty acts, captured in the most lusciously saturated Technicolor in the business. In fact, Freed/Minnelli's post-classical integrative approach made the postwar Grables (from *Mother Wore Tights*, 1947 to *The Farmer Takes a Wife*, 1953 on) better than the war ones, most especially the period *The Shocking Miss Pilgrim* (1947). In this amazingly uncompromised feminist tract, jotted by director Seaton and brightened by Gershwin, Grable is Boston's first "female typewriter" and unflappable suffragette. A holdout for nonconformity, she lays down the law to her fiancé: marriage as well as career. Coherent books, real-life situations (not just showbizzy ones, either), characters tailored as much along the lines of the new postwar female as Grable's saucy-but-nice persona, and the casting of singer-dancer Dan Dailey (not the non-musical male mainstay) made her work eminently watchable. Additionally, *State Fair* (1945), featuring R/H's only original movie score, *Centennial Summer*

(1946), and *Three Little Girls in Blue* (1946) were able to hang out with Freed's finest.

With *Call Me Madam, Gentlemen Prefer Blondes* (both 1953), and especially the R/H connection, Fox led the way with stage adaptations which went into high gear by the mid-fifties. The R/H set were graced with topical relevance, addressing xenophobia (*Oklahoma!*, 1955),[3] the male in crisis (*Carousel*, 1956), sexism (*The King And I*, 1956), racism (*South Pacific*, 1958), and acculturation and the generation gap (*Flower Drum Song*, 1960), which Universal wrested away from Fox. In *Carmen Jones* (1954), a black American update of George Bizet/Prosper Mérimée's opera *Carmen*, Hammerstein demythed the genre with its fable of an AWOL soldier committing a crime of passion for a femme fatale factory worker in the deep South. Yet, none was cinematically reimagined in the *On the Town* manner. Seemingly, only Donen could do the trick, eventually adding models *The Pajama Game* (WB, 1957) about a labor-management tug of war in a Midwest sleepwear factory and *Damn Yankees* (WB, 1958), a contemporization of *Faust*.

At WB, a musical stable reassembled (the Berkeley dispensation had ended around 1938) in imitation of MGM. Occasionally, the MGM magic worked. *On Moonlight Bay* (1951) was no *Meet Me In St. Louis*, and *She's Back On Broadway* (1953) couldn't hold a candle to *The Band Wagon*, but *Calamity Jane* (1953) was the genuine article: much better than its inspiration *Annie Get Your Gun* (1950). Frontier mythology and postwar sexism/gender-bending bolstered James O'Hanlon's antic yet touching tale of "Secret Love." Reversing the usual trend of leads playing sincere while supports did knockabout, Doris Day as Calam', and Howard Keel, *Annie's* Frank Butler borrowed from MGM to play Wild Bill Hickcock, were the comics, counterpointed by straight supports Allyn McLerie and Philip Carey. Director David Butler and choreographer Jack Donahue's integration of the fine Fain and Webster score was seamless. The rip-roaring "Deadwood Stage," for example, takes us through the credits on the wide open plains into town, winding up inside a saloon hall, establishing setting and mood, introducing characters, locking in the conflict. And Day's aggressive interpretation of the legendary pistol-packin' mama never lost the ability to break our hearts, as when she tells her beloved Carey to ask McLerie to the ball even though she knows, mistakenly, alas, that he wants to take her.

The musical drama *A Star Is Born* (1954) was just about as integrated and real as one got and a sterling exception to the usual mediocre run of musicalizations of past movies. Nodding to Selnick's 1937 version, Moss Hart's take-no-prisoners script sharply trashed Hollywood in its pitting one rising star against a falling one. Ex-MGM Garland held the screen as the naïve, masochistic singer whose success is more nightmare than dream, even when opposite the always consummate James Mason as the alcoholic, self-destructive burnout. With the know-how of the visual designers, director Cukor painted the CinemaScope/ Technicolored frame noir, giving the musical a uniquely somber look respon- sible for a downhearted feeling in the audience's guts. Black shadows vied with scarlets, dark blues, and greys. Most of the scenes occurred indoors and at night and were underlit; a couple of these scenes were red- and chartreuse-filtered. Outdoors was smoggy; a sunset and dawn looked like rust. Off-centering, split framing, the privileging of diagonal and jagged lines in staging enforced the hysterical, venomous, and ultimately tragic proceedings. Composer Harold Arlen and lyricist Ira Gershwin's score was gorgeous, with the 13-minute "Born In a Trunk" production number, a singer's equivalent of a dream ballet. Ten months in production at a shocking $6 million, the dymythed musical pre- miered at 3 hours. With the box-office coin stalling, honcho Warner took scissors to Garland and husband Sid Luft's independent production.

Young at Heart (1955), a musicalization of *Four Daughters* (WB, 1938), also struck a demythological chord, notwithstanding Sinatra's demanded upbeat ending (his character's suicide is unsuccessful). In this low-key, heavyhearted piece, two problematic males – a sleekly efficient, smug, slightly cold but good- looking composer (Gig Young) and his morosely self-pitying, cynical ugly duck- ling arranger (Sinatra) – turn a white-picket-fenced home of father, aunt, and three daughters (Elizabeth Frazer, Dorothy Malone, and Day) into a hotbed of suppression, wasted and misplaced energy, and eventual splintering before the forced back-together-again finale. *Pete Kelly's Blues* (1955) also played it lowdown. Between sets of a twenties jazz band, a society girl (Janet Leigh) has it bad (and that ain't good) for a cornet-playing bandleader (Jack Webb) while an alcoholic singer (Peggy Lee) is beaten up by her chiseling protection racketeer agent (Edmund O'Brien).

Paramount, Columbia, Universal, RKO, and UA's contributions were gener- ally dismissible. Paramount's typical Crosby crooners were like revues: songs galore dotted with comic specialties and enlivened with an imported dancer. Crosby's *White Christmas* (1954), however, was a cut above, a merry meringue with Danny Kaye, Rosemary Clooney, and ex-MGM Vera-Ellen whipped up by ex-WB director Michael Curtiz who also dished up the demythed *King Creole* (1958), Herbert Baker and Michael V. Gazzo's blistering rendition of Harold Robbins's tough proletarian novel with a surprisingly effective Presley. Also, recall that *Funny Face* was a Freed musical that eventuated at the studio.

For every A musical, Columbia produced three Bs. But its As never burst through. Its 1955 musicalizing of *My Sister Eileen* (1942),[4] admittedly, had moments: ex-MGMers Janet Leigh and Betty Garrett's performances as the McKenney sisters from Ohio taking up residence in Greenwich Village, Bob Fosse's choreography with an eye for CinemaScope space as in the standout "Give Me A Band and My Baby," a Jule Styne/Leo Robin story-sensitive score, but the piece fizzled in the last quarter as if director-co-writer Richard Quine (with Blake Edwards) just gave up. The trendsetter *Pal Joey* (1957) was misguided from the get-go, a bowdlerized version in which a louse emerged, under producer/star Sinatra's control, as a basically nice guy who meets with a happy end.

Even when Universal hired outside talent and upped the budget to make musicals like MGM, the results were dismally lifeless (*So This Is Paris*, 1955, was a far cry from *On the Town*; *The Second Greatest Sex*, 1955, was a poor man's *Seven Brides*). It was, however, *Meet Me at the Fair* (1952) that clicked, a B entry by Sirk who enlisted period and new ditties, taps and shuffles, and the detailed Americana visuals in the service of a touching story of an orphan who finds a home with a traveling medicine man (Dan Dailey) and his black partner (Scatman Crothers) against a background of political corruption in a small Midwest town of 1904.

RKO's rare musical excursions were lame-brained (*Two Tickets to Broadway*, 1951). *The Girl Most Likely* (1958), a musicalized *Tom, Dick and Harry* (1940) with ex-MGMers Jane Powell warbling Martin and Blane's songs and dancing to Gower Champion's beats, did show considerable savvy. Releasing through RKO until the early fifties, big spender Goldwyn insisted on a solid book but forgot other important matters: too much Kaye shtick in *The Kid from Brooklyn* (1946), derived from the Harold Lloyd farce *The Milky Way* (P, 1936) and *A Song Is Born* (1948), descended from the Wilder–Brackett social satire *Ball of Fire* (RKO, 1941); and the $4-million schizoid *Hans Christian Andersen* (1952) with every top-of-the-line collaborator pulling out all the stops though, alas, in different directions. Goldwyn placed "prestigious" director Mankiewicz in charge of his $5-million *Guys and Dolls* (MGM, 1955). He got a rewrite that made the relationships between high-roller Brando and Salvation Army miss Jean Simmons and hustler Sinatra and chorine Vivian Blaine more affecting, but lyrically palsied camerawork and cutting. He cast non-singers Sidney Poitier and Dorothy Dandridge, dubbed them, and replaced original show director Mamoulian with Preminger, who was more racially sensitive than musically attuned, for the $6.5-million *Porgy and Bess* (C, 1959).

At UA, musicals, unsurprisingly, were rare. Its first adaptation *Top Banana* (1954) had the dubious distinction of being a filmed transcript of the 1951 stage show shot at Broadway's Winter Garden Theater, while its second, the road-showed *West Side Story* (1961), distinguished itself by being the highest grossing musical ($19.6 million on a $6-million budget) and most Oscar accoladed of this period (10, including Best Picture). Yes, leads Natalie Wood and Richard Beymer were dubbed and Beymer, in particular, came across as light on his feet, but Oscar-winning supports Rita Moreno and George Chakiris were planted firmly on the earth. Also, Ernest Lehman's cinematic adaptation of Arthur

Laurent's libretto retained the punch-in-the-gut power of Shakespeare's *Romeo and Juliet*, this time with a backdrop of New York City gang warfare. The expressive–realist visual look straightaway and strikingly established this world. Wise's socially sensitive and original choreographer Jerome Robbins's melodic and kinetic codirection, as well as the beat-conscious editing of the untampered Bernstein and Sondheim score, pumped up audience adrenaline.

17.2   Musical Biography

Musical biography recounts the life, cradle-to-grave or the most significant chunk, of an invariably American musical entrepreneur/composer/performer whose real name is used. The biographee's catalogue of work provides the respective film with its numbers and, by implication, demonstrates the talent and the reason this talent warrants recognition. The genre continued with every studio, except RKO, making its fair share. *The Jolson Story* (C, 1946), with Larry Parks as the "World's Greatest Entertainer," was the most popular, even necessitating an almost-as-successful sequel *Jolson Sings Again* (C, 1949). Audiences did not seem to mind its unclassical non-reconciliation of the biographee's career and love life, a harbinger of things to come. The MGM series (*Till the Clouds Roll By*, 1946/Robert Walker as Jerome Kern; *Words and Music*, 1948/ Tom Drake as Rodgers and Mickey Rooney as Hart; *Three Little Words*, 1950 with Astaire as Burt Kalmer and Red Skelton as Harry Ruby; *Deep in My Heart*, 1954 with José Ferrer as Sigmund Romberg) resembled personality revues: texts crammed with an overly generous amount of numbers performed by just about every available musical contractee, interrupted by inaccurate bits of the respective biographee's private life. The first black musical bio *St. Louis Blues* (P, 1958), with Nat King Cole as W. C. Handy, took the same route. Director Curtiz and writers Melville Shavelson and Jack Rose varied the formula somewhat in *I'll See You in My Dreams* (WB, 1952) in which Day as the ambitious, goading wife of lyricist Gus Kahn (Danny Thomas) seized most of the limelight, thus setting a postwar busy bee against the first half of the twentieth century.

However, with *Young Man with a Horn* (WB, 1950), the genre realistically redefined itself, setting up an alternative blueprint still in vogue. Co-adapted by soon-to-be-blacklisted Carl Foreman and Edmond North from Dorothy Baker's novel, the film was a disturbing portrait of jazz trumpeter Bix Beiderbecke's[5] fanatical devotion to art; his *amour fou* for a rich, pathologically neurotic bisexual that upends his relationship with a nurturing bandsinger; his bout with alcohol; his abandonment of his friend/mentor/surrogate father; and his mental collapse. That the biographee's guide was black, that many sequences took place in black establishments, that the film acknowledged Beiderbecke's debt to black music were also new (*The Jolson Story* made only a slight concession in this regard).

The material was right up director Curtiz's (1888–62) alley, delving as was his wont into the ambivalent nature of ambition, soured love, the privately erected hells that cut people off, and the possibility of self-sacrifice. Moreover, Curtiz rendered the film in a visually exciting b/w documentary realist–expressionist mode and bittersweet tone, characteristic of him but not of the genre. Also refreshing was the complex level of performances. Kirk Douglas as the trumpeter was, as all obsessives, both frightening and childlike. Though Harry James dubbed the trumpet solos, Douglas's fingering and lip maneuvers were picture perfect. Lauren Bacall's femme fatale elicited pathos. Day's altruistic bandsinger was sweet yet aggressive; Juano Hernandez's guide, benignly stern. The bookended direct address to the camera by the trumpeter's colleague (Hoagy Carmichael), who tells the story throughout while participating in it, was likewise innovative. The ending, atypically, eschewed closure of the trumpeter–singer relationship. The lack of period flavor, except for the vintage songs, and the skipped-over dramatization of the trumpeter's resurrection which, incidentally, flies in the face of the real-life Beiderbecke's death at 28, were the only missteps in another career benchmark, among countless others.[6]

Having worked in his native theater as an actor and then in various European film industries since 1912, all along imbibing the au courant style of expressionism, Hungarian Jew Curtiz was brought out by Warner in 1926, after having a look at his *The Slave Queen* (1924) that out-DeMilled DeMille. Anchored at WB for 30 years, his prolificacy, versatility, and artistry went unmatched. In fact, back in 1942, Curtiz varied the musical bio with his switch from classical European to popular American composer as subject with another beacon, *Yankee Doodle Dandy*, with Oscar-winning Cagney as George M. Cohan.

Love Me or Leave Me (MGM, 1955) aesthetically and commercially clinched what had already been laid out in *Horn*. Here was a searing take on the bruising, sadomasochistic May–December relationship of ambitious twenties song stylist Ruth Etting and ruthless mobster Marty "The Gimp" Snyder, whom she used to get ahead. The trailblazer took in a whopping $4.1 million in rentals and spun off a bestselling soundtrack album and hit single "I'll Never Stop Loving You."

In the classical versions, the name–fame–fortune and production motifs were joined and pitted against romance, spawning a career-vs.-love conflict, ending with a reconciliation that embodied the American Dream while depicting showbiz as a heaven on earth. Often, a note of personal tragedy was thrown in to make the triumph of the finale even more resounding: Jane Froman/Susan Hayward's smashed legs in *With a Song in My Heart* (TCF, 1952) or Marjorie Lawrence/Eleanor Parker's polio in *Interrupted Melody* (MGM, 1955).

17-2   *Love Me or Leave Me* (MGM, 1955, p. Joe Pasternak)

In this demythed musical biography, gangster Max Snyder (James Cagney) lashes out at songstress Ruth Etting (Doris Day) after being slighted at her Ziegfeld Follies' opening.

Though still jam-full of numbers, the refurbished musical bio foregrounded the pressures leading to, or concomitant with, name–fame–fortune (betrayal, dishonor, gangsterism, substance abuse, divorce, sex as commodity, etc.). Moreover, the depiction of these pressures resulted, despite the numbers, in a portrait of celebrity and showbiz as a hell on earth. No longer heroically admirable, protagonists were ambivalent, sometimes downright unsympathetic. More: they were given an inner life. These switches plumbed the versatility of musical personalities and attracted dramatic actors. *Love*, advertised as the "Dawn of a new Day," proved a dramatic stretch for Day as Etting while Cagney, as her obsessive protector and lover, delivered the performance of a lifetime as a revoltingly uncouth, insecure man who was so much in love with the young, lithesome beauty, that it had the element of torment all over it. More: Cagney never lost the Jew in his rendition and did not hide the disability of a gimp leg. Though Americans still inhabited the form, all flagwaving, unlike in the classical renditions, was absent.

Chronology was still clodhoppingly inaccurate, but the writing was textured enough to play without the numbers (Daniel Fuchs won the Oscar for *Love's* story). Though the numbers still arose from creative sessions, rehearsals, and performances, they were dramatically contextual: they meant something at that point in the story (again, "integration"). Note: the nightclub set "You Made Me Love You"/"Stay On the Right Side, Sister," is the songbird's uneasy self-remonstrance and glib self-recrimination. The numbers, in fact, are an analogue of Etting's subjectivity, except for the finale's title song. The switcheroo is an indication of Etting's understanding, too late in the game, of Snyder and his side of things, which the selfish Etting blocked out for almost all of their relationship. Over her song, Snyder, too, at the bar weighing an ashtray in his left hand (as if he wanted to smash her face or his with it) finally sees it her way as he admits to the agent: "You got to give the little lady credit. The girl can sing. About that, I was never wrong." In this ironically sad windup, she understands him and he her but now at a distance whereas, when side by side, their obsessive, solipsistic perceptions collided.

This knockout was directed by Hungarian Charles Vidor (1900–59) who, having been educated at the Universities of Budapest and Berlin in civil engineering and the arts and having worked as an assistant editor/director at UFA, came to America in 1926. Six years later, he directed his first feature. After working his way from Bs to As at Columbia between 1939 and 1948, he went independent. In *Love*, he brought a shadowy, claustrophobically dense, splintered-frame visual style (very German expressionist) to a form usually lit in high key, shot in bright, carnival colors and visually soothing. Vidor and crew transposed noir's b/w palette to a color key where purple, magenta, deep crimson, and dark blue, with an occasional forest green (heavy, oppressive hues) dominated. No other MGM film or any film looked like this. Exceptional in its demythology, its contextualization of the numbers and visual look, *Love* also flecked its Beauty and the Beast variation with the myth, conventions, and iconography of the gangster film.

Shaped in the *Young Man with a Horn/Love Me or Leave Me* mold were *The Joker Is Wild* (P, 1957), with Sinatra as singer-turned-comedian Joe E. Lewis, directed by Vidor; *The Helen Morgan Story*, with Blyth as the warbler and Newman as her gangster-lover, which was Curtiz's attempt to do a *Love Me Or Leave Me*, which, ironically, was MGM imitating WB's Curtiz; *The Gene Krupa Story* (C, 1959), with Sal Mineo as the drug-beset jazz drummer; and *Song Without End* (C, 1960), with Dirk Bogarde as a Liszt embroiled in women, the Church, and professional problems. Vidor died during the production of *Song*, completing about 15 percent of the picture, which was taken over by Cukor.

Notes

1 3-D was negligible as far as its effect on the musical. The three musicals photographed in the process in 1953, *Those Redheads From Seattle* (P), *The French Line* (RKO), and *Kiss Me, Kate* (MGM), in most engagements were shown flat.

2 Less than a year later, Freed was planning a location shoot for *Pagan Love Song* (MGM, 1950), with Kauai eventually substituting for Tahiti, the musical's setting.

3 While the Magna Corporation distributed *Oklahoma*'s roadshow engagement, Fox held the continuous performances, at popular prices, saturation booking CinemaScope rights.

4 *My Sister Eileen* was an indication of Harry Cohn's cheap modus operandi. One in a steady stream of cost-saving musicalizations of former properties, it also showed his penuriousness in a further way. The first musicalization of *My Sister Eileen*, which saw the light of day in *The New Yorker* and was adapted on the stage by Joseph Fields and Jerome Chodorov who also adapted it on the screen starring Rosalind Russell and Janet Blair, was *Wonderful Town* (1953). With Comden and Green libretto and lyrics, Bernstein music, Donald Sadler's dances, Abbott's direction, and starring Rosalind Russell and Edie Adams, *Wonderful Town* was a Broadway smash. Though Cohn owned the original property, he refused to shell out any money for the remarkable Broadway score, commissioning new songs and a book.

5 As with the Dorothy Baker novel upon which the film was based, the protagonist was known as "Rick Martin," an exception to the form's *de rigueur* use of real names.

6 Among them the social problem film *20,000 Years in Sing-Sing* (1932), gangster thriller *Angels With Dirty Faces* (1938), female melodrama *Four Daughters* (1939), adventure *The Sea Hawk* (1940), romance *Casablanca* (1943), and mystery thriller/female melodrama *Mildred Pierce* (1945).

18

Social Problem Film and Courtroom Drama

18.1 Social Problem Film

America in transition begot a host of societal problems that were addressed in the social problem film, a genre that focuses upon a harmful condition of society and its effect upon the individual, or an individual problem shared by countless others in a society that caused or encouraged the problem.[1] Specifically, a victim/crusader/victim-crusader (the protagonist) goes up against the problem (conflict), after undergoing some education or enlightenment and show of support (usually from a female, if the protagonist is male; a male, if the protagonist is female). Sometimes, the female may thwart the protagonist's struggle but, in the end, joins the fray. Implying that the problem can be licked by social reform/treatment or begin to be alleviated by its acknowledgment, the genre ensures an upbeat conclusion. Though hardly subversive, the social problem film was particularly scrutinized by HUAC and the PCA.

The genre allowed practitioners to push the medium's thematic boundaries further, often destabilizing censorial codes in the process. For many independents, remember, this was a desired goal. Moreover, the genre was cheap to produce; for one thing, it did not cotton to the new technologies. Content, not technology, was the genre's marketing gambit. The genre was also a way of letting off some steam for the increasing number of industry liberals and a sign, in their minds, that the medium was growing up now that it unearthed, not escaped, society's problems. And with the embrace of the documentary realist style (to be seen), the genre material came across as more immediate and trenchant. At Oscar time, the genre invariably walked away with a fistful of nominations and awards.

VP Warner continued on this track. (In the classical heyday, his studio was a genre devotee and made the very best examples.) Shoulder to shoulder with

Warner stood Fox's VP Zanuck, whose industry roots germinated at WB. Zanuck was now sobered by the war experience, as was new MGM VP Schary. UA's Krim/Benjamin welcomed scripts on current issues. In fact, UA was leader of the genre pack, with WB close behind and MGM third. Producers John Houseman and Buddy Adler; producer-directors Kazan, Kramer, Preminger, Robson, and Rossen; directors Brooks, Lumet, Wyler, and Zinnemann; and writers Carl Foreman, Abby Mann, and Jerome Weidman shared an activist state of mind. Seasoned players James Cagney, Henry Fonda, and Ray Milland and rookies Marlon Brando, Glenn Ford, Susan Hayward, Burt Lancaster, and Gregory Peck gravitated toward the genre's material. The bracing number of films was testament to the genre's ferment as well as its topic accommodations and convention tunings, with the period-defining, ironically titled *The Best Years of Our Lives* (RKO, 1946) the flower of the flock.

Goldwyn commissioned poet/ex-war correspondent MacKinlay Kantor to turn a *Time* article on the readjustment difficulties facing World War II veterans into a story. Kantor delivered a 268-page novel in blank verse entitled *Glory for Me*. Personally connecting with the material, director Wyler (1902–81) climbed aboard. Born in Mulhouse, Alsace of Jewish–Swiss/German parentage, the self-taught Wyler had entered the industry a year after his arrival in the USA in 1920. He had already undergone a 10-year apprenticeship at Universal (1926–35) and now was chomping at the bit to complete his contract with Goldwyn, for whom he had been working since 1936. Wyler enlisted three-time Pulitzer Prize-winning playwright Robert Sherwood to pen the script.

Three protagonists, each from a different branch of service and class (class stratification was a Wyler hallmark), united by their similar problems, were centered. Air Corps recruit Fred (Dana Andrews) is working class; Navy enlistee Homer (Oscar-winning support Harold Russell), lower middle class; Army officer Al (Oscar-winning Fredric March), upper middle class. All feel uncomfortably adrift in a land different from the one they left. All fear the future as they search for jobs (Al is unsure about resuming his bank position). Defensive, evasive, sarcastic, seemingly overwhelmed, Fred grapples with recurring nightmares of the trauma of war. Homer must come to grips with the prosthetic hooks that have replaced his hands. Al must face up to his ever worsening drinking problem, which aggravates his cynicism, self-pity, and boredom.

But their problems also involve women. Fred has to rethink his spur-of-the-moment marriage to Marie (Virginia Mayo). While away, Marie got a job in a club and fooled around – she even introduces her current beau to her husband. Aggravating the situation, Fred is forced to deal with falling in love with Al's daughter Peggy (Teresa Wright). Homer must discern whether his fiancée Wilma's (Cathy O'Donnell) promise to stick by him comes from pity or love. Al's 20-year-old marriage to Peggy (Myrna Loy) is still stagnating in a miasma of habit and dullness and it cries out for his attention.

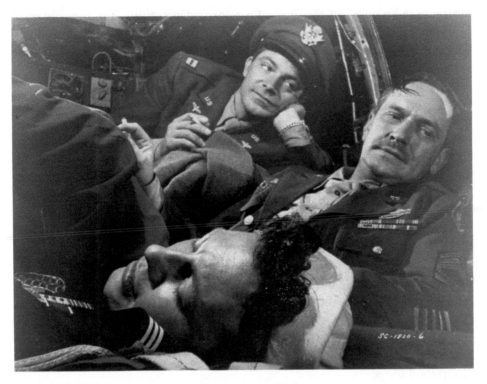

18-1   *The Best Years of Our Lives* (RKO, 1946, p. Sam Goldwyn)

Director William Wyler and cinematographer Greg Toland's composition-in-depth of the three protagonists – foreground sailor (Harold Russell), middleground army officer (Fredric March), and background Air Corps recruit (Dana Andrews) – in the social problem film.

Here was a portrait of the trauma of returning soldiers, a prime example of the crisis in masculinity and one of the most gripping concerns of postwar Hollywood. Wyler's preoccupation with the betwixt-and-between state of the male came into its own here and would continue up to his finale in 1970. Here, too, was a picture of the postwar female: fiercely independent, unafraid, forthright, and vocal. Marie, however, is amorally harmful while Peggy, who has no qualms about telling of her plans to break up Fred's marriage, is morally suspect. Marie destabilizes her man, while Wilma, Millie, and Peggy are sources of stabilization, crusaders in their own little way. Wilma does not flinch at Homer's hooks. Millie unabashedly tells her daughter of marital hardships: "How I had to convince myself that I didn't hate him..." and in doing so, shows her strength and intelligence and steadies her husband throughout. Strong, liberated, even amorally and immorally willful women, always part of Wyler's gallery, would remain so.

Best Years also noted the disarrayed state of the family, another thing on postwar Hollywood's mind. In addition to Fred and Marie's childless coupling and Fred's alcoholic father who lives in an on-the-edge-of-town shack with

Hortense, who gives off the aura of a reformed prostitute, the film observed Homer and Wilma's reserved, somewhat incommunicative parents and Al and Millie's two-decade union. As expected, the soldiers form a substitute family with Butch's bar their metaphorical abode. Problematic families, homosociality, and sacrifice-demanding friendship run through Wyler's work.

The film backgrounded other concerns: a corporation's choke on the little guy; the allure of glamour; conspicuous consumerism; the black market; job paucity; the difficulty of a Polish Catholic farmer with four kids to qualify for a loan due to lack of collateral; anti-Semitism; the presence of blacks in an all-white city; and alcoholism. Hovering over it all was the problem of the public's unconcern for the vet. America, it was shown, just did not give a hoot about the vet or the war for which he sacrificed his life.

As such, the film contained an unparalleled texture of the time and space of its setting (the fictitious Boone City, modeled after the real Cincinnati). Rendered by Wyler and his trusty cinematographer Gregg Toland in long-take, in-depth vertical, horizontal, and diagonal compositions, which preserved the temporal and spatial reality of every event, the film looked like a documentary. Glamorous close-ups (backlighting, soft-focus), canted angles, and forced perspectives were eschewed. No other Wyler–Toland collaboration before this had displayed such specificity, or for that matter, few, if any, other previous Hollywood films.

The film was formally anti-classical in other ways. In addition to the degree of texture achieved in the writing and directing, the film dealt with three (not one) ambiguously complex protagonists, their families, and their workplaces, intricately crisscrossing three, six, or was it seven (Fred's father) stories? Moreover, the experimental narrative was filled with the mundane day-to-day activities of typical Americans for all of its 172-minute running time – there were no suicides, robberies, fires, or earthquakes. Wyler's thirties work often tilted with classical codes, but not to the extent as it did here.

Yes, it was a social problem film, one of the best of its kind (as with those WB's social problem films of the thirties, from *I Am a Fugitive from a Chain Gang*, 1932, to *They Won't Forget*, 1937) but without their characteristic frenzied, furious, right-in-your-face, and loaded feeling. All was presented matter-of-factly, non-judgmentally, in a way that allowed the audience to make up its own mind. Even the ending's optimism was tempered; no rah-rah cheers here. At Homer and Wilma's wedding, Wilma tells her husband that she'll let him know about his hands in time; Al is still drinking; and Peggy is warned by Fred before the final kiss. The film also contained graftings from family, male, and romance melodrama.

The ensemble acting was matchless; no star turns whatsoever. Wyler's ability to show actors how to move, how to build a performance, how to react, all along paying prodigious attention to gesture, pitch, and volume of the voice, was part of the director's seamless style. Males wore no makeup and the females wore very little, except for Mayo, whose character called for it. In one scene, however, Mayo is deglamorized as she pulls off her eyelashes. Loy and Wright were given their clothes weeks before production began and told to wear them so they would have a worn look. Exteriors were location shot. In some scenes, hidden second-unit cameras recorded the actual people (not extras) on the location. Sets were constructed actual-size rather than the usual larger-than-life variety. The set dressing made the rooms feel lived in. Atypically, actual brand names of products, as in the drugstore scene, were used.

Wyler opted for a documentary realism, best seen in the unselfconscious descriptions of Homer lighting a cigarette, being undressed for bed and playing the piano, and putting a ring on the bride's finger. Wyler's approach was influenced by his own World War II experience. This respected and commercial filmmaker (his MGM loanout *Mrs. Miniver* had already won him an Oscar and was 1942's most financially successful film) was commissioned as a major in the US Army Air Force where he made two documentaries (*Memphis Belle: A Story of a Flying Fortress*, 1944, and *Thunderbolt*, 1947) and received an Air Medal, the Legion of Merit, and promotion to Lieutenant-Colonel. *Best Years* added to Wyler's laurels (seven Oscars, including ones for Best Picture and Director, and a return of $10.5 million on a $2.1 outlay).

Pride of the Marines (WB, 1945) with Garfield; the Zinnemann-directed, Foreman-written *The Men* (UA, 1950), hybridized with the male melo and recording Brando's debut as a paraplegic veteran; and the Robson-directed *Bright Victory* (U, 1951) with Arthur Kennedy also depicted the readjustment of men after World War II and Korea. *The Search* (MGM, 1948) took up the plight of displaced persons. As with *The Men*, Zinnemann crossed the film, which took a story Oscar, with a male melo, focusing on the ravaging effects of the problem on his people's psyche and identity and their struggle to break through. Its documentary realist look with its exteriors and interiors shot in the US-occupied zone of Germany was as unique as its unsentimental performance of debuting Clift as the GI and Ivan Jandl as the Czech boy.

Producer Kramer, director Robson, and writer Foreman's *Home of the Brave* (UA, 1949), where the problem of racism displaced the novel's anti-Semitism angle; *Intruder in the Dust* (MGM, 1950), whose black man was not the customary self-effacing one with white sensibilities (Juano Hernandez); and producer-director Kramer's *The Defiant Ones* (UA, 1958) tackled racial bigotry toward blacks – its original script won Oscars for Harold Jacob Smith and Ned Young; its b/w photography an Oscar for Sam Leavitt.

Anti-Semitism reared its ugly head in Kazan's Oscar-winnng *Gentleman's Agreement* (TCF, 1947) with Peck and Garfield and *The Vicious* (UA, 1948). The civil liberties of a small-town librarian (Bette Davis) are infringed when she refuses to remove a communist book from the stacks in *Storm Center* (C, 1956), a strong slap against HUAC. Reform was called for at *So Young So Bad*'s (RKO, 1950) female reformatory and *Unchained*'s (WB, 1955) prison. Alcoholism was treated in *Come Fill the Cup* (WB, 1951) with Cagney; *The Voice in the Mirror* (U, 1958) with Richard Egan; and *Days of Wine and Roses* (WB, 1962) with Jack Lemmon and Lee Remick. *The Snake Pit* (TCF, 1948), with Olivia de Havilland, examined mental illness. Drug addiction was profiled in Preminger's *The Man with the Golden Arm* (UA, 1955) with Sinatra and Zinneman's *A Hatful of Rain* (TCF, 1957), hybridized with the family melodrama. Exceptional children were handled in Kramer's *A Child Is Waiting* (UA, 1963), Abby Mann's ex-teleplay directed by documentarist John Cassavetes with Lancaster as a radical principal of a private school. *A Lion Is in the Streets* (WB, 1952) with Cagney and *The Best Man* (UA, 1964) with Henry Fonda exposed political corruption and chicanery. Director Kazan and writer Budd Schulberg's *A Face in the Crowd* (WB, 1957), hybridized with male melodrama in which the protagonist goes unregenerated, took up media hype and the collusion of politics and big business as a reporter (Patricia Neal) creates a Will-Rogers-type Frankenstein of the airwaves (volte-faced Andy Griffith). Through a TV writer's guidance, she destroys the monster by leaving the sound recording on after a taping, disseminating his off-the-cuff contempt for the "idiot public." Kazan's untraditional penchant for *in medias res* scene openings and cutting a scene at the start of its emotional wallop, as well as Schulberg's polemical lines ("The masses need to be guided with a strong hand by a responsible elite"), kept the movie bristling.

Of the juvenile delinquency cycle (*Knock on Any Door*, C, 1949 and producer Kramer's *The Wild One*, C, 1953, with Brando), writer-director Brooks's *The Blackboard Jungle* (MGM, 1955), crafted from Evan Hunter's novel set in an inner-city high school, was top of the heap. Its depiction of extremely sensational incidents of the problem (the rape of a teacher) was graphic. As a sop to HUAC, the film began with a written foreword declaring that the school depicted in the film was not your typical American high school and included a contrasting sequence in which the teacher/crusader–victim (Ford) sought out his former professor at a model suburban school. Ford's pregnant wife (Anne Francis) at first persuades him to give up (unlike the usual female enlightener). At the end, though, she encourages her husband to stay and lick the problem. Opening (and closing) with the jittery strains of "Rock Around the Clock" to which a boy dances with another boy while another simulates masturbation by stroking a soda bottle in front of his groin as a female passes by, the cheaply made film grossed $5.25 million.

Ransom (MGM, 1955), again with Ford, broached the question of capitulation to kidnappers. After Wyler gently laid out the diurnal details of life on a

Quaker farm in southern Indiana during the Civil War, *Friendly Persuasion* (AA, 1956) raised the issue of going to war. The film was also exceptional in bucking the genre's unalterably contemporary setting. *Slander* (MGM, 1956), a Jerome Weidman original, took off on the rise of the scandal magazines (here *Real Truth*), their blackmailing tactics, the postwar culture's infatuation with celebrity "dirt," and that aspect of capitalism that will do just about anything for a buck. Refusing to trade some smut about a famous Hollywood star whom he grew up with, kiddie TV puppeteer's (Van Johnson) ex-convict status is plastered over the tabloid's cover. The exposé leads to the loss of his job and son's death. The victim turns crusader, appearing on a TV show to tell how the tabloids are "poisoning" society. The film contains three soul-searching debates (a genre convention) wherein the protagonist, along with others, weighs the situation and plans strategy.

18.2   Courtroom Drama

Structured in terms of preparation for the trial (gathering evidence and witnesses; studying former cases), the trial itself, verdict (climax), and aftermath, the courtroom drama, a spinoff from the social problem film, uses crime (usually a murder) to unleash a character-revealing debate from all sides about the negative and harmful societal conditions or attitudes that brought about the crime. Didactic speeches, expectedly from the liberal defense, not conservative prosecution, came with the territory.

The Robson-directed *Trial* (MGM, 1955), which Don M. Mankiewicz unswervingly adapted from his own novel (save for the reform school in lieu of a hanging sentence), pushed many postwar buttons. A black judge (the first ever in a Hollywood film, played by Juano Hernandez) presides over a case involving a 17-year-old Mexican youth (Rafael Campos) accused of murdering a white girl (she actually died of a heart attack due to rheumatic fever while supposedly being assaulted). A communist lawyer (Arthur Kennedy) steps up to the bar, putting in an idealistic neophyte law professor (Ford) to argue the defense. The commie wants the professor to lose the case so the youth can be a martyr for the cause, hopefully accumulating donations and supporters to fight a racist America. The professor's enlightenment comes in the form of a disillusioned "fellow traveler" (Dorothy McGuire).[2] *The Young Savages* (UA, 1961), a close rendering of Evan Hunter's novel directed by Frankenheimer, with Lancaster as a DA seeking the death penalty for three Italians who stabbed a blind Puerto Rican, also unearthed racism, political chicanery, and media abuse. *The Rack* (MGM, 1956), a redo of Rod Serling's teleplay, dealt with a Korean War captain (Newman) accused of collaboration with the enemy. The stage-derived *Time*

Limit (UA, 1957) substituted a military investigator's office for a courtroom as he (Richard Widmark) prepared the court-martial of a major (Richard Basehart) accused of collaboration with the enemy while a POW in a North Korean camp. The Lumet-directed *Twelve Angry Men* (UA, 1957) stayed within a jury room. Here, 11 jurors, angry at being unable to take the easy way out by relying on their preconceived, entrenched notions, go up against the twelfth (Fonda), angry at finding himself among such men. In weighing the guilt of an 18-year-old Puerto Rican accused of patricide, Fonda (an individual) has the 11 (a conforming group) weigh their own biases.

This powder keg of a movie was leftist Lumet's (1924) calling card. Lumet's upbringing in an orthodox Jewish household in Philadelphia placed him on this ideological path early in life. His experiences as a child actor at the Group Theater, and later at the Federal Theater Project in the thirties, his studies at Columbia University, and his army duty only encouraged the journey. After about a dozen years in TV, he accepted Hollywood's invitation, but always kept his distance. *Twelve*, independently produced by fellow lefties Fonda and Reginald Rose from the latter's teleplay, was shot in 20 days on location in New York City for a measly $340,000.

In *Twelve*'s jury room and his subsequent work (*The Fugitive Kind*'s cluttered five-and-dime or *Long Day's Journey into Night*'s overstuffed summer house), Lumet choose enclosed spaces, made more claustrophobic with the presence of many people in each other's faces. Ironically, though, they are unable to get through to each other. Violence, verbal and physical, takes the place of interaction. As such, Lumet's people are all, metaphorically, isolated. Remarkably, too, was Lumet's opening of the teleplay's one-room setting, not in terms of departing outside it (except for the brief opener and finale outside the courthouse and washroom scene) but in terms of performances, lighting, and camera behavior.

In Kramer's period *Inherit the Wind* (UA, 1960), a thinly disguised rendition of the famous "Monkey Trial" of 1925, the questions of religious bigotry and free speech were discussed. Nathan E. Douglas and Harold Jacob Smith's restyling of Jerome Lawrence and Robert E. Lee's play featured Spencer Tracy as the defense counsel, Fredric March as the prosecutor, and Gene Kelly as the iconic reporter. In Kramer's long-winded (190-minute) *Judgment at Nuremberg* (UA, 1961), another Abby Mann-adapted teleplay, the issue of the guilt of four German judges (one played by Lancaster) brought out a spectrum of different positions on the Nazi war crimes. Kramer's (1913–2001) roots in the US Army Signal Corps during 1943–5 where he started making training films came to fruition in postwar Hollywood. Just about every time out, this independent producer who turned director in 1955 blazoned a relevant social issue (some new to film) and embraced the documentary realist style. Obvious, biased, preachy, with the plot standing still every now and then for characters to descant about the social problem, his films were, at best, interesting, gravely performed, and smartly crafted. They brought out public picketing and the industry's respect (*Judgment* received Oscars for Best Actor – Maximilian Schell – and Adapted Script). Despite peer recognition, Kramer was unable to walk that tightrope between the dramatic and the didactic, a feat that must be pulled off if the courtroom drama or social problem film is to be engrossing.

Preminger's (1906–86) equilibrium, on the other hand, was perfect, as his mesmerizing *Anatomy of a Murder* (C, 1959) showed. In bringing Robert Traver's bestseller to the screen, perceptively adapted by Wendell Mayes, Preminger insisted the novel's sensational language remain intact. And insist he could, since he was now independent, having paid his dues as a contract director at Fox from 1936 to 1953. What also served the picture well was the Viennese Jew's law and theater traditions.

Anatomy's trial was also lurid and fraught with offbeat characters. A seedy, not-in-demand country lawyer (Stewart), who spends most of his days fishing, goes up against a chillingly cynical city prosecutor (George C. Scott) in the defense of a sullen, pathologically jealous army lieutenant (Ben Gazzara) who killed a womanizing tavern owner for supposedly raping his sexually footloose wife (Lee Remick). Throughout the proceedings, various attitudes toward the law and justice system are self-reflexively arrayed, eschewing the usual route of courtroom drama's debate on the societal ills that caused the crime. The attitudes expressed are not only of the complexly written principals but the lawyer's alcoholic, mightily fired-up colleague (Arthur O'Connell), his sarcastic, out-of-pocket secretary (Eve Arden), the witnesses both for and against, the locals, the military, the shrinks, and especially the judge who suffers no fools.

Preminger's presentation of the various takes on the law remained objective while his presentation of the defendant's innocence or guilt remained up for grabs. As such, *Anatomy* was a perfect illustration of a Preminger movie which, in whole or in part, literally or metaphorically, centered on a trial in which the film audience was the ultimate jury, attempting to discern in an unbiased manner and coming to a decision on the controversial issue presented and his typically controversial people presenting. Such an approach presumed a level of sophistication in the American audience not often found in classic Hollywood picture-making. Moreover, performances were never pushed. Sam Leavitt's fast-stock, grainy b/w location photography of Michigan's upcountry, skewed expressionistically at times but always insistent of spatial wholes even when two people conversed, thus eschewing the typical shot/reverse shot trope, shivered with reality. (Leavitt was *the* photographer of courtroom drama and the social problem film.) Duke Ellington's cool jazz riffs caught the sizzle of the situations. Trumpeted by Saul Bass's cutout credits design of a segmented body,

Anatomy was something startling in a genre that tends to be explicit and loaded.

Notes

1   Disagreement as to the genre status of the social problem film is still voiced. That it is too various in plot strategies and thematic considerations as well as the transgeneric element of social consciousness are oft-cited reasons for its exclusion. Its inclusion here invokes the precedents of Peter Roffman and Jim Purdy, *The Hollywood Social Problem Film* (Bloomington: Indiana University Press, 1981) and Charles J. Maland, "The Social Problem Film," in Wes D. Gehring (ed.), *Handbook of American Film Genres* (New York: Greenwood Press, 1988), though the latter scholar seems somewhat conflicted on this issue. Nevertheless, I am indebted to Maland for the basis of my definition of the genre.

2   *Trial*, lo and behold, opened at Radio City Music Hall and earned a profit.

19

Suspense Thriller

During sound's first decade, the thriller, except for some gangster films, was considered a lower-case genre, something to keep the B mills at the majors running *(Mr. Moto Takes a Chance*, TCF, 1938) and a staple at the minors (*Sabotage*, R, 1939). Remember, the genre-iconic spies from Greta Garbo in *Mata Hari* (MGM, 1931) to Dolores Del Rio in *Lancer Spy* (TCF, 1937) were embroiled primarily in romantic troubles caused by the male, not the mission, and, as such, were essentially female melodramas.

Why the second-class citizenship? The thriller is chockablock with accident-informing events, seeming contradictions, contrarieties, plot holes, and loose ends. This risky approach to storytelling assailed the linearity of classical plotting (beginning/middle/end; cause-and-effect progression; spatial contiguity/ temporal continuity between scenes). Moreover, the thriller's purview of the world's irrationality and absurdity was not in keeping with classical Hollywood's usual happily-ever-after ending, with tensions reconciled, the triumph of good, and the restoration of order. The thriller's effect of stressing out the spectator was also problematic. Such an effect, though not considered base, was certainly not on the level of soothing the emotions, affording relaxation and relief from everyday cares. These were the pleasures, classical Hollywood thought, that a few hours at the movies should promise and deliver.

The thriller's preference for action (especially chases), which ran the risk of eclipsing or at the very least slighting character, also foiled classic Hollywood's character-in-action approach. Its star-dominated visual construction of a shot or scene (close-up; shot/reverse shot; backlighting; centering; level angling; visual design that outlined the star in the frame, etc.) was likewise severely compromised. The thriller's formal strategies, by and large, were stretched in the opposite direction (extreme long shot, close-up detail of an inanimate object, chiaroscuro, decentering, canted angles, exaggerated wide angles, etc.). Such modes, in their self-reflexive way, privileged technique and could undermine the star's persona and performance. Invariably, stars stayed away.

With *Night Must Fall* (MGM, 1937), based on Emlyn Williams's international stage triumph and touting Robert Montgomery's career-switch as a psychotic murderer, *Confessions of a Nazi Spy* (WB, 1939), directed by Anatole Litvak and starring Edward G. Robinson, and especially independent Selznick/Hitchcock's *Rebecca* (UA, 1940), a Best Picture Oscar winner with Laurence Olivier and Joan Fontaine, the suspense thriller as an A genre began to germinate and came to fruition in the war/postwar years while the B thriller continued strong and got aesthetically better. The genre's strategizing of a protagonist's physical, emotional, and intellectual confrontation with a world gone awry took on psychologically complex characterizations, morally fuzzy situations and solutions, and sociological resonances (the problem of male definition). It flirted with forbidden topics (aberrant sexuality, sadomasochistic violence). It began to ally itself with other genres. The genre, with its usual male controlling the action, made room for the female protagonist. And, all the while, it became humanly recognizable and timely.

Why the ferment? The assessment and reevaluation of World War II and the immediacy of the Cold War provided subject matter and setting while rendering the icons of the spy, the FBI, and the newly created CIA trenchant. The Cold War thriller was also a sop to HUAC.

Capturing a wide audience, print, radio, and TV's coverage of crime facts and fiction became incessant. Feeding as it did the postwar frenzy for exposé, the coverage offered a vicarious, societal-safe satiation of the attraction for the illicit and the dangerous. This attraction, of course, was part of the human makeup, but, at this time, functioned also as a relief from the dull, boring safety of conformism that the culture idolized. As a competitor, movies were impelled also to cash in.

The rise in mental/spiritual problems in which the mind/psyche posed a threat and the world in crisis came down to a private one, given shape by Freudian psychology, offered new terrain. Instancing this condition were the "personalization" of crime, the destabilized male and psychopath as protagonists, and the implication in many works of the surface/substance dialectic as a metaphor for postwar life.

The crystallization of the transgeneric noir style (1940–60), epicentered in the thriller, provided a vocabulary for the creation of suspense and thrills, as we shall see. Of course, suspense and thrills are components in varying degrees of every Hollywood plot, no matter what the genre. Horror and sci-fi rely heavily on them; the musical and love story not as much. In the thriller, however, suspense and thrills occupy a place of centrality in the construction of the story, mobilized as they are to represent a world that is tumbling down; an out-of-control protagonist whose response to that terrifying situation is up for grabs; and a conclusion that is anything but foregone. All the while, the specta-tor's visceral sensations are stirred. The genre, in fact, takes its name from its privileging of these literary methods and desired effect.

Finally, in place were a host of craftsmen and artists, sensitive to society's undercurrents which, they knew, could best be set in the thriller mold (and masked, if need be). Hardboiled writers Sidney Boehm, W. R. Burnett, Jay Dratler, Steve Fisher, and David Goodis, among many others, wrote in the vein of the influential Dashiell Hammett, Raymond Chandler, James M. Cain, and Cornell Woolrich, whose works were ready for adaptation and imitation now that the code was in a conciliatory mood. Photographers John Alton, Burnett Guffrey, and Nicholas Masuraca's (to name a few) expressionistic and/or loca-tion-shot visuals rendered the thriller's foreign, exotic, native underworld and workaday turf palpable. Taut, muscular-action directors with a cynical point of view found the sinister in motion of any kind, including Richard Fleischer, Jules Dassin, and Don Siegel. In addition, a quintet arose who used the genre as a vehicle for their personal demons: European émigrés Hitchcock, Fritz Lang, Robert Siodmak, Billy Wilder, and homegrown Orson Welles.

With the genre's classy redefinition that, moreover, reeked with social signifi-cance, no actor could resist. And every major studio wanted to be – and was – part of the action with WB, TCF, RKO, and UA leaders and P, C, and MGM not that far behind, while U brought up the rear.

19.1   World War II and Cold War Thriller

The spy, whether a professional or layman, watching secretly and under false pretense, and being watched, takes up residence in the World War II/Cold War subtype. The spy goes up against a foreign power that conspiratorially threatens national or global interest or a set of values the spy stands for and defends. Conventions comprise disguises and the telling of lies; close calls and accidental slips immediately covered up; worked-out codes and signals; excessive travel; information-gathering and relaying, compounded by the difficulty of remaining in touch with control; the final discovery and seizure of the spy; and the elabo-rate escape. Invariably male (atypical *I Was an American Spy*, AA, 1949, saw Ann Dvorak aiding Filipinos as the Japanese march in), the spy, on occasion, has a romantic consort who may or may not be on his side. Set during a war, usually on foreign soil, the spy displays courage, patriotism, and an ability to perceive accurately (the subtype is also a study in perception).

Though the number of films produced was not as high as would be expected, these thrillers, following the seminal documentary realist *The House on 92nd*

Street (TCF, 1945), were competently routine as, for example, *13 Rue Madeleine* (TCF, 1947), the follow-up from *House*'s creators: VP Zanuck, ex-newsreel producer Louis de Rochemont, and genre-loyalist director Henry Hathaway. This time, however, the film, with James Cagney heading a group of Allied agents locating Nazi files in France to discover the whereabouts of a rocket-projectile site, was an A production. A detailed, documentary-like examination of an occupational process (training a spy in *13 Rue Madeleine* or operating a spy unit in *O.S.S.*, P, 1946) appeared as part of the storylines, usually based on factual material taken from government files, newspaper articles, and fictional accounts of actual events. Mankiewicz's *Five Fingers* (TCF, 1952) was notable in switching the point of view from American/Ally to the enemy. Downstage was the venal spy "Cicero" (James Mason), a valet in Ankara's British Embassy who sells microfilm of "the most secret" documents to the Nazis. The Litvak-piloted *Decision Before Dawn* (TCF, 1951) targeted a German soldier (Oscar Werner) turned Allied spy in the hope of saving his country.

The Iron Curtain (TCF, 1948), dealing with communist espionage activity in Canada in 1943, inaugurated a series of Cold War thrillers. Bringing Red activity home were *Woman on Pier 13* (RKO, 1949), *I Was a Communist for the FBI* (WB, 1950), *Big Jim McLain* (WB, 1952), the dialogue-less *The Thief* (UA, 1952), and *The Atomic City* (P, 1953). The most wallopingly immediate of them all was director-writer Samuel Fuller's *Pickup on South Street* (TCF, 1953), where a "three-time loser" (Richard Widmark) foils an FBI attempt to track a prostitute (Jean Peters), unknowingly delivering a microfilm of a chemical formula to the reds by picking her pocket. The dire consequence of this misfire on the subway turns Manhattan into a battleground of pummelings, pursuits, and gun blasts in which the cops, the recidivist, and a necktie-selling stoolie who hoards her dough for a proper burial (heartbreaking Thelma Ritter) smoke out a commie network. HUAC, of course, legitimized the informer, a recurring character in this cycle.

Some films transcended the naïve simplicity of these early efforts which depicted "our" side as heroic and the commies as thugs with no chance to voice what attracted them to the "other" side. In the Hathaway-shaped *Diplomatic Courier* (TCF, 1952), an agent of the US State Department's communications branch (Tyrone Power), sent to Trieste to retrieve papers stolen from a murdered agent, finds that his own government can be as dishonest and brutal as the enemy's. *Night People* (TCF, 1954) was writer-director Nunnally Johnson's depiction of the shell game practiced by both sides as a counter-intelligence Lieutenant Colonel (Peck) re-kidnaps an American soldier from East Berlin. Writer-director George Seaton in his World War II-set *The Counterfeit Traitor* (P, 1962) went even further in this demythological regard, delineating how the "unfeeling" British "blackmail" the reluctant oil importer (Holden) into becoming a spy. In the process, the entrepreneur is forced to turn on some friends and use others, while putting all of their lives at risk. No matter, the British recruiter proclaims, for their lives are "expendable." With the appearance of the businessman's co-conspirator (Lilli Palmer), the issue of the Allies and their spies' morality begins to be questioned. Realizing that her information has caused hospital and school bombings resulting in the deaths of many civilians, she suffers guilt. Her conscience not allowing her to continue to spy, she seeks the sacrament of penance and God's forgiveness.

The Manchurian Candidate (UA, 1962) also demythed the subtype, as adapter George Axelrod exacerbated the hipness of Richard Condon's nerve-hitting novel of an Army major (co-producer Sinatra, with twitching eyes and mouth) who pieces together (with consort Janet Leigh) a communist plot to take over the government. The scheme had been planted while he and his buddy sergeant (Laurence Harvey) were brainwashed POWs during the Korean conflict and springs to life through the mere flick of the queen of diamonds playing card. *Manchurian* was all the while blackly humorous of the country's Cold War paranoia, HUAC (the McCarthy-like senator is ironically Moscow's puppet), and the family unit with mom (Angela Lansbury) as a castrating, murderous communist operative who sends her son on his assassination mission with a lingering, full-mouthed kiss. It was soberly allegorical as well, with its illustration of the dangers of extremism in politics and of American society as robotized. Director Frankenheimer's usual documentary realism and TV news styles, accented by expressionistic noir, proved a masterful way to ground this absurdly surreal nightmare.

19.2   Crime Thriller: Lawmen and Criminals

19.2.1   *Lawmen: private detective, police detective/cop, G-man, layman*

The investigation and discovery of something secret, involving a crime of some sort, is the stock in trade of the detective thriller. Hammett (1894–1961) and Chandler (1888–1959), along with other contributors (especially Carroll John Daly) to the *Black Mask* pulp magazine, contemporized the classical Sherlock Holmes-type gentleman sleuth into one tough cookie. An independent, he is in practice for himself. Alone and alienated, he has no social or home life to speak of. He operates in a corrupt, meaningless world where the client cannot be trusted and the law can be on his tail as he goes about his business. His professionalism, demanding the use of fists and guns as well as smartness and an adherence to a personal code, momentarily assuages deep-down fears and existential doubts and is a self-defining test in the "process of masculinization."[1]

The shadowed, grimy city (the favorites being Los Angeles and New York) takes the place of the classical detective's stylishly sedate lodgings. Character and problems inherent in human nature are at the heart of the matter, not an intricate puzzle (though the delight in unearthing clues and putting the pieces together is never abandoned). The female is fatale, not fragile. Moral certainty is an anachronism.

Hammett, whose novels were written between 1929 and 1934, was represented with remakes of *The Maltese Falcon* (WB, 1941), with Huston and Bogart reinterpreting Sam Spade,[2] and *The Glass Key* (P, 42), with Stuart Heisler in charge of Alan Ladd as Ned Beaumont.[3] Chandler, whose works spanned 1939–58 and whose alter ego Philip Marlowe was a humanizing of Hammett's creation ("Down these mean streets, a man must go who is not himself mean"), turned up six times. *Farewell, My Lovely* first appeared at RKO as *The Falcon Takes Over* (1941) with George Sanders and memorably as *Murder My Sweet* (1944) with Edward Dymtryk anti-typing Dick Powell. *The High Window* was also made twice at Fox, as *Time to Kill* (1942) with Lloyd Nolan and *The Brasher Doubloon* (1947) with George Montgomery. Titles intact, *The Big Sleep* (WB, 1946) emerged with Bogart under Hawks's direction, and *Lady in the Lake* (MGM, 1947) with Robert Montgomery directing himself. The Hammett/Chandler imitations were legion, none better than *The Dark Corner*'s (TCF, 1946) wretched gumshoe (Mark Stevens) who, just released from jail after being framed for a crime by his ex-partner, subsequently becomes a pawn in a scheme to murder a wealthy art dealer's wife's lover, or *Out of the Past* 's (RKO, 1947) private eye (Robert Mitchum), guilty over running away with a gangster's mistress, whom he was to locate and bring back, and ashamed in becoming her fall guy.

Descendant Mickey Spillane's (1918–2006) Mike Hammer loomed thrice at UA: the 3-D *I, the Jury* (1953), *Kiss Me Deadly* (1955), and *My Gun Is Quick* (1957). Only the second entry made a blistering impression. Blame it on Ralph Meeker's pickled portrayal of the brutish, solipsistic, intransigent dick with a cowlick who makes his living by divorce frame-ups. Just as culpable were A. I. Bezzirides's frenetic, staccato narrative (not the classically smooth unfolding of a story), earmarked by the credits in reverse and, above all, director Aldrich's groveling in the sordid violence of Spillane's people and places.

Aldrich (1918–83), after an economics degree at the University of Virginia, forayed into show business as a booker of big bands. Hollywood, 1941 found him a production clerk at RKO and eventually a director of shorts and feature assistant director. After a few years directing TV series, he was turning out B features by 1953. Underrated, Aldrich's work, no matter the class (A or B) or genre, was a pronounced break with classicism. Protagonists were semi/anti/non-heroic: each obsessive in varying degrees; some insane; most parentally damaged; most misogynistic. The representation of corrupt institutions including the family and the military was unrelenting. The usual solutions to a happy life that Hollywood held out for in its stories (fulfilling career, fighting on the side of law, heterosexual love, duty to one's country, religion, etc.) were just about absent. Relationships took on a tormented–tormenter cast, resulting in sadomasochistic violence with foreground obstructions suggesting his people were locked in prisons. Edging the situation with the new black humor, Aldrich took no sides but merely observed. His baroque images were busily and energetically multi-planed, often in the form of a facial profile in the frame's foreground edge with a full facial in the frame's background or a high-angle overview of the situation's participants.

By the fifties, the police detective/cop eclipsed the private eye, taking on his traits. Though part of a group, the cop comes off as separate from the other members of the force. He's more obsessive about his work than his fellows, or is a loose cannon, or feels his superiors are dragging their feet, or has a gnawing suspicion that they are part of the corruption. Rarely does he have a home life. The cop can also be conflicted in the pursuit of his quarry, due to some unexpected personal involvement.

Preminger's *Laura* (TCF, 1944) was the harbinger, fixing on a police detective's (Dana Andrews) transgressive obsession with a corpse and then suspect in a murder among the insular Park Avenue crowd. Glum, nervous, he smokes incessantly and plays with a baseball puzzle on the job. He's angst-ridden and repressed. With a shinbone shot full of silver from a gangster, he's unable to serve in the war and has never had a relationship: "A doll in Washington Heights got a fox fur out of me once." From the same file came the burnout, on-the-edge-of-a nervous-breakdown cop (Robert Ryan) sent out of town on a rape/murder case in the Ray-directed *On Dangerous Ground* (RKO, 1952). The assignment had been punishment for a display of brutality on a former job. Complications arise with the cop's feelings for his prey's blind sister. Undaunted hawkshaw (Sterling Hayden) who, discharged from his duties because he accused an "innocent" businessman of the murder of three cops, trails the suspect to Mexico in *Naked Alibi* (U, 1954). The spin in Richard Fleischer's neat B *The Narrow Margin* (RKO, 1952) was adroit. The embittered lawman (Charles McGraw), guarding a gangster's widow set to testify at a grand jury investigation, is himself being overseen by a female internal affairs cop (Marie Windsor) to determine if he is "legit." To make the train trip bumpier, the police detective is made to believe the female cop is the widow. Writer-director Fuller's *House of Bamboo* (TCF, 1955) set its sights on an army cop (Robert Stack) infiltrating a band of ex-GIs turned racketeers in postwar Tokyo. In a number of movies (*Jigsaw*, UA, 1949; *Illegal*, WB, 1955), a DA stood in for the cop.

Many films portrayed the cop as psychologically unhinged, owing to childhood trauma, some past guilt, job stress, and/or being criminally crooked on account of uncontrollable lust and/or greed. Preminger's *Where the Sidewalk Ends* (TCF, 1950) tracked an unstable, violent officer (Andrews) who accidentally kills a robbery suspect, making it appear a gangland murder. The cop's brutality is a compensation for his one-time mobster father. Joseph Losey's *The Prowler* (UA, 1951) was even more cynical. An all-American patrolman (Van Heflin), a former school athlete who drinks only milk and reads *Muscle Power* magazine, is ensnared by material success. He seduces a suburban housewife and kills her rich husband, staging the murder as self-defense. In *Pushover* (C, 1954), a sexually obsessed police detective (Fred MacMurray) even kills a fellow detective who witnesses his murder of the boyfriend of his thieving inamorata (Kim Novak). With crime not paying still on the Code's books, the crooked cop either confessed, after moral regeneration typically urged by a woman, and/or died ignominiously.

All kinds of G-men, molded along moral crusader lines and allied with an institution and sometimes a backgrounded home life, also infiltrated the territory. The FBI (Mark Stevens et al.) ferreted out a robbery gang (*The Street with No Name*, TCF, 1948). The *The FBI Story* (WB, 1959), based on Don Whitehead's nonfiction work, recalled an agent's (Stewart) war with a deranged bomber, the Ku Klux Klan, Prohibition gangsters, Nazi spies, and postwar commies. The epic work (covering 4 decades in 2½ hours), soberly directed by Mervyn Le Roy, came off as a well-informed historical document of one's man work at the bureau and its unsettling effect on his family life which, truth to tell, did sabotage the film's suspense-thriller effect. Treasury agents broke up a counterfeiting ring (the Anthony Mann-directed *T-Men*, EL, 1948) and smashed an international opium cartel (*To the Ends of the Earth*, C, 1948). US and Mexican immigration agents (George Murphy and Ricardo Montalban) nabbed a rancher smuggling Mexicans with phony work permits into California (Mann's *Border Incident*, MGM, 1949). A narcotics agent (Howard Duff) induced a convict to help smash a drug ring (*Johnny Stool Pigeon*, U, 1949). A postal inspector (Ladd) checked out a local robbery gang (*Appointment with Danger*, P, 1951). A federal agent (Robert Taylor) went up against a ring dealing in contraband war surplus materials (*The Bribe*, MGM, 1949) and, uncharacteristically, fell victim to romantic angst.

In most lawmen films, part of the narrative was given over to a documentary depiction of the latest facet in the investigative process, as in the John Sturges-maneuvered *Mystery Street* (MGM, 1950), where the science of forensics is shown as abetting the two detectives in the solving a murder. Such scenes plugged into the techno craze, thus warming the hearts of technophiliac America while sending a presumed warning that it was harder and harder to get away with crime.

Laymen of every stripe also turned detective. All were vulnerable, such as the avenging ex-GI (a limping Robert Ryan groping toward self-redefinition in Zinnemann's *Act of Violence*, MGM, 1949), an alcoholic lawyer (Tracy in Sturges's *The People Against O'Hara*, MGM, 1951), a naïve, curious housewife (Teresa Wright in the Siegel-stamped *Count the Hours*, RKO, 1953), an amnesiac (John Hodiak in Mankiewicz's *Somewhere in the Night*, TCF, 1946). A Pandora's Box of crimes (murder always) occurred, sometimes further entangled by a lethal romance, as these stalwarts took the law into their own hands, connected the dots and, only in the nick of time, were supported by the law. *D.O.A.*'s (UA, 1950) intriguing variation had a poisoned CPA (Edmond O'Brien) hunting down his own murderer.

The discovery of being framed, whereupon the wronged man/woman turns detective to extricate him/herself, was a popular variant. Popular, no doubt, since the pattern could be seen as a metaphorical indictment of the country's Red Scare cavalier accusations. In the same stew were a returning vet (Ladd) in the Chandler original *The Blue Dahlia* (P, 1946), a prison escapee (Dennis O'Keefe) in Mann's *Raw Deal* (EL 1949), an ex-con turned florist-delivery driver John Payne in Phil Karlson's *Kansas City Confidential* (UA, 1952), and the blonde tootsie (Barbara Payton) who sees the very man she was supposed to have murdered on her way to prison in *Murder Is My Beat* (AA, 1955). In Woolrich's *Fear in the Night* (P, 1947), remade as *Nightmare* (UA, 1956), a dream turns out to be true, ultimately revealing the suspected murderer to have been framed (DeForest Kelly in the former; Kevin McCarthy in the latter).

Sometimes a fellow with poor judgment and a yen for dough is tagged for a job and finds himself mired in a miasma of crime from which he must find a way out, as the lone-wolf gambler fresh from a short stretch in jail (Mitchum) in *His Kind of Woman* (RKO, 1951). Slyly astonishing is the film's modernist finale – a crosscut between Mitchum's being pummeled and whipped and a ham actor (Vincent Price) performing at commandeering a skiff full of hotel guests and Mexican police while reciting Shakespeare in a theatrical cape. Director John Farrow's juxtaposition of the farce undermined the extremely violent serious actions, actually satirizing the thriller's climactic to-the-rescue convention.

19.2.2   Criminals: gangster, prisoner, psychopath, hustler, middle-class felon

In the criminal subtype, law offenders (not upholders) are central. These films chart the threat and/or actual havoc that the lawless perpetuate in going up against the established society, its norms and values. Propelled by the American drive toward accomplishment and acquisition (things as well as people), these invariably modern urban folk are scarred by a deep psychological insecurity. They meet with fatal consequences at the end (and only at the end) from the hands of the lawful. Some self-destruct.

Freudian-limned portraitures marked the postwar gangster film, eliciting performances that riveted. Trumping Barry Sullivan's portrayal of the neurotic Shubunka (*The Gangster*, AA, 1947) and that of Edward G. Robinson's fascist Rocco destroyed by disillusioned vet Bogart (the Huston co-written/directed *Key Largo*, WB, 1948) was a pair of Cagneys.

In *White Heat* (WB, 1949) Cagney is Cody Jarrett, head of a gang of robbers that includes his beloved Ma (a creepy Margaret Wycherly). Ma soothes her boy's blinding headaches (a ploy, since childhood, to gain her attention) and eggs him on to higher criminal goals, while reporting Big Ed's (Steve Cochran) treacherous moves on Cody's oversexed wife Verna (Virginia Mayo) and Big Ed's ambition to become leader. Though the film spends a good deal of time on the T-men's ploy of planting one of their own men (Edmond O'Brien) in Cody's prison cell and latest surveillance technology in tracking the Jarrett gang, resulting in a double narrative, it is Cagney's Cody who steals our gaze and heart. For one thing, his recognizably human ways are garlanded with deliciously perverse bits (gnawing on a chicken leg, he shoots holes in a car's trunk that hides a treacherous comrade to give him air). For another: he was a unique individual, a straight-shooter in a world of hypocrisy (including the law agent and members of his own gang), and a man who, singlehandedly (not bureaucratically and minus the latest technology) got things done, and done fast. This trait, too, took the conformist audience's breath away. *White Heat* was a trailblazer in making a violent psychopathic outlaw, with an Oedipal fixation and insanity in the family closet, scary and sympathetic. (Cagney's thirties WB gangsters only flirted with audience ambivalency while Bogart's hood in *High Sierra*, WB, 1941, with a sentimental core – taking in a mutt; falling in love with a clubfooted girl whose corrective surgery he pays for, etc. – is indeed sympathetic, but he ain't scary.) Here was another instance of substance (Cody as a testament to individualism) crashing through the surface (the law's capture of a gangster). Along with Cagney's dynamite turn, Ivan Goff and Ben Roberts's terse, rough-hewn script full of chilling brutalities (a train engine's steam scalding a face) and the most mundane vulgarities (Verna's spitting gum out before bussing Cody) as well as Walsh's propulsive, tension-ridden direction (dense medium shot-frames that never linger to press a point; direct cuts) helped fortify the film's disturbing undertones. Its dingy look and the sound design of brusque hardboiled talk, grating effects, and a pounding Max Steiner score equally unnerved.

Kiss Tomorrow Goodbye (WB, 1950) was even nastier. Firmly handled by Gordon Douglas and sourced in hardboiled Horace McCoy's novel, *Kiss* traced the rise of the unrelentingly ruthless Ralph Cotter, a prison farm escapee, who, through murder, stealing, and bribery, takes over a small town. Cagney's Cody was unwittingly funny. His Ralph was just plain mean.

Formula mutation involved the citizen who deliberately (sometimes accidentally) gets involved with gangsters, succumbing to the temptation of easy money or immediate career advancement and, in the end, wondering whether the end justifies the means. In the Ray-steered *Party Girl* (MGM, 1958), Robert Taylor is an ingeniously cunning lawyer for a Chicago mobster. Born in the slums and crippled since age 12, the lawyer has attained his goal: respect, power, and the good/bad things money can buy.

Yet another shift settled on the gangster's henchman or professional killer, indelibly accounted for in the doosie *The Line-Up* (C, 1958), inspired by the TV series "San Francisco Beat." The tyro (Eli Wallach), who "had a father but never saw him," studies English syntax to disguise his uncouth trade while his partner-mentor (Robert Keith), who has never fired a gun in his life, collects dying men's last words. That the hit men, struggling to retrieve three separate parcels of heroin smuggled into San Francisco, were flesh-and-blood idiosyncratic and completely mesmerizing characters whereas the two police-detectives on their trail were boring stick figures was audience-agitating. After all, whose side were we supposed to be on anyway? It was one of Don Siegel's best: taut, crisp, and personally signed: the race against time on the part of the lawman and/or criminal, the psychopathic tendencies of his people, the betrayals and ironic twists around every corner, the use of violence to communicate, the tension between conformity and freedom, and a world that isn't what is seems. Siegel (1912–91) entered the industry in 1934 as a WB librarian, moved up to the insert, then montage department. Under the tutelage of f/x expert Byron Haskin, he began second-unit directing of action scenes until he manned his first feature in 1946.

Surprisingly, the gangster film made only a few concessions to the teen market. (Even the juvenile delinquent as criminal did not compensate for this lack, being addressed in only a few films: *City Across the River*, U, 1949, Siegel's *Crime In the Streets*, AA, 1956, and *Cry Tough*, UA, 1959). *They Live by Night* (RKO, 1949), Ray's first directorial job, with Farley Granger as an escaped prisoner and Cathy O'Donnell as the girl who cares for him after an auto accident, tapped into the thirties Bonnie and Clyde legend, even using a rural, not the genre's usual urban, setting. The legend also clung to *Gun Crazy* (UA, 1950), boasting Millard Kaufman and MacKinlay Kantor's nutso script and an equally wigged-out rendering by B-maestro Joseph Lewis. Ever since a kid, a farm-orphan (effusively smiling John Dall) has been fanatical about guns but, ironically, doesn't like to kill anything or anyone with them. The county-fair sharpshooter (condescendingly pinched-puss Peggy Cummins), on the other hand, gets off on violence. Heart-stoppingly different, the film contained a sadomasochistic interaction with the girl in the saddle, talk with the speakers' backs to the audience, cockeyed staging (the guy's face hogging the foreground as it looks through a car's back window), and weird perspectives (the camera, from a car's floor, capturing the driver through the steering wheel) and jump cutting. The *pièce-de-résistance*, however, was a bravura single-shot long take of a bank robbery and escape with the camera locked on a car's backseat.

The operation of the businesslike "syndicate," which began to exist alongside and eventually eclipse the ragtag band of outlaws, was also part of the scene. World War II had taken the heat off Abe Reles's 1940 revelation of the existence of a national crime syndicate and New York D. A. Burton Turkus's smashing of a national murder organization ("Murder Inc.") in 1941. But Senator Kefauver's 1951 committee investigation of organized crime turned up the flame. *The Enforcer* (WB, 1951) was the first major film to deal with the syndicate, with Bogart portraying Turkus. *The Captive City* (UA, 1952) was another, mapping a couple's journey to the senate committee to expose organized crime in their hometown. The uncharacteristically period *Black Hand* (MGM, 1949) had anti-typed Gene Kelly take on the Mafia, responsible for his parents' death, in 1900s New York City. In this "anti-syndicate" cycle, criminal and layman shared the center. Adding momentum to this stream were Jack Lait and Lee Mortimer's series of exposés which made "crime syndicate" a household word (*New York Confidential*, WB, 1955), as well as the public's image of the faceless syndicate as "alien," thus tapping into the era's xenophobia.

A focus on a detailed analysis of a crime, comprising mobilization and explanation (who, how, why), demonstration (rehearsal, commission, the thwarting of unforeseen obstacles), and unpredictable aftermath created an off-shoot called the "caper" or "heist" film. This was another, and most elaborate, example of the documentary-influenced depiction of a process filling out the plot line. The caper film's popularity was due also to its "inherently noble theme – men working together toward a goal . . . stress[ing] teamwork and [drawing] from each participant a performance of skill and courage."[4] Four directors made the formula their own, each blasting classicism to kingdom come.

The Asphalt Jungle was director/co-writer Huston's uncompromised reworking of W. R. Burnett's tough novel. Following six protagonists in an alternating fashion, emphasizing character over plot, and giving the enterprise an absurdist tweak, the film emerged as a sardonic study, set perpetually indoors at night, of a group of semi-professional criminals who undertake a jewel robbery: the power-plays within the group, the double-crosses, the steady disintegration. The caper film was one of Huston's typical "adventures," as corrupt mastermind lawyer (Louis Calhern) tosses off: "Crime is only a left-handed form of human endeavor." *The Killing* (UA, 1956), director/co-writer Stanley Kubrick's coolly ironic adaptation of Lionel White's novel, analyzed how the perfect crime, in this case a racetrack robbery, comes apart because of the human factors among the robbers, including an ex-con, corrupt cop, track bartender, betting-window teller, chess-playing wrestler, and sharpshooter. Symmetrically structured in terms of each crook's preparation for, then actual participation in, the master plan, the film used a disembodied narrator who introduces each participant (B actors all) and sets the time of the action. The multiple viewpoints and achronology in which time was flashbacked, overlapped, and repeated pummeled classical narrative. *Violent Saturday* (TCF, 1955), Fleischer's gangbusters' direction of Sydney Boehm's tidy adaptation of William L. Heath's novel, likewise played ingenious variations. The uses of CinemaScope, which made the location-shot copper-mining town space open and vast, and Deluxe Color, which rendered the almost constant daytime scenes even brighter, were the least of them. It was the narrative that truly thrilled. For the film's first hour, the three bank robbers' meeting and machinations play on the edges of six sets of the townsfolk's interpenetrating lives. Then, in the film's last half-hour, the robbers' commission of the deed centrally explodes into the lives of these townsfolk, changing them forever. Wise's *Odds Against Tomorrow* (UA, 1959) used the caper to discuss racism which, in part, unravels the scheme. This caper's trio comprised a gay, crooked ex-cop (Ed Begley), a racist, Southern ex-con (Robert Ryan), and a black nightclub singer (Harry Belafonte). The film's first hour of its 96 minutes' running time was given over to a detailed characterization of the males' occupations, personal lives, and reasons for robbing a small-town bank. All along, the film noted the males' attendant desperation, stress, and wacky neuroses, especially concerning the race issue.

Another cycle, from the late fifties on, was the Freudian-tinted, documentary-realist retelling of legendary Prohibition and Depression criminals. The strung-out antiheroes of these Bs, which took so much of their inspiration from TV crime shows that they looked like them, included the Siegel-directed *Baby Face Nelson* (UA, 1957) with Mickey Rooney, *Machine Gun Kelly* (AA, 1958) with Charles Bronson, *The Bonnie Parker Story* (AA, 1958) with Dorothy Provine, *The Rise and Fall of Legs Diamond* (WB, 1960) with Ray Danton, *Pretty Boy Floyd* (Continental, 1959) with John Ericson, *Al Capone* (AA, 1959) with Rod Steiger, *Portrait of a Mobster* (WB, 1961) with Vic Morrow as Dutch Schultz, *Mad Dog Coll* (C, 1961) with John Chandler, and *King of the Roaring 20's: The Story of Arnold Rothstein* (AA, 1961) with David Janssen, which eschewed the documentary approach.

Also populating the crime thriller were prisoners, rioting under sadistic conditions (Siegel's *Riot in Cell Block 11*, AA, 1954) or escaping (Dassin's exceptional *Brute Force*, U, 1947, penned by the soft-heart Richard Brooks). *Brute's* breakout and riot provided the five-minute climax to intricate character studies of four cellmates (among them, Lancaster): who they are, how they got here, their girls on the outside (in flashback), as well as the editor of the prison rag (Charles Bickford). *Brute*'s time was also taken up with the prison's administrative echelon, bristling with virulent power-plays among an insouciant governor; an ineffectual, confused warden; a dipsomaniac, caring doctor; and a fascist, psychopathic guard captain who beats a prisoner with a lead pipe while listening to classical music (Hume Cronyn). A ploy in some prison-break movies was the innocent inmate forced to participate (*Canon City*, EL, 1948). Frequently, the subtype focused on the escaped con seeking revenge on the very people who set him up (*The Threat*, RKO, 1949).

Also unique were stories of prisoners taking refuge in a family held at bay while unleashing locked-away tensions within/between family members. This thriller–family melodrama hybrid emblematicized the cultural fear of the stranger and the family's precarious state. *He Ran All the Way Home* (UA, 1951), capturing John Garfield's last performance, and *The Desperate Hours* (P, 1955), Joseph Hayes's popular novel/play/script and Bogart's last criminal role placed in Wyler's sure hand, were exemplary.

Included in this rogue's gallery were recidivists (*I Walk Alone*, P, 1948), and those who, despite the odds, went straight (*Crime Wave*, WB, 1954). The Hathaway-directed *Kiss of Death* (TCF, 1947) incorporated both types in its story of an ex-con (Victor Mature), apprehended in a robbery, opting for a reduced sentence by informing on other criminals. *Kiss*'s character probe took precedence over the action.

Caged (WB, 1950), written by Virginia Kellogg and Bernard Schoenfeld and directed by John Cromwell, rang a couple of changes. The protagonist is a sweet 19-year-old girl (Eleanor Parker) whose actual hardening behind bars we become privy to. Apprehended as an accessory in her husband's robbery of a gas-station, where the husband is killed, she is sentenced to one to fifteen years. Learning the politics of the joint and taught how to shoplift by the lesbian vice queen herself, who has sexual designs upon her, she makes a deal to get out. Giving up her baby, she's ready to meet the world: "From now on what's in it for me is what all that matters." An expensive car, parked curbside, with three smoothies inside (one puts his hand on her knee), waits to whisk her away. Educated, yes; repentant, no.

The crime thriller also made room for the mentally disturbed, whose psychopathology resulted in all kinds of mayhem. In Wise's *Born to Kill* (RKO, 1947), Lawrence Tierney "goes nuts about nothing," knifing his girl, her date, and his best friend as well as shooting the woman who falls under his bravado spell. An actor's (Oscar-winning Ronald Colman) star turn as Othello eerily spills beyond the footlights in *A Double Life* (U, 1948). A technician (Richard Basehart), extremely talented yet certifiably insane, lies, steals, and kill cops in *He Walked by Night* (EL, 1949). On the distaff side, a kleptomaniac (Lorraine Day), in need of psychiatric help, wreaks havoc on the men she loves in *The Locket* (RKO, 1946). Sexually twisted daughter (Jean Simmons), in love with her father and despising his second wife, makes a clean sweep by dispatching her stepmother and father (accidentally), and finally driving backwards over a cliff with her about-to-split boyfriend (Mitchum) in Preminger's *Angel Face* (RKO, 1953).

Also profiled was the hustler who passed over the criminal line. Returning vet (Garfield) resumes big-time extortion in W. R. Burnett-scripted *Nobody Lives Forever* (WB, 1946). An insidious carnival barker (anti-typed Tyrone Power) becomes a "nightclub mentalist," bilking the wealthy in *Nightmare Alley* (TCF, 1947). Losing fame and fortune, the fake winds up as a drunken, mentally impaired geek in a circus sideshow, tearing apart live chickens and eating their flesh. Most pitiable was *Night and the City*'s (TCF, 1950) club tout (a slimy Richard Widmark). Perpetually running and sweating in the pursuit of a get-rich-quick scheme, this scapegrace "who wants to be somebody" chokes on his own fast-talking/lying words when he "attempts to control wrestling in all of London." On the way to his self-destruction, director Dassin backgrounds the city's criminal element: forgers, black marketeers, scamming beggars, clip-joint proprietors, monopolistic promoters, and unfaithful wives.

Middle-class felons were a breed apart. PCA-passed adaptations of James M. Cain's (1892–1977) novels *Double Indemnity*, *Mildred Pierce*, and *The Postman Always Rings Twice* cast the mold that caused palpitations of recognition in the hearts of many Americans. Bitterly lucid about the myth of the American Dream (loving marriage, family joys, self-fulfilling job, peaceful suburbia) falling far short of the reality, the Cain corpus also encapsulated the suppressive aspect of middle-classness, dealing as it did with the desire to transgress and people's hypocrisies to cover up what they did not want known or did not want to face. And everywhere, sex and violence, eroticism and crime were fated to be mated.

One paradigm dealt with the corruption of a male white-collar or blue-collar worker. This protagonist begins as a solid citizen, respected, often a family man. His fall from grace results from something setting off suppressed desires within him: the problem is not so much in the stars as in his soul. As such, the motif reflected the muddle of the postwar male, wrestling with his masculinity in regards to law and desire. In *Nora Prentiss* (WB, 1947), a successful San Francisco doctor/family man (Kent Smith) becomes passionately involved with a caring, sensitive (not the usual aggressive, castrating femme fatale) nightclub singer (Ann Sheridan). To flee his life's withering routine, the doctor fakes his own death with the corpse of a heart-attack victim who has expired in his office. He then follows the singer to New York, where he succumbs to self-pitying, jealous alcoholic bouts, winding up on death row, convicted of the murder of none other than himself. A mailman (Farley Granger), wanting to give his pregnant wife "the finer things," steals an envelope filled with cash from an office on his route in *Side Street* (MGM, 1950).

Another paradigm was the crime of passion: jealous psychoneurotic vet (Joseph Cotten) strangles his slutty wife (Marilyn Monroe) and sends her young lover over Niagara Falls in *Niagara*, TCF, 1953. Yet another was the power drive gone berserk: ambitious editor (Broderick Crawford) drowns his wife who threatens to expose him in *Scandal Sheet*, C, 1952. *The Unknown Man* (MGM, 1951) was distinctive in that the middle-class felon was a wealthy lawyer (Walter Pidgeon) whose murder of the crime commissioner, discovered to be the Mr. Big of the racketeers, is elicited by an adamantine sense of justice. The justice also extends to setting himself up to be killed for his crime by the very suspect who was erroneously found guilty of the death of the commissioner but who, previously, was erroneously found innocent of the robbery and murder of a locksmith's son. Having defended the suspect at both trials and knowing full well that the verdicts were wrong, the idealistic lawyer is certain, this time, the young man's murder of him in his prison cell and presumed guilty verdict will ensure the triumph of justice.

The bourgeois felon cycle was female-gendered, too, a reflection of women's postwar empowerment. The woman-*causing*-distress pattern housed mostly greedy murderesses. A "beautiful, smart, hard" wife (Lizabeth Scott), being "middle-class poor unable to keep up with the Joneses," shoots her husband and poisons the chiseler to hold onto the bag containing $60,000 cash in *Too Late for Tears* (UA, 1949). The woman-*in*-distress pattern focused on female victimization at the hands of the male and her law-trespassing, morally problematic struggle to turn the tide, usually to hold the family together, sometimes just to save herself. *The Reckless Moment* (C, 1949) of a mother (Joan Bennett) comes down to her hiding the body of a shady older man with whom her daughter had taken up and for whose death she's partly to blame. The Woolrich-based *No Man of Her Own* (P, 1950) saw a down-at-heel pregnant woman (Stanwyck), abandoned by her womanizing boyfriend, assume the identity of a daughter-in-law of a rich family. When blackmailed by the returning boyfriend, she shoots him. *Sorry, Wrong Number* (P, 1948) caught the female in both situations. Here, a rich, selfish woman (Stanwyck) aggressively pursues a younger, virile nobody, snatching him from the arms of his sweetheart who also happens to be her friend. After marriage, she emasculates him, thwarting his every attempt to make something of himself. Frustrated, he steals drugs from his father-in-law's pharmaceutical factory to sell. The enterprise soured, he contracts for his wife's death to collect the insurance money. "Neurotic cardiac" that she has become, she is now a bedridden invalid all alone by the telephone when the killer comes to call.

Towering over all the nerve-rackers during/after his tenure was Hitchcock (1899–1980). The "Master of Suspense" reached Hollywood in 1939 after working smashingly in England in the silent/sound periods where the genre was indisputably grade A. His contributions were legion. With his psychological underpinnings, he made an essentially extrovert genre also introvert. His immersion into character subjectivity deepened the genre's emotional heft. And by making the world in crisis inextricably generative of a moral crisis in the protagonists who, ahead of the trend, were female as well as male, he made an initially simplistic genre complex.

Through an adventure, which could be accidentally thrust upon them, or make them curious, or waken what lay dormant, Hitch's protagonists were caught up, intrigued, or anticipatory but at the same time repulsed and fearful. In adventure, his protagonists grappled with the antagonist *outside* of themselves. Through romance, equally riddled with attraction and fear since intimacy ran the dangers of trust and responsibility, the protagonists grappled with the antagonist *alongside* themselves. These wrestlings were an analogue of the turmoil inside, the antagonist *within* themselves. As such, his morally ambiguous people underwent the sheer terror of losing physical, emotional, or intellectual control, educing perception problems, panic, guilt, even psychosis at times. It was a veritable dark night of the soul. Would they fight through or be crushed? Would they realize their resources, hitherto ignored or unused, or be paralyzed? Law or any other institution usually did not help, though the confession of the tumult with a romantic consort could ease the burden. No, the journey to achieve, or, at the very least, locate some patch of order was theirs and theirs alone.

With romance a large part of the picture, Hitch made the genre sensual and erotic and was undeterred, despite censorship, in delving into romance's outré side: obsession, sadomasochism, voyeurism, scopophilia, fetishism. He deepened the form's sociological strain with both urbane and vitriolic satire. He made the connection between the thriller and farce in terms of each's sense of fragmentation and absurdity. Humor, too, had a thematic implication. To get through the turmoil, his people needed, quite simply, a sense of it. It had a technical function as well. Humor was needed to sustain suspense.

But comedy was not the only genre hybridized. Hitch nonchalantly honeycombed the thriller with the pícaro adventure, horror, the female/male/family/romance melodrama, the social problem film, and political allegory. He also mixed and matched thriller subtypes within a work.

Hitch, with his God-given eye, told writers what, where, and how it would transpire: "I've been the writer of the design of my films . . . I lay out the whole film from beginning to end. The writer goes away and elaborates on it. He'll characterize the people and write the dialogue." He relished narrative experimentation, a surefire suspense-grabber, and insisted on production values.

Hitch cast stars – naturally, they gravitated his way because he gave them something to play. He embraced a star's persona, enabling the audience to identify with the character (the first necessity of suspense) while, at the same time, subverting it, another suspense shoo-in. In *The Man Who Knew Too Much* (P, 1956), Day's focused, resourceful, sunny all-American-career-girl persona, the equal if not better of men, is threatened. Having given up a successful stage career in deference to her Midwest doctor husband (Stewart), she has become, over the course of a decade-long marriage, nagging, argumentative, and paranoid. He makes fun of her suspicions, tells her to be quiet (at one point, he sedates her with valium), and leaves her out of things. In the end, though, the Doris we know and love is back. She supplies the puzzle's missing link: "Ambrose Chapel's not a man, it's a place." Her scream disrupts the assassin's aim. Her Oscar-winning "Qué Será Será" ferrets out her kidnapped boy while dispelling that other bit of Hitchcockian sabotage where she merely watched a performance at the concert hall.

Hitchcock's knowledge and extension of film technique to create suspense and thrills coined the genre's vocabulary. Moreover, his use of technique, even the most bravura, was thematic. In *Strangers on a Train* (WB, 1951), baby-faced Robert Walker's departure after strangling a woman occurs against a background of a sparkling, bright amusement park with its ferris wheel going around to the tune of "Baby Face" and the sound of revelers' merriment. The ironic visual and sound design raised the oft-heard Hitchcockian cry of cosmic indifference.

Hitch's undaunting exploration of technique took on a self-reflexive turn. Each work became also a meditation on the nature of film, the director's function, and the spectator's role. Through the audience's bond with character by means of the writing, casting, and direction (the alteration of an objective, then subjective tracking medium shot of a character), he put the audience through his people's suffering. This procedure became a large part of his thriller's meaning, efficacy, and enduring appeal. His people's moral ambiguity, of course, elicited ambivalence, making the audience stress out even more.

Hitchcock made the genre, in a word, personal. His thrillers held emotional truths and mordant ironies that came from the deep-down recesses of his soul, particularly his almost pathological fears of disorder, the unexpected, the loss of control. Where there is brilliant technical know-how, where form is content, and where that content has a distinct signature, there is art. That he toiled in the Hollywood commercial film, making movies to entertain the masses, made this achievement even more awesome.

In 1946, Hitchcock was some half-dozen years into his American period. He held onto his tradition of German Expressionism with its concentration on subjectivity and working within the frame (introspective acting, thematic visual design, and staging/framing/photography). He continued to practice Russian Constructivism with its emphases on working from frame to frame (editing) and striving in any way for thematic and/or formal collision. And he never abandoned the British documentary influence, with its concern for the objective description of the social scene and attention to detail.

Already among his medals was the Hitchcock–Selznick masterwork *Rebecca* (UA, 1940). Sourced from a Daphne Du Maurier international bestseller and adapted by famed playwright Robert Sherwood and Hitch's lieutenant Joan Harrison (among others), *Rebecca* was at once a mystery with two detectives: one lay (the "I" protagonist/Joan Fontaine), one professional; a woman-in-distresser; a May–December romance; a ghost story about the living dead; and a reworking of the fairy tale *Cinderella*.

On loanout from Selznick to indie Walter Wanger, Hitch assembled *Foreign Correspondent* (UA, 1940). Under Hitch's eye, writers Harrison and Charles Bennett, lauded novelist James Hilton, and humorist Robert Benchley made the nonfiction source material a Joseph's coat of many colors. At once mysterious (it's a spy thriller) and exciting (it's a pícaro adventure), the film's also socially satiric. It's romantic and comedic with Joel McCrea and consort Lorraine Day in a battle of the sexes, and propagandistic as well (Europe is at war and McCrea is an uncommitted reporter sent over to cover the European front).

Another loanout, *Suspicion* (RKO, 1941), emerged a mystery/romance melodrama/woman-in-distresser that Harrison, Samuel Raphaelson, and Hitch's wife Alma Reville refashioned from Francis Iles's novel. It was constructed around the relationship of a masochistic woman (Oscar-winning Fontaine) with a playboy (Grant). Censorship and commerce forced Hitch to skewer the ending, which, *o felix culpa*, actually aggravated the film's equivocality. Though Fontaine doesn't drink the milk which is not poisoned (originally, it is), there is no indication her paranoia will ever cease. It springs, after all, from a severe lack of self-esteem, initiated and perpetuated by her father. In fact, Hitch ended the film on another instance of her paranoia – Grant's drive along the coast. Further: there is no indication that either Grant's masquerading or manic behavior will cease either. Moreover, Fontaine would not want it any other way, tearfully begging Grant to return home with her rather than face prison for his bad debts.

Universal's first invitation produced the spy thriller/pícaro adventure *Saboteur* (1942), with glints of romance, comedy, and political allegory. For this Peter Viertel/Harrison original, Algonquin wit Dorothy Parker was brought in to make the dialogue crackling for Robert Cummings and Priscilla Lane. The second culminated in the superlative *Shadow of a Doubt* (1943), an original Gordon McDonnell story given to Pulitzer-Prize-winning playwright Thornton Wilder and then *New Yorker* writer Sally Benson, wherein detective and woman-in-distress thriller elements filigreed a family melodrama.

Two protagonists shared *Shadow*'s center, a charming sociopath Uncle Charlie (Joseph Cotten) and his peevish niece Charlie (Teresa Wright). Hitch's most extreme use of doppelganger thus far insisted upon the good and evil in each and the portrayal of uncle and niece as two sides of the same coin. Big Charlie never grew up, never changed, and is worse for it. Little Charlie's afraid of growing up and changing, as she experiences, for the first time in her life, the presence of unmitigated evil right in her small town of Santa Rosa, right in her own family, right in a person she has most looked up to and loved – her uncle. Doubling became the visual–aural structuring motif–metaphor throughout, extending to the use of the two visual styles, jet-black noir and bright Columbia Capraesque.

Fox next got Hitch's services for an original about a group of survivors (among them a glamorous photojournalist played by stage legend Tallulah Bankhead) adrift in the Atlantic on a *Lifeboat* (1944), the only remains of a Nazi-torpedoed ship. During the stressful sail, the group fishes a slippery Nazi from the waters. What to do? John Steinbeck, MacKinlay Kantor, and Jo Swerling all had a go with the spy thriller/adventure/political allegory wherein the suspense rose more from the dynamics of the group than the issue of survival, while Hitch had an experimental go with a single set.

Spellbound (UA, 1945), the second Selznick production, was a Ben Hecht re-creation of a John Leslie Palmer and Francis Beeding novel about an asylum doubling for a coven of witches. Out came a psychiatric tale, at once a detective thriller intertwined with a love story with the elements of psychiatry solving the murder and identity loss while cementing the love of a psychiatrist-detective (Ingrid Bergman) and patient (Peck). Hitch's most erotic film thus far with an approach to dream sequences atypical of Hollywood (thanks in part to Salvador Dali) was underlined by Oscar-winning Miklós Rózsa's concerto.

From the start, Hitchcock was a self-conscious thematic and formal experimenter, a modernist whose innovations both encouraged and were energized, and hence proceeded more boldly and assuredly, by postwar Hollywood's gradual slide from classical configurations. As, for instance, the perfect *Notorious* (1946), a Selznick package sold to RKO. Hecht's *Saturday Evening Post*-inspired tale about smoking out plutonium-possessing Nazis in Brazil (the spy thriller "text") became one of Hitch's most endearing love stories and one of film's great romances. During the mission, the FBI agent (Grant in an astonishingly complex dramatic key) and planted spy (Bergman) play a lethally foolish game of waiting for the other to give the word, the taunt of trust all lovers must initially play and damaged lovers like these continually play (the "subtext"). The romance, including a third-party frisson (Claude Rains), more than anything else commanded the breath-holding suspense, unnerving thrills, and $5 million purse.

The Paradine Case (SRO, 1947), the third and last Selznick, was a courtroom drama–mystery with lawyer (Peck) as the detective, complete with a triple romance. The lawyer detective falls in love with his murdering client (Alida Valli), who's head over heels in love with the groom-valet (Louis Jourdan) who, in turn, loved her dead husband. Three other couplings flecked the proceedings: the lawyer and his betrayed mate (Ann Todd); fellow lawyer (Charles Coburn) and his lesbian daughter (Joan Tetzel); and corrupt, mean-spirited judge (Charles Laughton) and his crushed wife (Ethel Barrymore). Hitch and wife Alma's first translation followed by Scottish physician turned playwright James Bridie's draft followed by an uncredited Hecht rewrite, along with Selznick's ultimate unfinished revision, turned Robert Hitchens's novel into a slightly overwrought affair. Hitch, nonetheless, moved the subplots deftly while the international cast delved into its deeply morally ambiguous characters.

Forming Transatlantic Pictures with English pal Sidney Bernstein and releasing through WB, Hitchcock had more control as the lollapalooza *Rope* (1948) evinced. Gay scribe Arthur Laurents gave Patrick Hamilton's British-set play, inspired by the 1924 Leopold and Loeb murders, a Freudian cast while Americanizing it. Hitch began the film immediately after the ghastly homicide of the college friend whose body is hidden inside a trunk standing in the center of the room. The trunk eventually doubles for a buffet table at a cocktail party hosted by the murdering Park Avenue lovers (controlling sociopath John Dall and manipulated Farley Granger). In attendance are the Nietzschean professor-detective (Stewart), also gay, as well as some of the victim's family and friends. As the party proceeds, questions about why the missing college friend has not yet turned up inextricably open up questions about the Nietzschean superman (and Nazi) ethic, morality, culpability, and, self-reflexively, the aesthetics of murder (and by extension, Hitch's movies). And the thriller takes on the onus of the social problem film, all the while being laced with a yummy black humor since the guests are, after all, eating off a corpse. From the credits' bottom-to-top roll-up through the seemingly one composition-in-depth-long-take visual structuring trope unfolding in one space in real time (actually, only 13 hidden cuts during the 80-minute party) to the director's first thematic use of color, *Rope* was another masterpiece. Garnering a respectable box office, it was also, thus far, the most sophisticated treatment of homosexuality à la Hollywood.

Under Capricorn (WB, 1949), James Bridie's redrawing of a Helen Simpson novel, was a mystery thriller set in 1831 New South Wales, Australia. Filmed in

19-1   *Rope* (WB, 1948, p. Alfred Hitchcock, Sidney Bernstein)

To craftsmen and star James Stewart (far right), auteur Hitch explains the maneuvers of the film's seemingly one long-take-composition-in-depth visual structuring trope.

Great Britain in Technicolor, this last of the Hitch–Bergman trilogy, with a fine supporting cast of Cotten, Michael Wilding, and Margaret Leighton, was a matter of extremely unstable people with egregious sins and secrets in their past whose present relationships are on the verge of being doomed.

Dispirited over *Capricorn's* box office, Warners demoted Hitch to in-house producer. *Stage Fright* (1950), Whitfield Cook's scripting of Selwyn Jepson's novel set in London and filmed there, was a mystery studded with social satire. It contained Hitch's most elaborate use yet of the theatrical setting with its illusion–reality dialectic as well as a lying flashback. Marlene Dietrich played the seemingly treacherous singer-actress; Jane Wyman, the short-sighted theatre student who eventually takes on the role of a detective; upcoming Richard Todd, the problematic male linked to both women. Alistair Sims was enlisted to play detective by his student daughter while Michael Wilding was the real one.

With *Strangers on a Train* (WB, 1951) the Hitchcock magic was back: breathtaking, coruscating, audience-friendly. Chandler and Czenzi Ormond revamped

Patricia Highsmith's mystery of middle-class felons to the master's specifications. *Strangers* emerged as a series of visual and verbal doubling, double-crossing, and droll riffs, set off by an unintentional, ever-so-slight toe-to-shin brush on a moving train. That accident sends four lives rushing to hell: the dour married tennis-pro playboy (Granger); his fun-loving, promiscuous pregnant wife (Laura Eliot); his mistress, a senator's daughter no less (Ruth Roman); and that delightfully daffy stranger who proposes to the playboy about swapping murders (Walker). As Hitch's best ever gentleman-clown psychotic and not-so-coded homosexual, Walker stole the show.

In *I Confess* (WB, 1953), an updating by playwrights George Tabori and then William Archibald of Paul Anthelme's play, a priest (Clift) is accused of the very murder a penitent has confessed to him but is indeed guilty of sinning in thought and desire, if not deed. Setting the ascetic Clift against the actual Catholic city of Quebec but without the characteristic humor, the film followed the priest's symbolic crucifixion, with his ex-girlfriend (Anne Baxter) unwittingly hammering in the nails.

Dramatist Frederick Knott adapted his own BBC/West End/Broadway success *Dial M for Murder* (WB, 1954) which Hitch shot in 3-D and (from now on) color. The morally problematic people included a greedy husband (Ray Milland), so obsessed with order and not getting his hands sullied that he rings up his wife's strangling; a rich, spoiled, beautiful wife (Grace Kelly) who has everything including a boyfriend; and a mystery-writer boyfriend (Cummings) who supplies a good deal of self-reflexivity to the proceedings.

Switching to Paramount and greater control as an independent, Hitch continued with middle-class felons. The *Rear Window* (1954), John Michael Hayes's recast of a Woolrich story, belongs to a recuperating, leg-in-a-cast photographer (Stewart). Through his camera lens, he peeks, pries, and probes into the inexplicable disappearance of the salesman's wife across the courtyard of his apartment complex. It's therapeutically entertaining. Vicarious, not actual, experience is what this guy's been about all his life. By trade, he records other people's lives. He's extremely skittish about relating to his girl (Kelly) who comes for an overnight stay armed with a red lobster and a peach peignoir. Also, the cavalier stance toward the neighbor gives him the illusion of power that he mistakes for reality. Innovative in its use of subjectivity, space (a one-room set), and sound, this marvel was Hitch's most explicit link between film spectatorship and voyeurism and most self-reflexive display of the art of directing. Audience adoration was in the $5.6 million range.

In a detective thriller–romantic comedy set against Oscar-winning Robert Burks's ravishingly rendered Côte d'Azur locations, Hitchcock set a thief (Grant) *To Catch a Thief* (1955), Hayes's take on David Dodge's novel. Below the surface intrigue of just who is the cat burglar, the mother–daughter relationship

(Jesse Royce Landis and Kelly) boils – all Hitchcock people are plagued with parent problems. The film also caught Hitch, Cary, and Grace at their risquely erotic and commercial ($4.5 million) peaks.

The Trouble with Harry (1955), Hayes's redo of John Trevor Storey's novel, was one of a kind. This detective thriller–black comedy had each one of a handful of isolated locals from a Vermont village solely taking responsibility for the murder of Harry, whose corpse continually appears, vanishes, and returns to the autumnal woods. The guilt and confession of each (character actors Edmund Gwenn, Mildred Natwick, and Mildred Dunnock, stage thespian John Forsythe, and Broadway dancer Shirley MacLaine) bring them together as a family. *Harry* marked the debut of Bernard Herrmann, who eventually provided eight musical landscapes in which Hitchcock set his images.

The link between the assassination of a prime minister at the clash of cymbals during "The Storm Cantata" at London's Albert Hall (text) and the fate of a shaky marriage between a control-freak doctor (Stewart) and his repressed wife (Day) vacationing with their son in Morocco (subtext) was part of the genius behind *The Man Who Knew Too Much* (P, 1956). Hayes's remaking of Hitch's 1934 work was elaborate with its grafting of a family melodrama onto a spy thriller.

Returning to WB and b/w for a film owed on his previous contract but taking the Paramount unit along (except for the production designers), Hitch assigned dramaturge Maxwell Anderson and writer-friend Angus MacPhail to bring Anderson's article to the screen as *The Wrong Man*. (The material had already cropped up on TV in 1951.) The triple-split narrative was given over, first of all, to a Stork Club bass player-family man (Fonda) who, though wrongfully accused of a robbery, is certainly guilty of some other things; secondly, to the man's wife (Vera Miles), whose guilt causes a nervous breakdown; lastly, to the unfathomable workings of Divine Providence. Also experimental was the absence of the second half of the usual descent–ascent movement. The thriller-family melodrama's thrust was all descent, harrowingly intensified, remorselessly implacable, starkly Bressonian. Except for the tacked-on coda that rings intellectually and emotionally false and unworthy of Hitch, everything about the film is assured.

Vertigo (1958), playwrights Alec Coppel and Samuel Taylor's outfitting of Pierre Boileau and Thomas Narcejac's pulp fiction, was a breathtaking spellbinder. At once a mystery thriller, a meditation on obsession passing for love, a ghost story, *Vertigo* was also the director's most autobiographical work yet in which a private detective (Stewart/director Hitchcock) plays God and makes a woman (Kim Novak/Hitchcock's actor) into his own image and likeness. From the dizzying credits through the predominance of music over dialogue to the non-closure, the narrative spiraled out of classical sight.

Respected Hollywood voice Ernest Lehman turned in *North by Northwest* (1959), the director's MGM outing, yet made with the Paramount unit. Raising his hand in the Oak Room of Manhattan's Plaza Hotel to summon a messenger boy, ad exec (Grant) is mistaken for a nonexistent CIA operative. Could this middle-aged mama's boy with two ex-wives continue to live as he traveled across America (here, Hitch plays with unlimited space), meeting up with the likes of a lying blonde (Eva Marie Saint), a suave academic commie spy (James Mason), and his bodyguard (Martin Landau) who's devoted to his master and quite possibly in love with him. That was the question. Part spy thriller, pícaro adventure, romance melodrama with two triangle situations (Grant–Saint–Mason; Mason–Saint–Landau), social satire, farce, and parody of the spy thriller genre, as well as Grant's persona and star status, Hitchcock's humdinger was the year's sixth highest grosser. Sure, comedy and thrills (specifically, the screwball romance/mystery combo) were allied most solidly with *The Thin Man* (MGM, 1934) and continued for over a decade with *Having Wonderful Crime* (RKO, 1945), one of the last examples. But the classical cycle was quite different in tone. There, the mayhem was light, jokey, and nonsensical with the comedy (jokes, pratfalls, etc.) gratuitously poured over the material. Here, the thriller's situations were taken seriously and presented ominously with the comedy arising dramatically from character and action.

Hitch's next two masterstrokes *Psycho* (1960) and *The Birds* (1963), the first of six films he would make for the MCA–Universal conglomerate, crossed the thriller with horror.

Another thriller-auteur, Fritz Lang (1890–1976), was one of the architects of German Film Expressionism, who fled Berlin when Hitler assumed command and eventually came to America in 1934. Though never receiving the recognition of Hitchcock, he was an influence on the master. Lang's vulnerable people found themselves in a pervasively threatening environment in which someone or some system, wresting enormous power, used that power to control them. What this evil situation did to the spirit of his Freudian-inscribed people, as gut reactions clashed with reasonable sense and change for the worse (not better) was all too possible, was the heartbeat of Lang's universe. For example, a war sweetheart who jilts her, a predatory painter of calendar girls who drugs her coffee, a columnist who wants an exclusive, a tattletale hamburger-joint owner, and the police are all part of the menace that traps a switchboard operator (Anne Baxter) into confessing to a murder she did not commit (*The Blue Gardenia*, WB, 1953). In the brilliant *The Big Heat* (C, 1953) a suspended homicide sergeant (Glenn Ford) is on a "hate binge." His pursuit of justice turns to revenge as he works outside the law to track down a potent gentleman gangster. His self-bruising pertinacity that takes the form of his incessantly choking and pulling a gun on people results in four women's deaths, including his wife. An ex-vet railroad engineer (again, Ford) becomes infatuated with a tart (Gloria Grahame) who wants him to kill her pathologically jealous thug husband (Broderick Crawford). A writer (Dana Andrews) aids a mighty newspaper-owner in working up a graphic case against capital punishment by allowing the magnate to spin a web of circumstantial evidence around him in the murder of a burlesque stripper. The writer, in turn, has done this to manipulate and control the investigation of his actual murder of the showgirl in question, who had been blackmailing him (*Beyond a Reasonable Doubt*, RKO, 1956). Formally, Lang was a master of unclassical narrative ellipse: cutting away before all the facts are laid out; skirting motivation and explications – the connection between reporter (Andrews) and serial killer in *While the City Sleeps*, RKO, 1956.

Perverse psychology fascinated Robert Siodmak (1900–73), another German expressionist expatriate, though born in America but raised in Germany, and another thriller doyen. His castrated, masochistic men, serpentine women, incohesive couples, and dysfunctional families suffered from frustrated or repressed sexuality. This sorry state also made Siodmak's people obsessive-compulsive: they never learned, driven as they were to retrace their missteps again and again, as with the apathetic Swede waiting for death in bed (*The Killers*, U, 1946), stewing over a moll and her gangster-lover's treacheries or the doomed armored-car guard seduced by his conniving first wife into a payroll robbery masterminded by her new husband (*Criss Cross*, U, 1949). To see the outgoing, strapping hunk Burt Lancaster (in both films) felled by a female, and a clearly vapid one at that, added an unbearable pathos. A lady from the right side of the tracks (Stanwyck) in *The File on Thelma Jordan* (P, 1949) so captivates a married district attorney (Wendell Corey) that he begins an illicit affair with her, conceals evidence when her rich aunt is murdered, and saves her from the death penalty by taking the prosecutor's brief and failing deliberately to make a case against her.

Thriller genius Wilder was yet another German expressionist exile. Salted by a scathing satire, his nasty, cynical thrillers added more haunting portraits of masqueraders whose inability to distinguish between reality and illusion ended in murder. An insurance salesman (Fred MacMurray) and a housewife (Stanwyck) are sexually aroused by the aphrodisiac of money as they collude and collide to bump off her husband and collect on his policy's *Double Indemnity* (P, 1944) clause. The egomaniacal, aging silent screen star (Gloria Swanson) takes young opportunist (Holden) into her decaying mansion on *Sunset Boulevard* (P, 1950), as her lover and co-writer of her comeback picture. Down-on-his-luck veteran reporter (Douglas) sets out to keep a Mexican-American trapped in a mine as a career move, his *Ace in the Hole* (P, 1951), but only goes to trap himself. In *Witness for the Prosecution* (UA, 1957), Wilder's fourth lulu, a wife (Dietrich) ultimately discovers that her all-consuming passion and

19-2 *Sunset Boulevard* (P, 1950, p. Charles Brackett)

Two residents of writer–director Billy Wilder's world: the con-artist (William Holden) and the incurably sick romantic (Gloria Swanson).

unswerving devotion to younger husband (Power) approaches sheer lunacy, for he is nothing but a womanizing rotter.

Wisconsin-bred Welles (1915–85) was also a thriller maven. Though the *Citizen Kane* (RKO, 1941) magic was never repeated, the spotlight of technical virtuoso Welles was still upon powerful individuals, unable to love or be loved, each with a problematic past, each nonchalantly Machiavellian, whose moral perversion brought themselves and others down. An ex-Nazi war criminal, now a college professor, is about to marry a society woman (*The Stranger*, RKO, 1946). A mysterious siren of the world's most famous criminal lawyer, *The Lady from Shanghai* (C, 1948), sets up an innocent to take the rap for murder and fraud. Richest man ever, *Mr. Arkadin* (WB, 1955), goes about destroying everyone who finds out about his sordid background as a white slave trader. Working the Mexican border, a stateside detective widower's MO is to frame suspects out of revenge, guilt, and fear of repeating his mistake of being unable to bring the man who murdered his wife to justice (*Touch of Evil*, U, 1958).

The autobiographical sting that came from Welles's own writing of these dimensioned, outsized characters and his flamboyantly performing them as well gave these modernist enterprises a reality within a world self-consciously constructed from all kinds of visual and aural frou-frou (*Touch of Evil*'s bravura opener with the camera doggedly tracking a time bomb planted in a car's trunk crossing the border until it detonates). As such, the characters and Welles's performances remained the most engaging elements in each of these wildly uneven works. For *Lady*, Welles, as an insignificant innocent, played against type while his then real-life wife Rita Hayworth essayed the evil figure of might.

19.3   Social Problem Thriller

A spate of films took up social issues (an "agenda") and a moral crusader approach to the protagonist, materials of the social problem film, and parsed it with thriller elements. The invariably male protagonist investigates (sometimes unwittingly) the problem and brings it to light while descanting from time to time about the problem. As such, he is both a detective manqué and lay sociologist. This hybridization was an inevitable courtship once the thriller appropriated the documentary realist style, though, it should be noted, while never abandoning its expressionistic roots.

Hathaway's *Call Northside 777* (TCF, 1948) took up the miscarriage of justice as an undeterred *Chicago Times* reporter (Stewart), discrediting the testimony of a key witness, springs an innocent man who has already served 7 years of his 11-year sentence for killing a cop. In *Crossfire* (RKO, 1947), director Dmytryk and writer Adrian Scott replaced the homophobia of Brooks's novel with anti-Semitism, as a police captain (Robert Young) probes two murders, discovering the "motive inside the killer." *The Dark Past* (C, 1948) called for the need to medically treat the psychopath. Hathaway's *Fourteen Hours* (TCF, 1951) warned against those situations that produced suicide. *No Highway in the Sky* (TCF, 1951) pleaded for safety in commercial air travel. *The Harder They Come* (C, 1956) shone a harsh light on the boxing racket. *The Quiet American* (UA, 1958), Mankiewicz's misguided overhaul of the complex Graham Greene novel, took a stand against the US involvement in foreign politics.

In the crown of works that unearthed racism (Losey's *The Lawless* P, 1950, Mankiewicz's *No Way Out*, TCF, 1950, *The Well*, UA, 1951), *Bad Day At Black Rock* (MGM, 1955) was the jewel. Millard Kaufman's cut-to-the-bone script opened with the arrival of a one-armed stranger (Tracy) on a streamliner into an Arizona whistle-stop. It closed with his departure 24 hours later. In between, he finds out what became of the Japanese father of his comrade who saved his life during the war. Melding the hybrid further with the western (setting; main street stand-off, etc.) and family melodrama (the outsider as community gadfly), director Sturges furthered showed a canniness in his use of CinemaScope and Eastman Color both to fracture and unify space, close it down, and open it up.

Best Picture Oscar went to Wilder's innovative treatment of alcoholism along thriller lines, *The Lost Weekend* (P, 1945). Yes, the reason for the protagonist's debilitating condition in Wilder and Brackett's redo of Charles R. Jackson's autobiographical work was switched from homosexuality to insecurity stemming from a stalled writing career. Yes, the book's downbeat ending becomes a tempered optimistic one (victim's best girl is a crusading force). Yet, the period-defining work emerged as refreshingly new. Up to this time, dipsomaniacs were hardly ever protagonists. If foregrounded, they were the stuff of farce. Here, however, the lush was presented in a serious fashion, a man like you and me, edging closer and closer to the brink of suicide, chased by the fiercest of demons, those within.

The tortured performance of light comedian Ray Milland (awarded an Oscar), who occupied the screen for practically all of the film's 101 minutes, documented the chaos of a mind unraveling: the retreat into the past, self-pity, lack of focus, specious reasoning, paranoia. The New York location shooting was strictly hold-your-breath, as when the camera followed alongside the unbalanced victim searching for a pawnshop to get money for his typewriter. Most harrowing was the subjective experience of a drunken stupor in which the hapless man observes a mouse nibbling his way through the apartment wall, a bat flying overhead and then, the bat eating the mouse's head as blood slithers down the white wall. Moreover, Wilder kept a cool, objective tone throughout: no sentimentality and no sermonizing.

Equally honored was Kazan's Oscar-winning *On the Waterfront* (C, 1954), an expose of labor racketeering along the docks. With Oscar-winning writer Schulberg adapting his own novel, Kazan was able to raise (and answer) another issue – naming names before HUAC. In so doing, Kazan salved his conscience since he himself did just that in 1952 to keep working. Unsurprisingly, he made the film's stevedore informant (Oscar-winning Brando) heroic. By going before the board and ratting, Brando completes his evolution from unfeeling slob to a man who acts with courage and knowledge of why he is doing what he does. The in-your-face authenticity of the Method performances and the blend of documentary realism and expressionism in the rendering of actual locations was the stuff of graven memories.

Notes

1   One of the main points in Frank Krutnik, *In A Lonely Street: Film Noir, Genre, Masculinity* (London: Routledge, 1991), p. 42, was that hardboiled fiction involved an "emphatic process of masculinization," most concerned as it was "with the aims, ambitions and activity of a male protagonist who proves and defines himself by his ability to overcome the challenges to his life and to his integrity."

2   WB first adapted *The Maltese Falcon* in 1931, with Roy del Ruth directing Ricardo Cortez as Spade, and tailored the property, now titled *Satan Met A Lady*, into a screwball romance-mystery in 1936, with William Dieterle directing Warren William, to cash in on the popular *The Thin Man*, sourced also in Hammett, which MGM introduced in 1934.

3   Paramount first filmed *The Glass Key* in 1935, with Frank Tuttle directing George Raft.

4   Expressed by Carlos Clarens, *Crime Movies: From Griffith to the Godfather and Beyond* (New York: W. W. Norton, 1980), p. 99, who went on to opine that four years of combat hardship and all sorts of foul play, more or less sanctioned by war, made crime seem less forbidding and remote.

20

War

For three years after the 1945 armistice, the war film, a depiction of American armed forces in combat with enemy forces during a war (usually World War II), lay low. It reconnoitered at the decade's end and went on to greater glory than in its 1942–5 blitz.

With time's anaesthetizing distance, the subject of World War II set off nostalgia in many men: the bonding, the focus, the élan, and expanse of heroism that came easily when the cause was undeniably right. The memory served as a buffer to the increasing splintering, heterogeneity, and perplexity of postwar America. The necessity of a group of men working concertedly, a generic motif, resonated with the postwar emphasis on consensus and uniformity. Equally, the war film, in its distinctly postwar embodiment, supplied a vehicle to understand, evaluate, and criticize the Cold War as World War II's legacy, corporate evil, authority, capitalism, race relations, and diminished individualism. Furthermore, many industryites who had served were now itching to tell of their experience, such as Frank McCarthy, ex-secretary to General George C. Marshall, instated as Fox executive in 1949; some even to question it. The Hollywood–London connection chimed in. World War II being one of the major subjects of the postwar British film, many co-productions (*The Purple Plain*, UA, 1955 with Peck) were war movies.

The genre's low financial outlay enticed. Casting did not exact bucks. Since the genre usually involved the ensemble, major male stars did not make a habit of volunteering. Van Johnson was drafted most; Wayne and Mitchum came next; and finally, Jeff Chandler, Frank Lovejoy, Aldo Ray, and Peck. Of this group only Wayne and Peck were major stars. Even when Wayne was involved, the screen time was shared by many others in the hope-to-be/never-were/unknown actor categories. With hardly any time for women, the genre did not have to shell out lucre for female stars. Also, unlike most other genres, its reliance on color remained sporadic.[1] And it did not call out for the large-screen format.

Additionally, the cooperation of the armed services – which provided equipment, material, and men – naturally kept costs down. The military saw the genre as a self-aggrandizing and recruiting tool. If the movie showed the military's best face and presented personnel, procedure, and events in an accurate manner (according to military perception), the brass gave it the go-ahead. If not, it flatly refused.

The British, German, and Russian war-documentary techniques, learned and practiced by Hollywood craftsmen during the initial run of World War II combat films, were refined for fiction (the opening of a map area of combat or terrain, prologue and/or epilogue, written/aural narration, outdoor shooting, actual combat footage inserts). True stories, unfabled incidents, and the lives of real soldiers from World War II provided plots. This documentary realist style and true-to-life subject matter gave the genre a scorching immediacy and appeal. Producer Schary and writer-director-actual vet Robert Pirosh's *Go for Broke!* (MGM, 1951) began with a foreword stating that Americanism is a matter of mind and spirit, not race. Its story of a Texas lieutenant (Johnson) heading a group of Nisei soldiers who go to Italy, then France, was based on the actual World War II 110th and 39th Battalions. Documentary footage was interspersed throughout. More graphic scenes of violence than those depicted in the 1942–5 lot hardly ever stirred the censors' wrath – historical status was justification enough. Finally, declarations of World War II had a special interest for vets Schary/MGM, Warner/WB, and Zanuck/TCF, who, after the war, became leaders in the production of the genre.

Six films flagged the genre's return. *Battleground* (MGM, 1949), producer Schary and writer Pirosh's pride and joy given over to longtime action director William Wellman, used the familiar patrol-caught-behind-enemy-lines pattern, in this case an army squad that became known as "the battered bastards of the Bastogne" during the Battle of the Bulge. Featuring some of the actual men who made up the famous "Screaming Eagles" 101st Battalion in bit parts, and ensemble contractees headed by Johnson, as well as documentary inserts and a foreword, the movie broke new ground in the realistic depiction of the personal feel of war on the part of dirty, weary, scarred riflemen from the airborne division.

Sands of Iwo Jima (R, 1949), directed by old-hand actioner Allan Dwan, was equally familiar with its tale of a hell-for-leather marine sergeant (Wayne) who whips his recalcitrant soldiers into a fighting machine, this time for the invasions of Tarawa, Iwo Jima, and Suribachi. Filled with documentary footage and how-to scenes (how to fold a flag, fight with a rifle, throw a grenade, bury a soldier at sea, etc.), the film also took time to detail the other side of this crack marine. He metaphorically parents a hothead kid in his troop who happens to be the son of his old buddy and gives his dough to a single mother who picks him up in a bar – compensations, no doubt, for a wife and kid who left him five years ago. The dimensioned role catapulted Wayne, along with his western turns in *Red River* (UA, 1948) and *She Wore a Yellow Ribbon* (RKO, 1949), to star status and iconized him, in the nation's collective mind, as the ideal soldier[2] and troubled postwar man who, come what may, followed through no matter what.

Fighter Squadron (WB, 1948) and *Task Force* (WB, 1949) also staked out the genre's timeworn, glorification-of-the-military terrain. *Squadron* emerged as Walsh's Valentine to the Air Force with Edmond O'Brien. For *Task Force*, writer-director Delmer Daves crammed a 27-year history of Navy aviation leading up to the branch's sterling World War II achievement of the Okinawa siege (in color) into 116 minutes. Narrated and performed by naval commander Gary Cooper, it seemed a recruiting poster.

Classically plotted but sporting the new documentary realist style, these films vividly etched the look of war: how war was waged, not why.[3] The stories unfolded from the points of view of the combatants, who comprised an ethnically, geographically, and attitudinally diverse unit of different ages, classes, and ranks[4] that exemplified a microcosm of American society. Occasionally, racial diversity was shown. Though the waging of war involved physical suffering and cost human lives, these films proclaimed that war made for adventures, friendships, and changes for the good in men. The films consistently climaxed in glorious victory or presaged a future victory if the film ended in a defeat.

Command Decision (MGM, 1948), William Laidlaw and George Froeschel's script from William Wister Haines's play, respectfully directed by Sam Wood, and *Twelve O'Clock High* (TCF, 1949), with Henry King in charge of ex-Air Force Commander Sy Bartlett's coadaptation of his novel, were something thematically new. These films took the audience into the rarefied higher branches of military power and decision making, while showing the war's psychological stress on leaders (anguished Gable; a mentally collapsed Peck, respectively) and the questioning of their authority by colleagues as well as the rank and file. The films also dispensed with the iconic combat scenes (*Command* records only a returning plane going up in flames and a montage of troops mobilizing; *High* has just one battle sequence).

Because of the sextet's winning grosses, the genre, both on a classical and aclassical demythological front, once again commanded attention. Regulation story patterns were reprised. A tough leader molded a regiment of reluctant soldiers (*Away All Boats*, U, 1955 with Chandler) or transformed raw recruits into experienced fighting men (Walsh's *Battle Cry*, WB, 1955 with Ray). The surly veteran (Wayne) went up against the compassionate second-in-command (*Flying Leathernecks*, RKO, 1951) or variant *Red Ball Express* (U, 1952), in which a lieutenant (Chandler) gets gas and ammo to the front while quelling the raging hostility of his top sergeant and the paranoia of a black soldier (Sidney Poitier) who accuses everyone of racism. Combat-romance with woman as threat provided the conflict of *Operation Pacific* (WB, 1951), with Wayne. The soldier proves himself by going from cowardice to bravery (the Civil War set, subjectively recounted *The Red Badge of Courage*, MGM, 1951).

Zanuck's *The Longest Day* was a culmination of yet another classical standard, the restaging of a military battle and a triumph of the documentary realist style. Directors Ken Annakin, Andrew Marton, and Bernhard Wicki so faithfully staged Cornelius Ryan's coadaptation (with assister World War II vet James Jones) of his widely read nonfiction work of the Allied landings in Normandy that production stills and actual photos taken on June 6, 1944 looked almost identical. Star cameos from the likes of Wayne, Mitchum, etc., that dotted the armies of extras (many actual military men), did not undermine the authenticity of the event unfolding, unconventionally, through the viewpoints of American, British, French, and German combatants (the dialogue of the latter two groups is subtitled). Photographed in CinemaScope/b/w in European locations, the opus ran for 3 hours.

Also, the film ended the easygoing military–industrial alliance that had existed since the infancy of film. Zanuck's use of actual troops stationed at the critical Berlin Wall, Mitchum's interview in which he cavalierly tossed off the remark that some soldiers were fearful of boarding a landing craft in high seas, and the reluctance of other military men to participate in filming, all sparked a Pentagon debate about the amount of men and equipment Zanuck received. When Zanuck refused to comply with the Defense Department's wish that a short scene of a Yank machine-gunning some German soldiers apparently trying to surrender be deleted, Defense reevaluated the military–Hollywood connection. The accident of an on-leave sailor killed while preparing explosives for use in *No Man Is an Island* (U, 1962) heated the debate. Effective, 1964: a new policy imposing stricter control over the cooperation process.

The new, aclassical patterns of a leader's trauma raising questions concerning his command and ability as well as the devastating effect of war also continued. In *The Caine Mutiny* (C, 1954), a translation of Herman Wouk's autobiographical Pulitzer Prize-nominated bestseller, the submarine setting gave way to a courtroom in the last third. Director Dmytryk captured Bogart's harrowing turn as the vessel's unhinged captain obsessively swiveling two steel balls in his right hand, Fred MacMurray's cool duplicity as the lieutenant, Johnson as an agitated mutineer leader, and not one combat scene.

The most deservedly accoladed of all was Oscar-winning *The Bridge on the River Kwai* (C, 1957). Within the traditional prisoner-of-war pattern, Carl Foreman and Michael Wilson's Oscared script from Pierre Boulle's novel,[5] directed by Oscar-winning David Lean, pitted the maniacally by-the-book

20–1   *The Bridge on the River Kwai* (C, 1957, p. Sam Spiegel)

By means of a box, intransigent, duty-bound Japanese captor (Sessue Hayakawa) lords it over the maniacally by-the-book British captive (Alex Guinness) in the jungles of Ceylon in director David Lean's demythed war film.

British captive Colonel Nicholson (Oscar-winning Alec Guinness) against his equally intransigent, duty-bound Japanese captor Colonel Saito (Sessue Hayakawa). Saito insists that British prisoners, including officers, build a massive bridge in the jungle of Ceylon (present-day Sri Lanka), photographed on location in CinemaScope/Technicolor. The martinet and control freak both come off as sadly foolish men.

   Bridge was also anti-war, with its images of war's uselessness and absurdity, none more so than the loony irony of the British throwing all their ingenuity and stamina into erecting a pivotal bridge for the enemy while another contingent of British is sent in to blow up the very same bridge. The film was ambivalent about Western technology, unlike the classical war film's typical celebration of it. Relentless in documenting war's brutalizing horrors, *Bridge* showed the waste of lives and resources. The Colonel, who has spent most of his adult life in the military, wonders, at one point, what the sum total of his life means. The inanity of trying to come to terms with ideological differences through fighting was also part of *Bridge*'s orders as was war's sad aftermath with both sides losing, a theme brought home by the final image of a hawk circling in a blue sky above the jungle, an image which rhymed with the film's first shot.

This storytelling device of bracketing metaphors was very anti-classical, demanding more from an audience than a typically classical film. What did the hawk mean? Audiences were meant to ponder and debate the meaning of the image as they left the theater. Certainly, as an image of freedom, it contrasted ironically with the story of physical and psychological imprisonment (a Lean trademark). Of course, there was the literal imprisonment of the Japanese prison camp. Furthermore and metaphorically, all the soldiers, both sides, were living a confinement since they had lost their individuality: they were part of a whole, ceasing to exist as an individual person. (Here *Kwai* also attacked the ethos of postwar conformity and loss of individuality.) Then, there was the psychological imprisonment: Nicholson is imprisoned by his absolute conviction to build a bridge while Saito is blinded by his own power. Holden, as the American Shears, is also imprisoned. Having escaped, he is forced to return to the military prison.

Bridge, with its multiple perspectives (British/Japanese/American), marked the postwar trend of unfurling the story from points of view in addition to and/or other than American. In the classical embodiment, the antagonist, more often than not, was faceless or sparsely shown. If the enemy were glimpsed, he was shown as stereotypically stupid. With the exception of *All Quiet on the Western Front* (U, 1930), the enemy was never afforded his side or say. In *Bridge*, moreover, while Colonel Saito speaks halting English with the British, his exchanges with the Japanese are in their language.

Even *Bridge*'s portrait of Holden as a cynical, solipsistic sailor, who in truth impersonates an officer because he feels they get better treatment in a POW camp, was an unflattering and thus, novel portrait of the American soldier. The addition of Holden to the international cast and the "Colonel Bogey March" hit single ensured victorious returns, despite neither combat nor romance and its 160-minute length.

Bridge brought together new trends that were in the air. The anti-military stance, especially in regard to leaders, began to crop only in the second half of the fifties when HUAC was winding down and America's suspicions of corporate evil were rife (along with the aforementioned *The Caine Mutiny*, Aldrich's *Attack!*, UA, 1956; Ray's *Bitter Victory* C, 1957; Kubrick's World War I-set *Paths of Glory*, UA, 1958; and Wise's *Run Silent, Run Deep*, UA, 1958). Except for Wise's work with its schizophrenic masking finale (pathologically obsessive Captain seeking revenge for a humiliation while jeopardizing his entire crew's safety is partially validated), all ended with a sadly ironic flourish.

By the mid-fifties, *Bridge*'s war-as-hell theme was also a constant.[6] Along with *Paths of Glory*, Walsh's *The Naked and the Dead* (RKO, 1958), Fuller's *Merrill's Marauders* (WB, 1962) and Siegel's *Hell Is for Heroes* (P, 1962) rubbed our noses in the slaughter of lives that war unmercifully exacts. *Bridge*'s diverse points of view had already appeared in Hathaway's *The Desert Fox* (TCF, 1951), cornering brilliant Nazi strategist Field Marshal Rommel; Wise's *The Desert Rats* (TCF, 1953), sighting the Australian contingent of the British 8th Army; *The Enemy Below* (TCF, 1957), pitting a Nazi U-boat commander against an American captain of a destroyer; and continued with Dymtryk's *The Young Lions*, with its German officer slant complementing those of two American soldiers; and *Under Ten Flags* (P, 1960), wherein a commander of a Nazi raider thwarts a British admiral. Dotted throughout *Run Silent, Run Deep* were Japanese officers' viewpoints, Japanese-spoken, English-subtitled. In these multiple and/or other perspective films, antagonisms were relaxed. Mutual respect was shown to the enemy for his courage and professionalism, even when the enemy's ideological beliefs were losing ground.

A cycle took the Korean conflict as subject, using old and new story patterns while introducing issues endemic to America's ambiguous position in Asia. Samuel Fuller (1911–97) mapped out the territory in 1951 with *Fixed Bayonets* (TCF) and *The Steel Helmet* (Lippert). In the latter, the surviving sergeant (Gene Evans) of a wiped-out platoon befriends a Korean kid and then a black medic, another lost corpsman. He finally hooks up with a patrol comprised of a mute, a Nisei, and an insecure, arrogant lieutenant. Through their arduous struggle to pass through enemy lines, Fuller raised issues of racial prejudice; war's dehumanization in turning men's fears and drives irrational (the furiously patriotic–distrustful sergeant is half mad); the questionable spoils of World War II (America rebuilding Europe/Asia); and America's ambiguity in playing cop, especially when the sides were no longer distinctly black and white.

World War II had interrupted Fuller's journalism (from 1924) and script-writing (from 1930) careers, serving as he did in the 16th Calvary of the First US Infantry Division from Africa to Czechoslovakia. This central experience of his life colored his subsequent career that included directing (from 1948) as well as producing (from 1951). Whether westerns, thrillers, or most significantly war films, Fuller's world view could be summed up by a line from *The Crimson Kimono* (C, 1959): "Life is like a battle. Somebody has to get a bloody nose." As with his alter ego protagonists, his mere 19 low-budget films, invariably Bs made at both the majors and minors, were blunt, grim, intense, idiosyncratic, and shockingly individual and crude. His films blasted classical traditions (the sparse, slogan-like dialogue: "You must be big to forgive"; presentational acting; choker close-ups; loopy perspectives as through a gun barrel; jump cutting;

schizoid tonal shifts; the overall lack of polish; the in-your-face confrontational, not comforting effect, for starters).

Other films based around the Korean conflict echoed Fuller's problematic sentiments in varying degrees and conveyed a fatalistically downbeat mood. Among the better: *One Minute to Zero* (RKO, 1952), with Mitchum; *Retreat, Hell!* (WB, 1952), the first Hollywood war film to image a major defeat (here, the Marine's 1st Battalion withdrawal from Changjin Reservoir), thus intimating the beginning of the end of America's foreign military supremacy; *The Bridges at Toko-Ri* (P, 1954), in which a psychologically destroyed navy flier (William Holden) questions his continuing in the war and America's presence in Korea; *Men in War* (UA, 1957); and *Pork Chop Hill* (UA, 1959). The equally downbeat *War Hunt* (UA, 1962), set during the last days of the conflict, offered a few more damaging perspectives of war, all which subtly raised the issues of war's morality. A replacement combat infantryman (Robert Redford, in his debut) is unnerved, unable to believe he's in the fray. He worries about the native farmers and their crops (a hand-held camera records his observations of them) and especially the fate of the unit's mascot, a 10-year-old Korean boy. He is so upset during a battle that he is unable to kill the enemy. Seasoned soldier (John Saxon), on the other hand, has become like a deranged serial killer, sneaking nightly behind enemy lines and slitting throats. No questions are asked. Even a ceasefire does not deter him. All along, the cynical officer makes his men aware that Korea is a politician's war: "We can't win . . . [it will] be settled around a conference table."

Some Korean conflict-set films, playing on communist fears, were in the traditional guts-and-glory mold: *Battle Circus* (MGM, 1953); *The Glory Brigade* (TCF, 1953); *Cease Fire* (P, 1953); and *Men of the Fighting Lady* (MGM, 1954), with Johnson.

Producer-director Robert Montgomery and writers Beirne Lay, Jr. and Frank Gilroy's independent assignment *The Gallant Hours* (UA, 1960), thematically innovative as previous war films, also brandished a strikingly unique narrative. The retirement of USN Fleet Admiral William F. Halsey, Jr. (Cagney, with darkened eyebrows as thick as his spectacles) frames the film. In between, the film eyeballs the most important mission in Halsey's World War II career, the crucial battle to take Guadalcanal, the point in the war that decisively reversed Japan's fortunes in the Pacific. No battle scenes, however, are shown. Rather the film spends its time on the introduction of the men involved, from commanders to privates; sessions where strategies are formed and second-guessing becomes a game; communiqués with government leaders; and, above all, the day-to-day routines and stress of living in the combat zone. Note: that both sides (American and Japanese) are depicted. As such, the film forgoes dramatic action, getting along with character sketches, patches of subjectivity, and explanations of wartime business.

Furthermore, the soldiers' introductions are accomplished by an off-screen narrator (director Montgomery for the American side; Art Gilmore for the Japanese). These verbal vignettes comprise facts of the respective fighting man's birth, education, and accomplishments (as we expect) as well as his habits, idiosyncrasies, and avocations (as we don't expect). Halsey's aide, we are told, is an expert at dancing the Charleston; Chief Yamamoto spends an hour every afternoon photographing flowers; the chaplain is a Vincentian who plays the fiddle. The profiles often include the proleptic mention of individuals' deaths, as with the private first class who "24 hours from now, a sniper's bullet will make . . . a paraplegic." Sometimes, the profiles include a future observation, as with the ace flier who will become the twentieth governor of South Dakota in 1955. These lengthy narrations, which also include explanations of business (the matter of codes, for example), play over incidents in which the actors' voices are dimmed.

Underlined by Roger Wagner Chorale's solemn chants, there emerged a tripartite textbook–chatty memoir–documentary of ordinary men meeting great challenges and war's sad mundaneness.

Notes

1   *Dive Bomber* (WB, 1941), *Captains of the Cloud* (WB, 1942), and *Thunder Birds* (TCF, 1942) were rare war film excursions into color during the classical period.

2   Previous Wayne portrayals of military men (*Men Without Women*, Fox, 1930; *Flying Tigers*, R, 1942; *Flying Seabees*, R, 1944; *They Were Expendable*, MGM, 1945) lacked Sands's impact.

3   Kathryn Kane, "The World War II Combat Film," in Wes Gehrig, ed., *Handbook of American Film Genres* (New York: Greenwood Press, 1988), p. 87.

4   Ibid., p. 90.

5   Since Foreman and Wilson were blacklisted writers; the script credit and award went to Pierre Boulle.

6   War movies with anti-war sentiments had appeared only sporadically in the silent and classical periods up to the mid-thirties (*The Big Parade*, MGM, 1925; *All Quiet on the Western Front*, U, 1930; *The Man I Killed/Broken Lullaby*, P, 1932; *The Eagle and the Hawk*, P, 1933), never constituting a cycle. Some, as with *The Dawn Patrol* (WB, 1930), were half-way houses, pacifist and anti-pacifist at the same time. Farce and musical passages undermined the remake *What Price Glory?*'s (TCF, 1952) questioning of war.

21

Western

The western, tackling the conflicts that arose as the American West forged a civilization out of the wilderness from the close of the Civil War in 1865 until the beginning of World War I in 1914, entered a mature phase. American myths, postwar, began to undergo a rethinking, such as the Frontier with its inherent racism, machismo, and stalwart family, whose head was the brave male and whose heart, the fragile female. Revisionism offered the genre the possibility of topical relevance and thematic sophistication while dramatically justifying graphic depictions of violence. The genre was easily able to accommodate the "with-it" psychological-sociological approach to character construction. These things undermined the classical conception of the western hero as a brave, just, courteous medieval knight of the plains, shifting and/or enlarging the story's concentration from a heroic male as protector of the community to a destabilized male in need of the community's help. The western was able to slip past the scrutiny of the censor (including that of HUAC), for the cavillous deemed the genre "safe" territory. In addition, the so-called "adult western" proved a way to compete with the genre's popularity on TV.

Location shooting, color, large-screen formats, and 3-D were conducive in the iconic celebration of the American land. Finally, a crop of actors (middle-agers Cooper, Fonda, Ladd, Stewart, Wayne, Randolph Scott, and Robert Taylor, along with newcomers Douglas, Heston, Lancaster, Mitchum, Peck, Glenn Ford, and Audie Murphy) were so excited about the departures from the form that they devoted a good part of their career working on the range. Directors Aldrich, Daves, Fuller, Hawks, Ray, Sturges, Budd Boetticher, Anthony Mann, and Sam Peckinpah refused to play by the rules of the game. Classicists such as Ford, Henry King, George Marshall, King Vidor, and Walsh had second thoughts, reworking their original commitments. All the major studios grazed the fertile land, with UA and U leading the herd.

Riddled with dark psychological strains was the Walsh-directed *Pursued* (WB, 1947). In this, Mitchum becomes quite unstrung upon learning he has been adopted as a child by the very man who murdered his parents. Moreover, he's in love with the man's daughter. The Hawks-helmed *Red River* (UA, 1948) saw a graying Wayne as a harshly irrational, unbalanced, controlling cattle baron and "father." Frantic during his drive of some 10,000 cows to market to make good his losses, he abuses his workers. Castigating his "son" (Clift) for his "soft heart," he vows to kill him when the son usurps his command. Wayne's violent ways are even questioned by one of his crew, who wonders why Wayne plugs disobedient subordinates with lead only to read the Bible over them. In *The Man from Colorado* (C, 1949), an ex-Civil War colonel turned judge (Ford) is certifiably psychotic, unable to stop himself from hanging men. His army buddy (Holden) asks the local doctor: "Could the war get . . . a decent man . . . so, well, sick that he can't stop killing?" As such, the film allegorically pondered the effect of World War II (and any war) on those who fought. The King-steered *The Gunfighter* (TCF, 1950) presented Peck as a "big, tough gunny," now old, tired, repentant. He is plagued by his legendary status that has made him uninvited in every town and a prey to every tough kid who wants to measure up to or surpass the legend. In *Johnny Concho* (UA, 1956) Sinatra grapples with his conscience after cravenly leaving town when his protector-brother is murdered. Marking the film debut of stage/TV director Arthur Penn, *The Left-Handed Gun* (WB, 1958), drawn from Gore Vidal's teleplay, caught Newman as a tortured, manic homosexual Billy the Kid, obsessive in his gunning down of his pal's murderer. In each, positive and negative impulses battled within the protagonist, indicative of the Frontier as well as postwar America's moral ambivalence, especially its males. Evil was pervasive: societal and individual. Contemplative passages wherein the protagonist took stock of himself appeared cheek by jowl with action sequences.

Such concerns as these closed down the genre's customary open spaces, curdled its usual rousingly optimistic tone, and reined in its expected robust pace. The Daves-guided *3:10 to Yuma* (C, 1957) was dispiritingly somber and measured. In its exterior scenes, the cracked earth was a constant reminder of the town's three-year drought; its interiors, where most of the film takes place, were shadowy. Outside and inside, what transpired was essentially a character-revealing debate between a pinched rancher-family man (Van Heflin), neurotically torn between his public and private duty, and an easy-going, affable bank robber-murderer (Ford). In *The Bravados* (TCF, 1958), inscrutably cold, sullen Peck, "with eyes of a hunter," mercilessly kills three men for the rape and murder of his wife, only to discover their innocence. The finale finds the mentally anguished avenger in a church pew, confessing to a priest: "I set myself up as judge, jury, and executioner." Not only in its male's deep psychic unmooring,

21–1   *3:10 to Yuma* (C, 1957, p. David Heilweil)
Locked inside a boxcar, outlaw Glenn Ford (left) engages in another debate with homesteader
Van Heflin in the psychological western.

the film diverged also in its foregrounding of the issue of the morality of
revenge. King's CinemaScope/Deluxe Color mirrored the alterity with decentering; closing down the immense space with shots through doorways and windows;
thick shadows splashed here and there; and a noticeable amount of silhouettes
and night scenes. With spatial minimalization and color shrouding, King also
played around with the usual way the large screen and color were used.

Director Anthony Mann (1906–67) provided some of the finest samples of
the genre's new slant. After Selznick nabbed him from the stage in 1938 as
casting director, talent scout, and supervisor of screen tests, Mann easily slid
into directing a series of poverty-row B films from 1942 to 1949, then moved
on to As. Bruised by some past happening, Mann's problematic hero populated
Winchester 73 (U, 1950), *Bend of the River* (U, 1952), *The Naked Spur* (MGM,
1952), *The Far Country* (U, 1954), and *The Man from Laramie* (C, 1955), all
starring Stewart. Stewart is out there going about his business (recovering his

stolen Winchester; leading a wagon train of settlers – *Bend*; taking a cattle herd to market – *Country*) and/or protecting the community (bounty hunting – *Spur*, or seeking men responsible for the sale of rifles to the Indians that caused his brother's death – *Laramie*). But something goes amiss, salting the sores of his past. His deeds are soon sparked by revenge that causes a fire in his belly. Neurotically obsessive, self-punishing, he begins to resemble the evil antagonist he attempted to stamp out (his murdering thief of a brother; the marauding Indians; a dangerous fugitive from the law; the powerful, greedy rancher and his deranged son and frustrated foreman; the thief who stole his cattle and henchman who killed his partner). Rarely does he enter the warm, comfortable space of a relationship with a woman and/or community, as, for example, Cooper in *Man of the West* (UA, 1958), a reformed bank robber, who, in protecting a card shark and tavern singer, comes face to face with his old gang, led by a sadistic brute who had raised him as his son and who rapes the singer. Blasting the gang away and realizing that his past will continually throw violent obstacles in his way, he, in the end, goes it alone, despite strong feelings for the singer.

The shaded hero is doubly out front also in Mann, Philip Yordan, and Russell S. Hughes's *The Last Frontier* (C, 1955) that, astonishingly, questions the "civilizing" of the Frontier, especially with its inculcation of the value of conformity and Christian practices. When a primitive fur trapper (Victor Mature) signs up as a Cavalry scout at a fort, he drinks more and more, talks to himself, becomes intimate with the commander's wife, and kills Indians with whom he had lived peacefully. He also loses his two beloved pals (one an Indian) whom he constantly touched and hugged. Furthermore, he is addled by the hypocrisy of the fort's inhabitants who have hurled recriminations at him when he honored their wish by abandoning the commander (Robert Preston) in a bear pit. The psychotic martinet, a West Pointer responsible for the loss of 15,000 men at the Battle of Shiloh as well as an additional 148 men and an entire fort to the Indians, is now, once again, trying to get it right and prove himself by foolishly attacking the Indians out in the open, thus sacrificing the lives of the people at the fort. Icy in his relations with his wife, obsessive-compulsive with his men (he adjusts their hats and buttons during a review), dismissive of his colleague's suggestions, the delusional leader is concerned only with his self-image, as civilization has taught him to be. With the trapper promoted to sergeant in a night ceremony amid falling snow (the final scene), the film subtly suggests, despite the congratulatory smiles all around underlined by the reprise of the jaunty title ballad by singer Rusty Draper, that his fate might be similar to that of the commander.

Budd Boetticher's (1916–2001) seven B films with Scott (four written by Burt Kennedy) that followed his classical warm-up at Universal (some half-dozen works, from *The Cimarron Kid*, 1950, to *Wings of the Hawk*, 1953) were also remarkable in this genre-renewal. *Seven Men from Now* (WB, 1956), *The Tall T* (C, 1957), *Decision at Sundown* (C, 1957), *Buchanan Rides Alone* (C, 1958), *Ride Lonesome* (C, 1959), *Westbound* (WB, 1959), and *Comanche Station* (C, 1960) unraveled yarns about solitary figures, still in the service of the town, addressing community issues, but, alas, never confronting the festering ones within. *Comanche Station*'s Cody, for instance, refuses to believe his wife, stolen by Indians very long ago, is lost forever. Fixated, he routinely goes about trading for the release of white women whenever he happens to hear of any who have fallen into the Indians' clutches. He's a frustrated father, too, instructing a young bounty hunter who's come under the thumb of an older bad man. "A man gets tired being all the time alone" is about as far as Cody goes in the expression of his feelings. The spare story line (Cody returns a wife captured by the Indians to her husband), Scott's underperforming, the setting's arid, rocky terrain, and the long takes of primarily endistancing long shots accentuated Cody's solitariness. Though in the 70-minute range, these Frontier miniatures unfold languidly.

The new western interbred with family melodrama, forming a distinct cycle imaging a Frontier family quite at odds with that in the classical version while echoing the rumblings in the nuclear unit. Memorably quirky were *Duel in the Sun* (SRO, 1946) and Mann's *The Furies* (P, 1950), both of which, daringly, also stripped bare female desire and boiled with sexual tension (a daughter for her father in the latter); Dymtryk's *Broken Lance* (TCF, 1954), where sibling rivalry and miscegenation take its toll; Wyler's *The Big Country* (UA, 1958) eschewing, in its 166 minutes, classical western action elements such as stage holdups, Indian massacres, drunken brawls, sober gunfights, etc., and instead concentrating upon people's interactions and reactions; *Gunman's Walk* (C, 1958), in which a father kills one psychotic son while disowning the other for casting his lot with a half-breed; and Huston's *The Unforgiven* (UA, 1960) and Siegel's *Flaming Feather* (TCF, 1960), where white households raise Indian children.

Shane (P, 1953) was the most unfadable of these interrogations of the Frontier family because of director Stevens's ability (here and in his melodramas) to make elemental characters, situations, and conflicts complexly real, their complexity never short-circuiting the directness of their impact. A. B. Guthrie, Jr.'s adaptation of Jack Schaefer's novel contained a greedy old goat with an array of gunslingers attempting to drive homesteaders off their land (among them the Staretts: father/Van Heflin, mother/Jean Arthur, and their 8-year-old son Joey/Brandon de Wilde). *Shane* also contained the intruder situation of family melodrama as solitary, mysterious, and laconic Shane (Ladd) comes upon their farm, where he stays on as a hired hand, as well as the genre's rite of passage embodied in Joey. From these patterns, Stevens culled resonating images: homesteaders' buckboarding to a skeletal town for supplies – en masse to protect themselves; a dog scratching his master's coffin as it is lowered into the grave; the father and the stranger competitively hacking away at an enormous tree stump. But the struggles were shown to be interior as well. Time and again, the mother keeps her growing romantic feelings for Shane to herself and tells her son, who loves Shane more than he does his own father, not to get attached to the stranger. Playing these diurnal sights and sounds against the majestic snow-capped Grand Teton Mountains (made to appear taller through the use of Loyal Griggs's 75 mm and 100 mm telephoto lenses) and Victor Young's full-blown stately score underlined the nobility of these simple folk. Simultaneously, the magnificent spaciousness and bittersweet melodiousness made the creatures seem vulnerable. With his talent for spatial contrast, Stevens was complexly polyvalent. A further example of Stevens's complex vision was holding out for values both of consensus/community and individuality at one and the same time. Lassoing a $9-million box office, *Shane* hit a cultural nerve.

Part of the genre's rejuvenation was the movement of women from supports to principals, sources of the story's conflict, sharers, sometimes even controllers of its point of view, as morally bedraggled as the menfolk (Maria Schell in Mann's *Cimarron*, MGM, 1960). Some were even forthrightly sexy (cigarette-smoking prostitute Joanne Dru in *Red River*, who'll give Wayne a kid if he'll stop pursuing his metaphorical son Clift, whom she has already slept with). Continents away from the frail damsels totally dependent upon the menfolk to protect their pure hearts from the lawless elements were ruthless ranch owner Veronica Lake (*Ramrod*, UA, 1947); Anne Baxter's "he-girl" Mike, raised by Indians (*Yellow Sky*, TCF, 1949); or boss-lady Stanwyck ("I was born upset") with a band of Fuller-brand *Forty Guns* (TCF, 1957). In many instances, these women themselves were the lawless elements (the anti-typed greedy Jeanne Crain in *Man Without a Star*, U, 1955; or Dietrich, ex-dance-hall gal, now owner of a horse ranch/haven for outlaws from whose pickings she takes 10 percent in Lang's *Rancho Notorious*, RKO, 1952). Aclassical, too, were *Rancho*'s narrative of three point-of-view flashbacks of Dietrich that keeps up the momentum of the increasingly psychotic criminal's search for the robbery, rape, and murder of his sweetheart; the silent montages with off-screen balladeer William Lee's "Legend of Chock-A-Luck" filling in the story gaps; and Dietrich's song-performance that stops the movie dead in its tracks as well as the occasional but noticeable jump cutting. Writer Yordan and director Ray reversed the classical western's male/female roles in *Johnny Guitar* (R, 1954). Saloon-keeper Vienna (Crawford), who wants part of the capitalistic pie by building a saloon outside of town where the railroad is to pass through, caterwauls and shoots it out with banker-landowner Emma (Mercedes McCambridge). Johnny (Sterling Hayden) and the Dancin' Kid (Scott Brady), on the other hand, occasionally lend support.

Darker images of the pioneer community appeared. Bravery, goodhearted-ness, probity, traits associated with the Frontier, were no longer in plain sight. *Johnny Guitar*'s law-abiding posse of townfolk, headed by a sheriff but run by Emma, is hypocritical and caluminous, taking up against Vienna so as their financial empire be not threatened, even making laws that are unlawful and forcing a false confession out of a young robber to indict Vienna. Such actions had a HUAC overtone to them. *High Noon*'s (UA, 1952) Hadleyville is peopled with cowards who turn away from supporting ex-sheriff Will Kane (Oscar-winning Cooper). Fearfully alone, Kane must face an unregenerate outlaw, arriving on the noon train and banding with his brothers, who is out to kill the lawman for sending him to prison. Even the sheriff's new wife (Grace Kelly) turns her back – well, up to the end, certainly. Adapted by blacklisted Carl Foreman from a short story, the film was an allegory of the industry's capitula-tion to HUAC and an indictment against conformity, as it pits the honorable individual against the ignoble group. To be expected, this dialectic was finely chiseled by director Zinnemann, who passionately shared Foreman's concerns.

No longer a place of expanse and possibility, the Frontier begun to appear as a dead end. Out of frustration with the way things turned out, some stalwarts turned opportunistic. Others looked for greener pastures. The Mexico of 1864 provided such a place in the Aldrich-guided *Vera Cruz* (UA, 1954), written by Roland Kibbee and James Webb. Here, for $50,000, an ex-Confederate colonel (Cooper), who "lost everything but his coat" in the Civil War, joins up with a horse thief (Lancaster) to transport a countess in a coach to the port city, accompanied by a band of scoungy gringos, a marquis, and European troops. The coach conceals $3 million in gold to pay for more European troops to keep the Austrian archduke on the throne. The secret out, everyone wants the gold for him/herself, even the peasant pickpocket who tags along. The journey alter-nates between battling the rebels and wheeling and dealing for the loot.

The westerner as opportunistic and/or dropping over the border and/or self-destructing was Sam Peckinpah (1926–85) territory. Peckinpah, from pioneer stock, received an MA in drama from USC and began as a regional stage actor and director. Some TV chores later, notably "Gunsmoke," Peckinpah crossed into movies in 1961 with *The Deadly Companions* (Warner-Pathé), fastening on a partially scalped Civil War vet's revenge complicated by his killing of a widow's small boy. With his second picture, *Ride the High Country* (MGM, 1962), an original by H. B. Stone, Jr., Peckinpah found his artistic voice. His absorption with superannuated people, out of joint, metaphorically lost, who easily slip from the side of law, is exemplified by a couple of aging ex-lawmen, the near-sighted Steve Judd (Joel McCrea) and the rheumatic Gil Westrum (Scott). Leg-endary for instilling law and order in towns, Steve and Gil are now anachronisms in a land they once built and maintained. Steve has landed a job transporting gold (a paltry $11,486, not the $250,000 he imagined) from a mining town to the bank. Having just bumped into Gil, who's running a shoddy carney game, Steve asks him and his sidekick Heck to go along. They accept because they intend to abscond with the cash.

Throughout the journey, Steve and Gil are conflicted between reason and unbridled feelings, another Peckinpah concern. Should Steve have taken the job? Should Gil steal? The questions of honor and personal code in a society that acts dishonorably arise when the old-timers allow a hormonal hoyden, escaping from her strict father, to join them and, later on, steal the girl from her abusive husband. When Gil comes clean, Judd arrests him. With his change of heart, Gil reclaims his sense of honor and duty.

The film makes us privy to other things that bedeviled Peckinpah: the importance of one generation's legacy or influence on another (the sidekick Heck); the hypocrisy of religion (a Bible-spouting father abuses his daughter and presumably killed his "whorish" wife whose grave he prays over); and the woman as whore (the farmer's dead wife and the females of the mining town). Even the hoyden has a cock-tease quality about her – after deliberately turning Heck on, she screams when he begins to have his way with her. According to Peckinpah, the Frontier, having made an uneasy alliance with civilization that subsequent generations have simply ignored or abandoned, was a battlefield.

The film, with its several protracted gunfights, one with a dolly into a bloodied face, and its depiction of the abusive treatment of the women at the hands of sexually repressed and/or inexpressive men, pointed the genre down the road of graphic, in-your-face violence.

All along, *Ride the High Country* demythed the genre, self-reflexively proclaiming its death. Simultaneously, however, the demythological tone had been informed with nostalgia for the genre's classical embodiment and what it represented. The final shot was the clearest example of this complex tone as McCrea's wizened face (foreground right frame) turns to take a last look at the mountain peak (background left frame) before expiring below the frame.

Such images clashed with the legendary Frontier, still memorialized by primitive artist John Ford (1894–1973). This first-generation Irish Catholic took to the Hollywood hills after high-school graduation in 1913, hopefully to work for his writer-director older brother Francis. Starting as a lowly Universal laborer, Ford, all along studying D. W. Griffith's achievements, worked his way up, debuting as feature director in 1917 with the western *Straight Shooting*. By the postwar period, Ford was the industry's poet laureate and by 1947 an independent producer as well.

Ford's males existed as examples to others, embodiments of moral lessons, the community's scapegoats and saviors and whose females, whether Virgin

Marys or Mary Magdalenes, were nurturing. Exemplifying this paradigm was *My Darling Clementine* (TCF, 1946), a retelling of Wyatt Earp (Fonda) and Doc Holliday's (Victor Mature) Tombstone days. Yet it must be noted that postwar piles supported the film's classic edifice. Earp is a befuddled man who has fallen in love for the first time and doesn't know quite how to act. Doc is a tortured, alcoholic consumptive, on the run from his profession, a woman who loves him, and himself. He has now taken up with a whore. A family of cattle-robbing murderers are on the loose until they are finally shot. Another family, an upright one, loses the two youngest sons. Ford's impressive Cavalry-triptych salute starring Wayne: *Fort Apache* (RKO, 1947), co-starring arrogant martinet Fonda; *She Wore a Yellow Ribbon* (RKO, 1949), awash with a protagonist's thoughts of aging and the memory of his dead wife; and *Rio Grande* (R, 1950), with a husband estranged from his family, also bear unsettling postwar markings. Blazing the classic trail, however, was *The Three Godfathers* (MGM, 1948), with Wayne as one of a trio of jailbreakers who sacrifices his freedom to tend a dying mother and child, the sixth remake of material that was filmed once before by Ford as *Marked Men* (U, 1919). *Wagon Master* (RKO 1950), an inspiring portrait of Mormons courageously making their way across the country, was also classically molded. In these the family, and by extension, the community, was sacred, and must be preserved, no matter the sacrifice. The memory and repetition involved in the holding to traditions and the commemoration of these traditions through rituals helped make the family and community cohere. With *The Searchers* (WB, 1956), however, there was a definite refocus.

At once an iteration and departure, *The Searchers*, trusty Frank Nugent's reworking of a LeMay novel, was a reevaluation and deepening and also an embracing of Ford's vision. Wayne is outsider-hero Ethan Edwards, ex-Confederate soldier, who shows up at his brother's Texan homestead in 1868 in Confederate cape, saber, and army britches. He never answers the question of why he didn't come home after the war. The freshly minted gold eagles that he gives to his brother suggest he's been robbing banks.

When his brother's family is murdered and two nieces kidnapped by the Comanches, this anachronism has finally something to do. Disrupting the funeral service (". . . no time for prayin'"), he sets off on a dogged search for his nieces, a search that will last many years. Even when it becomes clear that his niece Debbie has been acculturated to the extent of becoming one of the chief's wives (the other niece Ethan found had been raped and killed), the quest persists. When Debbie refuses to leave the tribe, Ethan is prevented from killing her by traveling companion Martin Pawley (Jeffrey Hunter). Though rescued as a child by Ethan and raised by his brother, Ethan refuses to consider Martin "family" because he's one-eighth Cherokee. All along, despite the truce, Ethan kills Indians (even shooting an Indian corpse's eyes out to prevent the Indian to reach, according to tribal belief, the Promised Land). He also relentlessly massacres their buffalo and eventually scalps the chief.

Assertive neighbor Laurie Jorgensen (Vera Miles), so desperate to marry shy Martin that she continually throws herself at him to kiss him, feels, as Ethan does, that Debbie is damaged goods and that it be better she had a bullet through her. But after the chief's death, Ethan does take Debbie home – to the Jorgensen household. The attempt at family solidity is problematic: Laurie's racism is still there and Ethan turns his back on them, wandering away.

The film was a vibrant metaphor for the postwar transition and the precarious state of its males. Ethan has fought in the Civil War, which is over. Upon his return, he has found his sweetheart married to his brother and a part-Indian considered family. During the search, he sees that his niece has accepted her lot among the Indians. Set in ways that counter the present reality, Ethan is out of sorts, adrift, holding on to conservative values at a time when they were being eroded by liberal ones, racist in still viewing the dark race as essentially threatening while the country itself was offering a second opinion on the race question. Ethan is also sexually repressed and frustrated, never attempting to move beyond his first love, even when she is found dead. Unable to change or consider new perspectives, he is a sad, lone figure.

The Searchers registered Wayne's most accomplished performance, the promise of *Red River* and *Sands of Iwo Jima* fulfilled. As Ethan, he conveyed an absolutizing instinct that was borderline pathological, holding us in fear about the character's next move and the next. The character's violation of the traditional Wayne persona disturbed, as did the absence of a love interest on the character's part.

Ford's narrative was experimental: the opening and closing scene chiasmus (the initial movement of Wayne sauntering from sunny exterior to dark interior of a home is reversed at the end); the middle section with Laurie's on-screen/off-screen reading from Martin's letter providing narrative thrust while linking the search's various stages; and the dropping in of farcical passages (Laurie's wedding) in a basically dark, brooding work. Furthermore, the many interlarded searches, each with its own story, brought about an atypical complexity: Ethan's search for his former sweetheart, now his brother's wife; Ethan's search for Debbie; Laurie's for Martin; Rev.-Captain Samuel Johnson Clayton for the chief's deadly contingent wreaking havoc on white settlers; and the chief's search to revenge the death of his two sons by the white military. Further, the mirror imaging of Ethan and the Chief disturbed. Number 11 among top box-office presentations that year, the film was dismissed by the industry and critics.

Ford's rethinking of native Americans in *The Searchers* (the description of the Indians' brightly hued clothes and artifacts speak of a distinctly rich culture), that culminates with his *Cheyenne Autumn* (WB, 1964), was part of the postwar revisionism of the Indian, traditionally represented as a redskinned savage who had to be wiped out for manifest destiny to fulfill itself. Launching this socio-logical cycle of enlightened portraits, swept along by the swelling civil rights wave, were the Mann-directed *Devil's Doorway* (MGM, 1950), with Robert Taylor as an Indian brave who returns from fighting in the Civil War to take up his people's plight after seeing their land sold to homesteaders of sheep and the Daves-directed *Broken Arrow* (TCF, 1950), dealing with the friendship between a pioneer scout (Stewart) and Cochise (Jeff Chandler) that quells the conflict between the whites and Apaches. The documentation of the Indian lifestyle throughout both films imaged the Indian as humane and cultured, while the inclusion of romance brought up the miscegenation angle, which the films liberally endorsed. In Aldrich's *Apache* (UA, 1954), Lancaster played a chief, dauntless in a last-ditch fight against the encroaching US army, while the Chey-ennes emerged as more human and braver than the Cavalry in *White Feather* (TCF, 1955). Some films lionized actual warriors of the past, such as *Taza, Son of Cochise* (U, 1954), *Sitting Bull* (UA, 1954), and *Geronimo* (UA, 1962).

The *Burning Hills* (WB, 1956) took up racism against Mexicans, while Ford's *Sergeant Rutledge* (WB, 1960) turned its attention toward blacks. *Cimarron*, at every stage of the settling of the Frontier, showed the presence of racism against Indians, from being prevented from sharing in the Oklahoma land giveaway to being barred from the redbrick schoolhouse. It also found anti-Semitism rife on the range. Socially sensitive Brooks's *The Last Hunt* (MGM, 1955) also attested to the western's new sociological sense by voicing the ecological extinc-tion-of-the-buffalo issue.

With all this redressing of the Frontier myth, it was inevitable that the western would wonder about the discrepancy between fact and fancy in the mythmaking process. As early as *Fort Apache*, Ford's Wayne put the best face on the intransigently cruel exploits of General Custer (Fonda) for the press. In *The Man Who Shot Liberty Valance* (P, 1962), Ford formulated the problem and ironically solved it: when there is a question of fact and legend, "print the legend."

Still arresting to many Americans, the essentially classical western continued. Yet, at closer range, postwar shadings were visible even in both the B- and A-range productions. Some notes: In *The Last Outpost* (P, 1951), ex-General Page is a white man who has become an Apache when the army didn't approve of his marrying an Indian and litanizes a series of injustices whites perpetrated against Indians. Sturges's *Gunfight at the OK Corral* (P, 1957) served up Earp (Lancaster) and Holliday (Douglas) wondering why they have to resort to vio-lence, while his equally violent *The Magnificent Seven* (UA, 1960) pondered what all their "magnificence" adds up to.

Rio Bravo (WB, 1959) was a Hawksian enterprise specifically to counter the psychological underpinnings, the lack of action, the dreary tone, the measured pace of the anti-classical westerns, particularly *High Noon*. The film does parade Wayne as a heroic sheriff, duets by sheriff's buddies Dean Martin and Ricky Nelson, dollops of farce, some extended fisticuffs and shootouts (in the film's first minutes, one guy is clubbed, another knocked out, and a third shot), and Warnercolor. But, alas, the oater also contains a series of males teetering on the brink of redefinition. The sheriff (Wayne) is inveigled into some mighty sexy verbal sparring with a crooked gambler (Angie Dickinson) who makes the usually laconic tall man talk and, uncomfortably, deal with his feelings. Sexually forthright, the gambler's always disobeying his orders. Revolt such as this brings the sheriff out even more. An ex-lawman now drunken bum (Martin) has been messed up by a woman (intimations of what will happen to the sheriff?). He must prove he deserves another chance and if he's worthy of palship with the sheriff. The cocky kid (Nelson) has to be brought down by a whiff of reality while the wizened, addled, insecure keeper of the keys (Walter Brennan), who walks with a limp, must be raised up by compliments and assurances that show respect. Well, the redefinitions are on their way to success as the four males and one extremely unprototypical female form, in a family melodramatic way, a substitute family. As such, in *Rio Bravo*'s 141 minutes of mainly character sketches and riffs eclipsing the already skeletal plot or, rather, situation (sheriff attempts to hold a murderer in jail until the arrival of the US marshal), we find another distinctly post-classical trend in picture-making. Still more: in lieu of the sunlit, wide-open spaces locations-backdrop of the traditional western, *Rio Bravo* opts for the predominantly studio-shot indoors (again, as in family melo-drama), with half of its scenes occurring at night.

Conclusion

Postwar Hollywood cinema stirred, rattled and, in some instances, undermined the mythology of genres that stabilized in the classic period. The world that emerged was a changed one. In short, a "larger-than-life" world was replaced by one "true-to-life." A relatively categorical, homogenous, and stable world gave way to one that was ambiguous, heterogeneous, fluctuating. Because "reality" was more difficult to understand and represent than the "ideal," the world that emerged was a lot messier.

People and their actions were just more morally ambivalent than before, be they shaded/anti/nonheroic protagonists or morally corrupt but somewhat heroic antagonists. And there were more of these kinds of people. Yes, the unadulteratedly morally good hero and totally decadent villain were still out there, but less so. People were also not consistently young, beautiful, white, and whole (some were physically handicapped). The reasons for actions weren't all that forthcoming and glib. Actions themselves did not come as easily as they did for their forebears. People were just not always in motion as before.

Differences, tensions, and contradictions between people or between people and institutions were as much reconciled as they were not. Things just always didn't turn out the way one wanted them to. The status quo was reaffirmed, but only after some degree of adjustment. Sometimes, though, it underwent an ironic tweaking; sometimes, an explosion.

Patriotism was invoked, but it was also questioned, especially in regard to war. The law and government were, more and more, not always seen as legitimate and capable systems of power. Institutions became, in general, less sound and benevolent. Often, the individual was left to his own devices to sort things out, although belief in God, religion, and now psychiatry were still seen as supports for some. Crime appeared as much overground as underground and it wasn't always crushed, though it still didn't pay. And it was not just a guy thing. Violence increased and became increasingly justified. Heterosexual eroticism and sexuality were now acknowledged and accepted as part of living, and they did not always guarantee a glamorously self-transcendent experience. Easily and frequently perverted, eroticism and sexuality could be dangerous, even lethal. In particular, the female was shown to have sexual desires. The homosexual was, at least, acknowledged as never before but, curiously, came across as asexual. The family unit was no longer consistently safe; marriage no longer an untarnished ideal; children no longer totally innocent. Even accounts of American history and legend began to lose their luster.

Part VI
Style

Introduction

Style is an often invoked and multivalent word in aesthetic circles. In the sense meant here, style is a manner of representation in which a film is conceived and rendered. As such, style also determines meaning. Hollywood cinema, since its inception, has been very eclectic. Some works are realist in their representation; others, formalist; still others partake of both modes.

Realism attempts a one-to-one correspondence between nature/reality and the way nature/reality comes to be depicted in film. Realism belongs to the mimetic tradition of art. Though practitioners claim pure objectivity in the depiction, subjectivity creeps in. Nevertheless, the realist keeps the subjectivity in check or, at least, hopes to do so. The realist likes to be seen as an effacer before reality.

Formalism strives to re-create reality in newly imagined ways. Formalism achieves its desired effect according to the interplay of the subjective impressions that the reality makes on the imagination of the renderer and the formal properties of film the renderer uses. As such, formalism belongs to the re-creative tradition of art. The formalist, no bones about it, imposes upon reality. Subjectivity enters to such a degree that reality is not so much imitated as reinterpreted.

Any practitioner of realism or formalism in the fiction film has an attitude of mind in choosing this or that mode. Attitude of mind, therefore, is another component of a style. This attitude carries over into the work, as say, in the area of genre. A realist would seek to do a social problem film or biography; a formalist, a musical or a science-fiction film. Though genres can be inflected in any style, certain genres are more at home with realism; others with formalism.

The realist believes in objective truth, that which can be verified in reality. As such, the realist tends to focus on the effect of a series of connected actions upon character. Moreover, since human beings are social animals, the realist generally places these actions within a social context. The character portrayed, furthermore, tends to be an example of the typical in the respective social context. The realist counts on this to instill the thrilling appeal of the recognition in an audience. The realist tends to be critical of the status quo and, depending upon the ardor of the realist, is unafraid to tread controversial waters. Moreover, in the construction of reality, all formal strategies used are never drawn attention to. How it is said (form) is at the service of what is said (content).

Conversely, the formalist believes subjectivity reveals more about truth than any mode that stays on the surface of phenomena, as realism. That is why the formalist banks on subjective perspectives and dauntingly stakes out the un/ subconscious, dreams and nightmares, anticipations and memories, and possible realities, in addition to conscious reality. Since the formalist's focus is upon perceptual insight and creative talent to revise reality in order to capture it in a deeper way than the realist, the form of the work is not only at the service of the content but also has a tendency to show itself off. Formal strategies are privileged in a formalist work, even at times to a self-reflexive extent.

Realism and formalism are relative terms. Culturally inscribed, each takes on the characteristics of the space and time in which they are located and defined. Therefore, different degrees of realism and formalism exist within as well as across national cinemas. The realism, say, in Hollywood's "photojournalism" of 1890 (Thomas A. Edison and W. K. L. Dickson's Kinetoscope shorts) is different from Hollywood's "classic realism" of the thirties, which, in turn, is not quite identical to the "documentary realism" of the industry's postwar years. The same can be said of the "psychological-sociological realism" of fifties Hollywood, World War II Italian "neo-realism," and Denmark's current "Dogma 95." It's the same old story with formalism. Within Hollywood, the postmodern "high-tech style" from 1977 on has emphases different from those deriving from the "style of expressive stylization" which held sway during the industry's 1963–76 fling with modernism, which, in turn, varies from the 1940–60 "noir." Across the ocean, France's turn-of-the-century "trick films," "German Expressionism" of 1919–33, or "Soviet Constructivism" of 1925–31 are phenomena distinct from Hollywood's formalist schools.

In *The Classical Hollywood Cinema: Film Style & Mode of Production to 1960*, the authors defined that style in Hollywood pictures from 1917 to 1960 as "the classic Hollywood style." A steel-trap of a style characterized by a stringent sense of unity and an equally rigid resistance to innovation,[1] the classic Hollywood style consists of the marshaling of all of a film's formal strategies in telling a story that "purports to be 'realistic' in both an Aristotelian sense (truth to be probable) and a naturalistic one (truth to historical fact)."[2] Moreover, the classic Hollywood style strives "to conceal its artifice through techniques of continuity and 'invisible' storytelling." "Comprehensible and unambiguous," the classic Hollywood-styled film contains "a fundamental emotional appeal that transcends class and nation."[3] Certain devices or technical elements are used to achieve this as well as a system of narrative logic, and systems of cinematic time and space that "almost invariably are made vehicles for narrative causality."[4]

In the classic Hollywood style/realism, the unity of formal elements, each element serving every other element and each serving the whole, go into the creation of a world. At this world's core is a character that has a goal and, furthermore, is able, more often than not, to achieve the goal which includes a heterosexual romance. (The character's public and private sides are addressed and fulfilled.) The character's goal-oriented actions are rationally caused and logically result in an effect, which, in turn, becomes a cause of another action, and so on and so forth. In linear fashion, the actions are hierarchically arranged to climax and resolve themselves in a finale. Behind this smooth operation wherein goals are achieved and things make sense is a romantic-idealist mindset. The post-Renaissance-inspired technique of balanced and centered compositions that privilege the main character/situation and the devices of continuity editing and decoupage (fragmenting a scene for thematic points and emotional high notes), both of which hold the world together, also belie an extremely optimistic disposition. Classic Hollywood style/realism's task of a "comprehensible, unambiguous" film that has a transclass/national appeal presumes the same attitude of mind. Such a noble task of appealing across the board, you see, necessitates dirty corners being swept out, cracks papered over, turning on lights in shaded areas, tying up things that hang in midair – everything in a proper perspective, everything in its proper space and on time.

The classic Hollywood style/realism did continue until 1960, even beyond that, and is still in evidence today. But, along the way, Hollywood embraced other styles that represented people/actions somewhat differently while emphasizing different formal strategies. Furthermore, these styles presumed a sensibility counter to the romantic-idealist mindset of classic Hollywood realism that was energized by the classical embodiment of genre. Postwar, three styles emerged – noir, documentary realism, and psychological-sociological realism – which gave Hollywood and its audience pause.

Some directors who worked in postwar Hollywood not only adopted these styles but went beyond, prefiguring what was to come. Hitchcock, Welles, Huston, Minnelli, Donen, and Tashlin, among others, plainly showed modernist tendencies. Tilting/questioning/toppling the thematic status quo, all were responsible also for new approaches to narrative that sabotaged the classic paradigms. All played around with subjectivity and point of view. Often their work self-reflexively reimagined cinematic space and time. These directors also engaged in intertextuality, incorporating within their respective works materials and structures from filmic as well as different discourses or signifying practices to create meaning. Minnelli referenced his own film *The Bad and the Beautiful* (MGM, 1952) throughout *Two Weeks in Another Town* (MGM, 1962). Donen resorted to nonfilmic intertextuality by making *Funny Face* (P, 1957) resemble a high-fashion magazine. Walsh used the nonaesthetic discourse of police procedural methods in *White Heat* (WB, 1949).

Occasionally, modernist tendencies turned up even in the least likely of places. In the B romantic comedy *Always Together* (WB, 1947), with a clever Henry and Phoebe Ephron/I. A. L. Diamond script, the girl is a movie addict, often seen at the movies with her boyfriend. From the movies on the screen, the couple derive their notions of what a relationship is all about, which they comment on. Furthermore, they attempt to live out these notions in their lives, which they also comment on. Thereby, they self-reflexively tell us which way the actual movie's plot will go, especially the ending. Producer-director William Castle in his B horror film–whodunit *The Tingler* (C, 1959) makes the movie screen within the film showing a silent film to an audience go blank, then dark and, in an extended sense, become the actual movie screen in the theater showing *The Tingler*. At this point, the protagonist Vincent Price warns, in voiceover in the dark, about the tingler on the loose, not only to the audience within the film, but to the actual audience watching the film, which has by now felt the jiggle from the vibrators placed under the seats. This gimmick was timed to go off at this point in the movie, convincing the actual audience that the tingler was, indeed, loose.

Additionally, self-reflexive instances of direct address to the camera on the part of the character within the film increased in postwar cinema. No longer only the terrain of comedian comedy, it appeared, for example, in the male melodrama *Edward, My Son* (MGM, 1949), where Spencer Tracy, at the film's start and finish, asks the moviewatching audience to answer the question: "If you have been me, what would you have done, ladies and gentlemen?" Other formal tropes arose (as we shall see), less determined by these new styles than by cultural and commercial considerations that, nevertheless, undermined the ironclad ways of classic Hollywood.

Notes

1   David Bordwell, Janet Staiger, and Kristin Thompson, *The Classical Hollywood Cinema: Film Style & Mode of Production to 1960* (New York: Columbia University Press, 1985), p. 3.
2   BST, p. 3.
3   BST, p. 3.
4   BST, p. 6.

22

Noir

Introduction

Noir coalesced roughly in 1940 and continued, as a pronounced strain, until about 1960, as far as its initial embodiment went.[1] Though heating up in 1940–5, its epicenter was the next 15 years, which roughly corresponds to the time when Hollywood, in earnest, stopped relying totally on its ancestry.

Noir's rupture with the formalities of classical Hollywood style and realism was not lost on BST, which acknowledged it as "an assault on psychological causality," "a challenge to the prominence of heterosexual romance," "an attack on the motivated happy ending," and "a criticism of classical technique."[2] But they go on to proclaim that "all forms of film noir's challenges none the less adhere to specific and non-subversive conventions deriving from crime literature and from canons of realism and generic motivation[3] . . . every characteristic narrative device of film noir was already conventional in American crime fiction and drama of the 1930s and 1940s."[4] True enough, but this school of detective fiction was itself a break with its classical embodiment, be it Arthur Conan Doyle's Sherlock Holmes or S. S. Van Dine's Philo Vance series. This renegade school (called "hardboiled") was a modernist redo, sporting new thematics (cf. Chapter 19) and new formalities (to be seen).

The psychological thriller moved in a new direction as well, which BST actually noted as going through a "rejuvenation" during the 1930s.[5] Writers (Patrick Hamilton/*Rope's End*; Francis Iles/*Before the Fact*; Emlyn Williams/*Night Must Fall*) made the genre contemporarily existential, thematically and formally upending its classical forerunner, the Gothic melodrama. The espionage thriller also went existentially modern in the early twentieth century with Erskine Childers's *The Riddle of the Sands* (1903), Joseph Conrad's *The Secret Agent* (1907), William Le Queux's *Spies of the Kaiser* (1909), and E. Phillips Oppenheim's *The Great Impersonator* (1920). Topicality, violence, eroticism, moral ambiguity, and the use of the genre as a vehicle for social issues entered with W. Somerset Maugham and his Ashenden series in the 1920s and 1930s; Eric Ambler's *Background to Danger* (1937), *A Coffin for Dimitrios* (1939), and *Journey into Fear* (1940); and Helen MacInnes's *Above Suspicion* (1941). But it was Graham Greene who most significantly revivified the subgenre with *Stamboul Train* (1932), *The Confidential Agent* (1939), and *The Ministry of Fear* (1943).

BST also contend that the stylistic features of noir were just as strongly motivated as those of classical cinema, since they fall under the rubric "realistic and genre motivations."[6] True enough, but many of these techniques never appeared in the classic B detective or A/B gangster thrillers or in scenes of dark doings in genres other than thrillers. Where, for example, is the precedent of having the protagonist, and star to boot (Bogart), recall incidents that initially sets the plot in motion, with his face completely blacked out (*Dead Reckoning*, C, 1947)? Or where is the gradual switching-off of the lights in the town till the frame is just about pitch black (*Storm Warning*, WB, 1951)? Or better still, where the use of deliberate underwriting, the professional killer-protagonist as cipher, the deadpan lead performance, a decentering in which the speaker's head is lopped off, and jump cutting that pummels classic spatial/temporal logic to bits, as in *Murder by Contract* (C, 1958)?

The 1940 releases *Rebecca* (UA), *Stranger on the Third Floor* (RKO), *The Letter* (WB), and the 1941 entries *Citizen Kane* (RKO), *Suspicion* (RKO), *The Maltese Falcon* (WB), *High Sierra* (WB), *Shanghai Gesture* (UA), *I Wake Up Screaming* (TCF), *Manhunt* (TCF), *Among the Living* (P), and *Strange Alibi* (WB) signaled noir's start while 1960's *Psycho* (P), its close. Within these historical parameters two relatively distinct modes, in most instances, overlapped: the pure expressionistic noir of, say, Billy Wilder's *Double Indemnity* (P, 1944) or Robert Wise's *The Set-Up* (RKO, 1949) and the more usual expressionist–documentary realist mix in Wilder's *Ace in the Hole* (P, 1950) or Wise's *Odds Against Tomorrow* (UA, 1959).

22.1   Determinations and Practitioners

America's cultural climate helped the sprouting of noir: the postwar certainly (see Part I) but also the World War II years (1939–45). The coming of the war (the several years prior to the Japanese surprise attack on Pearl Harbor on December 7, 1941 when America entered the war) divided the country into isolationists and liberals. This division, especially on the heels of Depression-era solidarity, caused tension. The war enabled America to get back on its financial feet after the Depression and after President Roosevelt's New Deal faced a dead end with its escalation of taxes, industrial regulation, the plethora of welfare agencies, and the carping from the business community which saw private enterprise, not government spending, as the means to a speedier financial recovery. This smell of money in the air created an "allure" of money. Loneliness, the experience of being in a strange land, the continual shelling, bombing, and omnipresent threat of death bummed out the fighting males. Some of the males at home turned insecure and despondent about being on the sidelines. Others were slackers. Some stateside males began to take advantage of the war and turned opportunistic. It was easy to get away with little things now that the nation had its mind on big things. Some females, if they weren't serving or part of the work force, began to share opportunistic ideas with the males or have their own. With the civilian introduction of penicillin in 1943, which cured syphilis, that opportunism included the sexual realm. Civilian populations moved to industrial locations; 11 million military lives were uprooted; family life underwent disruption. After the repeal of prohibition (1919–33), industrial racketeering took hold. During wartime, when the federal heat was off, racketeering dug deeper into the American soil.

Other forms of leisure activities kicked in. The hardboiled school of letters (the use of an unsentimental, tough-shelled protagonist making his way through a miasmic American city while relying on his own physical stamina and inner sense of what is right, rendered in a vividly vernacular prose) cannot be over-estimated. The pulp magazine *Black Mask* was a magnet and repository of hardboiled writing, notably Hammett, Daly, and Chandler with their creation of the existential urban private eye and his sallies into middle-class crime. Cain, Woolrich, and McCoy likewise contributed to this school which also involved experiments in a distinctively American prose style (the preference for the concrete; the detached, cynical tone; emphasis on subjectivity and point of view). Paperback outfits reprinted these short stories and novels while welcoming acolytes such as Steve Fisher and Jim Thompson.

Radio shows from the mid-thirties on ("Crime Busters," "Suspense") were further determinants. The protagonists were crime fighters, not gangsters, necessitated by the fact that radio was an in-home and sponsored medium. The stories were cut to the bone; the tone matter-of-fact; the narrative often pouring forth from first-person subjectivity. By 1945, radio stations broadcasted 90 minutes of crime shows every day. TV, of course, extended radio's influence by the early fifties.

Cinematic traditions, such as German Film Expressionism (1919–33), added to the mix. Part of Continental Europe's aesthetic revolution at the turn of the twentieth century, expressionism switched the axis of representation from the mimetic and objective to the re-creative and subjective. Whether "street films" that depicted the common citizen in this political, economic, social, and moral upside-down era (G. W. Pabst's melodrama *The Joyless Street*, 1925) or the

22–1   *The Dark Corner* (TCF, 1946, p. Fred Kohlmar)

Expressionism of the noir style dominates the tension-filled frame, as diagonal lines in the bottom half interrupt the verticals of art dealer Clifton Webb within the door frame as he comes upon his silhouetted wife in the arms of her lover.

"shudder films" (thrillers, horror, or sci-fi such as Robert Wiene's *The Cabinet of Dr. Caligari*, 1919; Murnau's *Nosferatu*, 1922; Fritz Lang's *Metropolis*, 1926), German expressionist cinema focused on man's psyche in an extremely stressed-out state. These films expressed the wild, transgressive subconscious, the dream life's release valves, the haunting nightmares, the illusions or delusions, even madness and possible alternative perspectives of their whacked-out, wasted individuals. The rendering was achieved through visually textured, expressive images that experimented with the spatial qualities of film: performance, visual design, and composition. The introspective acting with more reaction than action; the use of hairstyle, costume, and makeup, décor, and lighting switcheroos with the amount and direction of light, all were to get us inside the character. Oblique, fractured, decentered framing and staging as well as the assiduous, diagnostic camera were actors too, revealing inner realities, anchoring points of view.

Pitching in also was French Poetic Realism, a film style appearing roughly between 1934 (Jean Vigo's *L'Atalante*) and 1945 (Henri-Georges Clouzot's *Le Corbeau*, 1943).[7] Reflecting the strain and sadness infecting the country during the thirties Depression and its ultimate capitulation to Nazism, this style showed the severe disaffection, immobility, and sense of fatality eating at the heart of the urban working class and/or classless protagonists. Love was outside of one's reach (Jules Duvivier's *Pepe-le-Moko*, 1937). Violent death was around the corner (Pierre Chenal's *Le Dernier Tournant*, 1939). Perhaps youth, with its new morality and a return to the soil, was an answer. Consciously breaking away from the French film's reliance on high-cult theatrical and literary sources and methods, the films went in for spare, concentrated observations of the human condition, usually unfolding from a single consciousness recalling the past (Marcel Carné's *Le Jour se lève*, 1939). As with German Expressionism, visual design, whether studio sets or location, expressed the contour of the soul.

Another determining antecedent, but one closer to home, was Viennese Jew Josef von Sternberg's (1894–1969) work. His sophisticated portraits of class stratifications in America (*Docks of New York*, P, 1928) and his plumbing of the criminal inferno (*Underworld*, P, 1927; *Thunderbolt*, P, 1929) seemed a dry run for noir. So, too, his capturing of the eroticism and degradation of heterosexual coupling, specifically the sex–death tango, and the insidiousness of the femme fatale (*The Last Command*, P, 1928, and the seven features made not so much *with* but *about* Marlene Dietrich, from *The Blue Angel*, UFA/P, 1930, 1931, to *The Devil Is a Woman*, P, 1935).

Warner Bros.' rough and tough, street-smart house style could be noted as a forerunner, seen in its shyster satires (*Lady Killer*, 1933), gangster thrillers (*The Public Enemy*, 1931), backstagers (*Wonder Bar*, 1934), social problem films (*I Am A Fugitive from a Chain Gang*, 1932), female melodramas (*Baby Face*, 1933), and B detective series (Perry Mason). The topical, political, and controversial matter, by and large, boiled down to the interaction of a proletarian urban guy with questionable social institutions. Interaction turned confrontational and generally spilled over into crime. Peppered with a cynically impassioned tone, the pictures were often ripped from newspaper headlines and/or taken from real incidents. Actors with ordinary looks (Paul Muni, James Cagney, Edward G. Robinson, Joan Blondell, Barbara Stanwyck, Anne Dvorak) embodied these people who, in some genres, talked a wise-crack-ese (or variant of hardboiled talk). The visual design and composition were at once extremely stylized (expressionistic at times) yet recognizably nitty-gritty familiar. The pace was pell-mell.

22–2   *Ace in the Hole* (P, 1951, p. Billy Wilder)

Noir's expressionist and documentary-realist features blend as foreground lift literally and meta-phorically imprisons manipulative reporter Kirk Douglas against the actual Gallup, New Mexico background.

Another formative antecedent included the Universal horror films of the thirties under German Jew Carl Laemmle and son's aegis who imported talent from Germany (*Murders in the Rue Morgue*, 1932). To a lesser extent, the detective thrillers at TCF (the "Bulldog" Drummond/Michael Shayne series) and at MGM (*The Thin Man*/Nick Carter series) left their marks.

The documentary style of filmmaking (certainly from 1945 on) energized and helped crystallize noir. The documentary method and attitude of mind, as we shall see, seeped into the commercial feature during the war and began infiltrating all genres to such an extent that it became a distinct type of realism not only practiced but preferred during the postwar period.

Still another determinant was the war/postwar popularization of Freud in all arts and media. War's trauma caused problems of mind and spirit, particularly in the physically and/or psychologically-scarred vets. Postwar, America's head-and-heart malaise expanded, as Cold War worries, the sense of dislocation and alienation from changing values and lifestyles, the desperation to keep up with the Joneses, the sadness from the realization that bread and circuses were not enough, swirled about.

To those unwilling to keep the lid on and let problems fester, Freud offered a vocabulary to express their anxiety. Further, he offered a solution through the practices of psychology and psychiatry. And as far as the Hollywood industry went, it was very chi-chi to have an analyst. Residents of Beverly Hills knew the Freudian setup from personal experience and were eager to spread the word.

With Freud's tripartite division of the human being (superego as the internalization of authority; id as the pleasure principle; ego as keeper of both extremes in tow), as well as his belief in the sexual ground of all actions, the recurrence of certain primitive tribal ceremonial patterns in one's life, and the importance of dreams, Freud key lighted a person's interiority. His construct evinced an interest in the problem of perception (the truth/illusion or delusion battle); mental illness; a person out of control; sexuality as motivating factor; the intrusive, primitive truth beneath the civilized veneer; dream as a clue to understand conscious reality; the past as a key to unlock the present; and the clinical situation itself.

With the homogenization of Freud, the Hollywood film extended itself by becoming more introvert. While never abandoning the classic preoccupation with man's extrovert side (as deed-doer and goal-achiever), interiority became a new dramatic site. True, psychological motivation was a classical building block of character and did determine characters' actions but the method hitherto had been practiced often superficially (the one-note, clearly apprehended character), disallowing the protagonist to possess dimension, heterogeneity, and ambiguity.

Transgeneric, this introversion was manifest in the use of the involuted and refracted narratives controlled by a single consciousness (*Lady in the Lake*, MGM, 1946) or many different consciousnesses, in which case the aggregate was an attempt to put a person together, like pieces of a puzzle, in order to understand him (*Inside Straight*, MGM, 1951). In either case, the spectator is inside a person's mind. This flies, of course, in the face of classical cinema's preference for objective, linear storytelling and godlike point of view.

The internal mechanism of a character (*why* he does what he does) began being privileged over the classical concern for action (*what* he does). *Spellbound* (UA, 1945) is about the unblocking of an amnesiac by a psychiatrist. Character was more likely to be constructed along lines of a double or multi-faceted split within one and the same person which, ironically, did not guarantee the spectator's complete understanding of the character (the money-loving reporter, unscrupulous yet daring, who inhabits *The Underworld Story*, UA, 1950). Often the "mysterious force of fate" was invoked to assuage somewhat this feeling of incompleteness. Classical cinema emphasized character consistency, which ensured an audience's grasp of character. Shadows of doubt, whenever they appeared, were usually wiped by the thoughts of God's hand, providence, or will.

Another Freudian imprint was the narrative flashback, an indication not only of the use of the past to explain the present, but also an indication of the compulsion to repeat, the mark of a neurotic person and an analogue of Freudian analysis itself (*Mildred Pierce*, WB, 1945). Classic films used flashback but not as much as their wartime and postwar descendants. Flashbacks were either visual (the audience saw the past) or verbal (the audience heard about the past). The prevalence of dream or nightmare sequences in films of this time (*The Snake Pit*, TCF, 1948) was also Freudian inspired.

The admittance of the fearful and guilty, the neurotic, the sadist and masochist, the psychotic, the schizophrenic, the psychopath, all capable of crimes and misdemeanors, to the ranks of protagonists (previously, they were around as antagonists or supports) in lieu of the idealized or normal/average/symptomatic principal was quite a shift and also part of the Freudian legacy. More often than not, the spectator was left ambivalent, not just sympathetic to the protagonist (the schizophrenic killer/Phyllis Thaxter in *Bewitched*, MGM, 1945). The figure of the psychiatrist, in addition to the classical priest and doctor, as a sign of authority, and the structuring of scenes or an entire film in terms of therapy sessions (in part, *Strange Illusion*, PCR, 1945; *Caught*, MGM, 1948; or in toto, *Double Indemnity*, P, 1944) were also something new and, incontestably, tributes to Freud.

Space was more often than not contained, cluttered, shadowy, emblematic of Freud's concept of the imprisoned mind. Classically, this rendering of space was also used, but not with such frequency. The representation of lust, eroticism, and sexuality went coded, as in classical cinema, but sometimes not (*Gilda*, C, 1946). Either way, there was still more of it.

Industrial factors must not be lost sight of in noir's germination. Directors (Wilder, Lang, Siodmak, von Sternberg, Preminger, Zinnemann, Edward Schoedsack, E. A. Dupont, Edgar G. Ulmer, Anatole Litvak, John Brahm, Curtis Bernhardt, William Dieterle, Charles Vidor, Jean Negulesco, Joe May, and Henry Koster) and other craftsmen (writers Hans Kraly and Curt Siodmak; cinematographers Karl Freund and Rudolph Maté, both of whom turned directors, John Alton, Theodore Sparkuhl, and Franz Planer; composers Max Steiner and Franz Waxman) began their careers in the twenties at UFA, Germany's leading production-distribution-exhibition outfit, where they in/exhaled the expressionist sensibility. With Hitler's ascendancy, all had fled to America (some stopped over in France, where they acquainted themselves with the style of poetic realism).

Hitchcock, the hope of the British film, also worked in the German film industry where he came in direct contact with expressionism. *The Blackguard* (1925), which involved Hitch in writing, directing the art, editing, and assisting director Graham Cutts, was shot at UFA where the observant neophyte visited the set of Murnau's *The Last Laugh* (1924). Quite taken with Murnau's subjective camera, Hitch acknowledged: "Almost the perfect film . . . it had a tremendous influence on me." The first two films Hitch solely directed in 1926 were also Anglo-German co-productions.

In 1913, a year after directing his first film in his native Hungary, Curtiz studied filmmaking at Nordisk, one of Europe's leading companies, which was a major influence on German Film Expressionism. By 1916, Curtiz was a leading figure in Hungarian cinema. Fleeing Hungary for Vienna in 1919 because of the communist government's nationalization of the film industry, Curtiz, a year later, became the premier director at Count Alexander Kolorvat's large studio, "Sascha," catapulting it into the top Viennese player. No surprise, Sascha's output bore the expressionist taint. At WB from 1926 to 1953, Curtiz substantially contributed to the studio style which anticipated noir.

On Hollywood shores, some of these expatriate directors started out humbly in the major leagues with their artistic roots and inclinations squelched and/or controlled. As their commercial and critical cachet grew and as the mood of America darkened, these directors' ingrained manner and sensibility came up for air. As for the ex-Europeans who landed in the minor leagues, where the matter of control was not as crucial as at the majors, some moved up while others stayed and, in time, were able to make even more personal works that reflected on their beginnings.

The B film at the major studios and poverty-row outfits and the double feature format also energized this style, as Paul Kerr smartly noted in his seminal article "Out of the Past? Notes on the B Film Noir."[8] Bs economized the mind of the director, Kerr observed, resulting in lean rather than florid plots and an emphasis on visual rather than verbal values. Kerr continued: fast, cheap production encouraged night for night shooting; with borrowed sets, a reconfiguration took place in terms of new angles and skewed perspectives. Of course, in case of a scanty set, shadows were a must. With the enlisting of B players, ex-stars, or wannabes, characters and situations of murky morality were possible, which no major star would countenance. Stars, in the main, wanted to appear noble and good; their fans, moreover, concurred. B pictures also encouraged jump cutting. B pictures encountered less interference from the front office and the Code. All this meant that there was a good chance that controversial, sensational, and/or forbidden material, skirting being frisked, could or would slip through. Finally, Bs were relegated to lower half of a double bill in a hot- and-cold-shower format. Since most As were light, optimistic, and escapist (certainly classical ones), Bs tended to be dark and pessimistic.

Independent production, more conducive to thematic and formal experimentation than the studio system mode, also invigorated noir. Lastly, censorship, in the throes of transition, was conducive to make concessions in the thematic area.

22.2   Noir and Genre

Though epicentered in the thriller, noir polluted all genres, whether adventure (*The Treasure of the Sierra Madre*, WB, 1948), comedy (*It's a Wonderful Life*, RKO, 1946), family melodrama (*The Bad and the Beautiful*, MGM, 1952), or romance (*Till the End of Time*, RKO, 1946); even the musical (*Blues in the Night*, WB, 1941) and western (*The Outcasts of Poker Flat*, TCF, 1952). When shadowed, the tensions in these off-centered genres found little, if any, erasure. A case in point: in the female melodrama *Possessed* (WB, 1947), the obsessive compulsive victim of *amour fou* (Crawford) loses her mind and contact with reality. Noir-muddied off-genres also invariably came with a dastardly deed (often murder), a mystery and a detective (usually metaphorical), and a piling on of suspense.

22.3   Mode of Representation and Attitude of Mind

As a mode of representation, noir's literary design involved, first of all, a plot characterized by complexity. This complexity was achieved in a variety of ways:

1   A mystery element.
2   A convoluted narrative in which the history of events were controlled by subjective points of view – the subjectivity drifting in and out of the past; repeating things over and over:
   - the rare first person off-screen or the disembodied voiceover throughout (*Lady in the Lake*, MGM, 1947; the first fourth of *Dark Passage*, WB, 1947)
   - a third person on-screen, usually introduced by a first-person voiceover, which may or may not be continued (*Rebecca*, UA, 1940)
   - two or more or multiple third persons (the dual-perspective of *Laura*, TCF, 1944; the multiple-perspectives of *The Killers*, U, 1946, including a newspaper report of a robbery read by an insurance head)

- an off-screen narration or written prologue attesting to the truth or importance of what is about to be seen (*He Walked By Night*, EL, 1948)
- a narrative told to someone within or outside the story to point a moral (*Leave Her to Heaven*, TCF, 1945; *Edge of Doom*, RKO, 1950; *The Unknown Man*, MGM, 1951)
- the appearance of dream or memory flashback sequences (*The Burglar*, C, 1958) or passages of projection (*Sudden Fear*, RKO, 1952).

In most cases, the point of view was not adhered to unswervingly. Spectators saw more than the narrator did or could see (in *Gilda*, C, 1946, the first-person memory off-screen and third-person on-screen perspective of Glenn Ford takes us into the bedroom of husband/George Macready and wife/Rita Hayworth when Ford himself isn't there, and later reveals Macready's planned rescue after supposedly being blown up in a plane over the ocean which Ford, miles away on the beach, could never see).

That the plot, made up of past events, was being narrated or repeated from a present-day perspective was another characteristic, emblematic of a journey or quest on the part of the narrator's mind, and by extension the spectator's, to understand.

3   A psychological dimension that explored or attempted to explore the "why" as much as or more than the "what" (*Criss Cross*, U, 1949).
4   The belief that accident or chance (not the classical cause and effect) were the fabric of human existence which created plot twists and turns which were not easily accessed by the spectator, nor were they meant to be (*Sudden Fear* foregrounds the protagonist's working out on paper her revenge scheme, sequentially item by item, with each item even numbered, and later, during the actual perpetration, finding every thread of her plan unraveling).

Another characteristics of noir plotting was the sometime sidestepping of the de rigueur heterosexual coupling (*The Line-Up*, C, 1958) as well as the happy ending (*Out of the Past*, 1947).

In the characterization of the male or female protagonist, noir welcomed the presence of the *passive* (*The Long Night*, RKO, 1947) in addition to the passive–active male. Men are constantly found brooding in bed (*This Gun for Hire*, P, 1942; *Shadow of a Doubt*, U, 1943; *The Killers*, U, 1946). The *active* female (*Jeopardy*, MGM, 1952) was embraced in addition to the passive–active one. Noir was responsible for a slew of dimensioned, real ladies that Hollywood classical style only rarely saw, especially in terms of their sensual, erotic natures.

Insisting on male and female ambiguity (positive and negative traits as well as active and passive personalities), the style trafficked in semi/anti/non-heroes/heroines as protagonists, creating an ambivalent response in the spectator. Villains, male or female, shared the center with the hero (*Shadow of a Doubt*); sometimes they were the center (*So Evil My Love*, P, 1948). In the conception of the villain, ambiguity was often sought, rendering the spectator's hissable response an anachronism (*The Big Clock*, P, 1947).

Hardboiled dialogue sounded like colloquial, urban, unequivocally American talk. The choice of words was limited, with a preference for the concrete as nouns and verbs (tootsie Audrey Totter to pickup John Garfield: "It's a hot day and that's a leather seat and I got a thin skirt on" in *The Postman Always Rings Twice*, MGM, 1946). Repetition of words and phrases (and naturally, actions), as a sign of neurosis, abounded. Slang and fractured grammar were no problem. The dialogue, usually laconic, was edged in an ironically cynical humor and given a matter-of-fact tone through the downplay of adjectives and adverbs. Metaphor helped insure brevity; simile, directness. Skipper John Garfield describes a lawyer in *The Breaking Point* (WB, 1950): "He's two pounds in a one pound bag." "I met a lot of hardboiled eggs in my life but you're 20 minutes," hot-to-trot wife Jan Sterling throws in the face of reporter Kirk Douglas who spurns her in *Ace in the Hole*.

Contemporary setting was usual; period rare. Night was as constant as daytime. Space, whether studio-shot or locations, tended to be boundaried, labyrinthine, and situated in America. Public spaces and the interior of vehicles cropped up more than private places (with a dearth of around-the-table eating scenes). Transition points (staircases, sidewalks, highways, docks, depots, filling stations) and edges or ledges of some kind (corner, ocean, border town, coast cities, window ledge, fire escape, cliff) persisted with city/suburbs eclipsing the country. If the country appeared, it set itself up as a contrast, a utopia impossible to live in (*Out of the Past*) or an unachievable dream (*The Asphalt Jungle*, MGM, 1950). Thus, man's condition was seen as impersonally cold and harsh, relentlessly rootless, and plagued with anxiety.

Makeup stressed female's eyes and lips which were accompanied by a good deal of business (applying lipstick, smoking), drawing attention to the mouth and lips. Fingernails were painted. Extremely stylized female hairdos (the ponytail, the peek-a-boo pageboy, the upsweep, the shoulder-length flow) were character signposts. Female clothes emphasized legs (short skirts or gowns with slits, high-heeled shoes with straps, shorts, and accompanying business such as putting on shoes, straightening the seams of nylons) and come the fifties, breasts. Men's clothes often had a rumpled look about them, with ties at half-mast that went hand in hand with unshaven faces and tousled hair.

The set, set dressing, and props overburdened the frame, especially in their foreground placement. Low-key lighting eclipsed high-key in terms of frequency. The traditional placement of the key, fill, and back lights were experimented with in every possible way to undermine the normal. In color films, the spectrum of colors analogized noir's prevalent b/w (forest green/jealousy, hot red/passion, and shadows of every shape blackening the frames of *Niagara*, TCF, 1953).

Constant visual tropes included decentering (Perkins on the porch watching the detective leave in *Psycho*, P, 1960); oblique framing (Bergman's morning-after glimpse of Grant in *Notorious*, RKO, 1946); and splintered framing (the prison grille between Ann Sheridan and Kent Smith in *Nora Prentiss*, WB, 1947). Such tropes destabilized and fragmented the frame. Mirror shots were constant (throughout *The Reckless Moment*, C, 1949), suggesting the split in the character who looked into one. In staging, the dynamic and tension-filled vertical, diagonal, and jagged lines were preferred, as was disruptive multi-planed composition (Granger's pursuit of Walker on the carousel in *Strangers on a Train*, WB, 1951). Weirdly extreme perspectives (Crawford's large orbs in *Sudden Fear*) and canted angles (the opening high angle of Dan Duryea on the street in *World for Ransom*, AA, 1954) were also routine.

Jump cutting created unease and sometimes a momentary inaccessibility as it shattered time, making it run down faster (throughout *Dillinger*, M, 1945). Dissonant sound effects (screeching tires, car crashes, taxi horns, gunshots, sirens, telephones ringing, prison doors opening and slamming shut, train whistles, slapping, punching, waves crashing on the shore) were dinned into the spectator's ears. The music was eclectic: Harlem jazz or blues (*Phantom Lady*, U, 1944); Latin tangos, sambas, rumbas (*Criss Cross*); or lush scores that, without a clue, halted, and then, just as unexpectedly, started up again (*Citizen Kane*), full of cacophony and musical phrasing that did not follow through (*The Killers*). Sometimes, a single instrument (*Murder by Contract*'s guitar) or one orchestral section (the percussive riffs of *Pickup on South Street*, TCF, 1953) were highlighted.

Such formal strategies represented an America different from the one of classic Hollywood realism. No longer an expansive frontier, the land came across as a cul-de-sac. The dream had curdled into a nightmare. A sense of stasis was pervasive with the past hanging over the present, obliterating it. Nothing was ever forgotten, forgiven, or over; the past was always lurking, ready to destroy the present. If there was a hint of a future (*Gilda*), the past was still baggage people would carry. Though accident or chance was seen as part and parcel of living, the accident was usually wished for, entertained, or anticipated consciously or unconsciously. As such, the awful outcome was in the stars as much as it was in the self. Once it befell, it triggered a series of events from which it was difficult to extricate oneself. This contrary determinism, which was and, at the same time, was not of one's making, also created a sense of stasis. Traditional supports and extrinsic codes to live by were generally absent.

Meaning must come from within, which was, as the noir character discovered, difficult to generate and sustain (here, Existentialism's imprint). The under-world, as already known and accepted, was corrupt; but the known world, whether its public (politics, law, business, pastimes) or private sides (families, lovers, friends, neighbors), surprisingly, came off as not much different. Lusting for power and control, fame, money, and flesh (sex was seen as destructive) gave rise to this corruption which involved deception and betrayal. Nothing was clear anymore; nothing was nice.

This essential aloneness of the noir figure, be he/she corruptor, or corrupted, or one who tries to ferret out the corruption or beat it, brought with it identity confrontation, for one knows oneself basically in and through the company of others, as exemplified in classic Hollywood realism. This led to a sense of despair and disintegration within the character. Less about action than introspection, less about commitment to family, community, or career than solitude, less about life than death-in-life, the style bared the existential pain of the American soul. Classical Hollywood realism showed what was wonderful or what needed fixing in America. What needed fixing, moreover, was indeed fixed by the film's end. Noir locked into what was wrong with America, a wrong that usually eluded a quick fix, or any fix at all.

Besides revealing an unflattering portrait of the land, noir's intense, self-reflexive stylization also was able, by necessity, to code it, at least the more controversial aspects. What noir represented was revolutionary and terribly non grata on the American screen up to that time, given the industry's ideology to foment the democratic ideal of country, family, and morality and to entertain in the sense of escape and given, too, the Production Code, a structure in place to see that the democratic ideal was preserved on film. (Though this structure weakened after 1946, the Code's general impetus, remember, was not at stake, such as the preservation of the democratic ideal of country, family, and moral-ity. It was the specific embodiments that were disputed.) Noir also had to go up against World War II, a time when a united front was sought to fight the fascist foe, and the postwar chill in which the America way of life had to be sold abroad and at home (especially through movies) because of the totalitarian threat. Finally, noir had to consider HUAC, sedulously on the lookout for any subversive rendering of the homeland.

Notes

1   The nature of noir is up for grabs. It has been defended as a genre, period, or movement in film, even a narrative voice.
2   BST, p. 76.

3   Ibid.
4   Ibid.
5   Ibid.
6   BST, p. 77.
7   French historian-critic Georges Sadoul, coiner of the term, limited the style from 1934 to 1940.
8   *Screen Education*, 32/33, Autumn/Winter, 1979–80, reprinted in Alain Silver and James Ursini, ed., *Film Noir Reader* (New York: Limelight Editions, 1996), pp. 107–27.

23

Documentary Realism and Psychological-Sociological Realism

Introduction

The "realism" of the classic style with its romantic idealist mindset deepened in terms of both "documentary realism," whose impetus largely came from documentary film, and "psychological-sociological realism," sourced from the New York stage, TV, and literary worlds, while altering its sensibility. Some films were still styled along classic lines while others simultaneously embodied both the old and new approaches. Still others wholeheartedly took up the new realisms. These films that boldly ballyhooed the new were, as one would expect, the most striking and influential representations of their times and again stirred the placid waters of classicism.

23.1   Determinations of a Deeper Realism

Many influences brought about these grittier degrees of realism with their accompanying darker sensibilities. World War II and the postwar shifting had a sober effect on craftsmen, critics, and consumers of movies. Other popular leisure pursuits witnessed a similar aesthetic move: TV (1948–56), melodramatic and musical theater, fiction. Predictably, since movies competitively appropriated from them source material, molds, and approaches, Hollywood marched in step. The mode of independent production, with its promise of saying and doing something personal or different, likewise helped. The popularity of travel also had its say. People, more and more, had been to the places in which a film was set and they would brook no studio-built facsimile – no, they craved the reality of location work. Censorship was ready to adjust to the new realisms' topical, controversial, and thus-far forbidden thematics. And technology was available to formally produce it: high-speed lenses, portable cameras (the lightweight Cunningham Combat Camera, the Arriflex), portable sound equipments and high-speed film to go on location.

With the postwar interfacing of American and European cinemas and the commercial imperative to sell Hollywood abroad (and thus give American movies "foreign appeal"), European film movements, grounded in some degree of realism, were also contributory. Italy's postwar renaissance was called "neo-realism." The documents of directors Roberto Rossellini/*Open City* (1945), Vittorio De Sica/*Umberto D* (1954), Alberto Lattuada/*Without Pity* (1948), and Luigi Zampa/*To Live in Peace* (1947), along with writer Cesar Zavatini, manifested a concern for the people of Italy, particularly the working class and unemployed, abandoned children, outcasts, bandits, and prostitutes, as they tried to rise again from the ashes of war. The reality of the streets peopled with actors and nonprofessionals, wherein an occurrence's actual duration and location were respected with lighting playing a minor expressive role, dictated the camerawork. Immediate and fervid as journalistic prose, neo-realist works exposed problems, while urging something be done about them.

Commercial filmmaking in England (David Lean, Carol Reed, Peter Glenville) embraced the social realist strain mapped out by thirties documentarist John Grierson's theory and practice. World War II intensified this strain when the commercial and documentary film units united in an effort to fight the war. Around 1955, England's social realism was compounded by a movement called "free cinema." A cry of dissatisfaction at the way things were, "free cinema" shored up British cinema's social realist moorings. These endemically British pieces focused on the common man and shivered with a topicality reflecting the entire country, not just metropolitan and southern English culture. The films brazenly scoffed at the status quo. Financed by the British Film Institute and supported by the equally anti-establishment Angry Young Men School of novelists and playwrights, the practitioners made ripples with short films (Lindsay Anderson's *Thursday's Children*, 1954; Tony Richardson's *Mama Don't Allow*, 1955; Karel Reisz's *We Are the Lambeth Boys*, 1958), then launched into features (Jack Clayton's *Room at the Top*, 1958; Richardson's *Look Back in Anger*, 1958; Reisz's *Saturday Night and Sunday Morning*, 1960; and Anderson's *This Sporting Life*, 1963).

In France, the residue of "poetic realism" hung over the literary and theatrical adaptations with their psychologically precise characterization, to which the postwar French cinema was devoted. Neo-realism also heavily influenced these works by Marcel Carne/*Thérèse Raquin* (1953), Jean-Pierre Melville/*Les Enfants terribles* (1949), and René Clair/*Gervaise* (1956).

In addition to the commercial tug, Hollywood actors, producers, and directors, marveling at what was being done in realist European cinema, took their cue. With independent production in the air, they were allowed to do just that: project more substantial, less fanciful images in an effort to say something meaningful. The exodus of talent and craft from European industries, bringing with them their respective cinema's ways of doing things, helped the natives realize the goal.

The collegian, college-educated young adult, and open-minded adult tuned into this fare. In fact, Hollywood's new degrees of realism helped to segment this audience type and its preference for the "adult" film, thus splintering the notion of the mass audience of the classic period.

23.2   Documentary Realism: Determinations and Practitioners

Documentary or nonfiction film was the chief force ushering in the documentary realist style. Actually, documentary and the documentary realist style had cropped up in thirties America among independents, mobilized to record the harsh realities of the Depression and the burgeoning optimism of the New Deal, such as Pare Lorentz, Paul Strand, and Leo Hurwitz's *The Plow that Broke the Plains*, 1936. Hollywood, however, coldshouldered this type and style. After all, the industry felt that they were indeed doing a similar thing with their 9-minute newsreels, a compilation of current global events that preceded the showing of its fictions. Since the war, however, things had changed.

Directors and various other craftsmen, including TCF's production chief Zanuck, had gone to war and/or had worked in the film division of the Office of War Information, Overseas Branch. By 1942, 25,000 civilians from the industry had signed up for duty on the front lines or offices. Most were exposed (to the point of studying) English, Russian, and German documentaries: their distinct realism, techniques, and use as communication, education, and propaganda. In 1941, "Documentary" was a category instituted by the Academy for its annual honors. Two years later, the category was split into "Documentary Short Subject" and "Documentary Feature."

Distinguished directors began making documentaries. Notable was Capra's instructive *Why We Fight* series. Seven in all produced in 1942–5, Capra's brand comprised snippets from features and combat footage, laying out the background of why America was at war and the issues involved. Ford, Huston, and Wyler filmed reports of various campaigns and their aftermaths. Ford's *The*

Battle of Midway (US Navy-TCF, 1942), Hollywood's first war documentary, received an Oscar, as did Ford's *December 7th* (US Navy, 1943). Distributed by the War Activities Committee of the Motion Pictures Industry, Huston's *Report from the Aleutians* (1943), *The Battle of San Pietro* (1945), and *Let There Be Light* (1946), set in the mental-therapy rehabilitation centers for psychoneurotic vets, impressed. Wyler's color-photographed *Memphis Belle: A Story of a Flying Fortress* (Army Air Force-P, 1944) was the most widely seen documentary in America thus far. George Stevens, made Lieutenant-Colonel in charge of combat photography for the Supreme Headquarters Allied Expeditionary Forces, documented the D-Day landing in Normandy and the liberations of Paris and the Dachau concentration camp. Lesser-known craftsmen were put in charge of combat photography, the *Army-Navy Screen Magazine* newsreel for troops, and countless instructive documentaries, such as *The Negro Soldier* (1944), whose point was to allay agitation over segregation in the armed forces. Postwar, these filmmakers' sensibilities changed to the point of wanting to do something different with movies. Furthermore, documentary showed them how.

Documentary realism entered the fiction film through the war genre. *Wake Island* (P, 1942), with John Farrow in command of W. R. Burnett and Frank Butler's script, was the eye-opener. The film documented an actual campaign on the South Pacific island two weeks after Pearl Harbor in which a US Marine garrison held a base against the better equipped and larger Japanese forces. Plotless, the film consisted of a series of episodes and used non-stars (Robert Preston, Brian Donlevy, MacDonald Carey) as part of its ensemble. The lack of a heterosexual romance; a finale that recorded a US failure; the matter-of-fact (not fiery nationalistic) tone; and the presence of an off-screen narrator also placed the film squarely in the documentary realist tradition. Further, actual war footage was matched with the authentically re-created scenes, shot by Theodor Sparkuhl and William Mellor on location in California's Salton Sea. A commercial and aesthetic hit, *Wake Island* sparked a slew of war films in the documentary realist style until 1945. The style also activated the war genre's revival in 1948/9.

After Zanuck's return, Fox's social realism, evident since *The Grapes of Wrath* (1940), went into high gear. It was inevitable since Zanuck who, as Jack Warner's VP/Production from 1927 to 1933, had contributed to WB's distinctive social realist slant, seeing to it that tabloid topicality and gutsiness in the reporting of everyday people in everyday situations became the studio hallmark.

Besides the social problem films that poured out of the studio in the social realist manner (*The Ox-Bow Incident*, 1943, blended with the western) and the slew of documentary realist war films (*Guadalcanal Diary*, 1943), Zanuck slated documentarist Louis de Rochemont's "semi-documentary thrillers" for production. De Rochemont had worked for W. B. Pathé and Fox Movietone News.

With Time circulation manager Roy E. Larsen, he had produced *The March of Time* series of 1934–43 and had turned out some independent war documentaries in the documentary realist style (*We Are the Marines*, TCF, 1942). With *House on 92nd Street* (1945), de Rochemont came up with a blueprint, in place at the studio until 'Scope/Deluxe Color's introduction in 1953. The expressionistic thriller, which was the genre's flavor since 1940, was now riddled with a documentary realism, depicting a shadow land not only as exotic but immediately authentic.

House faxed a case from the FBI files about fully operational fifth-columnist activities in the nation's Capitol. Writers Charles G. Booth, Barre Lyndon, and John Monks, Jr. strung together the episodes, characterized by extensive documenting of the scientific crime-detection process by means of an off-screen narrator who also asserted the veracity of the proceedings. (The device was an analogue of expressionistic noir's flashback.) Norbert Brodine's location-shot, fast-stock, grainy images alternated with stock FBI footage. B players William Eythe and Lloyd Nolan and actual G-men in bit parts comprised the cast. The use of a typewriter font spelling out the opening credits, which also noted the full cooperation of the FBI, piled on the realism. House director Henry Hathaway (1898–1985), who began as a child actor and worked his way up to director in 1932 at Paramount before switching to Fox in 1941, where he was promoted to Zanuck's action-movie mainstay, brought the film home within a driving 88 minutes.

The blend of documentary realism and expressionism in the thriller not only galvanized Hathaway's subsequent works, such as *Call Northside 777* (1948), with its initial intertitle: "This is a true story . . . photographed in the State of Illinois using, wherever possible, the actual locales associated with the story," but also other Fox action directors such as Andrew Stone/*The Steel Trap* (1952) and Samuel Fuller/*Pickup on South Street*, who also worked the topography of war in similar fashion.

Every studio imitated the Zanuck–de Rochemont style of thriller, most significantly, ex-journalist turned Universal producer Mark Hellinger with *Brute Force* (1947) and the all-location-shot *The Naked City* (1948). Tops in Schary's MGM collection were *Jeopardy* (1952) and *Border Incident* (1950). *Union Station* (1950) and *The Turning Point* (1952) were Paramount entries. At RKO, *Armored Car Robbery* (1950) not only documented how a stickup in front of Wrigley Field transpired but also how the detectives tracked down the culprits, while *Roadblock*'s (1951) final sequence analyzed how the police staged a roadblock in Los Angeles to trap the cheating insurance detective in the city's river bed. Columbia's B thrillers from *The Mob* (1951) to *City of Fear* (1959); Republic's *The City that Never Sleeps* (1953); and Eagle-Lion's *Canon City* (1948) followed in kind. At WB, *White Heat* (1949) spent much time documenting a police

23-1 *The Naked City* (U, 1948, p. Mark Hellinger)
A semi-documentary thriller with Don Taylor, shot entirely on location in New York City.

procedure in apprehending a crook. Siegel, who had directed two shorts for de Rochemont in 1945 (*The Star in the Night; Hitler Lives*), got so caught up with the documentary realist location work of *The Big Steal* (RKO, 1949) that the B thriller turned into a scenic trip across Mexico. He redressed the fault in *The Line-Up* (C, 1958). Its nastiness is not only set against but played within the settings of San Francisco's docks, Opera House, and Hall of Justice (where police procedures are detailed in depth), Seaman's Club, Mark Hopkins Hotel, Aquarium, Sutra's Museum, and a freeway under construction, transmogrifying the romantic city into a forbidding metropolis.

Other documentarists came on the scene, emboldening Hollywood's documentary realist frame of mind as they worked in genres other than war and the thriller, making the style transgeneric. Matthew Brady's actual Civil War photographs inspired Zinnemann's western *High Noon* (UA, 1952), with its starkly arid look featuring washed-out skies and flat lighting coming from in front or above, rather than behind the subject, and with its avoidance of filters and soft focus for the close-ups. Moreover, the film's actual running time of 85 minutes corresponded to the story's time frame. John Sturges's frontiers in *Escape from Fort Bravo* (MGM, 1953), *Gunfight at the OK Corral* (P, 1957), *The Law and*

Jake Wade (MGM, 1958), and *The Magnificent Seven* (UA, 1960) emerged rugged, harsh, uninviting. Jack Arnold's locations grounded the horror–sci-fi happenings of *It Came from Outer Space* (U, 1953). Fast-stock location photography and an ambient soundtrack gave Irvin Kerschner's biography *The Hoodlum Saint* (UA, 1961), Irving Lerner's (1909–76) male melodrama *Studs Lonigan* (UA, 1960), and Denis Sanders's male melodrama-thriller *Crime and Punishment USA* (AA, 1958) credibility. All these works disclosed their respective directors' roots in documentary.

Some directors followed this trend, coming as they did from journalism, the sphere of prose reporting, or documenting: Hellinger, Fuller, and Brooks/the male melodrama *Deadline – U.S.A.* (TCF, 1952) and his social satire-family melodrama *The Catered Affair* (MGM, 1956). Brooks, along with Sturges, Mann, and ex-Fox contractee Andrew Stone, found a niche at MGM due, in large part, to Schary's self-proclaimed socially conscious, documentary realist bent. In fact, that's exactly the gambit Schary offered the investors, halting MGM's financially losing streak. After Mayer's resignation in 1952, Schary had the field to himself. As a result, the next four years saw more than half of the MGM product, wonder of wonders, socially conscious in a documentary realist mode.

The documentary realist style also guided the new generation of socially conscious directors. In step were Robert Rossen's male melodramas, such as *All the King's Men* (C, 1949) and *The Hustler* (TCF, 1961) with its Midwest pool hall, buck-and-a-half fleabag, and wee-hours-of-the morning bus terminal whose emptiness edged all sounds with a slight echo. George Seaton responded to the clarion call with his internationally-set pieces. For the true story of *The Counterfeit Traitor* (P, 1962), Seaton's international cast featured only one American actor (Holden); a location shoot in West Germany, Denmark, and Sweden; fast color stock that imbued the images with a newsreel immediacy; and Holden's voice-over throughout that both bridged and explained the innumerable procedural episodes. Except for composer Alfred Newman's omnipresent accents, the expressionism of this spy thriller was kept in check. The style also mobilized producer-director Stanley Kramer for the courtroom drama *Judgment at Nuremberg* (UA, 1961) and the social problem film *A Child Is Waiting* (UA, 1963); and Kramer's protégé Mark Robson for the family melodrama-social problem *I Want You* (RKO, 1951).

After a decidedly expressionistic noir period, ex-RKO/Fox contractee Robert Wise (1914–2005) tried on the documentary realist mode (though never totally abandoning his formalist roots), as in the female melodrama *Until They Sail* (MGM, 1957), with its camera detailing the wartime activities in the location-shot New Zealand town, seven radio broadcasts and a loudspeaker every so often blaring out war news, and the large wall map on which four female protagonists chart the war's progress. Wise, in fact, had spent a year in college as journalism major before the Depression forced him to leave school for work, which he found at RKO where his brother toiled in the accounting department.

Walking the same road as Wise were Preminger/the bio *The Court Martial of Billy Mitchell* (WB, 1955), the historical spectacle *Exodus* (UA, 1960), and the metaphorical family melodrama *Advise and Consent* (C, 1962); Mankiewicz/the European-shot social satire *The Barefoot Contessa* (UA, 1954); and Dmytryk/the war film *The Caine Mutiny* (C, 1954), the male melodrama *The Left Hand Of God* (TCF, 1955), and the adventure *The Mountain* (P, 1955). Nicholas Ray eventually joined up with the tempered documentary realist crowd with the family melodramas *The Lusty Men* (RKO, 1952), *Rebel Without a Cause* (WB, 1955), and *The Savage Innocents* (P, 1960), and the adventure *Wind across the Everglades* (WB, 1958), flecked with documentary footage of the flora and fauna of the location-shot Everglades, and the historical spectacle *King of Kings* (MGM, 1960). Anthony Mann, too, was a convert. The documentary realist sequences of the country's latest fifties jets that carried atomic bombs eclipsed the domestic side of the bio *Strategic Air Command* (P, 1955). The new aesthetic, in fact, enlarged Mann's canvas, as witnessed in the western *Cimarron* (MGM, 1960), with its periodic descriptions of the progress of a one-street town into a metropolis.

Hollywood's engagement with documentary realism also galvanized the style of some social realist vets: ex-journalist King Vidor/social problem film *Japanese War Bride* (TCF, 1952); Walsh/war-romance melodrama *Battle Cry* (WB, 1955); Mervyn Le Roy/the male melodrama *Toward the Unknown* (WB, 1956); and William Wellman/the war film *Battleground* (MGM, 1949), westerns *Yellow Sky* (TCF, 1949) and *Westward, the Women* (MGM, 1950), and adventure *Island in the Sky* (WB, 1953), with its off-screen narration. The style solidified Wyler's postwar work.

Past masters such as Curtiz, King, Stevens, Huston, and Hitchcock, whose styles were a blend of both expressionist and realist modes, began privileging the realism after the war. Note: under the same WB roof and in the same generic molds, Curtiz's male melodrama *Kid Galahad* (1937) and western *Dodge City* (1939) were much more formalist than his postwar counterparts *Trouble along the Way* (1953) and *The Boy from Oklahoma* (1954). King's classical Fox war and adventure products *A Yank in the R.A.F.* (1941) and *The Black Swan* (1942), and his subsequent *Twelve O'Clock High* (1949) and *King of the Khyber Rifles* (1953) recorded the same difference. Along these lines, compare Stevens's female melodrama *Alice Adams* (RKO, 1935) with his family melodrama *The Diary of Anne Frank* (TCF, 1959), or Huston's first couple of WB efforts (*The Maltese Falcon*, 1941; *In This Our Life*, 1943) with his first postwar WB film *The Treasure of the Sierra Madre* (1948) or better yet, his postwar independents (from *The African Queen*, UA, 1952, onward). But then, Stevens and Huston, who also dabbled in journalism, took up documentary filming during World War II. Hitchcock's *To Catch a Thief* (P, 1955) is larded with more than the master's usual amount of descriptive scenes, including several sections of aerial views from a moving plane. In *The Wrong Man*'s (WB, 1957) pre-credit sequence, Hitch himself, whose style always resonated with British Grierson's documentary aesthetic, no matter the film, alerted us to something new: "this time, I would like you to see a different [picture]. Its difference lies in the fact that this is a true story, every word of it . . ." Techniques that Ford used in his wartime documentaries became part of his postwar fictional output. Consider the snippets from an actual military training film and World War II battle footage inserted into Ford's bio *The Wings of Eagles* (MGM, 1957), which contains location shooting as well as the devices of voice-over narrator, movie newsreels, radio broadcasts, newspaper headlines, and a clip from the biographee's own scripted film (*Hell Divers*, MGM, 1931) to bridge the elision in the rangy, episodic structure of incidents.

As with the old guard, postwar newcomers Robert Aldrich, Sam Peckinpah, Stanley Kubrick – who began his professional life as a photographer for *Look* magazine and a maker of documentary shorts – and, after his first couple films, John Frankenheimer, who also worked in documentary shorts, blended documentary realism with expressionism throughout their work.

Old-time and novice formalists George Cukor and Blake Edwards occasionally tried on documentary realism. Cukor's romantic comedy-melodrama *The Marrying Kind* (C, 1952) and his social satire *It Should Happen to You* (C, 1954), both with their proletarian protagonists, overlapped dialogue, and extensive Manhattan shoots, are representative. *The Marrying Kind*, likewise, is chock-full of rarely-if-ever-seen-on-the-screen details, such as husband and wife brushing their teeth before retiring. Even the classically stylized way of transition from reality to dream (the out-of-focus image or the superimposition of shimmering water) is eschewed. A simple cut suffices. *It Should Happen To You* went on to foreground the style by having a documentary filmmaker as one of its protagonists and the documentary he made become a plot point. Cukor's Pakistan-lensed female melodrama *Bhowani Junction* (MGM, 1956), tellingly, chanted the mantra. Cukor interspersed documentary footage of Hollywood hoopla throughout the musical *A Star Is Born* (WB, 1954). Edwards's social problem film *Days of Wine and Roses* (WB, 1962) proved he was eclectic. The musical/melodrama/comedy's supreme stylists Minnelli, Donen, Sirk, and Walters, except for location shooting and the use of a process as a structuring device (the insertion of a how-to sequence), remained impervious – well, almost.

In an exceptional way that went beyond its locations in Holland and France, Minnelli's *Lust for Life* (MGM, 1956) evinced a documentary influence in its unique narrative and tone. The Van Gogh biography is a composite of three alternating series. Instructional passages predominate, whether it be Van Gogh's explanation of breaking the wall between what is felt and how one expresses it; a discussion on Impressionism; Gauguin's disquisition on art; and even the psychiatrist's diagnosis of Van Gogh's condition. Additionally, repeated counterpointings of the reality that Van Gogh observes and its re-creation on canvas appear. Finally, montages of Van Gogh's paintings are interspersed throughout. The episodes are held together by brother Theo's voice-over reading of Vincent's letters explaining himself and his actions, which is yet another form of instruction. In a dramatically engrossing way, the film purports, as documentary does, to teach and enlighten.

23.3   Psychological-Sociological Realism: Determinations and Practitioners

The renaissance in postwar theater, its reciprocal relationship with TV's dramatic anthology series, along with bestselling fiction, were the progenitors of the style of psychological-sociological realism. The style ribboned the O'Neill-influenced playwright (Williams, Chayefsky, et al.); the Method actor (Brando, Woodward, et al.), a God-sent incarnator of these playwright's characters; the simpatico director (Kazan, Ritt, et al.), a perfect conduit for the text's materializations; and the Marxist/Freudian-tinged bestselling novelist (Sloan Wilson, James Jones, et al.). With adaptation fever in the air, the East coast talent was cajoled to go west while the LA crafters were told to do like the New Yorkers. The postwar exodus to Hollywood, to a great extent, involved the New York stage/TV director/actor/writer.

Kazan was the style's captain in both its initial b/w flat screen pronouncement *A Streetcar Named Desire* (WB, 1951) and its easy color/ 'Scope accommodation *East of Eden* (WB, 1955). But Kazan's style was eclectic, embracing noir's expressionism-documentary realism mix in his Fox thrillers *Boomerang* (1947), *Panic in the Streets* (1950), and *Man on a Tightrope* (1953). And Kazan would never relinquish expressionism. For example, along with long-take compositions-in-depth, *Eden* is fraught with shadowed frames; skewed perspectives of the father–son confrontations; and the manic shot–reverse shot between two people in which both are fully in the frame at the same time.

Joshua Logan was Kazan's lieutenant. But he preferred the color/'Scope format (*Picnic*, C, 1955), unlike practically all of his colleagues, who went with b/w flat. The honor guard numbered Sidney Lumet (*The Fugitive Kind*, UA, 1960; *A View from the Bridge*, Transcontinental, 1961; *Long Day's Journey into Night*, Embassy, 1962); Daniel Mann (*Come Back, Little Sheba*, P, 1952; *About Mrs. Leslie*, P, 1954; *The Rose Tattoo*, P, 1955; *Hot Spell*, P, 1958; *Five Finger Exercise*, C, 1962); Delbert Mann (*Marty*, UA, 1955; *Desire under the Elms*, P, 1958; *Separate Tables*, UA, 1958; *Middle of the Night*, C, 1959; the Technicolored *The Dark at the Top of the Stairs*, WB, 1960); and Martin Ritt, who alternated between both formats (*No Down Payment*, TCF, 1957; *The Long Hot Summer*, TCF, 1958; *Black Orchid*, P, 1958; *The Sound and the Fury*, TCF, 1959; *Hud*, P, 1963).

Epicentered in family melodrama (and a reason for the genre's status), psychological-sociological realism also appeared in the female melodrama (Lumet's *Stage Struck*, RKO, 1958); the male melodrama (Daniel Mann's *The Last Angry Man*, C, 1959; Joseph Anthony's *Career*, P, 1959); romance melodrama (Logan's *Bus Stop*, TCF, 1956; *Sayonara*, WB, 1957; Lumet's *That Kind of Woman*, P, 1959); biography (Daniel Mann's *I'll Cry Tomorrow*, 1955); the social problem film (Method actor turned director Karl Malden's *Time Limit*, UA, 1957; Lumet's *Twelve Angry Men*, UA, 1957); and social satire–male melodrama (Delbert Mann's *Bachelor Party*, UA, 1957). Even farce (Anthony's *The Matchmaker*, P, 1958) and the western (Arthur Penn's *The Left-Handed Gun*, WB, 1956) were not exempt. Penn, as with Kazan, mixed expressionism in everything he touched.

23.4   Mode of Representation and Attitude of Mind

Though documentary realism was less stylized than psychological-sociological realism and each came with different emphases, there were correspondences in terms of their mode of representation and attitude of mind. Some films (*On the Waterfront*, C, 1954) embodied both styles. The styles' impact in changing the industry and audience's traditional notion of movies was another common trait.

A telling characteristic of literary design in both styles was the preference for episodic structure in lieu of the tightly interlocked space/time, cause/effect linked scenes that constituted the linear structure of the classic Hollywood style.[1] Why? Consider the sources. Documentary filmmakers eschewed linear narrative, which was, they continually stated, a stylization that undermined the integrity and immediacy of the reality shown. As far as the stage went, the playwrights wrote character studies, not plot pieces. Character concentration, which usually evolved from a confrontation between people or the family environment, lent itself to blocks or episodes of space and time, separated by acts and scenes within those acts. TV's segmented programming of the teleplays with a commercial break every 10 or 15 minutes pitched in. And too, the increased breadth and scope of the postwar fiction, with their multiple plots and/or subplots and array of characters, was pretty hard, if not impossible, for novelists to pull off within a linear plot. Foreign models of filmmaking (*The Bicycle Thief* or *Roshomon*) reinforced the phenomenon. *A Tree Grows in Brooklyn* (TCF, 1945), *King Solomon's Mines* (MGM, 1950), *Carmen Jones* (TCF, 1954), *Rebel Without a Cause* (WB, 1955), *Not as a Stranger* (UA, 1955), *Damn Citizen!* (U, 1958), *God's Little Acre* (UA, 1958), *Cimarron* (MGM, 1960), and the documentary realist-expressionist mix *War and Peace* (P, 1957) and *I Want to Live!* (UA, 1958), all time-, studio-, and genre-resistant, were only a mere handful of movies episodically constructed. This type of structure, of course, presaged what was to come with the intense narrative fragmentation of films from Hollywood's modernist period, anticipated already in the pervasively anatomizing structure of *All the King's Men* (C, 1949) and that of *Odds Against Tomorrow* (UA, 1959), which also employed jump cutting as the preferred mode of transition between episodes.

Much more than in the 1929–45 period, episodes bypassed a heterosexual romantic line of action, an almost invariable convention of classical plotting.[2] *He Walked by Night* (EL, 1949), *Battleground* (MGM, 1949), *Caged* (WB, 1950), *The Adventures of Robinson Crusoe* (UA, 1954), *Attack!* (UA, 1956), *Lust for Life* (MGM, 1956), *The Bridge on the River Kwai* (C, 1957), *Twelve Angry Men* (UA, 1957), *Anatomy of a Murder* (C, 1959), *Lawrence of Arabia* (C, 1962), and *Hud* (P, 1963), a mere sampling, go without. Also, the pure "action" scenes were progressively more deemphasized or left out, as with the kidnapping of the albino for divining purposes in *God's Little Acre*. *The Left Hand of God* is pretty much unconcerned with the escape of a Yank airman from a remote Chinese village in 1947, burrowing into as it does his soul-searching anguish and guilt. Fleischer's expressionist-edged *Compulsion* (TCF, 1959) dispenses with the robbery and murder, concentrating rather on the psychological effects of these crimes on the two collegian culprits, especially their sadomasochistic relationship. (Announcing itself as a horror of personality, the film shifts in its last third to a social problem film pleading against capital punishment.) Endings were often ambiguous (*The Nun's Story*, WB, 1959). Closure was disregarded (*Anatomy of a Murder*).

Whether or not the film involved Method actors, directors attempted to make the actor come across as simply behaving rather than acting. To do this, overlapped dialogue became more and more frequent (*The Bachelor Party*); improvisation, rarely discouraged (*The Search*, MGM, 1948). Of course, behaving rather than acting was the goal of the Method actor.

Along with the casting of the Method-trained or Method-inspired actor (Elizabeth Taylor, Burt Lancaster), the new realisms, by and large, held out for Europeans, Asians, and Hispanics to play their respective fictive counterparts, even speaking at times in their native language, as with Sophia Loren as the mail-order bride from Italy in *Desire under the Elms*, Sessue Hayakawa as the Japanese commandant in *The Bridge on the River Kwai*, or the Mexican handyman Ricardo Montalban in *The Man I Love* (MGM, 1952). Sometimes, an enlightened white man talked the language of the setting's people (guide Stewart Granger invokes various dialects of native Africans in *King Solomon's Mines*).

The exodus of foreign players into Hollywood and their landing leading roles were a significant switch from classical times. People of color increasingly played people of color in romantic leading parts (Pedro Armendáriz as the jilted suitor in *Tulsa*, EL, 1949; Harry Belafonte as the West Indian activist in *Island In the Sun*, TCF, 1957). They shared center stage as the protagonist's buddy (Sidney Poitier in *Edge of the City*, MGM, 1957) or were an equal part of a group protagonist (Belafonte in *Odds Against Tomorrow*, UA, 1959; Bernie Hamilton as one of a trio of convicts in *The Devil at Four O'Clock*, C, 1961). Black people began to appear as support/bit/supernumerary in positions classically unassociated with blacks, best pal/partner (Juano Hernandez) of the fishing-boat owner whose kid plays with the white owner's girls in the expressionist-tinged *The Breaking Point* (WB, 1950); one of the policemen at New York City's 21st Precinct in *Detective Story* (P, 1951); a judge (Hernandez) in *Trial* (MGM, 1956); an army psychiatrist in the expressionist-tweaked *The Manchurian Candidate* (UA, 1962). Black people were sometimes given points of view in the narrative, even when they played servants (the ubiquitous Ethel Waters in *Pinky*, TCF, 1949, *A Member of the Wedding*, C, 1953, and *The Sound and the Fury*). Such casting maneuvers solidified the "reality" on the American screen. *Requiem for a Heavyweight* (C, 1962) went so far as to pull an ethnic–racial switch in its big screen translation by changing the teleplay's Irish Caucasian protagonist McClintock to Mexican Mountain Rivera, essayed by Hispanic Anthony Quinn.

Another salient congruity between the styles was the working within the frame on the part of the director. Long-take composition-in-depth became the preferred mode of visual structure. Not surprisingly, since this visual trope came naturally to these new realists, who had previously worked in documentary film or the stage, where the space/time continuum was preserved. More importantly, it was a trope, as the directors knew, that compounded the sense of the reality of what was being represented since, as in life, it kept intact the contiguity of space and the continuity of time.

The visual trope also ensured a performance in rhythm (not broken up by cutting) which added to the reality of the character, while attesting to the

23-2   *Picnic* (C, 1955, p. Fred Kohlmar)

Actors Arthur O'Connell and Rosalind Russell (center middle ground) and Reta Shaw and Elizabeth W. Wilson (a bit to the left middle ground) surrounded by actual Midwest locals at one of
the Labor Day festivities in this location-shot family melodrama.

integrity of the performer and performance. If the director happened to have
one of those new Method actors in the role, the director wanted to privilege the
performance and performer and the fact that this new kind of acting was a
change from the presentational/pantomimic and representational performative
modes that constituted Hollywood's classical heyday. The director was able to
do just that by holding the camera on the actor.

Expectedly, the glamorous, intensely backlit facial close-up against a neutral
background, completely abstracted from the surrounding space, a staple of the
classic Hollywood style, was eschewed more often than not. Less fanciful and
more real, the medium facial close-up, incorporating the background and/or
sidereal setting, which may or may not include other characters, was
preferred.

When a director did resort to rapid cutting, it was for an intensely critical
movement or one of those pure "action" scenes, which was being devalued at
this time. Zinnemann used rapid cutting only three times in the 118 minutes

of *From Here to Eternity* (C, 1953): Prew's fisticuffs with a fellow soldier; Prew's early morning taps-eulogy for Maggio; and the Japanese surprise attack on Pearl Harbor. Ritt did likewise in the 112 minutes of *Hud* where rapid cutting occurred during the pig contest; the near-rape of Alma; and the shooting of the hoof-and-mouth-diseased herd. Even BST conceded that "long-take filming became more common after the war . . . and post 1952 films average fewer shots per sequence," though, alas, they chalked this up to the options within the classical paradigm.[3]

Location shooting, often with the use of the actual people from the respective environment, was the way to go. Notwithstanding the three lead actors, the cast of *King Solomon's Mines* were African locals and natives. Actual soldiers, who had to be trained in using World War II-issue rifles, played the extras in *From Here to Eternity*. Frequently, location shoots involved faster film stock, compact light sources, and source lighting to achieve a grainy, seemingly unstylized real-life aura (Lionel Lindon's tabloid-like lensing of *I Want to Live!* or that of Arthur Ornitz's *Requiem for a Heavyweight*).

Documentary footage of the place and action was often inserted into the theatrically staged scenes. *Twelve O'Clock High* flaunted its use of actual World War II aerial dogfight footage. The incessant shots of wild animals in their habitat, along with the impressive stampede caused by a brush fire as well as native rituals, made *King Solomon's Mines* an exceptional adventure. Actual rodeo footage generously sprinkled throughout *The Lusty Men* provided the viewer with a textbook of various events of the sport (bulldogging, riding a Brahman bull, roping a steer, saddle branching, etc.) accompanied by an announcer's explanation. Actual holiday celebration footage of Midwest locals, seamlessly blended with that of the actors on location, added texture to *Picnic*.

In both styles, more bedroom-set scenes appeared than ever before, as well as hitherto avoided, if ever seen, bathroom/locker set scenes, allowing for private moments and various states of undress. *Easy Living* (RKO, 1949), with its two locker scenes of football players undressing, was a timid harbinger of the daring scene in *East of Eden*, in which James Dean asks to borrow money from an investor in the gymnasium locker room while the investor showers and then dries off, or those eye-popping ones in *Splendor in the Grass* (WB, 1961), with Warren Beatty cleaning up in the locker room and Natalie Wood settling her nerves in a hot bathtub. Anthony Mann, in *God's Little Acre*, constructed a scene in which Buddy Hackett's head peeps into an outdoor tub where Fay Spain sponges her nude body.

Underclothes, shorts, bathing suits, and towel-wraps became a consistent part of a film's costume design. Men went shirtless (Brando in *Viva Zapata!* TCF, 1952; Aldo Ray in *Miss Sadie Thompson*, C, 1953; Newman in just about

23-3   *Pillow Talk* (U, 1959, p. Ross Hunter)

Even Doris Day borrows from the deeper realism's iconic use of underclothing for the opening scene of this romantic comedy.

every picture). The objectification of the male torso on the screen crystallized. Women in slips with severe décolletage were seen time and again, often straightening out the seams of their nylons (Taylor in *Cat on a Hot Tin Roof*, MGM, 1958; the intro of Natalie Wood as *Marjorie Morningstar* WB, 1958), shimmying off their panties (Lizabeth Scott in *Easy Living*), or putting on a girdle (Magnani in *The Rose Tattoo*). Female butts were also in vogue (Monroe paddle-balling in *The Misfits*, UA, 1961). In *Odds Against Tomorrow*, after Robert Ryan answers Gloria Grahame's request of how it feels to kill someone so as to get sexually aroused, he pulls on the belt of her bathrobe, revealing a black lacy bra and half-slip. The tearing of someone's clothes, revealing some part of the human body, became an iconic gesture/action. The minimal dress code often provided the logo for the movie's marketing and advertising: Brando's ripped T-shirt (*A Streetcar Named Desire*); Holden's torn shirt and Novak's revealing décolletage (*Picnic*); Taylor's slip (*Cat on a Hot Tin Roof*). Both male and female clothing often resembled items bought off the rack or at thrift stores; many were.

Male and female makeup, on the whole, tended to be more natural, less ethereally stylized than before, a procedure that even influenced the expressionist works. A star's unflawed look was abandoned. The very switch is self-reflexively foregrounded in the documentary-like process sections of the essentially expressionist musicals *A Star Is Born* (WB, 1954) and *Funny Face* (P, 1957). The everyday quality of the subject matter and the average-guy type character of these styles called for deglamorization. Also, the Method or Method-influenced actor, on the whole, was interested more in his/her craft and performance than appearance. Compare the looks of Gregory Peck playing professional men (a missionary priest in one; an army squadron leader in the other) and being made up by the same studio artisans in the classically realist *The Keys of the Kingdom* (TCF,1944) and the documentary realist *Twelve O'Clock High*. Owing to the common-man status of the jurors (and the actors' limited availability due to their simultaneous appearances on the New York stage and TV), the players in *Twelve Angry Men* wore no makeup. One-minute exposures to a sun lamp were used to darken their faces for the camera.

The new realisms impacted on music design. To fortify the probability of *The Day the Earth Stood Still* (TCF, 1951), composer Bernard Herrmann experimented with an electric score that favored an electronic violin and bass, and two high and low electric Theremins, four pianos, four harps, and a very strange section of about 30-odd brass instruments.[3] The infrequent use of spare background shadings (*Hud*'s guitar inflections) and the use of source music (*Hud*'s country and western blaring from Lon's pocket transistor) supplanted, to a large extent, the traditional symphonic scores with full-bodied arrangements. In general, wall-to-wall scoring was eschewed even with A films (*I Was a Male War Bride*, TCF, 1949; *Titanic*, TCF, 1953; *Twelve Angry Men*). Often, music backgrounded opening titles and seeped through only in the last couple of shots in *Call Northside 777*, *Detective Story* (P, 1951), and *Twelve Angry Men*, where music is also used only twice in the film. *Executive Suite* (MGM, 1954) and *The Defiant Ones* (UA, 1958) had no score whatsoever, though the latter film contains some swinging jazz from a truck radio (source music) and Poitier's folk-song that bookends the film.

More and more, regional music, indicative of the piece's setting/class/ethnic/racial complexion, underlined scenes. Native a cappella chants, the beating of drums, and the sound of animals provided the aural landscape of nineteenth-century Africa in *King Solomon's Mines*. Alex North's blues and jazz conveyed the plangent mood and the ominous, claustrophobic atmosphere of *A Streetcar Named Desire*'s New Orleans tenement. Joseph Brun's jazz backgrounds for *Odds Against Tomorrow* were as fractured, shaky, and shrill as the caper thriller's three protagonists and events. Rock and roll informed the racially mixed high school of *The Blackboard Jungle* (MGM, 1955); gospel for the Georgia fundamentalists of *God's Little Acre.* Henry Mancini merged rock and roll with Afro-Cuban music, appropriate to *Touch of Evil's* (U, 1958) clash of cultures.

The new realisms appropriated from the documentary tradition intertitle prologue ("Schofield Barracks/Hawaii/1941" of *From Here to Eternity* or "agricultural town of Salinas" of *East of Eden*) and/or voice-over narration (*Peyton Place*, TCF, 1957), attesting to the veracity of what was presented. These techniques cropped up more frequently than before.

At times, a film opened with an on-screen narrator introducing us to the unusual subject matter and assuring us that it was based in fact, as with *He Walked by Night* or Arizona's Governor Garvey's letter verifying the authenticity of the tale of the prospector's $20-million cache of ore in the Superstition Mountains in *Lust for Gold* (C, 1949). Alistair Cooke's opening commentary continued throughout *The Three Faces of Eve* (TCF, 1957), albeit off screen. At the start of the *The Ten Commandments* (P, 1956), producer-director De Mille prattles about the importance of the subject matter, invoking the Old Testament as his source. In some instances, the writer of the actual source of the film became a minor character in the film (played by an actor), as if to authenticate what was being presented: the novelist Barry Storm in *Lust for Gold*; the correspondent of the San Francisco paper who covers the Barbara Graham case in *I Want To Live!*; the character of biographer Thomas E. Gaddis in *Birdman of Alcatraz*. Offscreen narrators were even more plentiful. DeMille himself guides us through *The Greatest Show on Earth's* (P, 1952) dissection of the circus, the machinations behind the show, and the show itself.

In documentary fashion, the new realisms also filled out the narrative line with extended description of the setting, detailing its geography, as well as the mores and rituals of a particular community endemic to the setting. *Clash by Night's* (RKO, 1952) preamble delineates trawlers unloading the sardine catch on the dock from where it is carted off to the packing plant where the sardines are cleaned and canned, thus immersing us in the blue-collar life of a tiny Northern California fishing town. This convention usually took the form of a camera panning the location from a moving vehicle (the fishing village of Cape Breton in *Johnny Belinda*, WB, 1948; the Florida back roads in *Under the Gun*, U, 1951) or a wobbly, seemingly hand-held lateral tracking shot (Aldo Ray rushing from his home to the closed Peachtree Valley Mill in the heart of town in *God's Little Acre*). Preminger's variant in expressionist-drizzled *Anatomy of a Murder* came down to an objective tracking shot in front of the upper Michigan judge on his Sunday-morning jaunt from the church (already in the background) through Main Street to the courthouse and on to its library.

Location shooting and color aggravated this stratagem. Often the sections were so elaborate that they took on a life of their own, self-reflexively (and unclassically) stalling the plot. *Moulin Rouge's* (UA, 1952) plot kicks in only after a 20-minute prelude that minutely describes the bistro's décor, doings, and denizens. The descriptive passages of *Niagara's* falls and attractions ("Maid of the Mist," "Scenic Tunnel," and "Cave of the Winds") self-reflexively high-lighted Joe MacDonald's Technicolor camera that got amazingly close to the raging waters (no one had before) and scoped out the amusements (even tour-ists donning boots and slickers), all the while notably contrasting with the expressionist bedroom/belltower sequences. For *Summertime* (UA, 1955), co-writer/director David Lean ripped out so much of the play's dialogue that about one-third emerged a Venetian travelogue. The lovers' first meeting, in fact, didn't occur until about 25 minutes into the film.

Large-screen formats chipped in too, as with the illustration of the granary process in *Picnic*. The intersecting romances in *Trapeze* (UA, 1956) were con-tinually played in front of and/or alongside the maneuvers of the actual Cirque d'Hiver and the re-creations of the circus troupe at the corner café.

The debt to documentary manifested itself in dotting the narrative line with details that documented a character's situation (the last minutes of Barbara Graham awaiting execution in *I Want to Live!*). In the expressionistically-flecked *Caged* (WB, 1950), based on an actual prison life, the opening move-ment was given over to a description of the prisoner's transition to the big house: the ride in the paddy wagon with its slit of a back window; the waiting room where papers are filled out; the medical exam; the wait in the isolation ward until the blood test comes back; the interview with the superintendent; the work detail; chow time; the roll-call; the shower; and lights out.

One half of *King Solomon's Mines'* 102-minute length was fraught with docu-mentary detail. Long-take shots of wild, exotic animals and their behavior, as when elephants carry off a dead member of their species, were legion. Next in frequency were the shots of actual native tribal rituals, as a warrior sewing and putting the sewing paraphernalia in a small case that he places in the large hole of his earlobe. These shots varied with descriptions of the land's scenic beauty (a rainbow-dappled waterfall). Such documentary details determined staging as well: a snake crawls in a tree (foreground) while the search party passes through the middle ground. The film was more an ethnographic documentary than a fiction about a wife in search for a lost husband. No wonder, since *Mines* was the first color film shot on location in Africa. Prior to this, only a couple of production units actually set foot on the continent to secure b/w location shots to be used for a rear-projection studio shoot with actors in front. *Around the World in Eighty Days* (UA, 1956); *Harry Black and the Tiger* (TCF, 1958), set in India; *Hatari!* (P, 1962), concerned with hunters in Tanganyika; and the Canadian–Greenland shot *The Savage Innocents* (P, 1960), about the Eskimo way of life, were similarly constructed.

That passages were devoted to the environment and an analysis (not merely description) of a character's work in a large number of films must also be credited to documentary's status. *Johnny Belinda* demonstrated how wheat is ground. *Slattery's Hurricane* (TCF, 1949) brimmed over with sequences showing how intrepid Navy pilots, working for the US weather bureau on Florida's East Coast, collect evidence from flying that is given to meteorologists to determine the when, where, and extent of hurricanes. A good third of the 79-minute running time of *He Walked by Night* is taken up with the actual police procedural process of finding a shrewd robber/cop killer, particularly the creation of a composite drawing. (To reiterate: police procedural sequences cropped up in just about every police-detective/cop and G-Men cycle of thrillers.) The second scene of *Deadline – U.S.A.* is a demonstration of the process of getting a newspaper out, comprising the various levels and people involved, from the printing-press operators in the basement through the reporters in the desk room to the managing editor in his towering office. Aldo Ray's rounds as a blue-collar handyman at a Manhattan post office, which includes undressing and dressing in the locker room with the boys, constituted a scene in *The Marrying Kind*. The expressionist-filigreed *Human Desire* (C, 1954) spent an inordinate amount of time in the train's cab with engineer-protagonist operating the train from the small town to the city and back again. *Not As A Stranger* (UA, 1955) inserted a direct-cut montage to show the cases that a young intern deals with in a hospital; later, another direct-cut montage brought home the patients, their ailments, and the respective care of a young doctor starting his small-town practice. The film also elaborately presented two procedures, open-heart surgery and the removal of an opened safety pin from a ribcage, thus taking the audience for the first time, in a Hollywood fiction, to places it had never been before. *Toward the Unknown* (WB, 1956) spent about half of its length on a test pilot working on a Bell X-2 rocket plane, made to travel at 1,900 miles per hour. The aviation fighting between American jet pilots and Russian MIGs during the Korean War made for awesome sections in *The Hunters* (TCF, 1958). Strange as it may seem, a notable amount of time in the B horror-mystery thriller *The Tingler* (C, 1959) is given over to an explanation of the work of the autopsist-scientist's experiments with the force of fear. The explanations, in fact, come down to two lectures, complete with visual demonstrations.

Sometimes, the film's entire narrative was an intentional documentary look at a process. *Big Leaguer* (MGM, 1953), for example, began with a reporter facing the camera and telling us that the film is about how professional baseball players are made (that is, the process). Throughout the film, set in a location-shot New York Giants training camp, the disembodied reporter's voice introduced us to each stage of the process: "This is the beginning of being a big leaguer . . . now you start choosing a team . . . this is batting practice . . . the big game . . . the final cut," etc. The process was intercut with a look at one proto-typical, documentary specific player, a second-generation Polish kid from a Pennsylvania coal town; his father back home who thinks he's in college; and his new-found girl, the coach's niece. Most of *The Greatest Show on Earth* was taken up with the operation of the circus: self-reflexive passages of setting up in a new town, tearing down, getting into the costumes and onto the floats, etc., as well as the recording of the many varied acts of the show itself. The film's male and romance melodramatic concerns actually came off as interruptions. The workings of the checks-and-balances process in American government, manifested specifically in the Senate's *Advise and Consent* to the President's nomination for Secretary of State, shared the center of the film's male melodra-matics. *The Unknown Man* (MGM, 1951) was set up as a demonstration of the concept of justice. The off-screen narrator, after opening remarks about justice, introduces us to the people involved and their professions and personalities. As the plot – in which the narrator is a district attorney – unfolds, sententious statements and debates about justice and the law thicken the dialogue. In the final scene, we find that the story has been part of a baccalaureate address to law graduates. These films' entertainment mission unabashedly mixed with an educative one, along with countless other works at this time.

Many films were structured, in good part, along the episodic stages of a process. *The Search* painstakingly took us through what was involved in uniting a World War II Czech refugee with his parents. *Red River* (RKO, 1948) elucidat-ingly recounted the problems inherent in the migration of an immense herd of cattle from its breeding and grazing grounds along the Chisholm Trail to its sale in Abilene. Practicalities abound, from forming campsites at night to the bar-gaining with the money men in town. Though these situations' dramatic merit might be rather negligible, the element of information was intense. *Not as a Stranger* followed the education of a medical student to practicing doctor though lectures, surgery demonstrations, internship, practice in a small town, etc. *Birdman of Alcatraz* particularized how a murderer in solitary became a renowned ornithologist. Sizable chunks of caper thrillers, as seen, unfolded in terms of a crime's planning and execution.

No genre was immune to the episodic structuring of a process, even the expressionist musical. *It's a Great Feeling* (1949), shot on the WB lot, had con-tractees Dennis Morgan and Jack Carson as themselves showing how to (or in this case, not) get a film off the ground with an unknown (Doris Day). *Singin' in the Rain* (1952), with the actual MGM studio standing in for the story's Monumental Pictures, demonstrated how a silent fustian swashbuckler was transformed into a merry musical with sound.

Psychological-sociological realism brought with it an emphasis on character and its delineation. Over and above dialogue and action revealing character, age, looks, gender, ethnicity, religion, race, class, regionality, dream life, past, erotic side, work (another reason for the proliferation of workplace scenes), recreation, and familial relationship were shown to be constitutive of character and integral to the story. Such a pinpointing gave rise to an environment marked by a host of other characters through which, as in life, the central character/s took on their respective psychological-sociological complexion. Character complexity and the foregrounding of semi/anti/non-heroes as protagonists inevitably resulted. Troubled, anguished antagonistic people, with reasons of their own for doing what they did, took the place of the classically constituted hissable villains, often sharing center stage, sometimes co-opting it. Many films in this style were constructed as character studies, downsizing, if not forsaking, the classically honored element of linear plot (*A Streetcar Named Desire*, *The Misfits*). Even geographic region was raised to the level of character, and more often than not, an adversarial one (Salinas versus Monterey in *East of Eden*). Psychological-sociological realism resulted in the indeterminacy of character, not the classical character determinacy. That is to say, determining details of character were so plentiful that indeterminacy of character resulted. Reasons for why a character said or did this were never-ending – perhaps this, perhaps that, perhaps something else. Further, a character's priorities were shifting all the time, just as with any human being. This indeterminacy, more than anything, gave off the rush of being in the presence of the real.

Method acting, another characteristic of psychological-sociological realism, also privileged character. The Method's insistence on the ensemble, in particular, undermined the star-performance and the frequent construction of a film around a star, a hallmark of the 1929–45 period, thus instilling further realism in the piece by insisting on reaction as well as action, listening as well as speaking. Passages of actors silent and still abounded in psychologically-sociologically styled works.

With the advent of the Method actor and the conversion of the Method-influenced actor, screen acting got a whole lot subtler. In general, dialogue and action were less spot-on, forthrightly delivered; their meaning less clear and direct. Apprizing each scene's complexity, the Method actor's playing was rarely on the beat, with the resultant meaning manifold and layered. Moreover, the styles' socially important thematics; the arrival of the ordinary-looking Method actor (beautiful Clift, Adonis Newman, and babe Beatty were exceptions) who were, in the main, appearance non-obsessive; and the deglamorized star who came under the style's spell (bespectacled Grace Kelly in *The Country Girl*, P, 1954; or a plump, slovenly Monroe in *The Misfits*, who goes on self-reflexively to dismiss an array of glamor photos taken early in her career as silly) allowed, nay welcomed, an array of talent in pictures who looked like the average Joes and Janes on the block. Part of the gang on the stoop were Shirley Booth, Ernest

23-4   *Twelve Angry Men* (UA, 1957, p. Henry Fonda, Reginald Rose)

A demonstration of the "ensemble" as lead Henry Fonda (second from left) listens and reacts to support Lee J. Cobb drive home a point with his forefinger amid other jurors in the psychological–sociological realist TV-to-film courtroom drama.

Borgnine, Tom Ewell, José Ferrer, Andy Griffith, Judy Holliday, Jack Lemmon, Shirley MacLaine, Karl Malden, Mercedes McCambridge, Ralph Meeker, Jack Palance, Aldo Ray, and Frank Sinatra, whose postwar renaissance had much to do with the new realisms' prestige.

As an attitude, both documentary realism and psychological-sociological realism preferred as subject matter contemporary societal issues, actual events with some having a national/cultural significance, stories of real-life people, and more often than not, the common man or the common in famous and infamous men. If the matter happened to be controversial or forbidden, there was no shrinking from its depiction, unlike the classic Hollywood realism in the post-1934 enforcement-of-the-code decade. Nor was there any shying away from latent or overt critique of the status quo. Expectedly, much of the subject matter was based on newspaper or real-event magazine articles, autobiographically tinged plays and novels, biographies, and tabloid exposés. The factual basis of the films was invariably used as an advertising/marketing device. Even if a film

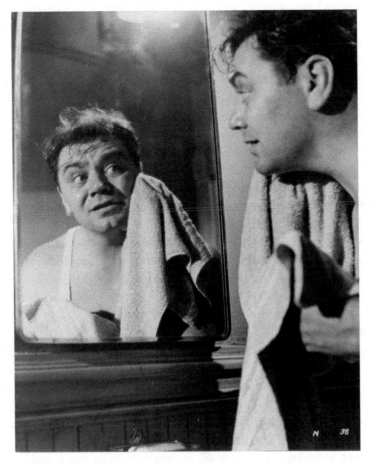

23-5　*Marty* (UA, 1955, p. Harold Hecht)

Average, man-in-the-street-looking physiognomies people postwar movies, as with the middle-aged, dumpy butcher Marty (Ernest Borgnine) in this social satire–family melodrama.

were a fiction, the selling machine insisted the film was about what was happening in every home (particularly, bedroom) in America now, notwithstanding its period setting (*Splendor in the Grass*). In addition to technology, the deeper realisms' sophisticated thematics, which reflected what was really transpiring across the land, was *another* selling ploy.

Depictions of sexual arousal and sexuality, with their attendant body exposure, were more frequent and daring because these situations were simply believed to be a part and a matter of living. *The Long Hot Summer* was primarily about sex. Repressed schoolteacher daughter (Woodward), who's been going with a gay man (Richard Anderson) for five years, hasn't had any sex and is all riled up when a lubricious drifter (Newman) hits town. One evening, the drifter, wearing nothing but a pair of white boxer undershorts, actually accosts the schoolteacher who's reading in bed – he does eventually put a pillow in front of his groin as the conversation gets heated. A brother and sister-in-law (Anthony Franciosa and Lee Remick) are continually seen in foreplay, so much so that the sister-in-law tells the brother he has to have other things on his mind because she is plum tired out. And a grand old widowed daddy (Orson Welles), when he's not upbraiding his daughter to fornicate because he wants grandchildren, pays nightly visits to a jovial old whore (Angela Lansbury). The dialogue, much of it replete with sexual innuendo, matched the action. Listen to the drifter commenting to the schoolteacher about her date with her gay boyfriend: "Your friend left early without even firing a shot." Incidentally, sexual innuendo was raised to a fine (or not so fine) art during this period.

Images of violence vied with those of sensuality and sexuality in frequency and graphic quality. Violence, too, was held to be a matter of life, and death. In the documentary realist-expressionist *Kiss Me Deadly* (UA, 1955), the detective's sadism in lingered over as he grinningly watches his attacker roll down a flight of steps or when he slams a drawer shut on a finger of a morgue attendant.

The psychological underpinning of character (a person's interior determining what he/she says and does) was probed as never before. This affected classic characterization and narrative in several ways. First, it shifted the emphasis from story as the primary interest in a film to character. Secondly, since the new realisms' probe admitted more psychologically teetering, unbalanced, messed-up, and deranged protagonists than in classic times, the possibility of characters with unclear, unknown, in search of, or bereft of goals was a reality, as much as characters with goals. And since life was more a matter of dangling and loose ends (as the new realisms implied) rather than the stuff of connections and closures (as the old Hollywood classic realism proclaimed), bleak, ambiguous, or tempered optimistic resolutions, which were part of the styles' purview, took their place alongside of Hollywood's usual optimistic ones.

The sociological dimension, which was tackled in a more profound way than in classic times (man's exterior spheres, as setting and class, determining what one says and does), gave rise to a diverse picture of regional America (and the world). Neither was as homogeneous as we were led to believe.

These styles' fractured, episodic structure, undermining the harmoniously linear building blocks of the classic style, compounded this sense of character fragmentation and diversity of land and class. The invoking of the episodic in fashioning the film world also occasioned the suggestion that accident and irrationality might possibly be the warp and woof of existence, not order or a provident God.

The styles' sophisticated thematics and self-conscious sense of saying/doing something and/or saying/doing something for the first time resulted in an earnest tone which, at times, could reach the level of a self-aggrandizing over-zealousness, as in a good deal of Kramer's work. This countered noir's matter-of-fact coolness and the classic style's generally optimistic, buoyant perspective on things.

Finally, the new realisms also resulted in a rethinking on the part of the industry mainly, but also on the part of the more sophisticated consumer, of the traditional notion of movies solely as entertainment (in the sense of escape or release) to movies as entertainment with a message, movies as a medium for entertainment as well as communication. (Even in the practice of location shooting, the industry gleaned an educative aspect.) This gave, in the industry's mind, a new importance and significance to its business and products, assuring it of its culturally prestigious standing. To the consumer, it was an acknowledg-ment of learning something from the movies in addition to the pleasure of getting away from one's life and problems for a couple of hours. This change of heart also brought with it a definition of movies that was more expansive, multi-leveled, dimensioned, and hence, more realistic. Also, with this new outlook, Hollywood began to departmentalize, imagining the possibilities of making certain movies for a selective audience while still dreaming of making movies, as in the good old days, with a clear-across-the-board appeal.

Notes

1   Cf. BST.
2   BST, pp. 61, 62.
3   BST, p. 16.
4   Ted Gilling, "The Color of Music: An Interview with Bernard Herrmann," *Sight and Sound* 41 (Winter 1971/2), 36–7.

24

Other Stylistic Devices

Other stylistic devices marked off postwar movies from their antecedents. These techniques were more a matter of cultural, commercial, and technological influences, less a matter of the push toward realism.

The use of multiple protagonists, each, more or less, with his or her own line of action that was intertwined with the other respective protagonists' lines of action, and its influence on the narrative configuration of alternating parallel or contrasting storylines and episodic structure were significant features of film-making after 1946. This strategy affronted the classic Hollywood style of "involving few characters in several interdependent actions instead of putting many characters through parallel lines of action."[1] The discussion of the determinations of this approach to narrative (the business practice of spectacular entertainment; the adaptation route which included the transferring of sprawlingly complex parallel-plotted and/or sub-plotted novels with a host of protagonists to film, as well as theatrical family melodramas with their house of characters, independent production with its embrace of formal experimentation, and the introduction of large-screen formats) has already been aired.

One immediate effect was that post-1946, the average length of an A film got longer, as we have also seen. Though BST granted that post-1946 films tended to have more sequences than their predecessors, they did not conclude that they had, average-wise, a longer running time.[2]

Another noticeable feature in the postwar movie was the frequent appearance of a pre-title sequence, another counter to the classic Hollywood style of initial action following the opening credits. Cottoning to all genres, this grab-the-audience device, determined partly by TV's commercial teaser as well as the desire to show off one of the large screen shapes and location shooting, was yet another instance of the period's preference for episodic structure. The ploy begins in earnest about 1952 with the romantic comedy *You and Me* (MGM). Director Aldrich practically made the trope a signature trait. The B-thriller

The Burglar (C, 1958) opened ingeniously on a full-frame World News newsreel featuring a segment about a recent heiress. A pull-back reveals we are in a crowded movie house. Only when customer Dan Duryea rises to leave do the credits appear. The male melodrama *Requiem for a Heavyweight* opens with a slow right-to-left pan across a line of gents at a bar watching a fight on a TV screen. A cut to a long-held subjective shot of the boxer's pummeling and exit from the ring, all out-of-focus, superimposed, and shaky images, plunges us into his physical and psychological state. When the boxer approaches the mirror of the corridor's cigarette machine, he – and we – see his gashed, disfigured face and the credits begin. The fantasy *Portrait of Jennie* (SRO, 1947), the musical *West Side Story* (UA, 1961), and the historical spectacle *Lawrence of Arabia* (C, 1962) have no opening credits whatsoever.

Still another period-marking stylistic difference, in keeping with the postwar phonograph boom and the studios' aggressive move into the phonograph and music publishing business as well as the advertising and marketing practice of media energization, was a song's insertion in a non-musical film sung by a usually known and sometimes unknown recording artist. The song could find its way in the film's title sequence (Eydie Gorme's title song for *Until They Sail*), anywhere during the film (a patron inserts a coin in the jukebox and Dolores Hanlan warbles the title song *A Kiss Before Dying*, UA, 1956, over the dialogue of the main characters at a restaurant), or at the film's finish (the reprise of Peggy Lee's introductory title song in *Johnny Guitar*, R, 1954).

Excepting film actors who came from and were still part of the recording business (Pat Boone, Bing Crosby, Doris Day, Dean Martin, Elvis Presley, Frank Sinatra), or actors who stretched their talent by singing (Audrey Hepburn), the recording artist usually did not have a speaking part in the film. If the recording artist did appear, it was in a cameo nightclub performance. Sometimes the musical talent appeared as him/herself. In *The Blue Gardenia* (WB, 1953), Nat King Cole sings the entire title song in a Chinese restaurant, even reprising the verse and refrain. Only two split-second shots of the protagonist at a booth cut away from the performance. Plot and characterization have just about come to a complete standstill. Cole's recording of the song is next heard coming from a phonograph during the murder scene and finally comes from a jukebox in a hamburger joint. During the titles, a separate card tells us that Nat King Cole introduces the song in the picture. At other times, the musical talent played a fictional background role, as with Duke Ellington and his riffing in a bar in *Anatomy of a Murder*.

Wherever it was inserted, the song was thematic. Frankie Laine's rendition of the title song from *3:10 to Yuma* (C, 1957), reiterated within the movie and at the end, encapsulated the plot. The character-defining "Moon River" turned up endlessly in *Breakfast at Tiffany's* (P, 1961). The songs, wherever placed and whoever sung them, unclassically broke the plot thrust, sabotaging the transparency of the Hollywood classical style. Invariably, spectators enjoyed the performance on its own (they were supposed to), while concomitantly wondering, especially if they really liked the song and/or singer, if the song had been recorded as a single or as part of a soundtrack album, in order to go out and buy it.

On occasion, the song thumbed its nose at thematic relevancy. In *Rio Bravo* (WB, 1959), for no dramatic reason (commercial, yes; thematic, no), Dean Martin, joined by guitar-plunking Ricky Nelson, duets to "For My Rifle, My Pony and Me," while John Wayne and Walter Brennan smile their approval. Nelson then obliges with "Cindy" (whoever she is). The plot has taken a breather.

Since a song was pre-recorded and sung to a playback, the sound emerged clearer, cleaner, and, above all, different in quality than the dialogue and effects recorded on the set. This resulted in another self-reflexive fissure in the film in which commerce again showed its remorseless puss. *Journey to the Center of the Earth* (TCF, 1959) even upped the stakes in the scene where Pat Boone serenades Diane Baker at the piano with "My Love Is Like a Red, Red Rose," doffing the character's Scottish brogue.

Another departure from the classic Hollywood style was the design of titles which rose to the level of an art form. Traditionally, titles appeared against a neutral background. Occasionally, an icon from the movie would appear in the frame, as with the drawing of a line of black-hooded/robed men for *Black Legion* (WB, 1937), or the sketch of Independence Hall for *The Philadelphia Story* (MGM, 1940). Sometimes, it was a genre-notifying image, as a thick book covered in velvet signaling a swashbuckling adventure. At other times, the titles comprised pages of a book (*Anthony Adverse*, WB, 1935) that simply denoted that film's source. Title sequences – elaborate, eye-popping, self-reflexively calling attention to themselves in a shameless way – supplanted these classic editions. Postwar title sequences were also thematic, their content and design dictated primarily by what was to transpire.

One avenue was the representational way, in which the credits appeared over the main action, putting the audience *in medias res*, as with Prew's arrival at Schofield Barracks during training practice in *From Here to Eternity*. With a battalion of soldiers marching horizontally across the frame and Prew walking vertically into the frame, the credits visually enunciated the film's central individual–conformity conflict. A series of railroad tracks randomly interweaving, crisscrossing, and then pulling apart in a switching yard from the point of view of the train engine's cab metaphorically stated *Human Desire*'s main topics: the sudden, accidental connection and equally sudden, accidental unraveling of human lives. In *Outrage* (RKO, 1950), the flash-forward credits of the rape's aftermath, which will occur 15 minutes into the film, is a way to pique our curiosity and draw us into the film. In *Stage Fright* (WB, 1950), a theater's safety curtain ascends revealing an actual St. Paul's Cathedral not, as expected, a stage set, clinching the film's illusion–reality contretemps while prefacing its structuring theater motif–metaphor.

Abstractionism was another way to go, either via typography (lettering characteristic of a genre or setting, as the typewriter font of *House on 92nd Street*) or graphics (the bouncy cut-and-paste newspaper clippings of *Teacher's Pet*, P, 1958). Sometimes, animation was preferred (the Bayeux Tapestry rendered in the UPA cartoon style for *The Vikings*, UA, 1958).

Design could be a combination, as *North by Northwest*'s (MGM, 1959) opener wherein black lines, spilling every which way from the edges of the frame, crisscross against a green background, eventually forming the girders of a modern glass Gotham skyscraper mirroring bustling New Yorkers. Against this, credits descend from above the frame, ascend from below the frame, and diagonally move across from the side frames, approximating the topsy-turvy nature of the plot and narrative to follow.

North's dazzling title sequence was the brainchild of Saul Bass, who helmed this mini-revolution in movies. A native New Yorker, Bass launched Saul Bass & Associates in Los Angeles in 1946 to create marketing graphics to sell Hollywood movies. His first film credits job was for Preminger's *Carmen Jones* (TCF, 1954): white letters against a black background with a central blood-orange flame burning with a rose silhouette. The credits presaged the first appearance of the protagonist in a black blouse and blood-orange skirt, with a rose in her hand; her character as a woman of inconsonant extremes (white, black, and red clash with each other); the story of passion/violence (red) and death (white and black are the absence of color) to follow. Preminger knew a good thing when he saw it and a professional relationship with Bass was cemented. An early Picasso-esque face with a tear falling from one eye emblematized the sad French narrator of *Bonjour Tristesse* (C, 1958). The Preminger jobs contained the Bass signature and method. Arrestingly simple, immediately symbolic, Bass's curtain raiser cut right to the heart of the movie's subject matter.

Bass worked for others. For the Mirisch Brothers' *West Side Story*, the credits took the form of graffiti scribbled in chalk appearing on New York's brick walls, doors, and street signs. Occurring at the film's end, they offered release from the finale's heartbreak while assuring the spectator that the problem was still out there. And, of course, Bass became part of the Hitchcock unit. For *Vertigo* (P, 1958), credits were thrust at us from the face, then eyeball of an unknown woman into which we plunge. Plunging, we witness the floating of animated spirals of different shapes. Plucked out of the eye, we return to her face. The female's mystery; the mixture of the reality of the face and the artifice of the animated designs; the use of a spiral (a problematic alternative for a circle, since a spiral seems to have no center) added up to our first instance of subversion. Subversion was one of *Vertigo*'s subjects, and best described Hitch's narrative method. The spiral also introduced us to the film's key structuring method.

Not only exploring the aesthetics of titles design in terms of setting up and defining a picture's thematic boundaries and of grabbing the spectator's attention immediately, the modernist Bass and producers also came to realize the significance of the titles design for marketing, advertising, and promotional purposes. Often the design became the logo chosen to sell the movie.

Conclusion

The noir, documentary realist, and psychological-sociological styles, the preferred modes of the postwar years, brought with them formal strategies and attitudes that countered what went before. The frequent use of multiple protagonists, the pre-credit sequence, the song-insert, and credit design also witnessed a Hollywood shaking itself from the standard mode and method.

Notes

1   BST, p. 16.
2   BST, p. 62.

25

Coda

By 1963, events occurred that brought about and/or augured significant changes from the postwar period. With the assassination of President John F. Kennedy, the country's mood got cynical, feverish, and loony. Vice-President Lyndon B. Johnson took the reins, seeing himself as keeper of Kennedy's promise in the accomplishment of an unparalleled program of liberal social and economic reform and stepping up the conflict against communism in Vietnam. Rumblings began to be heard from the white middle class and college students. Two and a half months before the year began, Pope John XXIII called an Ecumenical Council (in the almost two millennia of the Church's existence only a mere 20 had convened before). It would be nothing less than a revolution in Christianity. TV, expanding its evening news from 15 to 30 minutes, became the major source of news for the nation. The Beatles began their concert tour in Scotland, then Britain. Their single "Love Me Do/P.S. I Love You" was released in Canada; "Please Please Me/Ask Me Why" in the USA. Their first album *Please Please Me* was released in England. Pop music would never be the same. MCA, Inc.'s takeover of Decca Records, which included Universal, was just about sealed. European co-productions went into high gear. From France, New Wave tenets such as "film as art" and the "director as auteur" crossed the Atlantic, and began to be discussed in college humanities' departments, film societies, and even studio conference rooms. Swinging London became the epicenter of a cultural revolution, rivaling Hollywood as the movie capital of the world. More and more, the industry resorted to the two-version syndrome (stateside and overseas) for controversial films (*The Victors* from Columbia) with Americans clamoring for the European rendition. The following year, the US Supreme Court would call into question the issue of "community standards" as a criterion for obscenity. TV movies of the week became the B movies of the previous era. (When the kickoff *The Killers* proved too violent and was eventually given a theatrical release in 1964, *See How They Run,* readied in 1964, was substituted.) The lion MGM began to lose its roar. Darryl F. Zanuck's son Richard became VP/Production at TCF at age 27. The NAACP threatened film and TV companies with a nationwide economic boycott and legal action to end discrimination in the hiring of black performers and craft workers as well as the screen representation of blacks as caricatures and/or "invisible men." Sidney Poitier won the Best Actor Oscar for *Lilies of the Field* (UA). The Parkway Twin Theaters opened in Kansas City, Missouri, coming to the cost-efficient rescue of the exhibitor with its concept of a twin theater: two theaters (one with 400 seats; the other, 300) sharing a common box office, lobby, projection booth, concession stand, washrooms, water fountain, and ushers, that could show different attractions. Fitted into a suburban Kansas City shopping center, which was now displacing downtown or city center as *the* site of retail, the company behind Parkway was equally savvy in putting the complex in a space already available, a space that gathered a lot of people together for the purpose of purchasing and consuming. Moreover, the space came complete with parking. Minimalist in design, the theaters were cheaply erected. The year 1963 also recorded the scantiest box-office receipts ever, an ominous forecast of what was to come in the next and financially shakiest period in Hollywood picture-making.

Finally, it was the films themselves, the Academy's recognition, and the populace's acceptance that signaled something new. Modernist all, they boldly and self-consciously played with thematic and formal experimentation, questioning the status quo and ushering in the style of expressive stylization with its awareness of film technique/a movie's construction/the medium as a director's medium in watching a movie. From London, director Tony Richardson's *Tom Jones* won best picture/director awards and other awards and nominations. The performances of Richard Harris and Rachel Roberts from the British Lindsay Anderson's *This Sporting Life* were nominated, as was that of Leslie Caron in Briton Bryan Forbes's *The L-Shaped Room.* From Italy, Federico Fellini's *8 1/2* won directing, writing (as did the Italian Nanni Loy's *The Four Days of Naples*), art direction-set decoration and costume Oscar nominations (ditto Luchino Visconti's *The Leopard*). France's *Sundays and Cybele*, Serge Bourguignon, was nominated for script and score honors. Jean Genet's play *The Balcony*, brought to the screen by Joseph Strick with music by Igor Stravinsky, was cited for photography. Hitchcock sent *The Birds* flying, continuing his modernist excursions and opening a new road of horror, that of the end of the world. The first of the Bonds appeared, the modernist-tinged *Dr. No* (UA). And Kubrick, now securely London-ensconced, unveiled *Dr. Strangelove* in the UK. Out of respect for President John Kennedy after his assassination, Columbia delayed its end-of-the-year planned release in the States until early 1964. Kicking off on September

1, 1963, the New York Film Festival acknowledged the burgeoning significance of the European film to Hollywood, all the while positioning foreign films as a serious form of expression, indisputably an art form. This perception would not go unnoticed in Hollywood.

Select Bibliography

Included are further selected readings in addition to the works cited in the introduction and endnotes in the various parts of the book.

Part I

Bordman, Gerald. *The American Musical Theatre*. New York: Oxford University Press, 1978.

Boyer, Paul. *By the Bomb's Early Light: American Thought and Culture at the Dawn of the Atomic Age*. Chapel Hill: University of North Carolina Press, 1994.

Caute, David. *The Great Fear: The Anti-Communist Purge under Truman and Eisenhower*. New York: Simon & Schuster, 1978.

Chafe, William H. *The American Woman: Her Changing Social, Economic and Political Roles, 1920–1970*. New York: Oxford University Press, 1970.

Hirsch, Foster. *A Method to Their Madness: The History of the Actors Studio*. New York: W. W. Norton, 1984.

May, Larry, ed. *Recasting America: Culture and Politics in the Age of the Cold War*. Chicago: University of Chicago Press, 1990.

Melinkoff, Ellen. *What We Wore: An Offbeat Social History of Women's Clothing, 1950–1980*. New York: William Morrow, 1984.

Mordden, Ethan. *The American Theatre*. New York: Oxford University Press, 1981.

Mordden, Ethan. *Broadway Babies: The People Who Made the American Musical*. New York: Oxford University Press, 1983.

Moss, Alfred A., Jr., and John Hope Franklin. *From Slavery to Freedom: A History of African Americans*, 8th ed. New York: McGraw-Hill, 1999.

Parfrey, Adam, ed. *It's a Man's World: Men's Adventure Magazines, the Postwar Pulps*. Los Angeles: Feral House, 2003.

Spigel, Lynn. *Made For TV: Television and the Family Ideal in Postwar America*. Chicago: Chicago University Press, 1992.

Part II

Anderson, Christopher. *Hollywood TV: The Studio System in the Fifties*. Austin: University of Texas Press, 1994.

Bernstein, Matthew. *Walter Wanger: Hollywood Independent.* Berkeley: University of California Press, 1995.

Custen, George F. *Twentieth Century's-Fox: Darryl F. Zanuck and the Culture of Hollywood.* New York: Basic Books, 1997.

Dick, Bernard R. *City of Dreams; The Making and Remaking of Universal Pictures.* Lexington: University of Kentucky Press, 1997.

Dixon, Wheeler, ed. *Producers Releasing Corporation: A Comprehensive Filmography and History.* Jefferson, NC: McFarland, 1986.

Finler, Joel. W. *The Hollywood Story.* New York: Crown, 1988.

Gomery, Douglas. *Shared Pleasures: A History of Movie Presentation in the United States.* Madison: University of Wisconsin Press, 1992.

McCarthy, Todd, and Charles Flynn, eds. *Kings of the Bs.* New York: Dutton, 1975.

McGee, Mark Thomas. *Fast and Furious: The Story of American International Pictures.* Jefferson, NC: Mc Farland, 1984.

Monaco, Paul. *The Sixties: 1960–1969.* Berkeley: University of California Press, 2001.

Schatz, Thomas. *Boom and Bust: American Cinema in the 1940s.* Berkeley: University of California Press, 1997.

Soloman, Aubrey. *Twentieth Century-Fox: A Corporate and Financial History.* Metuchen, NJ: Scarecrow, 1988.

Wallis, Hal, and Charles Higham. *Starmaker: The Autobiography of Hal Wallis.* New York: Macmillan, 1980.

Part III

Belton, John. *Widescreen Cinema.* Cambridge, MA: Harvard University Press, 1992.

Salt, Barry. *Film Style and Technology: History and Analysis.* London: Starwood, 1983.

Part IV

Bernstein, Matthew, ed. *Controlling Hollywood: Censorship and Regulation in the Studio Era.* New Brunswick, NJ: Rutgers University Press, 1999.

Black, Gregory. *The Catholic Crusade against the Movies, 1940–1975.* Cambridge: Cambridge University Press, 1997.

Couvares, Francis G., ed. *Movie Censorship and American Culture.* Washington, DC and London: Smithsonian Institution Press, 1996.

Part V

Basinger, Jeanine. *The World War II Combat Film: Anatomy of a Genre.* New York: Columbia University Press, 1986.

Belton, John. *American Cinema/American Culture,* 2nd ed. New York: McGraw Hill, 2005.

Brill, Lesley. *John Huston's Filmmaking.* Cambridge: Cambridge University Press, 1997.

Canham, Kingsley. *The Hollywood Professionals Volume 1: Michael Curtiz, Raoul Walsh, Henry Hathaway*. New York: A. S. Barnes, 1973.

Carroll, Noel. *The Philosophy of Horror*. New York and London: Routledge, 1990.

Casper, Joseph Andrew. *Vincente Minnelli and the Film Musical*. Cranbury, NJ: A. S. Barnes, 1977.

Casper, Joseph Andrew. *Stanley Donen*. Metuchen, NJ and London: Scarecrow Press, 1983.

Casty, Alan. *The Films of Robert Rossen*. New York: Museum of Modern Art, 1969.

Ciment, Michel. *Kazan on Kazan*. New York: Viking Press, 1974.

Clum, John M. *Paddy Chayefsky*. Boston: Twayne, 1976.

Cunningham, Frank R. *Sidney Lumet: Film and Literary Vision*, 2nd ed. Lexington: University Press of Kentucky, 2001.

Denton, Clive, and Kingsley Canham. *The Hollywood Professionals Volume 5: King Vidor, John Cromwell, Mervyn LeRoy*. New York: A. S. Barnes, 1976.

Denton, Clive, Kingsley Canham, and Tony Thomas. *The Hollywood Professionals Volume 2: Henry King, Lewis Milestone, Sam Wood*. New York, A.S. Barnes, 1974.

Dick, Bernard F. *Billy Wilder*, updated edition. New York: Da Capo Press, 1996.

Dowdy, Andrew. *The Films of the Fifties: The American State of Mind*. New York, William Morrow, 1973.

Eisenchatz, Bernard. *Nicholas Ray: An American Journey*, trans. Tom Milne. London: Faber & Faber, 1993.

Fordin, Hugh. *The World of Entertainment: Hollywood's Greatest Musicals*. Garden City, NY: Doubleday, 1975.

French, Philip. *Westerns*. New York: Oxford University Press, 1971.

Garnham, Nicholas. *Samuel Fuller*. New York: Viking Press, 1971.

Gehring, Wes D. *Handbook of American Film Genres*. New York: Greenwood Press, 1988.

Gehring, Wes D. *Populism and the Capra Legacy*. Westport, CT and London: Greenwood Press, 1995.

Geist, Kenneth L. *People Will Talk: The Life and Times of Joseph L. Mankiewicz*. New York: Charles Scribner's Sons, 1978.

Gow, Gordon. *Hollywood in the Fifties*. New York: A. S. Barnes, 1971.

Grant, Barry Keith, ed. *Film Genre Reader*. Austin: University of Texas Press, 1986.

Gunning, Tom. *The Films of Fritz Lang: Allegories of Vision and Modernity*. London: British Film Institute, 2000.

Halliday, Jon. *Sirk On Sirk*. New York: Viking, 1972.

Harvey, James. *Movie Love in the Fifties*. New York: Knopf, 2001.

Hardy, Phil. *Samuel Fuller*. New York: Praeger, 1970.

Harvey, Stephen. *Directed By Vincente Minnelli*. New York: Harper & Row, 1989.

Herman, Jan. *A Talent for Trouble: The Life of Hollywood's Most Acclaimed Director, William Wyler*. New York: Da Capo Press, 1997.

Higham, Charles, and Joel Greenberg. *Hollywood in the Forties*. New York: A. S. Barnes, 1968.

Johnston, Claire, and Paul Willemen, eds. *Frank Tashlin*. Colchester, England: Society for Education in Film and Television, 1973.

Kaminsky, Stuart. *John Huston: Maker of Magic*. Boston, Houghton Mifflin, 1978.

Kanin. Garson. *It Takes a Long Time to Become Young*. Garden City, New York: Doubleday, 1978.

Kerr, Walter. *Tragedy and Comedy*. New York: Simon & Schuster, 1967.

Kitses, Jim. *Horizons West/Anthony Mann, Budd Boetticher, Sam Peckinpah: Studies of Authorship Within the Western*. Bloomington and London: Indiana University Press, 1969.

Kramer, Stanley, and Thomas M. Coffey. *A Mad, Mad, Mad, Mad World: A Life in Hollywood*. New York: Harcourt Brace, 1997.

Lang, Robert. *American Film Melodrama: Griffith, Vidor, Minnelli*. Princeton, NJ: Princeton University Press, 1989.

Leaming, Barbara. *Orson Welles*. New York: Viking, 1985.

Leitch, Thomas. *Crime Films*. Cambridge: Cambridge University Press, 2002.

Levy, Emanuel. *George Cukor: Master of Elegance*. New York: William Morrow, 1994.

Luhr, William. *Raymond Chandler and Film*. Tallahassee: Florida State University Press, 1991.

Mast, Gerald. *Howard Hawks: Storyteller*. New York: Oxford University Press, 1982.

Mast, Gerald. *Can't Help Singing: The American Musical on Stage and Screen*. Woodstock, NY: Overlook Press, 1987.

McBride, Joseph. *Searching for John Ford: A Life*. New York: St. Martin's, 2001.

McGee, Mark Thomas. *Roger Corman: the Best of the Cheap Acts*. Jefferson, NC: McFarland Press, 1988.

Pratley, Gerald. *The Cinema of John Frankenheimer*. New York: A. S. Barnes, 1969.

Pratley, Gerald. *The Cinema of Otto Preminger*. New York: A. S. Barnes, 1971.

Robertson, James. C. *The Casablanca Man: The Cinema of Michael Curtiz*. London and New York: Routledge, 1993.

Rubin, Martin. *Thrillers*. Cambridge: Cambridge, University Press, 1999.

Sayre, Nora. *Running Time: The Films of the Cold War*. New York: Dial Press, 1982.

Schatz, Thomas. *Hollywood Genres: Formulas, Filmmaking, and the Studio System*. New York: Random House, 1981.

Schickel, Richard. *Elia Kazan: A Biography*. New York: HarperCollins, 2005.

Shadoian, Jack. *Dreams and Dead Ends: The American Gangster Film*, 2nd ed. New York: Oxford University Press, 2003.

Shuman, R. Baird. *William Inge*. New York: Twayne, 1965.

Silver, Alain, and James Ursini. *David Lean and His Films*. London: Frewin, 1974.

Skenazy, Paul. *James M. Cain*. New York: Continuum, 1989.

Spoto, Donald. *Stanley Kramer: Film Maker*. New York: G. P. Putnam's Sons, 1978.

Spoto, Donald. *The Style of Alfred Hitchcock: Fifty Years of His Motion Pictures*, 2nd ed. New York: Anchor Books/Doubleday, 1992.

Whitaker, Sheila. *The Films of Martin Ritt*. London: British Film Institute, 1972.

Wright, Will. *Sixguns & Society: A Structural Study of the Western*. Berkeley: University of California Press, 1975.

Watts, Steven. *The Magic Kingdom*. Boston: Houghton Mifflin, 1997.

Wood, Michael. *America in the Movies or "Santa Maria, It Had Slipped My Mind"*. New York: Dell, 1975.

Wood, Robin. *Hitchcock's Films Revisited*. New York: Columbia University Press, 1989.

Yacawar, Maurice. *Tennessee Williams and Film*. New York: Ungar, 1977.

Zinnemann, Fred. *A Life in the Movies: An Autobiography*. New York: C. Scribner & Sons, 1992.

Part VI

Jacobs, Lewis, ed. *The Documentary Tradition: From Nanook to Woodstock*. New York: Hopkins & Blake, 1971.

Nolan, William F. *The Black Mask Boys: Masters in the Hard-Boiled School of Detective Fiction.*
New York and London: The Mysterious Press, 1985.

Silver, Alain, and Elizabeth Ward, eds. *Film Noir: An Encyclopedic Reference to the American Style.*
Woodstock, NY: Overlook Press, 1979.

Siska, William. *Modernism in the Narrative Cinema: The Art Film as a Genre.* New York: Arno
Press, 1976.

Appendix

Hierarchical Order of Postwar Hollywood's Top Ten Box-Office Stars (1946-62)

(From 1932 onward, Quigley Publications asked US exhibitors to name each year's winning ten movie stars, the results being based on a respective player's movie/s grosses. It is an approximate rather than scientific indication of the tastes of American moviegoers.)

1946: Bing Crosby/Ingrid Bergman/Van Johnson/Gary Cooper/Bob Hope/ Humphrey Bogart/Greer Garson/Margaret O'Brien/Betty Grable/Roy Rogers

1947: Bing Crosby/Betty Grable/Ingrid Bergman/Gary Cooper/Humphrey Bogart/Bob Hope/Clark Gable/Gregory Peck/Claudette Colbert/Alan Ladd

1948: Bing Crosby/Betty Grable/Abbott and Costello/Gary Cooper/Bob Hope/ Humphrey Bogart/Clark Gable/Cary Grant/Spencer Tracy/Ingrid Bergman

1949: Bob Hope/Bing Crosby/Abbott and Costello/John Wayne/Gary Cooper/ Cary Grant/Betty Grable/Esther Williams/Humphrey Bogart/Clark Gable

1950: John Wayne/Bob Hope/Bing Crosby/Betty Grable/James Stewart/Abbott and Costello/Clifton Webb/Esther Williams/Spencer Tracy/Randolph Scott

1951: John Wayne/Martin and Lewis/Betty Grable/Abbott and Costello/Bing Crosby/Bob Hope/Randolph Scott/Gary Cooper/Doris Day/Spencer Tracy

1952: Martin and Lewis/Gary Cooper/John Wayne/Bing Crosby/Bob Hope/ James Stewart/Doris Day/Gregory Peck/Susan Hayward/Randolph Scott

1953: Gary Cooper/Martin and Lewis/John Wayne/Alan Ladd/Bing Crosby/ Marilyn Monroe/James Stewart/Bob Hope/Susan Hayward/Randolph Scott

1954: John Wayne/Martin and Lewis/Gary Cooper/James Stewart/Marilyn Monroe/Alan Ladd/William Holden/Bing Crosby/Jane Wyman/Marlon Brando

1955: James Stewart/Grace Kelly/John Wayne/William Holden/Gary Cooper/ Marlon Brando/Martin and Lewis/Humphrey Bogart/June Allyson/Clark Gable

1956: William Holden/John Wayne/James Stewart/Burt Lancaster/Glenn Ford/ Martin and Lewis/Gary Cooper/Marilyn Monroe/Kim Novak/Frank Sinatra

1957: Rock Hudson/John Wayne/Pat Boone/Elvis Presley/Frank Sinatra/Gary Cooper/William Holden/James Stewart/Jerry Lewis/Yul Brynner

1958: Glenn Ford/Elizabeth Taylor/Jerry Lewis/Marlon Brando/Rock Hudson/ William Holden/Brigitte Bardot/Yul Brynner/James Stewart/Frank Sinatra

1959: Rock Hudson/Cary Grant/James Stewart/Doris Day/Debbie Reynolds/ Glenn Ford/Frank Sinatra/John Wayne/Jerry Lewis/Susan Hayward

1960: Doris Day/Rock Hudson/Cary Grant/Elizabeth Taylor/Debbie Reynolds/ Tony Curtis/Sandra Dee/Frank Sinatra/Jack Lemmon/John Wayne

1961: Elizabeth Taylor/Rock Hudson/Doris Day/John Wayne/Cary Grant/ Sandra Dee/Jerry Lewis/William Holden/Tony Curtis/Elvis Presley

1962: Doris Day/Rock Hudson/Cary Grant/John Wayne/Elvis Presley/Elizabeth Taylor/Jerry Lewis/Frank Sinatra/Sandra Dee/Burt Lancaster

Index

Note: Entries in italics refer to illustrations.

Lightning Source UK Ltd.
Milton Keynes UK
UKHW031838130220
358685UK00007B/259